What's New to This Edition

Global Journalism has established itself over a quarter of a century as a trusted authority on international media. The new edition carries that reputation further into the twenty-first century for a new generation of journalism and media scholars, students, and media professionals. Specifically, the book

❶ Highlights the continuing changes in global media over the past decade, featuring developments in the field of media technology, portraying the ever-changing role of international journalism. Topics covered include the impact of blog and iPod journalism; e-mail and Web sites from the Middle East to the Far East and in-between, and the legal impediments involved therein.

❷ Incorporates new discussions and examples showing how physical, cultural, and economic barriers impede media development and explores how countries work to overcome barriers caused by repressive governments and the challenges of globalization.

❸ Covers the major philosophical, problematic, and controversial issues of global journalism and presents informed discussions on how it is practiced around the world by today's global journalists and media organizations.

❹ Features the work of 25 national and internationally published authors, including some of the world's foremost scholars in specialized areas of research.

❺ Discusses and presents a case study regarding the ethics of how journalists and the media deal with news in a diverse, multicultural, and globalized world.

❻ Examines the issue of news presentation and the "skewing" of foreign news through "double misreading" when "tourist journalists" fall prey to the manipulation of spin doctors.

❼ Explores new developments in different media system across the globe, from emerging media markets in the East, and South East, to the way media and politics intersect in Latin America and Africa's developing democracies.

PEARSON

FIFTH EDITION

Global Journalism

Topical Issues and Media Systems

Edited by

Arnold S. de Beer
Stellenbosch University, South Africa

Preface by

John C. Merrill
University of Missouri, U.S.A.

Boston   New York   San Francisco
Mexico City   Montreal   Toronto   London   Madrid   Munich   Paris
Hong Kong   Singapore   Tokyo   Cape Town   Sydney

Acquisitions Editor: Jeanne Zalesky
Series Editorial Assistant: Megan Lentz
Marketing Manager: Suzan Czajkowski
Production Editor: Karen Mason
Editorial Production Service: Rebecca Dunn, Preparé Inc.
Manufacturing Buyer: Debbie Rossi
Electronic Composition: Preparé Inc.
Cover Administrator: Joel Gendron

For related titles and support materials, visit our online catalog at www.pearsonhighered.com.

Between the time Web site information is gathered and then published, it is not unusual for some sites to have closed. Also, the transcription of URLs can result in typographical errors. The publisher would appreciate notification where these errors occur so that they may be corrected in subsequent editions.

Library of Congress Cataloging-in-Publication Data

Global journalism : topical issues and media systems / [edited by] Arnold S.
   de Beer, John C. Merrill. -- 5th ed.
        p. cm.
   Includes bibliographical references.
   ISBN-13: 978-0-205-60811-9
   ISBN-10: 0-205-60811-6
   1. Journalism. I. De Beer, A. S. (Arrie) II. Merrill, John Calhoun, 1924-
PN4775.G56 2008
070.4--dc22

                                        2008022185

Printed in the United States of America.

10 9 8 7 6 5 4 3 2 1   12 11 10 09 08

CONTENTS

4 BARRIERS TO MEDIA DEVELOPMENT   48

PAUL PARSONS / GLENN W. SCOTT / RICHARD LANDESBERG

5 FREEDOM OF THE PRESS AROUND THE WORLD   65

LEE B. BECKER / TUDOR VLAD

14 EASTERN EUROPE, EURASIA, AND RUSSIA   214

ALLEN W. PALMER

15 THE MIDDLE EAST AND NORTH AFRICA   253

ORAYB AREF NAJJAR

16   SUB-SAHARAN AFRICA   293

MINABERE IBELEMA / TANJA BOSCH

Finding Perspective in an Ever-Changing Global Media World

We live in an exciting world of ongoing communication and media transformation. The world of the twenty-first century is hurrying along at a rapid pace, and so is journalism. This is even more the case with global journalism. Not only did September 11, 2001 change the way we look at international affairs, but it also influenced the way we perceive the media that bring us news and opinions about peoples and countries far and wide. More and better educated global journalists are needed to communicate and make sense of a perplexing array of news events that fill the 24-hour news cycle, from continuing political upheaval in the Middle East, Iraq, Serbia and Kosovo, and Zimbabwe to the changes brought about by globalization in the media and other spheres.

Modern communication and media innovations bring the world to us in ever increasing, more technologically sophisticated ways. In the process, the age-old dictum that the media brings the news to its audience is also falling more and more by the wayside. The audience itself is now also producing, or at least repeating, information on a wide scale through e-mail, SMS, and Web sites such as Facebook and MySpace and even contributing their own input into news channels such as CNN, with cell phone pictures and videos, as was evident during the 2008 earthquakes in China. In the process the traditional and not so traditional media, such as online newspapers and 24-hour international news services, invite the public to become part of the global news process. The student who had his cell-phone recordings of the massacre at Virginia State University in 2007 beamed and published around the world was but yet another startling example of so-called digital citizen journalism.

However, it is not only a case of picking up a camera and start shooting international news events. We have to realize that we live in a world where clear, solid journalism is often drained away by communication pollution and information overflow. Propaganda, biased information, superficial journalism, vulgarizing streams of crime and sex, focus on celebrities *ad nauseum,* unbridled reputation-destroying stories, opinion camouflaged as fact, "spinning" assertions of expertise—all these, and more, tend to put global news populations into a kind of drug-like stupor. A media-created world of puzzling shadows distracts the eyes, and syncopated sounds of war and violence deafen the ears. The communication waters are polluted and not enough is being done to clean up the mess.

Governments and business leaders of the media far too often use journalism as an instrument for self-aggrandizement and skewed social direction. Responsible journalists, as the cleaning crews, are undermanned and seldom concerned enough about the mental and psychological damage caused by global media pollution. This is, indeed, a pessimistic picture and many readers will consider it unfairly negative, but one that needs to be addressed by communication literature.

Writers of the chapters that follow present both rays of hope and optimism that shine on some parts of the world and indicate how various media systems serve their audiences rather well. Others describe the infrastructure of regional media systems that are challenged by serious impediments and restrictions. And still others see in revised theoretical media models and philosophies hope for a revitalization of international communication.

Since the early 1950s, I have been interested in global media and have studied it both up close and from a distance. Looking back, I realize that I have always been disappointed by three aspects of international journalism: the mind-dumbing emphasis on the sensational, the negative and the superficial; the tendency of media to escape from freedom into states of conformity, and the general unconcern of most media with raising the educational and intellectual standards of the public.

Just how serious the media problems are we really cannot know. But it does not take an abundance of sophisticated empirical research to show that, by and large, the media around the world are providing information and analysis unsatisfactory for human progress in the twenty-first century. Little doubt exists that a large part of the world's media is offering a titillating fare of entertainment and/or inviting their audiences to spend more money on goods and services necessary to lead a good and productive life.

Obviously, there is a counter side to this negative view. There are great media outlets around the world that strive to uphold high moral principles of responsibility and aspire to present only the best journalism. It is to this part of the media equation that this book speaks.

The editor of this fifth edition of *Global Journalism, Topical Issues and Media Systems,* Arnold de Beer, has consequently gathered an eminent group of writers who, because of their individual expertise and experience, provide valuable insights into and descriptions of the various media issues and systems around the world. The editor, who is from South Africa, is a scholar who looks beyond the Western perspective of journalism and is able to see the potential of media development in relatively unexplored territories. He has gathered contributors who are equally open-minded and cosmopolitan. The publishing of a book such as this is a daunting enterprise due to its vast and encompassing subject matter and the constant media flux throughout the world. It does, however, introduce the reader to the problems and general parameters of global journalism in one accessible volume, and it offers perspectives on a world of news that is more often in turmoil than in peace. As such, I hope that readers will find it a worthy contribution to global journalism literature.

JOHN C. MERRILL
Professor Emeritus of Journalism
University of Missouri, USA

ABOUT THIS BOOK

Now in its fifth edition, *Global Journalism* aims to provide the reader with a broad overview of the major issues facing global journalism and to describe some of the main dimensions and trends that characterize international media systems, news, and related issues.

With the continuing changes taking place in the field of global journalism, we wanted more than simply a superficial revision, because that would have defeated the object of looking at the world stage of journalism from the perspective of the ever-changing present. Consequently, all chapters have been revised to address issues pertinent to the mass media world of today and tomorrow. A new chapter has been included on critical media philosophy, while some of the other chapters have been replaced with new content by both previous and new authors.

The book consists of three interlinking sections. In **Part 1: Global Journalism: Theoretical Perspectives**, two authors offer different perspectives on the issue of how to approach global journalism from a theoretical point of view.

John C. Merrill in **Chapter 1: Introduction to Global Western Journalism Theory**, by way of an introduction to the book, sets a foundational stage for a broad discussion of the world's journalism and media systems. The chapter departs from the traditional Western theoretical approach of government–media relationships, with its emphasis on responsibility and freedom. It discusses how the mission of global media systems, in terms of government–media relationships, relate to the practical aspects of journalism and how the various philosophical differences among national media systems are determined.

In the new **Chapter 2: Critical and non-Western Press Philosophies**, Herman Wasserman offers a different theoretical point of view on how we theorize about global journalism. He critiques the centrality of government–media relations as the primary defining feature of media systems and argues for a more complex, multileveled approach to global media systems. A critical view is offered, with the emphasis on the place of media in global power relations, and the cultural and economic dimensions of global media.

Part II: Challenges and Barriers to Global Journalism offers an overview of some of the main barriers and challenges that confront global journalism.

International news reporting is about the way news flows within countries and intercontinentally. In the updated **Chapter 3: Global and National News Agencies,** Terhi Rantanen and Oliver Boyd-Barrett review the activities of the major international and national news agencies and discuss how the agencies have responded to the challenges of new technological and other changes that have developed in recent years. The chapter concludes that news agencies were challenged, competitively and financially, by the arrival of the Internet in the 1990s and the early years of the twenty-first century. However, there are signs that many, if not most, news agencies are weathering the threats of the Internet. Most agencies have appropriately readjusted their business models and have learned not only to live successfully with the Internet and other modern electronic media, but to become leaders in Internet and technological convergence.

Chapter 4: Barriers to Media Development makes it clear that barriers to media freedom and development have arisen in surprisingly different forms around the world. Some media are independent, others government controlled. Some are technologically sophisticated, others rather primitive. Some are economically strong, others are on the edge of survival. Using recent examples for this strongly revised chapter, Paul Parsons and two new co-authors, Richard Landesberg and Glenn W Scott, identify six factors that serve as barriers to media development: Physical barriers such as geography; cultural barriers such as societal taboos; economic barriers such as poverty and an uneducated workforce; governmental barriers such as licensing or censorship; media barriers such as poorly trained journalists; and technological barriers that highlight the disparity between media-rich and media-poor nations. These six barriers account for the most observable differences among media systems in the world.

The concept of press freedom is a contentious one. Fundamentally, the issues are: freedom from what and freedom for whom? In the Western world historically, much of the attention has been on freedom from government control. Critics around the world challenge the Western media's—and particularly the American media's—commercial base, arguing that the media are dependent on powerful forces in society that greatly weaken their independence. In the entirely rewritten **Chapter 5**: **Freedom of the Press around the World**, Lee Becker and Tudor Vlad elaborate on these issues by tracing some of the historical discussions of press freedom. Their chapter also shows how press freedom is monitored by major agencies around the world. It ends with a discussion of challenges to press freedom, with particular focus on those challenges resulting from revolutionary changes in the ways journalism is practiced within the context of new communication technologies. The authors dedicate this chapter to a renowned international scholar, the late Robert L. Stevenson, who wrote this particular chapter in the previous editions.

How do journalists approach media ethical issues, and how do they deal with ethical issues relating to media in today's globalized world? Questions approached in the entirely rewritten **Chapter 6: Global Journalism Ethics** by new author Herman Wasserman include: "Is it possible to construct an ethical code for journalists around the globe; how should journalism ethics account for the plurality and diversity in a multicultural, globalized media environment; what challenges do new media technologies pose for journalism ethics?" In addressing these questions, this chapter offers global perspectives that are too often absent from scholarly debates of media ethics that take place in North America and Europe. A special case study is also included.

Technology and turmoil in various parts of the world meant an almost complete rewrite of **Chapter 7: Global Advertising and Public Relations** by Doug Newsom. Technology has shifted the balance of communication power from the origins of public relations and advertising messages to the recipients. Messages in blogs, e-mails, and Web sites are sources of unmediated messages that challenge critical thinking and organizational credibility. The chapter shows how turmoil—economic, political, religious, and social—has heightened the need to communicate, yet, in many places, complicated if not actually impaired the process.

Chapter 8: Continuing Media Controversies by Paul Grosswiler features a new section on the Internet; citizen journalism; Weblogs; and other forms of new communication technology, such as Global Voices Online and Hometown Baghdad. The section on the World Summit on the Information Society has been expanded to include assessments by representatives of civil society groups and scholars since the WSIS concluded in 2005. Information on global media ownership has also been updated. The chapter retains its focus on renewed efforts to address global media controversies in the context of the New World Information Order movement in the 1970s and 1980s, including the rise of citizen advocacy groups in response to the intensifying problem of neo-liberal globalization of the traditional media and the Internet at the present time.

Mark Deuze in **Chapter 9: Global Journalism Education** analyzes and updates the changing field of journalism education to the present. Four main changes or challenges facing education programs in journalism worldwide are identified and discussed: increasing recognition and awareness of cultural diversity in society; the merging of entertainment and media industries, genres, and formats; the convergence of digital media technologies (multimedia); and the internationalization of media, journalism, and news flow. None of these trends have lost their relevance for the work and training of journalists, but several recent developments suggest that the complexity of today's media ecosystem has created a sense of urgency in the ways they are coalescing.

The important issue of who journalists are is taken up in the entirely rewritten **Chapter 10: Journalists: International Profiles** by new author Beate Josephi. In the age of blogging, the chapter attempts to define who is a journalist and what can be considered as the main characteristics of this amorphous group, generally called journalists, whether they work in "traditional" or "new" media. Based on new detailed data from four continents, it traces the trends with regard to gender, age, education, professional values, and aspects of the job.

In the revised **Chapter 11: Reporting Foreign Places,** Eric Louw unravels the problems associated with the reporting of foreign places. It discusses both the way in which "media reality" is sometimes deliberately skewed, such as when Anglo-American propaganda was fed to journalists in the Iraq War, as well as how on other occasions, the skewing of foreign news is derived organically from the limitations of journalistic storytelling, not the least in the case of the "missing weapons of mass destruction" in Iraq. The chapter examines the way in which present-day foreign news can be seen to produce a "double misreading," and the way in which "tourist journalism" can lend itself to manipulation by spin-doctors.

News is not what it used to be. Arnold de Beer argues in Chapter **12: Global News** that the simplistic days are gone when journalism textbooks rattled off a list of "criteria" or "attributes" washing-line style, as though it would suffice understanding one of the most complex terms and issues in modern media. This revised chapter not only looks at the historical origins of news, but also shows its evolution to a modern-day information phenomenon that is often difficult to grasp, and even more difficult to describe sufficiently, not only in a scientific style, but also in a way that would make sense from an academic point of view in the "real world or news practice" presented by twenty-first century new media and new concepts about news.

A new author, Byron Scott, opens **Part III** of the book, **Global Journalism in the World's Regions**, with his analysis in **Chapter 13: Western Europe** of how the "old Europe" has become a world center of communications technology, media conglomerates, and accompanying accomplishments and threats to press freedom. Western Europe includes some of the world's most respected journalistic institutions and is praised for a history of free expression. But censorship and such issues as immigration, terrorism, and national rivalries pose new challenges. The European Union's growing role in shaping policies and the European identity is emphasized. The chapter chronicles the slow retreat of Western Europe's traditional system of public broadcasters and state-subsidized newspapers. The current problems and prospects of 21 regional nations are reviewed.

In **Chapter 14: Eastern Europe, Eurasia, and Russia**, Allen Palmer shows how the development of mass communication has been turbulent and uneven in Eastern Europe, Eurasia, and Russia, especially over the last two decades. Much of the promise of the development of democracy has over the last number of years been sidetracked by the combined forces of tabloid sensationalization, as well as intimidation, violence, and low professional standards of journalists themselves. This strongly revised chapter tracks the continuing turmoil and progress of media development in the far-flung region. Of particular interest have been the media consolidation, privatization and disputations in Russia, where the intimidation and murder of journalists—at least a dozen in Russia since the early 2000s, including Anna Politkovskaya—has captured the attention of the world human rights community.

Chapter 15: The Middle East and North Africa by Orayb Aref Najjar has a new section on the importance of political blogging in the Arab world and on the response of various governments to this development. This chapter deals in particular with recent changes in media law in various Arab countries, as it is affected by the changes in the Internet environment and as a response to the rapid increase in the number of Internet users. The chapter also provides Web site information on the region's media in addition to an extensive bibliography.

As the euphoria of democratization in the 1990s waned, the African press has settled into the challenges of democratic consolidation. However, as Minabere Ibelema argues in **Chapter 16: Sub-Saharan Africa** the African press in general continues to thrive in an increasingly liberalized political environment, but that does not mean that African governments have completely shed their repressive past. More challenging for the press, however, is the reality of surviving in a highly competitive marketplace in which independent newspapers and broadcast stations have proliferated. This revised chapter with a new co-author, Tanja Bosch, shows the continent and its media at a different and challenging frontier by the end of the first decade of the twenty-first century.

Jiafei Yin, in the revised and extended **Chapter 17: Asia and the Pacific**, takes a specific holistic look at the historical development of the press across the Asian continent by emphasizing the common themes of the missionary press and the vernacular press for national independence. This path traveled still influences the news media in Asia today when they are often used as political tools in free or controlled societies. The chapter also explores the new driving forces behind the explosive growth of the press in China and India in contrast to some declining press trends in the West. However, it also points to the emergence of troubling signs in strong press environments, such as Japan and South Korea, where mass-circulating national dailies are fighting an increasingly tough battle against new media and free papers—just as in the West.

Chapter 18: Australasia revised by Stephen Quinn and new co-author John Tidey, highlights the major changes in media ownership and structures in Australia and New

Zealand. It details the significant impact of digital media on traditional media, and suggests ways in which media are evolving in each country.

With one of the authors returning from the fourth edition, **Chapter 19: Latin America** discusses the main themes and issues relating to journalism and media in the region. However, it is a newly written chapter by Rick Rockwell especially tracking more recent developments, such as media and free expression. Also new is the discussion of key events, such as the battle between the Venezuelan government and that country's broadcasters and the deployment of the Mexican army to guard newspapers from attacks by drug cartels. More theoretically, this chapter now also examines the resurgence of the state (in Venezuela, Ecuador, Argentina, and elsewhere) in an attempt to counter the growing power of the media.

The revised **Chapter 20: North America** by William Briggs examines the media environment of the two large North American democracies, Canada and the United States. The chapter demonstrates how the two nations, often perceived as identical, are actually quite different in their media as well as in many other characteristics. The chapter traces the historical media evolution in these two nations, setting the stage for the current legal and business climates. The chapter updates such topical issues as cross-border communication, convergence, multiple ownership of media, newspaper readership decline and the corresponding growth of the Internet and other new media technologies, media conglomeration, and the expansion of advertising and public relations.

The editor and authors hope that this new edition of *Global Journalism* will meet the expectations of readers who are interested in the role of global journalism in modern-day communication systems: in terms of a philosophical approach to this field; some of the major issues confronting global journalism; and the way media systems around the world work.

As editor, I wish to thank each and every one of the contributors for bringing their knowledge, expertise, but also their time and energy, to this project. Some have gone through extremely difficult times in the preparation of their chapters, be it in health or otherwise. All have done much more than an editor could reasonably expect for a book of this kind. All have produced sterling work. Without their goodwill, endurance, and patience, this book would not have come about. A word of thanks is also due to all the main authors for their input into this introduction.

However, this edition was also made possible by those colleagues who have worked on all the previous editions, from the first to the fourth when I took over as co-editor with Prof John Merrill. In this connection I especially want to thank the authors who contributed to the fourth edition and who were not involved with the fifth edition, but whose work help made it possible for the fifth edition authors to move ahead: the late Robert L. Stevenson; also Dean Kruckenberg; Katerina Tsetsura; David H. Weaver; Lianne Fridriksson; Catherine Cassara, Gregg Payne, Peter Gross; Mitchell Land, Lyombe Eko; Elanie Steyn and Donn Tilson. I would also like to thank and acknowledge the authors who contributed to past editions of *Global Journalism*.

It was only a pleasure to have worked with Jeanne Zalesky, Acquisitions Editor: Communication of Pearson/Allyn & Bacon in Boston, USA. Her unwavering support, skillful input, and good sense kept the project going from day one. I am indebted to her and to Megan Lentz, Pearson/Allyn & Bacon editorial assistant, for not flinching when we encountered hassles on the road to receiving all copy against shifting deadlines. I am also especially grateful to Rebecca Dunn and her team at Emilcomp in Italy for taking such good care of the copy editing and composition. My thanks also goes to Karen Mason, the production editor at Pearson/Allyn & Bacon; as well as to Christine Wilson for compiling the index, a valuable addition to this edition of *Global Journalism*. It says something about the process of globalization and Internet connectivity to have had this book produced with authors and production staff spread over four continents.

Most, if not all, of the authors got involved in this project through the stature and the academic acumen that Professor John C. Merrill has brought to this book, which he edited from the first to the third edition, when he got me on board as co-editor for the fourth edition. This was a singular honor for me. I trust that he will not be disappointed in this edition, and I thank him for writing the preface and introductory chapter. To my mind, John Merrill is the embodiment of being a *Mensch,* a true scholar and a role model. As an academic he has always pushed against complacent conformity, and he ever strives to set the highest standards possible. We can all learn from him.

ARNOLD S. DE BEER
Department of Journalism
Stellenbosch University
South Africa

PART ONE

Global Journalism: Theoretical Perspectives

Introduction to Global Western Journalism Theory

JOHN C. MERRILL
University of Missouri, USA

This book offers the reader a survey of the fascinating and complex field of global journalism, together with the topical issues that permeate media systems in the different regions of the world.

The press philosophies of global journalism and media systems throughout the world tend to gravitate and cluster toward two basic models: (a) monolithic and state-controlled entities and (b) more pluralistic, open entities. Developing countries, as well as present and former Communist and other authoritarian countries, normally fall in the first category, and Western developed countries in the second.

Today, with satellites beaming down information worldwide, with the Internet and cell phones enabling millions of previously silent people to speak and be heard, with television available around the world, and with newspapers and journals designed for almost every preference, the quantitative reach of the global media is a miracle of human vision and technology. Yet, this continuous information growth and reach remain spotty, and in some areas of the world the people are still poorly served.

Big international news agencies such as Reuters, Agence France-Presse, and the Associated Press continue to serve media everywhere, and their networking with regional and national agencies provides global media with a wealth of news and commentary. This is not to say that the media necessarily *use* all that much agency copy, but the news *flows* regularly and abundantly across national borders. Media systems use the material they get, and make it consistent with their media theories, some reflecting free-ranging and pluralistic approaches whereas others are regimented and monolithic.

The world has so many media systems that we should all be as happy as kings, to rephrase the late media scholar Robert Louis Stevenson's optimistic words. But are we? Moreover, we might ask, does a journalism and media system contribute substantially to human happiness? If so, what kind of press system makes the greatest contribution? And is happiness the supreme aim of media systems? This book attempts to present some generalizations about these and other related questions. This is a huge undertaking, made especially difficult by the need to bring it all together within the covers of one book. Consequently, the editor and authors of the chapters that follow fully recognize the necessary limitations of their analyses and commentary. In spite of such limitations, this book, written by specialists in their fields, provides an informed overview of world journalism and should prove very helpful to the reader.

The Machiavellian Pull and a Word on Media Ethics

Global journalism does not operate in a vacuum. In spite of forces such as globalization, varying moral, ethical, and religious values are still be found around the world.

Global ethics is also in the realm of global journalism, and though it is a serious issue, it will not be dealt with at length here. Suffice it to say that, in spite of some common or universal moral standards, different ethical norms are manifest in the various media systems around the world. To a large degree, journalistic ethics must be considered to be relative. Some philosophers and psychiatrists would even say that nothing substantive or scientific can be said about ethics. This issue gets us into the old debate about what is "truth" or what is the truth about ethics—a debate that gets us nowhere. But interestingly, positivist philosophers (e.g., Carnap and Wittgenstein) maintain that it is useless to talk about ethics—that ethics is simply subjective. Positivists deny any moral truth, claiming that ethical propositions cannot be proven either true or false.

Positivists would say that an expression such as "You were unethical in printing the name of the young woman in that story" is to say nothing more than that you did something. And behavioral psychologists generally deny the possibility of ethics altogether.

Most thinkers dealing with responsibility believe that a person is responsible even when he or she is not punished. Osama bin Laden in 2001, for example, is guilty of (or responsible for) Muslim terrorism even if he has not been apprehended. For the strict behaviorist, however, even if bin Laden were to be executed for his acts, he could not be said to be "guilty," only that he was apprehended, tried, and executed. And finally there are the absolute determinists among psychiatrists, followers of Sigmund Freud, who say that if a person did what he had to do, it is not worthwhile to discuss whether or not he ought to have done it.

Most ethicists would not agree with the absolute determinists, thinking that it is indeed worthwhile to talk about ethics as a substantive topic and to strive to be more ethical. Back in the mid-twentieth century, D. Elton Trueblood (1963:52), for example, maintained that we can talk competently about "objective truth" (the truth in a situation that we discover rather than invent), and although we do not possess this truth "beyond a shadow of doubt," we can make an effort to possess it through "the intelligent assumption that it is." Trueblood states further that "when men differ about moral standards, it does not mean that they should give up the struggle to learn what they ought to do. Instead it means that they must go on thinking and learning from one another" (265).

Ethics is self-enforced and does not depend on some outside power or even financial expediency to coerce a certain kind of media action. Many journalists and scholars around the world (and UNESCO as an institution) would like to see a greater agreement on what is ethical in journalism and what is not. A global code of ethics has been suggested, in addition to various national codes, and scholars have surveyed the world for *common or universal ethical standards* (Christians & Traber, 1997; Ward & Wasserman, 2008). Such a global code is, however, a controversial mechanism, seen by many as unachievable and, by some pure libertarians, as inappropriate for journalists seeking maximum freedom of expression.

There is one dominant perspective, however, that affects every press system: *Machiavellianism.* A basic desire that seems pervasive in the media is to *succeed in achieving a specified and overriding purpose.* This desire might be, variously, to reach national progress or supremacy; to achieve party objectives; to cooperate with or contend with government; to make profits for the institution or an individual person or family; or to propagate certain perspectives or values. But whatever the purpose, the wish everywhere is to *succeed*—and, what is more, to succeed often by using whatever means will work.

This Machiavellian emphasis in journalism (described at length in Merrill's *Princely Press,* 1998) permeates the world and poses a real danger to nonpragmatic or moralistic (principled) media approaches to global journalism. Such an amoral emphasis is, of course, related to the increase of politicization and with it, state power.

Modern journalists, like Machiavelli himself in Renaissance Florence, prefer to use normal, respected, and traditional "private" ethics if it can achieve their purpose, but they have little or no reluctance in using more "practical" (public or institutional) ethics when needed. Terrorists, and their journalistic apologists, for example, would not normally justify the suicide bombings and other acts that kill civilians; but when they find that attacking soldiers only or diplomatic endeavors do not bring them political and social success, they retreat from humanistic ethics. And so, analogously, liberal democracies and traditional theocracies bend their normal ethics as they try to achieve their ends. Both parties, however, are damaging their loyalty to religious and humanistic theory and to civil rights and legal guarantees. World crises serve as a catalyst for nations to become more Machiavellian and thereby increase their power.

Machiavellian instrumentalism bestows on the media various objectives, duties, or ends with a kind of positivist disregard for conventional ethics. The business of the press is often to achieve certain ends, for example, national security and stability, social development, financial gain for owners and corporations, and the viability and consolidation of the power of ruling elites. As will be shown in the global survey presented in the following chapters, the world's journalism is, in one way or another, an instrument of power, controled by the various elites that guide their societies. And subsumed in this concern with ends is an uneven pattern of truly ethical concern dealing with such issues as freedom, values, accuracy, significance, and respect.

In the midst of this instrumental, pragmatic, Machiavellian journalism in the world, indeed, slivers of moral concern are in evidence. A new demand (at least rhetorically) for media ethics, though voiced largely among journalism academics, is manifesting itself. Although this concern is as yet culture-bound, it is trying to break with Machiavellianism, of whatever source, and in some places it is even proposing a global code of journalism ethics. Yet it cannot avoid the instrumental conformity of achieving predetermined ends— an all-embracing ethical code being one of them. Laws regarding the media are increasing, evidencing a need for more media control. Could it be that a state-driven ethical code on one hand, or a socially sanctioned one on the other, will be a further step?

At least five centuries before Machiavelli, a political adviser in India named Kautilya proposed harsh, sometimes ruthless, techniques for the state. But he mixed pragmatism with compassion for the poor, for women, and for slaves. He became a very early example of moral concern—at least in some areas. His major work, *Arthashastra,* is unique in Indian literature for its open advocacy of *realpolitik* and its clear arguments. Although he is seen as a forerunner to Machiavelli, Kautilya, unlike Machiavelli, had as his ultimate purpose service of the public welfare rather than protection of the sovereign. And Kautilya, unlike Machiavelli, did not justify the principle of "any means" (to achieve ends) against anybody. He clearly forbade (Chunder, 1970:184) the application of devious methods against "good and virtuous people," and he advised the king to use duplicity in his military efforts only when peaceful methods failed.

So we can see that Machiavellianism, like so many other European philosophies, really originated in the East. It has remained a powerful force in the world and lends potency today to the idea of state power and authoritarianism—however much the rationale of public service may be attached to it. Increased consideration of the benefits to society obviously decreases the emphasis on individualism and plays into the hands of those advocating big government. And big government always has an impact on how journalists can do their work and how the media can play their role in societies around the world.

A New Hope: Communitarianism?

The noted American sociologist, Robert Nisbet, has warned persistently against increasing state power. In his *Twilight of Authority* (1975), he pointed out the incessant loss of individual liberties to state power, and, in his Preface (xi), he noted that "something like a vacuum obtains in the moral order for large numbers of people."

The communitarians of today, of whom Nisbet is an example, are trying to reestablish community and values, to put the society above egoistic individualism, and to stress social obligation rather than an obsession with personal freedom. Communication theorist Clifford Christians (1993, 2002) has been a prominent voice in instilling communitarianism in journalism and public communication. Proposing "community conversation" and greater citizen involvement in civic society, Christians has been a leader in championing and popularizing journalistic communitarianism. Although it has met with some opposition in the West and not permeated the far reaches of the globe (and how could it in unfree societies?), communitarianism's media offspring, *public or civic* journalism, has reared its head especially in the United States and has been praised widely in both academic and journalistic circles (Lambeth, 1992). Public journalism proposes to democratize journalism by involving the public in the daily editorial decision making of the media.

A contributor to this belief in community "conversation" has been the German sociologist Juergen Habermas (1999). According to Clifford Christians (2002:65), Habermas "understands language to be an agent of culture and social organization" and stresses that "moral consciousness must be nurtured [in spite of] conditions of technocracy and institutional power that stifle autonomous action in the public area." Adding much to the concept of a "democratic" press, Habermas proposes a reason-based, census-forming public discussion forum in what he terms the "public sphere"—a space existing between the economy and the government where public opinion develops.

It is from this public opinion that the people can supervise government. They, in a sense, can take the place of the self-centered public media today.

All this suggests two main traditions of citizenship—at least in the West—emanating from Plato and Aristotle. Plato stressed the unitary state—the power center of the society—and believed that having loyalties other than those to this state was counter-productive. In contrast, Aristotle believed that individual citizens, through thought and common virtue, could best assure the progress and security of the state.

A Platonic Future?

According to Nisbet (262), the Platonic tradition has come down through Hobbes and Rousseau to today's social and political scene—and, logically, to today's journalistic scene. Nisbet notes that today the state (in some countries I would add big business) is the form of Hobbes's Leviathan and has "become the overriding form of oppression and exploitation." It is also quite possible that the press too, as a part of big business in its giant corporate and internationalized power, has become a mental and an emotional form of Leviathan that oppresses and exploits. It certainly has "the last word" in any critical debate or situation, and it sets the agenda for global dialogue.

Thomas Hobbes, a key figure in modern political thought, believed that a strong authority was necessary to avoid anarchy and to maintain social order. People tend to become Hobbesians when they face danger and the prospect of social disorder.

Around the world some spokesmen for journalism would view such a premise as absurd, seeing the press as basically pluralistic and generally weak and splintered, virtually powerless as an agent of either change or oppression. This view is more akin to that of Aristotle, the second main tradition: that of the pluralist nature of society. Aristotle posited that there is a point "at which a state [or a press system] may attain such a degree of unity as to no longer be a functioning entity—like 'harmony passing into unison, or rhythm which has been reduced to a single note" (Nisbet:262). Unity versus dispersion, statism or big media versus individualism and pluralism: this is the fundamental question of global media systems.

In one way or another, in spite of its size and development, the world's journalism is in the service of accumulating and bestowing power. At least the critics believe so. According to media scholar Robert McChesney (2002:15), journalism has proved to be "a superior propaganda organ for militarism and war." He proceeds (17):

> The historical record suggests we should expect an avalanche of lies and half-truths in the service of power. Journalists, the news media, should be extremely skeptical, demanding evidence for claims . . . and asking the tough questions that nobody in power wants to address. . . . [There is] control of our major news media by a very small number of very large and powerful profit-seeking corporations..[and] most journalists [see their] primary role as stenographers for official sources [and] do not recognize it as a problem for democracy.

The final half of this quotation, of course, deals with capitalistic press systems, but the first part applies equally (or perhaps more) to the more authoritarian, state-controlled countries. Power, in whatever form, tends to corrupt—journalists, political leaders, parties, corporations, and individuals all are vulnerable. Global journalists (unless they love paternalism and fear personal freedom), then, must be alert to oppose government power, but at the same time they must realize that media power can be just as harmful to the people.

Global Media Cultures

Media cultures in the world are, as Mao Zedong would say, like a thousand or more flowers blooming (and withering). Certain soils are producing some kinds of media cultures, and other soils are producing quite different ones. One of the main, if not the most important, determining ingredients is freedom—or lack of it, as was discussed earlier. Another ingredient is national security—or lack of it. Another is economic development—or lack of it. Another is a basic moral philosophy—or lack of it. And yet another is a democratic proclivity—or lack of it.

Freedom cultures are hard to find. They are related to individualism and to a desire of the people to impact their society, to lead, to progress, to express their own spirit and creativity, and to converse without inhibition with their neighbors. Generally, this kind of culture calls for a high degree of education, a tradition of antipaternalism, a sense of competition, and a respect for diversity. People, generally, are social animals, relating to the group, the community, the society, and the state. They feel a sense of security in escaping from freedom, as Erich Fromm has described it, and retiring into the anonymity of a group, crowd, party, ideology, religion, corporation, or state.

A growing global tendency in the media today is caution in exercising great freedom. In the present atmosphere of terrorist activities, or uncertainty in personal and group safety, the ideal of press freedom is hardly flourishing. Wars, military skirmishes, destructive incursions, constant threats, suicide (homicide) bombings, nuclear dangers, biological and chemical attacks, and other horrors are looming on every side.

The new century, which can be said to have had its true beginning in September 2001 with the airliner terrorist attacks on the World Trade Center and the Pentagon, anticipates ever more dangers that are leading to ever more restrictions on a free press around the world. Freedom, it seems, must take a back seat to national security.

Antifreedom or controlled media cultures certainly existed long before the modern splurge of national insecurity and international terrorism. Dictatorial governments and strongman leaders have been harnessing media systems to their own ends since such systems have existed. Especially in regions not predominantly liberal such as Asia, Africa, and the Middle East, political and religious elites have exercised firm control over the media. As we shall see in the later chapters of this book, the futures of these regions have been, and generally are, unimpressed by democracy and media libertarianism.

Even in countries like the United States, growing numbers of intellectuals have become skeptical about older liberal verities such as individualism, the free marketplace of ideas, and the strong emphasis on media freedom. For them, the public, or civic journalists among them, social responsibility and the community must take precedence over freedom.

Freedom is therefore having a hard time, both among dictatorial egoists in many less developed countries and among altruistic antiliberals in more economically advanced countries.

State ownership of media, threats, imprisonment or exile of journalists, murder, destruction of press property, control of newsprint, and licensing: all are bad signs for improved media freedom. Even in so-called democratic nations where the state itself is slow to dictate to the press, there are terrorist groups, drug lords and their "hit men," religious authorities, various "mafias," global cartels, and consumer groups of all kinds exercising their power over the press. The global press is always limited by influential persons or groups that have reason and power to see the press go in certain directions.

Some countries have basically an information culture, based on much raw data and very little interpretation. Others have "entertainment" media cultures in which the populace is kept relatively passive by submerging it in popular culture. And yet others, being submerged, are mixed cultures floundering about in a sea of information and entertainment. We can even point to others that have media cultures, which might be called "bulletin board" cultures whereby at least a portion of the citizens get governmental policy and official memos on a regular basis. In all countries, the media do little or nothing to stimulate citizen participation in government. It might be said that, by and large, the global media distract people from serious matters and self-rule and transport them into a mediated world of paradoxes, superficialities, conundrums, exciting escapades, atypical people, threatening situations, and unrelated vignettes.

Politics and economics are other important factors in the existence of various media cultures. It would seem that autocratic or nondemocratic national cultures are prone to have much less freedom. We can see this in Latin America (e.g., in Venezuela with Hugo Chávez in 2007–2008) where military regimes seem to succeed one another periodically. We can also see it in the so-called Third World generally. Politics is perhaps more important than economic development. An example might be in legalistic and autocratic (but developed) Singapore. Another highly developed example is in the expanding free-market nation of the People's Republic of China where the Communist Party keeps press freedom imprisoned. In the more democratic nations of Europe and North America, on the other hand, media systems tend to have much more freedom from government controls. It might be added that most, if not all, of these democratically inclined nations with maximum freedom are capitalistic or free-market countries, where other constraints, such as those imposed by advertisers, are placed on the media.

In the modern world, journalists *must* take various cultures into consideration. Things become difficult for everyone, for example, if a libertarian journalist tries to insert his or her values into an authoritarian society. It is natural to expect trouble. Common sense, it would seem, would militate against such counterproductive attempts, but common sense too often defers to nationalism and personal ethnocentrism. Among other intercultural scholars, Novinger (2001:156–157) stresses the need to know and respect other cultures and their rules. As for the communicator, she states that it is necessary to be motivated to communicate; to have a deep desire to overcome ethnocentrism through education; to have knowledge of a culture's communication styles, and to be positive, adaptable, and responsible.

Freedom and Responsibility

A major problem associated with talk about press freedom is "semantic noise"—the inherent difficulty of a common understanding of terms by the communicants. For example, multiple meanings can be read into the term *press freedom*. Intellectual classes, at least in more liberal rhetoric, seem to be in favor of press freedom. For one thing, it sounds good: talk about freedom and democracy tends to put one on the bright side of a darkening world.

Listen to a cacophony of mutterings worldwide about press freedom: Our press is free to support the policies of the state. We have a free press: one that is free to ignore the will of the people. Our press is not free of social pressures and tradition. Our press is free, but we have codes of ethics. Our press is free except for various press laws. Our press is free except for the will of the stockholders, directors, and editors. Our press is free but limited by advertisers. Press freedom belongs to the people, not the press. Freedom of the press belongs to the press, not the people. Our press is a democratic press. Our press cannot be free and democratic. Our press is free from vulgar and immoral material. Our press is free from profit-hungry entrepreneurs. Our press is free from global media oligarchies and greedy plutocrats. And on and on we could go.

In the United States, people simply say that press freedom is guaranteed in the First Amendment to the Constitution. So American journalists surely must know what press freedom is. This is not quite the case, however. A quick look at the First Amendment reveals that Congress will make no laws to abridge freedom—and not a clue as to what "freedom of the press" is; not a clue as to what limits there might be to freedom; not even a clue as to what the "press" is or might be.

But somehow, possibly due to the power and impact of American journalistic philosophy on the world, a fairly well-defined concept of press freedom has enthroned itself globally—and it is largely the American model. And this has developed in spite of the semantic fog that surrounds the use of the term. The U.S. core definition is this:

Press freedom is freedom from government interference   Note that Americans seldom talk about interference by corporate powers, advertisers, civil pressure groups, publishers, editors, et al. The concern is with government and with the press being autonomous—independent of government control.

But wait: the U.S. Constitution does not assure freedom from government. It says only that "Congress" should not dictate to the press through *laws*. It says nothing about "Government"—about the executive and the judicial branches. Constitutionally, the president and the courts can have a merry old time abridging the press's freedom. So when people around the world talk of press freedom in the "American sense," they seem to be talking about freedom from government, but really they are talking about freedom from press *laws*. No laws and the press is free? Not by a long shot. As we look at the press globally, we see very quickly that a press system may be throttled in many ways other than legally. Every military regime knows that. Every theocratic regime knows that. Every dictatorial ruler or king knows that.

Millions of words have been spilled trying to define press *responsibility*. But nobody seems to know what it is; it is a term as nebulous as "freedom." Press responsibility sounds fine and is often said to coexist nicely with freedom. But behind the glittering vagueness of the term lies the hidden loss of freedom. The basic questions are: Who determines press responsibility? Are these determinations free of personal (political, religious, etc.) bias? Is not "responsibility" a relative term? And there are other questions: Is not responsibility in the eye of the beholder? Can a press system be responsible to some and irresponsible to others at the same time? Is responsibility the same as ethics? There seems to be no universal meaning for the term *press responsibility.* From a U.S. perspective, this type of reasoning gives the green light to any and all Third World nations to insist that their press systems are "responsible" to their society and their culture. Empiricism may well show that many Third World media systems *actually do harm the society and can be called irresponsible.* But most critics calling a press system irresponsible base their verdict not on valid research, but on personal and ethnocentric bias.

One aspect regarding the issue of freedom and responsibility should again be underlined: *It cannot be assumed that if one has a free press, one has a responsible press.* It can be said that the freer the press, the more likely it is to spawn irresponsible units. At any rate, we know that freedom is like fire: it can be helpful to society, and it can also be harmful. In the United States, it is often said that Americans want a free *and* responsible press. Unfortunately, however, Americans, like people in the rest of the world, do not really know what either type of press system would be like in ideal circumstances.

Press and Democracy

Around the globe today there is much talk of democracy, even in the current atmosphere of the post–9/11 world, which has spread a cautious fear in government and media circles. Protection of the society and community has forced the media to take a more cooperative stance toward antidemocratic governments and to retrench themselves in an older more paternalistic position. Government controls in many parts of the world are being justified by the prevalent need for "national security." Government systems that were opening up to some degree are reverting to older tactics of intimidation, new press laws, imprisonment, and even violence against journalists in order to prevent dangerous excesses and irresponsible acts that endanger social stability.

The increased globalization of the media, however, has increased media mutterings about democracy and the role of the media in fostering political democracy. Yet, when we look closely at the various press systems in the regional chapters that follow, we will note that the press is doing little or nothing to bring larger and larger portions of the societies into active participation in governmental decisions. Governments are increasingly being run by plutocratic elites and bureaucracies, with the average citizen being dragged along without any substantial power to change the situation. This is even true in the more liberal West. This situation may not always be bad, writes Robert Kaplan in the *Atlantic Monthly.* He believes that if the citizens of a country are not well informed and in reasonable health, democracy can be not only risky but also dangerous (1997:55–80). Other factors, he notes, are needed for democratic development: notably, a solid educational system, national stability, a healthy economy, and good infrastructure and communications.

In the media itself, giant conglomerates are stretching their power around the world, heading toward a *truly global media system,* placing increasing emphasis on the business side and less emphasis on the purely journalistic (news–views) side. Media barons sit far-ther and farther from the newsrooms, participating in various enterprises and, in many countries, even in government itself. Journalists the world over are adjusting to the group-related media, to the community-oriented press, and are adapting to the proclaimed need for social responsibility and national "development." Stock prices and social restraints are dictating the editorial policies of media everywhere, and even in the more libertarian coun-tries the older concept of the press as "a watchdog on government" is being transformed into a "lapdog of government."

If democratization is really important in today's media world, the media will begin to stress ways the people can have greater impact on governmental decision making, and also how they (the media) can share their own decision making with the public. As has been shown in Iraq and other Middle Eastern countries, democracy cannot be forced on a peo-ple; the people must want it, and the media must support and promote it. However, it may well be that the people (and media and governments), especially in these difficult times, do not really care about expanding democracy and are anxious even to limit it for security, financial, and political reasons. For the government, and to a lesser extent, the media, talk about egalitarianism, a handmaiden of democracy, implies the giving up of media and state power and a special elite status.

Equality does not exist today, either in or out of the press, and there is no reason to expect it to emerge in the future. Intriguingly, however, many serious thinkers are accepting and encouraging that possibility. John Rawls, a Harvard philosopher, is one such person. His very influential *Theory of Justice* is a landmark work for those who are proponents of egalitarianism. Rawls, at least for some like sociologist Robert Nisbet (Templeton, 1979:191), equates justice with "fairness" and then concludes that justice and fairness are *equality*. Rawls indicates that he believes in equality, not just equality of opportunity. He contends (191) "that all men of reason and good will, when liberated from the misconceptions and prejudices of the social order they live in [illustrated by Rawls's technique of putting them into what he called the original position or behind the veil of ignorance], will easily reach the conclusion that society is built on the rock of equality."

The big problem with the media's democratization is that journalists like to think they are the determiners of news and the distributors of views. That's why many of them are in journalism. And as regards the governments' democratization ambitions, journalists are spokespersons and action agents *for* the people. Because the people cannot make these difficult political decisions (they are not inclined to or qualified to), the political elite (a plutocratic oligarchy) must do it for them. Certainly, the official rhetoric from government and the press would not contain anything as blunt as the above. For a free press's necessary relationship to democracy is well-engrained in modern thought. Even Karl Marx, especially in his younger days, saw press freedom as "the pre-requisite for a democratic way of life" (Hardt, 2001:26).

Today such optimism is not so strong, due largely to the authoritarianism that Marx himself spawned. But one big hope that "new journalists" around the world have thrown out is the potential of the Internet and other electronic marvels (including satellites) to involve increasing masses of people in global communication. Now, it is said, we can all be journalists. But it should be remembered that any meaningful democracy must be based on sound, verifiable information, and such information coming from the unchecked computer is hardly that. Also, elites can manipulate electronic communication, something that to a large degree is already being done by those with the requisite power and predilection.

Overly optimistic media leaders should remember the story of Prometheus who, in his argument with Zeus, provided his people with a kind of blind faith that kept them from foreseeing their own destruction. Here is what Darin Barney (2000:6) said in his *Prometheus Wired*:

> The story of modern technology is the story of Prometheus's people writ large: the story of humanity blindly wielding instruments to command and transcend that which is given, in hope of creating its own future.

Because computers are mainly calculating machines, Barney believes that they are devoid of "philosophical thought, ethical action, and, ultimately, wisdom itself." (220). He concludes (267) that whether network technology can aid democracy is problematic. In fact, he says, "If computer networks are to be involved in democracy at all, they are likely to be instruments of democracy at its worst, rather than at its best." In *Republic.com*, a book on the subject published in 2002, Cass Sunstein, like Barney, questions the value of the Internet and warns that Web technology to tailor the news may indeed cause democracy to suffer due to the proliferation of idle chatter, unchecked information, and a multitude of personal biases.

Not everyone shares Barney and Sunstein's thoughts about computer journalism. Many see this new technology as a way for more direct democracy to take place, for pluralism to increase, and for the state to lose some of its power over citizens. This assessment is based on two main assumptions: (a) that information put on the Internet by the average citizen will be accurate and worth sharing with others, and (b) that the information will be of the kind that will give citizens more political power and impact.

The argument in favor of the benefit of the Internet is strong. Anthony Kuhn, *Los Angeles Times'* correspondent in Beijing, maintains that in China the Internet is changing the face of the news, making it easier for the people to express themselves and harder for the government to censor (*Global Journalist,* 3rd Quarter, 2001:8). Other regions of the world have reported the same sentiment. But the matter is more complicated than that. Even in China there are provisions against "subversive material" and endangering national security and stability. It should also be noted that in China commercial Web sites are not permitted to report; they can only distribute news from official sources. While this situation does indeed help get news to more people, it is questionable whether that permits greater freedom of the press.

The sterile and outward signs of pseudodemocracy (where simply voting is equated with democracy) around the world are quite discouraging to true democrats. In spite of much rhetoric and the proliferation of technology, the future does not look bright for significant and enhanced "people participation" that permits greater numbers of people to have a meaningful part in their government or their media. Talking to one another or even voting is one thing; having a part in the actual business of the media or the government is quite another.

In the next decade or two, increasing critical attention is likely to be given to the part the world press actually plays in democratization. During the twentieth century there was little more than the assumption that media play a large role. Perhaps the twenty-first century may bring some kind of systematic grading of the media's performance in this area. And beyond that, the press may help to suggest some new kind of participatory government that goes beyond an authoritarian plutocracy.

The next few years will likely see information increasing a millionfold, but the questions we should ask are: Will it be significant to the people's needs, and will it be credible? The idea of every citizen becoming a journalist and thereby democratizing journalism is a fascinating one but is beset with an interesting problem. If journalism is the province of everyone, then there is really no need for journalism education (schools and departments) or even for the term *journalist,* which sets a group of people apart.

This brings us back to the question of accountability mechanisms, which, as Bertrand (2002) has pointed out, are seen in abundance throughout the world. The problem, again, is the tension between responsibility and freedom, as well as the whole matter of the nonscientific nature of ethical action. Freedom is at risk as these accountability mechanisms proliferate, and as ethical actions seem to diminish, fewer of these mechanisms are available.

Basic Journalistic Stances

Given what has already been discussed in this chapter, it will come as no surprise that several basic journalistic orientations can be found among the world's press systems. They might also be called perspectives or stances or, perhaps better, world views (from the German *Weltanschauung*) of journalists.

World journalists, generally speaking, have two main "superstances", which are reflected in the kind of journalism they wish to practice and the kind of press system they want for their countries. These are the *serious–analytical* and/or *popular–superficial* stances. Many persons may see the first as no "journalism" stance at all, but rather as a more elitist literary or philosophical stance. Perhaps this is true. But there are journalists, as found in the top quality newspapers and broadcasting outlets, who know they should provide substantive, interpretive, thoughtful news and views from a meaningful historical perspective. And the world is full of mass-appeal, popular journalists whose populist inclinations direct them into more superficial, entertainment-oriented, and polemical journalistic practices. Their basic formula is: scandal, sex, crime, gossip, and photos.

Innumerable other stances help define journalists globally. There are the artistic and the prosaic journalists; the existential and the rationalist; the liberal and the antiliberal; the egoistic and the altruistic; the communitarian and the individualistic; the libertarian and the authoritarian; the adversarial and the cooperationist; the religious and the secular; the objectivist and the subjectivist; the optimistic and the pessimistic; the egalitarian and the meritocratic; the ethical and the unethical; the realist and the idealist, ad infinitum. In truth, journalists everywhere are a mixture of all of these.

The artistic journalists, for example, seem to combine the stances of the existential, religious, subjectivist, cooperationist, communitarian, and idealist. In these journalists, the authoritarian strain is strong. They are found mainly in the Middle East, Asia, Latin America, and Africa. Then there are the more prosaic journalists, who tend to be more objective, realistic, scientific, and rational, as well as more adversarial and libertarian and more meritocratic. These journalists are found mainly in Europe and in North America—with some pockets on the Pacific Rim.

Obviously, these journalistic stances are correlated with media systems found throughout the world. It could be the old chicken and egg problem—did the journalists' stances cause the press system, or vice versa? Or did the nation's history and culture cause the journalistic stance and then the press system? We will not attempt to answer such questions in this brief introduction, but they are worth scholarly consideration. We do know that some journalists are inclined toward neutrality and passivity—so-called objectivity—and others tend to be more biased, opinionated, involved, propagandistic, and subjective. Neither stance is ever "pure," and the nature of a government and/or society always synthesizes their basic inclinations to some degree.

In short, global journalistic life is always one big compromise. A journalist is ever tied to his or her society, to the values, traditions, ideology, and political realities. This makes world journalism something of a mystery—a large puzzle forcing audiences to try to separate fact from opinion, compromise from authenticity, reality from myth.

Journalistic stances, it would seem, are a result of a combination of genetics and experiences. They are impossible to eliminate, although various power groups are doing what they can to limit their variety and to develop a more homogeneous journalism. The libertarian will say *vive la difference,* and the social engineers will continue their attempts to harmonize and coordinate journalistic stances and activities.

Media Accountability

Should global media systems and individual media be accountable for their messages? Though a basic and simple question, it requires more than just a "yes" or a "no" answer. Most (but certainly not all) journalists the world over would say that media should certainly be accountable. But accountable to whom? For which of their messages? And, most importantly, *how* will they be accountable?

Since about 1950, we have heard a lot of talk coming from national press systems and from global organizations such as UNESCO about the media's social responsibility. If the press is to be "responsible" to society, then it must in some way be accountable. In authoritarian countries, mechanisms of accountability are lodged with the government, the military, and sometimes rebel armed forces. In more libertarian countries, such mechanisms are found in public opinion, audience acceptance or rejection, pressure groups, and mainly in certain laws (e.g., libel law) that hold media accountable.

Theoretically, the freer and more open a country is, the fewer accountability mechanisms there are. Or at least, those that do exist are rather vague, seldom used, and in need of interpretation. As a country inclines toward authoritarianism or dictatorship (in whatever form), its accountability mechanisms become more blunt, brutal, and bellicose. Laws are more specific and unambiguous, and they are used more frequently to control the media.

One communication educator in France (at the University of Paris), Claude-Jean Bertrand, has probably given more attention to accountability mechanisms than any other scholar. He has developed what he terms "a strategy for democracy," which is a rather exhaustive list of ways media can be held accountable. He calls his list M*A*S—Media Accountability System—in which he maintains that a journalist's "moral conscience is not enough."

Bertrand (2002:18–23) refers to various "internal" and "external" accountability mechanisms. Internal M*A*Ss would include a common creed or code of ethics, correction boxes, in-house critics , readership surveys, and self-regulation. External M*A*Ss are such things as alternative media, journalism reviews, press councils, ethics courses, critical books and articles, and opinion surveys on the media. In addition, Bertrand mentions "cooperative" M*A*Ss, which include letters to the editor, ombudsmen, ethics coaches, continuing education, and prizes and rewards.

As Bertrand himself admits, the main objection to his M*A*S is a possible loss of freedom, which could only be dealt with in societies where voluntary and accepted accountability mechanisms are at work. His M*A*S instrumentalities will not function in societies with blatant and brutal methods of restriction.

Media responsibility (i.e., what the media should do) is quite subjective and semantically difficult. Accountability is more objective and operational. It is not always "fair," but it can open the media to criticism and more direct action that can (though not always) cause the media to reevaluate their policies and actions with the aim of bettering them.

Quality Journalism

Even if people generally had the desire and power to impact their government substantially, would global populations live in more efficient and safer societies? Perhaps. But it would assume that wisdom accompanies the public input.

At any rate, the question is academic, for there is little evidence that the masses worldwide harbor a deep desire for quality journalism. The global scene today shows the existence of only a handful of truly serious, sophisticated, high-quality media. The "advanced" Western journalists contend that there can be little quality in journalism unless the media system is capitalistic. Less developed countries see this attitude as one of arrogance and believe that quality is largely culturally defined. In spite of such scattered contentions, the virtual consensus is that quality in media systems does, in fact, depend on the degree of national development. Moreover, the majority of media scholars believe that most of the world's media are spreading their superficial, popular, lurid, sensational, and negative messages to audiences that seem basically satisfied with the fare. At least no evidence has emerged that populations (other than intellectuals) are demanding more serious fare.

Typical of the recent criticism of media quality is *Good Work: When Excellence and Ethics Meet* by Howard Gardner et al. (2001). Based on completed questionnaires from journalists, the authors conclude that the integrity of journalism has been compromised in recent years and that good reporting has declined. A reviewer of the book for *Nieman Reports* (James Carey, 2002:79–80) has summarized the basic media faults developed in the book as the following: Journalists work for market share rather than for truth and significance; values and ethics have declined; there appears to be a need to play to "vulgar" audience interests, and the media are filled with entertainment and sensationalism disguised as news. And there are many more critics. Until his recent death, Dr. Carey was CBS Professor of International Communication at Columbia University; he saw some signs of improvement, but they were few and not so bright.

The calls for better journalism, though well articulated and numerous, are like voices crying in the wilderness: they seem to have no effect. International journals such as *IPI Global Journalist, Journal of Global Mass Communication, Gazette, Ecquid Novi: African Journalism Studies, European Journal of Communication, Index of Censorship, Publizistik, Asian Journal of Communication,* and *Freedom Forum News* provide more than enough examples of poor or low-level journalism.

People are basically illiterate—either "attitudinally" or "functionally": they simply don't like to do much serious reading or thinking, and they are hooked on entertainment. One only need look at the media in whatever country to see this "opiate" of the masses at work. Thankfully, one can find small oases of quality in the midst of the vast desert of blandness, but a BBC, PBS and NPR program, a *National Geographic,* a *New York Times,* a *Neue Zürcher Zeitung,* a *Le Monde,* or an *El País* is not easy to find among the strident and shallow voices of the world's media.

Obviously, different concepts of journalistic quality (in newspapers or other media) exist in the world, but underneath the nationalistic and ideological variations we find a rather firm sense of media significance and value. Several studies related to global concepts of quality newspapers (e.g., Merrill, 1968; Merrill and Fisher, 1980) have pointed to a common core of requisites for a quality newspaper and a general conception of what the highest quality newspapers of the world are at a particular time. Enduring criteria for a "great" or quality international newspaper found in these studies mentioned are the following:

- Read by opinion leaders globally.
- Found in leading libraries of the world.
- Read by diplomats in various countries.
- Quoted in journalistic and literary circles.
- Used in speeches of world leaders.
- Good and effective typography and makeup.
- In-depth and serious content.
- Emphasis on international relations and politics.
- Emphasis on economics, science, religion, and ideas
- A cosmopolitan and interconnected approach to news
- Audience feedback and guest essays
- Emphasis on social criticism, literature, art, and music.

It is little wonder, then, that elite newspapers do not reach mass audiences. Populations the world over are either media illiterate or "attitudinally illiterate" and, if they do read, they avoid such serious and heavy journalistic fare. In the United States (and it is probably true elsewhere), young adults and the younger part of the baby boom generation, show the greatest decline in newspaper reading of any kind. What they do read is not politics, economics, religion, and international and cultural affairs—the big items of the quality newspapers. Research by organizations such as the Pew Centre in the USA and Media Tenor in South Africa show that most readers rather prefer to read about crime, community items, sports, and health, and less about "serious" news topics such as international news, science-technology, and religion.

Although these findings do not bode well for elite or quality journalism in the early decades of the twenty-first century, some notable examples of serious international newspapers around the world do exist, providing hope and direction for both journalists and readers seeking a journalism of substance. These newspapers include the following:

> *ABC* (Spain); *Al Ahram* (Egypt); *Asahi* (Japan); *Ashahi* (Japan); *Borba* (Yugoslavia); *Christian Science Monitor* (U.S.A.); *Dagens Nyheter* (Sweden); *El Norte* (Mexico); *El País* (Spain); *Frankfurter Allgemeine* (Germany); *Globe & Mail* (Canada); *Guardian* (U.K.); *Independent* (U.K.); *Le Figaro* (France); *Le Monde* (France); *Los Angeles Times* (U.S.A.); *Mail&Guardian* (South Africa); *Mainichi Shimbun* (Japan); *Miami Herald* (U.S.); *Neue Zürcher Zeitung* (Switzerland); *New York Times* (U.S.A.); *Osservatore Romano* (Italy); *Süddeutsche Zeitung* (Germany); *The Independent* (U.K.); *The Times* (U.K.); *The Wall Street Journal* (U.S.); *Washington Post* (U.S.A.)

Typical of the well-informed elite, "saving remnant" of the world's journalism, these papers are proof that journalism can meet high standards if there is a journalistic will and a growing desire by populations to raise their sights. These elite papers serve as examples of good journalism and should inspire journalists—even if merely out of a sense of envy—to raise their standards.

Envy is usually regarded as negative and harmful, but it can be a positive influence too. It can challenge a monopoly of power; it can help propel innovation; and it can be a significant motivating factor for quality. The envious publisher or journalist might well strive to elevate his medium onto an elite level. According to Helmut Schoeck (1966:416–417), envy can turn into "an agonistic impulse," seeking to outdo others, and thus become a value-enhancing force.

The fact is that future and current journalists *should* envy the quality media of the world and aspire to attain that kind of journalism, for only then can global media improve. Contrary to those who insist that the media should simply provide what the people want, journalism must fill a deeper need. This position may perhaps only reflect one's Western ethnocentrism, but examples of journalistic quality are indeed to be found, rising like mountains above a dry and intellectually suffocating media desert. And these mountains must call all serious journalists to their lofty, though often dangerous, heights.

The Future

If the present global media picture provides any clue to the future, that future does not appear to be one that inspires respect and confidence. The volume of voices will increase far beyond their need or value. It will become harder to find credible information, and high ethical standards will be the exception as the bottom line further devours authentic journalism. Television and movies will increasingly deliver entertainment, superficial news, and vulgar displays of sex and violence. Bias in the media will be standard fare, and public interest publishing and broadcasting will be found in fewer and fewer elite journals and broadcast channels. Publishing groups will continue buying up the media, especially in the West. Advertising will continue to swallow up larger portions of space and time in the public media. Autocratic leaders in most of the world will continue to control information.

Timidity, spawned by a growing sense of "political correctness," will emasculate authentic journalism. Politics and journalism will further merge their interests, and the people will cease to recognize credible information even when it periodically appears.

Education for journalism and communication will become ever more political and biased in its progovernment stance. In the West, giant corporations will make further inroads into academic enterprises, building their edifices and giving them grants, and this financial largesse will discourage impartial classroom teaching. The same will be true of increased government educational grants tied to specific expectations. If the trend is not reversed, journalism education will be directed by big business and big government, and the students, indoctrinated in paternal and/or patriotic dependency, will inject this philosophy into their media.

In the Third World or developing (usually noncapitalistic) countries, the traditional autocracies will continue to direct the media, using them basically as instruments for social control. The rationale for such authoritarianism is usually that "tribal peoples" want it, that national security demands it, and that civil harmony requires it, or that the masses lack the desire or knowledge to rule. It seems a rather common belief, following after Thomas Hobbes, that humankind's natural condition is "war of all against all"; it was against such anarchy that a powerful state (Leviathan) was needed to impose order. People everywhere, believes Francis Fukuyama (1999:145), tend "to become Hobbesians when faced with the prospect of disorder."

Authoritarianism is seductive: it possesses a beguiling quality and a disciplined aura, providing a lure for orderly minds who want structure and social engineering, and a sense of security and institutional stability. It is a potent sociopolitical magnet that pulls unceasingly at nations and people—and also at journalism. It implies authority, and it satisfies the desire of the masses for leadership. In many countries, even journalists feel comfortable when they know strong hands are at the editorial tiller.

The futuristic scene also offers some optimistic pictures. First, a few outstanding, quality or elite journals will likely persist against the surge of informational mediocrity and crassness. Newspapers such as the *New York Times, Neue Zürcher Zeitung, El País, Le Monde, The Independent,* and the *Frankfurter Allgemeine Zeitung* will continue to improve and to provide credible information. Fortunately, a few newspapers will provide the serious reader with a synthesized view of the world's growing complexity and will move away from the splintered, isolated news snippets that characterize journalism of today. A world leader in this new context of integrated journalism has been the innovative *Independent* of the United Kingdom. "So what?" will take its place alongside "what" and "why" as the main question in future news stories in quality newspapers.

A few outstanding, serious channels will do the same for TV viewers. Above the superficial chatter of most television programming will be perhaps a dozen leaders in quality throughout the world. The British Broadcasting Corporation airs a number of thoughtful and educational programs, and in the United States outlets such as the History Channel and programs similar to Bill Moyers' *Journal* and the *Jim Lehrer News Hour* provide springs of clear water in the growing deserts of vulgar and polluted broadcast journalism.

A new information world existing alongside institutional journalism will be the domain of the bloggers and other Internet individualists, who will substantially add to the quantity of information. Their pluralism and freedom, if unrestrained by governments, will undoubtedly lead to more "democratic" information systems in the West. This new cyberspace journalism in the Third World, however, will be expunged of its freedom in due time and will be tailored to fit the authoritarian agenda.

Information and journalism (institutional and private) may well combine and form something perhaps called "informatics" that will be quantitatively monumental. Technologically, the "word" will be with us everywhere we go. We will have a surfeit of information. These questions, however, will linger: Just what can we believe? What does it all mean? Hopefully, the reader of this book will find answers to some of these perplexing questions.

BIBLIOGRAPHY

Barney, D. *Prometheus Wired: The Hope for Democracy in the Age of Network Technology.* Chicago: University of Chicago Press, 2000.

Bertrand, C.-J. "A Strategy for Democracy," *Media Ethics* 13, No. 2 (Spring 2002), 18–23.

Carey, J. W. "What Does 'Good Work in Journalism Look Like?" *Nieman Reports* 56, No. 1 (Spring 2002), 79–81.

Chen, G., and Storosta, W. (eds.). *Communication and Global Society.* New York: Peter Lang, 2000.

Christians, C. G., and Bracci, S. L. (eds.). *Moral Engagement in Public Life.* New York: Peter Lang, 2002.

Christians, C., G., Ferré, J. P. and Fackler, P. M. *Good News: Social Ethics & the Press.* New York: Oxford University Press, 1993.

Chunder, P. C. *Kautilya on Love and Morals.* Calcutta: Jayanti, 1970.

Freedom House. *Freedom of the Press 2004.* Karin Deutsch Karlekar (ed.). New York: Freedom House, 2004.

Fukuyama, F. *The Great Disruption.* New York: Simon & Schuster (Touchstone), 1999.

Gardner, H., Csikszentmihalhi, M., and Damon, W. *Good Work: When Excellence and Ethics Meet.* New York: Basic Books, 2001.

Habermas, J. *The Structural Transformation of the Public Sphere.* Cambridge, MA: Polity Press, 1989.

Hardt, H. *Social Theories of the Press.* Lanham, MD: Rowman & Littlefield, 2001.

Holmes, S. *The Anatomy of Antiliberalism.* Cambridge, MA: Harvard University Press, 1996.

Kaplan, R. "Democracy Just for a Moment." *Atlantic Monthly* (December 1997), 55–80.

Kuhn, A. "China: Internet Boom Changes Face of News." *IPI Global Journalist* (3rd Quarter 2001), 8.

Lambeth, E. *Committed Journalism.* Bloomington: Indiana University Press, 1992.

McChesney, R. W. "The US News Media and World War III." *Journalism* 3, No. 1 (April 2002), 14–21.

Merrill, J.C. *Media, Mission, and Morality.* Spokane, WA: Marquette Press, 2007.

———. *The Elite Press: Great Newspapers of the World.* New York: Pitman, 1968.

———. *The Princely Press: Machiavelli on American Journalism.* Lanham, MD: University Press of America, 1998.

Merrill, J. C., and Fisher, H. *The World's Great Dailies.* New York: Hastings House, 1980.

Merrill, J. C., Gade, P., and Blevens, F. R. *Twilight of Press Freedom: The Rise of People's Journalism.* Mahwah, NJ: Lawrence Erlbaum, 2001.

Nisbet, R. *Twilight of Authority.* Indianapolis, IN: Liberty Fund, 1979.

Novinger, T. *Intercultural Communication: A Practical Guide.* Austin: University of Texas Press, 2001.

Oakeshott, M. *Hobbes on Civil Association.* Indianapolis, IN: Liberty Fund, 1975.

Schoeck, H. *Envy: A Theory of Social Behavior.* Indianapolis, IN: Liberty Fund, 1966.

Spencer, H. *The Man Versus the State.* Indianapolis, IN: Liberty Fund, 1984.

Sunstein, C. *Republic.com.* Princeton, NJ: Princeton University Press, 2002.

Templeton, K. S., Jr. (ed.). *The Politicization of Society.* Indianapolis, IN: Liberty Fund, 1979.

Trueblood, D. E. *General Philosophy.* Grand Rapids, MI: Baker Book House, 1963.

Ward, S. J. and Wasserman, H. (eds.). *Media Ethics Beyond Borders: A Global Perspective.* Johannesburg: Heinemann, 2008.

2 Critical and non-Western Press Philosophies

HERMAN WASSERMAN
University of Sheffield, UK

Global media today are developing rapidly due to technological advances that have led to paradoxical outcomes: while media are truly global in their reach, they have also become more personalized and interactive, leading to an increased fragmentation of audiences and to a blurring between producers and receiver of media messages, to such an extent that one might have to refer to the latter group as "people formerly known as the audience" (Rosen, 2006). Classifying media systems in such a fluid, changing environment is a difficult task.

Yet the global media's reach and their inclusivity are also illusory in many ways. New media technologies, while changing the way journalism is practiced, consumed, and even defined, are not the free-for-all the surrounding rhetoric makes them out to be. In many parts of the world, as well as within some of the richest countries on the globe, people remain excluded from these technologies because they lack the material and social means of access these technologies require. Nor does the enabling power of the new media mean that journalism can now be practiced without fear or favor across the world, as the regular reports (for instance, in 2007 from China, Africa, and the Middle East) about journalists being killed, harassed, tortured or imprisoned attest.

Culturally, global media are increasingly central to our lives. Especially in the so-called developed world, media have become "environmental" (Silverstone, 2007). The world today is perhaps more interdependent and interconnected than ever before, thanks in large part to the pervasive role global media play. In a world where the local and the global combine and are interlinked, one could perhaps say that all journalism is global journalism. But the fact that global media enable us to know more about people in far-away countries, regions, and cultures has not necessarily led to greater understanding of or empathy for them. One of the central moral dilemmas in this era of global media has become the question of "proper distance" (Silverstone, 2007). How close should the media bring us to the Other without invading their privacy or make voyeurs of us? When are the media not bringing us close enough, allowing us to remain apathetic to the lot of the poor and destitute around the world?

In thinking about journalism in this era of global, environmental media one should avoid the temptation of simplistic dichotomies, static systems, and familiar models. New thinking is needed in the contemporary era. On the other hand, the often glib and celebratory rhetoric about the new media that rapid technological changes in the global landscape have occasioned is not very helpful either in helping us understand how geopolitical power relations and global inequalities inherited from, say, colonialism and the Cold War, still persist today. Similarly, the demise of the nation-state in favor of cosmopolitan perspectives (e.g., Rantanen, 2007) can also be exaggerated to such an extent that geopolitical power imbalances remain masked (cf. Sparks, 2007).

What is clear is that the role of media and journalism in the contemporary world has become much more central to society than ever before. Media and journalism now impact our lives not only on a political level, but increasingly also on cultural, economic, and social levels. And while global journalism plays an important role in politics around the world, as Josephi (2005) has pointed out, simply equating journalism with democracy would eclipse the role of journalism in many of the world's nations that do not meet the normative description of democratic, pluralistic media in its Western incarnation. The distinction between *quality journalism* in its latter (normative) form and supposedly lesser variants elsewhere, such as information, entertainment, and bulletin board cultures (Merrill, in this volume) tends to neglect the way in which political, economic, and social life are increasingly intertwined by way of global media. Big media empires like Google and News Corp are powerful economic players on the world stage, not simply critical spectators keeping governments in check. Political interests are linked to these economic interests, as several examples, including Google's self-censorship in China (more about this below) and *The Sun*'s (owned by Murdoch's News Corp) support for New Labour in the UK, have again illustrated in the last few years. Increasingly, new media technologies have extended the very definition of journalism itself. The blurring of the divide between news consumer and producer has led to the rise of *citizen journalism,* in which people formerly known as audience members now contribute news and photographs through cell phones, sometimes beating journalists working for mainstream news outlets to the story (as in the case of the Virginia Tech Massacre, for instance—Editors Weblog, 2007)—even if what is gained in terms of speed of coverage is sometimes lost in terms of depth or technical quality.

In the context of the rapidly evolving, shifting, and interactive global media context, today one would have to define *press systems* in a more dynamic, complex way than differentiating between them primarily on the basis of state-media relations and using nation-states as the unit of comparison. Appadurai's (1996) well-known framework for understanding the global cultural economy in terms of mediascapes, ethnoscapes, technoscapes, financescapes, and ideoscapes places media in an interdependent relation to other dimensions of globalization. Global press systems in the age of globalization can therefore no longer be understood in terms of older, Western-biased models of center-periphery, or in one-dimensional terms, such as state/government-media relationships.

In this contemporary scenario, the tension between established normative ideals for press systems around the world, as discussed by Merrill in this volume, and the descriptive reality of a multileveled and dynamic global mediascape, seems to increase. As Josephi (2005) has shown, journalism studies have always been marked by a tension between descriptive accounts and normative models, and normative theories for the media have not always reflected the changing dynamics of journalism and media. This is not to say that normative theories should mirror the descriptive reality of global journalism—indeed, normative theories pose an ideal for journalism globally. But the slippage between normative and descriptive should not result from ignorance of the developments of journalism in a contemporary world. An attempt to analyze and evaluate global press systems today should at least start from the acknowledgment that normative debates in journalism studies have been dominated by Western-centered frameworks, and that a "tiny handful of countries" were made to represent the whole of the world's press systems (Curran and Park, 2000:3). To overcome this Western bias, more perspectives from around the world need to be included when analyzing global press systems. However, it is important to note that this should not merely take the form of measuring "other" press systems against the normative measure of an American version of press freedom that has "enthroned itself globally" (Merrill, in this volume). A truly global perspective on press systems will have to consider the role of global journalism today in terms of its various dimensions and how these interrelate with and interconnect to each other. It is not the aim of this chapter to attempt such an analysis, but to point toward the various dimensions of global journalism that would need to be taken into account in the reevaluation of press system models. In the remainder of this chapter, some of the main features of these various dimensions are outlined in an attempt to map the terrain on which a rethinking of such a media theory could take place. These dimensions should be seen as interdependent and complementary, and a classification of global media systems in the contemporary global arena cannot be made on the basis of one of them in isolation.

Political Dimensions

Although the demise of the nation-state (as a result of, inter alia, increased migration and the stronger role of multinational financial institutions over and above national governments) is widely regarded as one of the consequences of contemporary globalization, the impact of state policies on media systems worldwide is far from negligible, as Merrill shows in this volume.

Recent examples of how the state can clamp down on media to meet their political ends are Zimbabwe and China. In Zimbabwe, it is extremely difficult for journalists to perform their newsgathering and reporting task critically and independently without falling foul of strict laws that can result in long jail terms or steep fines (AMDI, 2006; MISA, 2005). In China, electronic media are heavily censored—for instance, the limits imposed on the search engine Google (BBC, 2006) and the video-sharing Web site YouTube (Stanway and Johnson, 2008). The desire of the state to align the media with its vision of the nation, and its power to do so, are therefore still very much present in many parts of the contemporary, globalized world. However, it is not possible to simply equate "economically sound and free" media with a democratic political culture as opposed to ones that are "financially struggling and largely controlled by their governments" (Merrill, in this volume). China's media has embarked on a "profound commercialization process" over the past decade and a half, without the media necessarily having the power to challenge the Chinese government's control of the media (Huang, 2007:402). While optimists believe that the commercially strong, economically liberalizing Chinese media might contribute in the long run to a political democratization, this process takes the form more of an ongoing negotiation (Huang, 2007:402) than an inevitable causal link, as conventional liberal democratic press system theory seems to suggest. And in the United States, economic pluralism is not a safeguard against government control of images or management of news—as in the case of the ban of photographs or footage of dead soldiers returning from Iraq (Harper, 2003).

But pitting global media in a struggle for independence against political power vested in the nation-state alone neglects the importance of regional formations and discourses through which political power is articulated, amplified, or undermined. In the aftermath of 9/11, the United States and the UK, along with its allies in the "coalition of the willing" formed a power bloc that also impacted on global media discourses (see, for instance, Kamalipour and Snow, 2004; Berenger, 2004). News networks like Al Jazeera in the Middle East, and TeleSUR in Latin America have started to provide contra-flows of news to the dominant Western networks like CNN. Even so, the relation between global media and these new power blocs are more intricate than merely a dichotomy between the West and the Rest, with political power-play internal to the regions also influencing media–political relations (see, for instance, how attempts to forge closer ties between Qatar and Saudi Arabia had repercussions for coverage on Al Jazeera; Worth, 2008).

In Africa, the New Plan for Africa's Development (or NEPAD) created a framework for a regional, pan-African identity to emerge within or against which journalists negotiated their occupational identities. In the process, the notion of African journalism came into tension with Western, liberal notions of journalistic roles as they had been imported into African nation-states (Kanyegirire, 2006; Wasserman, 2005). In this process, we can observe, as Sparks (2000a:79) writes, "the erosion of the power and influence of the state-based media on the one hand, and a parallel strengthening of both the local and the global media."

The globalization of media can thus have a range of different influences on media on local, national, regional, and global levels. This process becomes especially evident in countries undergoing transition, when the local-national-global nexus gets rearranged. A case in point is post-apartheid South Africa. With the demise of apartheid, the country emerged from isolation, and its media industry was opened up for the entry of foreign media behemoths like the Irish multinational Independent Group. At the same time that global media entered the country, the forces of globalization were met with a renewed awareness of the local—for instance by the development of community media to provide an alternative to commercial national and global media.

In the light of these considerations, one could agree with Merrill (in this volume) that the American model of press freedom has "enthroned itself globally" as a normative concept that is also used as an indicator of where countries rank with regard to how successfully they have conformed to a circumscribed discourse of "freedom." Yet, as Hallin and Mancini (2004) have shown (and also reiterated by Josephi, 2005), significant tensions exist between this globalized, American-inspired normative notion of media-state relations and the descriptive reality of different models in existence in various localities and regionalities across the world. Simply accepting the former as the only, or correct way to view global media, neglects a slippage between ideal and reality.

In this contemporary global political arena, the media's role vis-à-vis political systems will therefore have to be seen more broadly than in terms of the nation-state primarily (which is not the same as discounting the continued influence of the nation-state, but to point to the need of considering other political power formations as well). Moreover, journalists often negotiate between various, often conflicting loyalties and occupational identities on local, national, and regional levels, resulting in hybrid positions depending on context (Kanyegirire, 2006). A view of global press systems can therefore not lapse into simplistic binaries or neat systems like authoritarianism versus liberal pluralism, but have to account for the multileveled, complex relationships between journalists and political power.

Economic Dimensions

The dominant liberal press system theory, exported via the United States to various contexts around the world (even though values such as truthtelling and independence are interpreted differently according to contextual factors), sees journalism's primary power struggle as directed against state interference in order to essentially protect individual freedom and access to information. While this struggle remains an important one, albeit it refracted through new political discourses as mentioned above, a press system theory for contemporary global media has to be based on a more complex understanding than a binary between state-controlled and free-market, pluralistic media systems. Apart from the fact that such a view raises paradoxes in the case of countries like China, where commercial media thrive economically within a restrictive political environment, it also underplays the control exerted over media by means of the "free" market itself, or by the more subtle workings of political hegemony linked with economic interests. In the United States, for example, the media operate in one of the most, if not the most, economically "free" environments in the world. Yet the market imposes its own limitations on the journalistic discourse. Why do major cable companies in the United States refuse to carry Al Jazeera? Is it only because there is "no market" for it, or is it because, according to the hegemonic political discourse in the United States, Al Jazeera is a propaganda tool for Islamic fundamentalism, and that therefore providing a politically dubious media channel on a cable bouquet would invite a backlash from politicians, interest groups, and subscribers, and therefore be "bad for business"(Al-Jadda, 2007)?

Furthermore, classifying press systems in terms of the economic dispensation within a given country or region neglects the way in which the global economy is now characterized by greater interdependence than ever before. The global media's central position in the global information economy necessitates a view of press systems not in terms of discrete nation-states or even regions, but complex global intersections between the local, national, and global. In this mediated globe, media, economic interests and political power are intertwined in ways that defy easy or neat categorization. For instance, decrying China as an example of an authoritarian media system might be accurate in terms of its political system, but the internal political power on the level of the nation-state is further amplified by global economic interdependence. The result may be new alliances between states whose press systems might seem very different when considered in isolation. This was exemplified by the controversial decision by the (U.S.-based) multinational media behemoth Google to introduce a browser in China that would self-censor searches in order to comply with the Chinese government's restrictions on information. In order to further its business interests, a company from the free-market, pluralistic U.S. media agreed to comply with Chinese censorship of sensitive topics like the Tiananmen protests and Taiwanese independence (BBC, 2006)

Examples like these confirm the assumption that the free market not only enables, but can also limit, the democratic freedom of the media. Propaganda is not only the prerogative of governments, as Herman and Chomsky (1988) have argued. On the other hand, a crude political economic criticism of economic influence over journalism can also lose sight of the way that journalists display agency in negotiating their professional roles within specific contexts where complete independence from economic interests may seem a naïve ideal. In some African countries, the practice of "brown envelope journalism" (called *gombo* in Cameroon; Ndangam, 2006), in terms of which journalists are paid per diems by their news sources, is often the only way in which to fulfill the newsgathering function of journalism in an environment with little infrastructure and constrained by dire poverty. But even in these dire circumstances, journalists are not mere victims of economic circumstances, but negotiate the tensions between their professional identities and their economic circumstances (Ndangam, 2006).

A view of press systems that dismisses outright the whole of sub-Saharan Africa because it does not conform to dominant Western notions of independence and pluralism, without attempting to understand the ways in which journalism functions within societies marked by high levels of poverty, or within cultural frameworks where communication takes on different social meanings, is not only biased but also analytically of limited use.

Cultural Dimensions

One of the problems associated with a static conception of media systems that focuses almost exclusively on formal aspects like a political dispensation and the legal framework, within which media operate, is that it does not allow for the fluid, dynamic ways in which people use media. Generalizations are often made that media systems in sub-Saharan Africa or Central Asia fail their duty toward the public because the content of their messages does not comply with dominant notions of credibility, substance, or neutrality. Such generalizations are made possible by focusing almost exclusively on what Stuart Hall (1973) referred to as the "encoding" moment of communication.

Almost exclusively, attention is directed at structural factors like political, legal, and economic factors impacting on the way that media messages are constructed. Yet, what is neglected in such a structural view of press systems is the way that people interact with media, or in Hall's terms, "decode" it. For such a broader view of media in global settings to emerge, a more dynamic, culturist approach to media would have to be adopted. Such an approach would correlate with what Couldry (2007) referred to as a comparative analysis of "media cultures":

> The analysis of "media cultures" can only develop through combining two types of comparison: first, a comparative analysis of the more "intangible", more subtle, aspects of the media environment in different places (for example, the relative social and symbolic status

given to celebrities, fans, media representatives, and so on); and second, the degree to which media rituals are embedded in wider belief structures, whether economic, political, religious or social. (Couldry, 2007:248)

Such an approach does not mean ignoring the structural factors. On the contrary, it would be "based on a rigorous analysis of the institutional structures and flows that sustain distinctive media cultures" (Couldry, 2007:249). Importantly, however, the analysis becomes more fluid and dynamic because what is analyzed is now not just "distinctive national systems," but also "nationally inflected but transnationally salient media flows," because "we cannot simply assume that national media systems magically secrete distinctive 'national' media cultures" (Couldry, 2007:249). Such a complex, dynamic, and open-ended approach is better suited to media in a postmodern, globalized world where boundaries and borders have become diffuse and reconfigured. This argument should not be mistaken for relativism based on the view that borders and boundaries have become obsolete, or that there is no difference between the media in, say, Venezuela and the United States, or between China and South Africa. As was mentioned earlier in this chapter, political, economic, and cultural dimensions of global media should be considered together, as they are interdependent. An integrated and culturally "thick" approach would therefore focus not only on audience agency to the neglect of structural (political and economic) factors. It would, however, result in a richer understanding of the ways in which media users interact with structural conditions and negotiate meanings within them.

In other words, journalists and their audiences (or those formerly known as such) will be viewed as having agency rather than being mere cogs in an overdetermined structure.

Of course, it is not a question of either structure or agency—it is exactly the interplay between structure and agency that will make dynamic analyses of global media cultures interesting and challenging. Such an approach would therefore not only condemn the media system in Zimbabwe because of the repressive state control over the press, but also consider how other, creative forms of journalism (for instance, in the form of popular music; Mano, 2007) emerge in such circumstances, or how audiences negotiate meaning "between the lines" of official discourse, or how alternative information seeps through the cracks of repression by means of clandestine pamphlets or broadcasting, or how they cope with repression through rumor, gossip, cartooning or jokes: what Nyamnjoh refers to as *radio trottoir,* or radio of the pavement (2005:23). Such forms of communication might not satisfy the purist normative media frameworks of Western liberal democracy that have become so authoritative globally, but taking them seriously will contribute to a more richly textured, thicker view of global journalism. Such a culturist approach will mean disposing of the long-standing strategy of elevating a certain elite style of "quality" or "serious" journalism to a norm to be followed universally.

The elitist view of "quality journalism," which has also led to the disparaging of popular forms like tabloid journalism, has perhaps more to do with safeguarding entrenched practices and journalism's adversity to change and its immunity (or one could say allergy) to critical self-reflection (Zelizer, 2000:ix, xi) than it has with contributing to the democratization of global journalism. Popular journalism, so disparaged and abhorred by "serious" journalists and journalism scholars, can often "offer journalism a bridge back to the public and the public sensibility which it is supposed to serve" (Zelizer, 2000:xi). While the basic question that remains is who decides what quality is and for whom, the hierarchy between high and popular culture has also become scrambled in an era when the predominance of the printed word has made way for a range of new media that have changed even the way "serious" news platforms convey the news. It therefore makes more sense, as Sparks (2000b:14) has done, to distinguish between different positions that newspapers (and other media for that matter) can occupy on a continuum (as opposed to a hierarchy), and where different outlets can avail themselves of different styles and approaches at different times, or even combine them simultaneously.

Conclusion

Media within the contemporary global landscape is constantly changing and developing, articulated through a diverse set of political, social, economic, and cultural relations globally. It is developing apace due to new technologies that allow it to change shape and broaden its reach in ways never imagined before. Yet within this brave new global media world, older legacies, power relations, and imbalances still persist. To capture the variety of forms that journalism can take within this world and to analyze it systematically is a daunting task. It needs flexibility, openness, and a dynamic approach. This chapter has just begun to outline some of the issues that such an approach will have to grapple with if it wants to be truly global in its reach, and contemporary in its scope.

BIBLIOGRAPHY

Al-Jadda, S. "Does Al Jazeera Belong in the USA?" *USA Today* December 19, 2007. Available: http://blogs.usatoday.com/oped/2007/12/does-al-jazeera.html. Accessed on 5 January 2008.

AMDI (African Media Development Initiative). "Zimbabwe: AMDI Research Report." 2006. Available: http://www.bbc.co.uk/worldservice/trust/researchlearning/story/2006/12/061208_amdi_zimbabwe.shtml. Accessed January 5, 2008.

Appadurai, A. *Modernity at Large*. Minneapolis: University of Minnesota Press, 1996.

BBC. "Google Move 'Black Day' for China." 2006. Available: http://news.bbc.co.uk/2/hi/technology/4647398.stm. Accessed January 2, 2008.

Berenger, R. D. (ed.). *Global Media Go to War*. Spokane, WA: Marquette Books, 2004.

Couldry, N. "Researching Media Internationalization: Comparative Media Research as If We Really Meant It." *Global Media and Communication* 3, No. 3 (2007), 247–271.

Curran, J., and Park, M.-J. "Beyond Globalization Theory." In Curran, J. and Park, M-J. (eds.), *De-Westernizing Media Studies*. London: Routledge, 2000.

The Editors Weblog. "US: Virginia Tech Tragedy Breeds Blog-style, Citizen Journalism from Mainstream Media," 2007. Available: http://www.editorsweblog.org/news/2007/04/us_virginia_tech_tragedy_breeds_blogstyl.php. Accessed January 2, 2008.

Hall, S. *Encoding and Decoding in the Television Discourse*. Stencilled Occasional Paper no. 7, CCCS, Birmingham. 1973.

Hallin, D. C., and Mancini, P. *Comparing Media Systems: Three Models of Media and Politics*. Cambridge: Cambridge University Press, 2004.

Harper, T. "Pentagon Keeps Dead out of Sight." *The Toronto Star*. November 2, 2003. Available: http://foi. missouri.edu/bushinfopolicies/transfertubes.html. Accessed on January 7, 2008.

Herman, E. S., and Chomsky, N. *Manufacturing Consent: The Political Economy of the Mass Media*. New York: Pantheon, 1988.

Huang, C. "Editorial: From Control to Negotiation: Chinese Media in the 2000s." *The International Communication Gazette* 69, No.5 (2007), 402–412.

Josephi, B. "Journalism in the Global Age: Between Normative and Empirical." *Gazette* 67, No. 6 (2005), 575–590.

Kamalipour, Y. R., and Snow, N. (eds.). *War, Media and Propaganda: A Global Perspective*. Lanham, MD: Rowman & Littlefield, 2004.

Kanyegirire, A. "Hybrid Journalistic Identities? Journalism(s) and NEPAD." *Ecquid Novi: African Journalism Studies* 27, No. 2 (2006), 159–178.

Mano, W. "Popular Music as Journalism in Zimbabwe." *Journalism Studies* 8, No. 1 (2007), 61–78.

MISA (Media Institute of Southern Africa). *So This Is Democracy?* Windhoek: MISA, 2005.

Ndangam, L. "'Gombo': Bribery and the Corruption of Journalism Ethics in Cameroon." *Ecquid Novi: African Journalism Studies* 27, No.2 (2006), 179–199.

Rantanen, T. "The Cosmopolitanization of News." *Journalism Studies* 8, No. 6, (2007), 843–861.

Rosen, J. "The People Formerly Known as the Audience." *Pressthink*. Available: http://journalism.nyu. edu/pubzone/weblogs/pressthink/2006/06/27/ppl_frmr.html. Accessed January 3, 2008.

Silverstone, R. *Media and Morality. On the Rise of the Mediapolis*. Cambridge: Polity, 2007.

Sparks, C. "The Global, the Local and the Public Sphere.", In Wang, G., Servaes, J. and Goonasekera, A. (eds.), *The New Communications Landscape: Demystifying Media Globalization*, 74–95. London: Routledge, 2000a.

———. "Introduction: The Panic over Tabloid News." In Sparks, C. and Tulloch, J. (eds.), *Tabloid Tales— Global Debates over Media Standard*, 1–40. London: Rowman & Littlefield. 2000b.

———. "What's Wrong with Globalization?" *Global Media and Communication* 3, No. 2 (2007), 133–155.

Stanway, D., and Johnson, B. "The Videos We Laughed, Winced and Wondered at Are blocked by China." *The Guardian*, January 4, 2008. Available: http://www.guardian.co.uk/technology/2008/jan/04/ youtube.video. Accessed January 4, 2008.

Wasserman, H. "Talking of Change: Constructing Social Identities in South African Media Debates." *Social Identities* 11, No. 1 (2005), 75–85.

Worth, R. F. "Al Jazeera No Longer Nips at Saudis." *New York Times*, 2008. Available: http://www.nytimes.com/ 2008/01/04/world/middleeast/04jazeera.html?ex=1200114000&en= b34 dee1780b4fa2c&ei=5070&emc=eta1. Accessed January 4, 2008.

Zelizer, B. "Foreword." In Sparks, C. and Tulloch, J. (eds.), *Tabloid Tales—Global Debates over Media Standard*, ix–xi. London: Rowman & Littlefield, 2000.

PART TWO

Challenges and Barriers to Global Journalism

3

Global and National News Agencies

TERHI RANTANEN
London School of Economics, UK

OLIVER BOYD-BARRETT
Bowling Green State University, USA

Prologue

From their first appearance over 170 years ago, news agencies have exhibited recurring patterns of change and crisis. Our analysis of continuities and discontinuities in news agency history identifies four discrete epochs. A defining theme is the changing relationship between the "global" and the "national" news agencies. A disciplined network of news exchange arrangements once constituted a multifaceted system for the gathering and dissemination of world news. This once-integrated global-national agency backbone of international newsgathering has now collapsed as a by-product of worldwide convergence toward a market-driven model of competition and entrepreneurship in news agency operations. In this chapter we explore the factors that account for these trends and their implications.

The Rupture

The global-national rupture was foreshadowed in the dialectic between communications media, processes of globalization, and constructions of national identity. Many media once identified as national were absorbed into multinational commercial media organizations. Some were originally state-owned or controlled but then privatized or deregulated to enhance their accessibility to international investments. Such trends reflected a deregulated transnational movement of capital and products; the disengagement of governments from activities they could transfer to the private sector; and new technologies that expanded media capacity for service extension. Previous agency missions of "national" service, nation-building, or development were no longer self-evidently meaningful objectives when clients were increasingly transnational, less committed to national public service ideals, preferring *à la carte* principles of news service and pricing structure, and more likely to compete directly with agencies for customers.

News Agencies from Early to Late Globalization

News agencies constitute the oldest electronic media, contributing to processes of globalization from the mid-nineteenth century. They transmitted news from multiple locations with the speed of electricity, contributing to the compression of time and space that is the hallmark of globalization (see Rantanen, 1998c). The relationship between global and national agencies is of profound importance in the constitution of modernity (Boyd-Barrett and Rantanen, 1998:5):

> The agencies were vital components in the armory of the nation state; then as now, the agencies were among the range of institutions which new nation states came to feel they had to establish in order to be seen to be credible as nations and in order to project or to control the dissemination of their "national image" on global markets.

Significant interdependency between global and national agencies developed with the emergent division between the small number of agencies that operated "globally," gathering news in most (known) countries of the world and selling news in most countries of the world, and those that principally operated "nationally," gathering news in single countries and distributing news within those same countries. Some "national" agencies have always had significant international activity (e.g., EFE of Spain; DPA of Germany; and the Press Association of Britain).

In nineteenth-century cartel arrangements, a global agency typically sold cartel news on an exclusive basis to a national agency, and a national agency delivered, either free or for a nominal price, its national news on an exclusive basis (after satisfying domestic clients) to a global agency (see, for example, Rantanen, 1998c). National agencies later began to subscribe to a range of global and international agencies, selling their national news to one or more such agencies, but the principle of interdependency between international and national was preserved. The news exchange principle persisted into the last decades of the twentieth century.

The balance of power between global and national agencies tilted ever more definitively in favor of the global. At the end of the twentieth century, some national agencies had collapsed, and the survival of some others was in doubt. The most resilient were those that had commercialized and transnationalized. This was indicative of transformations in the apparatus of national image construction for the reproduction of the nation-state (the burden on news agencies in this respect had diminished), neo-liberal dismantling of barriers to trade and investment flows, and regional concentrations of political identity (e.g., European Union).

A transition occurred in the 1990s from an interdependent global news system toward a looser, more individualistic, and less predictable arrangement. Some observers, including Pigeat (1997) and White (1998), considered that the global agencies themselves were in crisis, although by 2007, we argue, the more powerful agencies were exhibiting signs of reconstitution, recovery, and stability.

The industrial division between news wholesalers and retailers, and their interdependency, was undermined when global broadcasting companies like Cable News

Network (CNN) appeared, followed by BBC World, Al Jazeera, and others, gathering news from client broadcasters and sometimes selling news to them, all the while operating as broadcast news stations available directly to the public by cable or satellite and later by multimedia Web sites directly accessible, free of charge, to individual users worldwide. The Internet added new sources of competition and also threatened older principles of news value, copyright, and organization, making it more difficult to define and price news. Yet by 2008 the major agencies had reconfigured their business models such that the Internet became central to their operations and constituted a major source of new business opportunity, as in sales of text and video to Internet portals, Web sites, and blogs.

In place of the more orderly, systemic, and comprehensive arrangement of yesteryear, a handful of global news organizations (including traditional news agencies, global news broadcasters, and electronic news sites) autonomously gather news worldwide, selling that news to other news media ("wholesale"), including news-related Web sites, and incorporating it within their own news products for mass audiences ("retail"). The global news organizations may or may not have exchange arrangements with their clients. They may or may not collaborate with any of the many national and regional news agencies.

After World War II, some scholars spoke of the "Big Five": Agence France-Presse (AFP), Associated Press (AP), Reuters, TASS, and United Press International (UPI). These agencies were headquartered in Paris, New York, London, Moscow, and New York, respectively. By the mid-1990s, there remained only two powerful *general* news agencies, Reuters and AP, and of these one, AP, frequently operated at a loss, while the other, Reuters, depended for revenue primarily on financial data and trading services to financial institutions. Even Reuters was about to enter a protracted period of decline. Both agencies had recovered by 2007. These two were followed by a third general news agency, the French AFP. Itar-Tass and UPI, meanwhile, had significantly reduced the scale of their operations. In the field of news agency television news, by 1998 there were only two significant contenders, Reuters Television News and AP Television News (APTN) (Boyd-Barrett, 1998).

To speak of a decline in the number of global news agencies is to privilege "general" over financial news. If the financial is included, then agencies such as Bloomberg and perhaps Dow Jones are among the top. By 1980–2000, successful business models in the news agency world tended to privilege banks, brokers, and other institutional clients for financial data and trading services, or simply rewarded entrepreneurship, flexibility, and commercialization in the delivery of new products for nontraditional markets. These trends focused global news agency power in North America (United States and Canada), which by 2007 was corporate home to AP (owned by 1300 U.S. daily newspapers), Bloomberg (whose founder is currently mayor of New York), Dow Jones (shortly to be acquired by News Corporation), and Reuters (shortly to be acquired by Thomson Corporation). There were powerful national and international agencies based in other parts of the world, including Xinhua of China and Kyodo of Japan. But whereas the powerful Western news agencies enjoyed substantial penetration of non-Western markets, the reverse did not generally apply, although innovative ventures such as Al Jazeera showed some promise in this regard.

Constructing and Dismantling the Global News System

News agencies are the oldest electronic media, having survived as a genus since the establishment in 1835 of the world's first news agency, Havas in France, followed by AP in the United States in 1846, Wolff in Germany in 1849, Tuwora in Austria in 1850, and Reuters in the United Kingdom in 1851. A national news agency soon appeared in almost every European country. Outside Europe, development was slower. National agency development was critically shaped by the evolution of the global agencies. In each of the developmental periods, the relationship between the national and the global has shifted. The periods are as follows:

- The hegemony of the European news cartel, 1870–1917
- The dissolution of the European news cartel, 1918–1934
- The hegemony of the Big Five, 1940s–1980s
- The dissolution of the Big Five, 1980s
- The Big Three and from turbulence to stability, 2000–2008

The Hegemony of the European News Cartel, 1870–1917

Three European agencies—Havas in France, Wolff in Germany, and Reuters in the UK—became the first agencies to claim global reach. They divided up the world's news market among themselves by signing cartel agreements. AP joined the cartel only in 1927, but earlier had expanded its markets to South America by extracting a concession from the cartel as early as the late nineteenth century (Cooper, 1942; Rantanen, 1990, 1992).

These four agencies, with the exception of Reuters, started as national agencies. Even Reuters worked in close partnership with the British national agency, the Press Association, which would later become, for a period, joint owner of Reuters with Sir Roderick Jones before World War II, and again, with the Newspaper Proprietors' Association, after World War II. The major agencies invested most effort in serving national markets rich in newspapers and institutional clients. To better serve those clients, they expanded their newsgathering activities globally. Even where their domestic markets were relatively large, it was their foreign activities—facilitated by the vast imperial and trade activities of their host countries—that created clear water between them and solely national agencies operating exclusively on domestic markets (Boyd-Barrett, 1980). The respective size of its global market explains the success of Reuters in relation to its German and French counterparts: the British Empire was bigger than the French or the German, and British trading activity exceeded that of France or Germany (Boyd-Barrett, 1980).

The relationship between national and global agencies, one in which national agencies provided their news to global agencies without charge and bought foreign news from them, centered on exclusivity in two different ways. First, the *market* was exclusive: only one agency in one country could receive the international agencies' news, whose news could only be used by clients of the domestic agency. Second, with the telegraph, *speed* became of paramount importance. Only the first users of news could enjoy its commodity exclusivity since news could only be used once before losing its value (Rantanen, 1997). Exclusivity often became a significant factor in establishing national monopolies that were based on either cooperative structures or on state subsidy (see, for example, Rantanen, 1998c). The global agency could determine which local contender was to be the national agency, and, not infrequently, proceeded to instruct its protégé in how to operate to its own standards (see Palmer, 1998).

National news agencies symbolized the awakening of nationalist sentiments. Yet paradoxically, a national agency could be owned by an international agency: the Spanish Fabra was acquired by the French Havas, and some early Scandinavian agencies were owned by the German Wolff. Several early agencies carried the name of their founder, later acquiring country titles, such as Suomen Sähkösanomatoimisto (Finland's Telegraph Agency, founded in 1887), thus emphasizing their status as national institutions. The first non-European agencies (after AP) were established in that period (such as the Japanese Shimbun Yotatsu Kaisha, in 1886, the Argentine Agencia Noticiosa Saporiti, in 1900, and the Canadian AP, in 1903). All such agencies were born as junior members of the cartel controlled by Reuters, Wolff, and Havas.

The dominance of a few major agencies quickly became a problem for some of the subordinate agencies, even though they felt compelled to work within the cartel structure. There were notable attempts to escape or undermine that system, sometimes taking the form of alliances between a national agency and a single global agency (such as Stefani, Wolff, and Korrespondenz Bureau in 1889) (Boyd-Barrett, 1980; Rantanen, 1991). The cartel system made it difficult for newcomers to achieve access in global markets. United Press Associations (UPA; later renamed United Press International, UPI) tried and achieved some early success, partly by establishing links with minor agencies in the countries of the cartel agencies (such as Central News in the United Kingdom; see Boyd-Barrett, 1980). Its success was an important factor in motivating AP to be more aggressive in overseas markets (Boyd-Barrett, 1980; Rantanen, 1992, 1994, 1998a).

A further difficulty lay in the relationship of agencies to their respective governments. Even where there was no formal link, news agencies, whether big and small, for temporary (such as in wartime) or more sustained periods, either solicited or succumbed to direct or indirect government support or subsidy, for revenues as for sources. At this level, then, one can say that both global and national agencies grew out of and were supported by nation-states.

The Dissolution of the European News Cartel, 1918–1934

The second period started in 1918, when the U.S. agencies, AP and UPA (1907), expanded into South America. As a result of World War I, the German Wolff lost its position as a member of the news cartel. There was growing dissatisfaction among national news agencies with the power of global agencies, leading eventually to the dissolution of the cartel in 1934, spearheaded by U.S. agencies (AP and UP/UPI) in alliance with other national agencies (especially the Japanese and the Soviet) (Rantanen, 1994). National agencies became free to contract with any international agency they liked, at the price, in some cases, of losing exclusivity on their home markets once competing agencies and clients could contract directly with different international agencies.

Collapse of the cartel inaugurated a more equitable era in relations between national and global agencies. It was a time of crisis: survival through war, the introduction of new wireless technology, and the collapse of one form of control of a global news market in favor of a less regulated and more competitive system. The finances of the European global agencies, Reuters and Havas, grew decidedly shaky. Havas was dependent both on government subscriptions and on sale of advertising space for newspaper clients. Reuters restructured its ownership to involve the British national news agency, the Press Association, and looked with increasing interest at possible sources of state support (Boyd-Barrett, 1980; Read, 1999). These developments raised further doubts about the ability and will of such organizations to maintain independence of government.

In the 1930s, many agencies again worked closely with their governments or were taken over by governments. For example, the German government already had 51 percent of the shares of the agency (CTC) that had succeeded Wolff, and the remaining private shares were transferred to the German government. CTC was amalgamated with another agency in 1933, and a new agency, Deutsche Nachrichtenburo, was founded. Although this was nominally a shareholder company, it came fully under government control (Reitz, 1991:213–216). As a result, there was little freedom for independent news transmission, and most agencies willingly served the "common cause" of their nations-state, many of them preparing for the coming war. News agencies were turned into propaganda agencies.

The Hegemony of the Big Five, 1940s–1980s

U.S. agency international expansion, which had started prior to World War II, was delayed by the war and accelerated with the peace, as U.S. agencies capitalized on market opportunities in war-ravaged countries of Europe (Boyd-Barrett, 1980). A new French agency, AFP, was founded as a public institution that was cooperatively managed by a board of media, government, state broadcasting, and staff representatives, and whose most important and wealthiest clients were ministries and other departments of state at home and in French overseas territories. Following the tradition set by its predecessor, Havas, AFP soon gained the status of world agency. The Soviet news agency TASS extended its activities in the new Communist countries of Eastern Europe. Across other continents (the Middle East, Africa, and Asia), where countries were achieving political if not financial independence from old colonial masters, successive waves of new national agencies appeared.

By the 1970s, over a hundred countries had national news agencies (Carlsson, 1981). The excitement of liberation in the postcolonial countries quickly gave way to tensions between developing and developed worlds, when it became clear that political independence did not guarantee economic independence. One area of contention was the perceived imbalance of news flow and the power of the developed world to determine the global media representation of the developing world. There was growing critical realization of the emergence of an international media system that was largely controlled by North American and Western European interests.

For the established agencies, this represented a moment of threat, which the Western powers were quick to rebuff through their withdrawal of support for UNESCO, which had done much to legitimize the critique of what some scholars had labeled "media imperialism" (Boyd-Barrett, 1977, 1998; Boyd-Barrett and Thussu, 1992). To the established international agencies, this debate was something of an irrelevance in their daily battle for survival: AFP was heavily dependent on government support, and neither Reuters (at that time) nor AP easily suited the UNESCO image of Western news agencies as capitalist predators. But it was during this period that Reuters pioneered the digitization of economic and financial news services, a process that converted it from an amiable, rather stuffy institution to that of multibillion-dollar, aggressive core enabler at the heart of capitalistic globalization.

The Dissolution of the Big Five, 1980s

The fourth period began in the early 1980s. This was the post-NWICO (i.e. New World Information and Communication Order) era, instituted by globalization, neo-liberal economics of media de-/re-regulation, conglomeration and convergence, digitization, commercialization, and "competitivization" (Hamelink, 1994; Boyd-Barrett, 2006). Processes of conglomeration hastened the further diminution of UPI (for a time owned by Saudi interests, then acquired by the *Washington Times*), and World Television News (WTN, finally bought by APTV). The collapse of communism brought about the relative demise of TASS (which became Itar-Tass, a Russian national agency without the status of global agency) in favor of more commercial operations. The end of communism also weakened or destroyed the old East European national agencies, which have been succeeded by new or reformulated enterprises that must struggle to find sources of revenue sufficient to compensate for the loss or reduction of state subsidies (Rantanen, 1998b). For example, two national agencies that died in the Baltic countries were replaced by a regional agency owned by a Finnish media company operating in all three Baltic countries.

Although three major agencies may be said to have survived, they did so in a very competitive environment (in general, broadcast and financial news). The deregulation movement undermined state-supported broadcast institutions (important clients for national news agencies) and intensified competition between ever fewer but larger media conglomerates (which grew more critical of the services they received from national agencies). The Internet was perceived as a significant threat because it had the power to reduce competitors' costs of access to news and to clients, although longer experience suggests that it may be only the major players who have the resources necessary to attract large audiences.

The Big Three in the Twenty-First Century

The major agencies of today, Reuters and AP, have survived as members of the "inner club" for many decades, followed some way behind by a third major agency, AFP, which is a natural successor to Havas. We may argue that Reuters was the leading global agency in the world at the start of the millennium, *as a combined general / financial and trading services agency.*

Reuters had been a global company from its beginning and never operated solely as a national agency. In the latter half of the twentieth century, it increasingly distanced itself from its British identity. By the late 1980s, staff was drawn from 160 nationalities, although British and Americans were overrepresented in senior management (Boyd-Barrett, 1980; Read, 1999). Fenby (1986), an ex-Reuters executive, remarked that AP and UPI were not international at all in terms of their priorities: "the home market dominates their activities . . . their essentially American nature has been disguised by their worldwide organization and reach." Read (1999) points out that by 1977, Reuters was earning approximately $78m in foreign revenue, compared with AP's $20m and UPI's $17m. AP's foreign income amounted only to some 20 percent of its revenue, whereas Reuters, by contrast, was earning only 16 percent of its revenue from the United Kingdom. In this way, Reuters was the only global agency whose home market revenues had become insignificant compared to its foreign markets.

Reuters secured its financial base by becoming independent of media. An overwhelming majority (over 93 percent in 1997) of its revenues derived from financial news. Unlike other agencies, global or national, it did not have to compete on its domestic market with its own media clients. The traditional media market was less important, although success depended in part on the interdependency of general and financial news throughout its operations.

Many of its media initiatives in recent years had been internally controversial, as in the case of the establishment of Reuters Television. Suspicions that Reuters was not really interested in the media market encouraged its major competitor, AP, to boast that AP was now the leading global news agency for media, as opposed to Reuters, which saw itself as an information agency for nonmedia clients. In the recession of 2001–2003 Reuters downsized its staffing significantly in response to competitive pressures from Bloomberg and stagnant market conditions.

While Reuters experienced boom conditions in the 1990s, AP was in trouble. In 1995 its losses totaled $25.8 million. Patrick White, a Reuters journalist (1998), argued that AP's difficulties reflected a declining position as a global agency and the loss of revenue from overseas. He argued this was due to two main factors: competition from Reuters and AFP (both were very active in Asia during the 1990s), and competition from newspaper syndicated services such as those of the *New York Times* and *Los Angeles Times*. On the other hand, as a cooperative agency that had become almost a monopoly on the U.S. market, AP enjoyed the relative luxury of being able to lift member assessments to help it pay its way. By 1994, 94 percent of U.S. newspapers received AP's service, while only 11 percent took UPI's declining services (White, 1998), which came to concentrate on certain niche areas such as health care or strategic arms (Richie, 1999). Both agencies faced a situation in which daily newspapers were struggling against declining circulations and advertising revenues, and the rising threat of the Web.

The French AFP lagged behind AP except in the number of countries it served. Although the French AFP continued to depend heavily on subscriptions from state agencies, now accounting for over 40 percent of revenue and 46 percent of clients, this was a reduction from over 60 percent dependence on the state for revenue in the 1970s. As many of its clients were foreign as were domestic, so that it had a fairly strong identity as a global agency. It was the only major non-Anglo-American news agency, and it devoted significant resource and space to its coverage of Asia, Latin America, and Africa (White, 1998).

The three global agencies had developed different strategies in their struggle for survival. Reuters had shifted most of its energies into financial information and electronic trading services for nonmedia clients, but proved vulnerable to severe economic recession. AP had entrenched itself in a virtual monopoly position on the domestic U.S. market, sustaining significant dependence on member assessments. even if at times the cooperative structure exercised a conservative restraint on business innovation. AFP had secured its financial position by continuing reliance on the state, enabling it to maintain and even expand its foreign coverage. But the state was not always sympathetic to the agency's need for technological transformation, and many external clients did not look favorably on the role of the state.

National Agencies

Many national news agencies exhibited signs of crisis at the turn of the millennium. This was especially apparent in the developing world and in Central and Eastern Europe, but also in parts of the developed world. For example, Scandinavian news agencies, operating in one of the richest media markets in the world, encountered serious financial problems during the latter half of the 1990s. The Swedish news agency, TT, converted from cooperative to private status in 1999. Scandinavian news agencies, like many other news agencies, typically received most of their revenues from media clients (80 to 91 percent) and faced difficulty in generating entrepreneurial revenue streams.

Where news agencies had been customarily supported by media cooperatives, tendencies toward concentration of ownership and conglomerization of newspaper chains encouraged some member newspaper groups to withdraw support and to compile alternative, more competitive, and sometimes cheaper group news services. In addition, in countries with a strong national press and national broadcast institutions, there was a diminishing public expectation that local media should devote much space to out-of-area news.

The situation in Central and Eastern Europe revealed the difficulties faced by the formerly state-owned and fully state-subsidized agencies in adapting to a new competitive environment in which the state was eager to maintain control and yet had substantial state subsidy (see, for example, Rantanen and Vartanova, 1995; Rantanen, 2002). Although attempts had been made to establish news agencies controlled by Parliament (for example, in the Czech Republic, Hungary, and Poland) instead of the government, governments still liked to maintain their influence over the agencies (Boyd-Barrett and Rantanen, 2000). National agencies in Central and Eastern Europe (CEE) were forced to reduce expenses, services, and staff. Some had also to compete with private or foreign agencies in their home markets (Rantanen, 1998).

Global agencies found it advantageous to sell directly to retail media and other clients in national markets, where earlier they had distributed indirectly through national agencies because of the latter's monopoly position. With the decline of national monopolies, there was less incentive to use national agencies as intermediaries to access retail media. National agencies increasingly served small and local media that belonged to larger chains, and these chains sometimes preferred their own services for news of the capital city over that of the national agencies.

News agencies in developing countries shared some of the problems as nations in the CEE. For example, SHIHATA, the Tanzanian news agency, had practically no operations in June 1996 and finally closed in 1999. Reuters had previously interrupted its services because of unpaid fees; only one telephone was in operation, and there were no regional bureaus. Fax and telex lines were also cut (Kivikuru, 1998). National news agencies of several African states either disappeared in the 1990s or became moribund. Many of their problems relate to the collapse in confidence that state support for news agencies was desirable. Even intergovernmental or nongovernmental organization (NGO) support for such ventures declined in the wake of the end of the Cold War. Furthermore, the combined forces of deregulation, commercialization of media operations, and democratic forms of government weakened enthusiasm for state protection of news agencies.

Many national news agencies in developing countries continue to face serious difficulties. These were the focus of a UNESCO-sponsored workshop in 2001 whose recommendations urged the cultivation of a more entrepreneurial climate within national news agencies to help them compete against other news suppliers and to identify new market opportunities; the elaboration of structures of separation between agency operations and political authorities; and the preservation of a mission to serve the information needs of the nation as a whole (Boyd-Barrett, 2001).

Turbulence to Stability, 2000–2007

For some 150 years, news media around the world depended largely on the major worldwide news agencies, including, almost from the beginning, AP and Reuters, and on the news-exchange practices that these agencies controlled for their supply of news. The business models that sustained these operations have undergone continual processes of adaptation and evolution in response to changing social and political contexts, market structure, new technologies, and competition. Most recently, the pressures for change have emanated from the following:

- Merger and acquisition among both the agencies themselves and their clients
- Weakening of the old distinction between "wholesale" news media (providing news solely for other media) and "retail" media (providing news directly to end-users)
- Blurring of the boundary between "national" and "global" news agencies
- Competition from emergent Web-based services and blogs
- Decline of support from traditional sources of revenue (including membership assessments in the case of cooperatively owned agencies, and government subsidies in the case of government-sponsored agencies)
- Intensified competition for new sources of revenue in such fields as financial information services and trading platforms, and specialist sports and weather information

Sources of revenue for traditional news agencies have generally extended beyond media subscriptions to include, at various times, government subvention, advertising placement, leasing of communications networks, and, most significant of all in the case of Reuters, financial information and trading platforms for institutions such as banks, brokers, and traders. In 2007 Reuters announced that the board of the Canadian Publisher Thomson Corporation had agreed to buy Reuters for approximately $US17.2 billion. The Thomson Corporation would control about 53 percent of the new company. The merger would intensify the business rivalry between Reuters and another leading supplier of business information and trading platforms, Bloomberg. Combined, Thomson and Reuters would control 34 percent of the market for financial data, and Bloomberg 33 percent. Also in 2007, News Corporation secured the consent of the owners of Dow Jones, publisher of the *Wall Street Journal* and of Dow Jones wire services, to News Corporation's bid for ownership. For the first time in news history, four of the world's wealthiest news agencies, AP, Bloomberg, Dow Jones, and Reuters would be controlled by businesses based in North America, specifically the United States and Canada.

By 2008, the world's largest news agencies demonstrated a measure of financial and structural stability following several years of market turbulence. Many agencies that looked fragile in 2001 were notably healthier by 2008. Worldwide, most news agencies, whether global, regional, or national had converged, in whole or in part, toward a market-based business model. In some cases, this was achieved through a radical change in ownership structure and/or business model, as in the case of the New Zealand Press Association (NZPA), which, under pressure of intensifying business rivalries among its increasingly concentrated owner-client newspaper base, transitioned from a media cooperative model to a conventional business model in 2006. The world's single most celebrated example of cooperative ownership, the not-for-profit AP, owned by most of the daily U.S. newspapers, was dependent on membership assessments for less than a third of its income by 2006. What had once been one of the world's most celebrated examples of government ownership and finance of a news agency, Xinhua, the national agency of China, depended on self-generated revenue for 50 percent of its expenditure already in 1985 (Xin, 2006).

Bloomberg, of which approximately 70 percent is owned by the agency's founder, Michael Bloomberg, reported sales in 2006 of US$4.7 billion, an increase of 14.6 percent over the previous year. Reuters showed strong signs of recovery from several years of decline or stagnation. It reported overall revenues of approximately US$5.1 billion, representing a growth of 6.5 percent over the previous year. Of total revenues, a modest 6.6 percent (approximately US$340 million) was earned by its media division. Dow Jones and Co. (whose Enterprise Media Segment competes the most directly with Bloomberg and Reuters), reported 2006 revenue of US$1.93 billion, showing a year-on-year growth of over 16 percent. For 2005, AP reported revenue of US$654.2 million, a 3.8 percent increase over the previous year. Whereas 94 percent of Reuters revenue came from non-media commercial services, the corresponding percentage for AP was 20 percent. The Thomson Corporation, which was due to acquire Reuters, reported 2006 sales of US$6.6 billion and net income of US$1.1 billion. Its Thomson Financial component, closest competitor to Reuters, reported US$1.9 billion sales in 2005.

Other major international and national news services also showed signs of recovery and innovative, profit-driven development. In 2006, Agence France Presse reported net profit of approximately US$3.9 million, contrasted with a corresponding loss the previous year, a result described by its CEO as the "best result since 1979." DPA, the largest news agency of Germany, reported 2006 sales of approximately US$124.4 million and earnings after tax of US$7.8 million, an increase of 30 percent over the previous year. Earnings in 2005 had registered the first increase in turnover in five years. The British Press Association (PA) increased its underlying operating profit in 2006 by 5 percent to approximately US$12.8 million, on turnover that increased by 15 percent to approximately US$173.4 million.

The Internet had initially seemed more threat than opportunity for news agencies, because it reduced the costs of market-entry for news-gathering and distribution. Yet by 2007 the larger news agencies had successfully accommodated to a multimedia universe. All the major agencies now ran Internet news and information services for direct client access, as well as news and information packages for client Web sites and mobile telephone services. Thus, the Internet had greatly expanded the number of potential clients for agency services, increased agency flexibility in generating novel information packages, and reduced the costs of distribution so that a greater proportion of expenditure could be dedicated to content and service quality. Many client media during this period reduced the strength of international newsgathering and came to depend more heavily on the major agencies. Among the new generation of alternative news sites and blogs, few had the resources to compete with major agencies, and most depended heavily on the news services, direct or indirect, of the agencies.

Not all improvements in financial stability or growth spelled improvements in quality in basic news services, although many did. Financial improvements were in some places achieved through reductions in personnel (DPA experienced a 20 percent reduction in editorial strength between 1999 and 2005); in others improvement came through reduction in diversity of content, as Ellis (2006) argues happened with the New Zealand Press Association, which also lost the benefit of pooled reports by members.

Large agencies continued to be large employers, their editorial strengths dwarfing all but the very largest retail media (e.g., BBC, with 2006 sales of approximately US$7 billion and a staff of 25,377). In 2005–2006, AFP boasted 4,000 staff members in over 165 countries, of which 110 hosted bureaus and 50 were covered by local correspondents. Of the 4,000, 1,250 were journalists, video reporters, and photographers. AP claimed to have more than 4,000 employees in 2006, working in more than 240 worldwide bureaus, covering 97 countries and serving 121. In 2006 Bloomberg had 9,500 employees, Dow Jones had 7,400, and Reuters had a total staff of 16,300, of whom 2,400 were journalists. The British PA employed 1,534 staff in 2005.

Conclusion

The history of both international and national news agencies demonstrates how the gathering and distribution of news are governed by institutional structures and alliances between the agencies, their clients, and governments. Study of these structures and alliances reveals significant continuities over time, as well as important disjunctures. One question that we have considered here is whether at the beginning of the twenty-first century there has been a radical disjuncture in relations between global and national agencies and whether this matters.

With respect to global agencies, we find evidence of greater concentration among the big players, in terms of both number and location (North America). While there is a proliferation of broadcast and electronic media, some with their own newsgathering resource, few organizations, to our knowledge, command anything like the scale of human resource dedicated to worldwide newsgathering and distribution as is committed by AFP, AP, Bloomberg, or Reuters. The spread of correspondents distributed by other media is typically smaller and more concentrated in geographical and topical range. We conclude that the global agencies, though fewer in number, exercise a profound importance in the distribution of knowledge of current affairs, although this role is not always visible in retail media or on the Internet. In national markets, national news agencies often but not always constitute the single best resource and geographically the most extensive networks of newsgathering and distribution.

National news agencies, especially in the developing world, face a difficult future. The rationale of "development" that inspired many of them has not proved a sufficiently coherent philosophy to sustain the loyalty of state and nonstate clients. Many developing country governments find themselves under pressure from the International Monetary Fund (IMF) to relinquish their involvement in activities that the IMF considers can be performed equally well by commercial operations. In areas of the world such as Europe that have been subject to increasing regionalization, clients may have less interest in "local" news as was once defined by national news agencies.

More generally, sources of funding have been undermined by a number of changes: reductions in state subsidy, decreases in aid from NGOs, the cooling of loyalty of media groups that have set up independent newsgathering networks, reductions in subscriptions by global agencies where these now have sufficient local resource to meet their own requirements, and competition from global agencies where these have set up financial news services that undermine the nationals' scope for entrepreneurial diversification or where they have even set up competing domestic general news services.

Both state-owned and cooperative modes of national news agency ownership have been threatened by one or more of these tendencies. Many agencies find it difficult to reconcile the clashing interests, first, of the state, which often wants a vehicle for the dissemination of announcements from state ministries; second, of national and global clients in receiving a service that is free of state pressure and responsive to their news agendas; and third, of the agencies' need for dependable sources of revenue.

Overused as the terms may be, this period has indeed proven a time of change and crisis in the world of news agencies. We have noted that in response to previous crisis, many of the larger agencies had successfully reconfigured their missions, operations, and revenue streams (see Boyd-Barrett, 2007). But convergence to more intensely commercialized business models will inevitably involve intense pressures for adaptability, innovation, and change.

BIBLIOGRAPHY

Boyd-Barrett, O., "Media Imperialism: Towards an International Framework for the Analysis of Media Systems." In Curran, J., Gurevitch, M. and Woollacott, J. (eds.), *Mass Communication and Society,* 116–135. London: Edward Arnold, 1977.

——. (1980), *The International News Agencies,* London: Constable.

——. (1998) "Global News Agencies," in Boyd-Barrett, O. and Rantanen, T., *The Globalization of News,* London: Sage, 19–34.

——. (2001) *Final Report of the Workshop on News Agencies in the Era of the Internet.* Paris: UNESCO.

——. (2006) Cyberspace, globalization and empire, in *Global Media and Communication,* Vol.2, No.1, 21–42.

——. (2007) *News Agencies in the Media Convergence Era: Strengthening and Promoting Asia Pacific Voice,* 13th General Assembly of the Organization of Asia-Pacific News Agencies (OANA), Jakarta, December 10.

Boyd-Barrett, O., and Rantanen, T. "The Globalization of News." In Boyd-Barrett, O. and Rantanen, T. (eds.), *The Globalization of News,* 1–14. London: Sage, 1998.

Body-Barrett, O. and Rantanen, T. 2000. "European National News Agencies—The End of an Era or a New Beginning," *Journalism Theory, Practice and Criticism* 1(1), 86–105.

Boyd-Barrett, O., and Thussu, D. K. *Contra-flows in Global News: International and Regional News Exchange Mechanisms.* London: John Libbey, 1992.

Carlsson, U. *Nyheterna och tredje världen: En översikt av det internationella Nyhetsflödet. Lund: Studentlitteratur,* 1981.

Cooper, K. *Barriers Down: The Story of the News Agency Epoch.* New York: Kennikat Press, 1942.

Ellis, G., "World War: Demutualizing the New Zealand Press Association." Master's thesis, University of Auckland, 2006.

"European National News Agencies: The End of an Era or a New Beginning." *Journalism: Theory, Practice and Criticism* 1 (2000), 86–105.

Fenby, J. *The International News Services.* New York: Schocken Books, 1986.

Final Report of the Workshop on News Agencies in the Era of the Internet. Paris: UNESCO, 2001.

Hamelink, C. *The Politics of World Communication.* London: Sage, 1994.

The International News Agencies. London: Constable, 1980.

Kivikuru, U. "From State Socialism to Deregulation." In Boyd-Barrett, O. and Rantanen, T. (eds.,), *The Globalization of News,* 137–153. London: Sage, 1998.

Palmer, M., "What Makes News." In Boyd-Barrett, O. and Rantanen, T. (eds.), *The Globalization of News,* 177–190. London: Sage, 1998.

Pigeat, H., *Les agences de presse. Institutions du passe ou medias d'avenir?* Paris: La documentation française, 1997.

Rantanen, T. "The Globalization of Electronic News in the 19th Century." *Media Culture & Society* 4 (1977), 605–620.

——. *Foreign News in Imperial Russia: The Relationship Between International and Russian News Agencies, 1856–1914.* Helsinki: Suomalainen Tiedeakatemia, 1990.

——. "Mr. Howard Goes to South America: The United Press Associations and Foreign Expansion." *Roy W. Howard Monographs in Journalism and Mass Communication Research,* No. 2. Bloomington: Indiana University School of Journalism, 1992.

——. "Howard Interviews Stalin: How the AP, UP and TASS Smashed the International News Cartel." *Roy W. Howard Monographs in Journalism and Mass Communication Research,* No. 3. Bloomington: Indiana University School of Journalism, 1994.

——. "After Five O'clock Friends: Kent Cooper and Roy W. Howard." *Roy W. Howard Monographs in Journalism and Mass Communication Research,* No. 4. Bloomington: Indiana University School of Journalism, 1998a.

——. "From Communism to Capitalism." In Boyd-Barrett, O. and Rantanen, T. (eds.), *The Globalization of News,* 125–136. London: Sage, 1998b.

——. "The Struggle for Control of Domestic News Markets." In Boyd-Barrett, O. and Rantanen, T. (eds.), *The Globalization of News,* 35–48. London: Sage, 1998c.

————. *The Global and the National: Media and Communications in Post-Communist Russia.* Boulder, CO: Rowman and Littlefield, 2002.

————. 1991. Foreign News in Imperial Russia: The Relationship between International and Russian News Agencies, 1856–1914. Helsinki: Federation of Finnish Scientific Societies.

————. 1997. "The Globalization of News in the 19th Century", *Media, Culture & Society,* No 3, 605–620.

Rantanen, T., and Vartanova, E. "News Agencies in Post-Communist Russia." *European Journal of Communication* 2 (1995), 207–220.

Read, D. *The Power of News: The History of Reuters,* 2nd ed. Oxford: Oxford University Press, 1999.

Reitz, J. "Das Deutsche Nachrichtenbüro." In Wilke, J. (ed.), *Telegraphenbüros und Nachrictenagenturen in Deutschland: Untersuchungen zu ihrer Geschichte bis 1949,* 213–264. Munich: K.G. Saur, 1991.

Richie, I. "MBC, an Arabic Global TV Satellite Service." Paper presented at Green College, Oxford, March 5, 1999.

UNESCO. *News Agencies: Their Structure and Operation.* Paris: UNESCO, 1953.

White, P. *Le Village CNN: La crise des agences de presse.* Montreal: Les Presses de l'Universite de Montreal, 1998.

Xin X. "A Quarter Century of Creative Chaos: Xinhua News Agency, 1980–2005." Doctoral dissertation, University of Westminster, 2006.

Other Sources Consulted

Agence France Presse corporate information and press releases, available on its Web site, http://www.afp.com/english/home/

AP annual reports, corporate information and press releases, available on its Web site, www.ap.org

DPA corporate information and press releases, available on its Web site, http://www.dpa.de/en/unternehmenswelt/index.html

Press Association Annual Reports, corporate information and press releases, available on its Web site, http://www.pressassociation.co.uk/

Reuters Annual Reports, corporate information and press releases, available on its Web site, http://uk.reuters.com/

4 Barriers to Media Development

PAUL PARSONS, GLENN W. SCOTT, AND RICHARD LANDESBERG

Elon University, USA

When we think of media, we may envision global television news networks, magazines with colorful ads, and an Internet with something for everyone. But media in many countries must develop without much money or technology, or under the thumb of authoritarian governments, or in the face of language and cultural barriers.

Media develop and evolve in a world that is constantly changing. For instance, amid longstanding Middle East tensions, a sitcom featuring an Arab family became a surprise hit in Israel (Gradstein, 2008). That reflects a cultural change. Ahead of the 2008 Olympics, China lifted its decades-old restrictions on the freedom of foreign journalists to interview people without obtaining government permission (Ford, 2006). That's a governmental change. In Singapore, an opposition party launched a podcast on its website as a way of bypassing state-controlled media (Podcast, 2005). That's a technological change.

In wartime, controlling the flow of information can be as important as battlefield victories. In its war against terror, the United States is raiding al-Qaeda media centers in Iraq. One north of Baghdad was a nondescript house that had 12 computers, 65 hard drives and a film studio. In 2007, the U.S. military captured six media centers, sharply curtailing the amount of video and Internet postings made by al-Qaeda, whose members film every attack they conduct and then add music for special effect to raise money and attract recruits. General David Petraeus, the top U.S. commander in Iraq, told Congress in 2007 that the "war is not only being fought on the ground in Iraq but also in cyberspace" (Michaels, 2007).

Media change within a nation is usually evolutionary, and sometimes revolutionary. News, photography, movies, and even music suddenly died in Afghanistan when the Taliban seized control a decade ago. Claiming it was creating the world's purest Islamic state, the regime gave residents 15 days to throw out their television sets, videos, and satellite dishes to rid themselves of "moral corruption" (International Press Institute, 2000). As an example, the Taliban publicly hanged TV sets and burned stocks of films.

Afghanistan spent five years as the most media-restrictive country in the world. All kinds of barriers were placed in the way of media development. Newspapers were shut down. Music could not be played on the radio. Afghans were prohibited from having Internet access. The Taliban banned photography of any living person or animal, and photographers were even arrested for attempting to take photos of a soccer match in Kabul.

Media restrictions, though, merely mirrored the great upheaval that swept through Afghan society. Women could not step outside their homes without wearing a full-body veil. All men were ordered to grow beards. Within their homes, Afghans were told to destroy all pictures of living beings (although shops in Kabul remained open for passport photographs). The only radio station allowed was the Taliban's Radio Sharia, beaming propaganda 24 hours a day. But from outside Afghan borders, the British Broadcasting Corporation (BBC) and Voice of America offered special radio programming in Afghan languages.

Foreign journalists were prohibited from entering private houses, and they could not hire taxis or private cars. When the hunt began in the mountains of Afghanistan for Osama bin Laden and his terrorist network, and war threatened the Taliban's grasp on the country, foreign journalists became targets. Four journalists were pulled from their car and shot to death on a road leading to Kabul. In all, 14 journalists have died while covering the Afghan war and the intensified violence in 2005 and 2006 (Committee to Protect Journalists, 2007).

Once the war ended and the Taliban lost power, the reconstruction of Afghanistan's media had to start anew. Based on UNESCO estimates, literacy in Afghanistan declined to a dismal 31 percent after a generation of warlords, poverty, propaganda, and civil strife. Yet Afghan media are coming back. The independent *Kabul Weekly* is publishing regularly after the Taliban shut it down for six years (Scott, 2002). Radio Afghanistan is back on the air and broadcasting music again, and satellite dishes have reappeared in parts of the countryside. Magazines have returned to the street stalls of Kabul, including magazines for women. Kabul University reopened, with journalism in its curriculum.

Despite the improvements, Afghanistan still faces many challenges. Extreme Muslim groups threaten the media. The Taliban have reemerged and periodically target journalists. The country is ranked 142 out of 169 in the 2007 world survey of press freedom by Reporters without Borders. While the international monitoring group recognizes great strides in Afghanistan, it says those strides remain fragile because of "deteriorating security, threats from warlords, conservative religious leaders, and an increasingly hard-pressed government" (Reporters Without Borders, 2007).

Afghanistan's problems are among the most severe, but all nations—from the struggling to the mighty—experience barriers to media development. Back in the late 1970s, when Afghanistan was just beginning its decades of civil strife, American scholars Ray Hiebert, Donald Ungurait, and Thomas Bohn were erecting a media systems paradigm on the theory that the relationship between media and societies is reciprocal: "A country creates a national media system, and this media system in turn modifies that society" (Hiebert, Ungurait, and Bohn, 1979:35). They identified six factors that influence the development of a nation's media system: (a) physical/geographic characteristics, (b) technological competencies, (c) cultural traits, (d) economic conditions, (e) political philosophies, and (f) media qualities. The authors contended that the interaction of these six factors, rather than their independent effects, is crucial in the evolution of a media system.

Updating their paradigm for the twenty-first century, this chapter reclassifies and expands on those six barriers to media development. But let's first define what is meant by the words *media, development,* and *barriers.*

Media is defined as a means of communication and comprises the technology for sending and receiving messages and the organizations for gathering, processing, and transmitting news and information to a mass audience. Global news agencies, newspapers, magazines, broadcast stations, and satellite networks are commonly identified as the media. However, vehicles of communication also include books, pamphlets, billboards, and computer sites. Taken together, these forms supply the informational needs of a society. Important in this process is the ability of the media to identify, create, manipulate, and spread public opinion. The media are the institution in society that not only informs the public but also can help move the masses in collective, purposeful, and productive action.

Development is defined as increasing the quantity and improving the quality of the available means of communication. Media development refers to improving the availability, diversity, and quality of news and other information to meet the needs of the audience. Development also includes improved individual access to the channels of communication for the purposes of sending and receiving messages from the mass audience. In short, media development facilitates the flow of information among and between individuals and institutions in any given community or society.

Barriers to media development occur in six broadly conceived forms. This chapter defines them as (a) physical barriers, (b) cultural barriers, (c) economic barriers, (d) governmental barriers, (e) media barriers, and (f) technological barriers. These barriers often account for observable differences in the level of development or sophistication among the media systems in the world. In fact, no media system—not even the world's most advanced media system, which is found in the United States—can accurately claim to be without any of these barriers that hinder the ideal conditions for communication.

Barriers may be too pessimistic a word, since it implies an almost insurmountable obstacle. Although some barriers to media development do seem insurmountable—think of communicating across the Sahara, or publishing in a nation of illiterates—other barriers related to government policies and economic systems are more like major challenges that in time can be overcome for the good of a nation and its media.

Physical Barriers

We begin with Earth's topography. In many parts of the world, mountains and other inhospitable terrain prevent the installation of telephone lines and block the reach of broadcast signals. For instance, Peru is a media-rich nation of newspapers and broadcast stations, yet that is true only for the 60 percent of the population who live within 100 miles of the Pacific Ocean. For people who live in the Andes or in the plains to the east of the mountain range, radio signals sent via mountain transmitters remain the primary means of mass communication.

Geography is an overwhelming obstacle in building a national media system. The vast distances between media centers and media audiences make communication difficult or impossible. This is the case in Russia, with its landmass spanning 11 time zones. News in the afternoon in Moscow is news in the dead of night in eastern Siberia. For the island nation of Indonesia, the ocean presents a physical barrier to convenient communication in a nation spread across 13,700 islands. If economically feasible, satellites and repeater stations provide the solution to bridging some of these distances, waterways, and obstructing terrains.

Other physical barriers include the lack of basic infrastructure such as roads for the transportation of printed communication and the equipment for broadcasting. In the West African nation of Mauritania, for example, the quickest way to travel from the capital of Nouakchott to the northern part of the country is to drive 100 miles along the beach at low tide—"and that's the easy part," according to a U.S. State Department spokesman, because that must be followed by almost 200 miles over sand dunes (U.S. State Department, 2002). It is an overnight trip by truck or four-wheel-drive vehicle to reach the nearest population center, if the tide is just right.

Even climate and soil conditions can be a physical barrier to media development. Film stock tends to deteriorate faster in the tropics than in temperate zones, so film companies in tropical areas must take this into consideration when setting up film production and distribution facilities (Hiebert, Ungurait, and Bohn, 1979:37). Some nations, like those in sub-Saharan Africa, are unable to grow the type of coniferous trees preferred for producing newsprint, so they must rely on newsprint produced in Europe, North America, and parts of Asia. This physical barrier hampers the development of their domestic print media and keeps them in a constant state of dependency on imported newsprint.

Cultural Barriers

Every society has its own norms, taboos, values, and unique ways. Sexual content in the media that is accepted in Amsterdam would outrage the people of Seoul. The freedom to analyze and criticize religious institutions in the United States would infuriate Iran. The cultural barriers to media development are perhaps the most difficult to overcome because the solutions often require a change in a nation's attitudes and deep-seated beliefs about religion, society, education, and culture.

Illiteracy is a prime cultural barrier to media development. In Pakistan, Bangladesh, and Nepal, half of the people cannot read and write a short, simple sentence about his or her everyday life, which is the United Nations definition for being literate. Adult illiteracy rates are even worse in Ethiopia and Mozambique (United Nations Development Programme, 2007). According to recent estimates, there are 774 million people in the world who are illiterate, and 64 percent are women. Such gender differences are common in many economically developing countries. In Egypt, 83 percent of men are literate, compared with only 59 percent of women (UNESCO Institute for Statistics, 2007).

The inability to read and write limits a person's capacity to communicate, and just as important, it limits the ability to learn and grow. Lack of knowledge of the world profoundly influences attitudes and beliefs, often in a negative manner. Literacy opens up the world to the individual and drives the desire for more and better communication content. Literate individuals are much more likely to make demands of the media that will force the media to achieve a higher level of development. The printed media can flourish only to the degree that a domestic population is literate.

Multilingualism in a nation complicates the logistics of serving the information needs of audiences from different language and ethnic groups. India, for instance, is awash in newspapers. Some 55,000 publish in two dozen languages, and nearly 2,000 of those are dailies that often are engaged in media wars for readership (BusinessWeek, 2005). In some African nations such as Nigeria, three or four languages are used for daily communication. The mass media therefore are faced with the challenge of providing content in each of these languages to meet the needs of the entire population. This is particularly true where the media are owned by the government and operate on a fixed budget that does not allow expansion of service for all who need it.

In nations with privately owned commercial media, it is common for media outlets to focus on the information needs of the largest or most profitable segment of the audience, whether that segment is defined by language or by other unique interests. If media organizations do not have the money or the will to cater to specific language or cultural groups, that segment of the population will go without daily communication. When Singapore became a nation in the 1960s, it decided to exist as a multilingual society. The small island nation, tucked between Malaysia and Indonesia, has four official languages: English, Mandarin Chinese, Malay, and Tamil (southern India), with media existing in all four languages. Singapore has since become a business and technology leader by being able to converse fluently with the Chinese and Indians in the East and the British and Americans in the West.

Meanwhile, China is aggressively seeking to educate its young in English. As the most populous nation in the world, China faces significant language barriers. The nation shares a written language, but the spoken Mandarin in the north of China and the spoken Cantonese in the south of China are quite different, and some 23 dialects exist in the Chinese countryside. As a result, multilingualism serves as a barrier to strengthening a national media system in China.

Another potential hindrance to media development is the reliance on interpersonal communication and public opinion leadership in some societies. Mass media have little or no effect on the daily life of the ordinary citizen when the population is geographically removed from the institutions of government and lacks contact with the larger society. Local authority figures such as village elders or wealthy individuals tend to dominate communication and control public opinion. These social hierarchy and community decision-making practices are particularly common in African and Islamic nations. What these opinion leaders and their circle of associates have to say matters most in the absence of mass media and the diversity of views that the media tend to contribute. These information elites have little or no incentive to foster development of the mass media because it would usurp their power and diminish their status.

Religious beliefs also may result in diminished reliance on mass media and less desire to improve it. In the United States, religious groups such as the Amish or Christian fundamentalists shun or disapprove of their members being heavy media users, because they consider the media to have corrupting or immoral influences on the audience.

Whether rooted in religious beliefs or broader cultural concerns, the fear of negative influences from media content is not confined to any single country or region of the world. This concern is at the heart of what critics call cultural imperialism. Asian nations in particular have erected barriers against imported media content. Malaysia, for example, limits the amount of Western television programming on its channels for fear that Western content could decimate the indigenous culture and replace domestic attitudes and practices with those embedded in the foreign media. Western entertainment is often the target for exclusion because many of the products, services, and practices it promotes—for instance, violence and sexual innuendo, or the use of alcohol, tobacco, and birth control devices— are anathema to the cultural norms of non-Western societies.

But it is not merely West versus non-West. Western European nations also make the same cultural imperialism argument in taking steps to limit or exclude American and other foreign-produced content from their domestic media. No nation wants to become home to U.S. news and entertainment, to the detriment of developing its own media system.

As media globalization continues, many observers have tempered their claims about harmful one-way cultural flows from the West and see a more complex process occurring. For instance, people may absorb imported media forms and adapt them to meet their own cultural values. In this process, importers of cultures also become exporters. All this leads to a new level of cultural hybridity. Consider as an example the worldwide popularity of Japanese animated movies and programs, called *anime,* or the widespread embrace of *telenovelas* produced in Latin American nations, or the growth of India's dynamic film industry.

Economic Barriers

Whatever the physical and cultural barriers to media development may be, money is a necessity, too. A sophisticated media system cannot thrive in economically impoverished nations. In the African nation of Chad, for instance, most of the population exists at subsistence levels. The country has one television station and only a dozen radio stations. Although use of cell phones is increasing, fewer than 1 percent of the people have access to the Internet (CIA, 2007). A poor country faced with hungry people will support a media system only to the extent that it is an asset to the nation's economic improvement, and capitalist countries are more likely to allow profit-oriented media.

Nations with strong national economies, stable monetary systems, and educated workforces tend to be the nations with well-developed media systems. The global economic order has a tremendous impact on the world's media. Unequal economic and trade relations hinder the development, or at least the equal development, of the media in many nations. In some countries, political and economic instability retards development of the media by preventing the enticement of much-needed foreign capital. Across Africa, AIDS is devastating the workforce; in Botswana, for instance, 37 percent of the adult population has HIV/AIDS, and the national life expectancy is about 50 years compared to 78 for those born in the United States (CIA, 2007). It is hard even to think about developing a strong media system in the face of such catastrophe.

Thus, poverty and inequality in the allocation of the world's resources block the development of the media in many countries. Even if the media are privately owned rather than government owned, and the owners have an economic incentive to improve the media in order to capture the largest possible audience, it still requires money to buy a color printing press or to install a transponder to relay broadcast signals or to start an Internet café.

On a large scale, the cost of national telecommunication systems and communication satellites puts a well-developed media system out of reach for all but the wealthiest nations. Only a handful of nations have the money and technical capability to build, buy, or launch their own communication satellites. These satellites have proven to be tremendous enablers of national broadcast networks, remote printing for newspapers, and individual communication via telephone, fax, and personal computers. Through the cooperative International Telecommunications Satellite Organization (ITSO), previously known as Intelsat, most of the world's nations gain access to satellite communication by leasing transponders and accompanying frequencies on orbiting satellites. But without the resources to purchase and operate their own full-time satellites, these nations operate on whatever time and services are available.

Meanwhile, those nations with satellite technology can earn additional money to further develop their capabilities and thus keep outdistancing the poor nations with increasingly sophisticated means of communication. The U.S. space program is a prime example. Only a few nations have the economic and technical ability to launch satellites, and the United States is the leader in maintaining them once they are in orbit. The success of NASA's repair missions will help the United States to maintain leadership in the world information economy for a long time.

For developing nations, the cost of building infrastructure to enable significant development of national media is indeed a formidable barrier, even after the decades of debates, diatribe, and development projects aimed at changing the old information order. Competition from imported programming and the increased availability of international broadcast media content weaken development of the indigenous media in many parts of the world. A University of Cyprus report calls international broadcasting "a major competitive source" in news and sports for the Cypriot stations (Mallouppas, 1998). Singapore wishes to limit the amount of programming secured from neighboring Malaysia in order to develop its own television and film industry. Because of economies of scale, efficiency, and expertise in production and marketing, larger nations can provide almost unlimited quantities of higher-quality media content at a lower cost than producers in smaller or developing nations. This economic barrier makes it difficult, if not impossible, to develop indigenous entertainment programs by local production companies in a competitive situation.

A new barrier in the West is the emerging trend toward the consolidation of media ownership and control in the offices of a few multinational corporations. Media consolidation reduces the diversity of voices. For example, 14 newspapers in Canada's major cities were required to publish the same editorial at least once a week because all of the newspapers had come under ownership of the same media giant. In Mexico and in the United States this decade, critics have objected to efforts to relax federal laws limiting cross-ownership of newspapers, television, and radio stations (IFEX, 2005). A decision by the U.S. Federal Communications Commission in December 2007 to allow more cross-ownership in the largest media markets raised concerns that fewer large corporations will dominate the flow of news. Others, however, suggest that, thanks to digitization, consolidation is less of a crucial issue. Some newspapers, for example, provide digital newscasts on their Web sites without bothering to join forces with TV operations; conversely, TV stations can be market leaders with print news via their online sites.

Overall, the U.S. media are increasingly consolidating, and the impact is felt internationally. For instance, Time Warner owns CNN and CNN International, but also owns book companies, movie studios, television networks, and international cable networks such as The Warner Channel, which operates in Latin America, the Asia-Pacific region, Australia, and Germany. Time Warner also owns movie theaters in more than a dozen countries and publishes magazines, such as *People,* with a worldwide circulation (Columbia Journalism Review, 2004). As William Hachten and James Scotton noted in *The World News Prism* (2007), media globalization has helped to bring communication infrastructure and investment capital for private ownership to many of the former communist countries of Eastern Europe and developing countries of Asia. But the influx of capital and investors has now meant giving up ownership and control of these domestic media outlets to media barons and corporations in distant and foreign lands. Control over communications content accompanies ownership of media channels, and absentee owners are less likely to sacrifice economic profits to support the social good derived from a civic-conscious media system.

On a smaller scale, the cost of starting a media operation or purchasing an existing one is prohibitively high for individuals in any nation, and more so for those in poor nations. The cost of radio and TV sets also limits individual access to receive communication. Even the cost of a subscription or a single issue of a publication puts mass media out of reach for many people in the poorer nations. In South American countries hit hard by recession, some newspapers in Argentina and Chile are being distributed for free, with the intent of recovering costs through higher advertising rates due to increased circulation.

Then there are scarcities. Many nations do not have the presses and other technology for printing mass copies of publications. They often lack the equipment for photographic reproduction, for printing in color, and for other advanced production processes that add to the quantity and quality of printed materials. The scarcity of available electromagnetic frequencies for broadcasting and of geosynchronous orbital slots for satellites are barriers to developing telecommunications systems. On a daily basis, poorer nations also face a scarcity of electricity, gasoline, spare parts, and other necessities of transportation that hinder media development.

Governmental Barriers

Freedom of the press and broadcasting has gained momentum in the twenty-first century. Freedom House, a nonprofit organization based in New York, declared that 18 percent of the world's people now live in a nation with a free media (examples include the United States, Norway, South Africa, Israel, and South Korea), 39 percent live in nations with some media restrictions (Bulgaria, Brazil, Indonesia, Uganda, and Jordan), and 43 percent live in nations with state control or other barriers to a free media (Burma, Cuba, Libya, North Korea, and Turkmenistan). This trendline has not improved in the past decade (Freedom House, 2007).

Freedom House notes that the twentieth century began with not a single nation granting the right to vote to all citizens, male and female, and ended with three-fifths of the world's population having democratically elected governments. Despite two world wars and the Holocaust in the past 100 years, former Freedom House chairman Bette Bao Lord said, "In the end, this has been democracy's century. If the world's community of established democracies embraces freedom as a major goal, the next century will be freedom's century" (Freedom House, 2002). More recently, as concerns over terrorism and political turmoil have arisen, Freedom House leaders such as Chairman Peter Ackerman have noted that the new century has brought "a time of great opportunity and also formidable challenges" (Freedom House Annual Report, 2005).

Media freedom is nearly universal in Western Europe, North and South America, and the Pacific region. Asia and Eastern Europe are in transition, with about half of the nations having free or partly free media. Africa and the Middle East remain heavily tilted toward state control or other barriers to media freedom. Herbert Altschull (1984) theorized that the media often serve as agents of power to maintain and perpetuate the sovereign. To maintain political power, the sovereign finds it effective to suppress, stunt, and otherwise stifle the means of communication for fear that they would be used to usurp him. In such instances, the sovereign resorts to making the mass media part of his dominion. In China, media have served as the official "eyes and ears" of the Communist Party since the Communist Revolution in 1949. Across Eastern Europe, Africa, and the Middle East, governments control radio and television stations as a way of controlling the flow of information.

Where government does not own the means of communication, it sets up barriers to control the private or independent press. Censorship, licensing, and the use of "insult laws" to protect the honor of public officials are common practices used by governments around the world who fear that free expression in an open media system could galvanize public opinion to change the status quo. Because of this potential for the media to promote or instigate political change, journalists are sometimes jailed, beaten, or killed by political leaders attempting to control communication and hold on to power. Organizations such as Amnesty International, the Committee to Protect Journalists, Freedom House, and other international organizations regularly document and publicize the human rights abuses, media suppression, and killing of journalists around the world.

Threats to life and limb are serious political barriers to media development, but so too is the self-censorship that often results from these threats. Journalists in Central and South America have been under the greatest pressure of practicing quality journalism in the face of unstable regimes, would-be leaders in guerrilla movements, and drug cartels. Although media self-censorship is psychological in nature, the very real consequences of being victimized by political violence are a significant barrier to media development, causing some journalists and media organizations to remain silent at times and to serve as the mouthpieces of government at other times. Political leaders also may disenfranchise opposition parties and minority groups to maintain power and privilege. These political tactics amount to barriers to media development because political parties and minority populations often sponsor organs of communication that augment and enrich the flow of information in any media system. These suppressed groups, in fact, may provide the only means of mass communication for a significant portion of the population in some countries.

Threats to media freedom come in many guises, from death to defamation, from intimidation to licensing. Some despots shoot or beat the messengers; others use legal means. Here are a variety of examples culled from sources that track threats to the worldwide media:

—*Intimidation.* Many African governments have a deep-seated antagonism toward the media. Nations such as Niger, Zimbabwe, and Sudan make use of their police and military to intimidate and harass journalists.

—*Defamation.* In Latin America, so-called *desacato* or insult laws protecting the honor of public officials remain on the statute books and are used to punish media criticisms. In Cuba, a media executive went to prison for six years for "insulting" President Fidel Castro. In Zambia, four journalists, including a student, were charged with defamation for reporting that the president was suffering from Parkinson's disease, an incurable brain disorder (IFEX, June 2002).

—*Tax investigations.* After imprisoning an editor for 30 months for violating so-called insult laws, Azerbaijan's national security ministry added charges that the editor of two daily newspapers had evaded paying taxes (Reporters Without Borders, 2007).

—*Licensing.* After permitting the first privately owned newspaper in Syria in 40 years, the government grew frightened and introduced press licensing as a way of maintaining government control. In Zimbabwe, the government announced it would issue only one license to a national radio broadcaster and only one license to a national television broadcaster, effectively maintaining a media monopoly (Bafana, 2002).

—*Censorship.* The Myanmar military government clamped down on public access to information following protests in fall 2007. The government temporarily blocked Internet access and stopped sales of foreign publications carrying news of the crackdown.

—*Closure.* Amid its fight for national control against an Islamist group, the Somali transitional government forced the closure of three independent radio stations in 2007. This action came in a setting where eight Somali journalists already had died seeking to cover the armed struggle (Freedom House, 2007).

—*Seizure.* The government of Kazakhstan seized all 100,000 copies of an edition of the country's leading opposition weekly newspaper, *Juma-Times,* in 2005. The edition carried a report on an alleged political corruption scandal involving a U.S. businessman's payments for oil contracts (Reporters Without Borders, 2007).

—*Travel restrictions.* The governments of Thailand and Myanmar, which are neighbors on less-than-friendly terms, each implemented travel bans on reporters from the other country in order to suppress critical reporting. In the United States, the Washington correspondent for the Arab television network Al Jazeera was detained on his way to cover President Bush when, according to the BBC, police told him Al Jazeera's credit card had been linked to activities in Afghanistan (Freedom Forum, November 2001).

—*Jailing.* The government in Ethiopia has routinely locked up journalists in recent years. In 2005, for instance, authorities rounded up 14 newspaper editors and publishers identified with opposition parties and kept them jailed more than a year (Reporters Without Borders, 2007).

—*Death threats.* In Mexico, a newspaper executive refused a governor's insistence that he support a certain political candidate. Water and electricity to his home were cut off, and police officers surrounded it. When the governor threatened his life, the editor fled to the United States (IFEX, January 2000).

—*Lack of protection.* In Indonesia, the Alliance of Independent Journalists estimated 58 cases of violence against journalists in 2006 and 2007. The group called on government officials to halt attacks, provide more protection, and to cease efforts to "criminalize" media activities (Alliance of Independent Journalists, 2007).

—*Death.* Because of dramatic photos, the shooting death of a Japanese photojournalist covering a protest in Myanmar highlighted the dangers of news coverage of political unrest. The photojournalist working for Agence France Presse had arrived in the country just three days before he died. In Russia, an investigative reporter was shot to death in an elevator at her Moscow apartment building. When prosecutors arrested several men whom officials depicted as members of an organized crime group said to include some law enforcement officers, her death underscored concerns about the safety of journalists looking into Russia's political and economic power struggles.

The year 2007 turned out to be the deadliest for journalists in more than a decade. At the end of the year, 65 journalists had been confirmed killed worldwide, with almost half the deaths coming in Iraq (Committee to Protect Journalists, 2007). Overall, 679 journalists were killed in the line of duty worldwide from 1992 through 2007, with almost three of four murdered and the rest killed in combat or other dangerous assignments.

Besides drug wars and shooting wars and political wars, legal barriers exist to media development. Guaranteeing human rights, including the right to communicate, is a moral belief. Where human rights are elevated, liberty and creativity of the human spirit abound, and so too do the need and the desire for well-developed channels of communication. An essential component of the ideal media environment is a legal right for the public and the media to have access to documents and information held by the government. Those nations that have laws guaranteeing access to public records and public meetings provide a great advantage for their media to develop and thrive. In the United States, public access is mandated through the federal Freedom of Information Act and similar state open meetings and open records laws (called "sunshine" laws because they require governments to operate in the light of day). The media in nations without such laws are usually devoid of the rich and important content that characterizes a quality information system. Sunshine laws create a climate that facilitates newsgathering. Government officials and bureaucrats are more likely to cooperate with journalists when there is a presumption of openness and a right of the public to information. Journalists often face a significant barrier in gathering the news because government sources refuse to talk to them or explain public policy.

While many governmental barriers to a well-developed global media remain, good news abounds in many countries. Mongolia has prohibited government control of broadcasting. Romania is liberalizing its harsh defamation laws. In Latin America, insult laws recently have been repealed in Argentina, Guatemala, Honduras, Costa Rica, Panama, Paraguay, and Peru, and partially repealed in Chile. And in China, home to one-fifth of the world's population, a most remarkable development occurred. Just a few weeks after China formally issued a list of media taboos, nicknamed the "Seven No's" (#7 on the list warns the news media not to violate party propaganda), *People's Daily,* the 2-million-circulation bible of Marxist-Maoist orthodoxy, published an editorial that endorsed the citizen's "right to be informed" by an honest and factual media system (Zeitlin, 2001). The march toward a freer media, while inexorably slow, continues one step at a time across the globe.

Media Barriers

Newsrooms around the world have their own shortcomings, such as poorly trained reporters and editors, lack of objectivity, greed, loss of credibility, and self-censorship.

Lack of journalistic training is a barrier to media development in many nations. Formal journalism education is embryonic or nonexistent in most of the newly independent and developing nations, where on-the-job training is the norm. Journalists in the former Communist nations needed retraining before they could work in the media with a new philosophical and ideological approach. Those who could not be retrained were purged to improve the credibility of the "new" media in the eyes of the public. A shortage of journalists resulted, and with the end of communism, the field was suddenly open to anyone who wanted to have a go at it. The experience of press freedom for the first time, or liberation after an era of suppression, led to a surge in the number and variety of media outlets. Experience in Eastern Europe and elsewhere has shown that the newness wears off quickly. New and inexperienced journalists often then turned their attention to partisan reporting with the newfound tool of a powerful press.

Some settings are so volatile that professionalism is extraordinarily difficult. Palestinians living in the Israeli-occupied territories of the West Bank and Gaza were long prevented by Israel from establishing their own media. When Israel and the Palestine Liberation Organization (PLO) formally recognized each other in 1993, the PLO quickly moved to begin the development of a media system operated by Palestinians to meet the information and entertainment needs of Palestinians.

In 2002, Israel strenuously objected to obituaries in Palestinian newspapers that honored suicide bombers. The death notice of a Palestinian man who blew himself up, killing an Israeli woman and her 10-year-old daughter, glorified the man and concluded, "We pray that Allah will grant a haven for the heroic Martyr with His plentiful mercy" (Palestinian Media Watch, quoting *Al Ayyam*, February 10, 2002). Similarly, the media watch group criticized a Palestinian TV children's program for portraying a young girl running with a schoolbag over her shoulder, interspersed with real news footage showing an Israeli helicopter firing a missile, and then the female actress falling dead with her books scattering. The media watch director observed, "One prominent objective of the Palestinian print and broadcast media is to promote hatred and fear by presenting Israelis, even to the youngest viewers, as monstrous, ready and willing to kill them at any time. I do not think it is possible to prevent this kind of programming. After all, we have allowed the Palestinian Authority control over its own media" (Palestinian Media Watch, 2001).

On the other hand, a pro-Palestine media watch group attacked news coverage by CNN, the Associated Press, and other Western news agencies as highlighting Israeli suffering while downplaying Palestinian suffering (Palestine Media Watch, 2002). As an example, the Palestinian media watch group criticized CNN for having on its Web site a memorial listing Israelis who had died at the hands of suicide-bomber Palestinians, but not of Palestinians who had died at the hands of Israeli military forces.

A barrier to media development in Russia is manifested by the selling of favorable news stories. The practice is called hidden advertising because it goes under the guise of being an honest news story. Two-thirds of the journalists responding to a survey by the Institute of Sociology of the Russian Academy of Sciences in St. Petersburg said they had sold favorable news stories more than once. A senior researcher lamented, "These figures indicate how easy it is to manipulate journalists in Russia. It is difficult for them to resist financial temptations because, just like most people, they have rather modest incomes" (Mater, August 2001). The practice, known as *zakazukha* in Russian, involved "price lists" that are discreetly circulated to public relations firms. Former Communist Party mouthpiece *Izvestia* reportedly raised $310,000 in "hidden advertising" in one month alone. Russia has not been alone in this practice. The same cash-for-story procedure has been common in Mexico and other Central American countries, although reforms are occurring (Rockwell, 2002).

Beyond the corruption of "hidden advertising" is the political power of real advertising. The World Bank reported that Bangladesh newspapers are captives of state patronage because a newspaper's profitability, even its survival, heavily depends on the allocation of government advertising. As a result, a newspaper that turns critical of the Bangladesh government may be quickly disciplined by the withdrawal of state advertising (IFEX, July 2002). This potential co-opting of the media may produce a self-censorship that robs the public of necessary information that any well-developed media system should provide.

These barriers to quality journalism feed the low status of journalists in society and the lack of prestige ascribed to the media in general. Accuracy and fairness are measures of professionalism that can add to the quality of news coverage and can generate credibility and trust in the eyes of the public. However, these elements are not found in media systems that practice partisan, advocacy, or sensationalist journalism. In a Eurobarometer public opinion survey conducted by the European Commission, the sensationalist-driven British newspapers were found to be the least trusted by their readers. Their trust level was a dismal 20 percent. The next worse result (39 percent) was in Italy, where the media were at the time dominated by a billionaire prime minister. Trust was highest in Belgium, Finland, and Luxembourg, at roughly 60 percent each.

The practice of journalism in the United States is closely watched around the world. When the United States asked its TV networks not to broadcast excerpts of Osama bin Laden via the Qatar TV station Al Jazeera, other countries took note. Singapore praised the "healthy guided censorship" it saw in the new U.S. information policy. Zimbabwe sought to justify its repression of independent journalism by noting, "If the most celebrated democracies in the world won't allow their national interests to be tampered with, we will not allow it too." In response, the World Association of Newspapers (WAN) criticized the United States for justifying its call for self-censorship and noted, "It is no accident that bin Laden operated out of a country which had totally outlawed free expression, information and debate, nor that the regimes most supportive of his and other terrorism networks are among the most repressive in the world" (IFEX, May 2002). WAN President Roger Parkinson said, "The international community should put all its political weight and money behind every effort to bring down the barriers and obstacles to the free flow of information and ideas."

Technological Barriers

Technology is both a barrier to media development and a potential destroyer of barriers. Technology is a barrier in the world of established media because newspapers, magazines, radio stations, television stations, and cable systems are expensive to start and to distribute. When technology is transferred from media-rich nations to the media-poor, that transfer usually means sending soon-outdated equipment to the poorer nations. Although this practice does help the recipient nations, the technological gap between rich and poor nations keeps increasing. There are obvious disadvantages, if not dangers, in this growing disparity, but it takes money to close the gap.

The Internet does not share the enormous start-up and distribution costs of established media, although its use does require a literate population with access to a computer and knowledge to operate it. As a result, the Internet serves, and will long serve, as a communication forum for elites and the educated young.

The Internet transcends geographical boundaries, which makes its potential to destroy existing barriers so intriguing. The nonprofit Freedom House organization noted that many repressive governments—among them Iran, Pakistan, Syria, and Saudi Arabia—place fewer restrictions on Internet access than they do on print and broadcast media. A Freedom House scholar observed, "The Internet's relative openness in some closed societies reflects the dilemma posed by the opportunities on the web for economic development, international trade, and cultural advances" (Freedom House, 2002).

As the Internet and other digital technologies become a means to overcome barriers, they also represent a challenge to authoritarian rulers. Maintaining political leverage over newspapers and broadcast stations once was relatively simple. Printing presses were expensive and easily detected by authorities bent on shutting down or controlling a newspaper or magazine. Television and radio broadcast equipment was likewise expensive, and accessible spectrum space was scarce. But for a modest investment, producers now can create content in print, audio, or video form and transmit it globally.

In extreme cases, the *vox populi* of the twenty-first century—bloggers—are being arrested. China jailed 50 "cyber-dissidents," Vietnam jailed eight, and Egypt sentenced one man to four years in jail for a blog critical of the president. Access to news on the Web is being controlled in China, North Korea, Thailand, Malaysia, and other countries. Especially in war-torn countries, totalitarian regimes often own and always control the media and access to mass communication (Freedom House Map, 2007).

The OpenNet Initiative, a collaboration between researchers at the University of Toronto, Harvard Law School, University of Cambridge, and Oxford University, identifies four basic ways in which governments censor the Internet. With *technical blocking,* governments try to keep certain Web sites from being accessed by blocking the Web address or the domain. Some countries are starting to block sites based on key search words or key words in a Web address site. These are indirect ways of blocking Web access. Some regimes collaborate with Internet search engines for *search result removals*. Sites that the regime deems harmful will not appear when searched for, making it difficult to find opposition or free speech sites. *Take down* is a method used when authorities have control over hosts for Web content. Governments can demand that some Web sites be shut down or even have the domain deregistered, making the Web site invisible to browsers aiming toward the site. Perhaps the most pernicious form of Internet censorship is *induced self-censorship*. Not limited to totalitarian regimes, this method is used to keep people from searching for and seeing certain Web content through threatened legal action, including arrest. There may be no written prohibition on searches or reading of Web sites, but there is the implied knowledge that the government is keeping track of Web searches and usage, and that which runs afoul of the government could have harmful consequences for the Web user (About Filtering, 2007).

By 2007, about three-quarters of a billion people worldwide had used the Internet, representing a 10 percent increase from the previous year (ComScore, 2007). Denmark had the world's highest rate of per-capita broadband use, at 32 percent, followed closely by The Netherlands, Iceland, Switzerland, and South Korea (International Telecommunication Union, 2006). Growth rates for Net usage are highest in countries where access had been limited, such as Russia and China. As for everyday use, the United States leads the world in the number of unique Internet visitors, followed by China, Japan, Germany, and the United Kingdom (ComScore, 2007). Finally, here is a statistic to highlight worldwide variance in Internet access: Five times more Internet users live in the United States, and two times more live in Japan, than all of the users in Africa (ITU, 2006).

Conclusion

Afghanistan has a long road ahead to rebuild its media system. Physical barriers include its harsh terrain and decimated communications infrastructure caused by three decades of war. Cultural barriers include a low literacy rate, a history of religious strife, and the backlash against the flow of modern, mostly Western, cultural programs and information. Economic barriers include rampant poverty, the disintegration of a national economy or international trade, and a scarcity of resources such as radios, printing presses, and digital technology. Governmental barriers include an effort to revive democracy and civic institutions amid assassination attempts, feuding tribes, and continued military struggles with insurgents and Taliban fighters. Afghanistan adopted a new press law in 2004 that provides for freedom of expression but at the same time prohibits information contrary to the principles of Islam or other religious beliefs. This continues to leave journalists in a difficult position of negotiating their autonomy according to practical constraints. Also as a practical reality, the media enjoy more freedom in Kabul, the capital city, than in many provinces under the political control of regional governors or warlords who impose more arbitrary standards. Although the number of media outlets has grown substantially in recent years, many survive on subsidies from the state, political parties, or international agencies. Digital technology remains elusive; just 1 percent of Afghanistan's population had access to the Internet in 2006 (Freedom House, 2007).

Despite these enormous barriers, journalists are at work in Afghanistan, trying to make their nation and their media system better each day. Physical and economic barriers are often the easiest to overcome because all it takes are resources, whereas the barriers erected by human attitudes and actions remain steadfastly immovable until a society and its people are ready to take the next step.

Hiebert, Ungurait, and Bohn's media systems paradigm is based on a reciprocal relationship between a society and its media system, each having a direct impact on the other. Rather than any single factor being the determinant, the evolution of a nation's media system is based on the interaction of physical, cultural, economic, government, media, and technological barriers. Every society is a mixture of stability and change, and the resulting tension between the two affects the development of the media in that society.

BIBLIOGRAPHY

A.C. Nielsen Media Measurement Services. "An International Survey of the Internet." Available: http://acnielsen.com/products/reports/netwatch/index.htm, 2000.

"About Filtering." Retrieved December 26, 2007, from The OpenNet Initiative: http://opennet.net/about-filtering.

AINA. "Publications and Projects: Malalai." Available: http://www.ainaworld.com/en/publication_malalai.html, 2002.

Alliance of Independent Journalists. "Stop Violence and Criminalization against the Press!" Available: http://blogaji.wordpress.com/2007/08/24/344/, August 2007.

Altschull, J. H. *Agents of Power.* New York: Longman, 1984.

Associated Press. "Kim Dae-jung's Uneasy Relations with South Korean Press." Freedom Forum online. Available: http://www.freedomforum.org. Accessed August 20, 2001.

Bafana, B. "Zimbabwe: Broadcast Blues." 2002. World Press Review Online. Available: http://www.worldpress.org/Africa/113.cfm

BusinessWeek online. "Read All about It: India's Media Wars." May 16, 2005. Available: http://www.businessweek.com/print/magazine/content/05_20/b3933075.htm?chan=gl

CIA World Factbook 2007. "Botswana." Available: https://www.cia.gov/library/publications/the-world-factbook/geos/bc.html

———. "Chad." Available: https://www.cia.gov/library/publications/the-world-factbook/geos/cd.html#Comm

———. "India." Available: https://www.cia.gov/library/publications/the-world-factbook/geos/in.html

CIA World Factbook 2002. Washington, D. C.: U.S. Government Printing Office, 2002.

Columbia Journalism Review. 2004. *"Resources: Who Owns What."* Available: http://www.cjr.org/resources

Committee to Protect Journalists. "Journalists Killed: Statistics and Background." Available: http://www.cpj.org/deadly/index.html

Committee to Protect Journalists. "Journalists Killed in 2007." Retrieved December 27, 2007, from Committee to Protect Journalists: http://www.cpj.org/deadly/killed07.html

ComScore. (2007, March 6). *Worldwide Internet Audience Has Grown 10 Percent in Last Year, According to comScore Networks.* Available: http://www.comscore.com/press/release.asp?press=1242

"CPJ Chronicles Crackdown on Iran's News Media." Freedom Forum online. Available: http://www.freedomforum.org

Ford, P. "Ahead of Olympics, China Lifts Foreign Media Restrictions." Christian Science Monitor online, December 1, 2006. Available: http://www.csmonitor.com/2006/1202/p00s01-woap.html

Freedom Forum online. Web site: http://www.freedomforum.org

Freedom House. "Map of Press Freedom." Available: http://www.freedomhouse.org/template.cfm?page=251 &year=2007

———. "Annual Report 2005." Available: http://www.freedomhouse.org/uploads/special_report/ 41.pdf

———. "Freedom House Gravely Concerned about Desperate Situation of Journalists and Human Rights Advocates in Somalia." Available: http://www.freedomhouse.org/printer_friendly.cfm?page=70&release=590, November 15, 2007.

————. "Press Freedom Declines in Asia, Ex-Soviet Region and Latin America, Study Finds; Warns of Growing Internet Restriction: 2007." Available: http://www.freedomhouse.org/

————. "Survey of Press Freedom." Available: http://www.freedomhouse.org/pfs2001/pfs2001.pdf, 2002.

Gradstein, L. "Arab Sitcom Becomes Surprise Hit in Israel." National Public Radio online. January 15, 2008. Available: http://www.npr.org/templates/story/story.php?storyId=18096454

Hachten, W. A., and Scotton, J. F. *The World News Prism, 7th ed.* Ames: Iowa State University Press, 2007.

Hiebert, R., Ungurait, D., and Bohn, T. *Mass Media II.* New York: Longman, 1979.

International Freedom of Expression Exchange (IFEX). Available: http://www.ifex.org

International Press Institute. "Afghanistan 2000 World Press Freedom Review." Available: http://www.freemedia.at/cms/ipi/freedom_detail.html?country=/KW0001/KW0005/KW0109/&year=2000

International Telecommunications Union. "ICT Levels around the World." Available: http://www.itu.int/ITU-D/ict/statistics/ict/index.html, 2006.

————. "Top 20 Economies by Broadband Penetration, 2006." Available: http://www.itu.int/ITU-D/ict/statistics/at_glance/top20_broad_2006.html

Mallouppas, A. "Cyprus Media Profile." *Euromedia '98,* Vienna, Austria, June 26, 1998.

Mater, G. "Most Russian Journalists Sell Favorable Stories as Hidden Advertising." Freedom Forum online. Available: http://www.freedomforum.org/templates/document.asp?documentID=14735, August 29, 2001.

Michaels, J. "U.S. Pulls Plug on 6 al-Qaeda Media Outlets." USA Today online. Available: http://www.usatoday.com/news/world/iraq/2007-10-04-Mediacenter_N.htm

Palestine Media Watch. Web site: http://www.pmwatch.org [pro-Palestinian]

Palestinian Media Watch. Web site: http://www.pmw.org.il/bulletins-191101.html [pro-Israeli]

"Podcast Bypasses Singapore Media Restrictions." The Age online (Australia). August 5, 2005. Available: http://www.theage.com.au/news/breaking/podcast-bypasses-singapore-media-restrictions/2005/08/05/1123125882622.html

Reporters Without Borders. "Afghanistan: Annual Report 2007." Available: http://www.rsf.org/country-50.php3?id_mot=269&Valider=OK. Retreived December 29, 2007.

————. "International Press Freedom Roundup 2007." Available: http://www.rsf.org/rubrique.php3?id_rubrique=50, 2007.

Rockwell, R. "Corruption & Calamity: Limiting Ethical Journalism in Mexico and Central America." *Global Media Journal* 1, 2002. [Online journal] Available: http://lass.calumet.purdue.edu/cca/gmj/OldSiteBackup/SubmittedDocuments/archivedpapers/fall2002/Rockwell.ht

Scott, B. "Reviving Afghan Journalism." *Global Journalist Online magazine.* Available: http://www.journalism.missouri.edu/globalj/index.html, 1st Quarter, 2002.

UNESCO [on-line news portal]. Web site: http://www.unesco.org

UNESCO Institute for Statistics. "Literacy." Available: http://www.uis.unesco.org/ev.php?URL_ID=6401&URL_DO=DO_TOPIC&URL_SECTION=201, October, 2007.

United Nations Development Programme. Human Development Report. Available: http://hdrstats.undp.org/indicators/3.html, 2007.

U.S. State Department. Telephone interview with State Department spokesman Callie Fuller, August 1, 2002.

"Waging War on the Media." World Press Freedom Review, International Press Institute. Available: http://www.freemedia.at/wpfr/intro_wpfr.htm#top, 2001.

World Press Review Online. Available: http://www.worldpress.org/profiles/Botswana.cfm

Zeitlin, A. "Is the Stranglehold Easing?" Freedom Forum online. Available: http://www.freedomforum.org/templates/document.asp?documentID=14850, September 10, 2001.

5 Freedom of the Press around the World[*]

LEE B. BECKER AND TUDOR VLAD
University of Georgia, USA

The concept of press freedom is a contentious one. Fundamentally, the issues are freedom from what and freedom for whom?

In the Western world, historically much of the attention has been on freedom from government control. Many in the United States take great pride in the First Amendment to the U.S. Constitution, which states that "Congress shall make no law . . . abridging the freedom of speech, or of the press."

Critics around the world, however, question the Western media's—and particularly the American media's—dependence on its commercial base, arguing that it greatly influences their product. These critics ask who is being served by a media system that largely caters to popular taste and rarely plays an educative role, infrequently attempts to resolve social problems, and often ignores the needs of the citizenry.

This chapter elaborates on these issues by tracing some of the historical discussions of press freedom. It also takes a look at how major agencies around the world monitor press freedom. It ends with a discussion of challenges to press freedom, with particular focus on those challenges resulting from revolutionary changes in the ways journalism is practiced with the new communication technologies.

Normative Theories of the Press

Perhaps no single treatise on press freedom has been more influential than *Four Theories of the Press,* first published in 1956 by American scholars Fredrick Siebert, Theodore Peterson, and Wilbur Schramm (Siebert, Peterson, and Schramm, 1956). Almost 50 years after the book first appeared, scholars referred to it as a "work that remains remarkably influential around the world" (Hallin and Mancini, 2004).

---

[*] This chapter is dedicated to the memory of Robert L. Stevenson, who authored the essay on this topic in earlier editions of this book and whose scholarship on press freedom has informed our understanding of the topic. We are struggling still to accept a world without Bob. He touched our lives in many important ways.

Siebert, Peterson, and Schramm identified four models or theoretical types of media. The first, historically, was the *authoritarian* type, where the government controlled the press through prior censorship and through punishment after publication. The printing press was born into this type of society, and governments sought to create constraints to manage it. The modern variant of the authoritarian model, according to Siebert and his colleagues, was the *Soviet Communist* type. States following this model also controlled the media and assigned them the responsibility of building a classless, Marxist society. The *libertarian* model was seen as the counterpoint to the authoritarian model. Its primary feature is the absence of government control and the view that truth will prevail in an environment in which media operate free of that control. The American prescription of an absence of a role for government, stated in the First Amendment to the U.S. Constitution, was seen as an embodiment of the libertarian model. The fourth model, *social responsibility,* holds that the media have obligations to society that accompany their freedom. One of these obligations is to provide meaningful information to members of society.

A number of analysts have argued that the classification is incomplete. Hachten (1981), among others, proposed the addition of a fifth model, called the *developmental* model, in which the press is seen as a building tool for national identity and economic development. Picard (1985) argued for inclusion of a *democratic socialist* press theory, which allowed for state intervention, particularly through economic controls, to protect citizens from press concentration and to provide for society's needs.

Despite its continuing influence, the *Four Theories of the Press* has been widely criticized. Nerone (1995), for example, argued that even the title is misleading, for the book does not present four theories, but one theory with four examples. The theory is that a communication system reflects in its structure, policy and behavior the society in which it operates. Prominent communication theoretician Denis McQuail (2000) contends that Siebert, Peterson, and Schramm's theorizing is particularly deficient in regard to the broadcast media, where state intervention has been seen as nearly essential. Many Western societies have gone far beyond intervention, however, to create public service broadcasting alternatives to commercial broadcasting that have enjoyed wide public support. Hallin and Mancini (2004) argued that there has never been much evidence that there are many media systems that actually fit the models. Nerone (1995), Hallin and Mancini (2004), Stevenson (2004), and others, have argued that there is little evidence to support the idea that the media actually reflect the larger society of which they are a part.

What is perhaps most important about *Four Theories of the Press* today is its emphasis on the idea of press freedom. For the authors, freedom of the press from government constraint was central. This is what they meant by press freedom. The authors saw the media's dependence on commercial support as the mechanism by which it gained independence from government intervention.

Denis McQuail (2000) has argued that this concept of press or media freedom is too limited. A broader, and more valuable, concept should include both the degree of freedom enjoyed by the media and the degree of access for citizens to media content. The media should have independence sufficient to protect free and open public expression of ideas and information, according to McQuail. Citizens have a right to expect a diversity of content, however, and this expectation is at odds with a concentration of ownership and monopoly of control, whether on the part of the state or as the result of commercial market forces.

Beate Rozumilowicz (2002) contended that the question of "who has control of the media?" is the critical consideration of media freedom. She argued that media freedom requires a diffusion of control and access supported by a nation's legal, institutional, economic, and social-cultural systems. Free and independent media can only exist in a structure that is effectively demonopolized of the control of any concentrated social groups or forces. In addition, the structure must guarantee citizen access to the media and to media content. In her view, a media structure that is free of interference from government, from business, or from dominant social groups is better able to maintain and support the competitive and participative elements that define the concept of democracy and assist in the ongoing process of democratization.

Rozumilowicz sees the ideal media environment as one in which there are two media sectors, a market-led media sector and a nonmarket sector. Within the market sector, advertisers are free to present their goods to target audiences, programmers can use fees provided by these advertisers to draw in audiences, and audiences are informed and entertained to the extent the market allows. The nonmarket sector provides balance by ensuring that the needs of nondominant groups are met. It also creates a forum in which a common discourse emerges and people are allowed to function within the society. For these two sectors to exist, there must be legal, institutional, and social-cultural support. For example, the market sector can exist only if laws are in place to protect media from government interference. Audiences also must be protected via defamation laws from media abuse. Also needed are antitrust legislation, ownership laws limiting concentration, licensing laws, and rules on advertising. For the nonmarket sector to exist, there must be legal and institutional support for the right to publish and the right of access. Citizens should be guaranteed the right to information, and the various voices in society should be guaranteed the right to communicate.

This ideal world of media freedom is reached only through what Rozumilowicz calls media reform, and she outlines four stages of reform. The first stage, labeled the *Pre-transition Stage,* lays the groundwork for subsequent change. During this change, there is an opening or freeing of a previously constrained media system. The regime signals a greater willingness to tolerate criticism and expressions of alternative points of view. In the second stage, the *Primary Transition Stage,* there is a systematic change within the formerly authoritarian regime. Statutes on access to information, defamation, ownership, and the like are passed. The culture of censorship is disrupted. The next stage is called the *Secondary Stage.* During this period, both politicians and journalists participate in training seminars to explain and clarify the new institutional and legal order. Networks of media professionals develop. Journalists receive training in new skills of investigative and responsible journalism. The final stage is called the *Late or Mature Stage.* At this point, legal and institutional questions have been resolved, and educational opportunities for journalists are well established. Instruction to provide support for open communication is incorporated in primary and secondary schooling. In this view, media freedom is an end state toward which a country can move. It also can fall backwards, as changes take place in society. Monopolization of media outlets as a result of market competition, for example, would work against media freedom.

Another prominent communication scholar, James Curran (2005), presents a similar, if more complex, picture of media freedom. He differentiates between a classical liberal perspective on media freedom and the radical democratic perspective. The classical focuses on the freedom of the media to publish or broadcast, whereas the radical focuses on how mass communications can mediate in an equitable way conflict and competition between social groups in society. For Curran, the ideal media system would contain as its core public service broadcasting of the sort common in European society. Here people can come together to discuss how the society is to be managed. The *public service core* features public affairs materials, impartial news reports, and content reflecting the diversity of society. It is inclusive rather than exclusive.

This public service core is surrounded by and completed by four sectors. One is the *private sector,* which responds largely to market forces and public tastes. The private sector would be complemented by *a social market sector* consisting of minority media supported by the state to promote media diversity. A third sector, a *civic society sector,* would be under the control of social and political groups, such as the political parties, unions, and social interest organizations. These groups would control media that support their own causes. These media would contribute to a diverse media mix. A final sector, a *professional sector,* would be made up of communication professionals, such as journalists and entertainment producers, and its content would reflect professional standards. For example, the journalists should be guided only by a desire to seek out and communicate what they see as "truth." Entertainment producers would create socially relevant, critical content. While Curran's model is an ideal type, he argued that all sectors except the professional sector exist in many societies today.

Empirically Based Models of Press Freedom

The four media types identified in *Four Theories of the Press,* as well as those identified by others who elaborated on this classic work, were ideal types. That is, the types do not necessarily exist in fact. The theorizing is called normative, for it prescribes what ought to be rather than what is.

Scholars Daniel Hallin and Paolo Mancini (2004) provided the first empirical analysis of press models in their book, *Comparing Media Systems.* In this work, they attempted to describe what actually exists rather than what might or should exist. From that description, however, they also created ideal types.

Hallin and Mancini examined in detail the media systems of the United States, Canada, and 16 Western European countries and classified these systems into three types, or models. These are the *Polarized Pluralistic Model* (found in the Mediterranean countries of France, Greece, Italy, Portugal and Spain), the *Democratic Corporatist Model* (found in the Northern European countries of Austria, Belgium, Denmark, Finland, Germany, the Netherlands, Norway, Sweden, and Switzerland), and the *Liberal Model* (present in the North Atlantic countries of Great Britain, United States, Canada, and Ireland).

In classifying these countries, Hallin and Mancini recognized differences among them. The goal was to focus not on the countries, but on what the media systems of the countries say about media types. From these observations, they defined each of the three models.

The *Polarized Media Model* is one in which the press is oriented not toward the masses but to the elite members of society. Circulation is relatively limited. The electronic media system is highly centralized. Freedom of the press is a relatively new experience for media systems of this type, as is commercialization of the media. Newspapers have weak financial footing, resulting in the need for government subsidies. The state is often owner, regulator, and provider of funding for the media. The media system closely mirrors political divisions in society, and the press focuses on political life. Commentary-oriented and advocacy journalism are important parts of the media mix. Government, political parties, and industrialists with political ties exercise strong control over the media. Professionalization of journalism is not highly developed, and journalism and political activism go hand-in-hand.

The *Democratic Corporatist Model* has a high level of newspaper circulation, meaning that much of the population is reached, rather than only the elite. Press freedom came early to these media systems and coexists with strong state support for the media and regulation of them. These media systems have a history of strong party newspapers and newspapers aligned with organized social groups, so that, in general, significant elements of the media reflect the political divisions of society. At the same time, components of the media system are commercialized. While commentary-oriented journalism exists, there is a growing emphasis on professionalized, neutral journalism focused on the reporting of information. Journalists tend to be highly organized. Parties and organized social groups play a role in broadcast governance that is counterbalanced by professionalism within those institutions.

The *Liberal Model* has had high levels of newspaper circulation reaching the masses rather than only the elite. Press freedom also developed early in the countries that help formulate this model. Commercialism dominates, and there is only a weak link between the media and the political parties and divisions of the society. Professionalism of journalism is high, but the journalists are only weakly organized. Information-oriented journalism is predominant, though commentary exists as well. In general, the role of the state is very limited, but it is more pronounced in the area of broadcasting, especially public broadcasting. Broadcast and even public broadcasting are isolated from political control. Overall, the market plays a stronger role than the state, and journalism is more influenced by commercial than political influences.

Hallin and Mancini (2004) observe that there is some evidence that the *Liberal Model* is becoming increasingly dominant around the world. Changes in Europe—such as the increasing commercialization of the media system, the emphasis on information-oriented, as opposed to opinion-based, content, and the professionalism of journalists—are moving toward the *Liberal Model*. The change in Europe toward commercially supported broadcasting system, often at the expense of the public broadcasting system, has been particularly pronounced. Many countries have lacked the political will to provide the needed support for the noncommercial systems in a world where commercially supported broadcasters deliver a variety of programming. While critics point out that the "variety" is limited in the commercial offerings, consumers often seem satisfied with the sameness of the commercial offering.

Despite the evidence of the dominance of the *Liberal Model,* Hallin and Mancini argue that the existence of countervailing forces limit homogenization of the media systems around the world. Variations in the legal and political systems of the countries are reflected in their media systems, they note. For example, they see no evidence that First

Amendment absolutism, as it exists in the United States, would ever overtake the demands of the European systems for a strong contribution to the education and betterment of society by their media. Politicization of the media—even in the United States, where the Fox Network has enjoyed significant success—could well be a significant counterforce to further development of the *Liberal Model*.

Technological change, as will be discussed below, also has the potential to alter many of the current assumptions about media systems around the world.

Monitoring Press Freedom

More than 100 organizations throughout the world engage in some form of media system assessment and evaluation or media freedom promotion. Many of these were formed in response to democratization in Europe and in Latin America. The groups describe their missions variously as promoting free and independent media through activism, monitoring media freedom violations, evaluating media systems through indices and written reports, and defending and protecting journalists working in conflict zones and under repressive governments.

A number of these organizations are either global or regional in scope, allowing for country-by-country comparisons of their findings and conclusions. These organizations fall into two categories—nongovernmental organizations, or NGOs, and international governing organizations. Three NGOs—Freedom House (U.S.), the International Research and Exchange Board (U.S.), and Reporters sans frontières (Reporters Without Borders) (France)—produce numerical indices that touch on press freedom and varying amounts of written analysis of the overall media environment. Other NGOs produce similar written reports, often known as country reports, and/or counts and descriptions of physical, psychological, and legal attacks on journalists and media organizations. Examples are Arab Press Freedom Watch (U.K.), Committee to Protect Journalists (U.S.), Center for Journalists in Extreme Situations (Russia), the European Institute for the Media (France, Germany), the Inter-American Press Association (U.S.), the International Federation of Journalists (Belgium), the International Press Institute (Austria), and the Media Institute of Southern Africa (Namibia). At least three international governing institutions—the Organization of American States (OAS), the Organization for Security and Cooperation in Europe (OSCE), and the United Nations—have formed special media freedom offices, which produce reports for review by the entire organizations. Those reports are usually country and regional reports, as well as comprehensive analysis of particularly urgent media issues or controversies.

In addition, foreign ministries of governments also monitor media freedom. For example, the U.S. State Department uses its overseas embassies and their contacts to produce extensive reports on media freedom, based on U.S. standards, to determine whether the United States should provide financial and other aid to nations. Under the 1961 Foreign Assistance Act, the reports are required to be submitted to the U.S. Congress. The UK government submits a human rights report, including coverage of media freedom, to inform Parliament of global conditions and UK efforts to promote human rights. (The work of these groups is not reviewed in this chapter.)

Four of these organizations produce numeric scores for the countries they rate, and these scores are widely used throughout the world by people who are interested in monitoring change in press freedom in countries across times. The oldest and best established of the organizations monitoring press freedom around the world is Freedom House, a nongovernmental organization based in Washington, D.C. Freedom House was founded in 1941 to promote democracy globally. Since 1978, it has published a global survey of freedom, known as *Freedom in the World,* now covering 193 countries and 15 related or disputed territories (Freedom House, 2007a). The evaluations Freedom House produces are widely used by policymakers, academics, and journalists. The organization is funded by private individual contributions, foundation awards, and grants from governments, including the U.S. government and the European Union (Freedom House, 2007a).

In 1980, as a separate undertaking, *Freedom House* began conducting its media freedom survey—*Freedom of the Press: A Global Survey of Media Independence*—which in 2007 covered 195 countries and territories (Freedom House, 2008).

To measure press freedom in these countries, Freedom House looks at 23 different criteria in three distinct categories (Freedom House, 2008). The first category is the legal environment for the media, focusing on the laws and legal institutions that restrict the media's ability to operate. The second category is the political environment, and here Freedom House examines the degree of political control over the content of the media. The third criterion is economic environment. Freedom House evaluates the structure of media ownership, media concentration, costs of starting and operating media, and the open competition in the market for advertising revenue. Regional experts and scholars and general editors make the actual classification of the countries in terms of these 23 criteria. The top 10 and bottom 10 countries in terms of the Freedom House measures are shown in Table 5.1 for years 2001 to 2006.

Reporters sans frontières (RSF), a registered nonprofit based in Paris, evaluates what it terms Respect for Media Freedom as part of its work to defend journalists and media outlets around the world. It does this by condemning attacks on press freedom worldwide, publishing a variety of annual and special reports on media freedom, and appealing to governments and international organizations on behalf of journalists and media organizations. On an annual basis, RSF publishes comprehensive regional and country reports that assess political, economic, and legal environments for media freedom. In 2002, RSF released its first Worldwide Press Freedom (RSF, 2002) report and ranking of individual nations. RSF is funded by the sale of its twice-annual albums of photographs and annual calendars, as well as by auctions, donations, membership dues, public grants, and partnerships with private firms (RSF, 2007).

RSF measures the extent to which legal and political environments, circumstances, and institutions permit and promote media freedom and the ability of journalists to collect and disseminate information unimpeded by physical, psychological, or legal attacks and harassment. To create the index, RSF sends out a 50-item questionnaire to in-country sources, usually members of domestic and foreign media as well as legal experts and members of NGOs involved with media freedom (RSF, 2007). RSF receives an average of three to four completed questionnaires for each country, and if it does not receive at least three, the country is not included. The questions fall into five categories: physical and psychological attacks on the journalists, legal harassment of and discrimination against

Table 5.1 Freedom House Top 10 and Bottom 10 Countries in Press Freedom

Rnk.	2001	Rnk.	2002	Rnk.	2003	Rnk.	2004	Rnk.	2005	Rnk.	2006
1	Iceland	1	Andorra	1	Denmark	1	Finland	1	Finland	1	Finland
	New Zealand		Iceland		Iceland		Iceland		Iceland		Iceland
	Sweden		New Zealand		Sweden	3	Sweden	3	Denmark	3	Belgium
	Switzerland		Saint Lucia		Belgium		Denmark		Norway		Denmark
	The Bahamas		Sweden		Finland		Norway		Sweden		Norway
6	Belgium	6	Belgium	6	Norway	6	Belgium	6	Belgium		Sweden
	Denmark		Monaco		Switzerland		Luxembourg	7	Luxembourg	7	Luxembourg
	Norway		Norway		New Zealand		Netherlands		Netherlands		Switzerland
9	Australia	9	Palau		Palau		Switzerland	9	Switzerland	9	Andorra
	Finland		SanMarion	10	St.Lucia	10	NewZealand	10	Liechtenstein		Netherlands
	Marshall Islands								New Zealand		New Zealand
178	D.R.Congo	184	Eritrea	184	Sudan	185	Belarus	185	Belarus	186	Belarus
179	Rwanda	185	Sudan	185	IOT/PA		Sudan	186	Equatorial Guinea		Equatorial Guinea
180	Sudan	186	Uzbekistan	186	Equatorial Guinea	187	Equatorial Guinea	187	Uzbekistan		Zimbabwe
181	Somalia	187	Zimbabwe	187	Eritrea	188	Zimbabwe		Zimbabwe	189	Uzbekistan
182	Libya	188	Libya	188	Zimbabwe	189	Eritrea	189	Eritrea	190	Eritrea
183	Turkmenistan	189	Turkmenistan	189	Libya	190	Libya	190	Burma	191	Burma
184	Burma	190	Burma	190	Burma	191	Burma		Cuba		Cuba
	Cuba		Cuba	191	Turkmenistan		Cuba		Libya		Libya
192	Iraq	192	Iraq	192	Cuba		Turkmenistan		Turkmenistan		Turkmenistan
193	North Korea	193	North Korea	193	North Korea	194	North Korea	194	North Korea	195	North Korea

Source: Freedom House (2007b). Freedom of the Press 2007.

Table 5.2 Reporters Without Borders Top 10 and Bottom 10 Countries in Press Freedom

Rnk.	2002	Rnk.	2003	Rnk.	2004	Rnk.	2005	Rnk.	2006	Rnk.	2007
1	Finland	1	Finland	1	Denmark	1	Denmark	1	Finland	1	Iceland
	Iceland		Iceland		Finland		Finland		Iceland		Norway
	Norway		Netherlands		Iceland		Iceland	3	Ireland	3	Estonia
	Netherlands		Norway		Ireland		Ireland		Netherlands		Slovakia
5	Canada	5	Denmark		Netherlands	5	Netherlands	5	Czech Republic	5	Belgium
6	Ireland		Trinidad & Tobago		Norway	6	Norway	6	Estonia		Finland
7	Germany	7	Belgium		Slovakia		Switzerland		Norway		Sweden
8	Portugal	8	Germany		Switzerland	8	Slovakia	8	Slovakia	8	Denmark
9	Sweden	9	Sweden	9	New Zealand	9	Czech Republic	9	Switzerland	9	Ireland
10	Denmark	10	Canada	10	Latvia	10	Slovenia	10	Hungary	10	Portugal
130	Iraq	157	Bhutan	158	Iran	158	Vietnam	159	Nepal	160	Uzbekistan
131	Vietnam	158	Turkmenistan	159	Saudi Arabia	159	China	160	Ethiopia	161	Laos
132	Eritrea	159	Vietnam	160	Nepal	160	Nepal	161	Saudi Arabia	162	Vietnam
133	Laos	160	Iran	161	Vietnam	161	Cuba	162	Iran	163	China
134	Cuba	161	China	162	China	162	Libya	163	China	164	Burma
135	Bhutan	162	Eritrea	163	Eritrea	163	Burma	164	Burma	165	Cuba
136	Turkmenistan	163	Laos	164	Turkmenistan	164	Iran	165	Cuba	166	Iran
137	Burma	164	Burma	165	Burma	165	Turkmenistan	166	Eritrea	167	Turkmenistan
138	China	165	Cuba	166	Cuba	166	Eritrea	167	Turkmenistan	168	North Korea
139	North Korea	166	North Korea	167	North Korea	167	North Korea	168	North Korea	169	Eritrea

Period is from September to August.

Source: Reporters sans frontières (2007). Press freedom index.

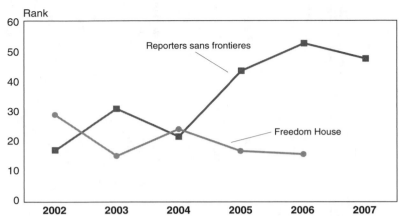

FIGURE 5.1 Press Freedom in the United States: Freedom House and Reporters sans frontieres Press Freedom Rankings
Sources: Freedom House (2007b). Freedom of the Press 2007; Reporters sans frontières (2007). Press freedom index.

journalists, obstacles to collecting and disseminating information, and government manipulation of the media. After questionnaires are returned, RSF staff members in Paris score the surveys. The top 10 and bottom 10 countries in terms of the RSF measures are shown in Table 5.2 for years 2002 to 2007. Discrepancies between Freedom House and RSF measures do exist, as Figure 5.1 shows.

The International Research and Exchanges Board (IREX) was founded in 1968 by U.S. universities to promote exchanges with the Soviet Union and Eastern Europe. A nonprofit organization based in Washington, D.C., IREX focuses on higher education, independent media, Internet development, and civil society in the United States and internationally. In 2001, IREX, in cooperation with the United States Agency for International Development (USAID), prepared its first Media Sustainability Index (MSI) to evaluate the global development of independent media (IREX, 2001). The report rates independent media sustainability in 20 states in four regions: Southeast Europe, Russia and Western Eurasia, Caucasus, and Central Asia. The final report included ratings and an extensive Executive Summary of regional findings as well as individual country reports. In 2005, IREX, with the support of USAID, the U.S. Department of State, and UNESCO, expanded its analysis to include 18 countries in the Middle East and North Africa (IREX, 2005). In 2007, IREX implemented for the first time the MSI for Africa. Media in 25 African countries were included. MSI Africa is supported by the Canadian International Development Agency, the World Bank Institute, and USAID (IREX, 2007b).

IREX does not attempt to measure press freedom, but rather independent media sustainability, or the existence of sustainable, independent media systems within the country. Specifically, it examines the extent to which political, legal, social, and economic circumstances and institutions and professional standards within independent media promote and/or permit independent media to survive over time.

ble 5.3   IREX MSI Top 3 and Bottom 3 Europe and Eurasia Countries in Free Speech

nk.	2001	Rnk.	2002	Rnk.	2003	Rnk.	2004	Rnk.	2005	Rnk.	2006
1	Croatia	1	Croatia	1	Croatia	1	Croatia	1	Croatia	1	Bosnia
2	Bulgaria	2	Romania	2	Montenegro	2	Bosnia	2	Romania	2	Croatia
3	Romania	3	Albania	3	Albania	3	Montenegro	3	Bosnia	3	Romania
18	Kazakhstan	18	Belarus	18	Tajikistan	18	Tajikistan	18	Kazakhstan	18	Kazakhstan
19	Tajikistan	19	Tajikistan	19	Uzbekistan	19	Uzbekistan	19	Belarus	19	Belarus
20	Belarus	20	Uzbekistan	20	Belarus	20	Belarus	20	Uzbekistan	20	Uzbekistan

urce: IREX (2007a). Media sustainability index Europe and Eurasia 2006–2007.

IREX assesses independent media sustainability using five criteria or objectives: (a) legal and social norms that protect and promote free speech and access to public information; (b) journalism that meets professional standards; (c) multiple news sources that provide citizens with reliable and objective news; (d) independent media that are well-managed businesses, allowing editorial independence; and (e) supporting institutions that function in the professional interests of independent media.

To determine how well a country meets those five objectives, seven to nine indicators for each of the objectives are assessed. To conduct scoring, IREX assembles in each country a panel of experts—local media representatives, members of NGOs and professional associations, international donors, and media development workers. Each panel is provided with the objectives, indicators, and explanation of the scoring system. Panelists review the information individually, then assemble to come to a consensus on scores. The panel moderator—in most cases a representative from one of the country's media or an NGO—prepares a written analysis of the discussion, which is edited by IREX representatives. IREX staff (in-country and in Washington, D.C.) also review indicators and objectives, scoring countries independently. The final score for a country is an average of the panel score and the IREX staff score. The top three and bottom three countries in terms of the IREX measures are shown in Table 5.3 for years 2001 to 2006.

The Committee to Protect Journalists (CPJ) was formed in 1981 by a group of foreign correspondents. The New York City-based organization reports and investigates attacks on journalists and lobbies domestic and foreign governments on their behalf. CPJ staff in Washington and New York monitor media in countries in five different regions: the Americas, Asia, the Middle East, Africa, and Europe. Developments are tracked through independent research, fact-finding missions, and contacts in the field. CPJ has published annual reports on attacks on the press since 1987. CPJ is funded solely by contributions from individuals, corporations, and foundations. It does not accept government funding (CPJ, 2007).

Annual reports are prepared by CPJ staff and sources in the country. CPJ checks each case from the field identified as a violation of press freedom by more than one source for factual accuracy, confirmation that the victims were journalists or news organizations, and verification that intimidation was the probable motive. Journalists are defined as people who cover news or write commentary on a regular basis. CPJ classifies abuses of journalists and the media using 10 definitions.

The report includes countries in which CPJ has intervened, as well as any other countries CPJ considers to have violated press freedom in a substantial way. Staff coordinators and researchers also rely for information on their own independent research, fact-finding missions to the countries, and contacts in the field, including government officials, human rights or press organizations, and individual journalists. In addition, CPJ publishes yearly evaluations of media freedom in various nations, which are known as country reports. Generally, the reports focus on the political, legal, and economic environments for media freedom. The CPJ counts across time are shown in Figure 5.2.

The Freedom House and Reporters sans frontières indices are based on similar concepts, namely, the existence of press autonomy and independence. The IREX Media Sustainability Index includes freedom of speech as one of its five components. The remaining four elements of the index are potentially quite distinct, incorporating the idea of durability of press operations in a competitive market. The Committee to Protect Journalists index focuses solely on attacks on press operations, rather than on support for them.

An empirical analysis of the numerical ratings of four of these organizations— Reporters sans frontières, Freedom House, IREX, and Committee to Protect Journalists— showed that at least the first three of these organizations largely come to the same conclusions about the media (Becker, Vlad, and Nusser, 2007). The correlation of the IREX measures with those of Reporters sans frontières and Freedom House was surprising, given that IREX tried to create a distinct concept, namely, media sustainability. The goal was a measure that incorporated press freedom, but focused more heavily on the eco-

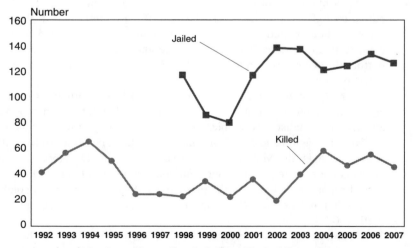

FIGURE 5.2   Number of journalists in jail or killed while on duty
Sources: Committee to Portect Journalists (2007). Statistics and background.

nomic and social environment of the country thought necessary for the development of a durable, independent media. A higher correlation of the IREX measure with Freedom House's measure suggested a nationality bias, as both IREX and Freedom House measures were the product of U.S. organizations, while RSF is a French NGO. This at a minimum raises a question about the independence of the evaluations of country perspectives on press freedom reflecting domestic political concerns. The analysis showed that the Committee to Protect Journalists, through its measures of attacks on the press, has gathered information that was not redundant with the RSF, Freedom House, and MSI indices. The CPJ counts of attacks correlates weakly with the first two measures and very poorly with the IREX measure.

The fact that Freedom House and IREX are funded in part by the U.S. government has raised suspicions of their findings by some critics. The RSF evaluations have been seen by many as an attempt to create a non-U.S. counterpart independent of U.S. influence. The overall similarity of the findings from the three different sources somewhat counters these criticisms of national bias. At the same time, the measurement of press freedom remains a human enterprise, and the selection of impartial evaluators in the individual countries is critical. It remains possible that the findings from the three different organizations are largely similar because they rely on the same observers or the same types of observers in creating their evaluations.

It also is quite clear that these measures of media freedom do not capture the full complexity of the concept of freedom discussed by McQuail, Curran, Rozumilowicz, and others. These measures focus heavily on constraints on media operation, rather than on citizen access and rights. Despite these limitations, these global measures of media freedom are important, for they give a sense of how constraints on the media have changed over time.

At the same time, it is important to recognize that media are very complex, particularly in large and changing countries. China and Russia give important examples.

Freedom House rated Chinese media as Not Free in 2007 and assigned the country a score of 84 (Freedom House, 2008). The media in China are all controlled by the government. At the same time, they are under tremendous pressure to commercialize, that is, to obtain revenues from the market through advertising and subscription fees. In order to gain audience attention (which is then sold to advertisers), the media must produce content that audience members want. As Thornton (2008) has reported, the Chinese media have discovered that investigative journalism attracts an audience. Thornton recounts a case in which a reporter for the *Chinese Economic Times* wrote about a taxi-licensing system that forced drivers to work long hours for low wages. The newspaper sold out almost immediately. The Central Propaganda Bureau banned other publications from reporting on the problem, and the city's Transportation Bureau ordered drivers not to read the article. The news spread on the Internet, however, and the public reaction increased. Eight days after the story was printed, then Vice Premier Wen Jiabao issued an official statement in support of the taxi drivers and directed that a report be prepared for then Premier Zhu Rongji.

Russia is another important example. Freedom House in 2007 also rated the Russian media as Not Free and assigned the country a score of 75 (Freedom House, 2008). Private ownership is possible legally, and, on paper, it exists. In fact, however, relatively few independent media voices operate (McFaul and Stoner-Weiss, 2008). The state either controls directly or indirectly all the national broadcast media and many print media outlets. Often the control is not transparent, because companies that are state owned, or that are owned by oligarchs closely aligned with the government, control the properties.

The crackdown on independent journalism in Russia also has been pronounced. On October 7, 2006, Anna Politkovskaya, a staff writer for *Novaya gazeta,* winner of Russian and international press awards for her courageous reports and stories about the Northern Caucasus, was shot dead in the entrance hall of her apartment building in Moscow. After this tragic event, the assumption was that the government and the society would be prepared to do everything necessary to prevent any other aggression against journalists. Unfortunately, on March 2, 2007, Ivan Safronov, a military analyst with the political daily newspaper *Kommersant,* died in unclear circumstances in the middle of his investigation on Russian military trade affairs with Arab states. And in April 2007, the offices of Russian Internews (renamed *Obrazovannye Media* following a new NGO law) were closed, following a visit and search by the police and prosecution officials (Azhgikhina, 2007). Internews in Moscow was the most prominent training program for Russian journalists. During the same month, the newspaper *Kommersant Daily* and *Ekho Moskvy* radio (the only national station to criticize the current regime openly) received official warnings from the state agency controlling the media about not reporting about, or even mentioning, an officially registered political party (Azhgikhina, 2007).

Antecedents and Consequences of Press Freedom

Stevenson (2004), long a chronicler of changes in media freedom around the world, asked, Does media freedom precede and bring about economic development and other types of social change, or does it follow it? In his view, the evidence has tilted in favor of the argument that development comes first and that this is followed by media freedom.

The same question can be asked about the relationship between media freedom and democratization, but here, the popular argument, particularly among government agencies and organizations interested in promoting press freedom, has been that press freedom comes first. A U.S. Agency for International Development report (USAID, 1999) stated that case strongly, arguing that free access to uncensored information is essential to a democratic system for four reasons. First, it helps citizens to make responsible choices. Second, the information ensures that elected officials uphold their oaths and represent the interests of those who elected them. Third, independent media strengthen the rule of law. Finally, press freedom contributes to transparent elections, giving access to all candidates. Despite that argument, the empirical evidence in support of it is far from complete.

As noted above, Nerone (1995), in his critique of Siebert, Peterson, and Schramm's (1956) *Four Theories of the Press,* argued the "theory" of the book is that a communication system reflects in its structure, policy, and behavior the society in which it operates. In other words, the characteristics of the society shape the press, not the other way around. In many ways, this was the starting point of the analysis of media systems by Hallin and Mancini (2004). So what did they conclude?

Hallin and Mancini (2004) do find considerable evidence that the characteristics of the political system are reflected in the media systems of countries. For example, those countries that have consensus patterns of government create public broadcasting systems that also focus on and are governed by consensus. Those countries that give deference to the rule of majority create public broadcasting systems with similar characteristics. Hallin and Mancini note, however, that the correspondence between social and political structure and media characteristics is not simple. Elements of the political structure work together, that is, interactively, not independently, to shape the media system.

What is most important is that Hallin and Mancini conclude that the connections between the political and cultural characteristics of society and the media are not one-way causal ones. The media systems are shaped by the social and political world around them. The media systems also bring about change in the political and social systems that surround them.

Public Satisfaction with Press Freedom

In 2005 and 2006, the Gallup Poll, based in the United States, asked approximately 1,000 adults in each of 128 countries around the world to report on the amount of confidence they had in the quality and integrity of the media in their countries. Gallup then compared those responses with the Freedom House's Global Press Freedom scores for each of those countries for 2007. The results are surprising and informative (Gallup, 2007).

Overall, Gallup found little correspondence between the level of confidence that citizens had in the media of their country and the level of freedom of those media, as judged by Freedom House, as is shown in Figure 5.3. Among those countries that Freedom House rated as Free (a score of from 0–30), on average, 47 percent of the population said they had confidence in the quality and integrity of the media. Among those that were Partly Free (a score of 31–60), the median score was 56 percent saying they had confidence in the media, and among those countries rated as Not Free (61–100), 50 percent on average had confidence in the quality and integrity of the media. One statistical measure of this relationship is a Pearson Product Moment Correlation Coefficient, which can vary from –1 to +1. The relationship between the percentage of respondents in the country who said they were confident in the quality and integrity of the media and the Freedom House Press Freedom score (where a high score is negative) was only 0.10.

Gallup also found that, although confidence in the media varied widely around the world, some regional patterns emerged. Confidence in the media was relatively high in Southeast Asia. Across countries surveyed, the median score was 64 percent. For the countries in Central America, South America, and the Caribbean, the media score was 55 percent. In Africa, the median was nearly the same, at 54 percent. In Europe, the median score was 42 percent. In North Africa and the Middle East, the median score was nearly the same, at 41 percent, but the range was quite extreme, with 77 percent of the respondents from the United Arab Emirates expressing confidence and only 25 percent from Turkey expressing confidence. In Asia, the median was 38 percent. In North America, the scores for the three countries were: Canada 56 percent, Mexico 53 percent, and the United States 32 percent.

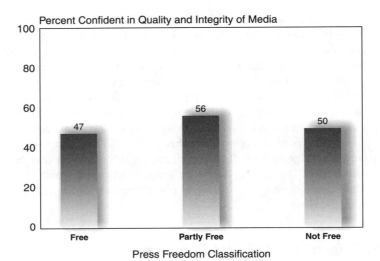

FIGURE 5.3   Public Confidence and Press Freedom
Sources: Gallup Poll (2007).

The biggest gaps in terms of confidence and the Freedom House scores for press freedom were in Taiwan, the United States, Slovakia, Estonia, Sweden, and Hungary, where press freedom is relatively high, according to the Freedom House measures, and confidence in the quality and integrity of the media is relatively low, and in Rwanda, Laos, Cuba, and the United Arab Emirates, where Freedom House rates press freedom as low but the citizenry has a high level of confidence in the quality and integrity of the media.

The editors of the Gallup Polls (Gallup, 2007) put it succinctly:

> Taken together, the results from Gallup Polls conducted in 128 countries worldwide and Freedom House's Global Press Freedom rankings paint a complicated picture of the media around the globe. While a country's press may be considered free, it may not be widely respected by the residents who live there. Further, media considered to have relatively limited press freedom may have the support of their people. These data suggest both measures, as well as others, should be considered by those seeking to assess and improve media worldwide.

Threats to Press Freedom

The discussion to this point suggests that there is a variety of threats to media freedom. They are a consequence of the country's political system, stability, economic development, and culture. A brief summary follows.

Censorship is a characteristic of totalitarian systems. Special institutions read the content of the newspapers and magazines before the publication and preview or listen to the broadcast content before it is aired. The senior editors and the news directors are appointed by the government and are charged with supervising the media content and eliminating materials that are critical of the political leadership. In most cases, the media in totalitarian countries are owned and subsidized by the government.

Self-censorship often occurs when journalists or media organizations make decisions not to investigate specific issues or not to publish or air stories resulting from those investigations. There are different reasons for these decisions, ranging from concern of retaliation from the political leadership or of losing an important advertiser to situations where the programming and the content are driven entirely by ratings. In the latter cases, media organizations might decide to eliminate unpopular, though accurate and important, materials.

Political instability also is a source of restrictions on media freedom. Under these circumstances, journalists and media organizations either take sides and lose their neutrality or avoid reporting for fear of potentially dangerous political developments.

Economic harassment or incentives are sometimes used by the government or business groups to control the media content. Government officials or big companies can manipulate the advertising of state-owned and private organizations to either reward or penalize media outlets for their favorable or critical attitudes. This type of manipulation is often found in emerging democracies, where the advertising market is not strong enough to support the increasing number of media outlets. Researchers have labeled this situation *hypercompetition*. The weak advertising market cannot sustain the large number of media organizations competing for those limited advertising revenues. The consequence often is low-quality journalism, compromises in terms of objectivity, and corruption within the media system.

Media concentration can affect media freedom. Businesspeople who have amassed fortunes during the transition from a state economy to a market-oriented economy (often known as "oligarchs") have created media groups. To do that, they established or purchased existing media organizations. In many cases, these media reflect the economic and political agendas of these oligarchs, rather than address the issues that are relevant for the general public and for the society.

Some governments also have used the *legal system* to restrict media freedom. These strategies include defamation and libel suits and jail terms for media organizations or journalists who publish or broadcast "inaccurate information," stories that are "insulting to the country," or information that "endangers the country's security." In addition to the type of laws that make reference to the media content, government officials in some authoritarian countries and emerging democracies have used other regulations to obstruct media operations, such as closing newsrooms for inappropriate fire alarm systems or for noise, restricting access to printing houses and denying licenses for "insufficient proof of financial resources."

Violence against journalists has also negatively affected press freedom. Journalists have been victims of attacks orchestrated by businesspeople, fanatics of all sorts, corrupt government officials, and drug lords.

Meaning of Press Freedom in Internet World

Over the last 30 plus years, a variety of technological changes, some small and some large, have radically altered the relationship between those who produce media content and those who consume it. On the one hand, the changes have increased the amount of material that is provided. On the other, they have given the consumer more control over that material, and particularly over how that material is used. The technological changes also have blurred the distinction between producer and consumer, as almost every consumer now also is able to be a producer.

These changes have had, are having, and will continue to have tremendous impact on discussions of the basic meaning of communication—and media—freedom. Media freedom can no longer be thought of simply as the freedom of newspapers, radio stations, and television stations to gather and disseminate the news. Media freedom must embrace those who produce messages for MP3 players, for cell phones, and for whatever other device enters the market.

The change has been dramatic, and it is likely to become more so shortly. The advent of broadband cable and satellites around the world in the last two decades of the twentieth century increased dramatically the means to reach the consumer, and new businesses emerged to take advantage of those technologies. The simple hand-held channel changer increased the consumer's ability to decide what to use and watch. Portable storage devices made every consumer of music a programmer who could produce a mix of music to suit his or her own tastes.

These technological changes affected the broadcast media first and most dramatically, but now the Internet and related developments are affecting all media. Newspapers and magazines and the other traditional media around the world are encountering challenges they have never encountered before. Included is competition for audience attention and competition for advertising revenue. Competition for content also has increased. The media no longer have exclusive access to and priority in dissemination of content. A moving image of a political rally that once only could be distributed by television now can be distributed on the Web and received by computers or mobile devices. A shocking still image that once could be distributed only by a newspaper or a paper can be distributed in a multitude of ways. The established media cannot so easily ignore or downplay what can so easily be distributed by others.

In a very basic way, these challenges raise the fundamental question: What is journalism? Historically, journalism has been what the journalistic media—and particularly those in newspapers and broadcast newsrooms—did. Certain patterns existed in those organizations. In the United States, and elsewhere where the Liberal Model was followed, for example, that meant that the journalist's voice and point of view were largely absent. The journalism was information-based rather than opinion-oriented. Journalists were neutral observers rather than involved activists. Of course, newspapers and broadcast stations also had editorials that presented opinions, they had columnists who offered their own points of view, and they had interpretative pieces that tried to integrate and make sense of the basic news. But these were generally labeled as such, and they were not the dominant part of the newspaper product or the news broadcast.

The Internet has changed everything. First, everyone can write and report, and everyone can express an opinion. Often, these are intermixed, as many of those who write Web logs—or blogs—have a point of view and are proud of it. They may report, but they can do so selectively and in service to their cause. They don't have the same organizational mandates of balance and fairness as the traditional newspapers and the broadcast stations. Often, the citizen journalists do not have the same training as the journalists working for those organizations. And they do not follow the same professional norms. In many ways, the Internet has mixed the role of advocate with the role of the journalist. It has made public relations and journalism more similar. It has made journalism more personal and given it more of a point of view.

That assumes that what appears on the Web, what is distributed via the mobile phone, what is spread via MP3 players, is journalism. Maybe it is not. Maybe journalism is only what trained journalists produce. Maybe the remainder of what flows around the Web is really something else.

In an important way, these changes in the media landscape have put a heavy burden on the consumer of information. In the past, a news report carried with it a type of certification when it was associated with an established newspaper or broadcast outlet. The traditions and biases of that organization were established and knowable. One could say, I trust the report because it appears on the newscast of a certain organization. Or one could say, I don't believe the report because it was included in the newscast of a different organization. Today, the consumer has to ferret out the background of the blogger or the Web page operator or the mobile device message producer. While documentation may seem to be more easily provided via links and scanned documents, these links and documents can be more easily fabricated than ever before.

If the "system" works—and that is a big "if"—the information providers that prove reliable over time will gather audience loyalty. That loyalty will be translated into continued use. That use will result in financial support—through advertising or subscription fees—for the information provider. The good information providers will survive while the bad will perish. In this optimistic view, feedback will be provided through fact-checking and counter-postings by the consumers. As a result, the audience will be knowledgeable enough to select and thereby will determine who the future providers of journalism will be.

The challenge of these dramatic changes in the media environment for those interested in promoting, monitoring, and studying media freedom is to adapt to this new world. Freedom House, Reporters sans frontières, and IREX already have incorporated into their analyses the presence or absence of Internet regulations. More will need to be done in the future. The very notion of media freedom has changed and will continue to change. The change is likely to be very rapid.

BIBLIOGRAPHY

Azhgikhina, N. "Landscape after the Battle: Russian Journalists between Past and Future." *Europe-Asia Studies* 59 (2007), 1245–1263.

Becker, L.B., Vlad, T., and Nusser, N. "An Evaluation of Press Freedom Indicators." *The International Communication Gazette,* 69, No. 1 (2007), 5–28.

Committee to Protect Journalists. *Statistics and Background.* Retrieved on January 10, 2007, from http://www.cpj.org/deadly/index.html

Curran, J. "Mediations of Democracy." In J. Curran and M. Gurevitch (eds.), *Mass Media and Society,* 4th ed., 122–149. London: Hodder Arnold, 2005.

Freedom House. *Freedom in the World.* 2007a. Retrieved on January 10, 2008 from http://www.freedomhouse.org/template.cfm?page=363&year=2007

Freedom House. *Freedom of the Press 2007.* 2007b. Retrieved on January 10, 2008 from http://www.freedomhouse.org/template.cfm?page=16

Freedom House. *Freedom of the Press 2007.* Lanham, MD: Rowman & Littlefield, 2008.

Gallup Poll. "Quality and Integrity of World's Media." 2007. Retrieved on January 10, 2008, from http://www.gallup.com/poll/103300/Quality-Integrity-Worlds-Media-Questioned.aspx.

Hachten, W. *The World News Prism.* Ames: Iowa State University, 1981.

Hallin, D. C., and Mancini, P. *Comparing Media Systems: Three Models of Media and Politics.* Cambridge: Cambridge University Press, 2004.

IREX. *Media Sustainability Index: Europe and Eurasia 2001.* 2001. Retrieved on December 12, 2004, from http://www.irex.org/programs/msi_eur/2001.asp

———. *Media Sustainability Index: Middle East and North Africa 2005.* 2005. Retrieved on March 10, 2007, from http://www.irex.org/programs/MSI_MENA/index.asp

———. *Media Sustainability Index: Europe and Eurasia 2006–2007.* 2007a. Retrieved on January 10, 2007, from http://www.irex.org/programs/MSI_EUR/index.asp

———. *Media Sustainability Index: Africa.* 2007b. Retrieved on January 5, 2008, from http://www.irex.org/programs/MSI_Africa/index.asp

McFaul, M., and Stoner-Weiss, K. "The Myth of Putin's Success." *Foreign Affairs* 87 (2008), 68–84.

McQuail, D. *McQuail's Mass Communication Theory,* 4th ed. London: Sage Publications, 2000.

Nerone, J. C. (ed.) *Last Rights: Revising Four Theories of the Press.* Urbana: University of Illinois Press, 1995.

Picard. R. C. *The Press and the Decline of Democracy.* Westport, CT: Greenwood Press, 1985.

Reporters sans frontières. *Press Freedom Index.* 2007. Retrieved on January 10, 2008 from http://www.rsf.org/article.php3?id_article=24046

Rozumilowicz, B. "Democratic Change: A Theoretical Approach." In Price, M. E., Rozumilowicz, B. and Verhulst, S. G. (eds.), *Media Reform: Democratizing the Media, Democratizing the State,* 9–26. London: Routledge, 2002.

Siebert, F. S., Peterson, T., and Schramm, W. *Four Theories of the Press.* Urbana: University of Illinois Press, 1956.

Stevenson, R. L. "Freedom of the Press around the World." In A. S. de Beer and J. C. Merrill (eds.), *Global Communication,* 66–83. Boston: Pearson Education, 2004.

Thornton, J. "Long Time Coming: The Prospects for Democracy in China." *Foreign Affairs* 87 (2008), 2–22.

USAID (1999, June). *The Role of Media in Ddemocracy: A Strategic Approach.* Washington: Center for Democracy and Governance, Bureau for Global Programs, Field Support and Research, Technical Publication Series.

6

Global Journalism Ethics

HERMAN WASSERMAN
University of Sheffield, UK

Introduction: Journalism Ethics between the Local and the Global

Journalists and their publics around the world struggle with the question: Is journalism ethics always contextually bound, or can we construct an ethical framework that we can apply globally? As one can gather from the Case Study on p. 86, this is not a simple and straightforward question to answer. In the light of the multicultural diversity that we are increasingly exposed to in a globalizing world, we should ask ourselves as journalists and students of journalism, whether we agree upon one set of ethical values for journalists everywhere, or should we take a relativist stance and accept the notion that journalism ethics will differ from country to country, culture to culture, religion to religion?

The questions posed above and brought forward in the case study, center on the complex relationship between the universal and the particular, a long-standing philosophical problem. Yet in recent years they have become more urgent on a practical, journalistic level. Globalization has increased our awareness of the "more intense mutual interdependence between countries through markets, communications, finance, crime and culture" (Bentley and Hargreaves, 2001:5). The events of September 11, 2001 have brought the question of conflicting sets of values and ideologies to the fore with a force that is impossible to ignore and have violently underlined the fact that Western liberalism as a moral framework is not accepted universally (Bentley and Hargreaves, 2001:6). Although not all Western media frameworks are rooted in capitalist, liberal individualism, the reminder that one set of values cannot be extrapolated and imposed globally also applies very specifically to journalism after 9/11, with new ethical challenges in terms of reporting on "us" and "them" (cf. Zelizer and Allan, 2002).

Although the new global landscape within which journalism finds itself is an uncertain and often precarious one, asking questions about how to find consensus on journalism ethics means that we at least recognize the need for a set of values to guide journalism through uncharted territory. Although the notion of universal norms and epistemologies has experienced a crisis in the postmodern era (Ang, 1998), the global acceleration of new media technologies and their increased reach has meant that the media play an unprecedented role in the lives of especially people in the developed world. The media have become "environmental" (Silverstone, 2007) to the extent that access to or exclusion of that environment has a profound influence on our material existence as well as our identities. These new technologies have in themselves posed new challenges for journalism ethics and the very definition of journalism (e.g., Singer, 2006; Lumby and Probyn, 2003). For all these reasons, an engagement with global media ethics is of vital importance. Such engagement should go further than merely comparing the occupational ideologies of journalists worldwide—although such a descriptive study can be very helpful in understanding how journalists worldwide see themselves and their work (e.g., Deuze, 2005; Hanitzsch, 2007; Weaver, 1998). An ethical framework for journalism in the age of globalization has to rest on a solid theoretical basis (Kruckeberg and Tsetsura, 2004:84).

CASE STUDY

Health Minister in Media Spotlight: To Follow African or Western Media Ethical Norms?

When the South African newspaper the *Sunday Times* published two front-page leads on consecutive weeks alleging that the South African health minister, Dr. Manto Tshabalala-Msimang went on a "booze binge" while in hospital (*Sunday Times,* 2007a) and calling her a "drunk and a thief" (*Sunday Times,* 2007b) after having obtained her medical records which showed that she had a liver transplant following liver cirrhosis, they were looking for trouble in different places. And they got it. Rumors surfaced that editorial staff's phone calls were monitored, and the minister in the presidency, Essop Pahad, threatened to withdraw all government advertising from the *Sunday Times* (Malan, 2007). Threats that the editor and journalists would be arrested were made (though never carried out), and the newspaper was forced by court order to return the copies of the health records to the minister's hospital (*Sunday Times,* 2007c).

The publication of the health minister's apparent actions in hospital and references to a time when she was apparently involved in stealing from patients while she was a nurse sparked much debate about the state of media freedom in the country and how the media's social responsibility should be understood. Published in an overheated political climate in the run-up to the succession race for leader of the ruling party (with the health minister's widely criticized policies on HIV/AIDS linked to her boss, President Thabo Mbeki's notorious denialist views on the pandemic), the reports in the *Sunday Times* triggered strong reactions that could also be read as being related to opposing political camps. While most of the media justified the publication of the medical records as being in the *public interest,* because it was "evidence of the minister's unsuitability" for public office, others called for introspection on the media's part for its *invasion* of the minister's *privacy* (*The Star,* 2007). One notable response came from a public broadcaster (South African Broadcasting Corporation or SABC) who withdrew from the South African National Editors' Forum (SANEF) after SANEF defended publication of the minister's medical report in the public interest. While the SABC has increasingly come to be seen as a government mouthpiece, and its response to SANEF's defense of the publication could also be seen in political terms, the SABC's response was also couched in cultural discourse. The SABC's chief executive, Dali Mpofu, said the *Sunday Times'* publication of the minister's health records was symptomatic of the "epidemic deterioration of journalistic ethics within your ranks and disrespect for our people":

> How inhumane and how far removed from the basic value of Ubuntu. Shame on all of you, especially those who have turned their backs on your own cultural values for 30 pieces of silver, pretending to be converted to foreign, frigid and feelingless freedoms. (Mpofu, 2007)

Mpofu's reference to the African ethical concept of "Ubuntu" (see p. 90) is reminiscent of earlier ethical debates about the South African media's publication of medical information (Wasserman and De Beer, 2006) in which African cultural values were also at the center of a dispute over the meaning of principles such as *human dignity* and *freedom of expression*. In both cases, the use of African values as a façade for an exclusionary political agenda was also critiqued (Leshilo, 2007; Fourie, 2007). These debates in turn form part of a larger discourse on the South African media's orientation toward Africa. President Mbeki has argued for a more "Africanist" orientation among members of the media and has criticized the media for perpetuating colonial stereotypes of Africans (Mbeki, 2003). This appeal is echoed by the South African journalism professor Guy Berger (2005:21):

> What's needed is for us South African journalists to see ourselves as African journalists. . . . 'Africa' also means giving South African audiences information on, and insight into, other countries on the continent, and not only stories that are negative. To have an African mindset implies understanding the commonalities across the sweep of the continent—and including South Africa—of similar colonial histories, peripheral economies, rural cultures, ancestral traditions . . . and also health challenges like HIV and malaria.

These debates about the media's ethical role in South Africa also became cultural debates about the renegotiation of post-apartheid identities (Wasserman, 2003). What these clashes seem to indicate is that media ethical values such as truth and human dignity have been interpreted through different cultural, political, and historical lenses, which often intersect with social and racial polarizations and hierarchies (Shepperson and Tomaselli, 2002). In short: an African view of journalism ethics emerged from these (politically charged) debates and was contrasted against a more conventional journalism ethical framework that was characterized as Western and therefore unsuitable for the African context.

A Theoretical Foundation for Global Journalism Ethics

When considering theoretical foundations for global journalism ethics, we have to realize that theories are constructed within social, cultural, and political contexts. The contexts that have shaped theories of journalism ethics have until now been predominantly located in the global North, more specifically the United States (Alia, 2004:4). When comparative case studies have been used, these examples of "ethics elsewhere" have mostly been incorporated into an overarching theoretical framework that had its origins in the North. This is true not only of journalism ethics, but of ethics in general.

[E]thics as an academic discipline in the West has been a biased undertaking in the past, and . . . one might want to use the term *global ethics* to distance oneself from this past. (Ladikas and Schroeder, 2005:406).

Constructing a theoretical framework for global ethics (which would include journalism ethics) will face challenges arising from cultural diversity in a globalized world, but also from political, economic, and social factors that impact on the construction of ethical theory. Ladikas and Schroeder (2005:407) list five challenges for global ethics:

- Global inequalities such as poverty/nutrition, HIV/AIDS, and gender bias
- Cultural differences in moral perspectives
- Difficulties in determining moral perspectives
- Lack of a relevant global decision-making body with enforcement authority
- Historical injustices

Without going into each of these challenges in detail, one can see how these challenges for ethics in a general sense could also apply to global journalism ethics more specifically. The search for global journalism ethics should have a solid theoretical base, but cannot be developed in isolation from real-life power relations, injustices, and inequalities. In our search for global media ethical values, we should not only be motivated by what Gikandi (2005:609) refers to as the celebratory narrative of globalization, but also by its counter-narrative, namely, that of crisis. Just as global media facilitate increased mobility across borders, the shrinking of the world, and cultural hybridity, they also form part of—and contribute to—a world that is starkly divided between those that benefit from globalization and those that remain on its margins. These power relations and global inequalities can influence the way that supposedly "universal values" are interpreted in different contexts. These interpretations might differ significantly from the currently dominant interpretation to such an extent that it undermines the dominant ethical framework into which these assumed universal values have been incorporated.

The above-mentioned example of how differently the ethical values of dignity, privacy, and public interest were defined by various role-players in the South African context, is an example of how local cultural frameworks, political exigencies, and social conditions impact on the interpretation of ethical values that have been globalized as professional norms and standards. Furthermore, the example showed how journalists in local contexts can interpret certain values differently from the way that they have been understood in the (Northern) theoretical frameworks from which they originate, but that among journalists in particular contexts these interpretations can also vary greatly, shaped as they are by cultural, political, social, and material conditions. In thinking about global journalism ethics, we should therefore not only pay attention to the global:local matrix in order to see how journalism ethics become "glocalized" in particular settings (Wasserman and Rao, 2008), but also acknowledge the heterogeneity of specific journalistic cultures and the hierarchies and power relations these particular journalistic communities display (Krukeberg and Tsetsusa, 2004).

So how should we proceed in thinking about global journalism ethics on a theoretical level? Journalism ethics is usually discussed under three different categories, and the negotiation of global journalism ethics should also take place across all these categories:

Meta-ethics

The question about whether ethical norms are universal/absolute or relative, or whether morality only applies in specific places and times, is a *meta-ethical* question, since it concerns the nature of ethics rather than the content of specific ethical norms. Meta-ethics is concerned with the nature of ethics, the meaning of ethical concepts and the validity of ethical claims. For instance, can moral truths be known (cognitivism) or not (noncognitivism)? Are moral judgments based on subjective preferences or objective facts? (Baggini and Fosl, 2007:98–99, 147–148). So when we ask whether an ethical theory can have global validity, and what the nature of such a theory would be, we are asking meta-ethical questions about the theoretical problem of universalism versus relativism (Ladikas & Schroeder, 2005).

In doing so, we can further distinguish between epistemological relativism and cultural relativism. Epistemological relativism is the position that we cannot make universal claims about truth, knowledge, or morality, because of the nature of language and the way it constructs our understanding of reality. Our knowledge of good and evil, right and wrong, is rooted in specific experience, and these truths cannot be universalized. This relativism has received increasing emphasis in poststructuralist thought, which critiqued the notion of language as a stable system within which universal truths and "grand narratives" can be constructed. These insights led to a crisis in Western culture and epistemology in the late twentieth century, as the "paradigm of immutable and universal morality" became discredited as belonging to the dominant gender and class (Christians, 1997a:4): "Transhistorical certitude has been replaced by philosophical relativism, that is, by the presumption that moral principles have no objective application independent of the societies within which they are constituted" (Christians, 1997a:5). The meta-ethical question here is whether it is possible to construct universal norms given a postmodernist understanding of rationality, knowledge, and communication. The second type of relativism has to do with our awareness of cultural diversity in a globalized world and the understanding that morality obtains its meaning within specific cultures, languages, and histories. This relativity is an attempt to respect cultural difference and acknowledge the history of discrimination and the setting up of hierarchies on the basis of cultural (and ethnic and racial) difference.

The shift in recent years toward greater recognition of cultural difference also has to do with the paradoxical countereffect of the process of globalization, namely, the assertion of the local in the face of the rapidly expanding global (Christians, 1997b:187). The meta-ethical question arising is whether we can construct journalism ethics that have their basis not in the Enlightenment views of moral truth based in universal rationality and yet are globally valid, while allowing for cultural relativity and difference, and allowing non-Northern value frameworks to "speak back" to the dominant center. One way of approaching the problem is to agree on certain "fundamental conditions for human flourishing" (Ladikas and Schroeder, 2005:408) that could be applicable across cultures, regardless of more specific moral norms (the example they use is that of female genital mutilation, in which the fundamental right to health comes up against the culturally specific moral value of chastity—if agreement can be found that health is more fundamental than chastity, that is). On a theoretical, meta-ethical level, the question that remains is on what presuppositions (our conceptions of the nature of human beings and their world) we are to base our fundamental principles and our moral precepts (Donegan, 1977:32) in order to make a distinction between fundamentals and culturally determined norms.

Normative Ethics

While meta-ethics is concerned with the nature of ethics and basic concepts, normative ethics pertains to judgments we make about particular issues (Baggini and Fosl, 2007:147). Normative theories are frameworks that guide our thinking about right and wrong and provide a foundation on which we can decide what moral action we should take. Normative theories provide justification for why particular actions are moral or not according to a logical argument about how actions can be judged.

In most scholarly literature on journalism ethics, normative theories are classified in five categories (Christians, Rotzoll, Fackler, McKee, and Woods, 2005:12):

- Virtue theory (Aristotle's or Confucius's Golden Mean)
- Deontological theory (Kant's Categorical Imperative)
- Utilitarianism (Jeremy Bentham and John Stuart Mill)
- Social contractualism (Rawls Veil of Ignorance)
- Ethics of Care (Judeo-Christian *agape* or feminist care ethics)

From the literature it is clear that the normative traditions that have been developed in the global North dominate journalism ethics scholarship. If journalism ethics is to become more inclusive of global diversity, normative journalism ethics will have to become more inclusive of other traditions, and not only explore the overlaps and commonalities between normative traditions, but also allow for non-Northern normative frameworks to provide a critique of dominant perspectives. Some exploratory work in this respect has already begun, but many challenges remain. Examples of normative theories from other traditions include Buddhist ethics; whose discussion in journalism ethics theory is a "natural response to the call in recent years to add non-Western voices to conversations about media ethics". Another non-Western approach is African ethics, with the late Francis Kasoma being one of its main exponents (e.g., Kasoma, 1996). The African concept of *ubuntu* (meaning a person is a person through other persons) has featured in recent debates about an indigenous African value framework. This concept has been used in a discussion of ethics in the general South African context (e.g., Shutte, 1993) and in relation to journalism and media specifically (Blankenberg, 1999; Wasserman & De Beer, 2006). Comparisons have been drawn between ubuntu and the normative tradition of communitarianism (Christians, 2004), but such a comparison has also been critiqued for its shortcomings when applied to journalism (Fourie, 2007). Critique of the dominant Northern theoretical frameworks within which normative journalism ethics continues to be couched has also been forthcoming from a related theoretical perspective, namely, postcolonial criticism (Rao and Wasserman, 2007; Wasserman, 2006).

International comparative studies of press systems (e.g., Bertrand, 2000) or press codes (e.g., Hafez, 2005) have provided a descriptive overview of journalism ethics globally, but these studies often remain descriptive and do not engage with ethical theory on a fundamental level in order to construct a new global framework. The tension between descriptive and normative journalism ethics (Josephi, 2005) therefore remains in place.

The international crisis following the publication of cartoons depicting the prophet Muhammad in the Danish newspaper *Jyllands Posten* in September 2005, underlined the need for more attention to Islamic normative ethics (see, for instance, Mowlana, 1989; Mohamed, 2008) within scholarship in the global North. In the wake of September 11, renewed polarization between and homogenization of the West and Islam has taken place in journalistic discourses, and a progressive journalism ethics that can open up the debate for more perspectives and dialogue is of critical importance.

What is crucial is that journalism ethics move beyond static and outdated normative theories like Siebert, Peterson, and Schramm's (1963) framework, *Four Theories of the Press,* which still has a strong influence on normative ethical thinking despite clearly being linked to Cold War thinking and being biased in favor of the West (Curran and Park, 2000; Wasserman, 2006). Such old dichotomies between the West and the non-West are passé (Kruckeberg and Tsetsura, 2004:85). Moreover, ethical theories that take the nation-state as their central basis of comparison are flawed in an era of globalization, with its complex flows and contra-flows. A dynamic theory of journalism ethics is needed for a dynamic era in global journalism.

Applied Ethics

Applied ethics is the branch of ethical thinking in which decisions are made about ethical action in actual cases. In journalism, these decisions often have to be made under great pressure and with very limited time available. For this reason, journalists should be well-versed in ethical theory and systematic decision making so that ethical cases can be argued under pressure without relying on "gut-feel" or instinct alone. In recent years, partly thanks to new technologies such as the Internet, comparative discussions of ethical case studies have become more commonplace due to a variety of media watchdog organizations circulating updates and alerts about journalism ethics case studies on Web sites and list-servs (e.g,. www.fair.org), as well as bloggers around the world that share their views of the media. While these opinions are not always based on sound argumentation or informed by journalistic ethical theory in the scholarly sense, they do serve to stimulate debate about good (or bad) journalism and create awareness of journalists' ethical responsibilities.

Internationally, journalists and media organizations practice self-regulation by means of ethical codes. Through organizations like the Organization of News Ombudsmen (www.newsombudsmen.org) examples of best practice can be exchanged, and precedents can be set for others to follow. Such comparative work does not necessarily solve the problem of dominant normative frameworks remaining in place, or the relation between the global and the local, but they can provide a space for dialogue and exchange between different points of view.

Conclusion: Is There a Way Forward?

It is clear that the challenges for journalism in the contemporary, globalized era are many. In a time when journalism is undergoing rapid change and media are impacting on social life globally on an unprecedented scale, the question as to how ethical journalism should be understood globally has become urgent. Is it possible to agree on ethical conduct for journalists around the globe? How should journalism ethics account for the plurality and diversity in a multicultural, globalized media environment? These are important, yet difficult, questions that will remain on the research agenda for ethicists for years to come.

While answers remain elusive, it is clear that journalism ethics will have to change if it is to become truly global. Theories developed in the North cannot masquerade as universal, nor will a superficial inclusion of different perspectives be enough if it is not accompanied by a serious attempt to revise ethical theory fundamentally. On the other hand, the demand for local values and cultural difference should not become a smokescreen for expedient political wrangling either, whether on the side of journalists or politicians, as seemed to be the case in the example from South Africa with which this chapter began— although global journalism ethics will also have a political dimension in its demands for social justice and global equality.

The debate about journalism ethics in the future will have to be inclusive, but also robust enough to encourage challenges from various competing perspectives. Such a debate will also have to include attention to the ways in which economic, social, and cultural power relations influence our understanding of journalism ethics. What is needed is a critical dialogue. Bentley and Hargreaves (2001:13) argues, in the light of the crisis of Western liberalism, for a more dialogic, negotiated approach to global morality:

> The moral discourse of the West in the last 20 years tells us that we need to reconsider the self-confident simplicities, the fundamentalisms of liberalism, in favour of bestowing more authority upon negotiated communities of interest, both at the national and international level.

Such an open-ended, negotiated approach, in which ethical values remain provisional and emerge from a critical dialectic between different ethical frameworks, is one through which we can hope to make progress on our way to global journalism ethics.

BIBLIOGRAPHY

Alia, V. *Media Ethics and Social Change*. Edinburgh: Edinburgh University Press, 2004.
Ang, I. "The Performance of the Sponge: Mass Communication Theory Enters the Postmodern World." In K. Brants, J. Hermes, and L. van Zoonen (eds.), *The Media in Question: Popular Cultures and Public Interests,* 77–88. London:Sage, 1998.
Baggini, J., and Fosl, P. S. *The Ethics Toolkit*. Oxford: Blackwell, 2007.

Bentley, T., and Hargreaves, I. "Introduction: The New Ideology." In Bentley, T. and Jones, D. S. (eds.), *The Moral Universe.* London: Demos, 2001.

Berger, G. "Current Challenges." In A. Hadland (ed.), *Changing the Fourth Estate: Essays on South African Journalism,* 19–26. Cape Town: HSRC Press, 2005.

Bertrand, J.-C. *Media Ethics and Accountability Systems.* New Brunswick, NJ: Transaction Publishers, 2000.

Blankenberg, N. "In Search of Real Freedom: Ubuntu and the Media." *Critical Arts* 13, No. 2 (1999), 42–65.

Christians, C. G. "The Ethics of Being in a Communications Context." In Christians, C. and Traber, M. (eds.), *Communication Ethics and Universal Values,* 3–23. London: Sage, 1997a.

———. "Social Ethics and Mass Media Practice." In J. M. Makau and R. C. Arnett (eds.), *Communication Ethics in an Age of Diversity,* 187–205. Urbana: University of Illinois Press, 1997b.

———. "Ubuntu and Communitarianism in Media Ethics." *Ecquid Novi* 25, No. 2 (2004), 235–256.

Christians, C. G., Rotzoll, K. B., Fackler, M., McKee, K. B., and Woods, Jr., R. H. *Media Ethics. Cases and Moral Reasoning.* Boston: Pearson, 2005.

Curran, J., and Park, M. J. "Beyond Globalization Theory." In Curran and Park (eds.), *De-Westernizing Media Studies,* 3–18. London: Routledge, 2000.

Deuze, M. "What Is Journalism? Professional Identity and Ideology of Journalists Reconsidered." *Journalism* 6, No. 4 (2005), 442–464.

Donegan, A. *The Theory of Morality.* Chicago: University of Chicago Press, 1977.

Fourie, P. J. "Moral Philosophy as a Threat to Freedom of Expression: From Christian-Nationalism to *ubuntuism* as a Normative Framework for Media Regulation and Practice in South Africa. *Communications: European Journal of Communication Research* 32 (2007), 1–29.

Gikandi, S. "Globalization and the Claims of Postcoloniality." In Desai, G. and Nair, S. (eds.) *Postcolonialisms,* 608–634. Oxford: Berg, 2005.

Hafez, K. "Journalism Ethics Revisited: A Comparison of Ethics Codes in Europe, North Africa, the Middle East, and Muslim Asia." *Political Communication* 19, No. 2 (2005), 225–250.

Hanitzsch, T. "Deconstructing Journalism Culture: Toward a Universal Theory." *Communication Theory* 17, No. 4 (2007), 367–385.

Josephi, B. "Journalism in the Global Age: Between Normative and Empirical." *Gazette* 67, No. (2005), 575–590.

Kasoma, F. "The Foundations of African Ethics (Afri-ethics) and the Professional Practice of Journalism: The Case for Society-centered Morality." *Africa Media Review* 10, No. 3 (1996), 93–116.

Kruckeberg, D., and Tsetsura, K. "International Journalism Ethics." In De Beer, A. and Merrill, J. (eds.), *Global Journalism.* Boston, MA: Pearson, 2004.

Ladikas, M., and Schroeder, D. "Too Early for Global Ethics?" *Cambridge Quarterly of Healthcare Ethics* 14 (2005), 404–415.

Leshilo, T. "Enemies of the People? Counterpoint." *Mail & Guardian,* September 7, 2007. Retrieved December 19, 2007 from http://www.mg.co.za/articlePage.aspx?articleid=318526 &area=/insight/insight__comment_and_analysis/

Lumby, C., and Probyn, E. (eds.). *Remote Control: New Media, New Ethics.* Cambridge: Cambridge University Press, 2003.

Malan, R. "80 Days That Rocked the Nation." *Empire.* November 2007.

Mbeki, T. "Address at the South African National Editors' Forum on the Media. April 12, 2003. AU, NEPAD and Democracy, Johannesburg. Retrieved on December 19, 2007 from http://www.dfa.gov. za/docs/speeches/2003/mbek0412.htm

Mohamed, A. "Journalistic Ethics and Responsibility in Relation to Freedom of Expression: An Islamic Perspective." In Ward, S. and Wasserman, H. (eds.), *Media Ethics beyond Borders.* Johannesburg: Heinemann (2008).

Mowlana, H. "Communication, Ethics and the Islamic Tradition." In Cooper, T. W., Christians, C. G., Plude, F. F. and White, R. A. (eds.), *Communication Ethics and Global Change,* 137–146. London: Longman, 1989.

Mpofu, D. "Enemies of the People? Point." *Mail & Guardian,* September 7, 2007. Retrieved December 19, 2007 from http://www.mg.co.za/articlePage.aspx?articleid=318519&area=/ insight/insight__ comment_and_analysis/

Rao, S., and Wasserman, H. "Global Journalism Ethics Revisited: A Postcolonial Critique." *Global Media and Communication* 3, No. 1 (2007), 29–50.

Shutte, A. *Philosophy for Africa.* Rondebosch: UCT Press, 1996.

Shepperson, A., and Tomaselli, K. "Ethics: A Radical Justice Approach." *Ecquid Novi,* 2, No. 2 (2002), 278–289.

Siebert, F., Peterson, T. and Schramm, W. *Four Theories of the Press.* Urbana: University of Illinois Press, 1963.

Silverstone, R. *Media and Morality. On the Rise of the Mediapolis.* Cambridge: Polity Press, 2007.

Singer, J. "The Socially Responsible Existentialist." *Journalism Studies* 7, No. 1 (2006), 2–18.

The Star "Time for Some Soul-searching." August 22. Retrieved December 19, 2007 from http://www.journalism.co.za/insight/time-for-some-soul-searching-2.html

Sunday Times. "Manto's Hospital Binge." August 12, 2007a. Retrieved December 19, 2007 from http://www.thetimes.co.za/News/Article.aspx?id=537601

———.   "Manto: A Drunk and a Thief." August 19, 2007b. Retrieved December 19, 2007 from http://www.thetimes.co.za/SpecialReports/Manto/Article.aspx?id=542808

———.   "Editor, Journalist to Be Arrested." October 14, 2007c. Retrieved December 19, 2007 from http://www.thetimes.co.za/PrintEdition/Article.aspx?id=586684

Wasserman, H. "Post-apartheid Media Debates and the Discourse of Identity." *Ecquid Novi* 24, No. 2 (2003), 218–224.

———. "Globalised Values and Postcolonial Responses: South African Perspectives on Normative Media Ethics." *The International Communication Gazette* 68, No. 1 (2006), 71–91.

Wasserman, H., and De Beer, A. S. "Reporting Ethically on HIV/AIDS: A South African Case Study." In Land, M. and Hornaday, B. (eds.), *Contemporary Media Ethics: A Practical Guide for Scholars, Students and Professionals,* 155–172. Marquette Books, 2006.

Wasserman, H., and Rao, S. "The Glocalization of Journalism Ethics." *Journalism: Theory, Practice, Criticism* 9, No.2 (2008), 163–181.

Weaver, D. (ed.) *The Global Journalist: News People around the World.* Creskill, NJ: Hampton, 1998.

Zelizer, B., and Allan, S. (eds.). *Journalism after September 11.* London: Routledge, 2002.

7 Global Advertising and Public Relations

DOUG NEWSOM

Texas Christian University, USA

An all-electronic communication world has given vitality to the long-lingering mass media discourse about "convergence." Print and broadcast media now exist without clear boundaries, so cross-training is essential. For advertising and public relations practitioners, digital thinking and working start with strategic planning, following through to execution and delivery and then analysis of results (Vranica, 2007).

Message conception for advertising and public relations must occur within the context of many cultures, a mix of legal systems, a global market where economic events can set off a tsunami of consequences and turn a kaleidoscope of ever-changing political climates. Reception and interpretation are also global—with estimates at 1.3 billion online users globally in 2007 and increasing daily. Although measuring online users is an inexact science, according to eMarketer, the largest user increases are expected in Asia since Western markets are almost at saturation points (eMarketer file, August 1, 2007).

The credibility of locally generated but globally received messages is an issue that has united advertising and public relations practitioners with news media writers and editors in efforts to link trust of information with transparency at the source (Bishop, 2007; Tsetsura, 2007; Rawlins, 2007; Edelman, 2007; Curtin and Gaither, 2007:246). There are a number of these organisations forstering better relations between the advertising, public relations and media sectors, such as the Institute for Public Relations, International Public Relations Association, International Communications Consultancy Organisation, Global Alliance for Public Relations and Communication Management.

Transparency is not the only issue, however. Another problem is that digital photography puts scenes on the Internet sometimes as they were and sometimes "enhanced." Ethical questions aside, the credibility of a message is always an individualistic interpretation. Advertising and public relations messages used to be designed for delivery to specific audiences, and their reception and potential impact were carefully researched. The existence of global media systems, mass and specialized, means that it is not possible to think in terms of restricting messages, commercial or otherwise, to particular audiences. Global access to messages, though, is occurring at a time when organizations of all kinds are trying to focus their messages more narrowly. While the original focus may be short-range and sharp, the effect is likely to be broad and diffused. Messages get through the clutter of competing media or ineffective delivery systems only through individual choice.

Message recipients are volunteer readers, listeners, or viewers. If something gets their attention, they may opt to receive the message. What is received, however, may not be a message intended for that audience, such as commercials and ads that come with imported media when the products or services are not available in that market. Or recipients' cultural experience may not give them the same frame of reference for the message, such as the romance and fantasy that surrounds much media content, especially advertising.

Results, in any case, are usually negative. Frustration occurs when products are not available or are too costly, perhaps because of import duties or the differences in monetary exchange rates. Sometimes there is bewilderment at not understanding the context of messages or themes for both editorial and advertising content.

Nevertheless, the Internet is both a primary information source and a communication tool, and as such it is the principal influence for changes in advertising and public relations management. Understanding the different prisms under which their efforts will be seen, advertising and public relations practitioners still must rely on carefully crafted messages and graphics designed for specific audiences to persuade them to accept a product or service or to support an idea. More unification of advertising and public relations has occurred over efforts at "branding" to gain recognition of and credibility for an institution and its services or products across borders.

Branding is not without problems. When multinational institutions, profit or non-profit, are branded in a way that ties them closely to their "nationality," or place of origin, other difficulties such as boycotts or sabotage occur with events or changes in the political climate (Al Shebil, Rasheed, and Il-Shammari, 2007). One source of misunderstandings occurs because the appreciation of "foreign" media content is usually limited to cultural elites, and not just in First World cultures. An example is the confusion among unsophisticated audiences about Web sites that appear to be connected to an organization but really are sites created by critics of the organization, its products or services or policies (Hill, Hill, and White, 2000; Guntarto, 2001). On these sites, misrepresentation or rumors often stir up trouble.

Global Communication

For advertising and public relations practitioners, global communication has increased the emphasis on issues management and crisis communication. Satellite broadcasting and the Internet create global awareness in times of crisis and are a major factor in the way crises are handled. Instant messaging across time zones occurs, and the world gets a mix of verified or verifiable information about events, along with the sheer fiction of an international version of urban myths.

Fax and phone, satellite broadcasts, and all of the electronic tools of the computer have indeed wired the world. In a crisis, those involved post news releases on their Web site first because that takes some of the international media inquiries off their e-mail, cell, and line phones. In addition, a crisis-struck organization usually gets out e-mail messages to employees in distant offices and posts information on the organization's intranet so that employees on site have the facts about the crisis firsthand. Although message delivery is instantaneous, global responses to crises and global campaigns are not exactly that. What public relations and advertising practitioners have relied on for years is a local contact, someone to guide their communication effort safely through the culture, which often includes religious and legal traps for the unwary. Lacking that local guidance can cause serious cultural clashes and, in a crisis, some critical misunderstanding. Handling crises and campaigns in a global environment requires culturally astute, careful, and committed practitioners where the message originates.

Crisis or not, technology gives presence to organizations and governments all over the planet, even if they don't intend to be there. To cope with this situation, large advertising and public relations companies have made connections with individuals and agencies or firms in different parts of the world. Often the companies have either hired their contacts or bought local firms with which they had an alliance. Experience in a locale also encourages multinationals to open a branch where contacts have been made. When global economic downturns have caused the closing of multinationals' offices in some areas, the result has not been the demise of this practice. Local firms have matured with more international commercial experience and even had an impact on governmental communication practices.

Changes in campaign strategies demonstrate what is occurring. Three strategic models for planning global campaigns are standardized, adaptive, and country-specific. In the standardized model, strategy is formed at the global headquarters and implemented in all operating areas. In the adaptive model, a basic strategy is adapted appropriately for each country where it will be implemented. In a country-specific model, the strategic planning is shaped to fit one country.

Research indicates that the standardized model is seldom used today. Although that might seem strange in a global environment where nations are exposed to campaigns in other countries, what it shows is that campaign planners adapt central message statements to different countries but make sure their messages are consonant. The increased sophistication of audiences from global exposure indicates that they recognize why one approach is used in certain parts of the world, although they know it would not be suitable for their own country. This is particularly true when audiences connect religious or cultural differences to the approach. Instead of a national approach, the present trend is a regional one, indicating that some recognition is now being given to the reality that separation by borders is more political than cultural. Curiously, while intentional messages, such as advertising and the more overt public relations messages, seem to be "filtered" by global audiences, that does not always happen with news. It is in news interpretation, rather than in intentional messages, that misperceptions seem to occur most often, with consequential "fallout" that advertising and public relations practitioners then must handle.

Campaigns have both commercial and noncommercial origins. Generalizations are risky, but in many countries the noncommercial communication function seems to have developed with a public relations emphasis in governmental and nongovernmental organizations (NGOs) as well as private voluntary organizations (PVOs) that have social missions (Coombs and Holladay, 2007). Ordinarily, the communication function takes on a marketing emphasis when focused on an industrial or commercial enterprise, but the lines between advertising and public relations blur into a general communication function with any persuasive effort. Government-directed social campaigns often use all media and a mix of advertising, publicity, and promotion. The advertising agencies involved in these social campaigns often developed a public relations segment. In addition, political candidates in democracies around the globe employed many such firms. The size of some of these campaign accounts attracted transnational and multinational advertising or public relations groups that have opened offices abroad to service them. These new multinationals soon attracted other clients from the commercial sector.

A proliferation of advertising and public relations people employed around the world have stimulated growth in professional organizations and education. Professional organizations for advertising and public relations are found in virtually every country, and there are international organizations too. Because these organizations began utilizing some professional upgrading and continuing education, they influenced education in their countries. Also, as multinational and transnational companies began looking for employees, they turned to the educational systems in these countries for graduates ready to come directly into the firm knowing what to do. There is little time today for on-the-job learning.

Whereas previously most universities outside of the United States of America preferred the European model of teaching disciplines, not professions (with the exception of law and medicine), many have now added courses in advertising and public relations and even majors. In nations where a tradition of teaching journalism already existed, such as India, the addition of public relations and advertising seemed to come easily. Giving support to these fledgling academic endeavors have been resident practitioners and their companies.

Growth in education for advertising and public relations is found in universities worldwide, and even governments that used to look at their development communications as journalistic or as information campaigns now recognize that this activity really belongs to the realm of public affairs. They best understand that when they have a crisis. Government Web sites are accessed by global audiences and greatly affect tourism, international business, public perceptions of their nation, and much more.

Asia and the Pacific

In Australia, New Zealand, Hong Kong, and Singapore, the maturity of these countries' advertising and public relations practice provides models for other countries where, for a variety of reasons, the practices are less developed. India also offers one of the more sophisticated regions for advertising/public relation practice, all the more so now that it has two high-tech states, Kerala and Andhra Pradesh. Countries to watch for accelerated influence in the fields of advertising and public relations are South Korea and Singapore, and the continuing development of China and India should also be noted.

South Korea, like many other Asian countries, is a high-tech nation generating business, entertainment, and community Internet services (Ha and Moon, 2007). Scholarship there is increasing too, as evidenced by the large number of publications authored by Koreans. One advantage of Korea's developments in advertising and public relations may be the relaxation of the foreign business ownership ban that has allowed for establishment of internationally recognized firms such as Burson-Marsteller (Curtin and Gaither, 2007). From a situation where previously the demand for public relations and advertising focused on technicians (Park, 2001), the influence of multinationals may transform that to more of a management function.

Indonesia and Thailand are moving forward, although the development is mostly in large cities. Much of this is driven by the explosive growth in the use of the Internet, especially by the young. Pakistan is caught up in its own government turmoil, exacerbated by the conflict in neighboring Afghanistan and its involvement in the Iraq conflict. Indonesia, like Malaysia, is focusing on education for its practitioners, as is China (see Ang and Lee, 2001; Ayaz, 2002; Rananand, 2001).

Singapore and China are places to watch for significant growth in advertising and public relations practices, as well as education. China's potential as a market has tempted traders for centuries, and no less so today. Singapore, also a trading center for centuries, today handles more tonnage than any other in the world and has an airline that sets the standard for luxury air-travel. The Lion-nation, Singapore, is losing some of its restrictive image, though it is still often called a "nanny state" because of its many government campaigns directed toward the behavior of its citizens. As its self-confidence increases, Singapore's government seems to be relaxing, however (Lamb, 2007). The island nation is striving to be a knowledge-based economy and so is technology driven. Business-to-business trade is strong there, with a corresponding impact on both advertising and public relations. Information technology (IT) continues to expand. Education in advertising and public relations is growing in Singapore, which benefits from being the base for a number of multinational advertising and public relations companies as well as many local firms with a long history. Furthermore, support comes from strong professional organizations that facilitate continuing education (Goonasekera, 2002; Liang, 2002). Singapore has strengthened its position in communication education by hosting international conferences and producing publications that include the scholarship of other Asian nations.

China's growth has increased with the location of major international advertising and public relations companies in Beijing, Shanghai, and Guangzhou. Now that China has World Trade Organization (WTO) status, Beijing has a new focus on technology companies and financial public relations. However, cultural and political land mines require a good guide. The media system, too, is a challenge because it takes weeks or even months to buy advertising space and to buy the services of journalists through the China News and Culture Promotion Committee to get publicity. Even so, public relations education continues to grow. The first program opened in 1985 at Shenzhen University, just north of Hong Kong, where the real practice of public relations began in 1981. Transparency remains a problem, especially in China's handling of crises such as the recalls of its manufactures in recent years and health issues such as SARS.

With its growing regional markets, China is the awakening giant in the area but it is experiencing significant troubles because its economy exploded, rather than expanded. The many multinational recalls of products from toys to foods, both pet and human, has been embarrassing to the Chinese government. China also has increased its nationalism to the point that multinational companies' criticism or even accidental "insult" arouses an indignant and defensive response, especially if unloosed on the Internet (PR Week, Global Special:17). A somewhat reluctant government has to deal with other advertising and public relations issues that come in from the Internet, although China, more than Thailand, polices the pervasive medium. China is less effective in its patrol of Hong Kong, which, like the Philippines, has a long history of advertising and public relations practice. At present, China is under considerable pressure to be at the top of its advertising/public relations game in hosting one of the biggest events in the world, the 2008 Olympics (Economy, 2007:49). Internally, it is promoting the use of the Mandarin language (as opposed to Cantonese) in the nation and in surrounding countries with significant Chinese populations, and it continues to focus on Confucian values.

One interesting facet of public relations practice in both Singapore and China that confounds other practitioners is something called *guanxi*. The practice involves using sometimes secret personal connections in a strategy. Some Western practitioners see it as not much more than networking or calling in favors, but it is different because it is tied to Confucianism. Guanxi is sometimes seen as being unethical, but its reconsideration in China may be in process as the country moves more toward strategic management of communication (Zhang, Shen, and Jiang, 2007). Another difficulty is the one created by what is sometimes referred to as Asian values of Confucian origin. Even Asians often see these values as an excuse for authoritarianism (Wu, 2002; Huang, 2000).

These two cultural manifestations, which do have an impact on public relations and advertising as well as the news media, are not as prevalent in "the other China," Taiwan. In Taiwan, most of the books used for education in universities for teaching public relations and advertising are Western texts. The practice, too, has a strong Western influence and has had since political democracy came to the country in the 1980s. International advertising and public relations firms are based in Taiwan, and the industry was growing rapidly early in the new century (Wu, 2001). Taiwan maintains a strong position in the international economy and often demonstrates its independence, as when it contracted a cooperative agreement with six other South Pacific nations in 2006 for financial aid, some of it going to promotions such as tourism (e.g. the Palau Declaration). Although promotions for tourism and commerce have strengthened, this part of the Peoples Republic of China remains cautious.

Government difficulties in both China and the Philippines have been a constraint. Nevertheless, for China, Hong Kong remains a significant marketplace for consumer goods; thus, the focus there is mostly on trade, as it is in Taiwan as well. In the Philippines, the government seems to be settling down, but still must deal with its rebellious minority population of Muslims, although this is not a new issue. The country has a long association with advertising and public relations connections with the West, especially the United States.

In Japan the status of public relations has improved and it is seen as strategic management, not just publicity (PR Week, Global Perspective, 2007:17). In the past, the nation has had few public relations firms, but the advertising agencies have public relations capabilities to offer clients within the 15 percent media commission system and are not now charging extra for public relations services. This structure makes it more difficult to charge for public relations work separately. Although public relations and Western-style advertising were introduced to Japan after World War II, the acculturation process has changed the practice considerably. Western-style approaches conflicted with the Japanese distaste for confrontation and braggadocio. Furthermore, there is respect for the creation of long-term relationships, especially with government and the media (Watson and Sallot, 2001). Advertising in Japan is subtle, and publicity is disseminated through press clubs, some of which are industry related. Other relationships are government oriented, and some are for political parties. Establishing relationships with the press clubs is the only way to get information to the news media unless reporters choose to take it from a company's Web site. News is generally announced through authorities, although this approach has not worked very well when Japan has had major crises, such as natural disasters or economic downturns. The government's slowness to act usually generates international criticism. Negative public opinion hits a nerve in the government. In particular, Japan's internal promotion of nationalism and efforts to soften historical versions of its World War II activities in the Philippines and China has created some discomfort, especially with its neighbors. Japan is nonetheless a major global player economically, especially in the automobile industry where its Toyota brand in 2006 gained the third largest share in the U.S. market, a first for any foreign car maker.

The public relations and advertising industries are growing, but they are still relatively small in Indonesia and Thailand and are likely to remain limited primarily to Jakarta and Bangkok, respectively, although of the two Indonesia seems more poised for development with its significant growth of the Internet, including online advertising. Cultural taboos also appear to be relaxing. In 2006, for the first time *Playboy* magazine went on sale in Indonesia, the world's most populous Muslim country, albeit with some more modified "exposure" of its models. In another Muslim country, Malaysia, advertising and promotion have always been subject to cultural restrictions. However, the growth of both public relations and advertising is more likely in Indonesia than in Malaysia, perhaps because of Indonesia's proximity to Singapore. The constraints in Malaysia originate with governmental regulation of media content and restrictions requiring the use of Malay firms, which is more of a control issue than protectionism. Because of the high involvement with government, public affairs practices are significant. The positive aspect is that increasing attention is being paid to education in the fields. Indochina reflects little development or growth, although technology may change that (Ahmad, 2001; Almatsier, 2001).

An increase in technology within the Philippines may be driving growth in advertising and public relations. If so, that would be a welcome change for a country that could lay claim to being the Pacific birthplace for public relations and a climate where advertising always has played an important role. The Philippines dates the "beginnings"of its public relations practice to the 1940s, and by 1955 it had a national public relations association. Constraints on corporate speech during the period of martial law under Fernando Marcos, 1972-1981, proved a setback, but by 1977 the government had authorized a bachelor of science degree in public relations. Universities that could support the degree were allowed to offer it. Also in 1977, an institute was established to serve as a liaison between education and practice. The country's weak economy has strapped its growth, but the technology sector is offering new possibilities. In the Philippines, public relations is growing faster than there are educated practitioners and senior practitioners to fill the jobs. A strong professional group has instituted a university degree in public relations, with public affairs as a major focus (Panol, 2000).

Although public relations education began in Australia at about the same time as in the Philippines, Australia is clearly the front-runner in the Pacific for both advertising and public relations practice. The country has major international firms that have been there since the 1980s, and a substantial number of well-developed local companies are doing well despite several economic recessions. In addition, the communication function appears in many companies, contrary to the situation for some of Australia's Asian neighbors, where it exists primarily in government or in advertising/public relations firms. Australia's educational institutions offer doctoral degrees in public relations, and undergraduate education has been available in public relations and advertising since 1970. The Public Relations Institute of Australia has been a significant factor in the spread of public relations education, as well as in setting standards for education and practice in the field. Public relations associations were first established in Australia in 1949 and 1952.

More recently, marketing efforts in Australia have turned more toward public relations than traditional advertising (PR Week, Global Perspective, 2007:17). Many of the same influences that have affected Australia have impacted neighboring New Zealand. And New Zealand, like Australia and the Philippines, reflects more of a Western-like practice of advertising and public relations (Singh and Smyth, 2000).

Westernized advertising and public relations practices also have been the model for India, although the nation's practitioners have been struggling to develop a more appropriate model for their nation, which still has a large rural population. Globalization and India's own national directive from Vision 2020 (future planning for the nation) have emphasized communications, especially the transparency aspect. Communication is becoming a strategic function as this world's largest democracy positions itself for global leadership. Aiding the nation has been its economic reforms of 1991, but a serious distraction has been the continuing trouble with Pakistan over Kashmir and the persistent internal difficulties with the Naxalites (Maoist terrorists).

India has a long history of public relations activity. Dr. C.V.N. Reddi has written much about its development in the Indian Public Relations Foundation magazine for which he is responsible, *PR Voice*. Dr. Reddi maintains that until India develops its own code of ethics and revamps education and continuing education for public relations practice, it will miss an opportunity to claim a place in world leadership in the field. The country's very active Public Relation Society of India (PRSI) has conducted continuing education seminars for decades. Also, India has transnational public relations and advertising firms, as well as many of its own local firms. Services remain mostly in the area of public affairs, business-to-business, corporate communications, and international communications (Sagar, 2002). India's cultural diversity creates many of the same problems that occur in the United States when the nation or some company tries to mount a campaign. Cultural glitches can occur unless care is taken to fine-tune the message for each segment, while being aware that the same group will be exposed to all of the campaign messages.

India has also been caught up in difficulties with Sri Lanka, which, like Pakistan, has transnational corporations practicing public relations and using advertising. In fact, local public relations practice in Sri Lanka remains a part of ad agencies and is not highly professionalized (Kundra, 2002; Singh, 2000). Sri Lanka has a highly literate population that makes considerable use of computers and the Internet, so it might emerge in the digital age. In Pakistan, the business sector is struggling under the military rule that has been imposed on this once democratic nation, although that may be changing due to international pressures over the Iraq and Afghanistan conflicts. Settling its governance problems may allow the nation to emerge as a major international influence since it has many local public relations and advertising agencies that have international affiliation with global firms and agencies. Transnational companies with internal advertising or public relations staff have made very little use of public relations or advertising within the country. The government, the impact of conflict, and a media that expects compensation for publicity all hamper communication in Pakistan.

In the Asian Pacific region, the real unknowns are Vietnam, Laos, Cambodia, and North Korea. Laos seems the most likely to develop its areas of advertising and public relations because of the strong influence from Thailand, although Laos's low female literacy and primarily rural economy may slow advancement. This is also true for Cambodia, although tourism is helping somewhat. Vietnam seems to be developing, albeit slowly. Government constraints have created a less promising climate in North Korea.

Technology is the driving force for commerce in the entire Asian Pacific region. As a whole, Asia is expected to lead the world in use of the Internet by 2012. Asian Pacific online advertising spending reached 54 percent of its total advertising expenses from 2005 to 2006, and several other nations are predicted to be top online spenders by 2009 ("Growth in Online Spending Rockets across the Asia Pacific Region," Microsoft Digital Advertising Solutions, January 21, 2007). In e-government rankings regarding lack of corruption, Singapore is third to Canada and the United States of America, and ahead of Japan, the UK, and Taiwan (see 2006 World e-Government Ranking by Waseda University Institute of e-Government, Japan, 2005).

Latin America and the Caribbean

Latin America has been beset by natural disasters of all kinds: earthquakes (Peru), volcano eruptions (Guatemala and Ecuador), and hurricanes on both coasts. The other crises have been over supplies of oil and natural gas and considerable political realignments. Nevertheless, the growth of advertising and public relations in Latin America and the Caribbean has much to do with the merging of economic initiatives both inside the region and globally (Starlach, 2001; Hirsch, 2001). Some nations are suffering from economic and political strife, and others are struggling to build a sufficient infrastructure.

Market alliances, some old and some new, tell the story because much of the advertising/public relations activity in this region is business-to-business and government-to-government. Most nations in the region have reestablished normal relations with Cuba, including all 15 nations constituting a 1975 market organization called the Caribbean Community and Common Market (CARICOM) in which Haiti's membership was restored in 2006. What seemed a possibility for the development of a more united marketplace for all of the Americas, facilitated by the 1994 North American Free Trade Agreement (NAFTA), is now being jeopardized by some global alliances of these countries and some hostility toward U.S. foreign policy, exacerbated by immigration issues with the United States. A major part of this market picture is the Southern Cone Common Market (Mercosur), which involves South American countries in a free-trade pact. Venezuela urges support for Mercosur, perhaps especially now since the economic organization has been at odds with the United States. Central America has had the Central American Common

Market (CACM) since the 1960s, and in 2005, at the fourth Summit of the Americas, U.S. President George Bush signed an agreement with the Central America-Dominican Republic Free Trade Association (CAFTA-DR). The agreement of these countries went into effect in 2006, but implementation was delayed in Costa Rica until a new president pledged to expedite the process there. A new group, anti-USA, was formed by Bolivia in 2006: Alternative for Bolivia and the Americas (ALBA), with co-signers Cuba and Nicaragua. Venezuela's president Hugo Chávez Frias said the new pact was designed to reduce U.S. influence in Latin America. Additional agreements are being made within the area such as Brazil with Belize. Nations with trade agreements outside of the Americas include El Salvador with Qatar, Honduras with China, and with others being planned.

Digitalization of communication, especially in advertising and public relations, has facilitated global expansion and provides the key to social and business development, although resistance is being demonstated in many countries by the poor who protest that they are being hurt, not benefited by globalization. A significant effort by this region's governments involves campaigns to promote ecotourism, improve social conditions, and attract investments, such as France's investment in improving sea- and airports in El Salvador. Panama is widening the Canal in anticipation of increased commercial as well as tourist traffic. In Mexico, a dramatic change in its economic and political systems opened up both internal and external communications. More openness has been a boon to public affairs and to commercial communication involving advertising and public relations (Díaz, 2002). However, there is increasing tension between Mexico and the United States over immigration issues. In addition, the economy's stability has been jeopardized by a disparity of resources—manifested internally by terrorists acts that have damaged industrial facilities, especially some transnational ones.

Mexico has a long history of being a home for international public relations and advertising companies. Some companies have been there since the 1950s. Others joined them in the 1960s, and in the 1970s Mexico's established some substantial local agencies and firms. As host to the first Inter-American Conference on Public Relations in 1960, Mexico facilitated the development of the Inter-American Public Relations Federation, which provides a framework for research on the growth of public relations activities in the area. More recently, the entry of more international public relations and advertising firms, the growth of business media, more cause-related marketing, and the public affairs activities of NGOs have stimulated the advertising/public relations field. The media have grown more independent, but public relations and advertising professionals still encounter corruption. Moreover, low literacy rates are limiting the use of media. Nevertheless, public relations practitioners have played a role though social engagement in stabilizing and strengthening Mexico's democratic systems (Molleda and Moreno, 2006:108).

Chile is a thriving advertising and public relations center thanks to its combination of democracy and solid market economy, as well its growing formal university education for the field. Brazil was the first country in this region to license public relations (in 1967) and require university education for practice. One of the first universities to offer public relations courses in Latin America was Peru's Pontifical Catholic University, although today many universities in the region offer courses, with some even offering majors in the field. In Peru, as in Panama, public relations practice is regulated.

Many of these countries offer an array of advertising and public relations services, as in the Central American country of Costa Rica and even more so in the Caribbean country of Puerto Rico. In South America, economic and political turmoil has upset the advertising and public relations business in Bolivia, Ecuador, and Venezuela. Political and economic challenges in Paraguay have been exacerbated by social problems, although the nation did host the 2001 Mercosur meeting. Both Paraguay and Uruguay have professional advertising and professional associations, together with a sound base for development. Most of these nations use their public Web sites for tourism and business sites for their business-to-business efforts.

Ecotourism is a major factor in much of these advertising and public relations efforts. The Galapagos Islands drive Ecuador's efforts, but also create controversy among other nations' claims to the Islands (Curtin and Gaither, 2007:88–93). Throughout the area, tourism accounts for more than half of their gross national product, even in Cuba, a fact that is putting pressure on the United States to change its relationship.

Mexico, Central and South America, and the Caribbean are all interconnected through trade confederations and professional associations. Furthermore, many professional advertising and public relations people are members of larger, international educational and professional organizations. Interaction is likely to improve communication relationships and skills, although each practitioner has to accommodate the political and economic vagaries of the nations in which each is working.

Sub-Saharan Africa

Globalization is not a tide that has floated all boats, and certainly that is true of Africa. Generally, Africa has lost ground in terms of per capita income. Although tourism and international events such as the Olympics are important, many global agencies simply cannot find enough business to function in poorer countries (Curtin and Gaither, 2007:241). In addition, literacy is a problem in all of these nations except in South Africa where both men and women have a high degree of literacy. Literacy levels are relatively high but unequal in both Kenya and Botswana. In most of the other nations, where three-fourths of the males may be literate, just a little more than half of the women are. Other problems such as corruption, health and human rights issues, political turmoil resulting in flights of refugees, international scandals, and crises such as the one in Zimbabwe have created a host of internal and external problems for the countries of sub-Saharan Africa (Kraft, 2002). The economic impact of these problems has disrupted tourism and trade, which, of course, affects the advertising and public relations industries. Universities have also been affected, as have communications facilities, creating yet more problems for the practice of advertising and public relations.

Botswana does rank as the least corrupt state in Africa, and the economy there seems to be improving, with resulting progress in the infrastructure. Nigeria has used public relations and advertising campaigns for nation-building (Curtin and Gaither, 2007:9) and has a strong emphasis on public relations education, with graduate programs at its universities. The Nigerian Institute of Public Relations was incorporated into the country's laws. In Nigeria, a full array of advertising and marketing services is available, as well as support services in the areas of market and opinion research and media analysis and evaluation. Public relations exists at the strategic level in some companies. International public relations and international media relations are specialties, as are financial public relations, integrated business communications, issues and crises management, lobbying and political communications, and government communications. Uganda has a Public Relations Association and is a member of the Eastern Africa Public Relations Association.

The Democratic Republic of the Congo has a Centre for Public Relations in Kinshasa, although political problems have caused disruptions in its activities. In Ghana, stability has come with the now proven transfer of power in a democratic process, although the country's record on transparency has not improved; its journalists are so poorly paid that they need remuneration in order to be able to attend news conferences (Curtin and Gaither, 2007:246). Ghana has an Institute for Public Relations, and Nairobi is the location for the Public Relations Society of Kenya. Kenya, endeavoring to work with Tanzania and Uganda in an East African economic community, faced economic setbacks and met with little success.

With all of these problems, it is not surprising that much of the advertising and public relations activities in this region are government initiatives. Some of this communication impetus comes from increasing demand for more accountability on the part of government. Those countries that are striving to achieve more transparency are using advertising and public relations talents, but often find the need to redirect such efforts to crisis communication. Increased literacy in parts of the area and the presence of the Internet have made public relations a more compelling need. However, much of the education for public relations still is "on-the-job" training, although some schools, especially *technikons,* are making an effort. After three years, *technikon* students can graduate with a national diploma in public relations.

Much of the training and continuing education still comes from the oldest and most sophisticated public relations organization in the area, the Public Relations Institute of South Africa (PRISA), which began in 1957 (Holtzhausen, Petersen, and Tindall, 2003). PRISA established an accreditation and ethics council in 1986 and has two certificate programs, one for public relations practice and the other for public relations management. PRISA also is the national external examiner for those who study three years for a diploma in public relations through distance learning. South Africa's "least corrupt" ranking, however, has slipped downward (Business iAfrica.com, November 7, 2007). On the other hand, South Africa boasts a highly sophisticated advertising and public relations sector that can compete with the best in the world. Both communication activities will play a major role in 2010 when the football World Cup is held in South Africa (for the first time in Africa).

The private sector, on the whole, has more professionally experienced advertising and public relations people who generally are trained abroad. These counselors and managers usually are are able to work across the cultures in this vast continent and cope with the increasing level of communication technology. Although technology has increased awareness and the ability to connect across the continent, cultural misunderstandings and power struggles provide serious barriers to professional performance.

Middle East and North Africa

Despite the turmoil in the Middle East, some advertising and public relations has continued to develop, especially in Turkey, Egypt, the United Arab Emirates, and Jordan, and to some extent in Saudi Arabia, Kuwait, and Israel. Smaller nations with advertising and public relations activity include Qatar, Bahrain, and Cyprus (see Shuriedeh, 2000). The turmoil in Sudan's Darfur over human rights has created an international crisis for the nation. Although there is a Sudan Public Relations Association in the country, strict government control over media and free expression have always been a restrictive influence.

The secular government in Turkey has attracted transnational advertising and public relations firms and has encouraged the growth of local communication companies. Turkey has a full array of services, including strategic counseling in public relations and advertising and marketing services as well as integrated business communications. Two public relations organizations exist, the Turkish Public Relations Association and the Public Relations Consultancies Association. As might be expected, research is important, with an emphasis on marketing and opinion research, and public relations is taught in universities. Other special areas of practice include finance, health care, the environment, arts and culture, education, entertainment, investor relations, public affairs, sports, sponsorships and fundraising, issues management, and crisis communication. These are in addition to the more traditional specialties of community relations, consumer relations, corporate communications, investor relations, media training, and public affairs. Turkey's international position as one that straddles Eastern and Western cultures makes it a centerpiece for the study of communication, especially the fields of advertising and public relations.

Egypt is the founding site of the Arab Public Relations Society, which began in 1966. Founder Dr. Mahmoud El Ghary also established the Public Relations Institute. Until the 1970s, most of the public relations practice there involved public affairs because most of Egypt's business was in government hands. After development of the commercial sector, a strategic communication function emerged. Neighboring Qatar's focus is mostly on public affairs and government campaigns rather than commercial efforts. In Jordan, the government's use of public affairs has increased, as has that by business management. As democratizing and privatizing activities continue, demand for skilled advertising and public relations talent will increase.

Saudi Arabia's public relations efforts primarily entail public affairs and corporate communications, although there are sectors of international public relations, issues management, community relations, and consumer relations. Advertising is local and national. The Internet has increased focus on this area, especially in the petroleum industry.

Kuwait has been involved in advertising and marketing communications for some time, as well as corporate communications, and has a national public relations association. With an increase in banking, tourism, and travel, it also offers market and opinion research, financial and investor relations, and community relations.

Although Israel has both an association and a counselors organization, it has been so caught up in conflict that its advertising and public relations efforts have been limited. Tourism, which affects both areas, is down, and many transnational corporations have recalled expatriate employees. When peace comes, it should resurrect what was once a large advertising and marketing industry and a comprehensive public relations complement with a wide range of specialties.

In the island nations of Bahrain and Cyprus, most advertising and public relations activities are either corporate or government; Bahrain has developed a technology focus.

Eastern Europe

This area, which includes East Central and Southeastern Europe, Russia, and the countries and regions of the former USSR, has been uneven in its development of advertising and public relations, but growth is apparent almost everywhere (McLeish, 2001).

East, Central and Southeastern Europe have made impressive gains both in the practice of advertising and public relations and in education. Some of the recent growth in the commercial and consultancy areas has come from the European Union membership of Hungary, Poland, Slovenia, the Czech Republic and the Slovak Republic, Bulgaria, Romania, Estonia, Lithuania, and Latvia.

Hungary and Poland began their advertising and public relations efforts almost immediately following the collapse of communism. Hungary has developed somewhat faster than Poland, which has lost some international advertising and public relations agencies. As a result of that pull-out, however, international agency trained people opened their own shops and are doing well (Laszyn, 2001). In some situations, they still engage in partner activities with the former "parent" firm. Hungary is a whole other story. Many multinationals and some international advertising and public relations firms have moved their offices to Budapest, which, like Vienna, is now considered a regional headquarters for business in this region.

Both the Czech Republic and Slovak Republic are also moving forward, helped to some extent by affiliation with and representation of some global transnational public relations and advertising companies and by an increase in tourism. The Czech Republic has benefited from the presence of multinational companies with Western-trained managers receptive to the idea of strategic as well as tactical use of advertising and public relations. The Slovak Republic is a bit behind the Czech Republic owing to the lack of as much foreign investment and a concentration of the advertising and public relations sector on promotion and publicity (Stransky, 2001). In both, however, a greater need for consultancy has arisen as a result of their membership in the European Union.

In Southeastern Europe, four nations have come to the forefront: Slovenia, Croatia, Romania, and Bulgaria. Advertising and public relations practices in Slovenia are much like those in neighboring Austria. Croatia, too, has a history of experience in the fields. Romania has been slow to recognize its potential, but some of its seasoned professionals founded a public relations association and are guiding the practice. The commercial sector is still limited, but public affairs offers many opportunities. Bulgaria was one of the first to celebrate its liberation by a spurt of private enterprise. High-tech and business-to-business as well as financial public relations practices are growing (Karadjov, Kim, and Karavasilev, 2001; also see Benova, 2001). Many of these nations have forged ties to Western educational institutions and have developed their own programs.

Among the countries and regions of the former USSR, the Baltics are the fastest developing in both the practice of advertising public relations and in education for the fields. On the educational level, Latvia has been somewhat more aggressive, but Lithuania has been almost as busy. Estonia is a full member of the WTO and has experienced very rapid economic growth, which is always good for advertising and public relations. The government is also committed to IT (Past, 2001). In all, the Baltics seem to be rushing to reconstitute their pre-Communist markets quickly and to move forward. Most of the firms and agencies in the Baltics are local, perhaps because of their languages. Although most know Russian and some speak German, they prefer to use their national languages. Although the Ukraine has potential, it has been slow in developing a marketplace for an advertising and public relations practice. The other states are having difficulty developing the infrastructure necessary for communications-related fields. One exception is Macedonia, which is working on its proposed membership in the European Union.

Russia has launched an impressive educational effort for these fields, including offering Russian-language editions of major U.S. public relations textbooks for use in its classrooms. Advertising took off right away with the advent of the market economy. Large transnational public relations and advertising firms opened offices in Moscow, and a professional public relations association has been founded based in Moscow. Professionals and students, now free to travel, are joining international professional associations and studying abroad in significant numbers. Public affairs no longer dominates the field of public relations practice in Russia, which offers as wide an array of specialties as do most Western nations. That is not to say that the practice is Western; it has been adapted for Russia. The transparency that is being called for in most Western nations as well as many Asian and Latin American countries remains an issue in Russia, despite the efforts of two professional public relations organizations, the Russian Public Relations Association and ICCO-Russia. The latter is offering instruction in public relations practice to second-year MBA students (Maslov, 2001).

Western Europe

Although most theoretical developments have occurred in the United States and Western Europe, an assumption that all public relations practice preceded by "Western" means homogeneity is not the case. What homogeneity there is has occurred because of large global public relations and advertising firms and multinational firms with global Web sites. Models for education and practice are drawn mostly from the Western world as a whole, and these nations tend to influence each other.

Western Europe originally defined public relations as "relationship management" because it fit the organizational model (Vercic, van Ruler, Buütschi, and Flodin, 2001). Another title frequently used for public relations in Western Europe is communication management, a title that has been exported to other parts of the world. At a time when U.S. practitioners were still resisting research, the British delved into it, perhaps because of the diversity of their European neighbors. In many of these countries, an integrated communication model has always been dominant. Public relations practice typically has been related to advertising and marketing because the practice was likely to be publicity and media relations, which morphed into branding. Although branding is strategic planning, it does not include what became a critical communication need, crisis communication. The increased impact of global media, especially the Internet and satellite television, has heightened sensitivity to issues and crises, especially in terms of global public opinion.

Much of public relations practice in Western Europe is business-to-business, with the EU serving as a major factor. The founding of the EU increased the need for public affairs in terms of business-to-government relations, although public affairs, in terms of government public relations, is by far the oldest and most traditional public relations model in all of these countries.

Public affairs and business-to-business practices are less costly than consumer contact operations, but that area has grown as well, as many of these countries emphasize tourism. The cost of pan-European campaigns comes from the need to adjust the presentation to Europe's many differences in culture, language, media, and national laws. An earlier solution—to locate the most effective agency or firm in each country—has now mostly given way to selecting the firm with the best connections to ensure linguistic, legal, and cultural acceptance.

Even though the EU has been the single biggest factor in the growth of public relations practice in Western Europe, standardization of public relations practice is far from the result. Education for the field also differs country by country, but continuing education usually comes through professional organizations. Professional organizations exist in more than 15 different countries, and some have more than one national organization. Although few European universities have public relations majors, increasing numbers offer courses. In Scotland and Finland, doctorates in public relations are available.

Finland has one of the largest and oldest individual membership public relations organizations, dating from the 1970s'. (In Europe, members may belong as individuals to professional associations, or they may participate in trade associations to which the major agencies belong.) Public relations and advertising expenditures in this media-rich country are high. As might be expected, with Belgium being the focal point for the EU, public relations practice is well developed and supported by two professional organizations. Neighboring Netherlands calls public relations communication management, although at the government level it is more informational or editorial in nature. Companies there function more at the management level and offer specialties, such as investor relations and crisis management. The Netherlands also has two professional organizations to offer continuing education and provides practical and theoretical education for the field (de Lang, 2000; van Ruler, 2000). As in most of the European nations, command of several languages is necessary in these three countries. Greece has a long history of public relations and, with its proliferation of media, offers ample publicity and advertising opportunities. Public relations firms in Greece offer an array of specialties, including integrated communication, which combines advertising and public relations (Papathanassopoulos, 2002).

Germany and France began public relations associations at about the same time, in 1958. Germany, as the EU's financial center, provides a wide array of public relations services and has traditionally attracted offices of the world's major public relations and advertising firms. The practice in France has always been less structured and more individualistic, as it has been in Italy. The growth in public relations in Italy prompted the president of the Italian Federation of Public Relations to say that it appeared that one in every thousand Italians was in public relations (Curtin and Gaither, 2007:1). In Italy, the personality of the Italian corporate owners and clients is reflected in the advertising and public relations style. Spain shares this style to some extent. The practice in Spain is really publicity and is subsumed under the marketing function. Most practitioners not educated on the job come to the field from marketing, commerce, or journalism. The educational experience is the same in Norway, although public relations courses at the university level began in the Norwegian School of Marketing in 1982. Norway offers a number of specialties, including financial, environmental, and crisis communication.

In Austria, the educational ties are to management rather than to marketing, which places the field more into the "strategic" area of practice. The preparation is reflected in the practice, which centers on issues management, crisis communication, corporate communications, and such. Their system is more like that in the United States, as is Portugal's. Strongly influencing Portugal was the fact that multinational Mobil has had public relations in house there since 1959. Portugal, as one of the founding members of the 1958 European Free Trade Association, also has close ties to Britain. Spain represents a situation often seen in other nations in which cities have a more highly sophisticated practice than the more rural regions (Huertas and Cavia, 2007).

Of all the Western European nations, Britain is closest to the United States in its advertising and public relations practices. The greatest educational difference between the two countries lies in the strict separation of vocational training from university education. After 1992, however, the only way to qualify for membership in the Institute of Public Relations in the United Kingdom was to pass an examination to receive the industry-controlled and industry-regulated Diploma in Public Relations. That training is offered through distance learning produced by the Open University for the Public Relations Education Trust. Britain now has university public relations courses at the undergraduate and graduate levels. In Scotland, university-level courses began at Stirling in 1987, largely due to the late Sam Black's IPRA Gold Paper on education of public relations, which has been a model for many nations.

On the whole, it is not realistic to talk about standards of practice for advertising and public relations throughout Western Europe. What is happening is the development of a sophisticated integrated model that focuses on "branding," giving a company instant identity and a greater strategic role for the whole corporate communications function due to issues and crises, which can get global attention in a nanosecond.

North America: The United States and Canada

The Internet commands the focus of advertising and public relations practitioners in North America, not only because it drives business in the United States and Canada, but also because many multinational organizations are headquartered in these two nations, including large conglomorates of advertising and public relations firms/agencies. The rapid growth of all new technology offers both opportunities and challenges. Electronic tools in the hands of individuals who are making their opinions known through blogs, joining others in virtual communities and placing their news experiences on the Internet, have dramatically shifted the powerbase from companies to consumers of information, products, and services (see "Top 20 Countries with Highest Number of Internet Users," InternetWorldStats.com, June 2007).

A shift in influence also has come from the significant growth in advertising and public relations activities around the world. In many cases, this growth has increased ties to major firms and agencies in North America, but in some areas of the world, the practices are expanding and developing within their own cultures. These firms and agencies, for their part, have been consolidating and restructuring as a result of changes in the global economy and the use of media, especially electronic media.

Disasters of all kinds, terrorist activities, and financial crises have focused attention on investor relations, public affairs, and the style and tone of advertising. Other major issues influencing practice are public health and climate concerns, such as global warming.

A benefit of this focus is greater emphasis on issue monitoring to anticipate crises, to take advantage of opportunities, and to place more emphasis on strategic thinking for longer-range goals and objectives.

Trends that have become staples in the practice are litigation public relations and more integrated communication approaches. The latter is interesting because what does not seem to be working is integration within advertising agencies or public relations firms, but large conglomorates such as WPP own both advertising and public relations firms, many of which are based all over the world. Apparently, few really understand the complexity of serious communication integration, which involves internal restructuring and rethinking problem solving with an array of tools from both advertising and public relations. The reality is that the lines between advertising and public relations continue to blur, not only in North America but also in other countries with which North American practitioners interact.

What does seem to be improving is the use of research before, during, and after projects, with greater emphasis on education for the field and continuing education for practitioners. Another change is increased requirement to know at least one other language. Many Canadians, especially in the eastern part of the country, know both English and French. In the United States, many people, especially those who living in the South and Southwest, know Spanish. The influx of Asians into both countries has created an awareness of the need for other language skills, and having clients abroad has emphasized the need for additional language skills. More advertising and public relations practitioners are getting experience abroad to give depth to the planning and counseling they need just to function at home (Hackley and Dong, 2001).

Both Canada and the United States have benefited from their own diverse populations, which has created a particular affinity for global interaction and an awareness of cultural differences. Both also have a long history of trade with other countries and with each other. NAFTA emphasizes these opportunities with its intent to create a total marketplace for the whole continent. Implementation has been challenged because of problems with illegal drugs and the need to consider security in light of terrorist activities. However, both issues actually offer the opportunity for greater interaction and enhanced relationships to fight common problems.

Technology makes a global environment unavoidable. Nevertheless, the local climate for the growth of advertising and public relations is directly tied to the country's type of government, freedom of expression, literacy, place of religion in the culture, and education.

BIBLIOGRAPHY

Ahmad, J. "Malaysia's Changing Face." *IPRA Frontline* 23, No. 2 (June 2001), 22.

Almatsier, R. "Indonesia's Struggling Image." *IPRA Frontline* 23, No. 2 (June 2001), 23.

Al Shebil, S., Rasheed A. A., and Il-Shammari, H. "Global Business, Battling Boycotts, When a Company Is Targeted Simply Because of Its Nationality, What Can It Do?" *Wall Street Journal,* April 28–29, 2007, R6,11.

Ang, P. H., and Lee, L. "Small Bang in the Singapore Media." *Media Asia* 28, No. 4 (2001), 204–207.

Association for Education in Journalism and Mass Communication convention papers. Available: http://convention2.allacademic.com/one/aejmc/aejmc07

Ayaz, B. "Pakistan's Expanding Marketplace." *IPRA Frontline* 24, No. 1 (March 2002), 24–25.

Benova, V. "Bulgaria's PR Landscape." *IPRA Frontline* 23, No. 3 (September 2001), 22.

Bishop, C. "Transparency and Human Rights on World Stage." *Media Law Notes, Association for Education in Journalism and Mass Communication* 35, No. 3 (Summer 2007), 5, 7.

Coombs, W. T., and Holladay, S. J. *It's Not Just PR: Public Relations in Society.* Malden, MA: Blackwell Publishing, 2007, 109–111.

Curtin, P. A., and Gaither, T. K. *International Public Relations: Negotiating Culture, Identity and Power.* Thousand Oaks, CA: Sage, 2007, 1,9, 88–93,114–116, 241, 246.

de Lang, R. "Public Affairs Practitioners in the Netherlands: A Profile Study." *Public Relations Review* 26, No. 1 (Spring 2000), 15–29.

Díaz, F. "Impressive Rate of PR Growth (Mexico)." *IPRA Frontline* 24, No. 2 (June 2002), 15.

Economy, E. C. "The Great Leap Backward? The Cost of China's Environmental Crisis." *Foreign Affairs* (September/October 2007), 38–59.

Edelman, R. Edelman Trust Barometer. www.edelman.com/trust2007/prior2006/FullSupplement_final.pdf

eMarketer. www.emarketer.com, file for 1 August 2007.

Goonasekera, A. "Communication Issues and Problems in the Asian Region." *ICA News* 30, No. 1 (January–February 2002), 9, 13.

"Growth in Online Spending Rockets across Asia Pacific." *Microsoft Digital Advertising Solutions,* January 21, 2007. Available: http://advertising.microsoft.com/asia/NewsAndEvents/News.aspx?Adv_News ID=199 (accessed September 16, 2007).

Guntarto, B. "Internet and the New Media." *Media Asia* 28, No. 4 (2001), 195–203.

Ha, J.-Y., and Moon, S.-J. "Digital Content Business in Korea," *Media Asia* 34, No. 1 (2007), 44–50.

Hackley, C. A., and Dong, Q. "American Public Relations Networking Encounters China's Guanxi." *Public Relations Quarterly* 46, No. 2 (Summer 2001), 16–19.

Hill, L., Hill, N., and White, C. "Public Relations Practitioners' Perception of the World Wide Web as a Communication Tool." *Public Relations Review* 26, No. 1 (Spring 2000), 31–52.

Hirsch, V. "A Continent Playing PR Catch-Up (South America)." *IPRA Frontline* 23, No. 4 (December 2001), 17–18.

Holtzhausen, D., Petersen, B. K., and Tindall, N. T. J. "Exploding the Myth of the Symmetrical/ Asymmetrical Dichotomy: Public Relations Models in the New South Africa (PRISA)." *Journal of Public Relations Research* 15, No. 4 (2003), 305–341.

Huang, Y.-H. "The Personal Influence Model and Gao Guanxi in Taiwan Chinese Public Relations." *Public Relations Review* 26, No. 2 (Summer 2000), 219–236.

Huertas, A., and Cavia, J. F. "Centre and Periphery: Two Speeds for the Implementation of Public Relations in Spain." *Public Relations Review* 32, No. 2 (June 2006), 110–117.

Karadjov, C., Kim, Y., and Karavasilev, L. "Models of Public Relations in Bulgaria and Job Satisfaction among Its Practitioners." *Public Relations Review* 26, No. 2 (Summer 2000), 209–236.

Kraft, D. "African Leaders Launch Alliance." *The Fort Worth Star-Telegram,* July 10, 2002, 7A.

Kundra, S. "A Teardrop in the Ocean (Sri Lanka)." *IPRA Frontline* 24, No. 1 (March 2002), 25.

Lamb, D. "Singapore, Peaceful and Prosperous, Southeast Asia's Famously Uptight Nation Has Let Its Hair Down." *Smithsonian,* September 2007, 100–112.

Liang, Q. C. "Practicing Public Relations in China." *Tips & Tactics, supplement of PR Reporter* 40, No. 4 (April 15, 2002), 1–2.

Laszyn, A. "Poland's PR Slowdown." *IPRA Frontline* 23, No. 3 (September 2001), 16–17.

Maslov, M. "Russian PR Grows, Sometimes at a Price." *IPRA Frontline* 23, No. 3 (September 2001), 19.

McLeish, A. "East of the EU." *IPRA Frontline* 23, No. 3 (September 2001), 14–15.

Molleda, J.-C., and Moreno, A. "Transitional Socioeconomic and Political Environment of Public Relations in Mexico." *Public Relations Review* 32 (2006), 104–109.

Panol, Z. S. "Philippine Public Relations: An Industry and Practitioner Profile." *Public Relations Review* 26, No. 2 (Summer 2000), 237–254.

Papathanassopoulos, S. "The Media in Southern Europe: The Case of Greece." *ICA News* 30, No. 6 (July–August 2002), 6–7.

Park, J. "Images of 'Hong Bo (Public Relations)' and PR in Korean Newspapers." *Public Relations Review* 27, No. 4 (Winter 2001), 403–420.

Past, A. "A Happy Return (Estonia)." *IPRA Frontline* 23, No. 3 (September 2001), 26.

"PR Week Global Rankings." *PR Week,* Annual.

"PR Week Global Special." *Global Perspectives,* July 2, 2007, 17–18.

Rananand, P. R. "The Internet in Thailand: Towards a Culture of Responsibility." *Media Asia* 28, No. 4 (2001), 183–194, 203.

Rawlins, B. "Measuring the Relationship between Organizational Transparency and Trust." International Public Relations Research Conference, 2007. IPRRC conference papers online.

"SA Slips Down Least Corrupt Ranking." Business iAfrica.com, November 7, 2006. Available: http:business. iafrica.com/news/389339 (accessed September 18, 2007).

Sagar, P. "The Need to Nurture Talent and Add Value (India)." *IPRA Frontline* 24, No. 1 (March 2002), 20–21.

Shuriedeh, M. J. "Public Relations in Jordan as an Expanding Field." AUSACE [Arab-US Association for Communication Educator] *Newsletter* 6, No. 2 (October 2000), 4.

Singh, R. "Public Relations in Contemporary India: Current Demands and Strategy." *Public Relations Review* 26, No. 3 (Fall 2000), 29–313.

Singh, R., and Smith, R. "Australian Public Relations: Status at the Turn of the 21st Century." *Public Relations Review* 26, No. 4 (Winter 2000), 387–401.

Starlach, J. "The Reunification of Latin America." *IPRA Frontline* 23, No. 4 (December 2001), 20–21.

Stransky, M. "Czech Republic and Slovakia." *IPRA Frontline* 23, No. 3 (September 2001), 20.

Taylor, M. "Media Relations in Bosnia: A Role for Public Relations in Building Civil Society." *Public Relations Review* 26, No. 1 (Spring 2000), 1–14.

"Top 20 Countries with Highest Number of Internet Users." InternetWorldStats.com, June, 2007. Available: http://www.internetworldstats.com/top20.htm (accessed September 15, 2007).

"Trends in the PR Industry across the Asia Pacific Region." *IPRA Frontline* 24, No. 1 (March 2002), 14.

Tsetsura, K. "The Study of Media Transparency and Payments for News Coverage Practices Worldwide." 2007 Study through International Public Relations Association and the Institute for Public Relations, 2007.

van Ruler, B. "Communication Management in the Netherlands." *Public Relations Review* 26, No. 4 (Winter 2000), 403–423.

Vercic, D., van Ruler, B., Buütschi, G., and Flodin, B. "On the Definition of Public Relations: A European View." *Public Relations Review* 27, No. 4 (Winter 2001), 373–387.

Vranica, S., "Managing the Digital Dilemma." *Wall Street Journal* (August 31, 2007), B3.

Watson, D. R., and Sallot, L. M. "Public Relations Practice in Japan: An Exploratory Study." *Public Relations Review* 27, No. 4 (Winter 2001), 389–402.

World e-Government Rankings by Waseda University Institue of e-Government, Japan." Waseda University Institute of Asia Pacific Studies, December 26, 2006. Available: http://www.obi.giti.waseda.ac.jp/ e_gov/2nd_rankings_en.pdf (accessed September 15, 2007).

Wu, M.-Y., Taylor, M., and Chen, M.-J. "Exploring Societal and Cultural Influences on Taiwanese Public Relations." *Public Relations Review* 27, No. 43 (Fall 2001), 317–336.

Wu, X. "Doing PR in China: A 2001 Version—Concepts, Practices and Some Misperceptions." *Public Relations Quarterly* 47, No. 2 (Summer 2002), 10–18.

Zhang, A., Shen, H., and Jiang, H. "Culture and Chinese Public Relations: A Multi-Method 'Inside Out' Approach." Paper presented 2007 Convention of Association for Education in Journalism and Mass Communication, Washington, D.C.

8 Continuing Media Controversies

PAUL GROSSWILER
University of Maine, USA

Negative media content, monopoly control of communication technologies, and an imbalanced global information current have been three continuing controversial issues in international mass communication, beginning with the creation of the European telegraph system in the mid-1800s and continuing until today. These three controversies have resurfaced at places like the World Summit on the Information Society (WSIS), initiated by the United Nations (UN); in countries such as Canada and France that are concerned about media imperialism, in advocacy organizations such as Voices 21; and at worldwide protests against the neo-liberal globalization policies of the World Trade Organization (WTO) and the Group of Eight (G8) nations, such as those in Seattle in 1999.

The burgeoning digital media—from the Internet and Weblogs to a dizzying proliferation of ever newer communication technologies, such as an array of "high-tech" cell phones—have led to greater citizen involvement in global media. These new media have both challenged and extended state and corporate global media controls. Traditional global media have co-opted digital media formats, and a vast variety of diverse voices around the world have emerged through these new media. The governments, organizations, and media have changed, but these three themes have persisted in various incarnations and developments throughout nearly two centuries of international mass communication.

At a preparatory meeting of the WSIS, Cees Hamelink (2002) noted that the summit was the third attempt since World War II to address global media issues. First, in 1948, the UN, despite crafting the Declaration of Human Rights, unsuccessfully attempted to draft global treaties on freedom of information. Second, in the 1970s and 1980s, the United Nations Educational, Scientific and Cultural Organization (UNESCO) engaged in a highly charged and politicized debate over the merits of a new global media structure, often referred to as the New World Information Order (NWIO).

Hamelink characterized the new WSIS challenge as encompassing issues such as equitable access, cultural diversity, the digital divide, rural communication, e-commerce, e-government, data protection, security, gender, and education issues. Initiated by the UN in late 2001, the WSIS faced the political challenge of fostering a democratic information society, the social challenge of creating an information society based on dialogue, and the regulatory challenge of adopting a universal declaration on the right to communicate.

At the conclusion of the first phase of WSIS, however, Hamelink—who had presented his vision of communication societies that are inclusive, open, and democratic—pessimistically wrote that the "aspiration of a common vision" had resulted in "blurred confusion" (Hamelink, 2004:281). The final texts of the WSIS lacked serious consideration of political-economic issues; it failed, for example, to link the global digital divide to the "global 'development divide'" (Hamelink, 2004:283). Despite the hopeful language of the WSIS, the global information society that is being created is fraught with problems. The problems of this information society include censorship of traditional media and the Internet; growing corporate media ownership of intellectual property rights; increasing dependence on wealth for access to information; further media conglomeration with minimal media accountability; the triumph of profits over human needs; and an increasingly limited public sphere (Hamelik, 2004:282).

Media scholar Victor Pickard linked the WSIS process with the "ascendance of neo-liberalism," arguing that WSIS bypassed economic issues, limited discussions to technical problems, privileged commerce over human rights, and abandoned the communication rift between rich and poor. A silver lining, however, may be found in the continued growth of citizen coalitions and in the work of progressive groups as they contest the dominance of neo-liberalism in global media and focus on cultural communication issues (Pickard, 2007:136). Sean O Siochru, too, described the "unique" WSIS process as one that offered a wide-ranging debate involving a spectrum of participants—but ended in "meager" policy outcomes favoring corporate and Western interests (O Siochru, 2007:27).

Global Media Controversies Today

Neo-liberal Media Globalization

The state of global media content, control, and current today underscores the steep challenges that movements like the WSIS face. The increasing neo-liberal globalization of media under the control of a few Western media industries raises serious concerns about global democracy. The list of the few media corporations that own most media globally changes as mergers and acquisitions have continued, including the mergers of AOL and Time Warner in 2001 and of Vivendi, Seagram's, and Universal in 2000. Thussu (2006) identified these transnational corporations, which were mostly based in the United States, as owners of most of the world's media in 2004: AOL-Time Warner, Walt Disney, Viacom-CBS, Bertelsmann, News Corp., Telecommunications Inc., Sony, and NBC, which partnered with Vivendi Universal in 2003, creating NBC-Universal (Thussu, 2006:99).

Before globalization, Thussu noted (Thussu, 2006:98), media owners stayed within limited boundaries. Disney, for example, produced cartoon films and built theme parks. With globalization, Disney, which is now the second largest media conglomerate, owns ABC TV, as well as 10 TV stations and more than 70 radio stations in the United States. Disney also owns ESPN and partly owns A&E Television, the History Channel, and E!, which reached 300 million homes in 120 countries in 2006. Disney's global presence includes Disney channels in Europe, Asia, and the Middle East, as well as Disney Channel Worldwide, with 120 million subscribers in more than 70 countries. Also involved in television and movie production and distribution, Disney owns Buena Vista companies,

Touchstone companies, and Walt Disney companies serving both media, as well as Miramax Films and Pixar. In print media, Disney owns Hyperion Books, Miramax Books, and more than 20 magazines. The conglomerate also owns several recording labels, including Hollywood Records and Lyric Street Records in country music. Despite all this growth, Disney has not abandoned its roots, having gone global with about a dozen theme parks, three dozen hotels, two cruise ships, and 660 Disney stores. Finally, entering the Internet age, Disney operated 40 Web sites in 2006 and was working on partnerships with Apple to provide ABC and Disney content for the iPod.

Decades before Disney's globalization, the negative cultural impact of Donald Duck and other Disney cartoons in Latin America was critiqued by Ariel Dorfman (1983) and Dorfman and Armand Mattelart (1975). Ben Bagdikian (2000) has been alarmed by the negative impact of media monopolies on public discourse in the United States for several decades, as corporate media monopolies have increased inexorably since his first edition of *The Media Monopoly* appeared in the early 1980s. At that time, 50 companies dominated U.S. media ownership. By the time the 2004 edition appeared, retitled *The New Media Monopoly,* that number had shrunk to five, including Time Warner, Disney, News Corp., Bertselsmann, and Viacom, followed by NBC (Thussu, 2006:110).

According to Thussu, U.S. and British newspapers and magazines continued to dominate global print media in 2005, including *Reader's Digest, Cosmopolitan, Time, USA Today, Wall Street Journal, Financial Times,* and *International Herald Tribune* (Thussu, 2006:125). Two U.S. and British news agencies, Associated Press (AP) and Reuters, dominate global news and information. Agence France-Presse rounds out the Big Three, which provide 80 percent of news globally (Thussu, 2006:130–131). Associated Press Television News (APTN) and Reuters Television, both of which narrowed global television news sources after AP bought Worldwide Television News from ABC/Disney in 1998 and Reuters bought Visnews, also dominate television news (Thussu, 2006:133). Cable News Network (CNN), whose CNN News Group reaches 2 billion people in 200 countries, and the British Broadcasting Corp. (BBC) are the leading international television news channels (Thussu, 2006:138).

Media globalization is amply evident in television, which relies on U.S.-based networks as the world's primary provider. Hollywood continues to dominate movie screens as it has since World War I, as well as the video market, while U.S. television programs like *Star Trek, Baywatch,* and *Sesame Street* spread U.S. popular culture to more than a hundred countries apiece. Advertising, too, is dominated by U.S. agencies and offers global services to the major conglomerates, of which the media are now part.

Thussu (2006:141) argues that Western media domination is more pronounced today than during the NWIO debates, promoting Western lifestyles and values through private global media and a market system that cooperate with governments to present a Westernized geopolitical view of global events. Robert McChesney (2001) asserts that global media do not represent U.S. cultural imperialism. Instead, these few corporate media owners globalize corporate and commercial values in a neo-liberal global media system that is stacked in favor of these giants and against small, independent, and local media. McChesney also identifies a second tier of 40 to 50 regional media giants, including Globo in Brazil and Televisa in Mexico, that support the dominance of the top Western media corporations and promote probusiness politics.

James Lull (2000) is more sanguine about the impact of media globalization, arguing that local audiences exert their own cultural power in culling meaning from media messages, regardless of ownership or content. Also, media scholars agree that people everywhere prefer their own media, in their own language, for their own culture. The new digital, satellite, and computer technologies that helped to create neo-liberal globalization are also helping to revive cultural identity in many Third World regions. Thussu (2006:183–184) offers as examples the role of Indian media televising serials based on Hindu epics and China's adaptation for television of the classic *Journey to the West*. Beyond state borders, diasporas of culture create audiences for local media from their home countries (Lull, 2000).

Internet Problems and Promises

The rise of the Internet raises the stakes of neo-liberal globalization and provides potential alternatives. The Internet is a decidedly U.S. and Western medium that is quickly being transformed into a truly global medium. In 2004, about 840 million people used the Internet, which was not much more than 10 percent of the world population, providing clear evidence of a "digital divide" between rich and poor (Thussu, 2006). Governments seek ways to censor the Internet, and corporate interests work to commercialize it. But the Internet has proved effective in promoting communication among organizations such as human rights groups, environmental activists, churches, labor unions, and political networks, including a worldwide network of activists coordinated by the Association for Progressive Communications (Straubhaar and Larose, 2002).

More recently, according to the U.S. State Department publication *eJournal USA* (Media Making Change, 2007:1), the World Telecommunications Union reports that about one-sixth of the world's population—or more than one billion people—uses the Internet regularly. Mobile telephone services have skyrocketed, too, with more than 2.7 billion subscribers. Citizen journalism sites such as OhmyNews.com, with more than 60,000 contributors globally (Pecquerie, 2007), and the Harvard University-sponsored Global Voices Online, which, according to its own description "aggregates, curates, and amplifies the global conversation online—shining light on places and people other media often ignore" ("Global Voices"), illustrate the transformative impact of the Internet and Weblogs on global media.

Communication technologies also are aiding emerging social movements opposing the neo-liberal globalization policies pursued by the WTO, the G8, and others. Centering on issues of environment, agriculture, labor, and peace, the protests against neo-liberal globalization have shaken the global economic planners since the late 1990s have used the Internet to communicate and bypass the corporate global media. The growing presence of online journalism practiced by bloggers from both within and outside the traditional media is also reshaping global media.

The stage appears to be set for a new struggle over the global media system's control, content, and current. In the neo-liberal corner, the global media corporations, supported by the United States, the WTO, and the G8 nations, will seek to preserve the status quo of unregulated global communication that favors the existing giants. In the other corner, the EU, the ITU, and the UN, allied with a host of Western and Third World countries, as well as a wide variety of advocacy groups, desire to reverse the corporate control of global media, democratize globalization, and preserve local media. The latter approach is described as the humanitarian regime (Hamelink, 2002) and the human rights framework of globalization (O Siochru, 2002). Perhaps at no other time since the rise of the old world information order has so formidable a challenge been mounted. But to assess this newest media controversy requires an understanding of the serious challenges the global media system has undergone in the last two centuries. (For a historical overview, see Merrill, 1995.)

UNESCO and the New World Information Order

Calls for a New International Order

Third World countries took issue with the international economic order in the early 1970s and also included cultural and communication matters in their objections. They expressed these objections primarily in UNESCO, but also in the UN, ITU, and Non-Aligned Movement. Third World countries had reason to be concerned about the imbalanced flow of media messages and the inability to stem the flow of television, film, news, and recordings from the West. In the face of this dominance, countries responded by setting up alternative news agencies, mostly after the NWIO debate began in the early 1970s, but the impact of these regional or southern news services remained negligible.

Western countries and media generally did not deny an imbalanced information flow or technology gap between the North and South, but they focused on technical aid through the World Bank and the ITU, while maintaining the free flow of information (Fortner, 1993). Third World countries found supporters in socialist countries that wanted to control the flow of information across borders for different reasons. Western media argued that state control of information was anathema, while the socialist and Third World countries argued that Western-dominated media did not provide free flow but served only Western media and audiences. The West saw information as a commodity, whereas the socialist and Third World countries viewed information as a social good. As a commodity, information flow prevented Third World countries from attaining independence. To balance the flow, suggestions ranged from alternative news systems to reserving satellite slots for future use and licensing journalists.

First Calls for NWIO

In 1970, UNESCO heard calls for a two-way information flow for Third World countries to preserve their cultures, and for national communication policies. UNESCO initiated research on news flow, cultural autonomy, and isolationism. UNESCO experts identified problems of "cultural neocolonialism" caused by new communication technologies (Galtung and Vincent, 1992). In 1973, the Non-Aligned Movement led to the establishment of a Third World news agency, the Non-Aligned News Agency. By 1976, the group had articulated the need to change the global communication system to decolonize information and create a new international information order.

In 1974, UNESCO called for a two-way flow of information and for a "free and balanced flow," and in 1976 UNESCO called for "liberating the developing countries from the state of dependence" (Mehra, 1986). In 1978, UNESCO unanimously adopted, with U.S. support, the Mass Media Declaration. This document affirmed freedom of expression and information, called for access and protection of journalists, and asked the media to help give a voice to the Third World. It asked the media to report about all cultures and peoples, exposing the problems that affected them, such as hunger, poverty, and disease. It asked the media to include the opinions of those who found the media prejudiced against them, and it sought correction of the imbalance in global news flow. The declaration also asked media professionals to include its ideas in their codes of ethics. UNESCO sought to promote "a free flow and a wider and better balanced exchange of information between the different regions of the world." In 1980, a resolution was adopted to implement the declaration, and a global congress was set for 1983.

The MacBride Commission

In 1976, UNESCO set up the 16-member MacBride Commission, headed by Ireland's Sean MacBride, to look at problems relating to the free and balanced flow of information and the needs of Third World countries. In 1980, the MacBride Commission issued its report, *Many Voices, One World,* containing 82 recommendations, of which 72 were unanimous. The remaining ones were opposed, with the West against anticommercial media suggestions, the Soviet bloc opposed to the abolition of government controls, and Third World countries seeking more balanced flow. UNESCO did not adopt the MacBride Report. Instead, in 1980 it created the International Program for Development Communication (IPDC) to help develop media systems in the Third World.

The MacBride Report called for "a free flow and a wider and better balanced dissemination of information." It also called for a "new, more just and more effective world information and communication order" (Galtung and Vincent, 1992). With recommendations on media economics, administration, technological uses, training, and research, the report also dealt with journalistic standards, but rejected the idea of licensing. It called for U.S. journalists abroad to receive language and culture training, and for gatekeepers in the West to be familiar with Third World cultures.

Among its other recommendations, the MacBride Report condemned censorship as well as the use of journalists for spying, and supported the need for national communication policies. It emphasized the media's role in helping oppressed peoples gain independence and the right to expression and information. It also called for reducing media commercialism. The report encouraged UNESCO to take a crucial role in carrying out the recommendations (Frederick, 1993).

New Efforts to Address Global Media Controversies

The confluence of several forces appears to be driving renewed efforts to address the recurrent problems of global media content, control, and current in the 2000s. The much greater visibility of neo-liberal media globalization raises social awareness far beyond the level of earlier decades. The shift of concerns about cultural imperialism from the Third World to developed Western nations brings these problems closer to home. Resistance to neo-liberal media globalization found an official home in the World Summit on the Information Society, representing a resurgence of efforts undertaken in the UN, UNESCO, the ITU, and other organizations. Although assessments of the WSIS from the perspectives of those seeking broader structural changes are mixed, newer voices have been added to the overall debate about the global media system.

The coalescence of socially activist professional and scholarly groups brings a new dimension, the voice of civil society, which was muted in earlier attempts. The enormous potential for democratic media change posited by the Internet and blogosphere helps connect all these forces. This network of new technologies empowers opposition voices to join together globally and provides a vision for democratic communication.

Concerns in the West

The cultural impact of neo-liberal global media on industrialized countries has caused increasing concern since the NWIO movement faded. In 1989, the European Union (EU) set domestic content quotas for its member states' media. In 1993, France succeeded in an attempt to exclude audiovisual media from the General Agreement on Tariffs and Trade (GATT). In 1998, groups of Western and Third World countries met in Ottawa and Stockholm to recommend ways to resist U.S. media influence and to exempt cultural products from WTO agreements. A number of countries throughout the world have instituted film subsidy programs to offset Hollywood imports. France and Canada have emerged as leading examples of Western efforts to combat U.S. media imperialism.

The WTO succeeded the GATT in 1995 as the arbiter of global trade, including trade in culture, knowledge, and communication. The umbrella term used for trade involving the media is "intellectual property," which the WTO describes as the important value of new technology products (World Trade Organization, "Intellectual"). The WTO's 1995 agreement on intellectual property rights attempted to create international rules to protect ideas and knowledge. Among the types of intellectual property added in 1995 were international copyright, trademarks, geographical indications, and patents. But as WACC notes, copyright and patents are Western concepts that run counter to traditional values of collective ownership of resources. Also, WTO support for liberalized trade in audiovisual products is allowing further consolidation of global media ownership (World Association for Christian Communication, "Key Issues").

It was at France's urging that the EU passed the 1989 television quota measure that required a majority of programming in member countries to be European (Gordon and Meunier, 2001). It was again France that led opposition to a U.S. attempt to apply free trade to cultural goods in GATT talks. As Gordon and Meunier concluded, the result was that GATT did not explicitly include cultural goods, so the EU in effect had the right to include them in its protectionist "Television Without Borders."

Gordon and Meunier note that between 1995 and 1998, Canadian and U.S. consumer groups, along with French media artists, opposed an effort in the Organization for Economic Cooperation and Development (OECD) to make it illegal to protect cultural investments in Europe in the Multilateral Agreement on Investment (MAI). The MAI was defeated in 1998 after France left the talks, marking the first victory for the anti-neo-liberal globalization movement combining cultural groups with others, such as farmers and intellectuals.

On the other side of the Atlantic, the French have a powerful ally in Canada, where more than 90 percent of movies in cinemas and on television, 75 percent of the music on radio, 80 percent of the magazines, and 60 percent of the books are imported, primarily from the United States ("Culture Wars," 1998). Canada has been formulating Canadian content (Cancon) rules since the late 1950s in order to protect and stimulate Canadian cultural production (Media Awareness Network, 2007).

The World Summit on the Information Society

The role of international government organizations since UNESCO debated the NWIO at first suffered a setback but reemerged in several initiatives in the UN, ITU, and UNESCO, which resulted in the UN World Summit on the Information Society. After 1985, UNESCO redirected its energies to avoid the politically sensitive issue of communication and reaffirmed its commitment to the freedom of the press, focusing on building infrastructures and training and education in Third World media systems. The goal of these technical programs is a balanced flow of information that attains a free flow of information (Galtung and Vincent, 1992).

O Siochru (2002) suggested that the WSIS could provide an opportunity to test the strength of the global governance structure. Together with the ITU, the UN at the end of 2001 initiated a call for the WSIS to address the whole range of relevant issues related to the information society (Hamelink, 2002). In mid-2002 in Geneva, the ITU took a lead role in the first of a series of preparatory meetings leading to the first phase of WSIS at the end of 2003 in Geneva and the second phase in Tunis in 2005 (ITU, 2002a).

Focusing on the digital divide in 2002, ITU Secretary-General Yoshio Utsumi told the UN in New York that action was needed to keep the information gap between haves and have-nots from growing (ITU, 2002b). Noting that 61 countries represent less than one percent of Internet use, Utsumi urged world leaders to create a more just, prosperous, and peaceful world. Calling on the WSIS to draw up an action plan for improving access to information technologies, Utsumi cited e-commerce in a Peruvian mountain village and an online African shopping mall as signs of positive applications. He counted among the WSIS goals guaranteeing the right to communicate and using information technologies to eradicate poverty.

In Geneva, Utsumi called on governments, UN agencies, civil society groups, and the business sector to work together to develop national policies, to represent diversity and development and to create material networks to benefit all people (ITU, 2002a). The agenda, themes, and outcomes of the WSIS suggested at the meeting included freedom of expression and the media; the needs of the developing world; access to information; the role of government, the private sector, and civil society; intellectual property rights; bridges between digital media, radio, television, the press, and the Internet; wireless technologies; consumer protection and privacy; affordability; gender; empowerment and democracy; e-health; and economic, social, and cultural development.

In contrast to these lofty goals, Hamelink's assessment of Phase One of the WSIS was highly critical. Despite the "promising language" of the WSIS meetings, the global information society under construction is one in which, Hamelink (2004:289) wrote:

- The fundamental human right to free speech is universally violated through forms of political and commercial censorship.
- The Internet—in particular—has become the focus of censorship initiatives.

- The rights to corporate ownership of intellectual property are greatly extended.
- The access to information and knowledge is increasingly dependent upon the access to purchasing power.
- The consolidation of power on information and knowledge markets is consolidated in the hands of only a few conglomerates.
- There is minimal public accountability from the corporate actors controlling most of the technologies and the contents of the information society.
- Profitability more than human security drives ICT developments.
- The public sphere is increasingly limited.

Hamelink (2004:189) argues that as long as control of the global system rests with the International Monetary Fund, the World Bank, the World Trade Organization, and others that serve the world's wealthy states, the WSIS is "destined to fail." Hamelink adds that with political control exerted by the "thoroughly undemocratic" UN General Assembly and Security Council, the global media system cannot be just. Regardless of the work of civil society groups, a new global structure, such as a world parliament, is needed to make needed changes.

Contextualizing the WSIS in relation to neo-liberalism, Pickard (2007:120–125) argues that the original impetus behind the WSIS—which included addressing the growing global digital divide—evolved into technical issues under the "neo-liberal economic logic" that shapes global media policies. During the first phase of the WSIS in Geneva in 2003, representatives from government, industry, and civil society identified issues to address such as Internet governance, free and open software, communication rights, intellectual property, human rights, and finances. Further meetings leading up to the second phase in Tunis, Tunisia, in 2005, were open to the same range of groups for a "pluralistic discussion".

A central issue that emerged was whether the Internet should continue to be governed by the Internet Corporation for Assigned Names and Numbers (ICANN), which is a private concern operating under the U.S. Department of Commerce. The alternative was to transfer this control to the ITU. This issue resulted in most of what little coverage U.S. media gave to the WSIS, while coverage was much more extensive in Europe, Africa, and Asia. The U.S. coverage was mostly opposed to the ITU taking over Internet regulation from ICANN, thus supporting U.S. dominance of global media. Although the European Union withdrew its support of ICANN for a time in 2005, the status quo maintaining ICANN's control of the Internet prevailed. According to Pickard, however, the United States' desire to unilaterally control the Internet will be met with continued opposition as the Internet becomes perceived more as a global medium (Pickard, 2007:125–131).

Social and cultural concerns at WSIS were shepherded by civil groups such as the World Association of Christian Communication, the Communication Rights in the Information Society coalition, the Association for Progressive Communications, and the European Communica, as well as many academics and activists. Among a dozen or more civil society documents addressing the needs of people with disabilities and indigenous people, for example, was one in particular cited by Pickard. Shaping Civil Society for Human Needs emphasized human rights, social justice, and sustainable development (Pickard, 2007:132; 136; 137).

In Pickard's postmortem analysis, the WSIS did not contest the neo-liberal economic order, limiting the debate to technical issues rather than addressing social concerns. The resulting policies favor corporate interests over human rights and global justice perspectives. Efforts to correct global communication gaps between rich and poor countries have mostly been curtailed. However, Pickard predicts, progressive groups that have represented voices of change for decades from NWIO through WSIS will continue to advance cultural and social concerns and seek systemic global media changes (Pickard, 2007:137):

> In light of today's neo-liberal orthodoxy, it is important and useful to recognize that diverse views were once seriously discussed, and there was once a wide range of serious debate and division among governments as to what a global communication regime should look like. For a brief time, there was a compelling promise of a new culture emerging with the rise of newly independent states. That promise of social transformation now seems more remote, but the possibility for resistance remains, though perhaps outside of WSIS.

Other WSIS participants give less pessimistic but still guarded evaluations. The International Federation of Library Associations and Institution, for example, has been participating in follow-up meetings in 2006 and 2007 to ensure that their interests remain on the WSIS agenda (Mincio and Lor, 2007). Although the United Nations, governments, and the private sector claimed success for WSIS, representatives of civil society called the results mixed (Toros, 2005). The Association for Progressive Communications viewed the WSIS as valuable, but its impact was uncertain, and it pronounced the outcome neither a success nor a failure. The inclusion of civil society groups in the Forum on Internet Governance was important, but control of the Internet was not wrested from the United States and the forum itself was to serve no management or oversight role.

Sean O Siochru, introducing the Global Information Society Watch 2007 Report, bemoans the "meager" policy outcomes of WSIS, and the challenges facing civil society organizations as a result of the limited opportunities afforded them in proposals favoring corporate and Western interests. Despite these constraints, WSIS afforded these groups an opportunity to share a forum and to learn about information and communication technologies together.

Civil Society Advocacy Groups

At the inception of the WSIS, O Siochru (2002) predicted that the inclusion of civil society groups in the WSIS debate would signal the emergence of media advocacy groups, such as the People's Communication Charter, the Platform for Communication Rights, the World Association of Community Radio Broadcasters, the World Association for Christian Communication (WACC), the MacBride Round Table, the Association for Progressive Communications (APC), and many others.

As the information order debate shifted in the 1980s after the demise of the NWIO, some of these groups filled the breach. For example, the media and international law were debated at a 1989 meeting of the Union for Democratic Communications and the National Lawyers Guild (Galtung and Vincent, 1992). Also in 1989, the WACC adopted a declaration focusing on communication as an individual right. The First MacBride Round Table was held that year, sponsored by the International Organization of Journalists, the Media Foundation of the Non-Aligned, and the Federation of Southern African Journalists.

Many of these groups have become affiliated with the Platform for Cooperation on Communication and Democratization, which formed in 1995, and a second umbrella organization, Voices 21, which formed in 1999. The first group emerged from a meeting in London of the APC, Article 19, the Catholic Media Council, PANOS London, the People's Communication Charter, Communication for Social Change, the International Women's Tribune Center, the MacBride Round Table, Videazimut, WACC, Worldview International, and Zebra (International Telecommunication Union, 1999). The platform agreed to work for the right to communicate to be guaranteed as a human right needed to democratize society. The platform also emphasized the democratization of communication structures, institutions, and processes.

Voices 21 called for an international alliance of groups to spur a new social movement based on an awareness of the growing importance of media and issues surrounding the concentration of ownership and control of media, as well as a concern that government censorship was being overtaken by subtle corporate censorship and a lack of public participation. Voices 21 suggested organizing activities around themes including media access; the right to communicate; diversity of expression; security and privacy; and the cultural environment (Voices 21, 1999). Voices 21's fears about current neo-liberal global media trends include the threats (a) to media diversity from homogenized programming; (b) to public understanding of the democratic process from the influence of media moguls and the corporate influence; (c) to economic development from the growth of global advertising; and (d) to cultural and social forms from the domination of English and the corporate shaping of media content.

Citizen Journalism, Blogs, and Other New Media

Arising in direct antithesis to the control of media by neo-liberal interests, the emerging new global media of citizen journalism, namely, blogs, and other new media such as cell phones provide new challenges to the continuing media controversies of control, content, and current.

At its annual International Symposium on Online Journalism in 2006, the University of Texas-Austin offered panels on blogging, citizen journalism, podcasting, and the digital divide—all central issues to the growth of global digital media (Garza, Kocurek, Fawcett, Gregoriades, 2006). Panelists expressed opinions that traditional journalists are changing their attitudes toward blogging and that the blogs are creating new spaces for journalists (Garza). As citizen journalism emerges globally, Yahoo.com does not rely on citizen journalists to produce entire articles, but instead involves them as community members (Kocurek).

Globally, online journalism is improving, although its growth is complicated by the digital divide (Fawcett). A survey of Latin American online newsrooms in 2004 found that most operated with fewer than eight journalists ranging in age from 20 to 30. Several years later, as Fawcett reported, almost a third of online journalists are over 30 years old and are gaining respect among print journalists. In Brazil, 15 percent of homes have Internet access, and three television stations are providing content specifically for the Internet.

The development of podcasting since 2004, which distributes audio or video files over the Internet, can assist print media in reaching a greater audience as podcasting following blogging as a trend in online media (Gregoriades).

Putting a U.S. government and media spin on the proliferation of global Web sites and blogs, the U.S. Department of State's *eJournal USA* has been examining the impact of emerging media. Faced with ubiquitous technologies of camera phones and bloggers, repressive governments are unable to quash dissent. Traditional media have been adapting to the new media, and individuals are developing strategies for using them, too. These media give individuals access to information and networks of people in order to further their own agendas, and influence nations around the globe.

Patrick Butler (2007) documents how the Internet, short-message service messaging (SMS), and cell-phone cameras have transformed the work of journalists and citizen journalists alike. In Egypt, new technologies were used to reveal corruption and organize protests; in Burma, cell phones were used to organize protests against the military in 2007, and to distribute video and photos of the government crackdown on protestors. Egypt responded by arresting a journalist/blogger, Burma by shutting down the Internet.

Countries like China and Iran have experienced more difficulties in controlling the Internet. With the second highest number of Internet users after the United States, China leads the world in arresting people for Internet uses, accounting for 50 of the 65 people in prison for Internet offenses worldwide (Butler, 2007). With 70,000 to 100,000 bloggers, Butler argues that Iran cannot keep pace with changing Web addresses and "proxy" sites that circumvent government controls.

Media corporations have assisted governments in their efforts to censor the Internet (Razook, 2007). For example, a search for "Tiananmen Square" on China's Google search engine reveals no mention of the 1989 massacre, in contrast to a similar search on Google.com, which lists the massacre in the top results. Other Internet companies such as Microsoft and Yahoo! yield similar results inside and outside of China.

Razook credits Amnesty International for linking U.S. companies, including Cisco and Microsoft, to China's efforts to control the Internet in 2002—an allegation the companies denied. In 2006, Amnesty published an account of how Yahoo!, Microsoft, and Google helped the Chinese government filter e-mail and censor the Web and blogs. Microsoft, for example, prevented bloggers from writing about topics such as Falun Gong and Tibet independence. Yahoo! was involved in providing information leading to the imprisonment of a journalist for sending an e-mail to a prodemocracy Web site in the United States. Responding to congressional inquiries, Yahoo!, Microsoft, Google, and other Internet companies have participated in developing voluntary standards of free expression and privacy.

Media companies also have sought to co-opt the blogosphere. For example, Time Warner's AOL division bought a producer of blogs on technology and automobiles. But because the financial cost of becoming a blogger is so low, the major media cannot succeed (Gillmor, 2006). Although blogging began in the United States, it has become global, with 5 million bloggers in China, 2 million bloggers in France, but only 60,000 throughout all of Africa.

The liberating potential of the global diffusion of new communication technologies is encompassed in the term *mobile democracy,* which Butler uses to describe events in the Philippines and Lebanon. Text messaging led to the fall of the Philippines president in 2001 and to the end of Syria's military presence in Lebanon. Butler cites Kuwaiti women using cell phones to earn the right to vote and run for office, South Koreans using cell phones to garner enough votes for an election victory, and Chinese using cell phones to facilitate labor strikes.

Despite these examples of positive political change, Butler also raises concerns that "mobile" democracy can turn into "mob democracy" to topple good leaders as well as bad, and that terrorists such as al-Qaeda can use digital media just as effectively as prodemocracy movements.

Another trend in global digital media change is the use of citizen-generated content by traditional media (Pecquerie and Kilman, 2007). The authors called it a "media revolution" when witnesses to the terrorist bombing of the London subway in 2005 deluged the media with 1,000 e-mails with videos. Other examples include CNN's use of student blogs and media use of cell-phone video in covering the shootings at Virginia Tech University in the spring of 2007. The leading French newspaper *Le Monde* is providing blogs to subscribers and urging readers to keep electronic travel journals that can be posted online at the newspaper. In Chile, a tabloid's circulation rose 30 percent after editors began using its most popular online stories to determine what to print.

One example of the professionalization of online citizen journalism is South Korea's OhmyNews.com. Journalist Oh Yeon-ho pioneered citizen journalism as an experiment with 700 reporters in 2000. In 2007, OhmyNews boasted a staff of 65 and more than 65,000 reporters in 100 countries (Porter, 2007). OhmyNews has imparted professional journalism ethics to its nonjournalist reporters, expecting them to identify themselves as reporters when covering stories; to desist from spreading false information; to not use offensive language; to inflict no damage to reputations by violating privacy; to use recognized methods of gathering information; to not use their position to seek personal gain; and to correct errors promptly.

Globally, Peskin and Nachison (2006) put the number of blogs at 1 million, a trend they identify as "We Media." With more than 2 billion people possessing cell phones and more cell phones capable of acting as still and video cameras, "global content generation" has been created with the ability to share all aspects of life, anywhere and anytime. We Media intensifies participation and changes the relationships between the We Media and the traditional media. Citizen journalism has moved from the periphery to the center, and the mainstream media find their control as gatekeeper threatened. In We Media, the authors contend, "the authentic, cultural expression" or voice of the individual is resurgent.

The blogosphere has been growing in Arab regions, with Internet access increasing dramatically since 2000 to 10 percent of the population, although the number of Arab bloggers is thought to be fewer than 25,000 (Beckerman, 2007). Arab blogs serve a variety of causes, from liberalizing Arab society to promoting groups like al-Qaeda. One Web site, Irabi 007, for example, disseminated videos of beheadings and attacks against U.S. forces in Iraq. Arabic blogs are now being augmented by English-language blogs, aggregated on portals such as iToot.net and enhanced by Ikbis, which functions like YouTube.

Many Arab bloggers need to remain anonymous for fear of reprisals for speaking out, but nonetheless more blogs have been emerging in Arab countries in the past few years (Beckerman, 2007). In Jordan, for example, bloggers have increased from a handful to several hundred. In Lebanon, blogs proliferated after the assassination of the prime minister and protests against Syria's military presence there in 2005, and again during the 2006 summer war with Israel. More conservative countries like Egypt have fewer bloggers, but even in Saudi Arabia the number of blogs tripled in 2006 to 2,000.

In the United States, a global blog indexer and aggregator based at Harvard University, Global Voices Online, was started by a former CNN international reporter and bureau chief, Rebecca MacKinnon (Lang, n.d.). Global Voices has a distinctly antitraditional media thrust, describing itself as a site that "amplifies the global conversation online—shining light on places and people other media often ignore." Its "manifesto" promotes values consonant with those sought by civil society groups at WSIS, although in no way related to those groups. With the motto "The world is talking. Are you listening?" Global Voices Manifesto in English and fourteen other languages announces that:

> We believe in free speech: in protecting the right to speak—and the right to listen. We believe in universal access to the tools of speech.
> To that end, we seek to enable everyone who wants to speak to have the means to speak—and everyone who wants to hear that speech, the means to listen to it.
> Thanks to new tools, speech need no longer be controlled by those who own the means of publishing and distribution, or by governments that would restrict thought and communication. Now, anyone can wield the power of the press. Everyone can tell their stories to the world.
> We seek to build bridges across the gulfs that divide people, so as to understand each other more fully. We seek to work together more effectively, and act more powerfully.
> We believe in the power of direct connection. The bond between individuals from different worlds is personal, political and powerful. We believe conversation across boundaries is essential to a future that is free, fair, prosperous and sustainable—for all citizens of this planet.
> While we continue to work and speak as individuals, we also seek to identify and promote our shared interests and goals. We pledge to respect, assist, teach, learn from, and listen to one other.
> We are Global Voices.

In a similar vein, a group called Chat the Planet inaugurated Hometown Baghdad on the fourth anniversary of the U.S. invasion of Iraq in March 2007. Hometownbaghdad.com was initiated to counter the "images of destruction that dominate our media" and tell the "untold story" of "the life of the everyday Iraqi." The online documentary follows three Iraqis struggling to survive as the crisis in Iraq deepens. Chat the Planet plans two more online documentaries, Hometown Jerusalem and Hometown Tehran.

Conclusion

The ultimate impact of alternatives such as Global Voices and Hometown Baghdad and citizen advocacy groups opposed to neo-liberal media globalization is difficult to predict. Sociologist Immanuel Wallerstein (1998) offers one way to assess historical alternatives, which he calls utopistics. Wallerstein has argued that the world is experiencing the collapse of the capitalist world system of the last 500 years and predicts that a new historical system will emerge after a 50-year "Black Period" of intense cultural and political struggle. During this period, he predicts, the privileged will attempt to preserve their interests through historically proven methods of repression and concession. Among the ways of protecting privilege in the transition to a new world system in the twenty-first century will be adopting the terms of the discontented, such as ecology, multiculturalism, and feminism. The oppressed will respond, Wallerstein predicts, with a variety of means, from violence to electoral challenge, theoretical developments in institutions of knowledge, and public appeals. He suggests that the only viable option is a rainbow coalition.

The current range of responses by global governmental organizations, Western and Third World governments, activist groups, and others aided by the Internet to the latest media controversies over control, content, and current of the global information flow may be viewed as emblematic of the struggle Wallerstein presents. The privileged global media owners and the powerful corporations and governments that they represent have in the past responded with concessions rather than systemic change. Challenges to the current order of neo-liberal globalization appear to be more globally widespread, better organized, and better communicated to global audiences than were the cloistered responses to media controversies in the past. The outcome could be a new historical system that will bring with it a global media system, with democratic control, content, and current.

BIBLIOGRAPHY

Bagdikian, B. H. *The Media Monopoly,* 6th ed.. Boston: Beacon Press, 2000.

Beckerman, G. "The New Arab Conversation," *Columbia Journalism Review* (January–February 2007). Available: http://cjrarchives.org/issues/2007/1/Beckerman.asp.

Butler, P. "New Technology, New Voices." *e-Journal USA.* (December 2007). Available: http://usinfo.state.gov/journals/itgic/1207/ijge/butler.htm

"Culture Wars." *The Economist,* September 12–18, 1998. Available: http://findarticles.com/p/articles/mi_hb5037/is_199809/ai_n18283722

Dorfman, A. *The Empire's Old Clothes: What the Lone Ranger, Babar, and Other Innocent Heroes Do to Our Minds.* New York: Pantheon Books, 1983.

Dorfman, A., and Mattelart, A. *How to Read Donald Duck: Imperialist Ideology in the Disney Comic.* New York: International General, 1975.

Fawcett, T. "The Global Digital Divide." International Symposium on Online Journalism, University of Texas at Austin, 2006. Available: http://online.journalism.utexas.edu/detail.php?story=150&year=2006

Fortner, R. S. *International Communication: History, Conflict, and Control of the Global Metropolis.* Belmont, CA: Wadsworth, 1993.

Frederick, H. H. *Global Communication and International Relations.* Belmont, CA: Wadsworth, 1993.

Galtung, J., and Vincent, R. C. *Global Glasnost.* Cresskill, NJ: Hampton Press, 1992.

Garza, N. "Blogging Grows as a Popular Section in Online Journalism." International Symposium on Online Journalism, University of Texas at Austin, 2006. Available: http://online.journalism.utexas.edu/detail.php?story=148&year=2006

Gillmor, D. "Bloggers Breaking Ground in Communication." *e-Journal USA.* (March 2006). Available: http://usinfo.state.gov/journals/itgic/0306/ijge/gillmor.htm

"Global Voices." Available: http://www.globalvoicesonline.org/

"Global Voices Manifesto." Available: : http://www.globalvoicesonline.org/about/gv-manifesto/

Gordon, P. H., and Meunier, S. "Globalization and French Culture Industry." *French Politics, Culture and Society* 19, No. 1 (2001), 22–41.

Gregoriades, C. "Podcasting: the New Salvation for Online Journalism?" International Symposium on Online Journalism, University of Texas at Austin, 2006. Available: http://online.journalism.utexas.edu/detail.php?story=154&year=2006

Hamelink, C. J. *Cultural Autonomy in Global Communication.* New York: Longman, 1983.

———. "Keynote at the Opening Session of the Civil Society Sector Meeting at the Prepcom 1 for the World Summit on the Information Society." Geneva, Switzerland, 2002. Available: http://www.geneva2003.ch/home/events/documents/gen_hamelink_en.htm

———. "Did WSIS Achieve Anything At All?" *Gazette: The International Journal for Communication Studies* 66, Nos. 3–4 (2004), 281–290.

"Hometown Baghdad." Available: http://www.hometownbaghdad.com/

International Telecommunication Union. "Enhancing the Capacity of the NGOs to Achieve Development Aims, Through the Use of Telecommunication." Document 2/085-E, Geneva, Switzerland, 1999.

Kocurek, C. "Citizen Journalism is Emerging around the World." International Symposium on Online Journalism, University of Texas at Austin, 2006. Available: http://online.journalism.utexas.edu/detail.php?story=146&year=2006

Lang, T. "Rebecca MacKinnon, Pretend Tourist No More." *Columbia Journalism Review.* Available: http://www.cjr.org/the_water_cooler/rebecca_mackinnon_pretend_tour.php

Lull, J. *Media, Communication, Culture: A Global Approach,* 2nd ed. New York: Columbia University Press, 2000.

MacBride, S., et al. *Many Voices, One World (MacBride Report).* New York: Unipub, 1980.

McChesney, R. "Global Media, Neo-liberalism, and Imperialism." *Monthly Review* 52, No. 10 (2001), 1–15.

Media Awareness Network. "Canadian Content Rules (Cancon)," 2007. Available: http://www.media-awareness.ca/english/issues/cultural_policies/canadian_content_rules.cfm

"Media Making Change." *e-Journal USA.* (December 2007). Available: http://usinfo.state.gov/journals/itgic/1207/ijge/ijge1207.htm

Mehra, A. *Free Flow of Information: A New Paradigm.* Westport, CT: Greenwood, 1986.

Merrill, J. C. *Global Journalism: Survey of International Communication,* 3rd ed. White Plains, NY: Longman Publishers, 1995.

Mincio, D., and Lor, P. "WSIS Follow-up Meetings in Geneva, May 2007." IFLANET (June 15, 2007). Available: http://www.ifla.org/III/wsis/MeetingGeneva2007.html

O Siochru, S. Social Dimensions of the Globalization of the Media and Communication Sector. Paper presented at a meeting of the International Labor Organization, Geneva, Switzerland, 2002.

———. "Introduction." Global Information Society Watch 2007 Report. Available: http://www.global-iswatch.org/files/pdf/GISW_Institutions.pdf

Pecquerie, B., and Kilman, L. "From Citizen Journalism to User-Generated Content." *e-Journal USA.* (December 2007). Available: http://usinfo.state.gov/journals/itgic/1207/ijge/pecquerie.htm

People's Communication Charter. "About the People's Communication Charter." Available: http://www.pccharter.net/about.html

———. "People's Communication Charter Text." Available: http://www.pccharter.net/charteren.html

Peskin, D., and Nachison, A. "Emerging Media Reshape Global Society. *e-Journal USA.* (March 2006). Available: http://usinfo.state.gov/journals/itgic/0306/ijge/peskin.htm

Pickard, V. "Neo-liberal Visions and Revisions in Global Communications Policy from NWICO to WSIS." *Journal of Communication Inquiry* 31, No. 2 (2007), 118–139.

Porter, C. "Every Citizen as a Reporter." *e-Journal USA.* (December 2007). Available: http://usinfo.state.gov/journals/itgic/1207/ijge/reporter.htm

Razook, E. "Governments, Companies Impede Free Internet Expression. *e-Journal USA.* (December 2007). Available: http://usinfo.state.gov/journals/itgic/1207/ijge/razook.htm

Straubhaar, J. D., and Larose, R. *Media Now: Communications Media in the Information Age,* 3rd ed. Belmont, CA: Wadsworth, 2002.

Thussu, D. K. *International Communication: Continuity and Change,* 2nd ed. London: Hodder Arnold, 2006.

Toros, H. "WSIS Ends on Mixed Note." TerraViva Online (November 18, 2005). Available: http://www.ipsterraviva.net/tv/tunis/viewstory.asp?idnews=408

United Nations. "Universal Declaration of Human Rights." Available: http://www.un.org/Overview/rights.html

Voices 21. "A Global Movement for People's Voices in Media and Communication in the 21st Century," 1999. Available: http://comunica.org/v21/statement.htm

Wallerstein, I. *Utopistics: Or, Historical Choices of the Twenty-First Century.* New York: New Press, 1998.

World Association for Christian Communication. "Key Issues in Global Communication." Available: http://www.wacc.org.uk/our_work/global_study_prog/resources/world

World Trade Organization. "Intellectual Property: Protection and Enforcement." Available: http://www.wto.org/English/thewto_e/whatis_e/tif_e/agrm7_e.htm

9 Global Journalism Education

MARK DEUZE

Indiana University, USA

Fast-paced developments in a changing social and professional economical environment, media-technological advancements, increasingly precarious or "atypical" (IFJ, 2006) working circumstances, and ongoing corporate colonization, coupled with declining prestige and credibility in the eyes of the public, are the main causes of concern and unrest within journalism worldwide. The dire situation the profession often finds itself in can be illustrated by this quote from Michelle Stanistreet, president of the British National Union of Journalists, at a conference on November 2, 1007: "Most media companies make big money—but they engage in round after round of cuts to increase their profit margins. Journalists are too often reduced to a cross between call-centre workers and data processors, stuck at their desks re-jigging press releases. Who knows what corruption, lies, and law breaking is going on in the corridors of power—no one has the time to look" (Journalism.co.uk, 2007).

The heavy or high modernistic and rather self-congratulatory view of journalism as being intrinsically objective, free, fair, and thus legitimate in itself is waning, particularly in well-established elective democracies (Hallin, 1992). Global journalism education has many different faces, but programs, schools, and courses in journalism across the globe face similar developments. This chapter tackles some of these issues in terms of their impact on contemporary debates regarding challenges and changes in well-established education practices worldwide, with a specific focus on the changing nature of work in professional journalism.

Global Journalism

In discussing global journalism education, it is first important to address what is meant here by global. As Morgan (2000) argues, ways of training and teaching journalists depend on culture and should be seen as a function of time and place. On the other hand, Reese and Cohen (2000) make a strong case for addressing issues in journalism education on a worldwide scale, claiming that in particular, the U.S. model of journalism education, in which journalism is taught as part of the university curriculum, more so than, for example, continental-European polytechnics or Anglo-Saxon on-the-job training traditions, has been widely adopted in schools often staffed by graduates of U.S. universities. Furthermore, international comparisons of journalist populations suggest that even though reporters and editors all over the world disagree on many issues, journalists in many, if not most, democratic countries share a history of continuing professionalization, culminating in a growing body of knowledge, a deeply felt commitment to autonomy in their work, and a strong awareness of the fundamental role journalism plays in the formation and sustenance of society (Weaver, 1998; Deuze, 2002). Research and education are connected to the ongoing professionalization of journalism internationally as the training of journalists evolves in formal and structural journalism education—a process that can be observed in widely differing stages of development across the globe (Splichal and Sparks, 1994; Gaunt, 1992).

Theoretically informed and empirically driven studies on journalism education are still rare (Deuze, 2006). At the same time, the field of journalism studies is growing in quantitative and qualitative significance. The contemporary research on journalism is inherently global in nature; therefore studies on journalism education need to identify shared questions and challenges rather than focusing solely on essentialized institutional or national particularities (Holm, 1997 and 2002; Fröhlich and Holtz-Bacha, 2003). As argued in the seminal work of Philip Gaunt (1992:2) on international journalism training: "Indeed, whatever the geographic area or socio-political context, journalism educators and media professionals have had to come to terms with the same problems." Using the cross-national comparative work of Gaunt (1992), Fröhlich and Holtz-Bacha (2003), and De Burgh (2005), one can define five distinct types of journalism education worldwide:

- Training at schools and institutes generally located at universities (see, for example, Finland, Spain, United States, Canada, South Korea, Kenya, Argentina, the Gulf States, and Australia; this is becoming the dominant mode of training journalists-to-be worldwide; some educators, particularly in Africa and Latin America, resist this model on the grounds that it has neocolonial features, making local programs increasingly dependent on global Western ideas and economies).
- Mixed systems of stand-alone and university-level training (France, Germany, India, Indonesia, China, Brazil, Nigeria, Turkey, South Africa).
- Journalism education at stand-alone schools (Netherlands, Denmark, Italy, countries in Africa, e.g., Ghana, Mozambique).
- Primarily on-the-job training by the media industry, for example, through apprenticeship systems (Great Britain, Austria, Japan; Australia started this way, as this is a typical feature of the Anglo-Saxon model).
- All of the above, and particularly including commercial programs at universities as well as in-house training by media companies, publishers, trade unions, and other private or government institutions (Eastern Europe, Cuba, North Africa; Southern Africa, and the Middle East).

Although we should not reduce regional and local complexities too much, the literature does suggest that most, if not all, systems of journalism education are moving toward the first or second model, indicating increasing levels of professionalization, formalization, and standardization worldwide. This is neither an inevitable nor necessarily a linear development. Yet this trend is not unique to journalism education, as systems of higher education worldwide are expanding rapidly, innovating and differentiating existing programs, and adding all kinds of new courses, curricula, or even disciplines.

Convergence Culture

There are four main changes or challenges facing education programs in journalism worldwide: increasing recognition and awareness of cultural diversity in society; the merging of entertainment and media industries, genres, and formats; the convergence of digital media technologies (multimedia); and the internationalization of media, journalism, and news flow. None of these trends has lost relevance for the work and training of journalists, but several developments suggest that the complexity of today's media ecosystem has created a sense of urgency in the ways they are coalescing—in the context of what Jenkins (2006) has termed a "convergence culture."

In today's digital culture, media work (Deuze, 2007) in general and journalism (Boczkowski, 2004) in particular can be seen as a stomping ground for the forces of increasingly differentiated production and innovation processes, and the complex interaction and integration between work, life, and play, all of which get expressed in, and are facilitated by, the rapid development of new information and communication technologies. This convergence is not just a technological process. Media convergence must also be seen as having a cultural logic of its own, blurring the lines between economics (work) and culture (meaning), between production and consumption, between making media and using media, and between active or passive spectatorship of mediated culture.

The ongoing merger of media production and consumption signals the emergence of a global convergence culture, based on an increasingly participatory and interactive engagement between different media forms and industries, between people and their media, as well as between professional and amateur media makers.

> Convergence is both a top-down corporate-driven process and a bottom-up consumer-driven process. Media companies are learning how to accelerate the flow of media content across delivery channels to expand revenue opportunities, broaden markets and reinforce viewer commitments. Consumers are learning how to use these different media technologies to bring the flow of media more fully under their control and to interact with other users. They are fighting for the right to participate more fully in their culture, to control the flow of media in their lives and to talk back to mass market content. Sometimes, these two forces reinforce each other, creating closer, more rewarding, relations between media producers and consumers. (Jenkins, 2004:37)

The role of the customer as co-creator of the media message increasingly finds acceptance throughout the cultural industries. Among creative and brand managers in ad agencies, the contemporary focus is on interactive advertising, which can be defined as the paid and unpaid presentation and promotion of sponsored products, services, and ideas involving mutual action between consumers and producers (Leckenby and Li, 2000). Marketing communicators brainstorm about the potential of "social" or "upstream," which refers to the strategic process of identifying and fulfilling consumer needs early in product development, up to and including customers and users at various stages in the total production and product innovation cycle. In journalism, editors of news publications actively consider adding what is called "citizen journalism" to their Web sites, allowing members of the audience to respond, comment, and submit their own news (Outing, 2005).

When combined with ongoing efforts throughout the media industries to develop multimedia formats (either through mergers and integrating different company units, or by the increasingly popular networking of the production process across numerous subcontracted business partners—a process which in the news industry tends to be called remote control journalism), producer-consumer convergence poses significant challenges to theorizing global media industries, understanding the role and function of journalism, impacting the way to teach and prepare the news workers of tomorrow. Some of the early research on multimedia journalism (Deuze, 2004; Singer, 2004; Quinn, 2005) and citizen news (Deuze, Bruns, and Neuberger, 2007) suggests the generally top-down, disruptive, challenging, and to some extent "depopulating" (as in coinciding with layoffs and casualization of labor) effects these developments have on the working environment of journalists. One other aspect of these trends is that they are mainstream; hardly any professional news outlets today are not affected by the shift toward some kind of technology-driven convergent, multimedia or cross-media production process, running parallel with initiatives to increasingly include the user, audience, or citizen-consumer in the way news gets gathered, selected, reported, and disseminated.

Global Models of Training and Education

Although change in journalism is nothing new, the current acceleration of threats and challenges to journalism in the context of a global convergence culture has caused scholars, publics, journalists, and journalism educators to reconsider their approaches, definitions, roles, and function in community and society. Journalism education in most countries around the world has traditionally covered the ground of practical skills and standards training, on the one hand, and general contextual education and liberal arts courses, on the other hand. Although the specific needs and demands of the media system differ from region to region and are largely determined by (and are a reflection of) the particular culture and foundation in law and history, the delicate balance between practical and contextual knowledge has always been the main area of attention within journalism programs worldwide (Gaunt, 1992). From analyses of programs and discussion about change in several countries and regions in the world regarding journalism (studies and education), three general conclusions can be drawn.

First, it still seems that much of the debate about journalism training issues takes place within the different national contexts, even though several schools or individual educators (especially in Western Europe, South America, Southern Africa, and the Pacific) are making formal or informal efforts to reach out to colleagues elsewhere. The generally nation-centric frame of reference of education innovation seems in stark contrast to the nature of contemporary media innovations and developments, which is distinctively international or "postnational."

Second, almost everywhere one can observe a heightened awareness and range of initiatives regarding journalism (further) training and education, a sense of urgency or even immediacy, which seems to be a sign of the times, particularly when it comes to reconnecting journalism with developing or established democracy (another system in turmoil) and when it comes to the implementation of new media strategies.

A third and most troubling conclusion must be a certain confusion and lack of focus regarding the overall pattern of media change, and little systematic response to media innovation in the professional (training) world. Changes and challenges abound, but at the same time, there seems to be a lack of vision, of strategies to master the current situation and work out a sustainable change model.

These three conclusions connect to a reevaluation of what journalism education in fact is or should be in the context of fast-paced developments and trends in society. Such concerns are articulated worldwide by national audits of journalism training and education programs and an almost feverish increase in the volume of more or less scholarly work in the field of journalism education. This is particularly noticeable in English-language scholarly journals such as the U.S.-based *Journalism & Mass Communication Educator,* the UK-based journals *Journalism Practice* and *Journalism Studies,* the South African-based *Ecquid Novi: African Journalism Studies,* and the Australian-based *Asia Pacific Media Educator.* Some prolific contemporary authors in the field include Frank Morgan (Australia), Jan Bierhoff (the Netherlands), John Herbert (United Kingdom), Arnold de Beer, Herman Wasserman, and Guy Berger (South Africa), Tom Dickson, Jeremy Cohen, and Stephen Reese (United States), and Claudia Mast (Germany).

Such audits generally assess the state of the art in a given national setting, contextualizing the report with one or more societal developments: new media technologies, further training wants and needs, globalization, convergence, and media differentiation. Some examples of such audits or studies (in alphabetical order) follow.

Australia

Mapping the field of communication and media studies in Australia, scholars concluded that particularly "newer" universities were innovating their curricula in order to meet the demands of a rapidly restructuring, broadening, and fracturing labor market (Putnis, Axford, Watson, and Blood, 2002). The journalism education model in Australia has evolved out of competing Anglo-European and American paradigms—generally framed as a culturist/positivist divide—and now includes a sprawling variety of course titles, job descriptions, and range of discipline areas drawn on. "Communication" is increasingly becoming a central organizing category for a variety of fields, including journalism, which development is similar to the one in the United States. Scholars such as the late James Carey (1996) have blamed this "colonization" of journalism by larger university departments of communication for the disconnection of journalism education and society. The Australian authors call for a clearer articulation of the skills that are being taught in the various areas of communication and media studies and an assessment of likely employment destinations of students. Their core concern seems to be the following question: Yes, we are all innovating and diversifying our fields and disciplines, but what are we training our students to become?

A particularly interesting development has been the integration of departments and fields of study as varied as literature and print media, visual and performing arts, music composition and publishing, new media, broadcasting electronic media and film into the "creative industries" concept, such as, for example, at the Queensland University of Technology's Creative Industries Faculty (QUT). QUT's John Hartley defines creative industries as an idea that "seeks to describe the conceptual and practical convergence of the creative arts (individual talent) with cultural industries (mass scale), in the context of new media technologies (ICTs) within a new knowledge economy, for the use of newly interactive citizen-consumers" (2005:5). It is in this context that journalism gets deliberately articulated with convergence culture.

Canada

Although Canadian journalism programs have emerged and developed largely similar to U.S. programs, a distinct difference has been the fact that the curricular line between journalism and other forms of media education such as public relations or advertising is much stricter in Canada (Johansen, Weaver, and Dornan, 2001). What the models in both countries share is an emphasis on three core components: news production practices, courses in media history and politics, and education in the liberal arts. The authors argue that, although there is greater curricular diversity in Canadian journalism programs than, for example, in the United States (partly because of the lack of an accrediting body), what seems to be lacking is a rich tradition in journalism research. Furthermore, the Canadian system lacks a unified approach because of its emphasis on regional journalism training in provincial, French, and British traditions (Johansen and Dornan, 2003).

Germany

Meyn and Chill (2001) offer an overview of journalism schools and training programs, concluding that most roads into the open profession in Germany focus heavily on down-to-earth practical skills. Their report singles out the increasing need for media companies to make a profit and the influence of the Internet (notably regarding the emergence of online journalism as a more or less distinct field) as developments having a particular impact on journalistic training and awareness. Although Germany has its fair share of journalism departments in universities and a range of specific training institutes offering short-term programs, the bulk of the journalistic workforce enters the profession via a *Volontariat* (internship) of one or two years. In an earlier book, Mast (1999) concluded that in recent years media companies have become increasingly specific regarding the qualifications they expect from newcomers to the profession. This has resulted in a wide variety of rules and ways of training within German media companies. In recent years, a gradual process of "academization" of German journalism education has taken place—even though the graduates of such programs are still expected to go through a process of in-house training and professional socialization (Fröhlich and Holtz-Bacha, 2003).

Great Britain

Herbert (2000:113) writes: "British journalism might have been at the root of the western and colonial tradition of newspapers and broadcasting, but its imperialism didn't extend to journalism education." The British media tend to rely on in-house training and a system of apprenticeships that could be considered to be similar to the German model, as in both countries roughly two-thirds of journalists enter the profession through on-the-job training. But in both countries growing numbers of journalists train through university journalism courses, which is a sprawling field of education particular to the second half of the twentieth century. This has resulted in many BA- and MA-level programs in new fields such as journalism ethics, or multimedia, or digital media journalism. According to Herbert, particular to this emerging field is a strong base in academic research, but without any direct involvement or collaboration with the industry for which these students are preparing. This to some extent was due to the fact that traditionally the news media controlled entry into the profession through in-house or otherwise industry-monitored training. Facing an increasingly competitive market, many organizations have now cut such programs, in turn leading to "an explosion of media and journalism courses in higher and further education which no one can oversee anymore" (Esser, 2003:233). Many of these new programs and courses are now effectively collaborating in different (and often quite informal) ways with local and regional British media organizations.

Europe

At the 2002 annual meeting of the Forum for European Journalism Students (FEJS) in Helsinki, Finland, Koskinen and Sederholm (2002) presented results of a survey of students in 51 educational institutions in 28 countries, concluding that most journalism schools have not innovated their programs to meet future demands of new media convergence, multimedia, and multiskilling of journalists. An earlier report by the European Journalism Centre showed that in Denmark, Sweden, the Netherlands, Austria, and Switzerland, widely varying approaches to journalism education and innovation persist, indicating a north/south divide (Bierhoff, Deuze, and De Vreese, 2000). Scandinavian countries seemed to be farthest along in adapting to a new media environment in contemporary newsrooms, while Central European countries were much more reticent in restructuring their curricula or in-house training projects. But, as shown in a 1997 survey of 56 schools belonging to the European Journalism Training Association, if schools do develop new teaching methods or programs, it is in areas having to do with new technologies (Loennroth, 1997). European schools for journalism tend to be almost exclusively oriented toward their national base, although that is now changing. Under new EU guidelines, there has been a feverish development of graduate (MA) and postgraduate courses and programs in journalism education, often with less than clear standards or methods. Recently, several countries have started accrediting councils to put a stop to this sprawling process. It is clear, however, that despite the problematic labor market and working conditions of journalism today, there are more and more places to get trained as a journalist in Europe than ever before.

The Netherlands

In a critical overview of media trends and developments linked to the status quo at Dutch vocational training schools (similar to recent publications in, for example, South Africa and the United States), Drok (2002) concluded that communication skills, ethics, analytical skills, and an unequivocal commitment to "the democratic mission" should guide any and all journalism education efforts. Although he signals technology and cultural diversity as important trends in society, Drok maintains that these emphasize core journalistic skills, rather than calling for a reconsideration or rethinking of additional skills for the contemporary media professional. Hagen, Manders, and Van Ruler (1997), in a historical overview of the Dutch system of vocational and academic journalism programs, write that the future particularly holds promise for lecturers to engage in more "applied research" and programs to engage in more cross-disciplinary collaboration. The key development in Holland in recent years has been a gradual dismantling of newsroom and in-house training programs and a rapid growth of new small-scale MA-level journalism programs at several Dutch universities.

South Africa

Two of the most striking conclusions of the 2002 South African National Editor's Forum (SANEF) National Journalism Skills Audit in South Africa were (a) a call for more "life skills," such as communication skills, motivation, professional commitment, and ethics, in tertiary training; and (b) an awareness that hierarchical, top-down styles of media management are counterproductive in today's newsroom (De Beer and Steyn, 2002; Steyn and De Beer, 2004). South Africa has a split system, comparable to that of the Netherlands, of journalism education programs at so-called technikons (offering vocational training) and at universities. The SANEF report explicitly mentioned the fact that most news media in South Africa lack the resources, time, or training policies to manage in-house training programs (such as is the case in Germany and Great Britain, for example) or to have more structured involvement in the technikon and university programs. A second national audit (Steyn, De Beer, and Steyn, 2005) on the news management skills of journalists in editorial offices showed a lack of managerial competencies and a high need for better education and training in this field.

Southern Africa

In an assessment of media training needs in Southern Africa—Malawi, Mozambique, Namibia, Lesotho, Swaziland, Tanzania, Botswana, Namibia, and South Africa—Lowe Morna and Khan (2001) found that the entry level for journalism training is gradually increasing everywhere. As the media industry booms, so are media training institutions in the region expanding. A wide variety of in-service training opportunities are available at existing national training institutions and in regional organizations such as the Johannesburg-based Institute for the Advancement of Journalism (IAJ; partnering with the U.S.-based

Poynter Institute) or the Maputo-based Nordic SADC (Southern Africa Development Community) Journalism Centre (NSJ). A specific problem for the region is the history of apartheid and colonialism; until the 1980s and 1990s, journalism training was restricted to small, generally white elite. In recent years, training programs for journalists have emerged throughout the region, resulting in a sprawling field of journalism education. The report concludes that the standard of education in all these programs, courses, and institutes is not very high, that the university courses tend to be too theoretical, and that most of these programs do not match the needs of the working environment, particularly when it comes to, for example, community media reporting. Yet, the media industry does not seem willing to invest in courses in content knowledge on issues particular to the region, such as covering HIV/AIDS or environmental issues. Lowe Morna and Khan also mention the effect of international (non-African) donors for these programs: donors want to influence course content, which results in programs that meet the needs of the international journalism community instead of Southern Africa's needs.

United States

In the major study, *Winds of Change,* by the Freedom Forum, Medsger (1996) wrote, "Though its roots in American universities are more than a century old, journalism education has the characteristics of an experiment—not a dynamic, evolving experiment, but a fragile, unsure, endangered experiment. Journalism is being de-emphasized, submerged or threatened with elimination on many campuses." This pessimistic discussion refers to the trend of journalism programs being incorporated into larger communication departments, a trend that many see as a potential threat, particularly regarding the skills-based training of journalism students. Medsger makes a strong case for demanding extensive professional experiences from print and broadcast journalism faculty. In a critical response to this report, Reese (1999) argued that the Freedom Forum report boiled down all issues facing journalism education to a "professional-academic" antagonistic dichotomy. He further criticized the report for being based on an unproblematized view of "the" profession, its mission, purpose, and its skills. This particular debate on theory versus practice, even though it has been around since the beginnings of formal journalism education, got new impetus when the president of Columbia University, Lee C. Bollinger (2003), convened a national task force to rethink the mission and future of journalism education before allowing the university's Journalism School to appoint a new dean. Bollinger published a much-debated statement, arguing for more investments in journalism education, particularly in stimulating the development of "an internalized value system" and "a sense of an identity as a professional" among students.

Worldwide

To conclude this overview of current debates in various countries and regions around the world, mention should be made of a special issue of the scholarly journal, *Journalism Studies* (No. 2 of 2001), where educators from South Africa, India, Slovenia, and the United States write about the issues they face in their countries. All authors called for more research to be done in the field of journalism, research that would be applicable to better journalism education. Furthermore, these educators critically addressed the notion of public service in journalism, as they invariably call into question the widening gap between the teaching and practice of journalism and its publics: the communities it intends to serve. This disconnect from segments of the public is a concern voiced by professional educators across the globe and most certainly relates to increased awareness of social complexity and the (re-)introduction of more critical-reflective and normative skills into the journalism education curriculum. (For a discussion of journalism education in the different regions of the world, see Section 3 of this book).

Discussion

Contemporary changes on the level of society, economy, and technology are well documented and apparent in most, if not all, elective democracies. Individualization, commercialization, fragmentation, and disintermediation are some of the key concepts used in this context to signal challenges to the way one defines journalism. What matters is not who a journalist is but who acts "journalistically" in the context of a local, national, or international news culture (Kovach and Rosenstiel, 2001; Deuze, 2002). The act or attitude of journalism is generally defined ideologically, using terms such as objectivity, ethics, public service, immediacy, and autonomy. But what do these terms mean for a journalist covering underprivileged communities? Or for a journalist facing political or commercial pressures? When public information can be just as easily disseminated by a blogger anywhere in the world, through someone's profile in an online social network, or via a professional, mainstream news outlet? How, in other words, can a journalist learn to cope with the myriad influences on daily work and still make a personal contribution to addressing the issues of contemporary society and thus democracy in a meaningful and responsible way? As Megwa (2001:283) writes, "Journalism education has too important a part to play in deepening and broadening the country's democratic processes for it not to be multisectoral, multicultural, and multiperspectival." Those ideals are lofty indeed, but also must be set against increasingly dire working conditions throughout the news industry and an exponential growth in courses and programs in journalism education, thus flooding the labor market.

As journalism and democracy have developed and become professionalized, journalism education has to act correspondingly. Professionalization brings organization, increased public self-criticism, constant evaluation, and standards for assessing quality. We must be aware of our own vocabulary and discourse as scholars and educators, which both enable and constrain us when we are considering what can or must change in our ways of doing things. Not only must the journalists of today work in a constantly changing setting and context, but the educators must also evolve to cope with a new and changing news culture as well. This is not a skills versus theory debate, but a cultural and ideological debate. Journalism education has national particularities, but as journalism and its practice of training and learning become professionalized, some more or less global issues arise that need international attention and exchange. To engage the changes and developments interrogated by national and international audits, one needs global awareness of best practices, identification of common problems, and an overview of practical implications from across the field. The biggest challenge worldwide seems to be to find ways to educate and train tomorrow's media professionals based on the need to regain, reconnect with, and join hands with a fragmented, disengaged, and increasingly critical public in the context of contemporary democracy. A worthwhile international step in this direction was taken with the first World Journalism Education Conference held in 2007 in Singapore under the auspices of the Association for Education in Journalism and Mass Communication (AEJMC, 2008).

BIBLIOGRAPHY

AEJMC, 2008. First World Journalism Education Congress to Be Held in Singapore. Available: http://aejmc.org/release/?p=10

Bierhoff, J., Deuze, M., and De Vreese, C. Media Innovation, Professional Debate and Media Training: A European Analysis [on-line]. European Journalism Center Report, 2000. Available: http://www.ejc.nl/hp/mi/contents.htm

Boczkowski, P. *Digitizing the News: Innovation in Online Newspapers.* Boston: MIT Press, 2004.

Bollinger, L. C. "President Lee C. Bollinger's Statement on the Future of Journalism Education." *Columbia University Record,* 25 April 2003, 8, 10. Available: http://www.columbia.edu/cu/record/archives/vol28/vol28_iss13/Pg8-2813.pdf

Carey, J. Where Journalism Education Went Wrong. Presented at the 1996 Seigenthaler Conference at Middle Tennessee State University, Murfreesboro. Available: http://www.mtsu.edu/~masscomm/seig96/carey/carey.htm. Accessed August 30, 2002.

De Beer, A. S., and Steyn, E. "SANEF's '2002 South African National Journalism Skills Audit: An Introduction and a Report Regarding the Media Industry." *Ecquid Novi* 23, No. 1, (2002), 11–86.

De Burgh, H. (ed.). *Making Journalists.* London: Routledge 2005.

Deuze, M. "National News Cultures: Towards a Profile of Journalists Using Cross-National Survey Findings." *Journalism and Mass Communication Quarterly* 79, No. 1 (2002), 134–149.

————. "What Is Multimedia Journalism?" *Journalism Studies* 5, No.2 (2004), 139–152.

————. "Global Journalism Education: A Conceptual Approach." *Journalism Studies* 7, No. 1 (2006), 19–34.

————. *Media Work.* Cambridge: Polity Press, 2007.

————, with Bruns, A., and Neuberger, C. "Preparing for an Age of Participatory News." *Journalism Practice* 1, No.4 (2007), 322–338.

Drok, N. *Drift & Koers: Trends op de Journalistieke Arbeidsmarkt.* Utrecht, the Netherlands: TUZE, 2002.

Esser, F. "Journalism Training in Great Britain." In Fröhlich, R. and Holtz-Bacha, C. (eds.), *Journalism Education in Europe and North America,* 209-236. Cresskill, NJ: Hampton Press, 2003.

Fröhlich, R., and Holtz-Bacha, C. (eds.). *Journalism Education in Europe and North America: A Structural Comparison.* Cresskill, NJ: Hampton Press, 2003.

Gaunt, P. *Making the Newsmakers: International Handbook on Journalism Training.* Westport, CT: Greenwood Press, 1992.

Hagen, P., Manders, H., and Van Ruler, B. "Nieuw Perspectief voor de Opleidingen Communicatie en Journalistiek." *Cahier* 8 (1997).

Hallin, D. "The Passing of the "High Modernism" of American Journalism." *Journal of Communication* 42, No. 3 (1992), 4–25.

Hartley, J. (ed.). *Creative Industries.* Malden, MA: Blackwell, 2005.

Herbert, J. "The Changing Face of Journalism Education in the UK" [on-line]. *Asia/Pacific Media Educator* 8 (2000), 113–123. Available: http://www.uow.edu.au/crearts/sjcw/APME/APME.html. Accessed November 5, 2007.

Holm, H. "Educating Journalists for a New Europe." In Bierhoff, J. and Schmidt, M. (eds.), *European Journalism Training in Transition,* 47–50. Maastricht, the Netherlands: European Journalism Centre, 1997.

————. "The Forgotten Globalization of Journalism Education." *Journalism and Mass Communication Educator* 56, No. 4 (2002), 67–71.

IFJ. "The Changing Nature of Work: A Global Survey and Case Study of Atypical Work in the Media Industry." International Federation of Journalists Research report, 2006. Available: http://www.ifj. org/pdfs/ILOReport070606.pdf. Accessed October 17, 2007.

Jenkins, H. "The Cultural Logic of Media Convergence." *International Journal of Cultural Studies* 7, No.1 (2004), 33–43.

———. *Convergence Culture: Where Old and New Media Collide.* New York: New York University Press, 2006.

Johansen, P., Weaver, D. H. and Dornan, C. "Journalism Education in the United States and Canada: Not Merely Clones." *Journalism Studies,* No. 2 (2001), 469–483.

Johansen, P., and Dornan, C. "Journalism Education in Canada." In Fröhlich, R. and Holtz-Bacha, C. *Journalism education in Europe and North America,* 65-92. Cresskill, NJ: Hampton Press, 2003.

Journalism.co.uk. Available: http://www.journalism.co.uk/staging/6/articles/530711.php. 2007.

Koskinen, P., and Sederholm, E. Survey on Journalism Education in Europe [online]. FEJS Report. Available: http://www.sockom.helsinki.fi/fejs/archives/00000082.htm. Accessed June 13, 2002.

Kovach, B., and Rosenstiel, T. *The Elements of Journalism.* New York: Crown Publishers, 2001.

Leckenby, J., and Li, H. "Why We Need the *Journal of Interactive Advertising.*" *Journal of Interactive Advertising* 1, No.1, 2000. Available: http://www.jiad.org/vol1/no1/editors/index.htm. Accessed November 5, 2007.

Loennroth, A. *Journalism Training in Europe.* Maastricht, the Netherlands: European Journalism Training Association, 1997.

Lowe Morna, C., and Khan, Z. *Assessment of Media Training Needs in the Southern African Region: Preliminary Findings.* Maputo, Mozambique: Nordic SADC Journalism Centre (NSJ), 2001.

Mast, C. *Berufsziel Journalismus.* Opladen/Wiesbaden, Germany: Westdeutscher Verlag, 1999.

Medsger, B. *Winds of Change: Challenges Confronting Journalism Education* [online]. Freedom Forum Report. Available: http://www.freedomforum.org/freedomforum/resources/journal-ism/journalism_edu/winds_of_change/. Accessed July 14, 1999.

Megwa, E. R. "Democracy without Citizens: The Challenge for South African Journalism Education." *Journalism Studies* 2, No. 2 (2001), 281–285.

Meyn, H., and Chill, H. "Journalistic Training in Germany." *Bildung und Wissenschaft* 4. Bonn: Goethe-Institut Inter Nationes, 2001.

Morgan, F. "Recipes for Success: Curriculum for Professional Media Education." *Asia/Pacific Media Educator* 8 (2000), 4–21. Available: http://www.uow.edu.au/crearts/sjcw/APME/APME.html. Accessed November 5, 2007.

Outing, S. "The 11 Layers of Citizen Journalism." Poynter Online, posted June 13, 2008. Available: http://www.poynter.org/content/content_view.asp?id=83126. Accessed November 5, 2007.

Putnis, P., Axford, B., Watson, L., and Blood, W. *Communication and Media Studies in Australian Universities.* University of Canberra, Australia: Lifelong Learning Network, 2002.

Quinn, S. *Convergence Journalism.* New York: Peter Lang, 2005.

QUT (Queensland University of Technology). Creative Industries. http://www.creativeindustries.qut.com/ 2007.

Reese, S. D. "The Progressive Potential of Journalism Education: Recasting the Academic vs. Professional Debate." *Harvard International Journal of Press/Politics* 4, No. 4 (1999), 70–94.

Reese, S. D., and Cohen, J. "Educating for Journalism: The Professionalism of Scholarship." *Journalism Studies* 1, No. 2 (2000), 213–227.

Singer, J. "Strange Bedfellows: The Diffusion of Convergence in Four News Organizations." *Journalism Studies* 5, No.1 (2004), 3–18.

Splichal, S., and Sparks, C. *Journalists for the 21st Century: Tendencies of Professionalization among First-Year Students in 22 Countries.* Norwood, NJ: Ablex, 1994.

Steyn, E., De Beer, A. S., and Steyn, D. "Obtaining 'Better News' through Better News Management." *Ecquid Novi* 26, No. 2 (2005), 212–227.

Steyn, E., and De Beer, A. S. "The Level of Journalism Skills in South Africa Media: A Reason for Concern within a Developing Country? *Journalism Studies* 5, No. 3 (2004), 387–397.

Weaver, D. H. (ed.). *The Global Journalist: News People around the World.* Cresskill, NJ: Hampton Press, 1998.

10 Journalists: International Profiles

BEATE JOSEPHI

Edith Cowan University, Australia

Who Is a Journalist?

Some 35 years ago Tunstall (1973:98) described "journalist" as "a label which people engaged in a very diverse range of activities apply to themselves." This dictum is more pertinent than ever. As Weaver (2005) points out, there are two main reasons why being a journalist is not a distinct profession. First, in most countries journalists themselves do not want to be restricted by having to be licensed as so-called professionals, and second, there is no one distinct educational pathway to becoming a journalist. To this reason can be added a third: that it is difficult to mark out the range of activities performed by journalists, and developments in technology keep adding to the scope.

Any definition of a journalist centers on the *function* the journalist performs and the *form* in which it is carried out. The function is defined as the collection, preparation, and distribution of news and related commentary and feature materials. Its form is through channels that reach an audience, such as the mass media. Most journalists' unions also emphasize that journalism has to be the main occupation of anyone wanting to be called a journalist. According to the International Federation of Journalists (IFJ, 2004), "a journalist is one who devotes the greater part of his/her working time to the profession of journalism and who derives from it most of his/her income being employed or working as a freelance."

The greatest challenge in the digital age to the definition of who is a journalist comes from blogging. The Internet provides a mass medium through which millions of individuals can distribute information and news-related commentary. In 2005 a California court had to decide when a blogger could be deemed a journalist. The court did not see a difference between publishing on online sites or in the traditional institutional media, and was therefore supportive of the proposition that people publishing information online should be entitled to the same constitutional protections as journalists (BBC, 2006). According to this ruling, it is first and foremost the function that makes the journalist rather than the form of distribution, or the fact of gaining income predominantly from journalism.

Who Are the Journalists Then?

It is harder than ever to defend news journalists working for the established or mainstream mass media as the only ones deserving the title journalist. This narrow definition of journalist has been swept aside by a tidal wave of bloggers whose activities have been made possible by the distribution capabilities of the Internet. As the California court ruling showed, there is no fine line between bloggers and journalists, as long as the blogger fulfills the function of publishing information (BBC, 2006). At times, as, for example, during the Iraq War, bloggers like Saddam Pax provided more insightful accounts for the public than did many journalists limited by the expectations of war reporting. Bloggers are challenging the traditionalist view of a journalist, and they have forced changes in journalism by making the amateur or citizen journalist an accepted member of the information-providing and commenting class.

Not only bloggers in their many millions make it problematic to establish who the journalists are. Some countries, like China, have two classes of journalists, licensed and unlicensed. Some countries do not distinguish between information and press relations officers and journalists, and elsewhere it is difficult to determine whether photographers, cameramen, radio magazine presenters and news readers are counted as journalists.

It is difficult enough to trace data on journalists, and it would be even more challenging to do so for those working outside the established mass media. It is the institutional journalists, the primary producers of the mass media (or MSM, as some bloggers call the mainstream media), who to date have been charted in surveys and who are the ones written about here.

The International Federation of Journalists, in the second half of 2007, claims to represent 600,000 members in 114 countries. This figure does not include China, which is not a member of the IFJ. According to official figures, China in 2007 had a total number of about 175,000 licensed journalists (Press Card Holders, 2007), of which less than 150,000 were considered actively working as journalists. Added to this total should be reporters who work in the media but are not licensed. This puts the number of journalists worldwide at well over three-quarters of a million.

In November 2002, the United States had an estimated full-time editorial workforce of 116,148 in the news media (Weaver et al., 2007). The figure for Germany in 2005 was put at 48,000 (Weischenberg et al., 2006), and in Australia the number was officially 22,800 journalists (DEWR, 2007). Any shrinkage of the number of journalists due to media convergence in the First World is more than made up by the expanding markets in Asia, Africa, and Latin America.

One of the best known comparisons of the basic characteristics and professional values of journalists (from 21 countries and territories) was carried out in the 1990s under the editorship of David Weaver (Weaver, 1998). The countries included were Algeria, Australia, Brazil, Britain, Canada, Chile, China, Ecuador, Finland, France, Germany, Hong Kong, Hungary, Korea, Mexico, New Zealand, the Pacific Islands, Poland, Spain, Taiwan, and the United States. The surveys were conducted between 1988 and 1996, mostly by mail and telephone, and included interviews with more than 20,000 journalists in total. This exercise led Weaver to conclude that "comparing journalists across national boundaries is difficult" (2004:142). Statements on roles and professional values largely depend on specific political and cultural settings, while it is easier to establish conclusive data on gender, age, and the educational background of journalists.

Demographic Profile

Changes have not only occurred in the production and dissemination of journalism; there also have been considerable global geopolitical and demographic shifts. A list of the 100 highest circulation newspapers shows that 75 of these are Asian, which includes South Asia (WAN, 2006). For the electronic media, no other continent can rival Asia in audience numbers, and it follows that Asia has more journalists than any other continent. When one is trying to arrive at the median demographic profile of the global journalist, it can therefore be assumed that he is an Asian male, about 35 years old, likely to hold a diploma, and working for a medium-sized news organization. More likely than not, he will work under conditions where media freedom is curtailed, given the fact that more than half the world's nations are seen as partially or not free in press freedom terms (Freedom House, 2006).

For the United States, the journalist's profile changed little a decade on from 1992, as reported in 2007:

> The typical journalist then was a White Protestant married male in his 30s with a bachelor's degree. In 2002, this average journalist was a married White male just over 40, less likely to come from a Protestant religious background, and slightly more likely to hold a bachelor's degree. But this journalist was still more likely to work at a daily newspaper than any other type of news medium in 2002, to have attended a public college or university, to work for a news organization owned by a larger company, and not to have majored in journalism in college. (Weaver et al., 2007:1)

Gender

Men are still more common in the newsrooms around the world than are women, though an almost equal distribution has been achieved in some countries, such as Finland or New Zealand. All the same, it cannot be said that the world moves progressively toward a gender balance in journalism.

In the United States, for example, "despite dramatic increases in women journalism students and increased emphasis on hiring more women in journalism in the 1980s and 1990s" (Weaver et al., 2007:6), the percentage of female journalists over the 20-year span from 1982 to 2002 has persistently stayed between 33 and 34 percent (Weaver et al., 2007:8). On the other hand, in Germany the percentage of women journalists is on a slow but steady increase. In 2005, the proportion of female journalists had reached 37.5 percent, up from 32 percent 12 years earlier (Weischenberg et al., 2006:350).

In Australia, the Department of Employment and Workplace Relations (DEWR) reported the percentage of women journalists in 2007 at 48 percent, which seems a steep rise from earlier findings of 33 percent (Henningham, 1998). However, the earlier figure related to women in full-time employment; DEWR puts women in full-time work at 35.3 percent and those working in journalism part-time at 12.7 percent. The Chinese data of the mid-1990s had the percentage of women journalists at around one-third of the workforce

(Chen, Zhu, and Wu, 1998), which, a decade later, according to official figures had risen to 37.7 percent (Press Card Holders, 2005a).

What is noticeable from the detailed U.S. data is that women dominate in the under 25 age group, where they make up 60.8 percent of journalists. This drops back sharply to 44.9 percent for the ages 25 to 34, and again to 24.8 percent for the 35 to 44 age group. To Weaver and others these figures suggest "that the demands of journalism may be more difficult for women who have childrearing responsibilities than are other occupations in general" (Weaver, 2007:11).

Age

In Western countries, the age of journalists is trending up. In the United States, in 2002 the median age was just over 40 (Weaver et al., 2007:1), a rise of four years since 1992 (Weaver, 1998:398). Also in Australia, the median age of journalists has risen to 38 years (DEWR, 2007), up from 32 years a decade earlier (Henningham, 1998). The situation is similar in Germany where 52.7 percent of journalists in 1993 were under 36 years of age. In 2005, only 32.4 percent of journalists were younger than 36 (Weischenberg et al., 2006).

In contrast, the median age of Chinese journalists may have dropped. In China, the terms *reporter* and *journalist* are not as interchangeable as in other countries. Press card holders, whether actively working or not, are deemed journalists, while young people who do the media fieldwork tend not to be licensed and are referred to as reporters, which helps to explain diverging data. The average of press card holders is about 38 years, whereas that of reporters was put at just 25 years of age (Wang, 2005). The low average age should not be surprising in a market that has expanded significantly and had to take on many young reporters. Similar developments can be assumed for African and Latin American countries.

The data for Western countries indicates that, as the media industry is static, if not contracting, job turnover is the major reason for vacancies in the industry (DEWR, 2007). In the United States, "many of the journalists hired during the boom period of the 1970s were still in their late 40s or early 50s in 2002, still quite a few years away from retirement" (Weaver et al., 2007:7).

We can therefore conclude that while journalism is a younger person's occupation, the age of journalists depends on periods of expansion in the media industry during which a large cohort of young journalists is hired, which then successively carries through, eventually pushing up the median age.

Education

There is an undeniable trend worldwide toward the "graduatization of journalism" (Splichal and Sparks, 1994). A report tabled at the first World Journalism Education Congress lists 1,859 degree programs worldwide. Counted were all programs known to the researchers from the University of Oklahoma, which could be classed as journalism-mass communication education (WJEC, 2007) Of these, roughly 25 percent were located in North America, 22 percent in Europe, 20 percent each in Asia and Latin America, 6 percent in Africa, 4 percent in the Middle East and 3 percent in Oceania. By beginning of 2008, this list has already grown to over 3 000 programs.

The figure assumed for China in the WJEC report, however, has already changed significantly. Data provided by the president of the China Association of Journalism and Communication Education (CAJCE) shows that China now offers more programs than the United States. According to the statistics provided by the CAJCE, more than 110 colleges and universities in China have offered a total of 661 undergraduate programs in journalism (209), broadcasting journalism (146), advertising (232), editing and publishing (50), and communication (24) as of May 2006, with an annual increase of 67 programs in the past five years. Total estimated student enrollment was about 130,000. The number of graduate programs has also risen fast in the new century. As of March 2006, China had approved 123 MA programs in journalism (60) and communication (63), while only 15 universities are permitted to hold a total of 21 Ph.D. programs, including 11 Ph.D. programs in journalism and 10 in communication (He, 2007).

The educational standing of Chinese press card holders, even without the rapid expansion of journalism programs, matches that of Western countries. According to official data, 54.8 percent hold a four-year bachelor degree, 38.5 percent hold a three-year diploma, and 4.8 percent a master's degree (Press Card Holders, 2005b). The site does not state the disciplines for which the degrees were awarded, but it has to be assumed that only a fraction of these came from the journalism and mass communication field.

Australia did not experience the explosion in the number of courses as did China, but its expansion in tertiary journalism courses well exemplifies the growth worldwide. In 1987, eleven tertiary institutions offered vocationally oriented courses at the undergraduate level. By 2001, 25 universities—representing two-thirds of Australia's 38 universities—offered some type of journalism course at the undergraduate and/or graduate level (O'Donnell, 2007).

While this increase in journalism courses does not mean that journalists are journalism graduates, it nevertheless coincides with a rise in the education levels of journalists generally. In the United States, in the period 1971–2002, "the proportion of full-time . . . journalists working in the mainstream news media with at least a college bachelor's degree jumped from 58% to 89%, but the proportion of those college graduates with a journalism degree increased only slightly from 34% to 36%" (Weaver et al., 2007:31). Similarly in Germany, 80.5 percent of journalists hold a university degree or have spent time at university, but only 13 percent hold a major or minor in journalism and another 17 percent has done communication or media studies (Weischenberg et al., 2006).

These figures are an indication that the media industry wishes for and welcomes graduates but is only partially convinced of the validity and usefulness of journalism degrees. All the same, the increasing levels of journalists' tertiary education globally are a sign of the strengthening professional position of journalists.

Professional Values

There is an assumption that journalists' professional values are an indication of the quality of the journalism they produce. But such a reductive equation cannot be made. While journalists are the primary producers, their autonomy is limited by the larger structure within which they work (Reese, 2001). Situated practice is strongly influenced by the political and cultural setting, which, in turn, influences the norms held high in journalism—be it a vision of journalists as the fourth estate or as essential elements in national development. This makes it impossible to ascertain any meaningful statement on professional values worldwide (Josephi, 2005:584).

Curran (2005:xii) attributes it to the American dominance in journalism scholarship that the "American model of fact based, neutral professionalism . . . [and] the libertarian, market-based model of organizing journalism" has been widely regarded as the norm. While the American model of factuality and neutrality, with its high regard for investigative journalism, is seen as attractive in many English-speaking and Nordic countries, the model of loyalty, as observed by Mancini in Italy (2003:97), can be found far more frequently worldwide: "What counts in journalists is above all the devotion, political and ideological loyalty, and the ability to create consensus regarding clearly defined ideas advocated by the newspaper or television channel for which they work."

However, there are no global studies of journalistic norms based on the model of loyalty. Nor have studies explored in depth the variations between the professional values held while at journalism school and those applied while working in the newsroom. Splichal and Sparks's *Journalists for the 21st Century* (1994) examined the motivations, expectations, and professionalization tendencies among first-year students whose norms and values had not yet been tested by day-to-day reporting. The most striking similarity that emerged was for these young people "to stress a desire for the independence and autonomy of journalism" (Splichal and Sparks, 1994:179). Splichal and Sparks remark that first-year students of journalism are at "the precise point in their development when one would expect to find the 'idealistic' conception of journalism as a genuine profession most strongly marked" and concede that "exposure to more realities of the occupational situation would lead to a moderation of these idealistic views" (Splichal and Sparks, 1994:182).

Splichal and Sparks's findings are encouraging with regard to values taught, but they also highlight that the organizational, political, and cultural setting has considerable influence on the professional values as practiced.

Roles

The most extensive research into journalists' perceptions of their roles has been done by Weaver (1998) in *The Global Journalist*, for which journalists from 21 countries and territories were surveyed. The questionnaire used in the various countries was based on Weaver and Wilhoits's (1986) study of American journalists. This has led to some curious results. As Hallin and Mancini (2004:303) have observed, their "research suggests that the differences in how journalists actually do their work are larger than the differences in survey responses, which are heavily shaped by cross-cultural normative expectations and aspirations." Only these cross-national aspirations can explain the fact that more Chinese journalists saw it as their role to investigate government than did French or German journalists (Weaver, 1998:466–467).

The most conclusive result from the surveys brought together in *The Global Journalist* is that getting information to the public quickly was seen as the most important function in almost all countries. With regard to other roles, there was little consensus. As Weaver wrote in the previous edition of this book, the analytical function of news media—providing analysis of complex problems—remained about the same in the United States during the 1980s, with about half saying it was extremely important. But among the 14 countries or territories where this role was measured, there were considerable differences, with journalists in Taiwan and France least likely to consider it very important and those in Finland and Britain most likely to say so.

With regard to providing entertainment, there was great disagreement among the 14 countries or territories reporting this role. Those journalists least likely to consider this very important were from Canada and France, whereas those most likely were from Germany and Chile. Clearly, this was one role where national differences in journalistic values were in sharp evidence. It seems that journalists from the Far East and North America were least likely to regard entertainment as an important function of journalism, but in Europe there were huge differences by country, suggesting that this is not a universal but possibly a Western journalistic role. A decade later, however, providing entertainment was seen as important by only 36.9 percent of German journalists, indicating a sharp decline from the previous 82 percent. The more recent result implicitly points to a certain degree of volatility in these surveys.

There was also disagreement on the importance of reporting accurately or objectively. The journalists least likely to say so were from Britain and the Pacific Islands, and those most likely were from Finland, Taiwan, and Germany. In Germany also a decade later the provision of precise and neutral information was seen as highly important by almost 90 percent of journalists.

Surveys similar to those in *The Global Journalist* have since been carried out in, among other countries, Tanzania, Nepal, and Uganda. The results in these three developing nations reinforce Weaver's earlier findings that providing timely information was seen as the most important role (Ramaprasad, 2001; Ramaprasad and Kelly, 2003; Mwesige, 2004). Beyond this agreement, the studies showed that the journalists' perception of their role was shaped by their countries' development imperative of educating citizens.

Ethics

What can be said about roles also has to be said about ethics. The surveys carried out for *The Global Journalist* took as a measure of ethics the kind of reporting methods journalists considered acceptable. Weaver (2004:148) found that on one point there was a high level of agreement among all journalists, suggesting a near-universal professional norm of protecting confidential sources. However, there was more disagreement than agreement over reporting practices generally. This led Weaver to conclude that, given these large divergences in the percentages of journalists who think that different reporting methods may be acceptable, it seems that there are strong national differences that override any universal professional norms or values of journalism around the world, and make it very difficult to talk about global journalistic ethics.

Aspects of the Job

Some scholars maintain that salary, job security, and chance to advance are less professional aspects of an occupation than editorial policies, ability to develop a specialty, autonomy, and helping people. It can be equally argued that salary can be seen as an indicator of the standing afforded to journalists. What has been said about Portugal (Pinto and Sousa,

2003:181) applies to many countries: "Traditionally, journalism has not been a prestigious profession. Censorship and the non-existence of specific academic qualifications made it a low-qualified and low-paid profession."

Even in countries where journalists are well paid, journalism is not an occupation that makes people rich. While there are high-profile media people in every country who contribute, somewhat falsely, to a glamorous image for journalists, there are many who do the daily grind. This leads to an uneven pay scale in journalism, not only between countries but also within a country. In the United States, according to Weaver et al. (2007:97), the estimated median personal income of journalists was US$43,588. Yet almost one in five journalists earned more than US$70,000 in 2001. At the same time, about the same percentage earned less than US$30,000. Journalists' estimated median incomes were higher than the 2002 U.S. median earnings for all white-collar workers by about US$4,500, but they were substantially below the US$51,480 median for all professional and technical workers. Also in Australia journalists are considered to be adequately paid. Their median income of A$57,928 per year lies above the average of A$46,800 per year for all occupations (DEWR, 2007).

German data show that just over half of the journalists were satisfied with their pay. The greatest source of discontent among German journalists was the lack of a clear career path. Only 30.2 percent felt that they had sufficient chances to move on in their job (Weischenberg et al., 2006). The chance to advance and job security are aspects of a journalist's occupation which, on the whole, are rated quite low.

For Britain, which until recently preferred on-the-job training for journalists, Delano (2000) had to conclude that there were no signs of improved job aspects in a hundred years of journalism. Data from the National Union of Journalists (NUJ, 2004) backs this up. Nearly half of all British journalists earn less than the national average wage of £26,151, and almost three-quarters of journalists earn less than the UK average wage of a professional worker of £35,766.

If this is the situation in one of the places of origin of news journalism, then understandably the situation in the developing world is worse. When the International Journalists' Network (2007) asked its members whether their pay seemed adequate, the overwhelmingly negative answers came mostly from Africa, the Arab world, Latin America, and South Asia. One e-mail put it succinctly: "In Malawi's case, most journalists resort to getting money from people they are not supposed to. This is because they are underpaid." Similar reports come from China (Columbia News, 2006) or Indonesia (IFEX, 2006).

Weaver's 1998 data showed that job satisfaction differed greatly even among countries with similarly poor pay, such as Brazil and Mexico. But this should not mask the fact that pay and conditions, especially journalistic autonomy, can be seen as tangible markers of journalists' standing in their respective societies.

Conclusion

For a number of decades journalists were measured by the degree of professionalization they were seen to have achieved. However, the debate about professionalization has somewhat abated. In a world that is more aware of all its parts than ever before, the American professional model, which had served as indicator, is no longer seen as representative enough in the global context. All the same, aspects of the United States' pioneer work are now firmly embedded in the professional ideal of journalists. As Joseph Pulitzer once wished, more journalists than ever worldwide have a college education. This is a very important, comparatively recent step, removing journalism from being viewed as a craft and its requisite skills taught on the job.

On one hand, we know more about journalists around the globe, yet on the other this increase in data is not so much clarifying the picture as adding to its complexity. Working conditions of journalists vary enormously—be these technological or political aspects. Many media systems around the world are in transition, thus making questions with regard to roles, ethics, and professional values even harder to ascertain.

What has remained a constant is that journalism, especially reporting, tends to be a young person's job. The percentage of women journalists is slowly trending up, but the higher number of females in the profession masks the fact that many of them work part-time. What has changed is the educational background of journalists, which clearly moves toward being college educated. This is a significant development. Only with an adequate education can journalists lay claim to theirs being the intellectual profession many perceive it to be.

BIBLIOGRAPHY

British Broadcasting Cooperation (BBC). "Why We Are All Journalists Now." June 5, 2006. Available: http://news.bbc.co.uk/2/hi/technology/5048556.stm

Chen, C., Zhu, J.-H., and Wu, W. "The Chinese Journalist." In Weaver, D. (ed.), *The Global Journalist: News People around the World*, 9-30. Creskill, NJ: Hampton Press, 1998.

Columbia News. "World Leaders Forum: Is China Moving towards a Fair and Balanced Press?" March 29, 2006. Available: http://www.columbia.edu/cu/news/06/03/wlf_china_press.html

Curran, J. "Foreword." In de Burgh, H. (ed.), *Making Journalists*, xi–xv. London: Routledge, 2005.

Delano, A. "No Sign of a Better Job: 100 Years of British Journalism." *Journalism Studies* 1(2000), 261–272.

Department of Employment and Workplace Relations (DEWR). "Journalists," August 28, 2007. Available: http://jobsearch.gov.au/joboutlook/

Freedom House. "Table of Global Press Freedom Rankings." Freedom House. Tables 2006. Available: http://www.freedomhouse.org/

Hallin, D., and Mancini, P. *Comparing Media Systems—Three Models of Media and Politics*. Cambridge: Cambridge University Press, 2004.

He, Z. President of the China Association of Journalism and Communication Education. E-mail Communication. September 1, 2007.

Henningham, J. "Australian Journalists." In Weaver, D. (ed.), *The Global Journalist: News People around the World*, 91–107. Creskill, NJ: Hampton Press, 1998.

International Federation of Journalists (IFJ). *IFJ Constitution*. May 29, 2004. Available: http://www.ifj.org/

International Freedom of Expression eXchange (IFEX). "Majority of Indonesian Journalists Vastly Underpaid: Aliansi Jurnalis Independen survey." September 5, 2006. Available: http://www.ifex.org/en/content/view/full/76840/

International Network of Journalists (IJN). "Journalism: Does It Pay Well?" February 5, 2007. Available: http://www.ijnet.org/Director.aspx?P=DiscussionArticle&ID=305957

Josephi, B. "Journalism in the Global Age: Between Normative and Empirical." *Gazette* 67 (2005), 575–590.

Mancini, P. "Between Literary Roots and Partisanship: Journalism Education in Italy." In Fröhlich, R. and Holtz-Bacha, C. *Journalism Education in Europe and North America. An International Comparison*, 93–104. Cresskill, NJ: Hampton Press, 2003.

Mwesige, P. G. "Disseminators, Advocates and Watchdogs." *Journalism* 5 (2004), 69–96.

National Union of Journalists (NUJ). "Half UK Journalists Paid Below Average Wage." November 8, 2004. Available: http://www.nuj.org.uk/inner.php?docid=840

O'Donnell, P. "Journalism Education in Australia—A National Report." Paper presented at the World Journalism Education Congress, Singapore. June 26, 2007.

Pinto, M., and Sousa, H. "Journalism Education at Universities and Journalism Schools in Portugal." In Fröhlich, R. and Holtz-Bacha, C. (eds.), *Journalism Education in Europe and North America. An International Comparison*, 169–186. Cresskill, NJ: Hampton Press, 2003.

Press Card Holders. "Age." 2007. Available: http://press.gapp.gov.cn/tongji/province_age.php

———. "Gender." July 2, 2005a. Available: http://press.gapp.gov.cn/tongji/province_sex.php

———. "Degrees." July 2, 2005b. Available: http://press.gapp.gov.cn/tongji/province_degree.php

Ramaprasad, J. "A Profile of Journalists in Post-Independence Tanzania." *Gazette* 63 (2001), 539–555.

Ramaprasad, J., and Kelly, J. D. "Reporting the News from the World's Rooftop." *Gazette* 65 (2003), 291–315.

Reese, S. "Understanding the Global Journalist: A Hierarchy-of-Influence Approach." *Journalism Studies* 2 (2001), 173–187.

Splichal, S. and Sparks, C. *Journalists for the 21st Century*. Norwood, NJ: Ablex, 1994.

Tunstall, J. "Journalism as an Occupation." *The Medico-Legal Journal,* Part Three (1973), 87–101.

Wang, Z. "Four in Five Reporters Want to Change Jobs, Says Survey." *China Daily,* August 11, 2005. Available: http://www.chinadaily.com.cn/english/doc/2005-11/08/content_492177.htm

Weaver, D. H. (ed.). *The Global Journalist: News People around the World*. Cresskill, NJ: Hampton Press, 1998.

———. "Journalists: International Profiles." In de Beer, A. and Merrill, J. (eds.), *Global Journalism: Topical Issues and Media Systems,* 4th ed. Boston: Pearson, 2004.

———. "Who Are Journalists?" In de Burgh, H. (ed.), *Making Journalists*, 44–57. London: Routledge, 2005

Weaver, D. H., and Cleveland Wilhoit, G. *The American Journalist: A Portrait of U.S. News People and Their Work*. Bloomington: Indiana University Press, 1986.

Weaver, D. H., Beam, R. A., Brownlee, B. J., Voakes, P. S., and Cleveland Wilhoit, G. *The American Journalist in the 21st Century*. Mahwah, NJ: Lawrence Erlbaum, 2007.

Weischenberg, S., Malik, M., and Scholl, A. "Journalismus in Deutschland 2005 (Journalism in Germany 2005)" *Medien Perspektiven* 7 (2006), 346–361.

World Association of Newspapers (WAN). "World's 100 Largest Newspapers [in 2005]," June 5, 2006. Available: http://www.wan-press.org/article2825.html

World Journalism Education Congress (WJEC). *WJEC Report*. June 2007. University of Oklahoma Gaylord College of Journalism and Mass Communication.

Reporting Foreign Places

P. ERIC LOUW

University of Queensland, Australia

The news we receive about foreign places is the outcome of multiple decisions by journalists, cameramen, editors, government spokesmen, and political spin doctors. Those concerned with the production of foreign news need to unpack the way journalists work; consider how foreign correspondents are enmeshed within the newsmaking agendas of their home organizations; grapple with how foreign policies of home countries can impact upon the news agendas of the journalists' home organizations; understand how journalistic stories are constructed within preexisting worldviews and discourses; plus explore the role played by journalism within the political process (Louw, 2005:Chapter 1).

Foreign news is a particularly complex product because it intersects with the political context of the journalist's home country; with the way journalists relate to foreign environments, and with the (shifting) relationships existing between home and foreign countries (Louw, 2005:Chapter 12). But it is a complexity worth exploring because the way foreign places are reported by the media can have significant impacts. For example, because U.S. power underpins the New World Order, the processes whereby Americans "make sense of distant places" now have real consequences for non-Americans. To a great extent, Americans form impressions of distant places, issues, and events from their news media. These impressions often translate into electoral pressure on U.S. politicians to act in certain ways toward distant populations. Hence, in a globalizing world, journalist coverage of foreign places increasingly impacts on the governance of these "distant places." For this reason it is important to pay attention to the practices associated with the reporting of foreign affairs.

Gaye Tuchman (1978) has argued that journalists construct a "window on the world" and has explained why this window is always a partial view (i.e., a skewed picture). For consumers of local news, a potential corrective exists for moderating the inbuilt skewing/distortion produced by news practices—namely, in the local context consumers (including politicians) can (to some extent) carry out their own "reality checks"—by comparing their own "lived experiences" and understandings with what is reported in the media. But when it comes to the reporting of distant places, such reality checks are not possible for the general public of media users. So news consumers virtually become almost entirely dependent on the news media to help them make sense of those distant places to which they themselves have no direct access. Furthermore, when distortions occur, they are generally not redressed because there is no pressure to correct them—given that distant audiences do not recognize the media distortions. As Wallis and Baran (1990:231) note, it is difficult for foreigners to redress reporting inaccuracies at a distance. For this reason, the emergence of international-government-directed efforts to influence foreign-news-driven "mediated realities" has inherent dangers, such as was the case with the embedded journalists in the Iraq War and the consequent news reports on the (missing) weapons of mass destruction, that turned out in the long run not to have been there in the first place.

Distance and Double Misreadings

Relying on the news media to understand distant places inherently produces a double misreading because journalists are generally not equipped to read distant contexts; and neither are their audiences. The result is a double misreading, as audiences with already limited understandings of distant contexts are forced to rely on partial/skewed journalistic reports to build up any kind of picture of foreign places. These "partial pictures" acquire a reality that then serves to frame the way the next generation of foreign correspondents and their news editors look at (and hence report) the distant places. Once a prejudice (whether negative or positive) has rooted itself within a newsroom culture, that prejudice will (unconsciously) inform future newsmaking about that particular group of people.

In a sense, if distant issues are not reported they do not exist, because only that which enters one's consciousness exists. Increasingly, television sets the agenda for what enters the consciousness of mostly people in North America, Europe, Japan, and Australia where there is wide access to television news channels. And when it comes to foreign contexts, this agenda-setting role is almost absolute. As regards the reporting of distant places "televisualized" agenda setting generates a particular variety of partiality—one often governed by emotive images. Television is very good at presenting visually sensational and unidimensional material; but it is a poor medium for dealing with complicated issues and contexts that require nonsensational analytic unpacking of their complexity. (For instance, in the run-up to the New Hampshire presidential primary in 2008 some of the big news TV media were selling the idea that Barack "Obama Mania" had gripped the country and opinion polls showed him ahead, but Hillary Clinton was the clear winner in that particular primary.) Watching television news tends not to leave audiences with a store of verified knowledge of the details and facts of what is happening, but rather with a blur of images.

Neuman et al. (1992:3) discuss how television news creates "common knowledge [which helps] people think . . . and structure their ideas, feelings and beliefs about political issues", and argue that television is good at putting obscure and distant events onto the agenda (Neuman et al., 1992:86). As Wallis and Baran note: "Radio and television are *immediate* and emotional media. The emotional prerequisite for successful communication in the broadcast media means that news, ideally, should be both informative and dramatic if it is to grip" (Wallis and Baran, 1990:246–247). Hence, foreign news selection tends to be geared to the highly visual, dramatic, and emotional because such news is more appealing to audiences. This also tends to leave audiences with very strong feelings about foreign issues that, ironically, are based on a highly limited repertoire of information.

Neuman et al. (1992:63–64) provide the example of intense antagonism toward white South Africans in the 1980s based on U.S. television coverage of the anti-apartheid struggle. A similar antagonism developed towards Serbs in the 1990s as a result of Anglo-media coverage of the Bosnian and Kosovo wars.

Television news compresses, condenses, simplifies, and eschews complexity and ambiguity. Wherever possible, television news production will reduce complexity to binary oppositions—mobilizing what Hartley (1982:21) calls "hooray" and "boo" words—because this makes for good emotive television that can attract and hold audiences. Foreign situations can be more easily simplified into facile "good guy" versus "bad guy" scenarios than local situations because audiences have no way of personally verifying reports on distant places. In this regard, General William Westmoreland's complaint that television news is simplistic is instructive:

> Television brought war into the American home, but in the process television's unique requirements contributed to a distorted view of the war. The news had to be compressed and visually dramatic. Thus the war that the Americans saw was almost exclusively violent, miserable, or controversial: guns firing, men falling, helicopters crashing, buildings toppling, huts burning, refugees fleeing, women wailing. A shot of a single building in ruins could give an impression of an entire town destroyed. . . . Only scant attention was paid to . . . the way life went on in a generally normal way for most of the people much of the time. (Westmoreland, 1980:555)

Sadkovich noted a similar process at work in reporting the breakup of Yugoslavia. He says:

> Television seems able to portray only a limited range of emotions because it lacks linear development and nuance. It homogenizes and reduces complex situations, events and emotions to simple standard items that are almost mythic. . . .Television precludes careful exegesis in favor of simple explanations of group conflict and reality in general. It invokes and evokes, it does not inform or explain.
>
> If television is a dream, it also decides what is real. . . .As the tube creates and idealizes some groups and ideas by focusing on them, it makes other[s] disappear by ignoring them. Because it is the key source of news for most Americans it has seriously distorted our view of reality (Sadkovich, 1998:60).

This skewed media reality is sometimes deliberately manufactured, such as with the Anglo-American propaganda fed to journalists preceding the Iraq wars. On other occasions it grows organically from the limitations of journalistic storytelling, such as seen in coverage of the post-2003 conflict in Sudan's Darfur region.

Sadkovich also drew attention to how U.S. journalists mobilized "name-calling" (1998:82) and/or emotion and drama during the Yugoslav conflict, such as the story of the Serbian boy and Muslim girl killed in each other's arms. "As drama the show was wonderful. As news, it meant nothing" (Sadkovich, 1998:68). Yet such visual dramatization has become the stock-in-trade of U.S. televisual coverage of distant places—dramatization that then spills into non-U.S. television. This often generates deep emotional responses among TV audiences, which can, in turn, produce emotion-driven foreign policy formulations.

Having recognized the power of negative TV images on foreign policymaking, the U.S. military developed a strategy for limiting them (see Louw, 2001:Chapter 8).

But it is not only audiences who misunderstand distant places; journalists regularly misread and misunderstand the foreign contexts to which they are sent. When journalists (and news editors) cover foreign contexts, they engage in their task with already existent pictures and discourses in their minds. These existent images determine the questions they ask and the images they seek. Hence, the partiality of news frames tends to be recycled and reproduced, so that discourses about foreigners and foreign places are resistant to change.

Journalistic Misreadings

Journalistic misreadings occur due to a number of factors. First, journalists arriving in a new context are foreigners and so are not rooted in the history or codes of the society they are expected to report. Journalists necessarily experience real difficulties when sent to cover societies grounded on unfamiliar religions (such as Anglo journalists in the Muslim world), or societies that are extremely complex (such as the Balkans, Russia, or Southern Africa). Van Ginneken (1998:125–126) notes how journalists often read the history and mores of their own societies into foreign contexts when trying to make sense of these places. In the process, they produce a distorted view of "the other." Karim, for example, notes how the Western media, when confronted with sociopolitical complexities they could not understand in the Caucasus and former Yugoslavia, simply produced a reductionist explanation based upon religious differences and irrationality (Karim, 2000:177).

When encountering "difficult" and "foreign" places, journalists often herd together into expatriate communities consisting of Western media people, businessmen, embassy and intelligence staffers, and NGO humanitarian aid workers (Van Ginneken, 1998:134). These expatriate communities tend to be cut off from the countries they live in, and so invent "closed-shop" interpretations or "scripts" (Van Dijk in Karim, 2000:179) to describe the difficult cultures surrounding them. It is these closed interpretations that the "folks back home" get to hear (via journalists and embassy dispatches). The reporting of post-Taliban Afghanistan and post-2003 Iraq are examples of this kind of reporting. The way in which Westerners and their Iraqi-allies retreated into Baghdad's Green Zone serves as a metaphor for such closed-shop understandings of foreign places. It is from within this Green Zone that the Iraqi script is produced. Van Ginneken suggests that once created, these scripts, or "prime definitions tend to stick" (1998:113) and be recycled.

Misreadings also occur because journalists carry their cultural biases with them when reporting on foreign contexts. Furthermore, they carry by extension the biases of their news editors—that is, journalists necessarily respond to requests and pressures from their home base to deliver stories conforming to "home needs" (see Cohen et al., 1995). In this regard, Karim (2000) and Said (1981) have discussed the anti-Muslim bias in Western media. Van Ginneken (1998:110) argues that journalists effectively judge others in terms of their own cultural biases. So foreigners operating in ways confirming the journalist's own cultural norms seem sensible and normal, while anyone operating outside these norms becomes "incomprehensible" or even "despicable." Attention is drawn to such "incomprehensible" and "despicable" behavior while "dark issues" in one's own culture are forgotten and blotted out (Van Ginneken, 1998:111).

Significantly, Anglo values have become something of a measure of normalness (or even truth) in the global media system, due in no small measure to the growing centrality of Anglo global-television such as CNN and BBC, and to the central position occupied by the United States within the New World Order. Consequently, Anglo journalists assume their values to be universally valid truths and uncontestable, partly because the New World Order is a de facto Anglo hegemony. Measuring other cultures against Anglo values is thus taken for granted. So, for example, the American trajectory of socioeconomic development is seen as a valid model for all to emulate, and the Anglo-American model for political modernization becomes a self-evident truth. This leads to the view that the United States has a right to export its vision of democracy to the world—as seen in George Bush's rhetoric about the Iraq War.

Greenfeld suggests that Americans have decontextualized their model of sociopolitical organization and transformed it into a "pan-human universalism" (Greenfeld, 1993:446). Anglo-American journalists now uncritically apply this pan-human universalism to all situations they encounter. Hence, when Americans believed in the melting pot, that became the measurement criteria for all. When multiculturalism replaced the melting pot, the journalistic measurement criteria shifted. Those not adhering to Anglo-American models of societal organization become despicable and/or incomprehensible. North Korea, Iran, Afghanistan and Libya have become such incomprehensible societies, as have all Muslim fundamentalists. Muslim fundamentalism has become a major boo word in the Anglo-global media.

Generally, African conflicts—for example, in Somalia, Sierra Leone, Rwanda, and Darfur—have also been presented as incomprehensible, although the opaqueness of these conflicts is often indirectly explained away by alluding to Western common knowledge of the inherently despicable nature of "darkest Africa." Similarly, ethnic wars in the former Yugoslavia were seen as despicable by the Anglo-global media, while the Balkan peoples become incomprehensible for failing to behave in a "civilized" (Anglo) way. In an earlier era, Afrikaners were deemed despicable for violating the Anglo model of sociopolitical organization. However, Anglo journalists tried to make Afrikaner actions comprehensible by equating apartheid with American white supremacy, slavery and Jim Crow laws (because the complicated Dutch *verzuiling* model of building and maintaining different social cohesive groups that underpinned apartheid was unknown to Anglos). If the global media are to be believed, Anglos fight wars, engage in conflict, and impose their will on others because they have "good reasons" to do so, whereas other people do so because they are despicable, uncivilized, or just plain odd. Thus U.S. counterinsurgency methods used in the War on Terror are condoned, while the same methods are condemned when used by Milosevic in Kosovo or by Putin in Chechnya. Effectively, Anglo hegemonies are routinely normalized; while non-Anglo hegemonies are routinely measured (judged) against Anglo norms, and/or in terms of their usefulness to Anglo hegemonies.

A third reason for the misreading of foreign contexts is the journalistic practice of deploying simplistic role labels. This takes place because journalists are often faced with the problem of rendering incredibly complex foreign contexts that are easily comprehensible for overseas audiences. Although the habit of shorthand labeling pragmatically achieves this end, it can also simplify to the point of distortion. In this regard, Wallis and Baran (1990:231) cite the BBC's deployment of race labels to describe 1980s South Africa. Van Ginneken (1998:105–108) looks at similar deployments in the case of Libya, Iran, and Eastern Europe. A similar pattern is evident in reporting post-2003 Iraq. Ultimately, the journalistic practices of labeling and seeking the visually dramatic and sensational necessarily eschews complexity in favor of decontextualized and dehistoricized reductionisms; for example, the complexity of Kosovo was reduced to the label of ethnic cleansing, and the complexity of South Africa was reduced to a struggle against white supremacy. The problem is that such reductionisms when applied to foreign contexts can become reality because the audiences have no direct knowledge of the context being described. Simplistic labels grow into truth for the audiences (and the editors) back home. They also become reality for the next generation of journalists sent to cover these foreign contexts; who then frame their questions in terms of such learned preconceived labels.

A fourth reason for journalistic misreading is that journalists routinely use binary oppositions when describing foreign contexts. Foreign places are peopled by good guys and bad guys. Some individuals and groups are idealized, while others are demonized and villainized. The process of demonization and idealization is frequently directly related to the foreign policy requirements of one's own hegemonic order. Hence, in an increasingly Anglofied global hegemony, it is the U.S. media's binary oppositions that have increasingly acquired a universalized naturalism. Recent examples are the demonization of leaders not acquiescing to U.S. interests (e.g., Saddam Hussein, Slobodan Milosevic, and Hugo Chávez); while leaders serving U.S. interests (e.g., General Pervez Musharraf) are idealized. Other examples of the demonization and idealization process are Serbs (bad guys) versus Kosavars (good guys), and Saddam's "henchmen" (bad guys) versus "ordinary Iraqis" (good guys). Not surprisingly, those demonized frequently become pariah groups whom one is not just "allowed" to dislike, but one is "supposed" to dislike. Over the past decades pariah groups have included Libyans, Iranians, Afrikaners, Serbs, and Muslim-fundamentalists. Of course, when the good guys fail to behave in ways that accord with media stereotypes, it causes great confusion and consternation—such as when "ordinary Iraqis" failed to welcome Americans as liberators and failed to embrace America's vision for Iraq.

Victim-Villain Discourse

The binary opposition model often slips into a victim-villain discourse, in which victims are portrayed as needing to be rescued from villains. This villain-victimhood discourse allows Nature to be the villain (in the form of natural disasters) and/or possibly some ill-defined villains who are discursively portrayed as bringing about climate change, which then causes natural disasters. Since the 1980s, the villain-victimhood discourse (in its various forms) has become very influential and has even produced a whole industry of NGOs, and aid and humanitarian agencies that specialize in helping "the weak." Those perpetrating the victimizing are often equated with the Anglo folk devil of Hitler. Once such a folk devil is successfully evoked, aggression against the villain can be easily justified (since it involves saving the weak from being victimized).

Not surprisingly, Western military planners and spin doctors have learned to mobilize both the villain-victim and folk-devil discourses. For example, Saddam and his "henchmen" were demonized prior to the 2003 Iraqi War. Similarly, before commencing the 2001 Afghanistan War, Pentagon spin doctors first popularized the idea of liberating Afghan women from the Taliban. These spin doctors recognized that a women's liberation discourse was a useful issue to piggyback upon because it has widespread currency and resonates well with many Western intelligentsia gatekeepers (e.g., journalists, teachers, and university intellectuals). Pentagon spin doctors understood the propaganda value of this theme in getting anti-Taliban stories picked up with minimal critical scrutiny from many Western journalists. For this reason, the head-scarf and grill (Chadri) was mobilized as iconic of Taliban repression of women—a symbol of victimhood justifying war against the Taliban. Similarly, before the 2003 Iraq War Saddam's victimization of Kurds was mobilized (although Turkish repression of Kurds over the border was conveniently ignored).

For the global media machine the most valuable foreign stories are those that can be cast as binary oppositions, in which the weak/victims are helped and/or the villains defeated. In a sense, such news provides a form of collective therapy (Van Ginneken, 1998:32). It is as if Western audiences need "good news stories" to make them feel better. This news as therapy is even more appealing if the audiences can be made to believe they have personally helped the victims (via donations to aid agencies or sending "their" troops to rescue victims). The fall of the Berlin Wall and the end of apartheid are two classic news as therapy stories, with Mandela's inauguration as South Africa's president being the classic example of such a binary opposition/good news/collective therapy portrayal, in which victims were miraculously rescued from villains. The 2003 defeat of Saddam Hussein (represented by the toppling of Saddam's statue in Baghdad) was a similar news as therapy story, until the therapy discourse was challenged by the emergence of Iraqi guerrilla activity.

But the binary opposition model also generates problem groups for the global media—that is, those groups that cannot be unambiguously idealized or villainized. This can happen because they are former pariah groups that now need to be rehabilitated (e.g., Russians after the Soviet Union collapsed and Afghan warlords incorporated into the post-Taliban government). Or they are groups of former allies, who have now become enemies (such as the Iraqis in the Gulf War, or the Indonesians during the Timor War). In such instances, the problem group is often divided into bad guys (supporters of Saddam and the Indonesian military) and good guys (ordinary Iraqis and civilian Indonesians). Other problem groups are allies with dark secrets (e.g., Iraq's and Turkey's repression of Kurds; Indonesia's massacre of Communists and its repression in West Papua, Ache and the Moluccas; and undemocratic allies in places like Pakistan and Saudi Arabia). These problems produce silence—no TV cameras are pointed in this direction.

Then there are problem groups formerly portrayed as victims, who begin behaving in ways that might call into question the old binary opposition model (e.g., repression, corruption, and mismanagement in many African states). The discomfort produced when the old binary oppositions unravel causes the media to fall silent—that is, uncomfortable issues disappear because they are taken off the television screens. The way in which Africa has generally fallen off the news agenda is an example of this, even with clear human rights violations in countries such as Zimbabwe still ongoing.

Similarly, journalists paid scant attention to the enormous post-Soviet social, religious, and ethnic tensions in Yeltsin's Russia, as well as the repression of Russians in some former Soviet states because such stories would get in the way of the preferred postcommunism good-news agenda. Only when the United States began criticizing Putin's undemocratic behavior did the Western media once again begin focusing on Russian transition problems.

Then there are foreign groups enmeshed with U.S.-issues, which prevents their media portrayal in a binary opposition format—for example, despite some striking similarities between Israeli and white South African aggression/repression, the Israelis were never unambiguously cast into the role of villains due to the strength of the U.S. Jewish lobby and Western guilt about the Holocaust. Further, binary oppositions routinely deployed by the media are sometimes shelved when using them would generate too much discomfort—that is, Karim (2000) argues, attention is always drawn to a religious binary opposition when Muslims can be cast as repressing Christians; but is dropped in favor of ethnicity when the reverse is the case.

A fifth reason for journalistic misreadings is that when sent to report on foreign contexts, journalists tend to (subconsciously) select contacts with whom they feel comfortable working—contacts who are as culturally close to them as possible and/or people who confirm their worldviews (Van Ginneken, 1998:91). For example, in non-Western societies, Western journalists generally cultivate contacts among Westernized elites because it is easier (and more culturally comfortable) to associate with and understand people who broadly mobilize the same discourses as oneself. Such contacts also tend to express views that confirm the cultural biases and prejudices of news editors back home (whom journalists have to please.)

Choosing foreign contacts who are culturally proximate to oneself necessarily skews the reports produced and can even build in biases that the journalist may not be aware of. An example can be found in the way Anglo journalists sent to cover South Africa have done their job—that is, for contacts they have favored white Anglos leaning slightly to the left (e.g., opposition politician Helen Suzman), or Anglofied/Westernized blacks (e.g., Anglican Archbishop Tutu.) Such people are culturally proximate to Anglo journalists and so confirm their worldviews. Significantly, foreign correspondents based in Johannesburg have generally lived in affluent suburbs (mostly inhabited by white Anglos and Westernized/Anglicized blacks), socialized with South African Anglos, sent their children to white Anglo schools, and routinely lifted stories from the local English-liberal press. Consequently, the perspectives of one (minority) local interest group gained a disproportionate airing on the international stage. This has necessarily skewed foreign news coverage of South Africa by inadvertently incorporating local struggles into the journalistic picture presented (in an unconscious and unacknowledged way). Ironically, because of this Anglo bias, the voices of the majority of South Africans have seldom been heard in an unmediated and authentic way.

Similarly, in Russia (and other East European countries), the global media have clearly felt more comfortable relying on liberal reformers as contacts and framers. This is partly because their interpretations confirmed what editors back home want to hear, and because the worldviews of liberal reformers tended to be more proximate to those of Western journalists than other Russian constituencies, whose perspectives tended to be rather incomprehensible from within a mainstream (Anglo) global media perspective.

A similar process unfolded in post-Taliban Afghanistan, where Western journalists relied on the interpretations of those inside the Kabul compound—Westernized members of the new government, aid workers, and UN staffers—while shying away from the majority of Afghans because they behaved in ways that were incomprehensible to Western journalists.

A sixth reason for journalistic misreading is that foreign issues are read in terms of home understandings and agendas. For example, the U.S. media have read South Africa's race relations as if they were simply equivalent to U.S. racial problems (Neuman, 1992:112).

Anglo journalists have also tended to assume that the outcomes of Western struggles over secularization, multiparty democracy, and gender equality have a teleological naturalness. Once such struggles are not seen as Western, but as universal, journalists assume they have the right to read (impose) their contemporary measurement criteria, their home battles, and their home agendas into foreign contexts. It also means journalists are licensed to be lazy because they do not have to seriously engage with the difficulties confronting overseas decision makers, but can simply judge them in terms of their home-base contexts. For example, much reporting of China's post-Communist reforms eschew the complexities, contradictions, and dangers confronting the reformers. Not only can this produce misreadings of societies with different socioeconomic trajectories from the Anglo world, but it also produces foreign resentments about Western misunderstanding and interference, as has manifested itself at various times, in locations like China, Iran, Malaysia, Indonesia, and Sudan.

Spin-Doctoring Journalists

When journalists are unfamiliar with an area, the potential for skewing increases dramatically not least because it becomes easier for spin doctors to steer the way journalists view the world.

Because U.S. power underpins the New World Order, the processes whereby Americans make sense of distant places now has real consequences for non-Americans. In particular, the impact of TV news on U.S. policymaking means non-U.S. players interested in impacting on U.S. foreign policy must now pay attention to how they can influence the journalists collecting information about their countries. Not surprisingly, one now finds groups in zones of crisis explicitly using the media (such as CNN and BBC) to try and appeal *directly* to Western audiences (Shaw, 1996:7). The notion of a passive periphery merely receiving information from the core and/or of the South being manipulated by the North cannot be seen as valid. In the emergent global communication system, it is simply wrong to assume the margins are always passive victims, because players on the peripheries also now actively engage in spin doctoring and manipulation of communication variables in an attempt to impact on decisions being made in the United States and the European Union.

Essentially, as the New World Order has shaped up, a number of processes have been modified, including the conduct of international politics, information flows, and the nature of news reporting. A new form of journalistic practice is emerging, driven by new technologies and a growing professionalization (and public relations) of news contacts. In the arena of foreign news, the relationships between newsrooms based in the Western core (USA/EU) and noncore areas have also shifted. New technologies have opened up the possibility of building "newsrooms without walls"—in which journalists and camera operators are free to roam widely, collect material relatively easily from remote sites; maintain regular contact with distant home bases; and easily download audio, visual, and written material into home computers from these distant locations. Air travel also means it is now relatively easy to deploy journalists/camera crews to distant locations to cover breaking stories. Thus it is becoming less important to base journalists in foreign locations, and so the phenomenon of tourist journalism is emerging—when camera crews/journalists fly in; cover stories and (thanks to satellite hookups) file these in real time with home newsrooms; and then fly out to the next story. Tourist journalism overlaps, to some extent, with parachute journalism from an earlier era; however, tourist journalists are in constant contact with their homebases (i.e., they virtually take their newsrooms with them), and piggyback on the comfortable infrastructure built for global tourism. So the new style is more voyeuristic than the old parachute journalists because increasingly, contemporary tourist journalists jet into foreign locations for very limited periods; spend much of their time in sanitized, air-conditioned hotels (where one can also watch CNN); and except for working with an organized industry of local spin doctors and public relations people, they hardly interact at all with the local natives/context.

On the one hand, tourism journalism means that news can (and does) now come from anywhere. It also provides even small governments with a potential communications vehicle with global reach. Nonetheless, this global news machine has an Anglo heart and a center that is very much geared to an American audience. After all, those who try to manipulate the global news machine understand where power resides in the new global hegemony—and so they use the global media machine to try to influence those who count, namely, those who drive the New World Order. Hence, CNN may wish to claim that it is not American and that its staff composition reflects an international focus; but the reality is that CNN has a U.S. homebase; its practices and discourses are Anglo-American; and CNN's influence and importance derive precisely from its status as a communicative conduit to the decision-making heartland of the New Word Order, which is de facto a Pax-Americana.

Tourist journalists can be more easily manipulated than local journalists because they spend short periods of time in unfamiliar places. And given the impact news images can now have on foreign policy formulation in the USA/EU, the tourist journalists necessarily become key targets for spin doctors and public relations operators. So, for example, many CNN staffers have reported an awareness of how governments around the world use CNN to distribute messages globally (Volkmer, 1999:153–155). Manipulation of the global news agenda is in no way unidirectional, although the center of the global news machine does set the broad parameters for what is considered newsworthy. Certainly, players all over the world (large and small) are able to influence this agenda, although to be successful at manipulating the global news agenda (i.e., selling their particular message, and/or successfully capturing the attention of the power brokers of the New World Order) requires playing in terms of the rules (discourses and practices) of the Western news machine (especially the Anglo-American machine). Ultimately, it is not only Western communication players (like U.S. military spin doctors) who are able to spin the global news system; the system can be spin-doctored by players on the margins as well.

A good example of spin-doctoring from the margins was the creation of the South African miracle discourse in 1994 (Louw and Chitty, 2000). A television spectacle was choreographed by South Africa's then ruling-coalition—the African National Congress and National Party (the party responsible for apartheid)—to sell the idea of a miracle transition to democracy in which the good guys won, the bad guys lost and justice triumphed. A scripted stage-managed show was organized (largely by Afrikaner bureaucrats) with tourist journalists in mind and geared to producing the sort of festive television event beloved by global TV news (see Dayan and Katz, 1992:5–12). Ultimately, the key target audience for this public relations spectacular were African Americans because it was hoped that South Africa could use this black constituency (much as Israel used the Jewish lobby) as a conduit to U.S. policymakers. Because most journalists jetted in for a short period (the elections and Mandela's inauguration), it was assumed they would not be in the country long enough to get on top of the situation, and so could be spin-doctored. The South Africans built an International Broadcast Center (IBC) to supply tourist journalists with quality images of the miracle transition, and the facilities for each TV crew to personalize these images with their own voiceovers. The IBC actually made it technically possible for tourist journalists to cover the 1994 elections without ever venturing out into the conflict-ridden South African community. The outcome was a tremendous spin-doctoring success, with almost the whole world watching the same pooled images and receiving the same public relations message—of a miracle, in which South Africans had found each other through negotiation, and in the process had created a social order worthy of foreign investment (Louw and Chitty, 2000:292–293). Within this media spectacular Mandela provided wonderful public relations material because he could be constructed as an icon of liberal reasonableness. For the South African choreographers, attaching to Mandela a saintly aura was invaluable public relations given the worth of "icons and symbolism within global television news" (Volkmer, 1999:106). At the end of the choreographed TV spectacle, the camera crews went home, and South Africa slipped off the global news agenda.

Conclusion

Overall it seems that tourist and other forms of instant international journalism have become a central fixture of the emerging global media machine and newsrooms without walls. For spin doctors on the margins, this can be a good thing, as it provides them with at least some opportunities for influencing the images reaching the key global cities. However, if nonskewed coverage of distant places is the measurement criteria, then the emergence of tourist journalism, festive television events, the televisualizing of diplomacy (and warfare), the closure of discourse through normalizing one set of discourses and practices (those acceptable to Anglo-Americans), and the widespread public relationizing of journalist contacts (Louw, 2005:Chapter 7) must be seen as less welcome developments. But for better or worse, this has become the nature of the new media environment and by extension now appears to be one of the given variables within foreign policy decision making.

BIBLIOGRAPHY

Cohen, A. A., Levy, M. R., Roeh, I., and Gurevitch, M. *Global Newsrooms, Local Audiences*. London: John Libby, 1995.

Dayan, D., and Katz, E. *Media Events: The Live Broadcasting of History*. Cambridge, MA: Harvard University Press, 1992.

Greenfeld, L. *Nationalism. Five Roads to Modernity*. Cambridge, MA: Harvard University Press, 1993.

Hartley, J. *Understanding News*. London: Methuen, 1982.

Karim, K. H. "Covering the South Caucasus and Bosnian Conflicts: Or How the Jihad Model Appears and Disappears." In Malek, A. and Kavoori, A. P. (eds.), *The Global Dynamics of News Coverage and News Agendas*, 177–196. Stamford, CT: Ablex, 2000.

Louw. P. E. *The Media and Political Process*. London: Sage. 2005.

Louw, P. E., and Chitty, N. "South Africa's Miracle Cure: A Stage-Managed TV Spectacular?" In Malek, A. and Kavoori, A. P. (eds.), *The Global Dynamics of News Coverage and News Agendas*, 277–296. Stamford, CT: Ablex, 2000.

Neuman, W. R., Just, M. R., and Crigler, A. N. *Common Knowledge. News and the Construction of Political Meaning*. Chicago: University of Chicago Press, 1992.

Sadkovich, J. J. *The U.S. Media and Yugoslavia, 1991–1995*. Westport, CT: Praeger, 1998.

Said, E. *Covering Islam*. London: Routledge & Kegan Paul, 1981.

Shaw, M. *Civil Society and Media in Global Crisis. Representing Distant Violence*. London: Pinter, 1996.

Tuchman, G. *Making News*. New York: The Free Press, 1978.

Van Ginneken, J. *Understanding Global News*. London: Sage, 1998.

Volkmer, I. *News in the Global Sphere. A Study of CNN and Its Impact on Global Communication*. Luton: University of Luton Press, 1999.

Wallis, R., and Baran, S. *The Known World of Broadcasting News*. London: Routledge, 1990.

Westmoreland, W. C. *A Soldier Reports*. New York: Dell Books, 1980.

Global News

The Fleeting, Elusive but Essential Feature of Global Journalism

ARNOLD S. DE BEER

Stellenbosch University, South Africa

Instant Digital News vis-à-vis Traditional News

In the first section of this fifth edition of *Global Journalism,* a number of issues have been addressed that affect foreign or global journalists worldwide. However, at the end of the day, global journalism is all about news. But what does this elusive concept mean? What does it consist of, and how can one define it; will there be universal acknowledgment if such a definition should exist? As Mowlana (1997:41) put it a decade ago: "The definition of news in many studies falls short of a comprehensive and universally accepted definition. In fact, there is doubt whether there can be a definition of what constitutes news which will be acceptable to all." We are still not closer to a satisfactory definition.

Developments in the digital media news field have not made it easier (see Campbell, 2004). Since 2000 "alternative public or citizen digital journalism" has changed the field of what was traditionally the domain of the formal news agencies, newspapers, radio and TV news stations. In the last year or so we have seen more and more ordinary folk going around their everyday business stumbling upon world breaking news—from school murders in the United States to earthquakes in the UK—and sending cell-phone images to international news organizations, which then send them around the world in a matter of minutes. Others, such as pressure, activists, or revolutionary groups have also discovered the value of even cheap hand-held TV cameras to beam news globally through any international news outlet willing to convey it. The short messages of Osama bin Laden since 9/11 by TV news channels have become known for this. These messages were sent from places where news organizations would traditionally have liked to point out the origin of the news to their audience, but which they could not, since bin Laden's whereabouts were unknown to these news organizations.

The tremendous explosion in Internet news, or rather information or entertainment through sites such as FaceBook, MyTube and You Tube, has also had a serious impact on news as we used to know it. Internet sites such as http://blog.reportwitters.com/archives/ scoop traditional international news outlets (such as was the case with the biggest earthquake in 25 years in February 2008, with Sky News being able to send images from the blog worldwide while a house was rocking in the quake).

The purpose of this chapter, however, is to shed some light on the concept of news and to come to grips with some of the main elements of this elusive term as it is found in traditional global, international journalism, or as it is still often called, foreign reporting.

The Origins and the Concept of News:
An Historical Overview

Over the years, media scholars and media sociologists have applied their minds to this intangible concept (see Tumber, 1999). The approaches range from the functional to the critical, from the biblical (the four apostles being the first great journalists of the present era) to the Marxist (news is produced by the bourgeoisie to enslave the proletariat; see Mowlana, 1994:353–368). In the last part of the previous century and earlier, a number of scholars have tried to shed more light on the term *news*. There were those who believed that news is made or *manufactured* (Cohen and Young, 1973; Roscho, 1975; Tuchman, 1978), and those who described how news is *discovered* (Schudson, 1973), *decided upon* (Gans, 1979) or *selected* (Epstein, 1981). Although not necessarily dealing with news as such, there were studies showing how difficult it is to capture the (news) reality. For instance, news is only the reflection or the image of an event (Boorstin, 1971), and even then it is a question of how real or true the reflection is (Watzlawick, 1977).

Other authors searched for the basic fundamental principles underlying news, including issues such as news values and news criteria (Cohen and Young, 1973; Merrill, 1997). Almost a century ago the German sociologist Max Weber discussed the role and function of journalists as disseminators of ideas in the form of news. A fellow sociologist, Albert Schäffle (1979), studied how people organize the reproduction of symbols (the unique feature of human civilization and the external reflections one perceives) in economically feasible and profitable enterprises called newspapers (Hardt, 1979).

Media and journalism theorists also tried to explain the idea of news by developing theories of the midrange. These include Elisabeth Noelle-Neumann's spiral of silence (1984) and models such as "agenda setting," "uses and gratifications," "information-seeking," and "gatekeeping," which try to explain how news works in society (see McQuail and Windahl, 1981; also see Schudson, 2003).

The question of what news is exactly, and how to define it in precise terms, was still not answered satisfactorily by the turn of the previous century, as the special editions of *Journalism Quarterly* ("How News Is Shaped," 2000:77:2) and "How News Is Constructed" (2001:78:3) testify.

On the other hand, all journalists and consumers of news do have a basic, or almost instinctive, notion of what news is, as the following short discussion of the history of news will show. However one looks at news, especially the international version of it, the idea, if not the modern concept, of news can be found throughout the centuries.

According to most sources, news (new information of topical interest) first appeared on a regular basis in the West when Julius Caesar had a written version of the Senate discussions, called the *acta senatus,* posted on the Forum outside the Senate building for the citizens of

Rome to read. At the same time (A.D. 59) Caesar ordered the daily posting of the *acta diurna* (daily acts). The content of the *acta diurna* was amazingly similar to the news in modern-day newspapers: about Caesar as head of state, about his family, birthdays and funerals of important Romans, trials and executions, wars, and even sports—the outcome of gladiatorial contests. A number of transcriptions were sent to other parts of the Roman Empire, making it the first kind of international newspaper (though it contained only official information).

It was not long before an enterprising Roman named Chrestus began collecting local and international information (from ships landing with merchandise to sell, to bumper crops, to the burning of witches at the stake) and selling these handwritten "newspapers" in local markets. He thus became one of the first journalists (from the Latin *diurnarius,* diary writer). Not unlike today, politicians and other important Romans, such as the writer Cicero (who died in A.D. 43), were very upset about the "sensational" news that Chrestus often "published" in his "newspapers." (For a more detailed description of the early development of international or global news, see Luykx, 1978.)

The first regular daily and weekly newspapers with local and international news appeared in the eighteenth century in Germany. As far as can be established, the very first doctoral dissertation on news (and especially international news) printed in newspapers appeared in 1690, when a German student, Tobias Peucer, published his doctoral dissertation "De Relationibus Novellis" ("On News Reporting") at the University of Leipzig. Apart from a cynical (but often correct?) definition of news being information to satisfy the curiosity of people by (publishing) unimportant and downright worthless material (think about the news of modern-day international celebrities in the tabloids), Peucer also defined news as the notification of a variety of matters that occurred recently in various places in the world (see de Beer, Van Ryneveld, and Schreiner, 2000:9; see also Atwood and de Beer, 2002). People's desire to learn things unknown to them (or thirst for the latest information, as Peucer puts it) was such that even 300 years ago, newspapers fulfilled the role of answering the basic question in journalism as researched by Peucer: *Ecquid novi*? ("What is new?" or "What is the news?" For a translation of this part of Peucer's dissertation, see de Beer, Van Ryneveld, and Schreiner, 2000:57).

Part of the problem of finding a generally accepted version of what news is has been the trend in journalism circles for the past few decades of regarding the practice of journalistic skills as more important and relevant than the development of sound conceptual and theoretical foundations of what actually constitutes news. Sometimes it seemed that journalists who could type fast and reach deadlines under pressure were more valued than those who would first stall the story to consider newsworthy issues on a more abstract and theoretical level (even if this was done for a mere few seconds of reflection; see later the discussion under "News Values"). Consequently, since there are no hard and fast rules of exactly what defines news, journalists tend to familiarize themselves with the concept of news and related aspects such as newsworthiness and news values through a process of "osmosis" or newsroom socialization (Breed, 1956; Tuchman, 1978). The theoretical study of news therefore often becomes quite esoteric, leaving journalists without credible criteria with which to define the concept news. (See later the discussion on news values.) As a result, although the planning, gathering, processing, distributing, and need for news as a specific variety of information have evolved on a high level over the past few decades, especially on a technical-practical level, academic journalism and the scientific analysis of the fundamental mechanisms of news still need to come to pass.

As foretold by Alvin Toffler in *Future Shock* (1977), Western civilization's most basic activity in the twenty-first century—communication—has been the subject of radical and fundamental transformations and alterations, as the third wave of change, the Information Revolution, came into existence (Toffler, 1980). The arrival of the agricultural age (the first wave of change) and the launch of the second wave (the Industrial Revolution) paved the way for the third wave, in which the development of electronic superhighways and information applications such as news have an impact on every level of everyday human activity. Naturally, these changes have influenced the media as a primary source of information (e.g., McQuail, 2000:Chapter 6). Journalism researchers, teachers, and students, therefore, not only should be versed in the art of technical journalistic competencies (such as finding, writing, and editing the news), but also should contribute to the science of journalism by conceptualizing and confronting communication challenges and problems on theoretical and critical levels. It remains an essential and often elusive ideal to educate potential journalists, and especially foreign correspondents, not only in the practicalities of news but also in the scientific analysis of news and all its related complexities. This is what this book purports to do.

One of the main problems media executives struggle with is how to present international news to audiences who are not really interested in news events occurring in countries whose names they cannot even spell (however, also see Rantanen, 2005). Another problem executives have to deal with is how much "uninteresting" global news they can afford to publish without losing their audiences and profits (see, for instance, Hoge, 1997; Seaton, 2002; Shaw, 2002). For example, researchers at Media Tenor, an international institute for media analysis, cite and analyze which stories are deemed more newsworthy than others, according to frequency in coverage and the tone in which individual stories are written and published. Year after year they find that in most Western countries international news takes a back seat to national and local news (see www.mediatenor.com; Malek and Kavoori, 2000; McCombs, 1997 on the issue of the media's agenda-setting function).

So-called "bad news," however (see Glasgow University Media Group, 1976) or events of conflict (see Gilboa, 2002), such as the attack on the World Trade Center in New York City on September 11, 2001, is always big news, especially when they are events that can be described and shown on television in detail (such as the continuing wars in Iraq and Afghanistan, e.g. Mellor, 2005). On the other hand, trends, such as the HIV/AIDS epidemic or famine, are more difficult to relate as news. This is demonstrated time and again by Media Tenor analyses of different media in countries such as the United States, the United Kingdom, and Germany. Foreign news is placed on the backburner unless it is related to events such as those described above (bad news events) or sporting events, such as the Olympic Games in 2008 in China and the Soccer World Cup in 2010 in South Afria (see *Media Tenor,* www.mediatenor.com, which analyzes global news on a daily basis).

Even so, news about the societal impact of sex workers, violence, and drugs; the role of the Internet in society and its effect on news; the relationship between news, terror, and conflict; and gender issues are recent trends that have made headlines (Bromley and Bowles, 1995; Kamalipour and Rampal, 2001; Ojajävari, 2001; Schechter, 2002). As Fulton (1998, quoting from Neil Postman) argues, it is not so much the topics of news themselves that cause problems but rather the way journalists see and experience news and the way media organizations present news to their audiences. In this regard, Postman argues that journalists have not adapted to the world they helped create. In the nineteenth century, the problem facing journalism was the scarcity of information. Today the problem is a glut of information.

The question is no longer how to get more diverse forms or topics of news in the media but how to decide what is significant and relevant information for the news process and how to get rid of unwanted information that will not make it to the news columns and broadcasts. The glut of information or unconnected data on personal digital hand-held and other computers make this an importan issue to investigate in future.

The Concept News

As we have seen, defining the phenomenon of news is not an easy task. News does not exist in reality outside of the individual and therefore does not qualify as an occurrence or event per se. Within the Western context, news is regarded as the reporting in the media of actual issues and events that occur before, during, or after actual incidents transpire.

News as a concept is not synonymous with an event, however. Instead, news can be seen as an attempt by individual journalists and their media organizations to capture the essential framework of particular events and trends by retelling them in the form of news reports. Such activities are usually carried out by journalists working within the context of specific news policies defined by particular cultural, political, economical, ethical, and journalistic frames of reference. The journalistic frames of reference are constructed by means of various factors that may include the nature of the publication, the policies of the institution, the policy of what is considered newsworthy or of special news value, the editorial organization of the publication, the quality of competition with other forms of media, the demographic profile of the readers, and the accompanying wants and needs of the publication's audience. All these elements should then again be considered against the background of societal forces, such as the political, economic, cultural, technical, geographic, and general media setup of a particular country (Hiebert, Ungurait, and Bohn, 1991; see, for instance, Wilson and Gutiérrez, 1995 on the way race and culture have an impact on what becomes news and what does not.)

Clearly, news cannot be reduced to a one-dimensional formula of practical knowledge and practices (such as the "definition" of news being that "when a dog bites the mailperson it is not news, but when the mailperson bites the dog, it is"). Our presence within the information age demands solid practical training in journalism, as well as journalistic scholarship with appropriate academic-theoretical approaches. Consequently, scholars of news often view the topic from their own specific paradigmatic point of view and treat it within a particular context, such as the Glasgow University Media Group's range of projects on bad news (see also Eldridge, 2000).

One rather easy way to solve the problem of what exactly one means by the word "news" is to consult a dictionary. *The South African Oxford Pocket Dictionary* (Branford, 1994:640) defines news as "information about important or recent events, when published or broadcast." This seems simple enough, but it does not address all the questions raised by such a definition. The *Dictionary of Communication and Media Studies* (Watson and Hill, 1997:116) defines news as the construction of reality by means of a production process providing "a familiar discourse, based on common sense and precedent."

And the common modern present-day source of information on all shades and shapes, Wikipedia.com, says news is "any *new information* or information on current events which is presented by print, broadcast, Internet, or word of mouth to a third party or mass audience."

The part about "word of mouth" has traditionally followed on the publication of news by the traditional media, but as we have seen earlier, more and more nonjournalists (see Chapter 10 in this edition) are becoming part of the news process as we used to know it.

Newspaper people also have their own versions of what news is. The British press baron Lord Northcliff once declared, "News is what somebody somewhere wants to suppress; all the rest is advertising," while a news scholar, such as Dennis MacShanj, sees news as "conflict; hardship and danger to the community; the unusual (oddity, novelty); scandal and individualism based on the latter attributes of news" (Watson and Hill, 1997).

Or perhaps news can be defined by a very simple notion: "News is what newspaper men make it," as Gieber (1964:180) wrote. But—and this is an important point in our quest for more knowledge about the concept of news—Gieber concludes that while news might be what newspaper people make it, "Until we understand better the social forces which bear on the reporting of news, we will never understand what news is" (Gieber, 1964:180).

We will now discuss a few of the approaches used by media scholars to understand and describe news.

Objectivity and Reality

One way to describe news is to state that it is an "objective" account in the media of a recent newsworthy event or trend. The Western journalistic tradition is one that, for the past century, has prided itself on practicing a custom that is based purely on objective news analysis and presentation. It is the journalistic claim that professionalism is seated within the ability to objectively judge and report on newsworthy events (Janowitz, 1975:618). According to this traditional perspective of objectivity, the journalist is an impartial observer who gathers, processes, and imparts news in such a manner that it can be vividly and concretely verified by the sensory capabilities of his or her readers (Atkins, 1977:27).

Although objectivity developed into the foremost trait to empower journalists (Tuchman, 1978:123), it is notable that journalists (and others) show very little awareness of what the concept truly entails. Objectivity in journalism has not necessarily established itself as a professional standard per se, but rather has developed as a kind of organizational imperative or belief by which journalists are required to perform their work. In reality, objectivity does not equal a professional tradition. Instead, it frequently involves a routine post hoc rationale by which journalists justify their professional behavior and activity.

For practical as well as academic journalism, the problem of objectivity presents two cumbersome questions: How do journalists evaluate news within reality, and what are the impact and the degrees of influence within reality that impinge on such evaluations?

Within the science of communication (and for a large part also within practical journalism) it has been suggested over the years that objectivity in journalism cannot qualify as a positivistic, verifiable concept (Drew, 1973; Atkins, 1977). As proposed by Cillié (1967:5), journalism does not exist as a neutral or an objective mirror image of reality as it often chooses to claim: "The newspaper, seen in its totality, is far more related to a portrait, an impressionistic portrait, than a mirror or a photo image. We select and accentuate; we cannot do otherwise."

For this reason researchers (Rivet, 1976:96) have concluded that objective journalism is not possible—that in fact it is a myth (Sigelman, 1973:133)—indicating that journalists move between two antagonistic poles (Heménus, 1976:102). On the one hand, there exists the inclination to report on reality in compliance with each individual journalist's value system (De Fleur,1973: 155–172). On the other hand, the pressures of factual circumstances influence the value systems and worldviews of journalists as they present themselves within the reality in which the journalists find themselves, and vice versa (Snyman, 1994). Therefore, one can assume that each journalist's interpretation of a news event is just as subjective as the reader's version of an article at the time it is read (Rosengren, 1978:42). One reason for this is that the journalist essentially decides what should and should not be perceived as news but always within the news policy of the media he or she works for and the circumstances surrounding the story (e.g., being in a war zone or working under political pressure.) It is suggested, then, that the arrangement (and omission) of facts on a news page or news broadcast reveals its author's opinions and intentions, as well as those of the news medium and the society in which the journalist operates.

Another basic difficulty in the process of structuring news is that the words used to convey and symbolize meaning are by nature haphazard. As stated by Richards (1936:69) and Brooks (1978:64), words themselves do not have meaning, but humans as communicators attribute meaning to words according to social and psychological factors. Each reader of a news article will also assign his or her own interpretation of its content—the principle of the so called active audience such as encapsulated in Hall's (1981) model of the encoding and decoding model, later applied in a classic study by Morley (1980) on the British program *Nationwide*.

For the disciplines of journalism and mass communication, the issue of objective, impartial reporting on the one hand and subjective, partial treatment of news events on the other thus involves an especially delicate and problematic situation.

News Values

Another way to look at news is to identify the different news values that constitute news. These "values" are the "professional codes used in the selection, construction, and presentation of news stories in corporately produced press and broadcasting" (O'Sullivan, Hartley, Saunders, and Fiske, 1983:153). As the old adage says, "Old news is no news." Therefore, in journalism variables such as time and distance play significant roles in what does and does not constitute news. As Christians (1981:64) puts it: "In reporting there is a premium on rapid decisions rather than on extended deliberation, on response rather than reflection. The person (journalist) of action is valued; the intellectual is frequently suspect." From this, one could conclude that Christians advocates that journalistic practices be oriented toward systematically investigating substantive issues, so as to gain more informed insight into the prevalence of such realities. The practice of merely processing information into news before a certain deadline is reached should be abandoned.

The German sociologist Albert Schäffle already wrote in 1881 (see Hardt, 1979:68) that the typical journalist lives only for day-to-day news and often feels and ponders on issues as the result of routine and mechanistic requirements of the trade, rather than critically developing and materializing intellectual thoughts. "News values such as its other sister concept–new–are ambiguous." As Hall (1973:181) stated: "News values are one of the most opaque structures of meaning in modern society. All journalists are supposed to possess it; few can or are willing to identify and define it." Yet, Hall argues, of the millions of events that occur around the world, only a very tiny portion become salient as "potential news stories." Of this small portion, a smaller fraction is actually produced as news.

A number of authors of journalism textbooks have made lists of news values that they believe constitute news. An example is that given by Harriss, Leiter, and Johnson (1992:27–33). According to these authors, the intrinsic characteristics of news values are as follows:

> Conflict (tension, surprise)
>
> Progress (triumph, achievement)
>
> Disaster (defeat, destruction)
>
> Consequence (effect of individuals or community)
>
> Prominence (the well known or famous)
>
> Novelty (the unusual or emotional)

In their groundbreaking work on foreign news, Galtung and Ruge (1965) identified nine elements or news factors that make up news selection, and these are still applicable today. These are:

- *Time span*: The event should best fit the time schedule of the news medium.
- *Intensity or threshold value*: Magnitude or sudden increase in the normal level of events.
- *Clarity/lack of ambiguity*: A story with clear facts would rather be published.
- *Cultural proximity or relevance*: The closer the event, the better.
- *Consonance*: Stories that are "expected"—for instance, corruption in certain countries—are more likely to be selected.
- *Unexpectedness*: The more unusual or unpredictable (also the reverse of consonance) will add to a story's news value.
- *Continuity*: Once a story is "running" there will be some momentum to carry it further.
- *Composition*: News stories should normally fit the overall balance of the medium.
- *Sociocultural values* of the society and the gatekeepers at the particular news medium.

These news values should be tied with the traditional journalistic 5 Ws and the H, or as Peucer showed 300 years ago (de Beer et al., 2000:17):

> The character in the event (who)
>
> The event itself (what)
>
> The cause (why)

The place (where)

The time (when)

The manner (how)

Elsewhere, de Beer (2000:257) has combined the different news values cited in journalism textbooks in a Distance-Intensity Scale: the nearer the news event and the higher the intensity of the event, the bigger the news value would be:

Distance Scale

Time (the closer to the event, the higher the news value)

Proximity (ditto)

Sociopsychological (ditto)

Intensity Scale

Status quo (the bigger the impact on the status quo, the bigger the news value)

Magnitude (single/plural; for example, one important politician versus many people dying in an accident)

Novelty (human interest, unusual events)

The higher the event scores on all or a number of these values, the more likely will the event "become" news. For instance, Iraq is quite far from the United States, but when loved ones are sent off to war in that region, it becomes very close in terms of the sociopsychological scale for people living in the United States. One general dying in such a war will be big news, bigger than the death of one GI. But a thousand GIs dying in one clash is likely to overtake the "story" of the general's death in terms of news value. And if one GI dies or saves a number of fellow GIs in an unusual event, this might also outstrip the death of the general on the news value scale. Fowler (1991:15–19, applied to the South African apartheid context by Oosthuizen, 2001:455) has pointed out that these news values are not ideologically neutral but can lead to a divisive view of society based on a distinction between "us" and "them," as was clear, for example, in the way different nations, organizations, media, and individuals viewed the U.S. stance on the war or invasion—depending on one's point of view—against Iraq in 2003 (see, for instance, McGuire, 2003).

News Preferences

The quantitative (and empirical) evaluation of news (elements) is a potentially fertile field for journalistic investigation to get closer to this elusive concept. Whether the professional actually addresses the reader's news preferences is a particularly worthwhile inquiry. Are journalists aware of what their readers want to know? More often than not there appear to be disparities between what the professional journalist deems an appropriate view on reality and what the reader perceives as a suitable explanation of reality (Bagdikian, 1973:134).

Reading Habits

Regardless of how the definition of news changes over the next few decades, the question that remains is whether people will in the future still satiate their informational hunger by getting "their news" through traditional media such as newspapers, news magazines, television, and radio.

The electronic age has introduced new modalities of communication, and the human activities that surround these innovations may also alter drastically (McQuail, 2000). One of the biggest threats to the survival of the printed media is readers' lack of motivation to engage in the "trouble" of reading or their inability to do so. Edwin Yoder (1981:A18), senior editor of the *Washington Star,* wrote more than two decades ago that one of the main reasons for the death of this renowned institution was the public's increased inability to read. This condition has nothing to do with the fact that electronic media such as television package news in a more attractive form, but rather stems from the fact that these media present news in an ever-increasing condition of pseudo-knowledge (Boorstin, 1971). In light of McLuhan's (1973) conception of the medium is the message, the illusion is created that by getting news from television one becomes more knowledgeable by looking at visual news images and listening to audio versions and that the need to read about these news events is becoming more and more obsolete.

Related to this phenomenon is the increasing tendency among children to spend time in malls or at home playing video games rather than reading. In fact, Yoder (1981:A18) believes that the *Washington Star* probably perished because of the growing number of cultures in which reading is performed without comprehension. Therefore, it is of the utmost importance to research such issues as reading habits in order to ascertain whether news presented in the traditional media still has a place within modern-day society.

New News Concepts

If we accept that in the modern industrialized age news can still be regarded as a particular form of information, which modern humans need for their survival, there is still the open question of whether the concept of traditional news will remain the conventional standard in the decades to come, especially in international news. Such is the case with so-called good news, which is still commonly regarded as none-newsworthy. Instead, the focus of newspeople and news organizations, with regard to foreign news as well, still seems to center on conflicts, the negative, and the abnormal.

This above-mentioned tradition has its roots in the custom of qualifying news according to longstanding news values, such as timeliness, changes in the status quo, and the peculiarity of events that make it potentially newsworthy. Often the end product, when it finally reaches the receiver, is an incomplete, summarized, and superficial representation of reality. It also remains an open question whether the "bad news syndrome" will continue its reign. In a period in which the individual is overwhelmed by enormous amounts of information (Toffler, 1980), it is essential to know whether the concept of conflict, rather than cooperation and harmony, will spur the making of a good story. Clearly, then, not only do news values need to be scrutinized, but also those themes that the profession considers newsworthy must be studied.

Training and Education in Journalism

An issue often mentioned when news is discussed is the training and education of journalists. South Africa offers a very clear example of this at the University of Natal, where Keyan Tomaselli and his group work very close to the lines taken by the Birmingham group. They consider news quite differently from, say, University of Northwest (Potchefstroom, where for a number of years news was seen and dealt with in a very functional, pragmatic, and eclectic paradigm. In the same fashion, Rhodes's journalism department is very much a part of transformation processes in the country, and during the apartheid years news was not necessarily considered within an Anglo-American objective "style" (de Beer and Steyn, 2002; de Beer and Tomaselli, 2000; Steenveld, 2002). In other words, students schooled in an anti-apartheid and transformational environment will have different views on news than those schooled within the apartheid or racist dogma (Jackson, 1993; Louw, 1993; Sanders, 2000; Switzer and Adhikari, 2000; see the special editions of *Rhodes Journalism Review* on racism in the media [2000] and the Internet [1995]).

But nowhere is a journalist's concept of news influenced more than in the way he or she is taught what is right and wrong, what is truthful and what is a plain lie. How far can one stretch the limits of one's own conscience (e.g., stealing a picture from a bereaved family in order to scoop competition with a front-page photo)? At a weeklong seminar in the United States on media ethics, attended by the author of this chapter, one senior media ethics scholar produced what he called "the tool box of journalism ethics." One of his tools was the lie, which he argued could be used very successfully under certain circumstances. Obviously, his students will approach his concept of news differently from students who are taught always to seek the truth and never to knowingly lie. The problem with this issue is that journalism ethics research receives very little attention at most universities. However, Starck (2002:142) shows that research supports the idea that students might think "more extensively and deeply" about ethical issues but that instruction does not change their moral values. The fact that journalism ethics receives relatively little attention at universities would also affect this.

Further complicating the issue is the question of whether there are ethical journalistic principles that may be universally applied when deciding on what is news and what is not. For instance, could the principle of truth-telling (see above) necessarily be applied across all cultures? For example, Starck (2000:140) describes how leading journalism and ethics scholars struggled with this concept when Thomas Cooper came up with three potential ethical elements as "candidates for universal status": the quest for truth, the desire for responsibility, and the call for free expression. Over the years, media ethics scholar Clifford Christians (Christians, Ferré, and Fackler, 1993) developed the idea of a community-based approach to media ethics. The basis of his argument is that the journalist should be led by a love for the human community in the form of *caritas* (agape) in searching for news. "We . . . are governed not by autonomous rationality, but by what we love most with our whole heart as whole persons" (Christians, Ferré, and Fackler, 1993:194–195).

Snyman (1994) elaborates on this idea in his deontological approach to media ethics and in the concept of the *liefdevolle persoonsbehartiging* (in German, *personen detreuing*). There is no easy and direct translation for this concept, but in general it relates to concepts such as caring for the other, looking after the other, showing concern or having consideration for the other, and even promoting, serving, or furthering the needs and interests of the other. Even though it is not exactly the same, *persoonsbehartiging* closely relates to the concept of personhood (Christians, Ferré, and Fackler, 1993:194–195). However, Christians and his co-authors warn that a "communitarian" approach to journalism (based on personhood) might become "Orwellian at the point where other institutions so constrain the press that it ceases to bear its own fruit and merely shades another pasture" (Christians, Ferré, and Fackler, 1993:7).

Media ethics scholar John Merrill (1997) devised a definition that journalists could apply when reporting on their own country or other countries. According to Merrill (1997:76), from a deontological departure of ethics and based on the TUFF outline, news stories should be Truthful, Unbiased, Full, and Fair. But this is not as easy as it seems. As Fuller (2001:8) quotes Kovach and Rosenstiel, truth is the "first and most confusing principle of journalism." What might look like light at the end of the tunnel for one journalist might be an oncoming train for another, and in war, as in international news about wars, truth is often the very first casualty.

In fact, it is not only journalists working in the "real world" who struggle with what is news and what is not. Journalism teachers, researchers, and authors face the same problem. Academic research journals around the world also struggle with the concept of news and present to their readers updated results of the elements that are argued to make up the news. In this regard *Journalism and Mass Communication Quarterly,* 2000 (vol. 77, no. 2) dealt with the topic of how news is shaped, while in 2002 (vol. 79, no. 1) the journal explored news content and consequences as special issue topics. Although coverage of international news can be traced back to the seventeenth century, unfortunately, relatively few research projects were turned into books (see, for instance, Fascell, 1979; Hachten, 1999; Malek and Kavoori, 2000; also see the special edition of *Ecquid Novi,* 1997 [vol. 18, no. 2] on news flow.)

One can also learn more about the content of news in a global or international context by looking at publications dealing specifically with news reporting from different continents and countries. (For example, see Harrison and Palmer, 1986; Mkhond, 1993; Peterson, 2000). Many of these studies relate to news flow projects (e.g., Malek and Kavoori, 2000).

In the long run, international reporters and foreign correspondents will ask themselves (mostly by instinct), How does this event score on the news level scale? Will my news medium, given its news policy (e.g., will it help sell the publication?) be interested in this story? Will other media carry the story or is it a scoop? Will it be possible to get the story out (of a war zone) in time to reach a deadline? And even with these questions answered in the positive, we have not yet touched on issues such as media freedom, media ethics, and media controversies dealt with earlier in different chapters. That's the fascinating and elusive nature of news.

BIBLIOGRAPHY

Atkins, G. "In Search of New Objectivity." In Sellers, L. S. and Rivers, W. L. *Mass Media Issues,* 203–243. Englewood Cliffs, NJ: Prentice-Hall, 1977.

Atwood, R. A., and de Beer, A. S. "The Origins of Academic News Research: The Case of Tobias Peucer's 'De relationibus novellis' (1690)." *Journalism Studies* 2, No. 1 (2002), 485–496.

Bagdikian, W. H. "Professional Personnel and Organizational Structure in the Mass Media." In Davison, W. P. and Yu, F.T.C. (eds.), *Mass Communication Research: Major Issues and Future Directions,* 122–141. New York: Praeger, 1973.

Boorstin, D. J. *The Image: A Guide to Pseudo-Events in America.* New York: Atheneum, 1971.

Branford, W. (ed.). *The South African Oxford Pocket Dictionary of Current English.* Cape Town: Oxford University Press, 1994.

Breed, W. "Social Control in the Newsroom." *Social Forces* 33 (1956), 323–335.

Bromley, R. V., and Bowles, D. "Impact of Internet on Use of Traditional Media." *Newspaper Research Journal* 16, No. 2 (1995), 14–27.

Brooks, W. D. *Speech Communication.* Dubuque, IA: Brown, 1978.

Campbell, V. *Information Age Journalism. Journalism in an International Context.* New York: Arnold, 2004.

Christians, C. G. "Journalism Ethics in a Double Bind." *Ecquid Novi* 2, No. 2 (1981), 61–68.

Christians, C. G., Ferré, J. P. and Fackler, P. M. *Good News: Social Ethics and the Press.* New York: Oxford University Press, 1993.

Cillié, P. J. "Koerante en Koerantmense Vir Ons Tyd" (Newspapers and Newspaper People of Our Time). Unpublished paper, journalism seminar. University of Stellenbosch, 1967.

Cohen, S., and Young, J. (eds.). *The Manufacture of News: Deviance Controversies, and Alternatives.* Englewood Cliffs, NJ: Prentice-Hall, 1973.

de Beer, A. S. "The Professional Teaching of Journalism as a Science Approach: An Introduction." *Ecquid Novi* 16, Nos. 1 and 2 (1995), 3–52.

———. "New Mirror in a New South Africa? International News Flow and News Selection at the Afrikaans Daily, Beeld." In Malek, A., and Kavoori, A. P. (eds.), *The Global Dynamics of News: Studies in International News Coverage and News Agenda,* 249–276. Stamford, CT: Ablex, 2000.

de Beer, A. S., and Steyn, E. F. "Towards Defining News in the South African Context: The Media as Generator or Mediator of Conflict." *South African Journal of Sociology* 27, No. 3 (1996), 90–97.

de Beer, A. S., and Steyn, E. F. (eds.) "Focus on Journalism Skills." *Ecquid Novi* 23, No. 1 (2002) (Special issue)

de Beer, A.S., and Tomaselli, K. G. "South African Journalism and Mass Communication Scholarship: Negotiating Ideological Schisms". *Journalism Studies* 1, No. 1 (2000), 9–35.

de Beer, A. S., Van Ryneveld, L. F. and Schreiner, W. N. "Leipzig: From Tobias Peucer's 'De relationibus novellis' (1690) to Ecquid Novi." *Ecquid Novi* 21, No. 1 (2000), 6–61.

De Fleur, M. L. *Theories of Mass Communication.* New York: David McKay, 1973.

Drew, D. G. "Attitude toward a News Source, Expected Reporter–Source Interaction and Journalistic Objectivity." Ph.D. diss., Indiana University, Bloomington, 1973.

Eldridge, J. "The Contribution of the Glasgow Media Group to the Study of Television and Print Journalism." *Journalism Studies* 1, No. 1 (2000), 13–129.

Epstein, E. J. "The Selection of Reality." In Abel, A. (ed.), *What's News: The Media in American Society,* 119–132. San Francisco: Institute for Contemporary Studies, 1981.

Fascell, D. B. *International News: Freedom under Attack.* London: Sage, 1979.

Fowler, R. *Language in the News. Discourse and Ideology in the Press.* London: Routledge, 1991.

Fuller, J. "Making the Truth an Idea That Journalists Can Believe Again." *Nieman Reports* 55, No. 2 (2001), 8.

Fulton, K. "A Tour of Our Uncertain Future." In Harper, C. (ed.), *What's Next in Mass Communication?* New York: St. Martin's, 1998.

Galtung, J., and Ruge, M. H. "The Structure of Foreign News." *Journal of Peace Research* 2 (1965), 64–90.

Gans, H. J. *Deciding What's News: A Study of CBS Evening News, NBC Nightly News, "Newsweek," and "Time."* New York: Vintage, 1979.

Gieber, W. "News Is What Newspapermen Make It." In Dexter, L. A. and White, D. M. (eds.), *People, Society and Mass Communications.* New York: Free Press of Glencoe, 1964.

Gilboa, E. (ed.),. *Media and Conflict: Framing Issues, Making Policy, Shaping Opinions.* Ardsley, NY: Transnational, 2002.

Glasgow University Media Group. *Bad News.* London: Routledge and Kegan Paul, 1976.

Hachten, W. A. *The World News Prism: Changing Media of International Communication.* Ames: Iowa State University Press, 1999.

Hall, S. "The Determinations of News Photographs." In Cohen, S. and Young, J. (eds.), *The Manufacture of News: Deviance Social Problems and the Mass Media,* 176–190. London: Constable, 1973.

———. "Encoding/Decoding." In Hall, S., Hobson, D., Lowe, A., and Willis, P. (eds.), *Culture, Media, Language.* London: Hutchinson, 1981.

Hardt, H. *Social Theories of the Press: Early German and American Perspectives.* London: Sage, 1979.

Harrison, P., and Palmer, R. *News Out of Africa: Biafra to Ban Aid.* London: Hilary Shipman, 1986.

Harriss, J., Leiter, K., and Johnson, S. *The Complete Reporter: Fundamentals of News Gathering, Writing, and Editing.* New York: Macmillan, 1992.

Heménus, P. "Objectivity in News Transmission." *Journal of Communication* 26 (1976), 102–107.

Hiebert, R. E., Ungurait, D. F., and Bohn, T. W. *Mass Media VI. An Introduction to Modern Communication.* New York: Longman, 1991.

Hoge, J. F. "Foreign News: Who Gives a Damn?" Available: http://cjr.rog/year/97/6/foreign.asp. Accessed October, 2002.

Jackson, G. S. *Breaking Story: The South African Press.* Boulder, CO: Westview Press, 1993.

Janowitz, M. "Professional Models in Journalism: The Gatekeeper and the Advocate." *Journalism Quarterly* 52 (1975), 618–626, 662.

Kamalipour, Y., and Rampal, K. R. (eds.). *Media, Sex, Violence and Drugs in the Global Village.* Oxford: Rowman and Littlefield, 2001.

Louw, P. E. *South African Media Policy: Debates of the 1990s.* Bellville, South Africa: Anthroppos, 1993.

Luykx, T. *Evolutie van de communicatie media.* Brussels: Elsevier, 1978.

Malek, A., and Kavoori, A. P. (eds.). *The Global Dynamics of News: Studies in International News Coverage and News Agendas.* Stamford, CT: Ablex, 2000.

McCombs, M. "New Frontiers in Agenda Setting: Agendas of Attribute and Frames." *Mass Communication Review* 24, Nos 1 and 2 (1997), 32–52.

McGuire, S. "What, Me Worry?" *Newsweek,* March 3, 2003, 10–14.

McLuhan, M. *Understanding Media: The Extensions of Man.* London: Sphere, 1973.

McQuail, D. *McQuail's Mass Communication Theory.* London: Sage, 2000.

McQuail, D., and Windahl, S. *Communication Models for the Study of Mass Communications.* London: Longman, 1981.

Mellor, N. *The Making of Arab News.* New York: Rowman & Littlefield, 2005.

Merrill, J. C. *Journalism Ethics: Philosophical Foundations for News Media.* NewYork: St. Martin's, 1997.

Morley, D. *The Nationwide Audience.* London: British Film Institute, 1980.

Mowlana, H. "International Communication Research in the 21st Century: From Functionalism to Postmodern and Beyond." In Hamelink, C. J., and Linn, O. (eds.), *Mass Communication Research on Problems and Policies: The Art of Asking the Right Questions in Honor of James D. Halloran.* Norwood, NJ: Ablex, 1994.

———. *Global Information and World Communication: New Frontiers in International Relations.* London: Sage, 1997.

Noelle-Neuman, E. *The Spiral of Silence: Public Opinion—Our Social Skin.* Chicago: University of Chicago Press, 1984.

O'Sullivan, T., Hartley, J., Saunders, D., and Fiske, J. *Key Concepts in Communication.* London: Methuen, 1983.

Ojajävari, S. "From Talking Heads to Walking Bodies: Challenging the Masculinity of News." In Kivikuru, U. (ed.), *Contesting the Frontier Media and Dimension of Identity,* 209–225. Göteborg: Nordicom, 2001.

Oosthuizen, L. M. "A Critical Assessment of News." In Fourie, P. J. (ed.), *Media Studies,* 447–468. Lansdowne: Juta, 2001.

Peterson, S. *Me Against My Brother: At War in Somalia, Sudan, and Rwanda.* London: Routledge, 2000.

Rantanen, T. *The Media and Globalization.* London: Sage, 2005.

Richards, I. A. *The Philosophy of Rhetoric.* New York: Oxford University Press, 1936.

Rivet, J. "Ecriture et journaliste: De l'opinion—Événement, l'ôpinion." *Communication et Information* 1, No. 2 (1976), 75–96.

Roscho, B. *Newsmaking.* Chicago: University of Chicago Press, 1975.

Rosengren, K. E. "Vertrekking in Het Nieuws: Methoden en Begrippen." *Massacommunicatie* 6, No. 2 (1978), 37–47.

Sanders, J. *South Africa and the International Media 1972–1979: A Struggle for Representation.* London: Frank Cass, 2000.

Schäffle, A. "The Nerves of Society." In Hardt, M. (ed.), *Social Theories of the Press: Early German American Perspectives,* 41–74. London: Sage, 1979.

Schechter, D. *Media Wars: News at a Time of Terror. Dissecting Media Coverage after 9/11.* Bonn: Innovatio, 2002.

Schudson, M. *Discovering the News: A Social History of American Newspapers.* New York: Basic Books, 1973.

———. *The Sociology of News.* New York: Norton, 2003.

Seaton, E. "The Diminishing Use of Foreign News Reporting." Available: http://asne.org/ideas/ seatonmoscow. Accessed October 13, 2002.

Shaw, D. "Foreign News Shrinks in an Era of Globalization." Available: http://www.commondreams.org/ headlines, 2002. Accessed October 13, 2002.

Sigelman, L. "Reporting the News: An Organizational Analysis." *American Journal of Sociology* 79 (1973), 132–151.

Snyman, P. G. "Media Ethics: A Deontological Approach." *Ecquid Novi* 15, No. 1 (1994), 43–70.

Steenveld, L. (ed.). *Training for Media Transformation and Democracy.* Grahamstown, South Africa: South African National Editor's Forum/Independent Newspapers Chair of Media Transformation, 2002.

Switzer, L., and Adhikari, M. "South Africa's Resistance Press: Alternative Voices in the Last Generation under Apartheid." *Freepress* 24, 4–6 (2000).

Toffler, A. *Future Shock.* New York: Random House, 1977.

Toffler, A. *The Third Wave.* London: Collins, 1980.

Tuchman, G. *Making News: A Study in the Construction of Reality.* New York: The Free Press, 1978.

Tumber, H. (ed.). *News. A Reader.* Oxford: Oxford University Press, 1999.

Watson, J., and Hill, A. *A Dictionary of Communication and Media Studies.* London: Arnold, 1997.

Watzlawick, P. *How Real Is Real? Confusion, Disinformation, Communication. An Anecdotal Introduction to Communications Theory.* New York: Vintage Books, 1977.

Wilson, C. C., and Gutiérrez, F. *Race, Multiculturalism, and the Media: From Mass to Class Communication.* Thousand Oaks, CA.: Sage, 1995.

Yoder, E. M. "Reasoned Dialogue of the Printed Word Remain Essential for Democracy". *The Washington Star,* August 7, 1981, A18.

PART THREE

Global Journalism in the World's Regions

13 Western Europe

BYRON T. SCOTT[*]

University of Missouri, USA

Recent Developments and Driving Forces

The time may be passing quickly when anyone speaks of Western Europe in anything except geographical terms. When a United States secretary of defense spoke of the reluctance of "old Europe" to participate in the 2003 invasion of Iraq, he was trying to suggest that European nations farther to the east were somehow more in touch with world opinion than France, Italy, and others to their west. Pan-European reactions emphasized that a number of trends, social, economic, and political, rendered Donald Rumsfeld's sarcasm simultaneously resented and inaccurate. Several of these trends, increasingly obvious in the latter part of the first decade of the twenty-first century, are discussed in this chapter as they relate to journalism and mass communication (however, also see Fridriksson, 2004 for the early 2000s). Among the relevant driving forces are cross-national audiences and ownership in the media industry itself, globalization driven by such seemingly diverse forces as technology, popular culture and human rights, and, unique to the rest of the world, the growing influence of the 27-nation European Union.

What the director of the European Journalism Observatory identifies as "a frightening concentration process" reflects a worldwide trend (Russ-Mohl, 2003:203). Such mass communication firms as Bertelsmann, Axel-Springer, Pearson, and Mediaset, all based in Western European nations, American émigré Rupert Murdoch's News Corp and others own multiple properties in multiple nations across the continent. "For 'the big guys' in the media industry, national borders obviously play a less and less significant role," Stephan Russ-Mohl observes, "They have been creating Europe for quite a while" (2003:204). Kiosks in the largest European cities long have carried prestige newspapers and opinion magazines in many languages, but now they feature tabloids as well as entertainment,

[*] The author acknowledges and thanks his students and colleagues at the Missouri School of Journalism and MU European Union Center who provided comments and assisted in research, especially: Michael Shulman, Jacob Stokes, Uthayla Abdullah, Wong Ye and Yvonne Yue Li. He is particularly indebted to his European colleagues whose analyses for the European Journalism Center's Media Landscape Project contributed to his understanding of the region.

hobby, and leisure periodicals. What was a public broadcast system dominated by government-owned or subsidized TV and radio stations now has significant independent competitors with electronic "footprints" stretching over multiple nations, often linked to satellites.

No modern media survey can ignore the influences of technology, but Western Europeans are arguably the most highly "wired" media consumers, with the possible exception of the Japanese. Household penetration of broadband in much of Western Europe now exceeds 70 percent. Satellite dishes have mushroomed across the facades of apartment buildings and manors alike, particularly since the mid-1990s. In several nations to be discussed, the number of cell phones exceeds the population. Particularly in northern nations it is possible to board a public tram, train, or subway and find the majority of your fellow passengers accessing the news, accessing messages, and conducting business on their cells. The Internet itself is increasingly populated by providers with URLs ending in national locations such as .uk (United Kingdom), .ch (Switzerland) or .eu, the new trans-Europe designation.

Without such technologies the influence of popular culture would be slowed across Europe. However, independent television, the World Wide Web, and burgeoning adoption of new technologies have rejuvenated the film and music industries. Events such as the annual pop music competition, Eurovision, find youthful audiences dancing and cheering in public squares as satellite images are fed to huge screens and fireworks crackle and boom overhead. As they are throughout the world, American movies, music videos, and TV shows are the chief competitors. Unable to restrict their influence, European entrepreneurs and even some governments are fighting back with their own products and delivery systems.

While many would argue the existence of "European culture," few would deny that many of the human rights emphasized in the Universal Declaration of Human Rights originated in the thoughts of Western European philosophers and leaders. Freedom of speech and of the press and access to information have been given new perspectives and fresh energies by such developments as the 1989 fall of the Berlin Wall and the subsequent events in former "Iron Curtain" nations that are now part of "new Europe," NATO, and the EU. In Western European nations this has been accompanied by heightened debates, further stimulated by such recent controversies as the Danish publication of images of Muhammad. Some of the most active press freedom advocates in the world are based in London (Article 19), Vienna (International Press Institute), Paris (Reporters Without Borders), and elsewhere in the region. Their critical reviews of media performance are not confined to transitional nations, but include their own publishers, broadcasters, and governments.

The European Union has become an increasingly significant-yet-contentious change agent in the media world. Scholars and commentators debate how supranational policies affecting modern media mesh with the visions of Jean Monnet and other pioneers of united Europe just over a half-century ago. Kevin Williams of Swansea University in Wales, UK, summarizes the situation neatly: "At the heart of EU media policy is a conflict between the desire to use the mass media to develop European identity and the economic priorities of increasing the industrial competitiveness of Europe's media industries" (Williams, 2005:115). Beginning in the 1980s with such initiatives as the Television without Frontiers Directive of 1989, the "Brusselcrats" and EU parliamentarians have fanned the embers of conflict anew with policies affecting broadcasting, print, and press freedom. If the future

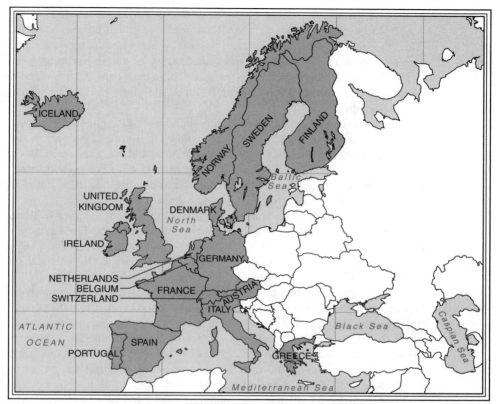

FIGURE 13.1 Western Europe as discussed for the purpose of this chapter

of the EU depends on a common understanding of what it means to be "European," the media have a critical, central role. Yet, despite hosting the largest press corps outside of Washington, D.C., many European journalists and their editors regard the activities in Brussels as "boring" (Harding, 2007:30).

The next sections examine these conflicting and overlapping forces in more detail.

Media Ownership Trends

In a region with rich traditions of individual, interpretative journalism, spiced with political partisanship, sales-stimulating sensationalism, and provocative criticism, it is depressing to recognize the forces of standardization and amalgamation. But most of the world's largest media companies have significant and growing representation in Western Europe. Because of their multicontinental reach, it is difficult to characterize many multimedia conglomerates as belonging to one nation or another, but several have deep European roots.

From a Gütersloh, Germany, Christian print and book shop in 1836, Bertelsmann A.G. has grown to a €20 billion a year multimedia corporation, operating in over 60 nations. Its divisions include Europe's largest magazine publisher (Gruner + Jahr) the world's largest trade book publisher (Random House), and biggest book and music club (Direct Group). It owns a majority of several business newspapers, principally Financial Times Deutschland. Arguably its most important presence in European journalism is the RTL Broadcast Group, which operates nearly 20 independent television and a like number of radio stations, primarily in Germany, France, Belgium, Hungary, Netherlands, and the United Kingdom.

Tracing itself back to a Yorkshire building and engineering company in 1844, London-based Pearson PLC is principally known in European journalism as the publisher of two prestigious periodicals, *The Financial Times* and *The Economist*. Both the daily *FT* and weekly *Economist,* as well as a growing number of online products and services, are global in reach and influence. Pearson also was a pioneer in satellite broadcasting but has recently concentrated its efforts in educational and trade publishing.

Europe's most controversial media magnate of recent memory is Silvio Berlusconi, thrice prime minister of Italy, whose family holding company, Fininvest, owns three large Italian TV channels and a variety of newspapers and magazines. Berlusconi has been criticized for using the broadcast arm, Mediaset, news shows for his personal political goals. His running editorial battle with *The Economist* magazine (which he calls "Ecommunist") is part of Europe's journalistic lore. Berlusconi's perceived media controls caused Italy to be isolated as the only Western European nation to be rated as less than completely free in the Freedom House world ratings, from 2003 through his departure from office in 2006.

There are a variety of other powerful European media companies—Hachette, Springer, Schibstedt, Vivendi, WAZ, and others—whose "colonizations" of Eastern European markets have created a media reach across the EU. But the power of Australian-turned-American media mogul Rupert Murdoch is most often mentioned by those who caution against conglomeration as a potential danger to free expression. Perhaps it is Murdoch's roots in sensational, tabloid journalism that fosters suspicions of the type that surfaced in 2007 when he purchased the largest and most respected U.S. business daily, *The Wall Street Journal*. But in Europe Murdoch's holdings are no less impressive; including perhaps its most prestigious "quality paper" *The Times of London* as well as *The Sun,* a tabloid with a huge circulation. Outside the UK, Murdoch's Sky Network of satellite television and radio is available across the continent and rivals CNN International and BBC for audience size and reach.

Although part of a worldwide trend, the fear that media empires will envelop Europe and suppress free expression is frequently voiced. In both Western and Eastern Europe, state-controlled or at least subsidized media monopolies were dominant until late in the twentieth century. Public service broadcasting, which reached its peak in the 1980s is now challenged or even dominated by independent stations. The state support of media that was a characteristic of Europe's media development now remains an important feature primarily in the Scandinavian nations. There and in the Netherlands subsidies are tied to maintaining a variety of voices in the media mix. McQuail and Van Cullenbert (2003) are among those who have described these changes and warn that a "paradigm shift" has taken place that challenges governmental and private institutions alike.

Technological Forces

Just as the offshore "pirate radio stations" of the 1970s and 1980s used small but powerful transmitters to break down the barriers of national controls on broadcasting, microchips have created a European independent media scene without borders. Broadband applications of the Internet and mobile phone technologies have turned the European media consumer into someone more engaged and diverse than the traditional stereotype of someone reading a newspaper at a sidewalk café.

Surpassed only by Japan in overall Internet usage and remaining slightly behind the United States in household penetration, high-speed Internet availability throughout Western Europe is increasing rapidly. "Three important success factors have become common," Macklin (2005:7) writes, "availability and choice, price and government support." In France, the United Kingdom, and Italy, this combination of factors created an 80 percent growth in household broadband in 2004 alone. These nations generally followed the example of Germany where Deutsche Telecom policies kept availability and rates attractive from the late 1990s. The expanding variety of services included digital TV, webcasts, and a variety of business applications such as real-time video conferencing. Internet cafés and hotel-based Web access services are now commonplace. Popular public applications included the Luxembourg-based Skype, which enables computer-to-computer voice phone calls at little or no cost, the Murdoch-owned MySpace.com, and such music download services as Napster. The latter company, saved from bankruptcy by Bertelsmann in 2000, was relaunched in 2007 after the German firm paid US$139 million in copyright infringement fees to music publishers.

Cell phones ("mobiles") are a major force in the changing patterns of European media usage. The world's largest wireless phone supplier, Finland's Nokia, dominated the worldwide market in 2007 with 39 percent of sales. Several Western European nations, including Luxembourg, Finland, and the United Kingdom, have more registered cell phones than people. All European nations operate under a single (GSM) wireless standard, which has increased the technology's popularity. In addition, the receiving party pays nothing. (In contrast, the United States has three competing standards and many services charge both parties.)

A 2006 study conducted by the London School of Economics and others outlined how mobiles have changed the media habits of younger UK users in particular:

> For young adults 18–24 years old, their mobile phone (26%) matters more to them than television (11%). Interestingly, among 18–24 year-old women, the proportion jumps to 32%, well ahead of television (11%). Men in this age group are not quite as attached to their phones as women, but 19% still name it as their most important technology product, well ahead of television. (*Cellular News*, 2006:1)

This does not necessarily translate to a more voluble set of mobile communicators, however. Users of all ages sent an average of 3.6 text messages compared to 2.8 voice calls daily. More than half of 18–24 year olds sent or received more than six text messages each day, almost three times their voice call frequency.

Commercial news services including Reuters and Yahoo! have an increasing number of broadband subscribers. The BBC "One-Minute News Service" is a popular mobile service. While Internet access and other data movement has been more expensive on mobile networks, the European Union has recently moved to lower tariffs to increase public access to mobile-adapted Internet sites.

Popular Culture Influences

With 23 official languages within the European Union alone, and ethnically and culturally diverse areas within individual nations such as Catalonia in Spain or across them as in Scotland/Wales/England/Northern Ireland, most observers despair of such a thing as "European culture." However, Western Europeans can find common identities beyond their cell-phone usage.

Aided by government subsidies and European Union-sponsored initiatives as well as the rise of independent and private broadcasting, the respected film industry has enjoyed a twenty-first-century resurgence. Their chief competitor in the European market is the United States. About one-quarter to one-third of films screened in European movie houses are European made. Principal producers are France, Italy, and the UK, particularly England. Here again, however, many film companies are owned and operated by multinational firms, from Bertelsmann to Disney.

Perhaps the oldest and most popular of the Euroculture events is the annual Eurovision competition, begun in Lugano, Switzerland, in 1956 under the auspices of the European Broadcasting Union. Aided by satellite transmission, the annual Eurovision television show has become a kind of World Cup final for European popular music groups. Billing itself as "an irreplaceable part of European culture," the competition now includes online and mobile phone balloting along with the traditional judging. Musical groups from 23 nations participated in the 2006 semifinal and final competition, held in Athens, Greece and won by Finland. The Eurovision broadcasts provide evenings of intense nationalism and pan-European pride, witnessed by millions watching in private homes, pubs and on giant screens in public squares.

Media Rights and Concern

As reflected in such documents as the United Nations Declaration of Human Rights, the philosophical arguments for such privileges as freedom of speech and of the press have distinctly European origins. Milton and Locke as well as Rousseau and Voltaire were Western Europeans; but so were Machiavelli and Marx who took somewhat different approaches to these entitlements. As in most other nations, events and policies contribute continuing debate in what John Stuart Mill called the "marketplace of ideas."

"Western Europe continues to boast the highest level of press freedom worldwide," according to the annual assessments of Freedom House, which has ranked the press systems of the world since 1980 and overall human and civilian rights since 1973. In 2007, Finland and Iceland tied for the top ranking among 194 nations, a position they traditionally hold. In fact, nine of the first 11 (because of ties) rankings went to Western European nations. Belgium, Denmark, Norway and Sweden tied for the third slot, followed by Luxembourg and Switzerland. The Netherlands battled Andorra and New Zealand for the 10th slot.

But not all of Western Europe's journalists practice in relative utopia. France and Austria have for some years lodged further down in the rankings, tied in 2007 for 39th a half dozen slots above EU newcomer Cyprus. While Greece and Italy teetered on the outer edge of the "free press" designation at 54th and 61st place respectively, Turkey languished at 101st, the only nation in this chapter to be designated by Freedom House only "partly free." Turkey's perennial bridesmaid status as a longtime candidate for EU admission is based partly on its recent history of press restrictions as well as arrests and assassinations of journalists. Some of these media problems will be discussed in the nation-by-nation media profiles later in this chapter. However, a common and growing difficulty is the inability of governments and journalists alike to deal with the pressures of immigration, particularly from nonwhite and non-Christian regions of the world.

An equally well-known media advocacy group, Reporters Without Borders (usually abbreviated RSF for Reporters sans frontières), based in Paris, began similar rankings in 2002 that are now quoted alongside Freedom House. RSF also lists Iceland as the most free press system in the world. In fact, all 15 of its top rankings in 2007 went to nations of Western or Central Europe. Yet it saw "noticeable problems" in France, Italy, and Spain where government officials and organized crime alike have clashed with reporters, including the new breed of online journalists and bloggers.

On May 3, World Press Freedom Day, the annual rankings released by Freedom House (FH) and Reporters sans frontières (RSF) create an annual international uproar. It would require too much space to compare the ill-understood methodologies, but readers should know that the two do not assess precisely the same things. FH tends to emphasize the actions of legal, economic, and governmental institutions, while RSF focuses on attacks and threats on individual journalists. In addition, the 2007 FH rankings included 195 countries while RSF ranked only 169, leaving out many small countries and including at least one not yet granted independence, Kosovo. (See Chapter 5 for more information on the rating of countries in terms of press freedom.)

EU Policies, Pressures, and Initiatives

Within the first decade of the twenty-first century, the European Union has grown from 15 to 25 to 27 nations. In Brussels, with periodic migrations to Strasbourg, the largest international press corps of Europe resides. Yet the institution and the media fight a continuing battle to understand one another. One longtime correspondent, Gareth Harding, presented the journalists' viewpoint succinctly:

> All too often the European Commission confuses information, which should be objective, with propaganda. The Commission is incapable of communicating in a language that ordinary people understand. The European Parliament has struggled to convey a strong message, hampered by the stranglehold that political groups hold on the information machine.

> The Council of Ministers faces a problem with the member-states: if there is a policy success, the governments take the credit, if there is a failure they blame the EU. The public, who don't know the difference between the institutions, are the losers. (Harding, 2002)

While this may not be much different from the problems faced by Washington, D.C. correspondents, Brussels-based reporters also must wade through multiple cultural and linguistic backgrounds as well as the EU's own rapidly evolving role. The failure of Dutch and French voters to ratify a European Constitution in October 2004 stimulated efforts at clarifying and explaining the EU's "message." On December 13, 2007, the signing of the Lisbon Treaty signaled a second effort to reform and expand the combined European efforts that the EU seeks to represent and media were challenged to help "take Europe into the twenty-first century." At the same time, the EU launched or intensified several initiatives to give a voice and identity to Europe.

"The European Radio Project" (ERP), a consortium of radio stations in 13 member states, was announced in the same week as the Lisbon Treaty signing. With the purpose of encouraging "the development of a European public area," ERP will produce daily news, features, and coverage of major European cultural events. Broadcasts initially will be carried on 16 participating stations and on the Internet in five languages—English, French, German, Spanish, and Polish—and translated into several others. The initial subsidy of €5.8 million will be increased as more stations and member states join. Participating stations represent a consortium of well-known public broadcasters, including Radio France Internationale and Radio Netherlands Worldwide and directed by Germany's Deutsche Welle.

Since the late 1990s the EU has subsidized the satellite channel, EuroNews, a seven-language pan-European public broadcaster that gives the news in 30-minute cycles. Originally an initiative of the European Broadcasting Union, EuroNews now has multiple owners with the majority of shares held by the UK-based Independent Television Network (ITN). In return for devoting at least 10 percent of its news to European issues, the channel receives an annual subsidy of €10 million from the EU.

Working through the Council of Europe, the European Commission, and its various directorates, the EU continues to concern itself with a variety of issues, primarily dealing with the historically strong but increasingly challenged public broadcasters. Examples of recent initiatives include the outlawing of tobacco advertising—a ban that most member states already had adopted. Media convergence in an increasingly digitized environment was a central initiative for both public and private sectors in the "eEurope" 2005 campaign.

European identity is not a dead issue for the media, but it is an underreported one. Jo Groebel of the European Institute for the Media calls it "an idea of our corner of the Earth, which somehow goes beyond history, the euro, politics, and everyday debates. We feel attached to our neighbors. . . . But we have no definite pictures, no myths, no media stories which would make the perceived fascination for Europe into a foundation for identity or at least for passionate interest" (Kevin, 2003:xiii). Stephan Russ-Mohl (2003:205) quotes a German editor who explains that local interests often crowd out regional, much less pan-European ones. "To put it in a more straightforward way: they are focusing on the local church towers."

Journalism Education

Until recent generations, most Western European journalists learned their trade in small, technical schools or on the job. Many still do. Scholars and critics of the discipline found themselves part of independent institutes or foundations. Many still are. But university-based schools and departments of journalism or mass communication are increasingly frequent.

Some of the best-established schools, combining practical, skills-based courses with theoretical overviews more typical of traditional European universities, include the Danish School of Journalism in Aarhus, the Netherlands' Hogeschool van Utrecht, University of Cardiff in Wales, and Sciences Po in Paris. The oldest postgraduate program is at London's City University ("the university for business and the professions"), which instituted journalism courses in 1976. There are now more than 60 university-based programs in the UK alone, most founded as part of the higher education expansion process initiated under Prime Minister Margaret Thatcher.

The European Journalism Training Association (EJTA), established in 1990, has about 50 institutional members in 20 countries. In common with universities in nearly 50 signatory nations, the EJTA focuses on creating standards and transferability to journalism education as dictated for all university-level disciplines by the Bologna Accords of 1999. EJTA educators formed the leadership core in the creation of recommended curriculum guidelines for journalism schools in transitional nations, issued by UNESCO in fall 2007.

Is There a "European Journalism"?

Characterizing European journalism is perhaps an even more difficult task. Following the demise of the late Robert Maxwell's newspaper, *The European* in the early 1990s, no major publishing effort has sought to engage Europe either as a culture or a journalistic demographic. Cebrian comments that ironically "The only paper [that] could aspire to do so with any chance of success . . . .is . . . an American paper the *International Herald Tribune* published in English, naturally enough" (1999:39). Now owned by the *New York Times,* "the *IHT*" is still headquartered in a Paris suburb and has been part of European journalism since 1887.

Patterns suitable for comparison and cultural linkages do exist across Western European media. Deirdre Kevin (2003) and colleagues at the European Institute for the Media in Düsseldorf are among those who argue that, eventually, the combined common interests of economics, politics, and national security will be critical in overcoming the barriers of history, geography, and language and that media will play a critical role in "Europeanization." One unappreciated aspect, they argue, is the role of the Internet and citizen-publishers working from blogs and Web sites.

Others despair, arguing that much of the policy debate is mediated by large, national "quality papers" such as *The Guardian* in the UK, Italy's *Corriere della Sera*, France's *Le Monde,* Germany's *Frankfurter Allgemeine Zeitung,* and Switzerland's *Neue Zurcher Zeitung*. While these opinion leaders maintain a general pro-European stance, they tend to become more nationalistic on specific issues. Williams acknowledges that:

"The contradictions of commonality and disunity are at the heart of any discussion of Europe and what is European. . . . The European mass media are no different." (2005:3).

The next portion of this chapter examines some of these commonalities and differences as they have surfaced recently in the journalism of 21 individual nations. Each profile includes that nation's press freedom status, as reflected in 2007 rankings and the recent economic, social, and political forces that are affecting how journalists do their work.

National Media Profiles

Austria

"Magnitude and power characterize the Austrian media landscape," writes Josef Trappel of the University of Zurich Institute for Mass Communication and Media Research, citing the high number of media among only 8.5 million consumers. "Power relates to the high degree of market concentration providing the dominating media actors with influence not only in their respective media markets but also in the political arena" (Trappel in Media Landscape, 2007) The result, he complains, is that "vested interests manage remarkably well to define the rules of the game."

A concentration of ownership that began shortly after World War II, strengthened by foreign investment, continues in contemporary Austria. Two national dailies, *Neue Kronen Zeitung* and *Kurier* account for more than half of newspaper penetration. The former's regional editions also dominate their markets. Despite a cartel law revised as recently as 1993, it is common for Austrian publishers to also own radio, TV, and cable markets, particularly in the provincial markets. Political influence is considered both a duty and right of media owners.

Since 1975 government subsidies have been available to all newspapers on request. In 2003 the structure and process of the subsidy program was liberalized to provide for cultural and ethnic diversity, particularly in smaller and specialized media and to encourage development of journalism schools.

Politicians and government officials alike make frequent use of strict libel and slander laws. The European Court of Human Rights overturned three defamation charges against the daily *Der Standard* as violating the free expression standards of the European Convention of Human Rights. In common with several of its European neighbors, Austria strictly bans any statements that deny the Holocaust or express anti-Semitic or pro-Nazi sentiments.

The historic dominance of Austrian Broadcasting Corporation (ORF) ended in 2001, and a number of commercial competitors, both national and regional, have entered the market, many owned by print publishers. Other channels, principally from Germany, also are part of cable and satellite viewership. ORF also dominates but no longer monopolizes Internet access, which is rising rapidly.

Considered among the most technologically advanced and entrepreneurial in Europe, the Austrian Press Agency (APA) serves all clients, public or private. The Austrian Press Council (*Presserat)* dissolved in 2002, declaring its respected Code of Ethics to be voluntary and self regulatory. The International Press Institute, a press freedom advocate based in Vienna, noted that self-regulation is a growing trend in European media. On the kiosks of Vienna and other Austrian cities, self-censorship battles against tabloidization in daily reporting.

Press Freedom Rankings: Freedom House (FH), 39th (tie with six other nations including France); Reporters Without Borders (RSF), 16th.

Belgium

In many aspects, the Belgian media landscape coincides with regional trends. In print, a *laissez-faire* approach to media ownership has led to concentration in the hands of a half-dozen corporations. On the broadcast side, a previously dominant public TV and radio system is fighting a grudging retreat to independent stations and competitors intruding via satellite and cable. An overstretched advertising market is creating declining media revenues. Newspapers and magazines pay no VAT (value-added tax), and declining national subsidies have parliamentarians searching for new support policies. "The neo-liberal policies of the EU and of the European media market have triggered commercialization," writes University of Ghent communications analyst Els de Bens, reflecting a concern seen in other Western nations. "Competition has become ruinous and this stimulated a tabloidisation effect on content. Public broadcast services, free from economic pressure, become more and more important" (Media Landscape, 2007).

Belgian public broadcasting (PSB) is an arguably unique system. In line with the nation's origins in 1830 as a federated state, Belgium has separate systems for French and Flemish audiences. Each has its own regulatory bodies and procedures, domestic stations, and even international broadcasting facilities. Although PSB retains the largest market share, it is losing its audiences to other media and independent, commercial stations. The first commercial radio license was given in 1985 and the first private TV license not until 1987. The state news agency, BELGA, also has completely autonomous French and Flemish units.

In 2005, responding to an international furor that embroiled the EU and brought protest by press freedom advocates worldwide, the Belgian Chamber of Deputies adopted a comprehensive law to protect journalists' sources. Police had raided the home of a Brussels-based German reporter, Hans Martin Tillack, searching for the identity of sources who had leaked sensitive EU documents. Because of the presence of NATO, the EU, and other international organizations, Brussels hosts the largest international press corps outside of Washington, DC.

Domestic politics are no less lively. Belgium's multiparty system is traditionally balanced along more or less ethnic lines. In 2007 parliamentary election results created a situation in which no official government coalition could be created for much of the year. Independence movements flare in Flanders and Wallonia. The 23 national newspapers are filled with political news and analysis on a daily basis. Reversing a European tradition, more than half of their circulation is on a subscription basis rather than kiosk sales. Partly in response to slipping circulation numbers, Belgian newspapers and magazines also are active on the Internet and compete actively online for breaking news. Brussels-based "webzines" such as http://thiseurope.com launched in 2007 are competing with traditional media in an increasingly competitive electronic environment.

Press Freedom Rankings: FH, 3rd (tie with three Scandinavian countries; RSF, 5th (tied with Finland and Sweden).

Cyprus

Despite the best efforts of the international community, including a classic rule-bending tactic by the European Union, there are two regions called Cyprus. The Republic of Cyprus, independent since 1960 and since 2004 a part of the European Union, reflects many of the trends in European media, including a lively print media and a public broadcaster threatened by independent competitors. The northern third of the island, occupied since 1974 by Turkish forces and known as the Turkish Republic of Northern Cyprus (TRNC), has all the media characteristics of a transitional society threatened by war. Only Turkey recognizes TRNC as a nation, and efforts continue to reunite the island. Despite its fundamental membership requirement that all border disputes must be resolved prior to admission, the EU chose to overlook the island's division; pleasing member Greece and infuriating candidate Turkey. When press freedom organizations such as Freedom House assess Cypriot journalism, they are careful to note that it is "the Greek side of the island" that is considered "free" (Freedom of the Press, 2007).

The tensions dividing the island nation provide a subtext for how the media operates as well as their news agenda. For example, for two weeks in the summer of 2007, Republic of Cyprus media made no mention of happenings in the TRNC, protesting frequent arrests of its journalists. In turn, Turkish Cypriot journalists complain of harassment by border guards and sometimes denial of access to the south.

The Republic of Cyprus includes a growing print environment with at least eight dailies, seven major magazines, more than two dozen weeklies, and even more fortnightlies and quarterlies. As elsewhere in Europe media ownership is increasingly concentrated, with the DIAS Publishing House controlling one of the two largest circulation dailies, popular radio and TV channels and several magazines. The print media are often openly affiliated with political organizations and filled with criticism and debate.

Originally established under British colonial rule, the Cyprus Broadcasting Corporation (CyBC) was a monopoly until 1990. Now a number of private broadcasters as well as cable and satellite broadcasts threaten its audience and advertising base. Most of the independent stations are affiliated with companies based in Greece. Parliamentarians have called for severe cuts in CyBC subsidies, which are derived from an electricity tax. There are more than 50 radio and TV stations, with 10 broadcasting nationally in Greek.

Newspapers are also popular on the Turkish side of the island. There are at least eight dailies, although editions "from the mainland" are reported to be more popular. There are also a number of weeklies and magazines. The Turkish Cypriot audience also prefers TV programming from Turkey, although several local channels exist, according to Myria Vassiliadou, media sociologist at Nicosia's Intercollege (Media Landscapes, 2007).

"No specific law in relation to the media can be found in the occupied north," Vassiliadou reports. "Journalists can be arrested, put on trial, and sentenced under . . . the so-called 'Criminal Code', concerning "Unjust actions", "The Courts", and "Military Adjudication" covering 84 items, all remnants of legislation from the British Colonial times and still in use." Journalists also may be put on trial in military courts for certain offenses.

Greek Cypriot journalists operate under constitutional guarantees and protections more typical of EU nations and are subject to civil suits. There is a published code of journalistic conduct and a 13-member Press Ethics Committee. But this body has no penalty or enforcement power, and most journalistic practice is self-regulatory. Private and public broadcasters have separate and independent regulatory authorities. Both have codes of conduct incorporated into their supporting legislation.

Press Freedom Rankings: FH 46th (tied with three others, including Spain); RSF 45th (tie with Cape Verde).

Denmark

The nation's historic free speech protections came under worldwide scrutiny in 2006 with the publication by the Copenhagen daily, *Jyllands-Posten,* of a dozen cartoons of the prophet Muhammad. Sometimes violent demonstrations in Muslim nations were accompanied by a boycott of Danish goods. Death threats and bomb threats were issued against the cartoonists and the editors, who apologized for causing offense to the Islamic faith. However, Prime Minister Anders Fogh Rasmussen declared the controversy a matter of free speech, protected by Danish constitutional law.

In the same year a lesser-known test saw two Danish reporters and their editor-in-chief prosecuted for allegedly publishing state secrets. The *Berlingske Tidente* journalists published a 2004 series based on unreleased reports from the Danish Defense Intelligence Service, questioning the reality of Iraqi "weapons of mass destruction." All three were acquitted in December 2006. A few months later a radio station, *Radio Hoger,* had its over-the-air license suspended for alleged violations of Denmark's laws against hate speech.

In an effort to maintain media diversity, Denmark remains one of the European nations that provide subsidies and low-interest loans to newspapers, regardless of political affiliation. The subsidies, in the form of VAT waivers and reduced postal distribution rates, are estimated at over 160 million euros per year. About 30 dailies continue to publish, with "no competition on the local newspaper markets, but increased competition on the national market during the past decade," according to Per Jauert of the University of Aarhus. Significant threats to both readership and advertising revenues have come from the popularity of free distribution. More than five million copies are distributed each week by more than 200 such papers, Jauert reports (Media Landscape, 2007)

Public broadcasting continues to survive and thrive despite increasingly frequent conflicts with the EU's policies to encourage independent competition. The Danish Broadcasting Company (DR) controls the largest and most popular national TV and radio services as well as many regional stations. Noncommercial radio stations qualify for government subsidies. Commercial radio came to the nation only in 2003. While satellite and cable services have provided additional choices to consumers, they remain largely loyal to DR programming. A larger threat may come in 2009 with the planned switch from analog to digital television, increasing dramatically access to bandwidth usage. "In general, the Danish Media market seems too small and maybe also too regulated to be attractive for foreign investments on a larger scale," comments Jauert (ibid.).

More than four-fifths of Danish households have Internet access, one of the highest penetrations in the world. All media, both print and broadcast, are active in the online world. Major newspapers have special e-sections accessible only to print edition sub-scribers. The most popular news sites belong to DR.

Press Freedom Rankings: FH 3rd (tie with Belgium and two neighbors); RSF, 8th (tied with Ireland and Portugal).

Finland

Although Finland's constitution was not revised to guarantee free expression and informa-tion access until March 2000, it long has been recognized at or near the top of any list of world democracies. Its credentials include the third largest newspaper circulation in the world, with 31 dailies among about 200 newspapers published. Transparency International ranks Finland as the least corrupt nation on the planet, making it also a prime investment market for all business, including communications.

Continuing its historic tradition of encouraging diversity of expression, the Finnish government in 2006 subsidized more than a dozen newspapers as well as party presses in Aland, its autonomous territory. The print subsidy program provides a counterbalance to the growing influence of two publishers, Alma Media and SanomaWSOY, which control most newspaper distribution.

As in most of Europe, public broadcasting once dominated the Finnish market. But now the Finnish Broadcasting Company, Yleisradio OY (YLE), competes with at least three nationwide commercial TV channels and nearly 70 commercial radio stations the first of which went on the air only in 1997. While broadcasting primarily in Finnish, some include programming in Swedish and the Lapp language, Sami. In 2007 Finland became one of the first nations to convert entirely from analog to digital transmission.

Internet access exceeds 60 percent. To encourage the medium's development, the Eduskunta, Finland's parliament, eliminated previous licensing laws. However, World Wide Web publications are required to identify their editor-in-chief and to archive posted materials for 21 days. Finnish law, which was one of the first to give every citizen a right to legal redress and reply, now includes the Internet.

Nokia is of course the nation's communications leader. The pioneer in cell phones now dominates the mobile market in most of the world.

Press Freedom Rankings: FH, 1st (tie with Iceland); RSF, 5th (tied with Belgium and Sweden).

France

Writing in the online journal of the French Joint Staff College during the suburban racial riots engulfing major cities in spring 2007, an officer of that nation's police wrote to remind his colleagues that press freedom has been part of the culture since 1789. While blaming self-censorship and economic difficulties which "pressure them into conveying new forms of propaganda and transmitting news which is sometimes wildly inaccurate," the gendarmerie officer reminded colleagues that journalists' rights needed continued pro-tection. (Formell, 2007) The nation that produced the Declaration of the Rights of Man and of the Citizen and backed it up with the first free press laws in 1881 continues its love/hate relationship with the media. The results often seem contradictory.

While in 2006 the minister of justice proposed adding a "shield law" to France's press freedom laws, police continued to raid newspaper offices and place reporters under investigation to reveal their confidential sources. In a nation where courts have cited the European Declaration of Human Rights protecting free expression—for example in a 2004 case charging *Le Monde* with racism—a 2007 law was adopted making it a crime to deny the early twentieth-century genocide in Armenia. While championing free expression as a historic right, public outcry forced the editor of *France-Soir* to resign after he republished the Danish cartoons of Muhammad.

For many France is the quintessential example of avid newspaper reading and lively subsequent discussions, but the French reading public is drifting away to other media. Overall circulation declined 15 percent in the period 1990–2005. Most of its newspapers are no longer linked to political factions. Major dailies are now owned in whole or part by Spanish (*Le Monde*), Italian (*Libération*), or German and Swiss publishers. French politicians have begun to call for domestic investors to step forward. Free-distribution papers are increasingly strong, with the presence in the market of three major distributors from Sweden and Norway as well as France. The "freesheets" are particularly strong in smaller towns and regions.

The state monopoly in broadcasting ended in a series of laws beginning in 1982. The result is an increasingly competitive marketplace: growing from three channels in 1980 to more than 200 today. There are more than 1,200 radio stations, most of them private but including a number still with Radio France or France Bleu public networks. By law, at least 60 percent of broadcast content must be of EU origin. The Conseil Supérieur de l'Audiovisuel (CSA) oversees these and a variety of other decisions, including licensing.

Public sector television remains strong, however. Three national public TV companies (France 2, France 3, and La Cinquieme) merged into a single group in August 2000. What is now France Televisions is financed almost entirely by the nation's audiovisual license fee, charged annually for each TV set. Freed of the necessity for advertising revenue, the public TV channels are being urged to develop their own programming in new, creative ways.

Agence France-Presse (AFP) remains arguably the most respected international news agency outside the English-speaking world. Founded in 1944, it is officially a national press agency and not a private company but is guaranteed its independence by law. AFP maintains employees in over 165 countries. About 40 percent of its annual budget comes from state funding.

Since the 1980s when France used a burgeoning videotext technology to establish its "Minitel" system, consumers have been accustomed to online communication. Just over 50 percent of the people access the Internet daily, although the percentage varies by age and social class. French newspapers, magazines, and broadcasters usually have online presences, with Web sites supplemented in some cases by archives dating back to Minitel. *Le Monde* and *Libération* offer free blogs, competing for teenage users with the popular "Skyrock" service.

The first ethical code for French journalists was adopted by its national body in 1918. Self-regulation has been a primary thrust for a series of codes by individual media companies and entities adopted with simultaneous legal protection in mind. Claude-Jean

Bertrand, the late University of Paris II media scholar, analyzed and advocated mechanisms for adopting and using ethical codes in France and throughout the world as a necessity for democratic development (Bertrand, 2000). His compilation of global ethical codes for journalists as well as guidelines for independent press councils remains online and maintained by the Missouri School of Journalism's Reynolds Institute (http://www.media-accountability.org/).

Press Freedom Rankings: FH, 39th (tie with six other nations including Austria); RSF, 31st.

Germany

As with the nation itself, the German media system remade itself twice in the twentieth century; once after World War II and again after reunification of the "two Germanys" in 1990. The system reflects German history and federalism as well as trends common to most Western European nations.

Press law not only forbids hate speech, Holocaust denial, and pro-Nazi sentiments, but it is even more sensitive than its neighbors to the intrusion of such statements from outside. International providers as well as those in Germany must agree to a policy titled "Voluntary Self-Control for Multimedia Service Providers." They are required to filter out or block any Web sites, primarily pornographic or sites advocating other banned topics, from a list provided by a federal department created for the purpose.

Following years of campaigning by German media and free press organizations, a Freedom of Information act went into effect in January 2006. However, it contains exemptions and a fee structure that journalists find excessive. This was only one of the continuing tensions between journalists and the government. In common with their colleagues in several European nations, German journalists saw their homes and offices raided by authorities seeking source materials on sensitive matters, particularly national security and "betraying state secrets." Another common experience with journalists of other European nations was the revelation that the German intelligence service was spying on journalists and tapping their phone conversations, as well as paying journalists to spy on their coworkers.

Print media include a surprisingly small number of national papers but a highly developed regional and specialized press. The prestigious national press includes *Bild, Süddeutsche Zeitung (SZ), Frankfurter Allgemeine Zeitung (FAZ), Welt, Frankfurter Rundschau (FR),* and *Tageszeitung (TAZ).* They compete for a slowly diminishing readership with the so-called boulevard press of tabloids and regional newspapers that are often highly political. Weekly papers like *Fie Zeit* and magazines, led by *Der Spiegel,* often contain investigative and interpretative reports designed to boost public discussion and kiosk circulation. The Axel Springer Group, itself one of the world's largest publishing companies, controls just under a quarter of the market.

German broadcasters compete under a dual system of public and private stations. In contrast to many other European nations, the public broadcasting system is healthy because the federation's states maintain a strong role. The German Federal Constitution gives sole broadcasting responsibility to the *Lander* (states.) The best known of the few exceptions is Deutsche Welle (DW), the national radio service that broadcasts almost exclusively outside Germany. Lander stations are financed by licensing fees to their users and may cooperate on national or international broadcasts such as the Olympics or the 2006 World Cup but are otherwise considered sovereign and independent. Only two commercial groups (so-called broadcast families or *Senderfamilien*) control most of private television: the Bertelsmann RTL group and Leon Kirch's ProSiebenSAT.1 Media. Their competition in turn comes from other stations on cable systems, available in just over half of German households, from a variety of international owners such as Disney, Viacom, or SKY TV.

Although digital programming has been available on German radio and TV for several years, the shift from analog has been slow. Disagreements among Lander broadcasters, government officials, and commercial providers centering on how digital programs should be delivered and decoded account for the delays. More than half of German households have access to broadband for Internet and other purposes.

The German Press Council (*Deutscher Presserat*) has functioned since the mid-1950s as a self-regulatory body of publishers and journalists. Public complaints are investigated, and newspapers are expected to publish the Council's results. However, its impact is limited by the fact that the majority of complaints come against the uncooperative "boulevard press." No such body exists to monitor broadcast ethics and practices.

Press Freedom Rankings: FH, 16th (tie with four other nations, including Ireland and USA); RSF, 20th.

Greece

After an economic slump ended the twentieth century, Greek media are enjoying growth that is linked to EU-stimulated improvements in the Balkans. Greek entrepreneurs are expanding services into neighboring Bulgaria, now also an EU member, candidate Macedonia, and elsewhere. At the same time in 2007 the EU asked Greek parliamentarians to ease their own provisions limiting international media ownership. Tensions relating to another EU candidate, Turkey, over Cyprus are providing complications.

Despite its EU membership, Greece continues to prosecute defamation as a criminal offense. However, journalists and authors charged in recent years have not been imprisoned. A growing number of independent newspapers and magazines nevertheless maintain critical coverage and investigative reporting. Freedom House (2007) has criticized media self-censorship, particularly on stories relating to ethnic minorities.

Newspaper circulation increased 26 percent during 2000–2005, almost recovering a similar drop during the economic troubles of the previous 20 years. In 2007 there were 87 national papers registered, along with 1,450 regional or local publications (Media Landscape, 2007). Only five publishing groups, all Greek-owned, dominate the market.

Multimedia ownership is restricted under Greek law to the "two-out-of-three" standard (print, radio, TV.) This has not prevented the development of more than 150 channels since the nation accepted the "Television Without Frontiers" provisions of the EU in 2000. Three public channels are operated by Hellenic Radio and Television (ERT), including a worldwide satellite service (ERT-Satellite). A fourth national public network, Vouli TV, was established for programming produced by the Hellenic Parliament. Nevertheless, private stations dominate the Greek marketplace, with only two channels, Ant1 and Megad, attracting over half of audiences and advertising revenues. Cable and satellite penetration is the lowest in the EU, hovering at less than 10 percent of households.

Radio remains an important and unusual feature of Greece's national media. Overwhelmingly local or regional and privately owned, only 35 of an estimated 1,156 stations had bothered to become licenses in 2007, according to Greek Open University analysts (Media Landscape, 2007) The National Council for Radio and Television (NCRTV) is an independent authority that may impose penalties, including license suspension or cancellation. However, self-regulation and *laissez-faire* remain the major characteristics of Greek media.

Although growing rapidly, access to Internet lags behind the EU average. Most major media maintain online Web sites.

Press Freedom Rankings: FH, 54th; RSF, 30th.

Iceland

The ingredients of Iceland's admired press freedom include national pride, tradition, concentrated media ownership, and, according to Freedom House analysts, a degree of self censorship. The nation's thriving independent media still are conscious that religious groups and doctrines are protected against heavy criticism or belittlement by statutes calling for fines and imprisonment. In common with many European nations, attacks on race, nationality, and sexual orientation are prohibited as exceptions to free speech.

Concerns about the effects of concentrated media ownership have caused considerable recent debate. One company, Nordurljos (Northern Lights) Corporation, controls or owns outright most of the private television networks and radio stations, and two out of Iceland's three national newspapers. In 2004 parliament passes restrictions on media ownership that were vetoed by the president. After a 2006 change in national leadership, the debate was renewed. For broadcasting, the autonomous Icelandic National Broadcasting Service (RUV) provides a leavening influence similar to that of Britain's BBC. Funded by licensing fees and advertising revenue, RUV was freed from state ownership in 2006 and became a "public limited company." RUV-supported broadcasters retain the obligation to promote the Icelandic language, history, and culture.

Despite operating in what is usually ranked the freest media system in the world, Iceland's journalists have been accused, by Freedom House and other press freedom agencies, of professional self-censorship for fear of libel and slander suits. It may be that the larger threats are the Icelandic media audience. Early in 2006, after a tabloid newspaper, *DV,* published a front-page story accusing a man of sexually abusing teenage boys, the subject of the exposé committed suicide. Public outrage included circulation and advertising boycotts. Parliamentarians suggested increasing damage limits for libel. By April the tabloid had to reduce its frequency to weekends only.

Internet usage in 2006 reached 87 percent of Iceland's population.

Press Freedom Rankings: FH, 1st (tie with Finland); RSF, 1st (tie with Norway).

Ireland

The "Irish Tiger" economy that took Ireland's GDP from far below the European average to more than 30 percent above it carried a media component. Fueled by EU and American investments, Irish journalism is thriving. Legal reforms to eliminate restrictions dating to British control and "the Troubles" have begun only recently. Censorship regulations and the Official Secrets Act are still on the statutes, though rarely enforced.

In August 2007 the first ombudsman representing the Irish press was named by a newly constituted Press Council. The first comments of John Horgan, a former Dublin City University professor, journalist, and parliamentarian, asked the government to reintroduce 2006 legislation to decriminalize Ireland's defamation and privacy laws. These laws, passed in 1961 to replace laws put in place under King Henry VIII, are thought to no longer reflect Irish media behavior. Horgan, who began work in January 2008, will be attempting to apply a new voluntary Code of Practice adopted by publishers. Both the independent ombudsman and the press council were part of the tabled 2006 media reform package of proposals. Their powers include publicizing their decisions and calling for retractions but not imposing financial penalties.

Ireland's print media include four national dailies, more than 60 local and regional newspapers, and a growing number of free newspapers based in major cities. British newspapers remain popular, particularly on weekends. One multimedia company, Dublin-based Independent News and Media, dominates more than 80 percent of the marketplace. Headed by Tony O'Reilly, Independent News is one of the world's largest publishers, owning more than 160 media properties, primarily newspapers in the UK, South Africa, India, New Zealand, and Australia as well as the Republic.

Since the 1920s, Irish broadcasting has been the province of public service broadcaster *Radio Telifis Eireann* (RTE), but private broadcasters are making inroads. In 2006 three new commercial channels joined the only existing one (TG 3) on the Irish spectrum. RTE operates two national TV services, RTE 1 and Network 2. A separate public channel, *Telefis na Gailge* (TG 4), carries programming in the indigenous language, Gaelic. As the first official language of the Republic, Gaelic media survive in Ireland primarily on broadcast and in two small-circulation weeklies. At the National Irish University in Galway, separate journalism courses are taught in Irish and English. Satellite/cable providers bring BBC and Sky as well as other international channels to an increasing percentage of households.

RTE also operates four popular radio stations across the nation that includes programming in English and Irish. By 2006 there were 54 licensed independent, commercial competitors. Internet penetration exceeds half of Irish households and includes several popular Web radio stations, operated by entrepreneurs who were unable to get or are still waiting for over-air licenses.

A major reform in the Broadcasting Act of 2001 sets standards for conversion to digital platforms for radio and TV. The renamed Broadcasting Commission of Ireland (BCI) also is drawing up standards and codes that will include Internet providers. The act follows tradition in setting up a separate broadcast authority, *Teilifis na Gaeilge,* for Irish-language broadcasts.

Press Freedom Rankings: FH, 16th (tied with four other nations, including Germany and USA); RSF, 8th (tied with Denmark and Portugal).

Italy

While most of the promised media reforms accompanying the election of the Romano Prodi government in April 2006 have yet to take place, press freedom organizations worldwide believe things are looking up for Italian journalism. Freedom House restored the "Free" designation to the nation's press after longtime premier Silvio Berlusconi failed to be reelected. However Berlusconi's family-owned Mediaset still dominates the marketplace, particularly on TV. (Author's note: He returned to office in spring 2008.)

The future of Italy's media might be in the hands of its consumers—literally. Mobile phone ownership far outnumbers house phones, and Italians clearly prefer to access news and entertainment on their cells, notes Fabrizio Tonello of the University of Padua. "Italians elected the cell phone as their favorite media already many years ago, almost taking over from Finland the world record," he writes, adding that broadcasting of more traditional sorts has long been more popular than print. Privatized in 1999, the telecommunications industry, which includes the Internet, has multiple providers with Pirelli by far the largest.

Circulation of the most prestigious newspapers, *Corriere della Sera* and *Repubblica,* continues a decline that began more than a decade ago, and their publishers are now concentrating on other opportunities, both online and in books and magazines. Many of the more than 150 Italian newspapers are owned by public trusts. As in many other European markets, free papers have found success in major cities, further undermining advertising revenues.

Much of the attention continues to be on Berlusconi and Mediaset, which owns three of the eight national TV channels. The complaint during his multiple terms as head of Italian government was that, together with the state service *RAI,* which operates three other channels, he controlled more than 90 percent of Italian viewers. A 2004 broadcasting reform law, adopted by the Senate, protected Mediaset by removing prior ownership restrictions. In 2006, shortly after the Prodi election victory, the EU notified Mediaset that it does not comply with its regulations on electronic communication. Although close to 800 regional and local broadcasters exist, the bulk of the advertising revenue comes to national TV. A serious competitor entered the market when Rupert Murdoch and the former Telecom Italia began a sports channel devoted primarily to football (soccer). The pay TV channel is now owned by Vivendi. Italian radio stations are heavily devoted to music, talk, and sports. The largest audiences are claimed by two RAI-affiliated stations, RADIOUNO and RADIODUE. Conversion to digital platforms was outlined in 2001 broadcast legislation that is being reconsidered under the Prodi reform movement.

In contrast to most other nations, Italian journalists must join a union or corporation to practice. To join *Ordine dei giornalisti* an individual must provide proof of employment with a recognized journalistic entity and take an admission examination. Recently, new journalism schools in Italy have been offering membership on graduation. The *Ordine dei giornalisti* also presides over ethical controversies and scandals in which journalists are involved as voluntary arbiters.

Once certified, the everyday life of Italian journalists may be complicated by changing and conflicting laws and government processes. Police have raided offices and homes seeking reporters' notes on sources to controversial stories. Online journalists are wary of a 2005 law authorizing government to conduct surveillance and to block Web sites on antiterrorist criteria, although the emphasis appears to be on foreign-based information providers.

Press Freedom Rankings: FH, 61st (lowest in Western Europe, tied with four other nations, including Israel); RSF, 35th (still lowest in region).

Luxembourg

With the highest per capita income of any world nation, Luxembourg is a thriving media and business market. Described by the former editor of a national newspaper as "an over-sized economy," it is home to Europe's largest private broadcaster, the RTL Group as well as its biggest satellite operator, SES Global. As a founding member of what is now the EU, it is home to a number of its institutions such as the European Court of Justice.

The nation's media serve an unusual audience: two-thirds commute from adjoining nations or are recent immigrants. Many of the nation's citizens commute to nearby Brussels. Newspapers are published in German, French, and Portuguese as well as Luxembourgish. While the general trend is toward private capitalism, the largest daily newspaper, *Luxemburger Wort,* is owned by the Catholic Archbishop of Luxembourg and an ally of the dominant Christian Social Party. RTL dominates the broadcast market, although a number of other stations exist and many more originate in neighboring nations. Internet penetration exceeds 70 percent.

Although Luxembourg lacks a Freedom of Information law, transparency is a praised government characteristic. Issues concerning journalists are those typical to a stable, prosperous democracy—wages, government deficits, and social welfare.

Press Freedom Rankings: FH, 7th (tied with Switzerland); RSF, not ranked.

Malta

The densely populated two-island Mediterranean nation is the smallest nation in the European Union but among the most crowded media markets. Maltese have access to more than 60 radio stations, five national TV channels, and a cable system serving over 80 percent of households. Five daily and two weekly newspapers in the official languages of English and Maltese are published. Broadband diffusion has been among the most rapid in the world.

Much of the media market depends on subsidies from political parties, trade unions, and the Roman Catholic Church, the nation's official religion. Coming from over a century-and-a-half as an English possession, Malta has a distinctly British journalistic style. Although it is one of only three EU nations lacking a freedom of information law, the articles in the *Times of Malta* and *Sunday Times* include investigative and critical analyses and partisan political commentaries.

Continuing controversies enlivening media coverage include Malta as a refuge for illegal immigrants from African nations, particularly Eritrea. Human rights agencies also have identified the nation as a stopover for human trafficking from Eastern Europe to Italy and Spain.

Press Freedom Rankings: FH, 22nd (tied with six other nations, including Canada); RSF, not ranked.

The Netherlands

Dutch journalists function in one of Europe's most rapidly changing media environments. In some areas the press and government work together closely to assist change, and in other areas to retard and control it. Netherlands broadcasting went completely digital at the end of 2006. Despite increasing concentration of ownership, several programs are working to maintain diversity for media audiences. At the same time the pressures of dealing with ethnic minorities, particularly Muslims, have caused public debates on the role of the press in national stability and security.

The 2002 murder of Dutch parliamentarian Pim Fortuyn, followed by the 2005 killing of filmmaker Theo van Gogh, shook society and fostered debate about how journalists cover crime and social issues involving the growing presence of recent immigrants to the Netherlands. Two journalists with the largest newspaper, *De Telegraaf,* were jailed for several days after refusing to reveal sources for stories about the Dutch intelligence service and the underworld. Charges were dropped. Subsequently, a government minister admitted that the reporters' telephone conversations had been monitored.

Two traditional features of the Dutch media world, independence and public service, are under siege. Three newspaper publishers that control 90 percent of paid circulation are owned wholly or in large part by Belgian and UK investors. In 2007 only seven independent publishers remained, down from 35 in 1970. The circulations of the seven national dailies and nine regional papers are slipping 2 to 4 percent each year. Two ubiquitous free papers, which entered the market in 1999, now distribute more than 450,000 copies daily. Publishers note that they are particularly popular with younger readers. The pioneering Dutch Press Fund remains active as an independent authority supporting print and online publications with loans and subsidies. The fund also encourages research and projects to improve minority media opportunities.

Since commercial broadcasting was first allowed in 1988, the share of Dutch public TV has diminished from two-thirds to about one-third of the audience. In addition to national TV, every province has its own public channel. Each organization is independent and is proudly described as private/public broadcasting. Programming is allocated according to political, religious, and social groups in each station's broadcast area. Cable penetration, most of it broadband, exceeds 95 percent, putting the Netherlands among the "most wired" nations in Europe. TV viewers get not only Dutch stations but those from Luxembourg and Belgium in their own language, as well as channels from Germany, France, Italy, the United States, and elsewhere. More than three-quarters of Dutch residents say they are regular Internet users. The radio situation is similar. Five of some 40 radio stations generally available are part of the Dutch independent public system. Licenses for commercial broadcasting are allocated through the Commission for the Media, whose specific charge is not to disturb the free market while simultaneously allocating broadcast time to public media.

In keeping with its history of independence, the Dutch press is self regulating. A national journalism council (*Raad voor de Journalistiek*) has the power to hear complaints and publicize its findings on its Web site and in a biweekly magazine of the association of journalists. However, the council cannot levy fines or sanctions. Unlike Sweden or Ireland there is no national press ombudsman, but several newspapers employ the arbiters who write regular columns about their findings.

Press Freedom Rankings: FH, 9th (tied with Andorra and New Zealand); RSF, 12th (tied with Latvia).

Norway

Stability is a word that the nation's analysts use to describe the Norwegian media environment. "The dominant newspapers, and magazine and book publishing houses were established 75 to 150 years ago, and they still play an important role," writes Prof. Helge Østbye of the University of Bergen (Media Landscape, 2007). The public service broadcasting system, *Norsk rikskringkasting (NRK),* founded in 1933, is still the major radio and TV force after 75 years.

Invariably cited among the freest press systems worldwide, Norway also prides itself as being at or near the top in newspaper readership. In 2007 there were 215 newspapers, with the most popular being *VG* and *Dagbladet*, both sold exclusively at kiosks (newsstands). Most of the other papers circulate by subscription or mixed systems. Official and public concerns have been expressed about a trend toward concentrated ownership nevertheless. British media conglomerate Mecom bought one of the three largest publishing houses, *Orkla Media,* in 2006. The other two, Schibstedt and *A-pressen,* remain owned by Norwegian interests. Together the three control more than 60 percent of newspaper circulation.

NRK was a broadcast monopoly until 1981. Three radio and two television channels remain state-owned. The government also owns a majority share in the major cable and satellite provider, Telenor, which also was a former state monopoly. There were several private TV competitors, two of them national.

Although advertising is an increasing economic force, it was banned from Norwegian radio until 1988 and from TV until 1992. In 2007 the government continued to ban political commercials, eliciting international protests (and perhaps private admiration) that they violated the European Convention of Human Rights. Restrictions already exist to bar cigarette and alcohol ads, prompting government debate on whether to also ban those for fast foods.

Digital broadcasting and radio is expected to completely replace analog broadcasting by the end of 2008. More than three-quarters of Norwegians have Internet access.

Buoyed by national tradition and a healthy economy that includes substantial North Sea oil exports, Norwegians support media with a number of social policies. Newspapers and books are exempt from VAT (value-added tax) levies, and are eligible for loans and subsidies financed by state funds. In 2005 Norwegian newspaper subsidies reached the equivalent of 40 million euro. Licensing, subsidies, and other official matters are administered by the Ministry of Culture through *Medietilsynet* (the Media Authority).

Conflicts and complaints about press performance are monitored by a Press Council that is independent and voluntary but in which all news media participate. A "Code of

Ethics for the Norwegian Press" was first adopted in 1936 and is updated regularly by the Norwegian Press Association.

Although public referenda narrowly rejected EU membership in 1972 and 1994, Norwegian media report that practices and policies are consistent with its membership in the Council of Europe and are supported by the European Court of Human Rights.

Press Freedom Rankings: FH, 3rd (tied with Belgium, Denmark, and Sweden); RSF, 1st (tied with Iceland).

Portugal

After generations of tradition and economic stagnation, change is clearly taking place in Portugal's media landscape. The direction of these changes is something less clear. Recent national administrations—since 2005 that of President José Socrates—have attempted to lessen state control and encourage investment, but with only mixed results. Initiatives to liberalize ownership have come to national legislators alongside proposals to enable courts to order journalists to reveal confidential sources and to allow publishers to reuse journalists' work for 30 days without additional pay.

Portuguese journalists are licensed, although analysts believe that recent unemployment trends find a high percentage in other professions (Media Landscape, 2007).

The circulation of free papers exceeded that of commercial dailies in 2005, with an associated weakening of the traditional press's circulation and advertising base. Portugal's print circulation already was in the bottom tier of European nations.

Media ownership is concentrated in four commercial groups, the state, and the Catholic Church. The church controls broadcast stations and newspapers primarily in the regions. Media Capital owned by the Spanish conglomerate, *Prisa,* is the only international presence in the marketplace.

The removal of state monopoly and progressive deregulation has created more than 100 private TV channels and radio stations. The remnants of public broadcasting (RDP) suffer from a lack of reliable funding as well as diminishing audiences and are strongest in rural areas. TV Cabo, the first TV cable system, also is Portugal's only satellite provider. It controls more than 80 percent of the 1.4 million customer-wired market, although significant over-the-air systems persist.

In the late 1990s both government and media owners were enthusiastic about the possibilities of media convergence, but multimedia experiments have largely failed or have not materialized. All major dailies have Web sites, however. Portugal's plan to convert to digital broadcasting is controlled by the state RDP which has not proposed a switchover target date. The ratio of mobile phone customers to Internet users is 11:1. The telecommunications industry is dominated by a single company, PT.

For more than a decade major dailies have employed ombudsmen. In 2006 the state RDP added ombudsmen for radio and TV, and commercial broadcasters are expected to follow.

Press Freedom Rankings: FH, 12th (tied with Liechtenstein and Palau); RSF, 8th (tied with Ireland and Denmark).

Spain

After the end of the Franco dictatorship and Spain's admission to the European Union, the country has maintained economic growth that is among the best in the world. Its media, however, have not fared as well. Readership is declining in newspapers and magazines, and Spanish public broadcaster RTVE has cut thousands of jobs. Nevertheless, the Spanish press is lively and often controversial, particularly when investigating governmental corruption and terrorism.

Civil defamation suits against journalists are not unusual in Spain. Local and national courts have accused journalists of illegal associations with terrorist groups, including al-Qaeda and the Basque separatist group, ETA (Spanish acronym for Basque Fatherland and Freedom). In turn, journalists covering ETA do so accompanied by bodyguards. Taysar Allouni, who interviewed Osama bin Laden for Al Jazeera Television, was among 24 individuals sentenced in 2005 for terrorist associations. He was sentenced to seven years of house arrest. Additional tensions surround a growing immigrant population, some coming illegally from Africa. One-in-ten individuals in Spain is foreign-born.

Readership of Spain's more than 100 daily newspapers "has not varied substantially in the last decade, but its percentage remains remarkably lower than that of other EU countries," according to a University of Navarra analyst, Ramón Salaverría. Although Internet usage is increasing, it also is among the lowest in Western Europe, hovering just above 40 percent. The most accessed Spanish Web site belongs to the national newspaper *El Mundo*.

The largest circulation newspaper, *20 Minutos,* is distributed free to more than 2.3 million people daily. The respected *El País* has a paid daily circulation of just over 2 million (Media Landscape, 2007). Unlike many other Western European nations, Spain has no media subsidy program with the exception of a limited interest in developing minority language press.

Television is growing, but the technological transfer from analog to digital is not expected until at least 2010. In addition to local and regional station, RTVE provides two national public service channels and there are three private national networks. In contrast, there are more than 4,500 radio stations, almost half of them transmitting without a legal license.

With journalists in over 100 countries, *Agencia EFE,* founded in 1939, continues as the largest Spanish-language news agency. As with RTVE it is a state-owned company.

Spain does not have a national press council, although several newspapers have ombudsmen.

Press Freedom Rankings: FH, 46th (tied with three other nations, including Cyprus and Poland); RSF, 33rd.

Sweden

Sweden's strong press freedom tradition, embodied currently under its Freedom of the Press Act and Fundamental Law of Freedom of Expression, is traced back to what is believed to be the world's first freedom of information law in 1766. Swedes also are generally credited with the *ombudsman* (representative) system for mediating conflicts between press and public, although the original 1809 usage was to settle disputes between government and citizens.

Considerable recent attention, both public and parliamentary, has been devoted to how new technology should be included in these protections. Public sentiment is strongly in favor. Swedish Foreign Minister Laila Freivalds resigned in 2006 amid criticism for her role in shutting down a politically right-wing Web site that had stated its intention to post the Danish cartoons of the prophet Muhammad. Major Swedish newspapers and magazines began developing strong online products in the 1990's in anticipation of the Internet's popularity among younger audiences. Public and private broadcasting followed suit. Nearly 80 percent of households have Internet access.

Newspaper circulation per capita remains among the highest in the world. More than 80 percent of adults say they read a newspaper daily. Most Swedish newspapers are regional, local, or specialized, although the largest are national tabloids concentrating on single-copy sales. *Aftonbladet* holds the largest circulation followed by *Expressen*. Free dailies are beginning to make inroads on the traditional, paid papers, particularly in advertising revenue. The largest multimedia firm in Scandinavia, Bonnier Group, is the dominant newspaper publisher in its home nation. The Stockholm-based company also owns papers in Poland, Denmark, Italy and the Baltic nations among others. Sweden offers government subsidies to ailing newspapers and also provides a reduced VAT obligation.

State-controlled public broadcasting, both with multiple national and regional outlets, still commands the largest audiences. Swedish Radio has about 60 percent of its market, while Swedish Television (SVT) has a share close to 40 percent. Private television and radio did not come to the nation until the late 1980s. A Broadcasting Commission supervises licensing. Digital conversion for Swedish broadcasting will take place in 2008.

The first Swedish Press Council was organized in 1916 and continues today as a cooperative among publishers and journalists. The national ombudsman system gained acceptance in the 1950s.

Press Freedom Rankings; FH, 3rd (tied with Belgium, Denmark, and Norway); RSF, 5th (tied with Finland and Belgium).

Switzerland

The Swiss political and linguistic structure places special requirements on its media. The nation's legendary lack of transparency in banking and trade conflicts with its deep commitments to free speech and diversity. Its historical independence—for example, it declined to join the European Union and agreed to become the United Nations only in 2002—contrasts to its role as a nexus for European media.

There are no national newspapers; rather, the Swiss press is characterized by regional publications, often owned by some of Europe's biggest media conglomerates, including Ringier, which owns the largest tabloid and Sunday papers. Concentration of ownership has caused many smaller papers to close. The Swiss version of the popular free paper, *20 Minuten,* controlled a quarter of the daily circulation by 2006. Owned by the multimedia firm Tamedia, based in Zurich, the free paper came on the market in 1999 and was an instant success.

There also are no national commercial TV channels in Switzerland. Although many international channels are brought into the marketplace via virtually total cable and satellite coverage, Swiss viewers rely heavily on local stations and the Swiss Broadcasting Corporation (SBC).

SBC's structure, mission, and daily operations are formulated for the nation's needs. It operates seven networks and 18 radio stations as an independent, public service entity that is nevertheless dependent on state funding from license fees, supplemented by advertising. An elaborate system of cross-funding ensures that each of Switzerland's 27 cantons can afford public service programming suited to its individual linguistic and cultural audience needs. Independent competitors find it difficult to compete, except in the largest cities.

Swiss TV is expected to complete conversion to a digital platform in 2008, followed by radio in 2009. With Internet access in some 70 percent of households, online users have increasing options to access digital radio as well as digital video services.

Complaints against the print press are primarily a matter for the courts. Hate speech, anti-Semitic statements or Holocaust denial are prosecuted. In April 2006 the European Court of Human Rights reversed a Swiss court conviction of two journalists charged with inciting a public official, whom they refused to identify, to disclose secret material. Adding to public debate about the journalistic right to protect sources was the arrest of two other journalists charged with publishing a fax from the Swiss Intelligence Service referring to CIA prisons in Eastern Europe. The journalists were to be prosecuted under the Swiss military penal code.

An elaborate investigative and appeal procedure exists for broadcasting complaints, however. The 11-member Independent Authority for Program Complaints (UBI) works with an ombudsman to mediate and adjudicate such matters. Its publicized final decision can only be appealed to the Swiss Federal Court.

Press Freedom Rankings: FH, 7th (tied with Luxembourg); RSF, 11th.

Turkey

As the only country in the region rated only "partly free" by press freedom advocates like Freedom House, Turkey stands out. Part of its status is wrapped up in its history and a larger part in its hopes for the future as a longtime candidate for European Union membership.

A 2004 revision of the Turkish press law, honed to meet EU requirements, was virtually reversed by new restrictions to the penal code passed the following year. In 2006, nearly 300 persons, many of them journalists, were prosecuted under the penal revisions, according to the Turkish press freedom NGO, *Biane* (Web site, 2007). Consisting of more than 100 Tujrkish newspapers, *BIA* was founded in 2003 with funding from the EU Initiative for Democracy and Human Rights.

Government charges have included "the denigration of Turkishness, insulting Turkish identity," and "inflaming hatred and hostility among peoples." Offending materials included articles on the Armenian genocide in 1915, the divided status of Cyprus, and continuing battles with Kurdish rebels on the border with Iraq. Charges were dropped against Turkey's Nobel laureate novelist, Orhan Parmuk, because his alleged criminal statements, criticizing Turkish denials of the 1915 Armenian genocide, were made prior to the penal code revisions. Commentators have placed much of the blame for the prosecutions on nationalism arising from continuing EU rejection of Turkish membership. Government officials have pledged to press parliament to revise these laws even while arrests on a variety of other charges, including defamation and consorting with terrorist groups, continue. Self-censorship is becoming more frequent in Turkish newsrooms, and Bianet and other press freedom advocates continue to protest.

Despite these conflicts, the size of the Turkish media world is impressive. There are more than 2,000 newspapers in Turkey, 40 of which have national circulations and are based in either Istanbul or Ankara. A small number of multimedia conglomerates control the preponderance of publications. The Doğan Group owns the two largest circulation "quality" papers as well as the best-selling "boulevard" tabloid and the largest English-language daily.

After the state broadcasting monopoly ended in 1993, hundreds of independent broadcasters came into the marketplace. Many were unlicensed and continue to broadcast in that way. The Radio Television Supreme Council (RTUK) was created to regulate private broadcasting but is under constant criticisms for the severity and political nature of its decisions.

Officially Turkey has two dozen national, 16 regional, and 215 local TV stations. The Turkish Radio and Television Corporation (TRT), begun in 1964, continues to broadcast over four channels, one of which devotes itself to the Turkish National Grand Assembly when it is in session. As part of EU-assisted reforms, two new public stations were begun in 2006, broadcasting to the Kurdish minority. There are more than 1,100 private radio stations in Turkey, and a substantial number already "simulcast" on the Internet.

Although Internet access is just past 20 percent penetration in Turkey, it is growing rapidly. Most media are developing Internet magazines and news sites to appeal to Turkey's substantial youth population. National movement to digital platforms is not scheduled until 2010.

Press freedom Rankings: FH 105th (tied with Argentina); RSF 101st.

United Kingdom

Just as it is increasingly difficult to generalize about Europe itself, the UK media can no longer be viewed as a unitary industry united by a common language. Michael Bromley of the University of Queensland points out that "there are distinctive English, Scottish, Irish and Welsh dimensions, reflecting the composition of the State itself, and heightened by devolution in the late 1990s" (Media Landscape, 2007). Still, the United Kingdom and its media focus on London, where recent governments and parliaments have liberalized laws, deregulated standards and encouraged global marketplace perspectives over traditional thinking.

Although none of the major media conglomerates is headquartered there, the UK contains major components of many of them. And many of the icons of the British press, including Reuters, the BBC, *The Times of London*, and even the nation's libel laws have changed and continue to do so. "Recent UK governments have attempted to bolster national media against competition from overseas predators. At the same time, it has been accepted that the biggest media are not national but global, and governed primarily by the market" (Bromley in Tergis, 2007:43).

The UK's libel laws, which formerly forced the burden of proof on the defendant, were reformed in December 2006. A major impetus to the Defamation Bill was the decision of the House of Lords Law court favoring *The Wall Street Journal Europe,* on the basis that the article subject was in the public interest. Points of legal tension persist, however. More than 40 percent of media requests under the recent Freedom of Information Act were rejected in 2006 for reasons ranging from public health and safety to national security. Following the July 2005 bombings of the London Underground, a Terrorism Bill was passed, reminding many of free speech restrictions during bombings by the Irish Republican Army in the last part of the twentieth century.

The UK press is anchored by 10 daily and 10 Sunday papers, all carrying significant circulations and weight in public discussions. However, there are dozens of respected regional and local papers. Media critics point out that only eight companies control virtually all of them, with the top four owning over 85 percent of the paid circulation. However, the largest daily circulation belongs not to *The Times, The Guardian, The Independent,* or any other of the well-known "quality" papers. Nor does it belong to any of the sensational "red-top" tabloids. The free paper *Metro,* begun in 1999 by Associated Newspapers, is the UK's circulation leader. Its more than 850,000 daily copies make *Metro* the largest free paper in the world. There are some 10,000 magazines published in the UK. Many, such as *The Economist,* also have substantial overseas editions.

The British Broadcasting Corporation (BBC), perhaps the most prestigious state-supported public broadcaster, continues its tradition of independent reporting. However, it has been under recent parliamentary fire for the size of its budget, generated by licensing fees for all consumers with televisions. The BBC "empire," as private competitors refer to it, encompasses 14 television channels and associated enterprises capturing more than a third of the UK's TV audience. Its radio arm includes five national channels, five others available in digital, regional stations in Northern Ireland and in Scotland and Wales, broadcasting in Scots and Welsh, and 30 local stations. Internationally, its crown jewel is the World Service, now heard globally in many over the air and digital delivery systems. Not surprisingly, commercial competitors have come to question if the BBC is stifling an almost mature marketplace. Those competitors include Murdoch's News Corp, which operates the Sky network as well as Classic FM, which operates the best-listened-to radio broadcasts after the BBC.

Reuters, the legendary news service, is converting itself to a primarily business news provider in competition with Murdoch's Dow Jones and Bloomberg. In common with most UK media, independent or state-supported, it has developed an impressive interactive, online presence. Traffic on The Guardian Unlimited Web site allows it to claim to be the most read paper in the world.

In 2005 and 2006, the UK boasted the fastest-growing broadband market in Europe. Nearly two-thirds of the population has Internet access at home. An announced government goal is to reach every UK home by 2010. The "dash to digital" began in 1998 and is expected to be completed for TV in 2008 and for radio shortly afterward.

Press Freedom Rankings: FH, 31st (tied with Latvia); RSF, 24th.

New Challenges

The next decades will be exciting for journalists and media consumers in "old Europe" as well as its neighbor nations. The change agents are now in place to destroy stereotypes and traditions alike: the Internet, free papers, mobile phones, and other new media, and importantly a new audience of young, online sophisticates demanding more and more from those providing information and entertainment.

In some nations public broadcasting systems are crumbling, and in the better economies of the Scandinavian nations they are being revised. What part state-supported broadcasting will play in the new European social welfare system is debatable. Global multimedia giants have an ally in European Union policies and regulations encouraging media independence and commercialization. By the middle of the second decade of this century, most of the broadcast systems will be digitized, opening opportunities for hundreds of new media products. Licensing battles are bound to rage as the possibilities for places on the spectrum increase.

While information delivery may increase, the journalists who create those products may have a more difficult job. Despite the region's overwhelming traditions of free expression, the forces of nationalism, threats of terrorism, and tensions surrounding immigration are increasing. Faced with unknown fears, the most freedom-loving citizens and their governments tend to see priorities differently. In particular, pressures for journalists to reveal sources or go to jail are increasing across Western Europe, as are government reactions to investigative reports that threaten vaguely defined national security.

Media scholars, journalism educators, and analysts will have an increasingly important role to play. Theirs will be the difficult tasks to understand, explain, and perhaps advocate and even shout warnings. Much of the world looks to Western Europe for positive examples of how a free and independent press benefits a free and open society.

BIBLIOGRAPHY

(Author's note: All Internet addresses (URLs) cited are current to December 2007.)

Bertrand, C.-J. *Media Ethics and Accountability Systems*. Paris: Transaction Publishers, 2000.

Beunderman, M. "EU to Fund Pan-European Radio Station." EUobserver.com, December 12, 2007. Available: http://euobserver.com/9/25306/

Cebrian, J. L. "The Media and European Identity." *New Perspectives Quarterly,* Boston, 16;1999, 39–42.

Europa, official Web site of the European Union, "Treaty of Lisbon." Available: http://europa.eu/lisbon_treaty/index_en.htm

European Journalism Training Association. Available: http://www.ejta.eu/index.php/website/

"Freedom of the Press," Freedom House, New York. Available: http://www.freedomhouse.org/template.cfm?page=16

Formell, M. "Freedom of the Press and Its Excesses in France." IDC Forum, April 2007. Available: http://www.college.interarmees.defense.gouv.fr/IMG/pdf/FORMELL_CE_B4_article_Tribune_v5_ENMT.pdf

Fridriksson, L. "Western Europe." In De Beer, A. S. and Merril, J. C. *Global journalism: Topical Issues and media systems*. Boston: Pearson/Allyn & Bacon.

Fröhlich, R., and Holtz-Bacha, C. *Journalism Education in Europe and North America: An International Comparison*. Cresskill, NJ: Hampton Press, 2003.

Harding, G. "Europe Must Get On-Message," *Centre for European Reform Bulletin,* Brussels, 22: February/March 2002. Available: http://www.cer.org.uk/articles/n_22_harding.html

————. "Nothing to Write Home About?" *E!Sharp,* July/August 2007,Brussels, 28-30.

International Press Institute, Vienna. Available: http://www.freemedia.at/cms/ipi/

Kevin, D. *Europe in the Media: A Comparison of Reporting, Representation and Rhetoric in National Media Systems in Europe.* London: Erlbaum, 2003.

"Largest Ever Social Study of Mobile Phone Usage." Cellular News, London. Available: http://www.cellular-news.com/story/18461.php

Macklin, B. "European Broadband Take-up Picks Up Pace." *New Media Age,* April 14, 2005, 7.

Media Landscape, European Journalism Center, Maastricht and Brussels. Available: http://www.ejc.net/media_landscape/

Media Resources. "Who Owns What, Columbia Journalism Review." New York. Available: http://www.cjr.org/resources/

Office of the Press Ombudsman/Press Council of Ireland. Available: http://www.presscouncil.ie/v1/portal.php?content=thepresscouncil.php

Russ-Mohl, S. "Towards a European Journalism?—Limits, Opportunities, Challenges." *Studies in Communication Sciences* 3, No. 2 (2003), 203–216.

"State's first Press Ombudsman Appointed." *The Irish Times,* August 15, 2007. Available: http://www.ireland.com/newspaper/ireland/2007/0815/1187036479260.html

Terzis, G. (ed.). *European Media Governance: National and Regional Dimensions,* Bristol, UK, Intellect, 2007.

"Turkey's Human Rights Status Discouraging." Bianet News in English. Available: http://www.bianet.org/english/kategori/english/103480/

Van Cullenbert, J., and McQuail, D. "Media Policy Paradigm Shifts." *European Journal of Communication* 18, No. 2 (2003), 181+.

Williams, K. *Get Me a Murder A Day! A History of Mass Communication in Britain.* London: Hodder Arnold, 1998.

————. *European Media Studies.* London: Hodder Arnold, 2005.

World Press Freedom Index. 2007, Reporters sans frontières, Paris. Available: http://www.rsf.org/article.php3?id_article=24021

14 Eastern Europe, Eurasia, and Russia*

ALLEN W. PALMER
Brigham Young Univeristy, USA

A Tenuous Road for Media Development

Development of mass media in Eastern Europe, Eurasia, and Russia has remained turbulent and chaotic throughout the first decade of 2000. Human Rights Watch (2002) affirms that the respect for media freedoms in the region has been tenuous and has followed "a rough path of ups and downs." While the media operate under the presumption of freedom in some areas, there are both excesses of tabloidization and uncertainty of economic support; elsewhere journalists have used the Internet and other communication innovations to challenge authoritarian powers, but liberalization of communication is still uncertain in many of the region's struggling nations. Especially among new member states in Eastern Europe of the European Union (EU), political and economic reforms of media will continue to evolve to match Western European standards.

The legacy of Communist-style governance continues to haunt those working for media reforms, especially in the Balkans, Eastern Europe, and the new independent states of Eurasia. In many places, threats and intimidation pose a threat to journalists' lives and independence. More often, media employees work without adequate economic support, which leaves them vulnerable to bribes, extortion, and other forms of payoffs.

Although some states in the region have remained authoritarian and largely unchanged, others have confronted many of the legal, economic, and political obstacles to democratic expression. Private media in Eastern Europe are now considered to be relatively free, as assessed by agencies such as Freedom House and Human Rights Watch, but governments increasingly have sought to impose serious legal limitations on the exercise of these freedoms. The new media are inventing themselves, searching for ways to assert political independence and economic viability in uncertain conditions. In Russia, the media are caught in the wild swings of public and political favor. Most media in the region exist in the shadow of political and economic threat, corruption, or intimidation. For the

* Research for this chapter was provided by Lois Bauman, Daniel Duerden, Valori Infanger, Christel Swasey, Jennifer Martin, Rita Somfai, Talita Stasevskas, Brett Stifflemire, Megan Stoker and Linda Tobler.

first time after the early 1990s, Russia was declared "not free" by Freedom House. The murder of journalist Anna Politkovskaya in 2007, together with other attacks on journalists in Russia, focused international outrage on the threats faced by media workers. Many observers wonder how such societies can cultivate a healthy and transparent relationship between government and the media (Gross, 2002).

The influx of venture capital from Europe and North America in Eastern Europe and Russia has been accompanied by sensationalized tabloid treatment of the news. More generally, the press there has seen a sharp decrease in circulation since the early 1990s, because of economic distress and because of lack of consumer confidence. The infrastructure of the print media (equipment, facilities, and distribution systems) remains generally inadequate.

Although many nations have enacted civil codes consistent with Western standards, the ambiguity of codes addressing "defamation," "libel," "ridicule," "derision," and "insults" allows courts wide latitude. This has the potential "chilling effect" of curbing bona fide reporting of malfeasance by elected or appointed public officials, civil servants, and politicians. Some observers of democratic developments in the region now ask whether a single model of reform and media development is reasonable. Those who track rapid changes point to the uneven and unpredictable evolution of the media.

Media Developments in Eastern Europe

The history of the media in the Eastern European nations of Albania, Bulgaria, Romania, Hungary, Poland, Czech Republic, Slovakia, as well as Yugoslavia, is a history of these nations' political roots deeply embedded in communism. While each nation eventually carved out its own destiny apart from the Soviet Union, each was dominated, from the end of World War II, by authoritarian regimes whose beginnings were fostered and entirely supported as puppet states or satellites controlled by the USSR. The media had no voice, but served as the publicity arm of the regions' respective regimes. Their purpose was that of propaganda, indoctrination, and disinformation. As authoritarian control within these entities ebbed and flowed with various political tides, so, too, did the media they controlled. But never did the iron fist of government entirely release its grip on the media machinery it harnessed to control its peoples. Vigorous censorship was enforced; outside media, particularly that of Western radio and television broadcasts, were not permitted. Strict obedience to party lines by the media was expected.

It was not until the region's political upheaval in the late 1980s and 1990s that private, independent media began to emerge. It emerged as economic reforms initiated to staunch economic ruin encouraged privately owned, capitalistic enterprises. It came about as an outgrowth of its citizens' demand for freedom of expression without reprisal. Even then, as a shift from authoritarian regimes to republics of democracy changed Eastern Europe's political landscape to one of greater freedom of expression, it was difficult for media practitioners, previously trained by and controlled by their governments, to let go of indoctrinated mechanisms of obedience. While some media have embraced the opportunity to criticize their governments and political leaders, others have timidly clung to their comfortable reticence of simply repeating the party line.

Much of these nations' media remain in the sphere of government ownership. Government-owned, these media continue as the "official" voice of the people. While Eastern Europe's nations have written constitutions guaranteeing freedom of expression and of the press, as well as information laws that offer journalists some access to government information, overt government control has been replaced with self-censorship, as well as political and financial pressures that create a difficult climate for journalists. In addition, "insult laws" that make it illegal to libel or defame the government, its politicians, or its citizens, in some cases, make it difficult to accurately report a government's doings. While no state mechanism officially controls the entire media landscape, journalists who publish counter to the government or political figures, or even other powerful figures face reprisal, sometimes in the severe form of beatings or murder.

The fortunes of the media of Eastern Europe are closely tied to the political fortunes of its governments. They, like their governments, are in an era of transition and upheaval as progress toward actual democracy, at times, is impeded or even slides back toward familiar authoritarian patterns. It remains to be seen, as many of these nations step onto the world stage as they seek membership or have joined the European Union, whether media and freedom of expression reforms, now part of their constitutions but unevenly supported by their governments, will one day be actual reality.

Former Yugoslavia and the Balkan States

Throughout much of the twentieth century Bosnia and Herzegovina, Croatia, Macedonia, Montenegro, Serbia, and Slovenia were tied together as the nation of Yugoslavia. The nation united much of the major South Slav groups of Croats, Serbs, Slovenes, and Bulgars. Governed by dictator Josip Broz Tito during Yugoslavia's Communist era, each nation was a republic under united central rule. Tito allowed each some autonomous governance, including that of the Kosovo and Vojvodina regions within Serbia.

This attitude of autonomy was also pervasive in the media throughout the Yugoslav region. In an exception to general Communist policy that the media is an instrument of indoctrination, the media was considered, instead, a source of information. Each region's media was specific to its location and was self-regulated. This partial autonomy bred journalists and writers that emerged in the 1980s to criticize the government and reflect ideas independent of the republic. As democracy took hold across Eastern Europe, demands for freedom of expression gained momentum in Yugoslavia as well. Democracy, however, did not come peacefully.

Although united under the Yugoslavia banner, ethnic, regional identity remained paramount among its peoples. Nationalistic sentiment and ethnic hatred fomented under Serbian dictator Slobodan Milosevic's manipulation of the media. As Yugoslavia fractured, Milosevic's dream of a Serbian homeland became a nightmare of ethnic cleansing. International peacekeeping forces eventually brought peace to the region, and Milosevic died an international prisoner charged with genocide. Once united, Yugoslavia became six nations, its media legacy stained with blood, having incited its peoples to mass killings, rapes, and ethnic cleansing.

FIGURE 14.1 Eastern Europe

Bosnia and Herzegovina   Now a democracy overseen by a host of nations, Bosnia and Herzegovina's legal framework for press freedom is codified in law. Libel and defamation are no longer criminal offenses as of March 2007. However, media reform has stagnated as reactionary forces within the government continue to grapple for influence over media content. Indirect methods, rather than overt control, are often used. "There are often threats made by a company or a political group controlling some company that they will stop advertising, if it is unhappy with the reporting of a certain media organization" (International Press Institute, 2006).

Croatia   As Croatia prepares to join the EU in 2010, it has embraced reformed media law. Its constitution guarantees freedom of the press and bans censorship, even as it also provides for the right of correction if published news violates legal rights. Newspaper circulation is in steady decline, spawning sensational tabloids in a struggle to attract and hold readership. "The heritage of communism, consequences of the war and interethnic antagonisms have resulted in a partial implosion of the concept of media freedoms and led to the appearance of propagandistic journalism" (OSCE, 2007).

Macedonia   The constitution of Macedonia guarantees freedom of expression, and in 2006 parliament decriminalized defamation. Defamation continues to be a criminal offense punishable with fines; however, journalists are no longer jailed (Reporters Without Borders, 2007). In Macedonia's changing media landscape, its journalists practice self-censorship as a result of political influence on media owners. Fearful of losing their jobs, media practitioners slant their news coverage toward their employers' political persuasions.

Serbia and Montenegro   In 2006, Serbia and Montenegro's voters approved separation into two nations. A struggle over media content and control has commenced in Montenegro, where most media outlets have close ties to political powers. Journalists here face reprisal, from beatings to murder.

Serbia's media climate is, by degrees, more hospitable. Libel is no longer punished with prison time, but with high fines and jail time, instead, if the fines cannot be paid. Serbian broadcast media, including radio, continues to be government-owned; a privatization deadline has been extended to 2008. Numerous private newspapers have emerged, but are highly dependent on advertising and have spiraled into tabloid sensationalism to attract readers.

Slovenia   The only former Yugoslav state to join the EU by 2007, Slovenia has 877 registered media outlets. Eight daily newspapers have a combined circulation of 263,000. The biggest of these are *Delo* and its sister tabloid publication, *Slovenske novice*. Fifty-four percent of households have access to the Internet. Although Slovenia's constitution contains guarantees for press freedom, that freedom is tenuous and its media landscape is bleak. "One of the biggest problems in the Sloveno media is how to assure editorial autonomy and protest journalists from the pressures of their editors, owners and politicians. Pressure is largely manifested through financial threats and even threats of dismissal" (International Press Institute, 2006). Political pressure also poses a threat to media independence. The Slovenian parliament's new Media Act, passed in 2006, assures the government the "right of correction." Incorrect information that is published is remedied with a correction in the same place and in the same time frame as the original, thus offering a de facto propaganda platform. The legislation has also raised the practice of self-censorship by media.

Albania

The Albanian government now generally respects freedom of speech and of the press provided by the Law on Fundamental Human Rights and Freedoms. There have been reports, however, of police assaults on journalists covering the news, and of journalists being attacked by unidentified assailants. Defamation trials against the media and political interference with allocation of state-funded advertising to media outlets also appeared as obstacles to media performance. The ability of Albanian journalists to initiate significant media reforms or to protest attacks on their colleagues has remained limited by professional disunity.

Belarus

Free elections in Belarus in 1994 brought Aleksandr Lukashenko to the presidency and a return to authoritarian government. Under Lukashenko's administration, censorship was reintroduced, independent trade unions were banned, and restrictions were introduced on who could run for election. Opposition politicians and journalists have withered. Information leaks from within the government indicate that the president's security force was behind several politically-motivated murders, but no action has been taken.

In 2004, Lukashenko eliminated restrictions on presidential power. He used his increased authority to stifle civil liberties even further, including freedom of association, assembly, religion, movement, speech, and the press. The neo-Stalinist philosophy of the Lukashenko government extends to economics. Belarus has initiated none of the economic reforms currently underway in many of the newly independent states. Instead, it continues to function with a centrally planned economy that is hostile to private enterprise and inhibits foreign investment. The country's borders are closed to print, audio, and video imports, and the independent media, which moved to Lithuania when they were denied the opportunity to publish in Belarus, have been forbidden to transport their papers across the border.

With the return to Soviet-style government, political information officers have been assigned to all state enterprises and offices. Official youth groups and trade unions have been reestablished, and even entry to university is under the president's control. In 1997 the Council of Ministers introduced strict regulations that held foreign correspondents responsible for any critical remarks made about officials of the regime and forbade them to report anything negative about Belarus.

Although the country's constitution and various amendments provide for a free press and free access to information, the provisions are not borne out in reality, and restrictions were tightened in 1998. Legislation includes prohibition against defaming the president, senior government officials, and other members of the ruling elite. It also allows the State Committee for Press to suspend a publication for a year without a court ruling. This law also banned imported publications.

The country's nine state-owned large publications receive government subsidies, in addition to subsidized printing, paper, and distribution. As a result, state media support government policies and attack the opposition.

While the constitution allows for independent media, recent measures by the Belarusian government have almost eradicated the independent press. In 2005, Lukashenko passed into law a bill that made it a criminal offense punishable by up to three years in prison to criticize the president or government. As of 2005, there was only one major independent daily in the country of Belarus, and it was crippled in 2006 when the monopoly publishing company owned by the government stopped handling subscriptions of independent newspapers. By 2007 most of the major printing outlets in the country were controlled by the government, leaving independent newspapers little choice but to close.

Belarus has 165 licensed television operations and 65 radio stations. The largest are controlled by the state. All of them are in competition with Russian media, which transmit signals into Belarus. Some stations have been suspended for critical coverage of the regime. But while government controls all of Belarus broadcasting, it has no impact on Radio Liberty, which provides independent coverage of Belarusian news.

The Belarus government has also curtailed Internet use. In 2005, Belarus had only one Internet provider, and people were required to show identity cards in order to gain access to Internet cafés. By May 2007, bloggers and independent media on the Internet were opened to criminal prosecution for slander and defamation.

Belarus has two organizations of journalists—the state-run Belarusian Union of Journalists with about 2,000 members and the independent Belarusian Association of Journalists with 750 members which is a member of the International Federation of Journalists. In October 2000 the Belarusian Association of Journalists tried to hold a festival celebrating the non-state-owned media, but the government suppressed the event.

Bulgaria

Hundreds of private radio and television stations began operation in Bulgaria after government changes in 1989, but a litigious climate in the Bulgarian courts and parliament affected the accountability of almost every journalist. The number of legal charges against journalists averaged about 100 each year. Through the efforts of journalists' organizations and human rights groups, a Bulgarian penal code relating to media libel and insult was changed in 2000, limiting the scope of criminal prosecution of journalists. The maximum punishment for libel and insult was changed to a substantial fine instead of prison.

After 1989, the Bulgarian print media were free of overt government control. As of October 2006, there were 15 national daily newspapers, but only one—*Dnevnik,* established in 2001—is considered a quality newspaper. In 2006, among four national weekly newspapers of substantial circulation, two—*Capital* and *Banker*—are considered "quality." The Bulgarian media market is dominated by "hybrid tabloids" that combine news with gossip, celebrity news, and sex. In response to this proliferation of tabloid content in the media, two self-regulatory ethics committees—one for print media and another for electronic media—were created at the end of 2005.

The Bulgarian News Agency (BTA) has a network of journalists and correspondents that serve as information sources for most media outlets. Parliament reworked a new law in 2002 to designate the news agency as "autonomous" and to define its role in distributing government information to media outlets. BTA is the most reliable and professional media source in Bulgaria.

Recognizing its financial potential, the Bulgarian government sought to impose a 20 to 40 percent fee on Internet service providers in new regulations adopted in November 1998. However, the proposed licensing provision was struck from the regulations after protests from the fledgling Bulgarian Internet Society. From 2000 to 2006, Internet usage increased more than 400 percent. Bulgaria became a member of the European Union on January 1, 2007.

Czech Republic

Until the breakup of the Republic of Czechoslovakia in 1939, Czech newspapers were partisan contributors to a vigorous political life. With the reforms of the 1990s, Czechs and Slovaks agreed to separate peacefully on January 1, 1993 into two countries: the Czech Republic and Slovakia. Today there is general independence and press freedom in the Czech media; however, there is still a significant amount of political and commercial pressure. Media owners in the Czech Republic are financially dependent on their investors, and they are careful not to jeopardize these relations.

In the Czech Republic, nearly all libel cases in the media since 1990 have been adjudicated according to the civil code instead of criminal statutes. Statutes concerning defamation of the president were revoked in 1997, but the laws addressing defamation of the republic itself remain in force.

In 2001, an alleged political appointment to the directorship of Czech Television sparked a revolt at the television station that led to the registration of the newly appointed general director, his dismissal of the Czech Television Council by the Czech parliament, and a change in media legislation that shifts the nomination of council members from the Chamber of Deputies to civic associations. The new law, however, allows the chamber to assume the television council's responsibilities and to appoint a new temporary director, thus leaving the future of Czech Television in political hands. A law that went into effect in the Czech Republic on January 1, 2000, provides freedom of access to information under the control of the state and local authorities, as well as under other institutions affecting the rights of citizens.

A new Access to Public Information Law was approved by the Czech parliament in September 2001, and the Czech Press Act gives journalists the right to protect their sources unless the sources are involved in a criminal act. Libel and defamation remain a criminal offense, and prison terms apply for journalists who do not obey. In 2005 there was a concern regarding government's limitations on the work of television and radio reporters.

The Czech Republic continues to be widely regarded as the home to the freest media of the region. Among the 60 dailies published, 8 are national newspapers. *Mlada fronta Dnes* ("The Front of Today's Youth") is the most widely read newspaper in the country;

however, it is often viewed as biased and superficial in its editorial content compared to leading Western newspapers. The tabloid *Blesk* has the largest market share among the Czech newspapers, followed closely by *MF Dnes* and *Pravo*.

The country's public radio operates three national networks besides other local and foreign broadcasting; there are about 100 radio stations on the air countrywide, the most important being a three-channel public radio network and two nationwide radio stations. A U.S.-owned company owns the most popular regional radio station. In addition, the country also hosts the global headquarters and transmission center of the U.S. Radio Free Europe/Radio Liberty. All main international press agencies have their representations in Prague. Czech audiences can access 150 television stations. Among them the public television CTV operates three channels: CT1 with 29.9 percent, CT2 with a 40.2 percent audience share, and a new news channel, CT24, which broadcasts online. Besides the public television network there are two major private stations with national reach, TV NOVA and TV Prima; TV NOVA has the largest share of the market. Cable and satellite channels attract over 6 percent of the audience.

Hungary

The first newspapers in Hungary were published in Latin and German. The first Hungarian language newspaper (*Magyar Hirmondo*) was published in 1780 in Pozsony (today's Bratislava, the capital of the Slovak Republic.) Censorship dominated the Hungarian press scene until 1859, when the three-month long Austro-French-Italian War marginalized censorship and journalism became more interesting. When Hungary became a sovereign state in 1918, a lively, highly politicized, literary press fed the fires of a rich political and intellectual life until fascism snuffed out both in the 1930s.

When Hungary emerged as a sovereign, democratic state in 1990, its authoritarian governmental habits continued in its attempts to manipulate and control the public service media. Hungary's media wars, which pitted reform-minded public service media leaders like Elemer Hankis and Csaba Gombar against the government and parliament, were emulated in Poland and Czech Republic.

Today, journalists in Hungary have legal access to government information as long as the documents do not compromise state security, but there is a prevailing mind-set of security that prevents government transparency. The Hungarian parliament debated a law in 1999 that would have required media outlets to publish corrections to false statements of fact and also opposite opinions. The International Helsinki Foundation called the proposal "the first step to censorship." The proposal was later dropped.

There are about 1,600 registered publications available to Hungarian readers, 33 of them daily newspapers. Hungary has 77 radio stations, one public service radio (Hungarian Public Radio) operating three national networks, and four main national commercial radio stations (Slager Radio, Juventus, Danubius Radio, and InfoRadio), four national dailies (*Nepszabadsag, Magyar Hirlap, Nepszava,* and *Magyar Nemzet*), and 35 television stations, according to the International Journalists' Network (IJNet). There are two publicly owned stations, with Hungarian Public Television operating two channels and a satellite channel Duna Television; and three privately held terrestrial stations RTL Klub, TV2, and Hir TV.

Publicly owned MTV reaches 97 percent of households. Privately owned RTL-Klub and TV2, both owned by foreign consortiums, each reach 86 percent of TV households.

A new law on electronic freedom of information was passed by the Hungarian parliament in 2005. The law specifies the public information that must be published on the Internet, such as court decisions, laws, and draft bills. In 2006, however, the Hungarian Civil Liberties Union took a position against the proposed law on restrictive classified data act, which was introduced by parliament in December 2005.

Numerous private publications throughout the country express a variety of views and are available to the public; the government generally does not interfere with their operation. Hungary's constitution provides for freedom of speech. However, the ruling party, the Hungarian Socialist Party (MSZP), is often criticized for influencing the state-owned media. Reporters and editors continue to face persecution because the processing of altered laws is slow. In 2004 government interference in media was a continuing concern for several state-owned stations governed by a state-appointed media oversight board. The commercial broadcast industry has flourished in Hungary inasmuch as the influence and popularity of public outlets have been significantly weakened.

The appointment of a new National Television and Radio Board by the ruling coalition government in February 2002 brought thousands of protestors into the streets of Budapest demanding the establishment of a truly independent board. With the enactment of broadcasting laws in 1995, Hungary established councils and boards to distribute licenses and regulate broadcasting. The Data Protection and Freedom of Information Law was passed in Hungary in 1992 and strengthened in 1995 with a parliamentary commissioner to oversee its implementation within eight days. In 1998, a law prohibiting the recording of government meetings, except for a summary containing the names of the participants and the agenda, put a damper on Hungarian journalists' access to information. In Hungary, as in most Eastern European states, the constitution generally provides for freedom of speech and press, and in general the government respects these rights, though not without some reservations.

In 2004 the government of Prime Minister Peter Medgyessy collapsed, marking the most notable event of the year, and was followed by the peaceable new government of Prime Minister Ferenc Gyurcsany. A year later the nation celebrated the fiftieth anniversary of the 1956 political uprising, and once again protestors gathered on the streets of Hungary in the worst antigovernment demonstration in 50 years against dishonesty and public lies following the elevation of Gyurcsany. An audio tape was broadcast of a private party speech given in May 2006 by Hungary's prime minister in which he admitted his party had lied to the public in order to win April's general election. Also, he publicly admitted to hiding the truth about the state of the Hungarian economy. "I almost died when I had to pretend for one and a half years as if we were governing. Instead, we lied in the morning, at night and in the evening." Gyurcsany eventually apologized for misleading the public, but he refused to resign despite thousands going to the streets demanding he leave office.

On several occasions the media found itself a target of the protestors. For instance, shortly after the prime minister acknowledged fault, protestors broke into the headquarters of the Hungarian Public Television, forcing it off the air. Hungary's political crisis raised a growing sense of uncertainty about the country's future direction, especially concerning the capacity of the mass media to produce unbiased and fair reporting.

The future of Hungary's media credibility depends in large measure on economic factors, but even more fundamentally on the evolution of its political culture and politics. Economic development, important in supporting a wide range of media outlets, does not guarantee independence from political pressures. Instead, what readers, listeners, and viewers demand of the media, and the direction in which journalism will develop, will be determined by their practical definitions of democracy and citizenship.

Moldova

In 2000, Moldova voted to become a parliamentary democracy. Its future status is uncertain, however, because while the western portion of the country is generally oriented toward Western Europe and is interested in reform, the eastern industrial region declared independence on September 2, 1990. This independent region, Transnistria, or the Dnestr Moldovan Republic (DMR), is an authoritarian state oriented toward Russia.

Moldova has a robust press, with a wide variety of newspapers and television outlets. Most media are affiliated with a party or political coalition. All Moldovan media are supposed to be licensed, but to avoid the tax; some publications are issued as supplements of already licensed organizations.

Moldovan press law protects press freedom, but no distinction is made between defamation of public or private individuals. Journalists found guilty of defamation can be fined amounts of money equal to 100 or 200 times the average monthly salary. Physical attacks against journalists also continue across Moldova, especially in Transnistria. A law that would have taken action against physical attacks on journalists was rejected in July 2005.

Teleradio-Moldova, the state-owned broadcasting operation, is the country's main source of television and radio programming; private television and radio stations exist that broadcast in local markets. In the DMR, the state owns the two major newspapers and restricts press freedom by harassing or closing the small independent papers. No papers from one side of the country are allowed to circulate in the other side.

Both sides of Moldova, like many of the newly independent states of Eurasia, have language issues. After independence, a new law required that 65 percent of all TV programming be presented in Moldovan, essentially a Romanian dialect; however, it is much easier for most stations to use Russian programming.

Economic problems have recently taken a toll on Moldova and its press. After the collapse of the Soviet Union, the economy of Moldova also collapsed and has yet to rebound. To escape harsh economic conditions at home as much as 20 percent of the country's active population is now working abroad, a third of which are the educated population of the country. Among those preferring to leave the country are many journalists. With Romania entering the European Union, this emigration problem has been exacerbated, and by late 2007 it was thought that one in eight Moldovan citizens had applied for Romanian visas.

Poland

The history of Poland in the twentieth century is one of triumph and struggle against a backdrop of Communist rule. As early as 1970, Poland's independent, underground press published and distributed uncensored opposition literature. The rise of this media expression mirrors, to some extent, the rise of Poland's Solidarity movement. Solidarity, the national workers' union, burst onto the national scene in 1980 through a series of strikes that forced the Polish government to recognize, and bargain with, an independent entity that demanded greater rights. Much of the opposition literature supported Solidarity, although by 1982, this literature had expanded to discuss a wide range of opposition viewpoints. While the Communist government increasingly tolerated unofficial media and the state media's increasing references to illicit publications, it was not until 1990 that state censorship was abolished. Poland transitioned to democracy in 1989.

In 2004, Poland joined the European Union and was obligated by its membership to follow the "Television Without Frontiers" directive to permit broadcasts from fellow EU states. Its state-owned television broadcaster, Telewizja Polska (TVP), dominates the audience market and advertising market with nearly 60 percent of market share. The Polish government also owns 5 national radio stations and 17 regional stations of the 235 stations nationwide. In contrast, its press is primarily privately owned, with 167 national and regional dailies, 827 weeklies, and 2,401 monthly magazines. Although a democracy, Poland's government continues to heavily influence media content.

While Poland's constitution guarantees freedom of expression, libel and defamation laws continue to hamper its media workers. Article 212 (2) codifies prison sentences for journalists who libel public officials (Reporters Without Borders, 2007). Article 135 (2) penalizes journalists who insult the Polish president with three years in prison. In 2006, according to this law, it became a criminal act, punishable up to three years in prison, to defame the Polish nation by "publicly charging the Polish Nation of participating, organizing or being responsible for Communist or Nazi crimes."

Romania

After the demise of the Nicolae Ceausescu dictatorship in late 1989, Romania's press freedom blossomed in the early 1990s, only to decrease to "partly free" through 1999. A Romanian law on state secrets, passed by the Romanian parliament in March 2001, could result in a further decline of media freedoms. Nineteen cases of legal and physical harassment of journalists were investigated by the Committee to Protect Journalists during 2000–2002.

Two Romanian daily newspapers, *Adevarul* and *Romania Libera,* reached a circulation of 1.5 million shortly after democratization began. By 2007, there were hundreds of privately owned publications. However, financial and political pressures undercut the general independence of most private newspapers. Between 2000 and 2004, the state supplied certain newspapers with large amounts of advertising money as a so-called masked subsidy, but with the new government this state advertising has stopped.

Many Romanian newspapers tend to focus on entertainment and novelty at the expense of investigative reporting. This sensationalized approach is still seen in the best-selling newspaper *Libertatea,* which is a soft tabloid. Media credibility has dropped among Romanian institutions, behind the Romanian Orthodox Church and the army.

After Romania was invited to join the European Union in 1999, there were significant media reforms, but parliament then considered various laws to limit, rather than promote, press freedoms. The Romanian constitution prohibits defamation of the nation, attempts to instigate wars of aggression, incitement to discrimination and public violence, and obscene conduct contrary to morality. Recently, the penal code of 1996 was changed, decriminalizing libel and slander. Despite its somewhat halting media reforms, those changes were sufficient for Romania to be accepted as an EU member state on January 1, 2007 (Horga & La Brosse, 2002).

The most popular form of entertainment in Romania is television, which reaches most Romanians via cable networks. Therefore, most of the nation's advertising revenue, almost 90 percent, is channeled to TV. A dual broadcasting system was introduced in 1992 that led to the creation of the Romanian Broadcasting Corporation and, in 1994, the Romanian Television Corporation, which transformed the state system into an independent, public service institution. Both private and public stations are regulated by the National Audiovisual Council, which awards broadcast licenses and regulates the airwaves.

Romanian TV programming is dominated by imported entertainment content, especially programs from the United States. The collapse of communism created a market for Western ideas and products, a demand that is filled through the vicarious experience of TV fantasies in imported programs. More than six million Romanians are Internet users, and online media are becoming increasingly accessible as broadband continues its rapid growth. Blogs are increasingly popular and influential.

Slovakia

The development of the Slovak media has followed a very similar path as its Czech neighbor since the fall of communism in 1989, and the liberation of the media has opened up to various mass media outlets. Although freedom of expression was guaranteed by the constitution, the authoritarian Meciar government (1992–1998) was successful in controlling, manipulating, and intimidating the media, even more so than in the Czech Republic.

Slovak television is dominated by privately owned TV Markiza, which covers over two-thirds of the country; it is followed in popularity by public service Slovak Television (STV), private TV JOJ, and TV NOVA and TA3. In addition, there are 78 terrestrial and cable television stations spread around the country. There are 94 commercial radio stations such as Radio Express, Radio Viva, and Radio Okey competing with public service Radio Slovak operating five national networks. In the Slovak Republic, the heads of Slovak TV (STV) and radio were dismissed for failing to guarantee objective and independent broadcasting, and in 1999 STV became editorially independent. STV had been heavily influenced by Prime Minister Vladimir Meciar. About 30 percent of Slovakians share the view that the choice of stories is influenced primarily by media owners, whereas 43 percent believe it is driven by the interest of politicians. The Slovak Republic adopted a comprehensive Freedom of Information Act in 2000 that grants all citizens access to almost all unclassified information.

By 2000, 1,465 publications were officially registered (up from 326 in 1989), among them 451 newspapers, while there were fewer than 20 dailies (half of them with a national reach, six regional, and three local.) The most popular newspapers are *Hospodarske Noviny, Novy cas, Sport,* and *Pravda.* Slovakia was significantly involved in the Danish cartoon controversy in 2006 when the Slovak regional court fined *Pravda* US$95,000 for three offensive published articles.

On March 17, 2004, the parliament approved and added an amendment stating that media representatives will not be allowed to work for either the Slovak intelligence service (SIS) or the military intelligence agency (VOS). Slovakia, along with other 10 other countries in the region, joined the EU on May 1, 2004.

Ukraine

November 28, 2004 was the beginning of the largest national movement in the Ukraine since it declared its independence in 1991. The Orange Revolution drew hundreds of thousands of people into the streets of the capital Kiev in support of presidential candidate Viktor Yushchenko. The West-leaning Yuschenko had emerged in the popular polls far ahead of his Eastern-oriented opponent, Prime Minister Viktor Yanukovych. Yushchenko's fortunes took an ominous turn, however, when it was widely reported by the international press that he had been poisoned by dioxin by his political opponents in a campaign laced with intrigue. On Election Day, however, Yanukovych was declared the new president, sparking cries of ballot rigging and corruption in government. What followed was a series of protests and demonstrations, culminating in January 2005 with new elections that declared Yuschenko president.

While it was widely hoped that Yuschenko would usher in an era of freedom and progress in the Ukraine, his presidency quickly fell apart as his prime minister left office, taking half of the party support with her. Yanukovych was reelected prime minister in August 2006, further splintering the government.

The Ukrainian public has expressed impatience with Yushchenko's government, particularly in his treatment of Gregory Gondgadze, an investigative journalist who was murdered on September 16, 2000. Gondgadze's murder was used as a rallying point during the Orange Revolution to highlight government corruption and repression of the media. However, by 2007, relatively little had been done to resolve the Gondgadze murder, despite the 2005 release of the Melchenko Tapes, which revealed that the decision to get rid of the murdered journalist was made on the highest levels of the Ukrainian government.

The fracturing of the Ukrainian government between Yuschenko and Yanukoyvch has paved the way for massive corruption in Ukrainian government and business. As of 2004, much of Ukraine's media were controlled by oligarchs who benefited from privatization of the steel industry. Journalists speaking out against corruption in Ukraine found themselves increasingly under threat of physical violence from economic, political, and various criminal interests, while the government has done little to stop such threats.

Ukraine has several major private television broadcasters with national signals, as well as four major FM radio stations. Given difficult economic times, television was the people's only source of reliable information. A 1999 survey found that 90 percent of the population watched television every day and that viewers were fairly evenly divided among the four top stations. However, research conducted a year later indicated that the broadcast outlets with the most credibility in Ukraine were the BBC and Radio Svoboda, sponsored by the United States.

Some influential independent media outlets have moved to the Internet, and by 2007, 35 percent of Ukrainians had Internet access. Internet freedom was restricted, however, when the Ukrainian government enlisted the help of several organizations to survey Internet content in order to protect national security and limit other forms of what it considered undesirable information.

Numerous layers of Ukrainian legislation include language to protect press freedoms, but the law and practice diverge. There is one area, however, in which the laws are followed to the letter. Ukrainian laws make no distinction between rights to privacy for private individuals and public officials, and these laws have been used repeatedly by politicians who have sued the media for large amounts. Efforts by journalists to persuade parliament to limit a newspaper's liability for damages have failed.

The Media in Eurasia

The story of the media in the newly independent states of Eurasia is the story of the struggles, successes, and failures of post-Communist democratization. Optimism over the transition to democracy and free-market economics has given way to recognition of the complex challenges such transitions present. For all these nations, democratization has been a struggle, and the development of both independent media and the civil and cultural climates to support it has been fraught with difficulty.

One of the most noteworthy aspects of the transition to life after communism in Eurasia is the difference in the experience of general groupings. Whereas all the nations of the former USSR have encountered challenges along the path to self-governance, there are qualitative differences between the experiences of the Baltic states, the Central European states, the Transcaucasian states, and the Central Asian states. These differences arise out of the different cultural and political differences that held and continue to hold sway in these countries before, during, and after communism.

The Baltic nations had long considered themselves as separate cultural, and to a degree, political entities from the Soviet Union, and their transition to life after its collapse has been relatively smooth. In the new nations of Ukraine and Belarus the transition has been much more traumatic. Although these countries had some sense of an independent identity prior to the collapse of the former USSR, they were nonetheless Slav and less inclined to see the Russian empire as something distinct from themselves. For them, the transition to new nationhood has been the struggle between entrenched forces from the old days and forces that would radically change governance. The countries of the Transcaucasus were more prepared for transition than other new nations. Given their established tribal and geopolitical identities, they were psychologically prepared for existence apart from the Soviet Union. Unfortunately, the very origins of such fierce independence have also meant that each of the three countries now face tribal and territorial disputes that sap their resources, deflect their political energies, and preoccupy their media. In Central Asia the fights are primarily for the right and ability to publish independently.

The very complicated challenges faced by the newly independent states, and especially by the smaller group of nations that are also members of the Commonwealth of Independent States, have prompted political scientists to question whether paradigms of democratization drawn from no Communist countries are relevant to the study of post-Communist political change.

Under Soviet rule, media were viewed as instruments of the state, and criticism or discussion was to be aimed at correcting the course of communism, not challenging the system or those in power. Under Gorbachev's control, the USSR and its republics were introduced to the concept of *glasnost,* which was intended to reinvigorate the Soviet Union by allowing freer public comment about issues of importance to modernization of the country. While *glasnost* opened windows and then doors to media coverage of formerly taboo topics, it did so without providing the rule of law or civil institutions necessary to support press freedom in the long term.

Thus, while each of the newly independent states has provisions for free speech and media independence written into its constitution, and many of those constitutions include provisions for due process in the courts should media behavior overstep the bounds of those laws, these laws are not necessarily recognized in practice. Recently, investigative journalists in Ukraine were killed, possibly for pursuing stories the government did not like, and a journalist in Kazakhstan was sentenced to hard labor for insulting the president. Outside organizations such as the International Freedom of Express Exchange, the Committee to Protect Journalists, Article 19, and Reporters sans frontières keep track and call attention to these kinds of incidents.

The struggles of the media in all of these countries have been carried on with extensive support from organizations in Western Europe and the United States. These include government-sponsored organizations, such as the Organization for Security and Cooperation in Europe, radio governmental organizations (such as the Organization for Security and Cooperation in Europe-OSCE, Radio Free Europe-RFE), and the U.S. State Department, as well as regional and international nongovernmental organizations (NGOs), such as the European Institute for the Media, the International Federation of Journalists, Human Rights Watch, and the Soros Foundation,

The Baltic States

The Baltic States—Estonia, Latvia, and Lithuania—are still troubled by lingering issues from the past, but they are aware of the other newly independent states, particularly in the area of media independence. While each of the Baltic countries has a mix of public and private media ownership, most of the broadcasting and newspaper outlets of the country are privately owned and free of government intervention. The problems that challenge Baltic journalists tend to cluster around issues of ethics and professional practices.

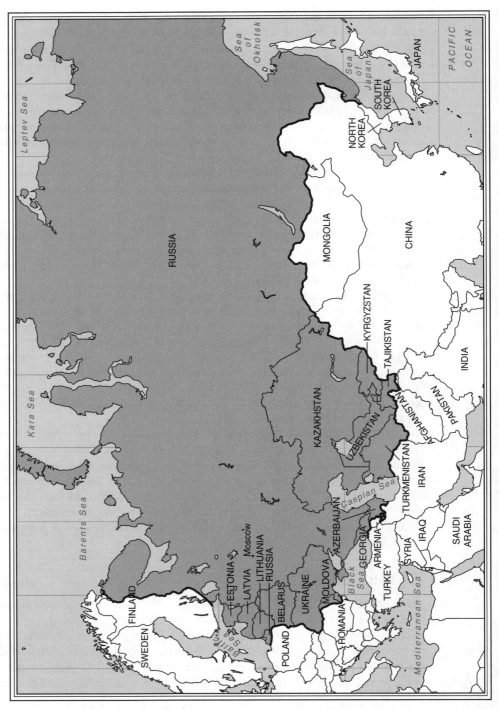

FIGURE 14.2 The new independent states formed after the collapse of the former Soviet Union

Estonia, Latvia, and Lithuania all rank high on the list of democratic countries and have enviable scores in both political rights and press freedom categories. All three countries have actively engaged in the economic and democratic reforms necessary to make them eligible for admission to the European Union.

Generally speaking, it is possible to assume that the Baltic States are going in the right direction to assure democratic rights and freedom of speech and press. Not only have they scored many achievements—for instance, their high rankings for freedom of the press have placed them with free developed democratic countries such as the United States and Germany—but they are still working on maintaining these achievements. However, these countries still face issues regarding nondemocratic acts and actions that violate freedom of the press principles.

Estonia   Estonia has a stable political and economic system and respects basic civil liberties, including freedom of the press. Corruption is not pervasive, and there is an active campaign to eradicate it.

All Estonian language dailies are privately owned and receive no financial assistance from the government. There are dozens of newspapers mostly financed by readers and owners. Although the government still owns the nation's printing facilities, they are managed privately without official interference.

Estonia has three national television stations that are private and one state-owned television station, which has the largest national audience. There are 30 private radio stations in addition to the state radio. Russian-language broadcasting is popular in Estonia.

More than 40 Estonian-language papers have united to form the Estonian Newspaper Association, which lobbies on behalf of its members' interests, defends member newspapers, and champions the interests and rights of Estonian media against violations of freedom of the press.

Fifty percent of Estonia's advertising expenditures go to newspapers; television follows, with 20 percent; and magazines and radio each get 12 percent, with the balance spent on other forms of advertising, such as billboards and posters.

Estonia has the highest Internet penetration of any country in Eastern Europe or the former Soviet Union. Twenty-eight percent of Estonians betweens the ages of 17 and 74 use the Internet, and projects are under way to make 80 public access sites available. The only constraint on Internet access remains the high cost of computers and connections.

In general, unethical reporting is less of a problem in Estonia than in either of the other two Baltic states. However, Estonia has not been exempt from press trauma. An Estonian publisher of the country's largest Russian-language daily and weekly newspapers was shot in 2001, a year after his son had been killed in the same manner. No suspects were identified in either case.

Latvia   Latvia is a functioning market economy with a democratic constitutional system. In general, the government respects freedom of speech. Latvian media express a wide range of critical views. It has no legal penalties for irresponsible journalism, and legal penalties are the same for libeling private and public people.

Most newspapers and magazines in Latvia are privately owned. The two most popular dailies have circulations of 70,000 and 65,000, respectively. A Russian-language paper is next most widely read, with a circulation of 15,000. There is one state-owned weekly and a second state-owned paper that come out four times a week. All major cities have their own privately owned papers. Private companies handle the bulk of newspaper distribution.

The country has two state-owned television networks and nine privately owned stations. The station with the largest audience is the privately owned Latvian Independent Television, which has nearly twice as many viewers as its closest state-owned competitor. Ten percent of Latvian viewers view satellite television. There are a large number of independent radio stations broadcasting in both Russian and Latvian, and 10 of those stations are located in the capital, Riga. The radio station with the most listeners is the major public radio station, Latvia's Radio 1.

Television gets the largest share of Latvia's advertising expenditures, with 43 percent, while newspapers receive 35 percent, radio 6 percent, and magazines 4 percent.

Latvian media problems tend to center around language issues, particularly as they impact the Russian-language press: the professional performance and ethics of journalists, particularly with regard to libel and slander; and the impact of Latvia's corruption problems on journalists who had written stories about smuggling through Latvian ports by the Russian mafia and were investigating alleged involvement of local officials in an illegal alcohol business. Latvian journalists are subjected to in-house pressures from owners and, as a result, tend to engage in routine self-censorship.

Lithuania   Lithuania continues to struggle with weakness in its judicial system, which undermines the rule of law.

The mass media in Lithuania inspire more confidence than all other institutions. Yet, in 2000 lawmakers passed legislation that would have created a national ombudsman to control the media. Although the president vetoed that provision of the bill, it was replaced with measures to beef up an existing commission charged with investigating journalism ethics.

Most of the Lithuanian media are privately owned, although the state still owns part of the dominant news services and all of the national radio and television public broadcasting Company. Private media are doing well, but state broadcasting has had a harder time paying its creditors.

Lithuania has three major newspapers and three major broadcasting operations. Newspaper distribution is privately owned, and few publications use the state-owned postal system. Two percent of Lithuanians directly subscribe to the Internet; 5 percent of the population report that they use it at available facilities, including work sites and Internet cafés.

Journalists working for state-owned radio and television face frequent pressure and intervention from the government. Russian-language journalists are more likely to feel beleaguered. All journalists have problems with access to government information, particularly information relating to military and security issues.

Lithuanian journalism has a reputation for sensationalism, scandal-mongering, and a disproportionate focus on violent crime. In addition, Lithuanian media are prone to periodic outbreaks of inflammatory content, whether nationalistic, anti-Semitic, or pornographic.

Lithuania has the harshest libel laws of the Baltic countries, with penalties including jail time, hard labor, or fines. In the mid-1990s, Lithuanian journalists experienced personal attacks and office destruction attributed to criminal sources.

Central Asia: Kazakhstan, Kyrgyzstan, Tajikistan, Turkmenistan, and Uzbekistan

Reporters Without Borders has ranked world press freedom in Turkmenistan, Uzbekistan, Kazakhstan, Kyrgyzstan, and Tajikistan among the least free in the world. Reporters Without Borders condemned Uzbekistan's "brutal repression of an independent press that is almost non-existent" and defined press freedom in Tajikistan and Kyrgyzstan as "extremely precarious."

The Central Asian post-Soviet states of Kazakhstan, Kyrgyzstan, Tajikistan, Turkmenistan, and Uzbekistan each ranked "not free" in 2007 in Freedom House's rankings. These rankings were based on the legal environment in which the media operated, the degree of independence of the news media from governmental ownership and influence, economic pressures on news content, and diverse violations of press freedom, ranging from the murder of journalists to extralegal abuse and harrassment by state and nonstate actors. Other international press freedom watchdog organizations concurred.

The Moscow Media Law and Policy Institute has pointed out that the existence of media freedom laws cannot guarantee the freedom of mass media, and the Committee to Protect Journalists (CPJ) has reported a pattern of diminishing press freedom in these countries: "Shielded by institutional secrecy, authorities make little effort to track down the killers. CPJ has documented case after case in Europe and Central Asia where investigators ignore journalism as a motive. Instead, they classify the killings as common crimes and label professional assassins 'hooligans.' Prosecutors open and suspend investigations, rarely informing victims' relatives and colleagues, who have to scramble for information or do their own forensic investigation. Detectives sometimes fail to study the dead journalist's notebooks, computers, and tape recorders. They fail to interview all witnesses, then ignore the testimony of those they do interview. Investigations are closed for lack of suspects despite glaring evidence to the contrary."

CPJ also reported that there is less press freedom in the region today than there was during the *glasnost* years in the late 1980s and 1990s in the Soviet Union. The CPJ cited the murder of 46 journalists in the former Soviet states over the past 15 years, with 90 percent of the cases unsolved and with governments hiding abuses.

Kazakhstan   From his one and only official Kazakhstan Web site to the legislation that gives him lifelong oversight over future presidents and governments of the country, it is clear that Nursultan Nazarbaev controls Kazakhstan. In fact, the Kazakh calendar has a month named after Nazarbaev and one named after his mother. And while Kazakhstan's constitution guarantees freedom of the press, it also provides special protection for the president.

Vast mineral and oil reserves make Kazakhstan attractive to the West, and Nazarbaev describes his country as an oasis of stability, a feature investors find reassuring. However, the resultant petrodollar income highlights the poor living conditions of Kazakh citizens and has triggered corruption and bribery scandals, which have caused massive capital flight.

Kazakhstan advances the rhetoric of democratization and political reform, but rhetoric bears little resemblance to reality. Control of all strategic resources and political power is concentrated in Nazarbaev, his family and relatives. Those strategic resources include the media.

In 1996 Dariga Nazarbaev, the president's daughter, took over the state-owned news agency. This change led to the closing of many of the country's media outlets. The president's daughter continues to run several television channels and controls two of the nation's leading newspapers. All prominent broadcast media are either state run or controlled by members and associates of Nazarbaev's family.

The Kazakh press experienced a brief spell of freedom in the mid-1990s. At that time, the country had a popular, professional newspaper that had its own broadcast operation. The company was driven out of business by raids, intimidation, tax audits, and arson. Finally, it was purchased by a business with close ties to Nazarbaev's son-in-law.

Since 1996, the government has cracked down on press freedom, and conditions for the media have worsened. In 1998 Nazarbaev's handpicked legislators passed a media law that officially restricted media independence. Then, in 1999, a law was passed that made it a crime for anyone to publish any information about the president and his family or their economic interests.

The 2005 election gave President Nazarbaev a new seven-year term, but opposition in the media resulted in a crackdown on the opposition and prosecutions for defaming him.

New legislative restrictions passed in 2006, imposing costly registration fees for journalists, broadening criteria for denying media outlets registration, requiring news outlets to submit the names of editors with registration applications, and necessitating re-registration in the event of an address change. Media watchdog groups such as Freedom House condemned these amendments.

Regular assaults on the independent media in Kazakhstan have prompted mounting expressions of concern from Washington and watchdog organizations concerned about antidemocratic developments in the country.

In 2006, following the murder of opposition leader Altynbek Sarsenbayev, journalist Kazis Toguzbayev published two articles on the Internet Web site (www.kub.kz) criticizing Nazarbaev's actions in the context of Sarsenbayev's murder. Toguzbayev, accused of undermining the reputation and dignity of the president, faced criminal charges.

Editor Yergalieva Gulzhan of Svoboda Slova received a 10-day prison sentence for saying President Nazarbaev and his daughter were behind the murders. Editor Kenzhegali Aitbakiyev of the opposition newspaper *Ayna-Plus,* which had reported on corruption allegations against Nazarbaev, was beaten and left unconscious in the street. Prosecutors failed to take meaningful actions after the beating. *Ayna-Plus* had been publishing under the name *Zhuma Times* until a court shut it down, having been sued for libeling Nazarbaev and ordered to liquidate. That newspaper was forced several times to change its name, as did other publications.

French journalist Gregoire de Bourgues, 24, was murdered at his apartment in Almaty. Reporters Without Borders sent a team to Kazakhstan to investigate and participate in the trial, having been granted interested party status by a judge in France. Following Sarsenbayev's murder in 2006, Culture and Information Minister Yermukhamet Yertysbayev said the state would restore full control over the Khabar media holding company.

Independent print publications are hampered by low circulation and government influence. In 2007, the printing company Dauir briefly refused to print seven Almaty-based opposition newspapers. Dauir's director was Svetlana Nazarbaeva, the president's sister-in-law. The Internet provided some refuge for Kazakhstan's beleaguered independent press, although there were reports of government interference in the form of monitoring and blocking opposition Web sites. The Kazakh opposition helps fund a Web presence in Moscow that has sought to expose corruption in the Nazarbaev regime.

Less than 3 percent of the Kazakh population has Internet access, and, as the Togyzbayev case shows, Internet authors are as vulnerable to the country's strict libel laws as other journalists.

In the mid-1990s, U.S. funding helped create exchanges that sent Kazakh journalists to spend time with American newspapers, and then offered them a workshop at home on American-style journalism. Other Western countries have also developed contacts intended to help Kazakh journalists learn the ropes of democratic media.

There were 400,000 Internet users in Kazakhstan in 2005, out of a population of 15.2 million. There are 2.9 million telephone lines, 4.9 million cell phones, 12 television broadcast stations with 9 repeaters, and three radio broadcast stations (AM60, FM 17, and shortwave 9.)

Kyrgystan   In the early 1990s, the West viewed the Kyrgyz as the most democratic people in Central Asia. The country had diverse representation in their parliament, their president had not been a Communist Party leader under the old regime, and the president tolerated media criticism, if not investigation of high-level corruption. In the intervening years, however, President Askar Akayev did his best to bring his country into line with its neighbors.

After the ouster of President Akayev in 2005, opposition forces that came to power advanced plans to transform Kyrgyz state television into a public broadcaster. The bill passed by parliament, however, was subsequently vetoed.

Media covering topics unpopular with the president find themselves at the mercy of tax auditors or burdened by crippling criminal libel judgments. Although Kyrgyz law protects freedom of speech and prohibits censorship, it is unevenly applied. Under Akayev, newspapers that are on the wrong side of the president have experienced paper shortages. Libel is considered a criminal offense, but the practice of filing libel suits against media outlets has become less common since Akayev's fall in 2005.

Although only 5 percent of the Kyrgyz population have access to the Internet, Kyrgyzstan has a lively selection of Internet news sites, blogs, and forums for political discussion. Foreign media are allowed to operate freely within the country, but foreign ownership of domestic media outlets is prohibited. Uchkun, the state-sponsored printing house, controls the primary means of publication in the country, but a U.S.-sponsored printing house, operated by Freedom House since 2004 provides publishers with an alternative.

Kyrgyzstan has 40 to 50 regularly printed newspapers and magazines. Most are private but not independent. E1 TV is ostensibly a public broadcaster but is subject to government control in practice. Kyrgyzstan has 5 major TV stations based in Bishkek: National TV, NTS, KOORT, Pyramida, and NBT. All broadcasters are subject to heavy government influence. The government ended NTS transmissions in a number of regions in 2007, citing the need to use the frequency for a new state channel.

The state media praise the president lavishly. Most of the private media try to provide balanced coverage, but there are outspoken critics among the private media, and they face harrassment. Journalists routinely engage in self-censorship to avoid repercussions from the government.

Advertising is restricted by law to 20 percent of print media space. Newsstands and kiosks were privatized in the early 1990s, but they still get all their publications from the state distribution operation. The government owns the printing plant for the state media.

Although broadcast services reach much of the country, their equipment is not powerful enough to make it possible to reach into mountainous regions. The law limits advertising in broadcasting to 25 percent of airtime. Broadcasting stations are required to pay for all supervisory functions of the National Agency for Communication. This agency, together with the minister of justice and the president's office, must approve all broadcast licenses.

The country has legal guarantees of press freedom, but there are many constraints and limitations. Media are not allowed to print false information, even in a direct quote. It is illegal to damage a subject's honor, or to publish articles that encourage war or incite ethnic or religious antagonism.

Res Publica, which has a circulation of 10,000, has repeatedly challenged the president and as a result has faced repeated court cases. Its reporters, copy editors, and even its chief editor have been imprisoned for their roles in producing derogatory stories about the state itself. Other journalists have been jailed for writing disapproved stories, and several journalists charged with printing state secrets were jailed and interrogated by government security forces. Journalists who interviewed opposition politicians faced fines for tax code violations and the repeated attentions of tax investigators.

In 1998 Akayev set up a Morals Commission made up of illustrious citizens and academics. The commission suspended three newspapers. All of them revised their approaches to the practice of journalism and reopened in 1999. Observers have suggested that it is only fair to note that Kyrgyz journalists tended to report stories based on rumor and unsubstantiated reports.

Independent Kyrgyz media faced considerable political and financial constraints during the 2000 election. Local officials filed libel suits in response to critical articles, the presidential administration triggered tax audits and criminal investigations, and while most private media got off without excessive trouble, the treatment of outspoken members of the press provided a clear warning to the rest.

Internet use is limited both because the citizens of Kyrgyzstan are poor and cannot afford service and because the infrastructure of the country does not make it possible for people who live in rural areas to get service. Internet use is estimated at 0.4 users per 1,000 population. There are no government restrictions on Internet use or access.

After Akayev's fall in 2005, government attempts to exert control over the country's media environment increased, leading to opposition demonstrations in Bishkek in 2006. Journalists at Kyrgyz state television and radio staged a protest over the appointment of an ally of president Kurmanbek Bakiyev as deputy director.

At that time, authorities blocked opposition leaders from appearing on state television, privately owned NTS lost power to its antennae, and hacker attacks made news Web sites akipress.org and 24.kg inaccessible for several days. An arson attack by hooded men damaged Pyramind, an independent TV station. Not surprisingly, government officials failed to investigate. Death threats came against the editor of the station. Also in 2006, a broadcast journalist was assaulted by progovernment demonstrators in Zhalalabat, and a television reporter was brutally beaten and sued after critical reporting on railroad corruption. In 2007, police forcibly prevented journalists from covering an opposition demonstration and seized control of newspapers.

The campaign to denationalize newspapers, formally launched in 2005, has resulted in the abrupt abandonment of the newspapers to free-market forces, terminating operations for most newspapers.

Tajikistan   The Tajik constitution provides for freedom of both speech and press, but these freedoms are more recognizable in the breach. As a matter of practice, Tajikistan restricts freedom of speech and press. The media are licensed, and editors practice self-censorship out of fear that their newspapers will be shut down. The country has no circulating daily newspapers. Most citizens received their news from the broadcast media. There are no daily newspapers because the economy is too weak to support anything beyond weeklies.

In 2005–2006, government efforts to reduce Tajikistan's media environment proved successful. Laws set five-year prison terms for criticizing the president publicly. A court suspended Tajikistan's Union of Journalists from April to July of 2007, arguing that its charter violated Tajik law. Internet news Web sites were blocked. The state maintained a strong presence on the media landscape through direct and indirect ownership, licensing requirements, subsidies, and control of transmission facilities.

There was no oppositional participation by broadcast and print media during the coverage of the 2006 reelection of President Emomali Rakhmonov. Before the election, Tajik authorities asked Internet providers to block Web sites that aimed to undermine the state's policies in the sphere of information, according to a letter obtained by Reuters. After a few days of shutdown, Internet sites were restored. The Websites were centrasia.ru, arianastorm.com, charogiruz.ru, ferghana.ru, and tajikistantimes.ru, all of which featured materials critical of Rakhmonov.

In 2007, the British Broadcasting Corporation's (BBC) FM radio broadcasts in Tajikistan were suspended in a dispute over registration requirements. The Tajik government claimed the suspension was not politically motivated. The BBC was denied a license for FM broadcasting but was able to open a bureau in Dushanbe.

The independent newspaper *Nerui Sukhan* remained closed in 2006. The newspaper's editor-in-chief received a two-year corrective labor sentence for illegal use of electricity. In 2006, the Supreme Court substituted a fine for the sentence.

Adolat, a struggling weekly opposition paper, vanished when its printing house, Shafei, refused to print the paper on short notice. Shafei purportedly received instructions from Tajik government officials not to print *Adolat.*

Despite the fact that the government maintained a near freeze on the registration of new media outlets, two new newspapers with political content registered in 2006. There were no reports of violence against reporters throughout 2006, but the murders of 29 journalists during the 1992–1997 civil war remained unsolved.

Rebroadcasts of Russian television and radio are widely available, and international media are allowed to operate relatively freely. However, many foreign broadcasts were only available via satellite links in 2006, and few Tajiks could afford that technology

The government controls all printing facilities and newsprint supplies, and subsidizes nearly all publications. Because of the government stranglehold on production and distribution, even independent papers are extremely dependent on the central government, and because of short supplies of newsprint, they cannot always publish. When uncertain conditions are coupled with low salaries, the result is low morale.

Television and radio are the most influential media in Tajikistan. Both are state-owned. The state also controls all broadcast licenses and subsidizes all broadcasting facilities. The only alternative media from outside are Russian, and a reported 78 percent of Tajiks watch Russian television.

Internet access in Tajikistan is growing, in part because of the efforts of the U.S.-funded Central Asian Development Agency. There are five Internet service providers in Tajikistan, but most of their customers are foreigners, since the cost of subscription is the equivalent of US$20, and monthly fees are US$4 to US$6 an hour—the equivalent of a Tajik's monthly salary. Government operations and research institutes also provide access to a small elite.

Independent journalists are routinely exposed to intimidation, harrassment, and violence. Reprisals are frequent, particularly punishment for investigative reporting into government connections with narcotics trafficking. The head of the Ministry of Interior Press Center was shot and killed near Dushanbe, apparently because of his investigation into the regime's involvement in the drug trade.

Turkmenistan   Turkmenistan possesses an abundance of natural resources: the world's fifth largest reserves of natural gas and substantial deposits of oil. Yet it is still impoverished, and since independence from the Soviet Union in 1991, it has remained largely closed to the outside world.

In 1996 President Saparmurat Niyazov declared himself Turkmenbashi, "father of the Turkmen," and was made president for life in 1999. He named himself founder and owner of all newspapers and magazines, and under Niyazov broadcast news generally consisted of the activities and speeches of the government, fostering a vision of the president as a benevolent father. The only criticism allowed on the news was the president's criticism of government officials.

The death of the autocratic Niyazov in December 2006 revived hopes for greater freedom in Turkmenistan. President Kurbanguly Berdymukhamedov was sworn into office in 2007, winning the election with 89 percent of the vote. Western diplomats, however, condemned the election as rigged. Among other promised reforms, Berdymukhamedov has sworn to introduce unlimited Internet access. Turkmenistan's media environment remains one of the most repressive in the world.

Weeks after the presidential election, Berdymukhamedov was chosen as chairman of the People's Council, Turkmenistan's highest legislative body. He was the only candidate.

As in past years, the government maintains an absolute monopoly over print, television, and radio, directly controlling media outlets, printing presses, and other infrastructure. Few foreign journalists are allowed to enter the country, and those allowed in are monitored and their movements are restricted. No private print or broadcast media are allowed in Turkmenistan. Several autonomous publications that existed under Soviet rule have closed.

Turkmen opposition groups in exile operate a number of Web sites that are harshly critical to Turkmenistan's repressive political system, with original and translated material in Turkmen and Russian. It is unclear whether these are accessible from within Turkmenistan, where the government controls and monitors the Internet. The cost is prohibitive for the vast bulk of the population, and less than 1 percent of citizens have access to the Internet. State television rebroadcasts some Russian entertainment programming, and satellite dishes remain available to citizens who can afford them.

Almost all print publications are based in the Ashgabat Press House in the capital. Government agents often seize Russian papers from travelers landing at the Ashgabat airport. Still, Russian and Western newspapers are often available at hotels in the capital.

The government budget funds all newspapers. Advertising and circulation sales provide meager income. The government imports and restricts access to newsprint, equipment, and supplies. Party functionaries hold most key posts in Turkmen radio, television, and newspaper operations. The state-owned National TV and Radio Broadcasting is the only domestic broadcaster. It operates two television channels. The first broadcasts in Turkmen and Russian. The second, in Ashgabat, broadcasts in Turkmen. The state broadcasting operation delays, censors, and rebroadcasts content from the Russian Public Television and the Russian radio station Mayak. The only independent broadcast content available to Turkmen comes from Radio Liberty's shortwave operation. Most of those who continue to report for Radio Liberty work under pseudonyms. Journalists have endured threats and surveillance, torture, and imprisonment. Some have been forced into exile.

In 2007, Radio Free Europe/Radio Liberty correspondent Ogulsapar Muradova died in police custody. She and two human rights activists had been arrested, given a closed trial, and sentenced to a six-year prison term allegedly for possessing illegal ammunition. Relatives who were allowed to view Muradova's body said it bore telltale signs of torture. Turkmen authorities refused to investigate the circumstances of her death.

Several state-run news organizations exist, however, police broke up a gathering of journalists planning to form their own organization.

There is very low Internet use in Turkmenistan, both because there is little access and because the state has few resources. Turkmentelecom and other state bodies control Internet access. Public usage in 2005 was estimated at 36,000 for a country with more than 5 million people. Server facilities are donated by the International Internet Registry in London.

The Organization for Security and Cooperation in Europe (OSCE) has described the lack of press freedom in the country as unprecedented. Canada-based International Freedom of Expression Exchange said Turkmenistan has one of the worst media climates in the world.

Uzbekistan   Uzbekistan is still run by its Soviet-era leader, President Islam Karimov. The Uzbek government does not respect freedom of speech or the press, despite nominal constitutional guarantees. It is an authoritarian state that holds zero tolerance for negative media coverage. The Committee to Protect Journalists named Uzbekistan as one of its 10 Most Censored Countries in the world at a UN press conference in 2007. The country has no private publishing houses or printing presses, and the establishment of new periodicals is subject to government approval.

A violent government suppression of a 2005 demonstration in Andijan further diminished media freedoms in Uzbekistan. Uzbek TV began to report the events of the Andijan massacre only following President Karimov's press conference, two days after the massacre. Karimov asserted that there had been no shooting of peaceful citizens protesting against mass repression and poverty; security forces had carried out a successful operation against Islamic terrorists who were being directed from abroad. Karimov urged journalists to believe only what they heard from the Uzbek prosecution service, namely, that the deaths in Andijan numbered only 169 and that peaceful citizens had been killed by Islamic terrorists, not by government troops. Karimov squeezed out all independent and foreign media and foreign, nongovernmental organizations following the massacre. International experts estimated that between 700 and 1,500 people, including women and children, were killed when Uzbek government forces opened fire on demonstrators in Andijan. The government ordered that the transmission of news broadcasts from Russian television, especially NTV and Ren-TV, be jammed immediately. Nongovernmental and cable television companies knuckled under; in early 2007, they had been forced under threat of closure to unite in a single network, the Uzbekistan Kabel Sistemalari, owned by President Karimov's daughter, Gulnara Karimova, and a family friend, Firdavs Abdukhalikov.

Karimov turned aside international calls for an independent investigation into the May 2005 killing of hundreds of civilians by government troops in Andijan. He accused the West of waging an information war on Uzbekistan, and his government continued to use trumped-up charges of terrorism and extremism to jail media critics, political opponents, and human rights advocates.

Karimov reacted defiantly to the World Bank's February decision to stop lending money to Uzbekistan. The president claimed the World Bank's decision had been based on incorrect information, and he warned Western nations to stop interfering in Uzbekistan's internal affairs. In 2006 the BBC, Radio Free Europe/Radio Liberty, and Voice of America remained unable to broadcast from within Uzbekistan.

Activist Saidjahon Zainabiddinov was reportedly sentenced to a seven-year prison term for speaking with foreign journalists about the Uzbek security services. Deutsche Welle correspondent Obid Shavanov was stripped of his accreditation for inaccuracies alleged in his reporting.

Harrassment prompted Alo Khojayev to shut down his independent news Web site Tribune-uz.info. Six journalists were fired from state-owned media outlets for freelancing for foreign publications. Independent journalist Ulughbek Haydarov was sentenced to a six-year prison term for extortion after reporting on government corruption. Sobirdjon Yakubov, a journalist with the newspaper *Hurriyat,* was jailed after calling for democratic reforms. An Uzbek court in 2006 suspended Freedom House's operations in the country for providing Internet access without a license. The Uzbek government has criticized foreign journalists—mostly Russian-based reporters for newspapers like *Nezavisimaya Gazeta* and *Izvestiya* and the news service Interfax—for reporting libelous stories.

Exile groups publish papers in Moscow and Istanbul and smuggle them into the country. Broadcast media are subject to a highly bureaucratic annual re-registration process.

The government denounces foreign-funded media as aggressors in an information war against Uzbekistan, portraying Western-style democratization as a plot to undermine Uzbek identity. With foreign-funded media banned from the country, the Internet was a critical source of information, and a number of Uzbek journalists were able to operate news sites from abroad with a focus on rights issues. However, the total number of Internet users was less than one million in a country of over 26 million people. Authorities block critical news and opposition sites. Some remain available through proxy servers.

President Islam Karimov continued his crackdown on the independent press, political opponents, and civil society groups. Karimov's regime expelled dozens of foreign-funded nongovernmental organizations, including those supporting local media. The few remaining independent journalists were forced to choose between severing ties to foreign-funded media or facing harassment, legal action, and imprisonment. A restrictive new law regulating the work of journalists for international media made it illegal for local reporters to contribute to foreign media outlets not accredited by the Ministry of Foreign Affairs.

To solidify its grip on Uzbekistan's battered independent media, the government tightened restrictions on local and international journalists working for foreign-funded media. The cabinet approved regulations in early 2007 that gave the Ministry of Foreign Affairs wide discretion to issue formal warnings to foreign correspondents, revoke their accreditation and visas, and expel them. Foreign correspondents are barred from "interfering in the internal affairs of the Republic of Uzbekistan." The broad language of the regulations does not define what constitutes interference in Uzbekistan's internal affairs.

Putting the new regulations to immediate use, the Foreign Affairs Ministry issued reprimands to three local correspondents for the German public broadcaster Deutsche Welle. Obid Shabanov, rebuked for filing allegedly inaccurate news reports, had reported on a January incident in which 30 people froze to death when their bus broke down in the desert. Yuri Chernogayev, charged with working with unaccredited journalists, had confirmed the accuracy of that report to a Reuters correspondent.

In a positive development, journalist Sobirdjon Yakubov was released from prison. A reporter for the state-run weekly *Hurriyat,* Yakubov had spent a year in jail on subversion charges based on allegations of religious extremism. A Tashkent court released him for lack of evidence. Another reporter remained in prison after being convicted of unconstitutional activities in connection with a *Hurriyat* article that questioned the compatibility of Islam and democracy.

U.S. lawmakers, including Senator John McCain, called for the suspension of U.S. funding to Uzbekistan until the country showed progress on human rights and allowed an international investigation into the Andijan killings.

On May 13, 2007, the two-year anniversary of the Andijan killings, the U.S. Department of State and the European Union issued statements condemning the crackdown and renewing calls for an independent probe. The state-controlled Uzbek press reacted by condemning the West's "information aggression" toward Uzbekistan, the U.S. government-funded Radio Free Europe/Radio Liberty said.

In September 2007, Dzhamshid Karimov, a former correspondent for the London-based Institute for War and Peace Reporting (IWPR) who wrote critically about local and federal officials, was forced into psychiatric confinement in the central city of Samarkand. Karimov, the president's nephew, had been under close government surveillance for months. Authorities had earlier cut his long-distance and international phone connections and seized his passport.

On September 8, a Tashkent court sentenced poet and singer Dadakhon Khasanov to a suspended three-year sentence after a closed-door trial in which the defendant had no lawyer. The charges stemmed from a song Khasanov wrote and recorded in commemoration of Andijan. The AP reported that the lyrics read in part: "Don't say you haven't seen how Andijan was drowned in blood. . . .The victims fell like mulberries, the children's bloodied bodies were like tulips."

Libel, public defamation of the president, and irresponsible journalism, especially reporting falsehoods, are all crimes under Uzbekistan's 1997 Law on Media.

Russia

Journalism in Russia has changed rapidly in the past three decades, reflecting the country's political, social, and economic changes. Today, Russian journalism has a new philosophy that is heavily rooted in the long tradition of this profession. The major turning points of Soviet and post-Soviet history of Russia as well as this country's political and economic turnaround have directly influenced the character of journalism in Russia at the beginning of the twenty-first century.

The development of journalism in Russia can be divided into three major parts: the pre-Soviet period, which includes the early days of journalism, nineteenth-century journalism, and journalism in the early twentieth century; the Soviet period, from 1917 until 1985, which includes the Soviet period as well as changes during *perestroika* and *glasnost*; and the Gorbachev and post-Soviet period, from 1985, when the Soviet Union collapsed, to the present.

Contemporary Russian journalism is very diverse. Today's Russian journalism took over a gigantic media system, divided it into parts, and made independent media out of these pieces. One of the major characteristics of post-Soviet Russian media is its human and material resources. New Russian media did not have to start from scratch: a journalism tradition and infrastructure were already available. At the same time, many media, such as the Internet, developed as a result of political and technological changes in Russian society. In this section we present general information on Russian media—print, broadcast, and the Internet—and then discuss journalism education in Russia.

Print Media   Even though many independent newspapers that were created in the early 1990s had to use grants from Western organizations to publish, and many editors and journalists of national newspapers split up to create their own media organizations, Russia had arrived at its independence with a strong foundation of diverse forms of journalism. Readers in the Soviet Union were active subscribers to major national and local newspapers (often it was a good sign of party citizenship to subscribe to *Pravda, Izvestia,* and others) as well as many special interest media. Young Russians read at least *Komsomolskaya Pravda* and *Rovesnik,* while teenagers had to follow news in *Pionerskaya Pravda* and *Pioner.* Elementary schoolchildren had their own magazines such as *Murzilka.* Readers of post-Soviet Russia have been not only economically disempowered, but also highly selective in their choice of media.

Segmentation of the audience is a central feature of modern Russian media. During the period from the late 1990s until the early 2000s, the annual circulation of Russian newspapers has declined by about 35 percent, but the number of newspapers published grew by 20 percent. The frequency and times when newspapers are published have also changed in the post-Soviet era. In 1989, 11 of the 34 national newspapers were published daily, and 15 were published once or twice a week. Of the 333 newspapers that were published in 2000, only 20 were published daily. In 2000, 5,425 regional newspapers were published, their circulation totaled 14.9 million copies, and they covered 94 percent of the total number of newspapers printed in Russia. In 2006, *The International Herald Tribune* became the first international daily newspaper to be published in Russia.

Many of the most popular newspapers in Russia are tabloid dailies, which include mostly entertainment, advertising, and sponsored press releases. The most popular national paper is *Argumenti i Fakti,* which has the largest circulation in the nation at 3.5 million and contains various sections on topics such as health, advice, and celebrities. *Moskovskii Komsomolets,* a paper with a daily circulation of 800,000, was once the official paper of Moscow's Communist Party and is now the preferred national paper of many educated readers.

Russian newspapers were traditionally divided into national, regional, *raion* (county), and other local, internal (usually factory-owned) newspapers, and specialized (such as economic and professional and leisure interest) newspapers. Many of these papers have changed their focus and now publish strictly informative or tabloid materials as well as reprints from national newspapers. This is especially true for local newspapers because of the lack of professional staff and financial flexibility required to cover local events.

Magazines have also experienced dramatic changes from Soviet to post-Soviet eras. In Soviet times, magazines of general and special interest were extremely popular in promoting the Soviet image. Today a number of magazines are Russian versions of Western publications such as *Cosmopolitan, Popular Mechanics, Men's Health, The New Yorker,* and *Newsweek.*

Broadcast Media   As with print media, broadcast media were a historic part of a larger Soviet system, and this structure allowed broadcast media to survive the collapse of the Soviet Union. Television set ownership by the public in Russia is high, with 73 percent of households in a survey of eight regional cities reporting owning a color television set since 1993; and 43 percent of households reporting owning two or more television sets (Internews, 1999). Estimates suggest that there are approximately 60.5 million televisions in Russia, or .42 sets per capita (Tenlab, 2002).

Russia has at least 7,306 TV broadcast stations. The most dominant TV stations are RTR, a state-controlled station; ORT, a station with 51 percent of shares held by the government, and 41 percent of shares held by regional governor and Russian oil tycoon, Roman Abromovich; and NTV, the only Russian station critical of government policies. Among the most popular newscasts are by Vremya on ORT, which has an estimated audience of 14 million viewers nightly (26 percent rating); Vesti, on RTR, and Sevodnya, on NTV. ORT has a much broader reach than RTR or NTV, mostly because of transmitter availability.

The majority of broadcast media in today's Russia is state owned. Most administrative regions in Russia have their own government-run TV stations as well as at least one independent station. Independent stations suffer from financial shortages and for the most part exist through grants from Western independent associations and private businesses. Because TV is the most successful medium to influence Russian publics, and most Russians get news and information from national television stations (ROMIR, 2007), federal and local governments pay particular attention to the content of TV stations. Although government might not dictate specific programming, it influences what and how events are reported.

Radio broadcasting also continues to be dominated by state-owned and state-operated stations, but more local independent radio stations are emerging. Among independent media that have emerged, the most popular are Ekho Moskvy, an independent station that provides a combination of news and talk radio in the Moscow region; the national stations Mayak and Radio Rossiya; and Europe Plus, a station that mostly broadcasts music.

The Internet   The European Media Institute projected that already by 2002, Russian Internet users would have reached 27 million, and this number has grown substantially since then, with about 14 percent of the population having access by 2005. Russian Internet users are most likely to be between the ages of 18 and 35, and have a higher education and income level than the average Russian (ROMIR, 2007).

Many problems of Internet access remain for a broad range of the Russian public. Internet cafés are the most popular places for Russians to surf the Internet because a majority of Russian homes do not have Internet connection. Public institutions, such as universities and libraries, often do not have a fast and reliable Internet connection because of their inability to pay for continuous use of a reliable connection (despite national programs funded by the Open Society Institute of the Soros Foundation.) In recent years, access to digital lines in Russia has improved, especially in urban centers, but a large demand for high-speed Internet access remains unsatisfied.

Major media organizations have invested in existing Internet-based publications and have also established their own. Many Web sites are mirror publications of already existing print or broadcast media (*Komsomolskaya Pravda, Izvestiya, Kommersant,* and others); others are original Internet media (Gazeta.ru, Lenta.ru).

The growth of Internet usage in Russia is most apparent in the current trends in the use of Weblogs and online journals. Although Internet usage in Russia lags behind that of many other countries (Russia ranks number 90 in a study of 220 countries), the number of blog and online journal users in Russia is behind only those of the United States, Canada, and the United Kingdom.

Journalism Education in Russia   The old Soviet form of journalism education remains largely unchanged in post-Soviet Russia. The ideological core of Russian journalism—coverage of news events in accordance with the Communist Party's view of the world—required a comprehensive liberal education with study of works by Russian writers and publicists. As Murray (1994:88) described: "The role of the Soviet press . . .was not simply to report in accordance with Marxist-Leninist logic. The journalist also had a duty actively to participate in the construction of future society." The Russian model of journalism favors an analysis of events, while the Western model favors informative reporting.

During the Soviet period, the most famous universities for journalism education were Moscow State University and Moscow Institute of International Relations, which mostly prepared journalists for work in national media. The capital city of each republic of the former USSR, as well as most major cities in several Russian regions, also had large state universities that offered journalism majors. Among the most popular and comprehensive were St. Petersburg State, Ural State, Voronezh State, Far-Eastern State, as well as Kiev State (Ukraine), Minsk State (Belarus), and Tartu University in Tallinn (Estonia). All these schools had a rich journalistic and literary tradition and the best faculty available. At the same time, these institutions were monitored closely by Glavlit and other party representatives and thus were highly conservative in their curricula.

When *perestroika* and *glasnost* were adopted, Russian journalism education went through a period of reestablishing and rethinking its educational practices. Faculty members were inspired by open discussion of previously banned publications and materials, and engaged in debate about modern journalism issues and the state of higher education.

Contemporary journalism education in Russia now faces several challenges. First, many faculty members have left universities in search of better paying jobs. In the Soviet Union, teachers were in a higher than middle-class salary range, but by the end of the 1990s, they hardly managed to cover basic needs for their families. Journalism faculty in Russia, in addition to full-time teaching, usually work in the Russian media, advertising, and public relations.

Economic problems are also evident in Russian schools in the lack of modern audio-visual and Internet equipment. Another problem occurs because many professors of the "old school" have retired, and undereducated professionals and those with little graduate training have taken their place. Many people who work for today's Russian media come from a variety of backgrounds and do not have any solid training in journalism writing. As a result, informational genres occupy the press and broadcast media, and a shift to a more Western model of media has become more evident. More journalists who have never received extensive training are working in the Russian local and regional media. This Western model favors purely informative reporting without the Russian model of journalism's analysis of events. Often, sensational tabloid journalism replaces quality writing on current subjects of political and economic importance.

In addition, Russian journalists do not have a full understanding of the concepts of freedom of speech, independence, and the principles of investigative journalism. When these principles are understood, Russian journalists may not know how to use them to empower media workers. Formal training at the university level does not solve the problem because Russia lacks the tradition of studying and examining the principles of freedom of expression and the press. Media marketing is also an underdog in journalism higher education: traditional liberal arts schools of journalism have a hard time finding faculty members who are properly trained and who completely understand media marketing and the principles of publishing in the new economic context.

Training seminars and workshops as well as internships in Western media are constantly offered to Russian journalists by independent organizations that guard freedom of speech worldwide. Among them are the International Federation of Journalists, the

International Journalists Network, the Open Society Institute of the Soros Foundation, and many others. In 2005, a Russian pedagogical journal, *Media Education,* was founded by leading Russian media educators. Fulbright grants also encourage U.S. journalism professors to come to Russia to teach a Western view of journalism (Aumente et al., 1999).

Contemporary Problems of Russian Journalism   Russia was abruptly categorized as "not free" in the 2007 Annual Survey of Media Freedom by Freedom House. Some important factors leading to this judgment involved political influence, economic dependency, ethical challenges, and self-censorship.

Political Influence   Freedom of speech was widely celebrated and acknowledged in the early 1990s and established 1989 through 1992 as a golden era of Russian journalism. However, by the middle and late 1990s, the euphoria of freedom of speech was overcome by the political influence that government officials had over the media, working from the old assumption that journalists should follow the party line. Many representatives of the Russian administrations, especially at the local levels, still had a Communist approach, though now they called themselves democrats.

Russian President Vladimir Putin has been actively criticized by international organizations for limiting opportunities for freedom of speech for Russian media and was named one of the "10 Worst Enemies of the Press for 2001." After Putin became president, the Russian state increasingly interfered with media autonomy (Becker, 2004).

Sanctions such as cuts in governmental subsidies and isolation from printing presses, which sometimes are also concentrated in the hands of local government officials, are effective means for government officials to exercise economic influence over the media. Often officials would use other sanctions, such as closing newspaper offices because they did not immediately meet updated fire requirement standards, and not renewing media licenses.

A question of editorial freedom is raised every time a newspaper is forced to stop publication, leave an occupied building, or pay substantial fees that may result in media bankruptcy. "In the overwhelming number of cases where perpetrators can be identified, it is the state that has committed facilitated acts of violence and repression against journalists" (Becker 2003:110).

Russia's legal system offers very little protection for the media, and "ever-flexible" laws permit the government to take selective actions against media organizations (Becker, 2004). In July 2006, Putin signed a law that expanded the definition of extremist activity now so broad that it allows authorities to use unchecked power against its critics, including the media (Walker, 2007).

Economic Dependency   The economic problems of Russian media began in the early to mid-1990s when the economy of the Soviet Union began to fail. Mass media faced the greatest challenge of how to stay alive during this financially unstable period. Many newspapers, for instance, were not in a hurry to obtain independence from the official administration for purely economic reasons: "Newspapers that were registered with official bodies were still entitled to a greater allocation of state subsidized paper from the state publishing committee" (Murray, 1994:51).

Independent newspapers had to buy paper at much higher prices, and this was one of the methods of indirect influence by the party-state apparatus used on rebel media (Murray, 1994). Another problem that outspoken Russian print media faced in the 1990s was the refusal of the state-owned retail distribution organization Soyuzpechat' to distribute the newspapers (Tolz, 1990). Hiring independent distributors rather quickly solved this problem. Some national newspapers organized their own circulation organizations, which were later used to sell many newspapers and magazines that were printed by publishing houses created by the newspaper leaders. The best example is a publishing house of one of the leading Russian newspapers Komsomolskaya Pravda, which now has distribution offices in almost every region of Russia.

Russian oligarchs and the government still use economic methods to control or silence the media. Ketter (2001) observed that officials still indirectly control the economy of the Russian media. More and more media in Russia are in the hands of oligarchs, and many scandals have arisen around the media and their editors directly from the scandals and disputes among oligarchs. In 2004, the state retained ownership of the two leading national broadcast channels, RTR and ORT, and much more of the country's media (Becker, 2004).

In the latter part of the first decade of the 2000s, it remained difficult to predict which way the Russian media market would develop. Globalization might minimize the *"peculiarities* of Russian media market" as Vartanova (2007) puts it, but it is also possible that the impact of domestic political developments might even influence the media economy even more.

Questions of Ethics   The question of ethical conduct among Russian journalists is often raised in relation to the economic dependency that individual journalists face today. Often, professional ethics are questioned when a journalist who works for one newspaper, magazine, or broadcast channel also works for an advertising or public relations agency. *Zakazukha* is a Russian slang word that can be translated as "pay-for-publicity." Holmes (2001) explains that this is "the payment to newspapers and individual journalists for media coverage." In Russian media, *zakazukha* simply is bribery that is offered to, or demanded by, journalists. This practice, prevalent in Russian television and print media, is in violation of Russian Federation Law 108, "Advertising," signed on July 19, 1995, which states, "Media information organizations are not permitted to take payments for placing advertising in the guise of informational, editorial, or authored material." Despite this law, *zakazukha* has become increasingly popular.

The problem of demanding and accepting money for news coverage has developed as a result of the unprofessional publicity policies of advertisers who label their media advertising tactics as publicity (e.g., Tsetsura, 2000, 2002; Tsetsura and Kruckeberg, 2004), but has not been substantially addressed in journalism research. Even though many Russian media have ethical codes of professional conduct and the Russian Association of Journalists has initiated its own code of ethics, they often remain on paper and are not enforced. One of the major reasons cited by Russian journalists as to why this practice occurs is the economic dependency of journalists. An average salary of a Russian journalist in regional newspapers hardly ever exceeds $200 a month and often is less than $100. Many journalists live in poverty and are forced to work in advertising and write *zakazukha* materials. The salaries of Moscow journalists working for national media are often compa-rable with the salaries of business and account managers of successful companies, yet the problem of *zakazukha* also occurs in Moscow media. Many argue that the practice will not disappear soon because of both poor economic conditions and low ethical standards.

National and international organizations are helping to prevent unethical journalistic practices. The project Media Transparency International, conducted by the International Public Relations Association in collaboration with the Institute for Public Relations and journalism leaders worldwide, aims to minimize the existence of cash for news coverage.

Self-censorship   Self-censorship is a phenomenon that came to play in post-Soviet Rus-sia in the late 1990s when political and economic sanctions as well as criminal charges were leveled against journalists and editors who tried to investigate corrupt officials and lucrative business. Self-censorship became quite popular among editors who did not want to get their media "in trouble."

Self-censorship stops journalists before they even begin investigations or new reports on certain subjects because of their fear of economic problems that their media could experience later, such as cuts in subsidies from the government or financial support from publishers. Economic problems are not the only reasons independent journalism has become onerous. Today, journalists often fear criminals' retributions against them if they investigate subjects or persons having criminal connections. The lives of journalists who dare to investigate governmental or business wrongdoings can also be threatened.

Many journalists and editors in Russia do not investigate or write materials that may potentially bring harm to their media and themselves. They most often fear economic sanc-tions and criminal retributions. Approximately 200 media employees were killed in Russia between 1991 and 2004, while many more local journalists were attacked and beaten (Tunstall, 2008). Harassment of journalists is not declining.

In the last decade, several famous journalists who worked for Russian media were killed as a result of their investigations. More recent prominent deaths include Dmitry Kholodov; Pavel Klebnikov, an editor who unmasked the super-rich of Russia; Anna Politkovskaya, Russia's most celebrated journalist who "wrote about things that mat-tered"; and Ivan Safronov, a Russian defense correspondent. Most of these attacks on journalists were not adequately investigated, several cases were closed as a result of unproven accusations, and many of these crimes were not even officially filed. Filed cases generally used the Criminal Code of Russian Federation (in cases of murder or harassment). However, civil cases on these grounds have not yet been filed. In cases where media rights were violated, courts were not active in analyzing the cases and mak-ing recommendations.

Many Russian newspapers today have turned into a tabloid-like press, publishing scandal materials about Russian movie stars and singers, sensational crimes, and disasters, as well as reprinting similar publications from the Western tabloid media. Some claim that many media interpreted the *glasnost* campaign as "an opportunity to indulge in forms of media sexism" previously associated with capitalist societies (McNair, 1991).

In lieu of reporting stories about corrupt officials and the country's socioeconomic problems, tabloid-like materials have been a huge success among a Russian public because they make no difference to Russians' reality and provide easy and fun reading.

Tabloid stories are actively promoted by newspapers and magazines that are formatted after popular Western mass media, such as *Cosmopolitan* and *Esquire*. Articles also are reprinted with permission of Western publishers, who have seen a big potential for such media. For several years, the country has been filled with Russian editions of *Maxim, Cosmopolitan, Playboy,* and Russian newspapers (like *Speed Info*) and magazines (like *Karavan Istorif*), modeled after Western tabloids. Regional media have followed this path and have come up with their own local versions of *Elle* and the *New York Post*. Typical examples of the Russian tabloid press are found in the newspapers *Moe!* and *Efir,* published in Voronezh.

Many nationally recognized newspapers have also turned to tabloid materials, and their journalism quality has declined. Among these media is the newspaper *Komsomolskaya Pravda,* which was the major newspaper for a young audience during the Soviet regime and was considered one of the most progressive and high-quality newspapers during the *glasnost* period. Now, *Komsomolskaya Pravda* is becoming more of a quality tabloid rather than a quality professional newspaper, expanding its tabloid empire, both ideologically and physically, to regional publications such as *Komsomol-skaya, Pravda-Voronezh,* and *Komsomolskaya Pravda-Don.*

Many researchers cite a rapid growth in the number of media and, at the same time, a formal decline in the journalists' responsibility for publications as the major reason for low professional standards. A crisis of trust has been progressing dramatically in the past 10 years. A low level of professionalism and journalists' widespread "selloff" (a formal word for *zakazukha*) are obvious to readers. These trends have lowered media consumers' loyalty to Russian media in general. Among the most trusted media today are television, even though the problems discussed earlier are also apparent there, and the Internet.

Legal Freedom of Speech in Russian Mass Media

Legal freedom of speech is a relatively new phenomenon in Russia, with a short but very rich history that is associated with events of the twentieth century. Analysis of some aspects of this phenomenon can help to understand its nature and modern state of existence. It is important to study freedom of speech in a country that has a long history but a brief democratic tradition. Those who study the concept of freedom of speech worldwide can benefit from examining how freedom of speech in Russia has helped to shape the democratic principles of that country and what obstacles freedom of speech faces today.

Freedom of speech has always been associated with freedom of expression in the mass media. Some research has focused on the Soviet mass media and the particularities of freedom of speech in the former Soviet Union and contemporary Russia. Usually, such analysis combines a discussion of issues related to freedom of speech with an analysis of Russian journalism and post-Soviet mass media. However, researchers have failed to closely examine the legal basis of freedom of information in Russia (Tsetsura, 2002; Reporters Without Borders, 2007).

Legal Aspects of Freedom of Information   The Russian constitution meets European standards of human rights, including the right to freedom of information. Article 29 of the constitution states, "Freedom of mass information is guaranteed. Censorship is prohibited."

Articles 41, 42, and 55 also provide sets of instruments to defend citizens' freedoms such as freedom of expression. However, these rights, supported by international laws, have never been applied in practical terms to court proceedings that involve freedom of information disputes (Simonov, 2000a).

The democratic Media Law of the Russian Federation, which is a main federal document that guarantees freedom of speech in mass media, has a number of provisions that form the legal grounds for freedom of speech. Several aspects should be considered when freedom of speech in mass media is discussed. First, the Media Law confirms that censorship is prohibited (Article 3). Second, Article 43 says that any citizen or organization has a right to request a denial in the media if false information concerning someone's honor and dignity has appeared. As one can note, honor and dignity are used here in relation to a person as well as to an organization.

The next point reflects the crucial difference from the American legal tradition in solving disputes between journalists and plaintiffs. The same Article 43 states that the burden to prove that statements are true first of all lies with the media: "if the editors of a mass medium do not have evidence to demonstrate that distributed information is true, they are obligated to refute such information in the same medium." This differs significantly from the ways in which such cases are presented in the United States, where the burden to show falsity is almost always on the plaintiff (Tedford, 1997).

Another article of the Media Law elaborates on the rights of journalists, specifically stating that any journalist has a right "to state his/her personal opinions and evaluation in materials to be distributed under his/her name" (Article 47). As the analysis shows, sometimes this statement is not taken into consideration and is bypassed in court.

Article 49 declares, "The state guarantees protection of journalist's honor, dignity, health, life, and property in relation to his/her professional activities." This statement is too vague and has not been cited in any of the decisions related to the cases of infringements of media rights. Often this right is neither cited nor addressed in legal charges. While the Russian constitution provides for freedom of speech and of the press, authorities are able to use the legislative and judicial systems to harass and prosecute independent journalists (Freedom House, 2007). Such harassments were made easier in January of 2007 when Putin signed into law new regulations that required stricter registration and reporting for nongovernmental organizations (NGOs). These regulations have given the government greater control over society as well as potentially restricting journalists from receiving information from NGOs (Freedom House, 2007; IPI, May 2007).

The penalties for violating the Russian laws in relation to freedom of information are identified according to the legislation of the Russian Federation, the Civil Code, and the Criminal Code. They usually involve filing other civil cases as a result of violations in relation to freedom of information (in successful cases, in which it is proved that the media were offended, journalists can continue filing cases as individual citizens) or in publishing a denial and paying some compensation (in cases in which it is proved that the media offended the plaintiff.)

Public Aspects of Freedom of Information   Freedom of information also struggles to find its place in public debates. First, Russians question the right to freedom of information that they have now, at the beginning of the twenty-first century. If at the beginning of *perestroika* the public was active and enthusiastic about promoting freedom of information and defending its rights (the public's protests in August 1991 and the support of Yeltsin at the time support this claim), today the public is less and less involved in the debates on freedom of speech. Some governmental actions have contributed to the public's disappointment and withdrawal. Media law often is not enforced and not supported in practice. Moreover, mass media stay uninvolved in public debates because of the self-censorship phenomenon.

According to a study conducted by the Glasnost Defense Foundation (GDF, 1999), several factors have contributed to the decline of public interest in issues of freedom of speech as well as increasing concern among media representatives about media rights to accessing information. Political pressure on the media, confusion in legal documents, and the media's economic dependency on their political orientation are among the factors identified.

Another big problem addressed in the GDF study is a poorly interpreted notion of media being "the fourth branch of power" in Russia, with no mechanisms to express and promote diverse opinions and defense of the public's interests. For example, recently the BBC's World Service Programs were told that they would no longer be broadcast in Russian (IPI, August 2007). Media, not having the actual power to pressure administrators and influence opinions, have lost the readers' trust. A disappointed public does not have an interest and confidence in freedom of information that is essential for successful public debates in the media (Simonov, 2000a).

BIBLIOGRAPHY

Aumente, J., Gross, P., Hiebert, R., Johnson, O. V. and Mills, D. *Eastern European Journalism. Before, During and After Communism.* Cresskill, NJ: Hampton Press, 1999.

Becker, J. "Keeping Track of Press Freedom." *European Journal of Communication* 18, No. 1 (2003), 107–112.

————."Lessons from Russia: A Neo-Authoritarian Media System." *European Journal of Communication* 1, No. 2 (2004), 139–163.

Freedom House (online). "Annual Survey of Media Freedom 2007a." Accessed on September 7, 2007. Available: http://www.freedomhouse.org

Glasnost Defense Foundation. *The Silent Regions.* Moscow: Sashcko Publishing House, 1999.

Gross, P. *Entangled Evolutions: Media and Democratization in Eastern Europe.* Washington, D.C.: The Woodrow Wilson Center Press/Baltimore, MD: Johns Hopkins University Press, 2002.

Holmes, P. "IPRA Moves Swiftly on Zakazukha; PRSA Stays out of the Nike Fray." *Holmes Report* 2 (March 12, 2001).

Horga, I., and de La Brosse, R. (eds.) *The Role of the Mass-Media and of the New Information and Communication Technologies in the Democratisation Process of Central and Eastern European Societies.* Brussels: International Institute of Administrative Studies, 2002.

Human Rights Watch. "The Cost of Speech" (online). 2002. Available: http://www.hrw.org/reports/2002/albania/index.htm

International Press Institute. Waging War on the Media: World Press Freedom Report 2001 (online). Available: http://www.freemedia.at/cms/ipi/freedom_detail.html?country=/KW0001/KW0003/KW0052/&year=2006

Internews. "A Survey of Russian Television" (online). 1999. Available: http://internews.ru/report/tv/tv1.html

Ketter, W. B. "Russia's New Media Struggles for Freedom." American Society of Newspaper Editors newsletter (online). August 2001. Available: http://www.asne.org/kiosk/editor/01-ianfeb/ketter1.htm

McNair, B. *Glasnost, Perestroika and the Soviet Media*. London: Routledge, 1991.

Murray, J. *The Russian Press from Brezhnev to Yeltsin: Behind the Paper Curtain*. Brookfield, VT: Edward Elgar, 1994.

Organization for Security and Cooperation in Europe (OSCE). July 27, 2007. Internet Censorship Spreading: OSCE Study. Available: www.osce.org.

Reporters Without Borders. "Russia—Annual Report 2007." Available: http://www.rsf.org/article.php3?id_article=20823&Valider=OK

ROMIR Monitoring Research Holding, 2007. Accessed at http://romir.ru on September 14, 2007.

Simonov, A. "Anatomy of Freedom of Speech." Glasnost Defense Foundation (online), 2000a. Available: http://www.gdf.ru/publications/simonov10.html

———. "Law Pressed Hard by Lawlessness." Glasnost Defense Foundation (online). 2000b. Available: http://www.gdf.ru/publications/simonov09.html

Tedford, T. L. *Freedom of Speech in the United States,* 3rd ed. State College, PA: Strata Publishing, 1997.

Tenlab Multisystem Video, 2002. Accessed at www.tenlab.com on September 14, 2007.

Tolz, V. *The Impact of New Press Law: A Preliminary Assessment*. RFE/RL Report on the USSR, November 9, 1990.

Tsetsura, K. Development of Public Relations Theory and Practice in Russia: A Geopolitical Perspective. Paper presented at the 5th PRSA Educators Academy International Interdisciplinary Conference, Miami, FL, March 2002.

———. Understanding Public Relations Terms: "Evil" Nature of Public Relations As It Is Seen by Some of the Russian Publics. Paper presented at the Third PRSA Educators Academy International Interdisciplinary Conference, Miami, FL, March 2000.

Tsetsura, K., and Kruckeberg, D. "Theoretical Development of Public Relations in Russia." In Tilson, D. J. (ed.), *Toward the Common Good: Perspectives in International Public Relations*. 214–232. Boston: Allyn and Bacon, 2004.

Tunstall, J. *The Media Were American*. New York: Oxford University Press, 2008.

Vartanova, E. (2007). "Russian Media Model: New Economic Structures". Accessed at http://www.helsinki.fi/aleksanteri/maisterikoulu/opinto-opas/luentokurssit/oppimateriaali/russian_media_model on December 14, 2007.

Walker, C. "Muzzling the Media: The Return of Censorship in the Commonwealth of Independent States." Freedom House (online). Accessed at http://www.freedomhouse.org on September 2, 2007.

15 The Middle East and North Africa

ORAYB AREF NAJJAR
Northern Illinois University, USA

The changes in the media landscape in the Middle East and North Africa (Figure 15.1) make the media almost unrecognizable from what they were only a decade ago. Many media organizations have embraced new technology, challenged sole government ownership of all means of communication, reduced their reliance on Western news agencies, and diversified their content. These changes have accelerated the pace of communication and enriched it, allowing people of the region to read each other's media, and, via the Internet, hear it and see it. The changes have also made internal and across-border censorship difficult and have prompted many countries to reconsider their information policies. Arab satellite channels, with their pan-regional fare, also have united the fragmented pan-Arab news market. Some satellite channels and some online newspapers have started providing video clips for their viewers and readers. Most importantly, Arab media have become a source of news to the rest of the world and reversed the direction of news flow about themselves, which used to travel mostly from West to East and from North to South. Blogging is becoming popular in the Middle East and North Africa and is often used by disenfranchised groups and human rights advocates to connect with the outside world. Internet use and Internet radio transmission are becoming important, which has led some governments to regulate them.

The acquisition of new technology has favored those who can afford it, shifting and rearranging influence between and among geographical areas within the Middle East and North Africa. Despite these changes, the most important issue facing the countries of the region has remained the same: how to adopt new technologies necessary for advancement while preserving their traditional values and culture. Each country has handled this issue differently, but not a single country has managed to avoid it.

Historical Highlights

The Ottomans ruled the Middle East and parts of North Africa for 400 years, until World War I, when they lost their empire to Western powers. Britain, in effective control of Egypt and the Arabian Gulf since the turn of the twentieth century, gained control over Palestine, Trans-Jordan, and Iraq through a League of Nations mandate. France, already

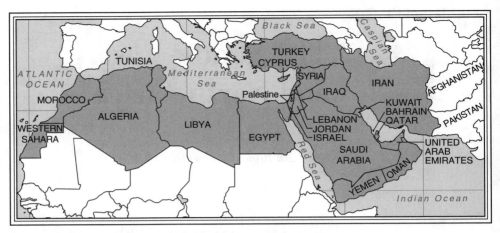

FIGURE 15.1 Middle East and North Africa

with colonial control over Morocco, Tunisia, and Algeria in North Africa, was granted mandatory powers over Syria and Lebanon. Although the mandate powers were supposed to shepherd the countries to independence, some powers were reluctant to leave, forcing Arabs into years of struggle to oust Britain and France from the Middle East and North Africa (Ismael and Ismael, 1999:131–133). Algeria earned the nickname of "the country of the million martyrs" for the number of Algerians who died fighting for freedom from France.

Modern Turkey was founded in 1923 from the ashes of the Ottoman Empire. First elected president in 1923, Kemal Atatürk admired the West and secularism and forcibly reduced the influence of Islam by attempting to turn Turkey into a secular Westernized country. The Turkish military exercises substantial but indirect influence over politics to protect the secular nature of the state. But Turkish nationalism and secularism have not yet replaced Islam in the hearts and minds of many Turks, as evidenced by the July 22, 2007 elections, in which Islamic-affiliated parties were returned to power.

In Iran's more recent history, the U.S. Central Intelligence Agency (CIA), in coopera- tion with British intelligence, plotted the military coup that, in 1953, returned the Shah of Iran to power and toppled Iran's elected prime minister, Mossadegh, an ardent nationalist. Both countries were fearful of Iran's plans to nationalize its oil industry. President Eisenhower had also approved the plan because of his fear of communism. *The New York Times* reporter in Tehran during the coup wrote, "The only instance since I joined *The Times* in which I have allowed policy to influence a strict news approach was in failing to report the role our agents played in the overthrow of Mossadegh" (Risen, 2000). To Iranians, however, U.S. meddling in internal Iranian affairs was a major failing that continues to haunt U.S.-Iranian relations.

Iranian cleric Ayatollah Khomeini, exiled after his arrest for speaking out against the Shah's relationship to the United States, returned to Iran in 1979 and established a govern- ment in the wake of the Iranian Revolution that forced the Shah out of Iran (Goldschmidt, 1988:216–221). Iran is still ruled by clerics who are suspicious of the West and of Western influence, especially in the press.

The founding of the state of Israel in 1948 was seen by Israel and most Western countries as a fulfillment of the nationalist-religious Zionist dream of return and as a refuge for European Jews fleeing the Nazis. But Palestinian history books call that same event "the disaster" because they say it led to the dispersal of an estimated 520,000 to 850,000 Palestinians and the creation of their refugee problem. The founding of the state of Israel in the middle of the Arab world also has resulted in a profound Arab public reaction to Western sponsorship of Zionism. Anti-Zionist and anti-imperialist rhetoric unified the Arab media and continues to do so. As Susan Sachs writes, "The Palestinian 'problem' has driven policy in the Arab world for nearly as long as there have been independent states. More than a preoccupation, it has had the force to undermine rulers, incite revolutions, circumscribe development and define patriotism" (Sachs, 2000). Since Egypt and Jordan signed peace treaties with Israel, and after the Palestinian National Authority entered into negotiations with it, the total boycott against talking to Israelis has been breached by Arab satellite stations, exposing viewers to the Israeli point of view for the first time since 1948.

Even though the Arabs had not been united since the fall of the Omayyad Dynasty in A.D. 750, they began to feel that people who speak one language should unite. Egypt's skillful use of its media, most notably Voice of the Arabs radio in the 1960s, gave concrete expression to that Arab nationalist longing. Pan-Arab nationalism became a dominant theme in regional political dynamics despite tensions between several countries (Goldschmidt, 1988:277). That same longing for unity is now being rekindled by pan-Arab satellite broadcasting. Arabism, however, is facing direct competition from the proponents of a pan-Muslim identity. It is also being challenged by what some Arabs and Muslims consider as an attempt by the United States government to impose a "New Middle East," which includes non-Arab states like Turkey and Israel, while keeping Iran at bay; a scheme lampooned in cartoons and depicted in the press as a revival of the failed Western-inspired "Baghdad Pact" of the 1950s.

Several recent events and trends have changed the dynamics of societies in the Middle East and North Africa and have had a profound impact on their media:

- The disintegration of the Soviet Union and the retreat of the Arab Left
- The rise of religious fundamentalism
- The change in media economics and content as a result of globalization and privatization
- The onset of the Palestinian-Israeli peace negotiations, which, despite their failure, changed the Arab world's media relations with Israel
- The accession to power of new young leaders relatively more open to freedom than their predecessors
- The growth of nongovernmental organizations that monitor government-press relations
- The fallout of September 11, 2001, which resulted in new "antiterrorism" legislation that was often used against the opponents of the rulers rather than to fight terrorism
- The 2003 invasion of Iraq and the divisions and religious forces it unleashed, forces that use the new media skillfully and may be seen on YouTube and on the Internet.

Print Media in the Arab World

Because of the liberalization of print media in some Arab countries, it is no longer possible to write about "the Arab media" as if they share the same media policies. There are 22 Arab countries, and their media differ in physical infrastructure, technical capability, and content. The level of freedom of speech each government allows, or each press body extracts through struggle, varies from one Arab region to the next. All of these countries, however, have one thing in common: All have witnessed the slow erosion of state power vis-à-vis the media. All have seen the rise of nonstate actors-cum-communicators.

Following is a description of each region's media (in alphabetical order) and the forces that drive them.

Print Media in Iraq, Jordan, Lebanon, Palestine, and Syria

Iraq   Iraq closed all private daily newspapers in 1967. Saddam Hussein's regime, which started in 1979, banned all political parties operating in Iraq at that time. Although the Iraqi government invited the public to form political parties in 1991, no one took the invitation seriously. A renewed call in 1999 to form "supportive" parties to the one allowed party, al-Ba'ath (Renaissance), resulted in failure to get the 150 signatures needed to register them because those parties were not allowed to enter the elections (Arab Human Rights Organization, 2000:39).

Until the fall of Baghdad to the American forces, Iraq's ministry of information and the journalists' union controlled the six daily and one dozen weekly newspapers. Uday, the son of President Saddam Hussein, headed the committee of editors-in-chief and owned *Babel,* the highest-circulation newspaper. *Al-Thawra* (Revolution) was the official mouthpiece of the Ba'ath Party (Russell, 2003).

The occupation of Iraq led to a scramble among various local and diaspora forces for the control of the hearts and minds of the conquered/liberated Iraqi people (according to differing perceptions of what happened to Iraq). The actors on the new media scene include returning Iraqi exiles, British and American officials, Iraqi former political parties, and various indigenous Iraqi religious and secular groups. The Iraqi Communist Party was the first to publish an eight-page weekly, *People's Path,* on April 20, 2003 (Russell, 2003). Shortly after that, 150 Iraqi newspapers were established (Al Jazeera). Very few of those papers are still publishing, for both financial and security reasons, but publications from various Arab countries circulate freely.

The new legislation governing the Iraqi press retained some of the more represssive elements of the previous era, and sanctioned the imprisonment and fining of journalists. The Kurdish parliament attempted to pass a similar restrictive law that would allow the imprisonment of journalists and add prohibitive fines as punishment, but Massoud Barzani, president of the Iraqi Kurdistan Region, said he intended to send it back to parliament for revision (Kurd Net, 2007). The revelation that the the U.S. military command in Baghdad has paid Iraqi newspapers to carry positive news about U.S. efforts in Iraq, through a contract with the Lincoln Group, has tarnished U.S. efforts to help foster a free press in Iraq. American officials, however, defended the practice "as part of a legitimate campaign to counter insurgents' misinformation" (White and Graham, 2005). Arab editorial writers and cartoonists were not impressed with that explanation. Some popular Web sites continue to use Abu Ghraib iconic photos of Iraqis being tortured by Americans on their Web pages as proof that the United States does not respect human rights and, by implication, should not be dictating human rights terms to other nations (Mahjoob.com, 2008).

It is extremely dangerous to practice journalism in Iraq, especially for Iraqi journalists who work as stringers for the Western press and go where others fear to go. In addition to facing the danger of being killed by militas of every stripe, they also face the danger of being jailed by American forces, as was the case with Bilal Hussein, an Iraqi photographer who had a hand in the Associated Press's 2005 Pulitzer Prize for photography (Arango, 2007). Between the start of the war in 2003 and until January 6, 2008, 278 Iraqi and 24 non-Iraqi media professionals were killed. Among them were 161 journalists/reporters, 22 cameramen, and 6 photographers (The Brussels Tribunal, 2008).

Jordan   Jordan, the host of Palestinian refugees in 1948 and 1967, always felt the need to shield itself from the fallout of the Israeli-Palestinian conflict with tough press legislation to curb hostility to its alliance with the West. The government tightened press regulations every time the country faced a major internal or external crisis (Najjar, 1998, 2000).

The regulations introduced after September 11, 2001 have reversed most of the positive changes in press law introduced since the 1989 liberalization. The Jordanian prime minister argued that Jordan's old code did not cover the current need "to face up to terrorist acts and punish them." The amendments to the code provided for the closure "permanently or temporarily" of publications with items that are "defamatory, false, harmful to national unity or the state's reputation" or that carry news that incites illegal public meetings or disturbing the public order, or news instigating acts of religious and racial fanaticism. The code imposed prison sentences from one to three years, instead of fines, for insulting the royal family. Furthermore, sensitivity to the growing clout of religious parties in Jordan has negatively affected the press. Two editors of the weeklies *Shihan* and *Al-Mehwar* were arrested twice to be questioned by a judge. *Shihan* reprinted three of the Danish cartoons of prophet Muhammad and called on Muslims worldwide to be "reasonable," and Al-Mehwar printed all 12 of them alongside an article about criticism of their publication. Both were charged with offending religious feelings and given two-month prison sentences on May 31, 2006 (Reporters Without Borders, " Jordan," 2007).[1]

Today, Jordan has a variety of publications that range from leftist to Arab nationalist to Islamist. The country also publishes two English-language newspapers, a daily and a weekly.

Al Ghad newspaper, an independent and private daily in Jordan, launched in August 2004, became one of the country's leading newspapers with a circulation of more than 55,000 just 18 months after its launch. Almost 70 percent of its readers are subscribers; an unusual figure for papers in the region (The Arab Press Network, 2006). The paper charges about half the price of other papers.

Despite laws that claim that Jordanians have a right to freedom of expression, the security services remain strong and practice pre-censorship, even though there is no provision for it in the media law. The Jordanian government continues to believe that it is unable to depend on the union-dominated Jordanian Press Association to express the government's point of view—thus its reluctance to allow freedom of the press (El Sharif, 2002). The Press Association also parts ways with the government on the state's policy of normalization with Israel before Israel withdraws from the territory it occupied in 1967 and deals with refugee issues. The association still threatens to expel any member who visits Israel.

Lebanon   The early arrival of printing in Lebanon enabled it to develop its press and export its journalistic expertise to several Arab countries. Lebanese journalists founded *al-Ahram* newspaper of Egypt and, later, publications in Sudan, Morocco, and Qatar (Abu Zaid, 1985). The period from 1943 to 1962 saw the proliferation of a vigorous political press that turned Lebanon into the capital of Arab journalism. Because of the wide margin of freedom Lebanon enjoyed, Arab leaders waged their political battles in the Lebanese press they directly owned or subsidized (Al-Alawi, 1981). To put an end to that trend, the Lebanese government stopped issuing licenses for new political publications in 1953 in an attempt to reduce the number of daily political papers to 25, and the number of weekly and monthly papers to 20 (Al-Ghareeb, 1978:70–71).

The Israeli invasion of Lebanon in 1982 to oust the PLO, and the 16-year Lebanese civil war, which ended in 1991, destroyed Lebanon's infrastructure and reduced the influence of the Lebanese press in the Arab world (Ellis, 1999).

Jihad al-Zein, op-ed editor of *al-Nahar* daily, says, however, that even though the Lebanese press has lost some of its pan-Arab appeal, it contributes trained cadres to the Arab media as well as ideas for debate (Al-Zein, Interview, 2000). During the civil war years, many regular publications either stopped publishing or published outside Lebanon, mainly in London. Those publications are now returning to the Middle East (Jarrah, 2008).

The Palestinian National Authority   The Palestinian press has experienced a curious development in the past few years. While the independent local press is thriving, the government press is more controlled than it has ever been. Legal protections granted to journalists since 1995 have been eroded by Palestinian infighting.

Since Hamas came to power in January 2006, journalists have faced problems from three different quarters: Israeli occupation forces who continue to treat Palestinian journalists as Palestinians first, and thus, restrict their movement and expose them to danger; and Palestinian factions belonging to Hamas or Fateh who clash and target each other's media and journalists.

In this lawless atmosphere, six foreign journalists were kidnapped. All were freed after being held between hours and several days. Two U.S. journalists of Fox News were seized in Gaza on August 14, 2006 and held for two weeks by an unknown group. The Palestinian government failed to investigate these kidnappings, but Reporters Without Borders "considered that in most cases they were not political but the work of individuals or isolated groups seeking publicity or sometimes jobs" (Reporters Without Borders, "Palestinian Authority," 2007). BBC reporter Alan Johnston was held hostage for four months in Gaza, leading the Fateh-led Arab journalists Union to demonstrate on his behalf and leading Hamas to work to free him (Reporters Without Borders, "Palestinian Authority," 2007) and (BBC News, 2007).

A poll of 1,531 Palestinians in the West Bank, including East Jerusalem, and Gaza found that three out of every four Palestinians over 18 said they trusted the Palestinian media outlets and followed the news on a daily basis. However, they faulted their own media for concentrating on political developments, but failing to cover cultural, athletic, and economic issues. Those polled also said that the local media coverage relied too heavily "on the opinions of talking heads having clear partisan agendas versus . . . those affected by the policies of the Israeli government, the Palestinian factions and the Western powers who have maintained a crippling economic boycott of the Territories since Hamas was democratically elected in 2006" (Abu Sa'da, 2007). The margin of error was around 4 percent.

Syria The establishment of the Ba'ath (Renaissance) Party in 1944 determined the political course of Syria. The party has secular, socialist, and Arab nationalist goals. Hafez al-Assad, who became president in 1970, signed a 20-year cooperation agreement with the Soviet Union in 1980, putting Syria at odds with the United States. The demise of the Soviet Union left Syria without strong allies (Lancaster, 2000) and made it more vulnerable to pressures to liberalize. Syria outlaws fundamentalist Islamists and has expelled their leaders following their struggle with the regime in 1982 (Jarrus, 2000). In 2004, however, Syria signed a strategic cooperation agreement with Iran, just as the United States was heating up its rhetoric against both countries.

Analysts have predicted that the new ruler of Syria, Bashar Al-Asad, will be more open to freedom of the press than his father, but liberalization has been slow. The Syrian government controls the press and distributes news through its official agency, the Syrian Arab News Agency (SANA).

Syria is taking cautious steps toward privatization in two areas: the Internet and advertising (Moubayid, 2000). Although several private publications were allowed to publish in 2000, including a satirical magazine, most are now closed because of content restrictions and a conflict with the government over distribution rights (Reporters Without Borders, "The Only Satirical Paper," 2002).

Several journalists were arrested in 2006 for interviewing exiled regime opponents, taking part in conferences abroad, and for criticizing government policies. They were subjected to lengthy legal proceedings before the Damascus military court, which, under a 1963 law, tries anyone considered to have undermined state security (Reporters Without Borders, " Syria," 2007).

Print Media in the Gulf States: Bahrain, Kuwait, Qatar, Saudi Arabia, and United Arab Emirates

The whole Arabian Gulf area was on the fringes of the Arab world because most countries were British protectorates until 1971 and were late in developing any type of media. Those countries were thrust onto center stage during the oil boycott following the 1973 Arab-Israeli War, a period in which the Gulf area became visibly linked to the Palestinian problem, and during the Iraq-Iran War and the Gulf War, when they became important as oil producers (Zahlan, 1998).

The Kingdom of Bahrain The Kingdom of Bahrain—called the state of Bahrain until it became a constitutional monarchy on February 14, 2002—was deprived of its real independence by a series of treaties with Britain. In 1967, Britain moved its main regional naval base from Aden to Bahrain. Bahrain gained its independence from Britain in August 1971.

Bahrain drew up its constitution on May 12, 1973, and elected its first parliament that year. In August 1975, the prince disbanded the National Assembly because the Parliament attempted to legislate the end of Al-Khalifa hereditary rule (there since the late eighteenth century), and the expulsion of the U.S. Navy from Bahrain (there since 1948). The constitution was suspended in 1975. Even though Bahrain was nominally independent, a Briton headed state security for some 30 years until 1998. He was instrumental in ruthlessly suppressing prodemocracy unrest in Bahrain, along with his deputy Adel Felaifel (Silverman, 2003).

Bahrain and the United States signed a Defense Cooperation Agreement in October 1991 granting U.S. forces access to Bahraini facilities and ensuring the right to preposition materiel for future crises.

Bahrain has built an advanced infrastructure in transportation and telecommunications, making it a regional financial and business center. The move toward a more open society came in 1999, when a generational change brought Shaykh Hamad bin Isa Al Khalifa to power after the death of his father. The constitution was amended and ratified on February 14, 2001. Parliamentary elections were held in October 2002, the first for nearly 27 years. Women were allowed to run for office (BBC News, 2007). A Bill called the Protecting Society from Terrorists Act, ratified in August 2006, gives an overly broad definition of terrorism by implying that any "political organization opposed to the Bahraini Constitution" could be perceived as a terrorist group. The Egyptian Organisation for Human Rights (EOHR) stated that "the bill restricts the right to freedom of expression including the right to seek, receive and impart information of all kinds" (IPI, World Press Freedom Review, "Bahrain," 2006.)

United Arab Emirates   The United Arab Emirates is a federation of seven states formed in 1971: Abu Dhabi, Dubai, Ajman, Fujairah, Ras Al-Khaimah, Sharjah, and Umm Al-Qaywayn. The UAE is one of the most liberal countries in the Gulf region.

Although the UAE was a late arrival on the Arab journalistic scene, it now has an established press. *Al-Ittihad*'s first weekly issue appeared on October 20, 1969. Initially, this government paper was distributed for free to avoid competition with the papers of other Arab countries. In April 22, 1971, however, the paper started publishing daily. It now has 32 color pages and a 16-page supplement. *Al-Ittihad* used satellite technology in 1981 to print the paper simultaneously in Dubai and Abu Dhabi. The paper has offices in various emirates in keeping with its name, "Unity." *Al-Ittihad* started publishing online on March 15, 1996.

The UAE has one private Arabic daily, *Al-Bayan*; and three English-language publications: *Gulf News* daily, *Khaleej Times* daily, and *Emirates Business* 24/7, which appeared on December 9, 2007. This newest publication reflects the business ethos of the Emirates. The daily bills itself on its Web site as "the first and only publication in the UAE providing the reader with what the region has been missing so far—first-rate business news that you can use." The UAE daily *Akhbar Al Arab* launched *Al Maraa Al Arabia,* a supplement for women. The supplement was so successful it managed to attract new advertisers and make money for the paper 18 months after it started, according to the Arab Press Network of September 28, 2005. This development was very timely. The Ministry of Justice is amending judiciary law to allow women to take up positions as judges and prosecutors at the federal level. Other Arab countries that already have female judges are Bahrain, Egypt, Morocco, Jordan, Sudan, Syria, and Tunisia (Salama, 2008).

Two of the Gulf countries, Kuwait and Saudi Arabia, are compared below for contrast.

Kuwait   Kuwait, one of the few monarchies in the Gulf with an elected parliament, enjoys a vigorous press with technical capabilities and experienced reporters who are respected in the Arab world. Kuwaiti journalists have a margin of press freedom other Gulf states do not enjoy. This difference can be explained by the fact that some Kuwaitis had flirted with leftist and Arab nationalist parties and ideas in the 1950s and 1960s, while other Gulf countries remained shielded from the intellectual currents of that era. Although Kuwaiti women got the right to vote only in 2005 due to pressure from conservatives, they have always enjoyed a higher level of education than women in some other Gulf countries, and they occupy important positions in the professions. It is expected that with their high qualifications women will gain more political power.

The 2006 press law did away with government monopoly on newspapers and allowed the private sector to obtain licenses. Unlike the 1961 press law, the new law allows those denied a license the right to appeal the decision. Furthermore, it prevents the cancellation of a license, suspension of a newspaper, or detention of a journalist without a court order. The law abolished imprisonment for journalists and did away with jail terms for insulting the ruler of Kuwait but increased the fines associated with both offenses. Article 19 of the amended press law prohibits blasphemy pertaining to "God, the Prophet, his Companions and the Quran," carrying prison terms of up to one year as well as heavy fines. Calls for toppling the regime carry penalties reaching a life sentence (IPI, World Press Freedom Review, "Kuwait," 2006). While some government officials continue to demand restrictions on the press, countervailing forces in parliament, within the legal system, and among intellectuals continue to fight restrictions.

Saudi Arabia   The state was created in 1932, and the Al Saud dynasty holds a monopoly of power. The kingdom follows the Wahhabi sect's strict interpretation of Islam, making it the most conservative Arab state. Unlike Kuwait, Saudi Arabia does not allow political parties. Although it has one of the most sophisticated media scenes in terms of equipment, it is also the most restricted in terms of content (BBC, Country Profile, "Saudi Arabia," 2008). Control is achieved through government input on who gets into journalism. The organizations are run by government-approved boards of directors. A censorship committee reviews and censors all national and foreign publications according to the policies of the state. A Saudi government policy statement of 1982 still forbids criticizing the government, the royal family, or the clergy and heads of state of friendly countries (Rampal, 1994:245–246).

The government owns the Saudi Press Agency (SPA), and newspapers tend to follow SPA's lead on whether or not to publish news on sensitive subjects. Observers have noted that the Saudi press has been able to publish informative articles that would have been censored in the past. On the other hand, the culture and information ministry told journalist Kinan ben Abdallah al-Ghamidi without explanation that he could no longer write in the government daily *Al Watan*. He had already been forced to resign as the paper's editor in 2002 after reporting that U.S. troops were using the country's military bases.

One positive development was the establishment of a private paper, *Shams,* which targets Saudi Arabia's 18–32 years demographic and has a circulation of 40,000. The fact that the paper is owned in part by Prince Turki bin Khaled has not shielded it from religious censorship when it dared publish one of the cartoons of the prophet Muhammad that appeared in the Danish daily *Jyllands-Posten,* even though the country's highest religious authority declared it permissible if the intent was to highlight the offense against Islam. Yet 20 days later, hard-line clerics pressured the authorities to close the paper. A compromise worked out through the Information Ministry allowed the paper to reopen if it dismissed its 32-year-old editor-in-chief (Reporters Without Borders,"Saudi Arabia," 2007). Saudi Arabia sponsors several major Arab newspapers in European capitals, especially London. These papers have a wider margin of freedom than papers in Saudi Arabia but are not very critical of Saudi policies (Jarrah, 2008).

Qatar   The government abolished the Ministry of Information and lifted controls over the press in 1995, paving the way for press freedom. The press has not yet established itself on the Arab scene, and self-censorship on matters relating to Qatar is still practiced. Qataris approved their permanent constitution by referendum on April 30, 2003, opening the way to democracy. By 2006, however, print journalism had not yet experienced the freedom experienced by Al Jazeera TV.

Print Media in North Africa: Algeria, Egypt, Libya, Morocco, and Tunisia

Countries formerly ruled by France, such as Algeria, Morocco, and Tunisia, were left with a legacy of French culture, expressed daily in the French-language press, which still carries a lot of weight and, some charge, gets the lion's share of government advertising.

Algeria   After a century of rule by France, Algeria became independent in 1962. Algeria is an interesting case of what happens when democratic reform is not inclusive. The first-round success of the fundamentalist Islamic Salvation Front (FIS) Party in the December 1991 balloting caused the army to intervene, crack down on the FIS, and postpone the subsequent elections. Islamists resented being kept out of power unfairly when the government allowed elections featuring progovernment parties and what it considered moderate religion-based parties to run for office.

After a long civil war in which more than 100,000 rebels, soldiers, and civilians were killed by both sides, FIS's armed wing, the Islamic Salvation Army, dissolved itself in January 2000, and many armed insurgents surrendered under an amnesty program designed to promote national reconciliation. But that period took a big toll on the press. Fifty-seven journalists were murdered between 1993 and 1996.

The Algerian press started to enjoy some freedom only after the Algerian constitution in 1989 introduced political pluralism and information diversity. Sixty-five political parties sprang up as soon as it was permissible, a fact that attests to the Algerian thirst for political participation. The 630 daily and weekly publications that rushed to appear were finally reduced to 45 daily French and Arabic papers in 2007, with a total circulation of more than 1.5 million copies. There are 20 domestically printed weekly publications with a total circulation of 622,000 and 11 monthly publications with total circulation of 600,000. In July 2006, President Bouteflika pardoned 67 journalists convicted of defaming or insulting state institutions. Critics point out that, according to the criminal code, insulting the president is still punishable by a prison sentence. Nevertheless, the pardon was widely seen as a significant step toward democracy (U.S. Department of State: Background Note, Algeria, 2007).

Areas of concern include the weight of the public sector in advertising. At 65 percent, it remains decisive in the success of publications. One quantitative study showed that government favors French papers with subsidies, even though they distribute fewer copies than the Arabic papers. This favoritism, they say, creates tension because it isolates the French-educated elite from the masses and delays the Arabization of Algeria. Five printing presses belong to the state (Diliou, 2000:58–61).

The most important issues now being debated in Algeria are the role of Islamists in the country and the debate over public acknowledgment of past human rights abuses.

Egypt The Egyptian press is not as influential as it used to be at the pan-Arab level because satellites now provide up-to-the-minute news from numerous other sources. There is, however, a vigorous tradition of investigative reporting and lively dialogue on internal Egyptian affairs not found in the rest of North African countries. For example, the press thoroughly investigated charges of corruption in the process of privatization under President Sadat and continues to do so.

The degree of freedom enjoyed by the Egyptian press has always been tied to the strength and diversity of Egyptian political parties, as the following brief background information on parties illustrates. In 1952, Egyptian President Gamal Abdel Nasser overthrew the Egyptian monarchy, under which there was a combination of private and party press. Nasser dissolved political parties in 1953 and closed four of their publications as well as 42 others appearing irregularly. The 1960 Law for Reorganizing the Press made it illegal for individuals, corporations, or political parties to own or run papers. Newspaper ownership was given to the Arab Socialist Union, which established three dailies. Although the papers sometimes published dissenting views, only a few trusted editors dared criticize the regime. Censorship was imposed on and off during that period (Abdul Rahman, 1989:18–38).

Despite the media restrictions, the regime enjoyed wide popular support. Pan-Arab nationalism, which stressed political unification, anti-imperialism, and nonalignment, became personified in Nasser's leadership. *Al-Ahram*'s column "Frankly Speaking," written by Nasser's confidant Mohammad Hassanein Heikal, was read and analyzed by world politicians and Arab masses alike (Al-Shalabi, 1999).

President Sadat showed his pro-Western orientation shortly after coming to power in 1970. Sadat lifted the direct censorship imposed since 1967. The 1977 Law No. 40 for organizing political parties allowed parties to issue papers without licensing. But Sadat closed some publications and transferred the staff of others in 1974 and 1977. Especially targeted were leftist publications that criticized his overtures to the West. Law 148 for the year 1980 restricted freedom of the press. Islamist power grew in Egypt with the suppression of the left.

President Hosni Mubarak came to power after Sadat's assassination by Islamists in 1981. He continued allowing most political parties to publish their own papers, and he also allowed some leftist publications suppressed under Sadat to return. But the imposition of martial law after the assassination gave the government wide powers over the press (Abdul Rahman, 1989:18–38, 67–72). Today, the Egyptian media are owned by the government, by political parties, or by the private sector.

September 11 has had a negative effect on freedom of expression in several Arab countries. Egypt, for example, renewed the state of emergency in April 2006 for an additional two years, providing a continued basis for arbitrary detention and trials before military and state security courts. By then, the state of emergency had been in effect for almost 25 years (Najjar, 2008). In May 2008, Egyptian MPs have approved a government request to extend emergency law for another two years, although President Hosni Mubarak had promised it would be lifted in 2006. The excuse given was that the anti-terror legislation that was supposed to replace the emergency powers—in force since 1981—is not ready. The emergency law allows detention without charge for long periods and searches without warrants (BBC News, "Egypt renews emergency law powers," 2008).

As a result of vigorous activism by Egyptian journalists, when 25 independent newspapers refrained from appearing for a day, the press law was amended to remove jail sentences for journalists for some offenses and to allow increased fines for those making defamatory allegations of corruption against officials. Prison sentences for "serious media crimes"—such as libeling the president and foreign heads of state—remain. And imprisonment for libel is left to judges' discretion rather than being banned altogether (BBC News, "Egypt MPs," July 10, 2006). Removing prison sentences from media law, however, does not remove them altogether because they are still tucked into the Penal Code. Furthermore, journalists are often tried in State Security Court, subjecting them to imprisonment as well as heavy fines (Baheyya, 2007). Since September 2007, the law has been utilized to jail 11 journalists for "offenses" ranging from criticizing Mubarak and his son Jamal to misquoting a government minister (AME Info, "Egypt Keeps Libel Laws," 2007).

Libya   Libya gained its independence in 1951. Since 1969, when Muammar al-Qaddafi came to power, three of the four leading daily newspapers have been funded through the General Press Office, an extension of the information ministry. The Revolutionary Committees Movement, a state-supported ideological group, controls the fourth newspaper (IPI, "Libya," 2006). One newspaper publishes in English.

After September 11, 2001, Qaddafi cracked down on Islamists and forbade anti-Western preaching in mosques. Islamists also happen to be among those who oppose his rule (IPI, "Libya," 2001). Very little has changed for the press since then.

Morocco   King Mohammad VI, crowned in July 1999 at the age of 37, has tried to reconcile with communities that were at odds with his father and liberalize the economy and the country. Many argue, however, that he has not gone far enough, despite the fact that the September 2002 parliamentary elections were thought to be honest. Even though elections were presented as part of the "democratic transition," journalists were summoned for interrogation or fined over articles they wrote.

The government is still able to exercise censorship because the press law passed by the House of Representatives on May 6, 2002, did not go far enough. Even though the law imposes fewer controls over starting publications and lighter penalties and smaller fines for journalists, it retains jail terms for insulting the king and the royal family (three and five years in prison, compared with between 5 and 20 years previously.) Article 29 retains the government's right to ban Moroccan or foreign newspapers if they are deemed to "undermine Islam, the monarchy, national territorial integrity, or public order." The Islamist fundamentalist media was also targeted.

The Moroccan courts imposed suspended prison sentences and exorbitant fines on the editors of five major weekly newspapers in 2006 in what were considered politically motivated prosecutions of independent newspapers. Suspended sentences have a chilling effect on the press. Furthermore, high fines threaten the financial viability of independent publications.

One publisher and editor of the independent weekly *Al-Ousbouia Al Jadida,* was charged with defaming the monarchy under Article 41 of the 2002 press law and faced three to five years in prison and a possible fine of approximately US$11,000. The charges stem from a 2005 interview with the daughter of Sheikh Abd al-Islam Yassin, head of the outlawed Islamist organization Justice and Charity, in which she suggested that Morocco should be a republic. An article published in the independent weekly *Al Ayyam* on November 6, 2005 about the royal harem existing under previous Moroccan monarchs got those who published it charged under Article 42 of the 2002 press law in which any insult to the royal family is punishable by a prison sentence of up to one year and a fine of around US$11,000. Truth is not a defense in Morocco under Article 41. On February 16, 2006, the independent weekly *Le Journal Hebdomadaire* was ordered to pay approximately US$350,000 for questioning the objectively of a government report. IPI reported that "[t]he disproportionate damages are equal to 138 years of a minimum salary in Morocco and was the largest sum of damages ever awarded against a Moroccan publication" (IPI, "Morocco," 2006).

Tunisia   Tunisia shook off colonial rule in 1956, but a French-language press continues to coexist with the Arabic press. The 1993 amendments to the press law gave journalists the right to use truth as a defense even if writing about a member of the government. Other changes forbade the administrative suspension of whole newspapers but kept the right to suspend the offending issue. "While there is no official censorship of the media, self-censorship has become a feature of daily life, as various types of government coercion have restricted the ability of journalists and political personalities to speak freely. Nonetheless, the high rate of literacy and the sizable middle class have helped to sustain an avid readership for the large number of periodicals (notably business and economics) that are published" (*Encyclopedia Britannica*, 2008). A fact-finding mission undertaken by the Tunisia Monitoring Group (TMG), a coalition of 16 members of the International Federation of Expression Exchange (IFEX), reported, "While in some small-circulation newspapers there is now an unprecedented amount of balanced reporting on local issues, the larger circulation official press continues to lack balance." The mission also commented on the self-censorship of journalists because of official intimidation (IFEX, 2007).

Print Media in Iran, Israel, and Turkey

The Islamic Republic of Iran   Iran in recent years has taken a two-pronged approach to the media: it censors media within its borders, it attempts to block some media from outside, but it also has become a major news source itself, in several languages. Press freedom and state regulation of the press have emerged as crucial issues in the struggle for power between reformists and conservatives. The issue of freedom did not come to a head, however, until conservatives lost the election on year 2000 elections, for the first time since 1979 (Middle East Review of International Affairs, 2000). Conservatives believe that the culmination of the Islamic Revolution in 1979 was itself a political, social, and cultural reform based on Islamic principles. So conservatives want to guard against the press becoming "a gateway for cultural invasion" (Human Rights Watch, "The Press Under President Khatami," 1999). The freedom of the press fostered by President Khatami and his supporters, however, exists only within the limits drawn by the clerical leadership. Those opposed to clerical rule still have no place in public debate in Iran (Human Rights Watch, "As Fragile," 1999). The government proposed a law in 2006 that would force media workers to register with the Ministry of Culture and Islamic Guidance. In 2006, 38 journalists were arrested and a dozen media outlets censored (Reporters Without Borders,"Iran," 2007). On March 21, 2007, two Iranian newspapers with large circulations were banned, and another newspaper was closed. Only around 40 publications have received licenses, even though 2,826 applications were awaiting approval. According to the official statistics of the Press Supervisory Board, since June 2006, 570 publications have had their licenses revoked, some because they did not observe Clause 16 of the Press Law, which requires new licensees to publish within six months from the date of issuance of their licence (Mofidi, 2007).

Despite the media restrictions, several authors of new books on the Iranian media argue that there is a vital press and dissident movement in Iran. Hossein Shahidi argues that the only segment of the Iranian media where independent journalism has had an opportunity to develop is online reporting (Shahidi, 2007). A book edited by Mehdi Semati sees Iran as "a complex society that has successfully managed to negotiate and embody the tensions of tradition and modernity, democracy and theocracy, isolation and globalization and other such cultural-political dynamics that escape the explanatory and analytical powers of all-too-familiar binary relations." The book argues that failing to appreciate the complexity, paradoxes, and contradictions that characterize life in contemporary Iran results "in a general failure to explain and to anticipate its contemporary social and political transformations " (Semati, 2007).

Israel The Israeli press has passed through several stages of development in terms of ownership, political control, and content. The early Israeli press was financed and controlled by political parties that also appointed their editors. The party press gave way to the private press in the 1980s and 1990s (Caspi and Limor, 1999:67–68). The Israeli print media provide news and feature stories in Hebrew, Arabic, Russian, English, French, Spanish, Amharic, Farsi, Ladino, and Yiddish (Ben-Rafael, 2001).

Newspapers in Israel reflect the ideological diversity in the country. Although Israeli papers are often accused of being leftist, David Newman writes that this is not the case. *Ha'aretz* is liberal and left of center, but other papers speak for the right; for example, *Mekor Rishon* (founded as a means of combating the perceived left-wing bias in the mainstream media), and *Hatzofeh* (the only Israeli daily associated with a political party, the extreme right-wing National Religious Party). *Davar* (the organ of the Workers' Movement) and *Al-Hamishmar* (the publication of the Israeli Communist Party) vanished as the demand for socialist-inspired newspapers decreased, along with the Trade Union Movement whose members received these newspapers. There are also two major mass-circulation tabloids, *Ma'ariv* and *Yediot Aharonot* (Newman, 2002).

A paper like *The Jerusalem Post,* which until the mid-1980s used to be edited by people close to Labor, turned conservative after being bought by the Hollinger Group, and underwent an almost overnight switch in editorial policy with respect to the Israeli-Arab conflict. Newman described its policies this way: "though it tolerates some diversity . . . [it] supports Israel's right-wing government, is largely anti-European, and has become more parochial in its focus on the Jewish world at the expense of a broader coverage and analysis of world news" (Newman, 2002). The Israeli press has been strengthened by reporters like Amira Hass, who insisted on covering the West Bank and Gaza by living there among Palestinians (rather than among Israeli settlers), and Gideon Levy, member of *Ha'aretz*'s editorial board, who told an interviewer that "somewhere in the Ha'aretz newsroom is a thick file of subscription-cancellation notices inspired by his coverage" [of Israeli excesses in the occupied territories.] He added that he was "less constrained in his punditry than most columnists are in the United States and Europe" (Glain, 2007).

In 1989, the High Court of Justice ruled that censorship may be applied only when the item in question will harm public safety (Limor, 1999). That ruling emboldened the Israeli press. The International Press Institute (IPI) noted that the weakening of the once stringent Israeli military censorship was dramatized in 1997 in the coverage of two fiascos involving the Mossad, the country's secret service (IPI, "Israel," 1998). The Israeli press exhibits much more willingness to discuss Palestinian issues vigorously and frankly than the more timid American press. Several online Israeli papers have added video to their daily news reports.

Israel has come under international criticism for its handling of the press since the beginning of the Palestinian uprising starting in September 2000. According to an April 2002 report by the Vienna-based IPI, 6 journalists have been killed and 59 have been injured by gunfire or shelling (IPI, "IPI Releases," 2002). Israel also destroyed television stations in the occupied Palestinian territories in 2002, as well as in Lebanon when it invaded the south in 2006. In both cases, it accused its enemies of incitement and bombed their facilities.

Turkey   Turkey has a diverse and lively press with an estimated 2,124 newspapers in circulation. Forty of these are national, 23 regional and 2,061 local. Among the national dailies (with their average daily sales), *Posta* (644,413), *Hürriyet* (522,880), *Zaman* (509,667), *Sabah* (445,679), and *Milliyet* (263,538) are the major ones. National media are stronger than the local. Turkey's media is heavily dominated by conglomerates such as the Doğan Group, Merkez Group, Çukurova Group, İhlas Group, Doğuş Group, and Feza Group. All the major commercial channels and newspapers belong to these multimedia groups. The distribution of the print media, too, is monopolized by Doğan Group's Yay-Sat and Merkez Group's MDP.

The mainstream (indeed nationalist-leaning) major dailies are *Hürriyet* and *Milliyet,* "the biggest selling" boulevard daily *Posta,* the quality paper *Radikal* (40,665). Merkez Group owns *Sabah,* which competes with *Hürriyet.* Remarkably, Liberal Islamic dailies *Zaman* (owned by Feza Group) and *Yeni Şafak* employ liberal and left-wing columnists and thus offer a relatively broader perspective, especially on the controversial issues. Turkey publishes three English dailies. The biggest selling magazines are the weekly "colorful and light" news magazines.

While overall readership of the local press is not large for a country of such a large size, the newspaper business is intensely competitive. Despite the government's restrictions, the media criticize government leaders and policies daily. The constitution provides for freedom of speech and of the press; however, the government sometimes limits these freedoms through a series of antidefamation laws.

Reporters Without Borders charged that "[d]espite the announcement of democratic reforms within the framework of Turkey's candidacy for membership in the European Union, prosecutions for beliefs and opinions are still systematically and severely punished by virtue of a repressive legislative arsenal aimed at protecting the state against demands by the Kurds, Islamists and the far left" (Reporters Without Borders, "Turkey," 2002). The 1991 repeal of the law prohibiting publications or communications in Kurdish legalized private spoken and printed communications in Kurdish.

That move promised to ease relations between the government and the Kurdish minority (Parsons, 2002). Because of the invasion of Iraq and Turkish fears of Kurdish separatist tendencies, however, Turkey has been fighting the Kurdistan Workers' Party (Kurdish: *Partiya Karkerên Kurdistan* or PKK) in Northern Iraq.

Broadcasting in the Arab World

Until recently, broadcasting in the Arab world was under the thumb of various governments, with the exception of Lebanon.[2] Current trends suggest that broadcasting is entering a new era characterized by channel and program diversity, technological sophistication, and sweeping commercialism. Yet while those countries have privatized entertainment for fear of losing the members of their audience to widely available satellite stations from several countries, many have not privatized news or political opinion. The demise of the Soviet Union, however, has eroded barriers to full-throttled economic globalization.

Radio is booming in the Arab world with 211 FM radio stations currently broadcasting in 18 Arab countries. The Arab World's FM radio boom continues with 36 new FM radio stations starting between late 2005 and January 2007. "State-owned radio stations in the Arab world are still more numerous than private radio stations, although the number of private ones is growing rapidly," according to Layla Najia, Arab Advisors research analyst. "There are currently 113 state-owned radio stations that cover the listed 18 countries, while there are 98 private stations" (AME Info, "The Arab World's FM," 2007.)

Not everyone in the region accepts the inevitability or desirability of privatization and globalization. Some insist that focusing too narrowly on efficiency criteria ignores fundamental questions about "the nationality of capital" (Pripsten-Posusney, 1999). Many fear returning their countries' strategic assets to foreign hands. But more importantly, some fear the erosion of their own values. Jordanian columnist Hussein al-Rawashdah laments the effects of the spread of foreign culture "that refuses all types of freedom except the freedom of commercial speech, and wages war on all values except the value of consumption" (Al-Rawashdah, 1997). Respected journalist Hisham Milhem says that "The media landscape has changed radically in a revolutionary way." He added that there were more than 250 satellite television stations and 19 new radio stations added only in the last few years. According to Milhem, the Arab world has "a different media reality . . . that powers-that-be cannot ignore" (Phillips, 2008).

Broadcasting in Iraq, Jordan, Lebanon, Palestine, and Syria

Iraq   Until it was occupied by the United States of America, Iraq had two channels: the official channel of Iraq Television and Youth Television, a private channel headed by Uday Hussein, the son of the former Iraqi president. On March 26, 2003, the United States bombed Iraq's main television station and other broadcasting facilities. Some charged that the attack came as a revenge for the broadcast of video of dead American soldiers, while the American military said it was to damage the regime's command and control capability" (Dworkin, 2003). Afterward, the United States sponsored several projects to create TV stations in Iraq.

Although Iraq was the first Arab country to have television in 1956, it was the last to have satellites, first because of censorship, and then in 1996, because American sanctions against it prevented the importation of satellites. In July 1998, Iraq launched its first satellite channel ("Satellite," 1999). Iraq's splintered political scene is reflected in Iraq's 30-plus terrestrial and satellite channels, the layout of which increasingly mirrors the country's turbulent scene, with stations cropping up to represent every sectarian and political trend similar to stations of Lebanon. Sectarian issues appear to be driving broadcasting and funding sources determine content and orientation. Al Salam TV relies on funding from Shiite cleric Muqtada Al Sadr, Ghadeer TV on the Higher Council of the Islamic Revolution, Al Masar TV on the Islamic Da'awa Party, and Ahlul Bayt TV on the patronage of Shiite cleric Ayatollah Hadi Al Moderassi. Baghdadia TV is considered a moderate Sunni channel and Baghdad TV, run by the Iraqi Islamist Party, is known as "Baathist TV" among Shiites who criticize its pro-Sunni agenda. Afaq TV shows video footage in support of the Sunni Iraqi Islamic Party and Muqtada Al Sadr (Cochrane, 2006).

The Coalition Provisional Authority (CPA) under Paul Bremmer, introduced Order Number 14 in June 2003, which prohibits media from broadcasting or publishing material that incites violence against any individual or group, "including racial, ethnic, religious groups, and women," encourages civil disorder, or "incites vilence against coalition forces." Violators, if convicted, will be fined up to $1,000 or sentenced to one year in prison (Prusher, 2003). Reporters sans frontières (RSF) called these legal formulations "vague terms whose interpretation by U.S. authorities could be used to crack down on the local media." The organization also criticized the detention of journalists of Al Jazeera while filming an anti-U.S. demonstration. Another Al Jazeera reporter described on Al Jazeera how he was detained for 24 hours and had his video confiscated after photographing the remains of a family in a burned car hit by American forces responding to attacks against them from elsewhere (Al Jazeera, The Correspondents, May 10, 2003).

Many wondered whether calling for the end of the U.S. occupation or longing for the return of the Al-Ba'ath Party as a substitute for the chaos in Iraq would constitute incitement. It appeared that under that law, it does. For example, the Interior Ministry shut down

Sunni TV stations Al-Zawra and Salah-Eddin on November 5 for broadcasting film of demonstrators waving pictures of former President Saddam Hussein and protesting against his death sentence. At least 30 journalists were arrested by Iraqi security forces during 2006, and four of them were still being held without charge at the end of the year. The U.S. army arrested eight media workers during the same period, and at year-end four of them were still being held without a stated reason (Reporters Without Borders, Iraq Annual Report, 2007).

Jordan   Despite partial privatization of television and the appointment of a Jordan Radio and TV board, the media, especially the channel that transmits news, remain under government control because entertainment, rather than news, was partly privatized. Critics charge that privatization cum capitalism defeats the original goal of privatization: to liberate news and public affairs programs from government control. Jordan's brief foray into the "idea" of private TV came when Jordan ATV, the first private TV terrestrial station and satellite station, was set to broadcast after two years of preparation, on July 31, 2007. The Jordanian Audio-Visual Commisison halted transmission on NileSat, citing lack of proper licensing as an excuse—an excuse few people bought. Jordanian columnist Batir Wardam called the halting of the TV "as the most damaging to the image of press freedom in Jordan "in" a long history of bad official decisions against press freedom in Jordan (Wardam, 2007)." He added that it was a case of halting "media investment in favor of the miserable, pathetic and controlled official TV we all know as JRTV."

The most positive development, however, has been the introduction of Internet radio to Jordan in the form of Amman.Net, the brainchild of journalist Daoud Kuttab, who started it by "doing something illegal, legally." He created radio programs, broadcast them on the Internet, and then, through an agreement with Palestinian private broadcasters a short distance away, had those stations rebroadcast them from the West Bank. Jordanians heard this local program in Jordan. The innovative part of Amman.Net is its concentration on local issues, human rights, women's issues and technology. Grants from the Amman Municipality and from UNESCO made Jordan a training location for Internet radio enthusiasts from different parts of the Arab world. Kuttab and his young staff members also transmitted parliamentary deliberations and created Web sites for some parliamentarians to connect them to their public. Kuttab eventually got a license to broadcast terrestrially (Najjar, 2007).

Lebanon   Radio broadcasting in Lebanon, which started in 1938 under the French Mandate, remained a government monopoly until the beginning of the civil war in 1975 (Dajani, 2003).

Lebanon is the only country in the region that saw television as a business from the start. Lebanon's view of the media as a private enterprise ensured its primacy in entertainment television, if not in political broadcasting. Private control created a freer climate for political criticism than that found in other countries with government-controlled media, but at the same time, it also led to government pressure to reduce critical reporting for fear of driving away potential investors.

When the government got involved in television, it was at the request of the two private stations that had started broadcasting in 1956 and 1959. A 1977 legislative decree legalized the official merger in a new company, the Lebanese Televison Company (Tele Liban), licensed it for 25 years, and gave it a monopoly until 2012. Tele Liban was to be managed by a 12-member board of directors, six representing the government, with the chair to be appointed by the government (Dajani, 2003).

The weakening of the central government in the mid-1980s ensured the failure of the idea of monopoly and encouraged some warring factions to establish their own pirate stations because they felt that Tele Liban was not doing them justice.

The government legalized the existing stations in 1989. Forty-six were set up in a few months, and 10 were on the air by the end of 1991 (Dajani, 2003). The new Audio-Visual Law adopted by the parliament gave 16-year licenses and classified television stations according to their content (news and politics, no news and politics, coded signals to subscribers, international satellite).

In September 1996, the council of ministers restructured private broadcasting on the recommendation of the National Council of Audio-Visual Media. Radio stations were reduced from 150 to 10. TV stations were reduced from 60 to 4 (in addition to Tele Liban) ("Lebanon," 1996). Lebanon's permitted TV channels reflect sectarian and boss interests. In 2006, there were six licensed television stations which operate as both terrestrial and satellite broadcasters: "The Lebanese Broadcasting Company International (LBCI, formerly LBC), which speaks for the Maronite Christians and represents the views of the right wing Lebanese Forces; Future Television, which addresses the Sunni Muslims and is owned by the family of former prime minister Rafiq Hariri; The National Broadcasting Network (NBN), representing one faction of Shi'ite Muslims and owned by the family and supporters of the speaker of the parliament; Al Manar, organ of the Shi'i Islamic Hezbollah Party; New Television (NTV), which began as an organ of the Communist Party, but is presently owned by opposition politicians; and finally, Tele Liban, which is managed by a board appointed by the government" (Dajani, 2006).

Al-Manar station, belonging to Hizbullah (the Party of God), was allowed to stay open. The station was established on June 3, 1991, while Israelis were still occupying 20 percent of the south of Lebanon. According to its Web site, it was not unusual for the south and Bekaa Valley to be under Israeli fire "while singers chant[ed] on numerous TV channels simultaneously. There had to be a TV that committed itself to put in images the suffering of our people in the occupied territories." But its effectiveness lay in waging "psychological warfare against the myth of the invincible Israeli" (Muhsen, 1998:63). Hizbullah statistics after the April 1996 conflict with Israel show that 1,200 journalists visited Hizbullah's information center. Hizbullah also issued 474 briefings and distributed 200 videos to news agencies (Muhsen, 1998:66–67).

A Catholic station, Tele Lumiere, continues to broadcast without a license, but with tacit government approval. The Holy Koran TV does the same.

Despite the sectarian origin of some of those stations, commercial self-interest has led them to reach out beyond their original constituencies. The government is less concerned about critical reporting on government officials inside Lebanon, but is very sensitive about the image projected abroad via satellite TV (Kraidy, 1999). The attitude of the Lebanese government contrasts with the attitude of other governments that are very concerned about public criticism of their policies or persons.

Palestinian Radio and Television   The West Bank provides an example in which media privatization has led to more local production rather than to corporate ownership. The government-owned Palestine Broadcasting Corporation (PBC) operates Palestine TV from Ramallah and Gaza. But a development unique in the Arab world has been the establishment of 70 private radio and TV stations alongside PBC and Hamas's TV station in Gaza.

When the Palestinian Authority, headed by Yasser Arafat, entered Gaza on July 1, 1994, it asked broadcasters who had worked at various PLO radio stations around the Arab world since 1965 to return and establish the official radio in the West Bank and Gaza ("History," 2000).[3] Listeners can hear the news every hour on the hour in Arabic, Hebrew, English, and French, in that order. The PBC also operates Palestine Satellite Channel.

But even before the autonomy was extended to the West Bank in September 1995, several Palestinian citizens had already established unlicensed small radio or TV stations starting in December 1993.[4] The broadcasters came from all sectors of society: the physics university student who experimented with the first transmitter that broadcast only around his house; the penniless print media veterans who found the new medium promising for hard-hitting documentaries on public issues and solicited funds from businesspeople who wanted to make money off advertising; and the leftist political party that wanted a voice in the political process (Farraj, 2000).

The introduction of TV to badly served towns in the north and south of the West Bank made broadcasting much more central to the lives of people in those areas than the centrally located print media whose concentration remains national. In April 2002, Israeli soldiers destroyed the equipment of various private TV stations. Donations replaced the equipment, and most stations are back in operation. Recently, Palestinians themselves attacked their own stations (Reporters Without Borders, Palestinian Authority-Annual Report, 2007).

The Ma'an News Agency (MNA; Ma'an means "together" in Arabic) is a Palestinian online News agency that publishes up-to-the-minute news in Arabic, English, and Hebrew. The MNA began operation in December 2004. The Ma'an Network (Ma'an) is composed of nine independent TV stations and production studios located in each major city of the West Bank and Gaza. Ma'an says it is "dedicated to promoting understanding of the Palestinian situation by strengthening cooperation between local and international media." It is funded by the Netherlands Ministry of Foreign Affairs and the Ministry of Foreign Affairs of Denmark, Danish International Development Assistance (DANIDA). (Ma'an, 2008.)

Syrian Radio and Television   The first official Syrian radio station launched during the French Mandate in 1941 was taken over by the Syrian government in 1946 after the French withdrew from Syria. A series of military coups beginning in 1949 increased the importance of radio for the different regimes, which strengthened its operation. By 1951, its service covered all the Syrian provinces as well as the neighboring countries, the Mediterranean region, and parts of Africa. Syria transmits programs in Arabic, French, Hebrew, Turkish, Spanish, and Russian (Dajani, 2003).

Syrian Arab Television is financed directly by government, which also controls its political content, as well as by advertising. It operates within the General Directorate of Radio and Television whose board is chaired by the Minister of Information (Dajani, 2003). Syria decided to allow private radio stations to be established starting in 2002 but did not allow them to broadcast news.

Syrian Arab TV commenced operations on July 23, 1960. In 1985, Syrian television started a second channel that concentrated on cultural programs (Syrian Arab News Agency [SANA], 2002, quoted by Dajani, 2003). Paradoxically, Syria's refraining from importing Western TV series, unlike its neighbor Lebanon, gave its own TV industry a boost by forcing it to rely on the active Syrian cultural scene (theater and dance troupes). Syrian historical drama and political satire shows are very popular in the Arab world for their good scripts and biting social commentary. Its Ghawwar al Tosheh program, a comedy that indicts Arab bureaucracy, ran in many Arab countries for years and was running in a flight on the Royal Jordanian Airline in 2008. Syrian drama is not afraid of treating gender and class issues in a serious but entertaining way. On the other hand, Syrian political and news talk shows have not distinguished themselves in the pan-Arab debate scene because political censorship prevents Syrian satellite TV from inviting guests whose views are radically different from its own. Syria does not restrict its citizens' use of satellite dishes, and Syrian callers and experts frequently participate in Al Jazeera satellite TV call-ins. Starting in 2004, analysts noted some improvements in the media landscape. Syrian TV is encouraged to carry political programs and occasionally airs interviews with opposition figures. Syria has set up a free media zone in Damascus and applications have been lodged for licenses for new private satellite TV channels. Those who take part will get tax breaks for buying equipment ("Minister Urges," 2004). Syria allowed Shams private TV to operate but closed it at the end of October 2008, eight months after it opened (Syrian Comment, 2006).

Broadcasting in the Gulf Countries: Bahrain, Kuwait, United Arab Emirates, Saudi Arabia, and Qatar

While Gulf countries have lagged in terms of print press freedom, they have distinguished themselves on the Arab information technology and media scene, in part because of their financial resources, but also because of a conscious commitment to move away from having oil as their only product. Dubai, which in the early 1970s depended on oil for 87 percent of its economy, hopes to reduce that to only 2 percent in 2010 ("Dubai," 2002). Qatar and Abu Dhabi have distinguished themselves in satellite broadcasting, and Dubai by luring Internet and communication technology to a special media zone it set up.

Bahrain Bahrain government-owned Radio and TV Corporation operates five terrestrial TV networks. Those consist of a general program in Arabic, a second program featuring cultural and local programs, a Koran program, a sports service, and the English-language Radio Bahrain. The long absence of elected government until October 2002 resulted in a press used to self-censorship or exile. The media have not yet developed as institutions capable of policing government. The 2006 elections may put them on the path of reform.

Kuwait The Kuwaiti Ministry of Information controls the radio and four terrestrial TV stations. Kuwaiti media are currently involved in a power struggle with Islamists who want to apply a more conservative policy to the state TV and radio ("Kuwaiti Minister," 2000). Despite that setback, Kuwait has a strong constituency for freedom of expression.

There are no private radio stations in Kuwait. Radio Kuwait is controlled by the Ministry of Information and broadcasts programs in Arabic and English.

Saudi Arabia   Saudi Arabia is an example of a country whose strict media policy is being eroded by the various Arab satellite programs that are picked up in the kingdom. But it is also a country that has created and funded a media empire for itself outside its borders, thus making itself an important media player in the Arab world (although not in political broadcasting until the establishment of Al Arabiya Satellite TV in 2003 to compete with Al Jazeera).

The state-owned Broadcasting Service of the Kingdom of Saudi Arabia (BSKSA) is responsible for all broadcasting and is directly controlled by the Ministry of Information.

United Arab Emirates   Abu Dhabi TV consists of three channels: the Emirates Channel, which focuses on the Gulf region; the Abu Dhabi Sports Channel, a pay channel, and the Abu Dhabi Satellite Channel, which is making its mark on the Arab media scene by competing with Al Jazeera by presenting political talk shows that draw large audiences. Even though Abu Dhabi TV does not get much coverage in the West, in the Arab world it is followed with attention. During the 2003 U.S. war with Iraq, all U.S. stations heavily used Abu Dhabi's coverage, as well as Al Jazeera's.

A Lebanese media critic described one of Abu Dhabi's satellite programs as a seamless performance in which the station interviewed the editor of *Oriental Studies* in Paris, then cut to its own correspondent in Bethlehem, then to its correspondent in Ramallah, West Bank, then to the United Nations, then to Tehran, then to Ramallah to interview some politicians, then to Damascus to cover demonstrations. The critic said that the Lebanese satellite stations, which dazzled Arab viewers when they first appeared, are now behind Gulf stations and should reconsider their coverage (Yaghi, 2000). Radio is owned by the government.

Dubai   Dubai is a perfect example of a country that adopted capitalism and globalization with a Middle Eastern twist that befits the country's background as the home of traders and seafarers. Unlike Abu Dhabi and Qatar, Dubai has shunned political broadcasting to avoid controversy, but has turned itself into a media hub by attracting 194 world-class computer companies to its Dubai Internet City (DIC) and the Oasis for electronic projects in 2000, and for inducing Arab companies that had migrated to the West to set up shop in Dubai alongside Western companies it attracted through tax breaks ("After the Opening," 2000).

Dubai Media City (DMC), launched on November 4, 2000, like DIC, accepts 100 percent foreign ownership and offers a 50-year corporate and personal tax exemption to "individual media people" as well as corporations. The vision is of a media community that will bring broadcasters, TV production companies, publishers, ad agencies, and public relations companies as well as individual journalists together in one 500-acre landscaped "media ecosystem."

Dubai has invested approximately $800 million in Media City, slightly more than its investment in Dubai Internet City. It provides cutting-edge technology, including production and transmission facilities. The strategic position of Dubai at the crossroads of the Middle East, Africa, and South Asia enables it to serve as a media hub for the region and to target an audience of nearly two billion people. The list of residents includes Indian channels like UNI TV, AsiaNet, the Iranian Soroush Multimedia, and Zen TV, a channel targeting teens. Sheikh Abdullah bin Zayed Al Nahyan, UAE Minister of Information and Culture said,"When I talk about media freedom, I do not mean it as an ambiguous and misleading phrase." A key role for Dubai Media City will be the development of indigenous talent within the Arab world. The Ministry of Information and Culture is establishing a special Media Institute in the city designed to encourage UAE nationals to move into the media industry (Dubai Media City, 2007).

DIC has already reportedly leased out 95 percent of its space, with IBM already breaking ground in DIC for a regional headquarters and with Microsoft, Oracle, Compaq, MasterCard, Sun Microsystems, and Hewlett-Packard among the more than 190 companies already licensed to operate in DIC.

Middle East Broadcasting Centre (MBC), the largest Middle East, pan-Arab broadcaster, has relocated to Dubai Media City from London. Other clients include Middle East Business News, producing for CNBC. CNN started operating out of Dubai Media City in early January 2002, doing two things: incorporating a regional news bureau there, and launching CNNArabic.com out of Dubai Media City. Reuters has relocated its operation and expanded it at Dubai Media City. Reuters is a major "anchor" client for Dubai Media City and, like MBC, has a building named for it (Schleifer, 2000).

DMC is intent on encouraging Gulf nationals to enter the media field by training them in the media professions. The industry side of the Dubai International Film Festival grew in 2007. Dubai Festival City (DFC) selected 15 film projects and brought the filmmakers together with producers, financiers, film fund spokespersons, distributors, sales agents, and broadcasters, then awarded grants of $15,000 to the three scripts judged to be best and accredited them to attend Cannes in 2008 (Quilty, 2007).

Qatar   Qatar's state television runs three channels: one main Arabic service, a Koran channel, and one English channel. Qatar has one private station, Al Jazeera, run by an independent board.

Al Jazeera Satellite TV: A Pan-Arab Voice in Qatar   The most important recent development for the Arab media was the establishment of the Al Jazeera satellite station in Qatar in 1996. That station put Qatar on the map of Arab politics, replacing Egypt as the main content provider and Saudi Arabia as the media bankroller.

Al Jazeera has introduced a new form of "Global Arab Village" not seen since the days of Voice of the Arabs radio from Cairo in the 1950s and 1960s. The station's most famous talk-show programs, *More Than One Opinion, The Opinion and the Other Opinion,* and *The Opposite Direction,* pit people from different political camps or countries against each other and invite listeners to call in, and they do—from every Arab country as well as from Iran, Pakistan, Europe, and the United States. Sparks fly and "red lines" imposed by governments are crossed because all the "forbiddens" are ignored (criticism of rulers and regimes, religion, and women's status). Al Jazeera is the only station that has a women's program that does not deal with cooking, childcare, or fashion. *For Women Only* discusses gender and work issues, as well as women's education and political participation.

Al Jazeera is constantly fielding protests from different countries. Al Jazeera says it has been the victim of an advertising boycott. It was bailed out by the ruler of Qatar in

2003 after racking up losses of £19 million. Hamad Ibn Khalifa, prince of Qatar, refuses to censor the station and continues to fund it (Wheeler, 2003).

Al Jazeera made its name in the West during the war in Afghanistan with exclusive footage that other channels around the world were eager to buy. In the process, it earned the enmity of the U.S. administration. Its office in Kabul was destroyed by American "smart" bombs two hours before the Northern Alliance took over the city. In 2003 the station broadcast bloody war scenes from the invasion of Iraq, images Western news organizations would consider too shocking to show. One showed the head of a child, aged about 12, that had been split apart, reportedly in the U.S.-led assault on Basra.

On March 23, 2003, Al Jazeera relayed footage of Iraqi television's interviews with five captured American soldiers, infuriating the Americans. Ali Kamal, the marketing director of Al Jazeera, defended the station's right to show pictures of dead bodies because the media have a duty to show the bloody price of war. He added that Arab media are under attack because they now have the "upper hand" over Western broadcasters. Kamal was in England receiving the Index on Censorship Freedom of Expression Awards for circumvention of censorship (Whitaker, 2003; Tryhorn, 2003). During the invasion, the Iraqi minister of information, Mohammad al-Sahhaf, asked Al Jazeera to replace two of its correspondents. Al Jazeera announced on air on April 2, 2003, that it "froze" the reporting of all eight of its correspondents in Baghdad (but said it will continue broadcasting live images of the invasion). The minister relented, and the station quietly resumed its operations. Francis Hasso said that "Al Jazeera's approach to covering the war . . . has seriously threatened the political projects of the world's most powerful." She added that Al Jazeera's coverage has contradicted American and British claims that the war was "bloodless, costless and clean." At the same time, the coverage "has reflected the Arab recognition that the Saddam Hussein dictatorship was a tragedy," even while it questioned the claim that Iraq was invaded to bring about democracy and liberation (Hasso, 2003). The fact that Al Jazeera's reporters and producers are drawn from various Arab countries adds to the station's pan-Arab appeal, enriches the station's programming, and makes it earn its slogans, "The Opinion and the Other Opinion" and "All the Colors of the Rainbow."

In 2003 Al-Arabiya was set up with Saudi money to counter Al Jazeera. Surveys show that Al-Arabiya is the market leader in Saudi Arabia, and it has done well in the Arab Gulf countries, but it is not as popular in Jordan, the Palestinian territories, Syria, and Egypt (Worth, 2008).

Broadcasting in North Africa: Algeria, Egypt, Libya, Morocco, and Tunisia

Only Egypt has opened up broadcasting to private investors, and those investors have so far not threatened the status quo because they are more interested in broadcasting as a business than as a political tool.

Algeria   Algeria has three national radio stations and two television channels, all state owned. The broadcasting sector has not been touched by the "liberalization" the government has boastfully promoted. In the framework of the Organic Law, a broadcasting regulatory authority will be created and will consider opening radio and television to the private sector. But, officials said, those plans "will initially exclude news bulletins."

Egypt   President Nasser understood the oral culture of nonelite listeners and distributed radios to rural areas. He used radio most effectively for developmental purposes, but he also used it to spread the idea of pan-Arabism and nonalignment as he cooperated with Asian and African leaders, among them Jawaharlal Nehru, prime minister of India, and Kwame Nkrumah, prime minister of the Gold Coast (later Ghana). Afro-Asian states hoped to strengthen their independence from Western imperialism while keeping the Soviet bloc at a comfortable distance. This strategic bloc was the beginning of what came to be known as the nonaligned movement and the Third World (Quest, nd). During that period, Egypt expanded its radio services to many countries, especially in Africa, and transmitted in several languages. Egyptian radio, "The Voice of the Arabs," however, lost its leading role after the 1967 Arab-Israeli war, when listeners criticized its lack of credibility in war reporting and Arabs turned to the BBC to learn of their defeat at the hands of Israel. The Egyptian place in political Arab media was further eroded after President Anwar Al-Sadat signed a peace treaty with Israel in 1979 and Egypt was expelled from the Arab League until 1989. The pan-Arab leadership in political media went unfilled until 1996, when Qatar established its satellite station, Al Jazeera, and Abu Dhabi established its satellite station.

The Egyptian Radio and Television Union (ERTU), which controls TV, is state owned. Television started in Egypt in 1960. It has two national terrestrial channels and six regional channels. ERTU launched its first satellite channel in 1990 (Reporters Without Borders, "Egypt: Annual Reports," 2001, 2002). Egypt was the first Arab country to acquire its own satellite (Nilesat 101). It now runs Egyptian Space channels ESC1 and ESC2, plus Nile TV International, which broadcasts some programs in English and Hebrew. Egypt is the leading television producer in entertainment in the Arab world because it is able to rely on its huge library of old Egyptian films. By announcing on January 17, 2000, that it was creating a free media zone, it was serving notice that it intends to capitalize on its TV production infrastructure to preserve that preeminence (Feuilherade, 2000). Egypt offers a variety of news talk shows and cultural entertainment, but its news still has the official look and concentrates too much on the comings and goings of the Egyptian leaders, although not to the same extent as the Saudi station.

In November 2001, Egypt launched the first private satellite network, Dream TV. The station disappeared in 2004 after several high-profile people, like veteran presenter Hamdy Kandil, who hosted a weekly political talk show "Editor-in-Chief," and Ibrahim Eissa, who hosted the popular program "In the Café" and former editor-in chief of the *Al-Ahram* paper, had their shows abruptly canceled or they themselves canceled them (depending on which version one accepts.) All three had been politically outspoken (Osman, 2004).

Libya   Libya's radio and TV are controlled by the government, but the first nonstate TV station, Al-Libiyah satellite TV, was launched in 2007. A new Libyan TV station, Al Badil, the alternative, whose name suggested that it was an alternative to the state-owned first TV channel, turned out to refer to "the alternative thinking or theory" as embodied by the Green Book or Third Universal Theory, of Libyan leader, Qaddafi. It turned out to be another vehicle for transmitting the speeches of the Libyan leader (BBC Monitoring, "Libyan Al-Badil", 2008).

Morocco   Both radio and TV in Morocco are controlled by the government. Following the dismissal of the interior minister, Driss Basri, in 1999, King Mohammed VI replaced the directors of the official news agency (MAP) and the main public television channel (TVM). These changes on the media scene were considered as signs of a "slackening" of official control over public media. But broadcasting has not yet provided alternatives to government-issued fare.

Tunisia   Tunisia has four domestic terrestrial channels. Tunis 7 and Canal 2 are both national public service channels operated by ERTT, which produces about 30 percent of its programming locally. Tunis 7 also transmits by satellite to Europe and neighboring countries. Tunis's domestic pay TV, Canal Horizons Tunisie (launched in 1992), is uncensored. The fourth channel is the Italian RAI-Uno. Tunisians can also receive by agreement Canal 2 of France, although Tunisians have in the past suspended relays (for example, during the 1999 elections). Two London-based opposition satellite TV channels can be received in Tunisia, *Al-Mustaqillah,* (The Independent), and the *Islamist Zeitouna* (Olive Tree) (Reporters Without Borders, "Country Profile: Tunisia"). The state maintains monopoly of radio stations.

Radio and Television in Iran, Israel, and Turkey

Iran   Iranians rely on television and radio because newspapers and print media have a limited circulation outside the main cities. Iran's radio and four-channel television are controlled by the state. Starting in 1993, and within a short period of time, satellite dishes started to proliferate in Iran. The ban on the installation of satellites, ratified on February 12, 1995 (*Official Journal,* No. 14468, March 6, 1995) slowed down but did not prevent satellite acquisition because of the difficulty of practical implementation. By 1994, about 500,000 dishes had been installed ("Cultural Satellite," 1995). Iranians, however, manufactured their own dishes in Iran and made smaller ones that avoid detection but get fewer channels (Arjomandi, 1999:4–13 passim).

The 1995 ban had largely been ignored since the 1997 election of President M. Khatami. In 2001, Iran once again enforced the law and confiscated thousands of dishes. Reuters quoted Defense Minister Ali Shamkhani as saying, "Bankrupt elements abroad are trying to use the satellite network to launch a political challenge (BBC News "Iran Cracks Down," 2001). He was referring to several expatriate TV channels, run by Western-based dissident groups, who were exhorting Iranians to riot after soccer matches ("Police," 2001). There are five Iranian–American TV stations in Los Angeles, which is the home of the largest Iranian population in the world outside Iran.

The decision to ban dishes engendered a great deal of discussion, with some officials arguing that it is better to adopt a policy of "cultural immunity" than to ban the technology because of some benefits on satellite TV ("Iran Confiscated," 2001). Some worry that, with the closing of newspapers, the bans and propaganda against reform by the state broadcast monopoly controlled by hard-liners could prepare the ground for a further crackdown. State radio and television chief Ali Larijani said he will expand official satellite, radio, and television networks to provide an alternative to foreign sources ("Iran Intends," 2000). Tehran has Al-Alam (The World), an Arabic channel that is avidly watched in Iraq. Its coverage of President Bush's trip to the Middle East focused on dissent. Iran's view of

President Bush, says CBS News analyst Reza Aslan, is a lot like the U.S. view of President Ahmadinejad. "The Iranian media sees the president of the United States as an out-of-control religious fanatic, pretty much the same way that the American press sees the president of Iran" (Phillips, 2008).

Israel   "The Voice of Israel," established in 1948, had its origins in the Palestine Broadcasting Service established by the British in 1936. In 1951, Israel's foreign-language broadcasting was extended to cover several languages to serve its immigrant population and Jews abroad. Initially, the government was determined to keep its monopoly of broadcasting. In the mid-1960s, the government controlled the Israeli army radio and the educational TV, while state radio and television became part of the public system. Starting in 1973, however, some challenged government monopoly by resorting to offshore broadcasting. The first such station was the Voice of Peace, 1973–1993. The offshore vessels represent various Israeli constituencies, from music-only stations to religious stations whose purpose was to "return people to religion."[5]

By the 1990s, 50 pirate radio stations went into operation (Caspi and Limor, 1999:125–126). Legal commercial local radio began only in 1995. The parliament legalized pirate stations that had been in operation continuously for at least five years as of January 1, 1999. The two meeting these criteria are Arutz 7 and Shas's Radio 2000, both religious. Petitions were submitted to Israel's High Court claiming that the law "rewarded criminals and discriminated against the legal operations of Israel's existing regional stations," which had to put up large financial guarantees and compete against other bidders in order to obtain licenses. Arutz 7 argues that it had to put up large sums to keep a ship offshore. In the mid-1990s, the Second Authority set up 16 regional radio stations, to be operated by private licenses. Radio 2000 was intended for the Arabs of Northern Israel and Kol Hay for Jewish religious listeners.[6]

Israeli radio is diversifying its content and using the latest technology. Netkaing has grabbed the musical niche by providing Israel's dominant digital radio station. Since its debut in early 2000, The Marker.com has become the favorite in business circles because it offers immediate Hebrew translation of the Wall Street column, thestreet.com. The English-language daily, *The Jerusalem Post,* launched Internet radio (JpostRadio.com) in an effort to encourage reporters to tell stories in more than one medium.

Israel started TV broadcasting in 1968 in response to a report that lauded the medium's educational potential as a way of integrating Israel's new immigrants into the culture, as well as a mechanism that would prevent Arabs who remained in Israel in 1948 and Arabs Israel occupied in 1967 from being exposed only to the televisions of the surrounding Arab countries (Caspi and Limor, 1999:146). Television was controlled first by the government and then by the Israeli Broadcasting Authority (IBA), which is controlled by a board of directors composed of political appointees. TV was initially financed from license fees but now accepts paid ads (Lehman-Wilzig and Schejter, 1994:115–119). The first venture to break away from government monopoly came from the owner of Odelia TV, which started broadcasting in June 1981. By July, the government had prepared a hastily proposed anti-offshore broadcasting law. On November 29 the station was temporarily closed. On November 30 the anti-offshore law came into force. Israel refused to cooperate with offshore broadcasters except in cases of emergency.

There was a great deal of resistance to the introduction of a second TV channel in Israel. Initially, National Religious Party ministers blocked even discussion of the issue. In 1990, Israel finally accepted the introduction of the second channel, "22 years after the inception of television in Israel, 13 years after the major parties included the demand in their party platforms, and nearly 4 years after the law was first proposed." Experimental broadcasts of the second channel, however, had started in 1986 in order to allow Israel to "seize" frequencies for the second channel before other countries of the region started using them (Caspi and Limor, 1999:152). The second channel turned commercial in 1993. Cable television started broadcasting in January 1991. The Cable Television Council divided the country into 31 areas. As a result, Israel is well covered by this local network (Lehman-Wilzig and Schejter, 1994:115–119).

Turkey   Turkish TV had a slow start as a government enterprise, but once it took off, broadcasting flourished and was later privatized. The Turkish government started broadcasting in 1968. Full-color transmission came on July 1, 1984. The single-channel era ended in 1986 when TRT-2 joined TRT-1. In the 1980s, people who had satellite dishes watched foreign channels. In March 1990, a private Turkish TV channel, Star 1, took advantage of a gap in the telecommunications law and started broadcasting from Germany. Another, Show TV, started in Paris in 1992 ("History of Turkish TV": http://www.creatonic. com/tv/history.htm). By 1992, Kamal 6, Flash TV, HBB, ATV, and TGRT had joined the television market. Private television channels debated Alevi religious practices, homosexuality, feminism, Kurdish nationalism, and other formerly taboo subjects. M. Hakan Yavuz observes that "the new communication channels have combined with a wave of Islamic movements to promote sectarian and ethnic minority consciousness by a fusion of local and global identities" (Yavuz, 1999:181). This fusion is also true in the case of Turks in Amsterdam (Ogan, 2001).

Around 1,100 private TV stations are now broadcasting in Turkey, and 100 of them are also available on cable. Of these 36 are national, 102 are regional, and 950 are local radio stations. Besides the radio stations owned by the multimedia groups there are also many independent radio stations (European Journalism Center, 2008). Touchy subjects for journalists include the relations between the secular and the religious, the status of Kurds, and Armenians. Radio and TV stations are sometimes suspended for airing sensitive material. Some of the most repressive regulations have been lifted as part of reforms intended to meet EU entry requirements (BBC News, "Country Profile: Turkey," 2002). Kurdish-language broadcasts, banned for many years, were introduced by the state broadcaster in June 2004 as a part of reforms intended to meet EU criteria on minorities. Some overseas-based Kurdish TV channels broadcast via satellite.

Foreign Countries Transmitting in Arabic

In an attempt to reach the Arab world, several countries have begun transmitting radio and TV news in Arabic. The first among them was Iran with al-Alam (The Word), a TV station Iraqis can watch without satellite dishes. The United States started Radio Sawa in April 2002, a radio that uses pop to appeal to youth. It also started Al-Hurra (The Free One) in 2004.

Germany started its Deutsche Welle TV in Arabic in February 2005. France launched its "France 24" on April 2, 2007 to transmit "a fresh new and objective outlook at world events from a French perspective." Staff members hail from various Arab countries, in addition to the channel's correpondents from all over the world (AME Info, France, 2007).

The different Arab nationalities will allow the channel to interact with Arab viewers while being aware of the culture and values of the Arab world, according to the channel. The French hope to increase the number of hours from 4 to 24 (Layalena, 2007). Rusiya Al-Yaum, which started broadcasting on May 4, 2007 has more than 500 staff members, around 100 of whom are drawn from North Africa and the Middle East. Its programs are also available online. The channel broadcasts 20 hours a day and concentrates on news and documentaries that give prominence to the history of Russian-Arab relations and the Russian viewpoint on current affairs with a perspective that is sensitive to the region's culture. Russia, which enjoys good relations with Arab countries, wants an opportinuty to explain how Russia understands international developments (Press Release, 2007).

The BBC World Service, which is restarting its Arabic-language television channel, hired away 25 of Al-Arabiya's senior journalists as well as some of Al Jazeera's. BBC World Service has appointed Salah Negm as news editor for its Arabic Television Service to be launched in 2008. Negm, a former BBC program editor, early in his career set up the news department for Al Jazeera and was appointed director of news of Al-Arabiya after its launch (Press Release, 2006).

While Western countries seek to reach Middle Eastern countries by broadcasting in their language, Iran is reaching beyond its borders in a show of assertiveness. In July 2007 it started broadcasting in English on "PressTV," a new 24-hour network to "counter" major international mass media like CNN or the BBC by offering programs that challenge the "biased, one sided, double-standard, distorted items projected by the Western media." Iran Analytical Report notes that Iran "is trying to win Muslim hearts and minds through its well-financed, expanding array of media outlets targeting the Middle East, Caucasus, and Central Asia. Tehran is attempting to . . . present its own view of world events. To the detriment of others, this retaliation seems to be making an impact" (Iran Analytical Report, 2007). On the other hand, Iran blocked the BBC's Persian-language Internet Web site on January 23, 2006. The site was receiving about 30 million page hits a month—about half of which are from inside Iran (Haeri, 2006). Iran has invested heavily in foreign-language channels—one broadcasts specifically to the Iranian diaspora, and another, Sahar TV, broadcasts in a variety of languages, including English, French, Kurdish, and Urdu. Iran's state-run radio station broadcasts in about 30 languages (Usher, 2006).

On the other hand, Al Jazeera English started transmission in 2006 and has grown beyond its wildest expectations. It already has 100 million viewers just a year after its launch, half a million of them Israelis. Al Jazeera English is the world's first global English-language news channel to be headquartered in the Middle East. "From this unique position," Al Jazeera English's press releases state that it "is destined to be the English-language channel of reference for Middle Eastern events, balancing the current typical information flow by reporting from the developing world back to the West and from the southern to the northern hemisphere. The channel gives voice to untold stories, promotes debate, and challenges established perceptions." The station has broadcasting centers in Doha, Kuala Lumpur, London, and Washington, D.C., and supporting bureaus worldwide.

Internet Penetration and Growth in the Middle East

Internet usage increased dramatically between 2000 and December 2007. The largest increase was in Iran, which saw a growth rate of 7,100 percent. The highest Internet penetration was in Israel, at 57.6 percent, but Israel's growth has plateaued at 191.3 percent. Internet penetration in The United Arab Emirates stands at 38.4 percent, and its growth rate has plateaued at 132.4 percent. Syria, whose Internet usage did not increase until the younger President Assad entered the scene, has a penetration rate of only 7.8 percent, but a very high growth rate of 4,900 percent.

The Saudi population, also a late arrival on the scene, is trying to catch up, with a 2007 penetration of 17 percent but with a growth rate of 2,250 percent. The other Gulf States that have developed their infrastructure, Qatar has an Internet penetration of 32.0 percent but a much larger growth rate of 866.3 percent as it tries to catch up with other Gulf States. Similarly, Kuwait, with a surprisingly low penetration rate of 32.6 percent, has a 444.5 growth rate. Other countries whose skill level is good but who suffer from low GDP have lower penetration rates. Jordan at a 13.2 percent penetration rate and 526 percent growth rate; Lebanon at 24.2 percent penetration but a 216.7 percent growth rate. Palestine has a penetration rate of 10.5 percent and a growth rate of 660 percent aided by grants from human rights organizations and the Europen Union, among others. Yemen's penetration rate remains low at 1.2 percent of the population, but the country appears to be attempting to increase its numbers with a growth rate of 1,700 percent. Only Iraq has a lower penetration rate at 0.1 percent and a growth rate of 188 percent (Internet World Stats, Middle East, 2007); both because of restrictions on the Internet before 2003 coupled with the American sanctions against Iraq and because of continued lack of security in Iraq. When it comes to Arab countries in North Africa, Morocco is rated second in the top 10 Internet users in Africa with a usage rate of 20 percent and a growth rate of 6,000 percent, followed by Egypt registered at a penetration rate of 10.5 percent in March 2008 but a high growth rate of 1,815.6 percent. Libya's usage rate remains low at 4.2 percent, but its use growth rate is high at 2,500. Morocco's penetration stands at 21.3 percent, Tunisia's at 16.6 percent and Algeria's 10.4 percent (Internet World Stats, Africa, March, 2007).

One Palestinian Weblog was established on 23 July 2007 on the Arabic Media Internet Network. By July 10, 2008, it had 681 bloggers at http://blog.amin.org in addition to the other bloggers that exist elsewhere. The Blogs have received 1,119,656 visitors.

Blogging in the Middle East

Blogging is starting to spread and has proved its usefulness as a means of social communication between the sexes (e.g., women and men in Saudi Arabia), political organizing (Egypt, Bahrain, and Kuwait), and an instrument of human rights activism (Palestine, Lebanon, and Iraq).

In Egypt, blogging has seen a surge from 30 blogs in January 2005 to 3,000 in early 2007. The practice emerged as an extension of existing popular movements like the Kifaya (Enough!). Kifaya successfully used the Internet for mobilization for petitions and demonstrations. Despite the low usage rate in Egypt, the content of blogs is important because it reaches influential people and because the private press prints its content. Arab satellite television also uses it as a source for its broadcasts. Says one blogger, "We are the children of Al Jazeera" (Azmi, 2007:13). Muslim Brothers on ikwanweb.net became active after 2005, with a new and more technologically savvy younger generation being less reticent than the older one in airing internal debates on personal blogs (Lynch, 2007).

Bloggers made major gains in 2007 when a cell-phone clip shot by two Egyptian policemen of themselves torturing a bus driver in police custody and posted by Egyptian bloggers on YouTube in November 2006 netted the guilty policmen a three-year jail sentence. The case is one of several exposed by Eactivist bloggers (BBC News, "Egypt Police Jailed," 2007). The availability of sites like YouTube has allowed the posting of clips critical of the relationship of Arab governments and the United States (a relationship the press is not allowed to tackle with frankness.) In the video, Ya 'Amm 'Arabi (Hey Arab Uncle [Leader]), http://www.youtube.com/watch?v=ZamJloNsokw, popular artist 'Abd al-Rahim castigates Arab leaders for allowing George W. Bush and Ariel Sharon to act as global imperialist bullies divvying up the Middle East pie between them (Grippo, 2006).

Despite the arrest of several Egyptian bloggers, the Administrative Judicial Court issued a decision on December 29, 2007 in which it rejected Judge Abdul Fattah Murad's request to ban 51 Egyptian Web sites. The court emphasized support for freedom of expression and the importance of not compromising the freedom of these Web sites as long as they do not undermine fundamental beliefs or public order (allAfrica.com, 2008).

The growing influence of the Internet in *Kuwait* is evident by the increased number of blogs tackling political and social issues. Online participants played a critical role in forcing the government to acquiesce to the Five Departments Acts when they initiated a strong online campaign in the last election (IPI, World Press Freedom Review, Kuwait, 2006).

Libyans have relatively free access to the Internet, but their online activity is closely monitored. In November, the Reporters Without Borders took the country off its list of "enemies of the Internet." However, a new cyber-dissident, Idrees Boufayed, has since been imprisoned for posting material on opposition Web sites (Reporters Without Borders, "Libya," 2007.)

Saudis censor the Internet for political and social and religious content and filters say openly that certain pages on a site have been censored by the authorities. In 2005 censors tried to completely bar access to the country's main blog-tool, blogger.com, but gave up after a few days and now just censor blogs. "Saudi Eve," the diary of a young woman who discusses her love life and criticizes government censorship was added to the blacklist in June 2006 (Reporters Without Borders, "Saudi Arabia," 2007). The BBC estimates that there are some 500 bloggers in Saudi Arabia, most of whom blog anonymously. In 2007, Fouad al-Farhan was the first blogger from Saudi Arabia to be arrested, allegedly for the content of his blog (Merrett, 2008).

One of the most colorful Arab Web sites is penned by a *Bahraini,* "Mahmood's Den: An Arab man's attempt at bridging the cultural gap" (http://mahmood.tv/). Mahmood, a one-time aircraft avionics maintenance engineer, is an ardent advocate of freedom of expression. He defends bloggers and others accused of "press offenses" by posting their photos with their mouths taped shut. He also conducts campaigns to free journalists harassed or imprisoned by the authorities. In addition, Mahmoud posts articles from the Bahraini constitution to remind the government that freedom of expression is protected. At least 24 websites were blocked in Bahrain in 2008. Two websites, (http://www.ba7rainss.com/vb) and (http://www/bahrainforums.com) were closed because of their "sectarian nature" based on Article 19 of the decree-law No 47 of 2002 because they "harmed the regime, the official state religion, morality or different confessions in a way likely to cause a breach of the peace" (IFEX, 2008).

Bashar al-Assad, who used to oversee the Internet before his father's death, has increased *Syrian* access to the Internet by increasing the number of phone lines available to the population and dropping cell-phone rates. Syria, however, continues to filter net content and did so after the Israeli invasion of Lebanon to stop "Israeli infilteration" of Syrian Web sites. Three people are in jail for criticizing the regime. The government blocks access to Arab-language opposition Web sites (Reporters Without Borders, Syria-Annual Report, 2007).

In *Tunisia* all the Internet cafes are state-controlled and under police surveillance. Web content is filtered. Web sites like Reporters Without Borders cannot be accessed from inside Tunisia. The security services also constantly harass independent bloggers and opposition Web site editors to ensure that self-censorship prevails. One cyber-dissident, Mohammed Abbou, has been imprisoned since March 2005 for criticizing the president in an online newsletter (Reporters Without Borders, Tunisia-Annual Report, 2007). Morocco blocks access to Web sites close to the Polisario Front and to the online publication of the Islamist organization Justice and Charity, which challenges the monarchy's legitimacy (Reporters Without Borders, Morocco-Annual Report, 2007).

Blogs in *Iraq* "are gaining momentum" but remain few in number. There were 268 blogs at the end of 2007, with 150 of them active. Some of the more influential ones written in English—including Treasure of Baghdad, The Mesopotamian, and Twenty-Four Steps to Liberty—are widely read by journalists and policymakers. Riverbend, a blog written anonymously by a young Iraqi woman, won a 2006 Bloggie Award and later was published as a book (*Baghdad Burning*) that won the Samuel Johnson Prize for best nonfiction; it "give[s] a rare glimpse of the mundane details of daily life in Iraq" (Beehner, 2006).

Netvision acquired *Israel*'s biggest blogging site, Israeblog, which was up in 2001. Some 5,000 new blogs are added each month, bringing the site's total to more than 300,000, although most are inactive (Haner, 2006).

There are several Web sites by people who are specialists in the Arab world; the best among them belongs to political science professor, Marc Lynch. He is the the author of two books, one of which is on the media (*Voices of the New Arab Public: Iraq, Al Jazeera, and Middle East Politics Today*). The book has extensive research on hundreds of Al Jazeera talk show programs Lynch has watched and analyzed. His Web site (http://www.abuaardvark.com/) presents, in English, a summary of the daily Arab press he reads in Arabic as part of his efforts to keep up with the Arab media. He also has links to Arab bloggers who write in English, like an excellent Egyptian Web site (Baheyya, http://baheyya.blogspot.com) that deals with freedom of expression and legal issues.

Prospects for the Future

Most rulers of the region have a different set of problems than the ones they had with the old media they easily controlled: how to keep their grip on power while some of the control of communication is out of their hands and beyond their borders (Reporters Without Borders,

"Enemies of the Internet," 2000). Some governments have adapted by liberalizing the media (e.g., Kuwait). Other governments are facing the prospect of having their state-run media become irrelevant because of competition from pan-Arab and regional satellites (Sakr, 2002).

Some countries are establishing their own news channels to directly compete with Al Jazeera (e.g., Al-Arabiya, a joint Saudi-Lebanese-Kuwaiti venture). Some satellite stations have gone into niche programming for groups not previously served in the Arab world— for example, teenagers and the religious community. More diversification is expected in the future. September 11 and the occupation of Iraq, however, have given some Arab governments the excuse to clamp down on anti-U.S. free speech in the name of security (e.g., Jordan). Furthermore, Arab information ministers passed a resolution at their emergency meeting in Cairo, February 7, 2008, to impose new and stringent restrictions on political programs in particular. They adopted those measures under the guise of banning the encouragement of depravity and protecting religion. But Arab human rights experts and political commentators agreed that the ban is designed to muzzle freedom of political speech (BBC Monitoring: "The Muzzling ...", February 8, 2008).

What is certain is that there are more media, more choices, and more outreach from and to the Middle East and North Africa than ever before. There is more radio and TV "chatter" about politics and sex. The Internet is the new location for dissent.

In the 1970s, the nonaligned countries criticized the Western monopoly of global news services, and the quality, quantity, and fairness of the news that developed countries produced about the developing countries. The debate resulted in a call for a plurality of sources, and a "New World Information and Communication Order" (Fore, 1982:442). That new order is upon us. The West is no longer seen as dominant in news, although it continues to be dominant in entertainment and is making enormous advances in infotainment. *New York Times* Columnist Bob Herbert put it best in a February 22, 2007 column titled, "From Anna to Britney to Zawahri."

Arab satellites are providing an alternative to the old flow of information by reversing the flow that used to travel mostly from West to East and from North to South. The number of Arab listeners depending on foreign sources has decreased at an astonishing rate, leading several major powers to try to recapture that "market" by broadcasting news in Arabic. The monopoly of foreign news agencies on news of the region has been broken. Different nations of the region are trying to reach each other as well as other countries in different ways and in different languages via satellite, the Internet, and blogs. The only thing that stands in their way is their own governments' attempts to stop them through new legislation.

NOTES

1. For a glimpse of a Jordanian cartoonist's comment on freedom of the press in Jordan, see http://www.mahjoob.com/archive/02/1/23/jan23.jpg. In the cartoon, a newspaper headline reads "Cloudy climate, lack of vision, need for caution, use reflectors, do not shine strong lights." "Weather bulletin?" one reader asks another. "No, it is the new information policy."
2. For a history of broadcasting in the Arab world, see Boyd (1999).
3. Palestinian Central Bureau of Statistics, "Media Survey 2000," conducted in the period of June 17–July 15, 2000, on a sample of 8,276 households. Available: http://www.pcb.org/press/media_su.htm

4. Information is culled from interviews with TV station owners in the summer of 2000: Issa abu al-Izz, April 30; Omar Nazzal, May 30; Tareq Jabbar and Rimah Kilani, June 8; Hamdi Farraj, June 12.
5. Information about offshore broadcasting is available from: Brand, M. (2008). Israeli Offshore Radio: A Comprehensive Overview by Mark Brand. Available: http://www.offshore-radio.de/israel/index.html
6. See Douglas Boyd, "Hebrew-Language Broadcasting during the British Palestine Mandate." Available: http://www.israelradio.org/history/pal-clan.html

BIBLIOGRAPHY

Abdul Rahman, N. "The Experience of the Algerian Press—Between Freedom and Bullets." Al-Mashrek al-Ilami, June 2000, 22.

Abu Aardvark: A Blog by Marc Lynch. Bush in the Middle East. January 9, 2008. Available: http://abuaardvark.typepad.com/abuaardvark/2008/01/bush-in-the-mid.html

Abu Sa'da, F. Palestinians Trust Their Media Despite Weak Performance. December 17, 2007. http://www.menassat.com/?q=en/image/2479-palestine-roadblocks-eddie-gerald-arabimages-com

"After the Opening of the 'Internet City' in the Emirates: The Launch of the Dubai Oasis for Electronic [Start-up] Projects," allAfrica.com.

Al Jazeera. The Correspondents, May 10, 2003.

"Al Jazeera Broadcasts to U.S." BBC, April 9, 2003.

Al-Rawashdah, H. "What Do We Do? What Do They Do?" Addustour, May 19, 1997.

Al-Zein, H. "Iraqi Satellite Covers the Palestinian Uprising: Nationalist Atmosphere Instead of Breaking News." As-Safir, October 6, 2000, 15.

Al-Zein, J. Interview, Beirut, Lebanon, October 16, 2000.

AME Info. "The Arab World's FM radio boom continues with 36 new FM radio stations starting between late 2005 and Jan 2007," February 21, 2007. Available: http://www.ameinfo.com/111362.html

———. "Egypt Keeps Libel Law." November 10, 2007. Available: http://www.ameinfo.com/137666.html

———. "France 24: The New International News Television to Launch Its Arabic Channel." March 29, 2007. Available: http://www.ameinfo.com/115236.html

Arango, T. "Case Lays Bare the Media's Reliance on Iraqi Journalists." New York Times, December 17, 2007. Available: http://www.nytimes.com/2007/12/17/business/media/17apee.html

Arjomandi, G. The Impacts of Direct Broadcasting Satellite (DBS) on the Iranian Media Sphere. Paper presented at the Article 19 International Seminar, Satellite Broadcating in the Middle East and North Africa: Regulations, Access and Impact, Cairo, 20-21 February, 1999.

Azmi, N. "Bloggers against Torture." The Nation, February 19, 2007, 11–16.

Baheyya. "The Death of Deference." 2007. Available: http://baheyya.blogspot.com/

BBC Monitoring: [Editorial: "The Muzzling of Satellite Television Channels and Incrimination of Their Employees"]. Al-Quds al-Arabi website, London, in Arabic 13 February, 2008. Available: http://www.arabmediasociety.com/arab_media_wire/?item=626

———. Libyan Al-Badil TV: A Brief Survey. January 2008. Available: http://www.akhbarlibya-english.com/index.php?option=com_content&task=view&id=319&Itemid=43

BBC News. "Country Profile: Egypt." BBC News. Available: http://news.bbc.co.uk/1/hi/world/middle_east/country_profiles/737642.stm.

———. "Country Profile: Libya," BBC News, 2008. Available: http://news.bbc.co.uk/1/hi/world/middle_east/country_profiles/819291.stm

———. "Country Profile: Saudi Arabia." BBC News, 2008. Available: http://news.bbc.co.uk/2/hi/middle_east/country_profiles/791936.stm

————. "Country Profile: Tunisia." BBC News. Available: http://news.bbc.co.uk/2/hi/middle_east/country_ profiles/791969.stm

————. "Country Profile: Turkey." BBC News, 2002. Available: http://news.bbc.co.uk/1/hi/world/europe/country_ profiles/1022222.stm.

————. "Egypt renews emergency law powers." May 26, 2008. Available: http://news.bbc.co.uk/2/hi/middle_east/7420133.stm

————. "Egypt MPs Amend Libel Law." July 10, 2006. Available: http://news.bbc.co.uk/2/hi/middle _east/5166666.stm

————. "Egypt Police Jailed for Torture." November 5, 2007. Available: http://news.bbc.co.uk/2/hi/middle_east/7078785.stm

————. "Iran Cracks Down on Opposition." 18 March, 2001. Available: http://news.bbc.co.uk/2/hi/middle_east/1228172.stm

BBC News. Timeline: Bahrain. October 9, 2007. Available: http://news.bbc.co.uk/2/hi/middle_east/817505.stm

Beehner, L. "Iraq's Press: A Status Report." Council on Foreign Relations. May 1, 2006. Available: http://www.cfr.org/publication/10574/

Ben-Rafael, E. "Israel: News, the National Obsession," *World Press Review,* Vol. 48, No. 12, December 2001.

Boyd, D. *Broadcasting in the Arab World,* 3rd ed. Ames: Iowa State University Press, 1999.

Campagna, J. *Princes, Clerics, and Censors.* CPJ Special Report, May 9, 2006. Riyadh, Saudi Arabia. Available: http://www.cpj.org/Briefings/2006/saudI_06/saudi_06.html

Caspi, D., and Limor, Y. *The In/Outsiders: Mass Media in Israel.* Cresskill, NJ: Hampton Press, 1999.

Cochrane, P. "The 'Lebanonization' of the Iraqi Media: An Overview of Iraq's Television Landscape." Transnational Broadcasting Journal. Vol. 16, 2006. Available: http://www.tbsjournal.com/Cochrane.html

Committee to Protect Journalists. "CPJ Condemns Israel's Destruction of Palestinian Radio and Television Building." January 19, 2002. Available: http://www.cpj.org

Cozens, C. "Europeans Flock to Al-Jazeera." *The Guardian,* March 25, 2003.

Gozaresh-e Film 26 (March 1995), 36–38.

"Cultural Satellite: The Fate of Satellite in Iran, Yes or No?" *Gozaresh-e Film* 26 (March 1995): 36–38.

Dajani, N. "The Re-feudalization of the Public Sphere: Lebanese Television News Coverage and the Lebanese Political Process. Transnational Broadcasting Journal." Vol. 16, 2006. Available: http://www.tbsjournal.com/Dajani.html

————. "CPJ Report, Picking Up the Pieces." June 13, 2002. Available: http://www.cpj.org/Briefings/2002/West_Bank_june02/West_Bank_june02.html

————. "The Media in Lebanon, the Status of"; "The Media in Syria, the Status of." In Donald Johnston (ed.), *Encyclopedia of International Media and Communications.* San Diego, CA: Academic Press, 2003.

"Dubai Internet City (TECOM)." Newsflash, April 21, 2002. Available: http://www.newsflash.org

"Dubai Media City," 2007. Available: http://setupservicesinmediacity.com/

Dworkin, A. "Iraqi Television: A Legitimate Target?" Crimes of War Project. March 27, 2003. Available: http://www.crimesofwar.org/print/onnews/brief-tv-print.html

Egypt: Court Rejects Request to Ban 51 Web sites. January 2, 2008. Available: http://allafrica.com/stories/200801040175.html

Egyptian Organization for Human Rights. "Emergency Laws Oppress the Country" (press release), March 2003. Available: http://www.eohr.org/PRESS/2003/3=0.HTM

Ellis, K. "The Struggle of a Small Country in a Regional Content." *Arab Studies Quarterly* 21, No. 1 (Winter 1999), 5–25.

El-Sharif, N. Interview, May 18, 2002. Cited in Orayb Najjar, "Jordan: Status of Media in." In *Encyclopedia of International Media and Communications,* vol. 4. San Diego, CA: Academic Press, 2003, 310–315.

Encyclopedia Britannica, (online). Available: http://www.britannica.com/EBchecked/topic/609229/Tunisia/257571/Media-and-publishing#tab=active~checked%2Citems~checked&title=Tunisia%20%3A%3A%20Media%20and%20publishing%20_%20Britannica%20Online%20Encyclopedia

European Journalism Center. Media Landscape—Turkey. 2008. Available: http://www.ejc.net/media_landscape/article/turkey/

Farraj, H. Interview, June 12, 2000.

Feuilherade, P. "Censor-Free Zones?" *Middle East International,* January 28, 2000, 13.

Fore, W. "A New World Order of Communication." *Christian Century,* April 14, 1982. Available: http://www.religion-online.org/showarticle.asp?title=1305

Glain, S. "Ha'aretz, Israel's Liberal Beacon." *The Nation,* September 6, 2007. Available: http://www.thenation.com/doc/20070924/glain/2

Goldschmidt, A., Jr. *A Concise History of the Middle East.* Boulder, Colo: Westview Press, 1988.

Grippo, J. "The Fool Sings a Hero's Song: Shaaban Abdel Rahim, Egyptian Shaabi, and the Video Clip Phenomenon." TBS 16 2006. Available: http://www.tbsjournal.com/Grippo.html

Haeri, S. "Iran Blocks BBC Persian Web site." January 24, 2006. Iran Press Service. Available: http://www.iran-press-service.com/ips/articles-2006/january-2006/bbc_persian-site_blocked_24106.shtml

Halabi, R. *"The West Bank Story."* New York: Harcourt, 1981.

Haner, L. "Netvision Buys Biggest Israeli Blogging Site." October 4, 2006. Available: http://www.haaretz.com/hasen/spages/770422.html

Hasso, F. "Who Covered the War Best? Try Al-Jazeera." *New York Newsday,* April 17, 2003.

Heil, A. L., Jr. "Rate of Arabic Language TV Start-ups Shows No Sign of Abating." May, 2007. Arab Media and Society. Available: http://www.arabmediasociety.com/?article=18

"History of Broadcasting" (radio seminar). Ramallah, Poetry House, May 14, 2000.

Human Rights Watch. "Egypt: Four Editors Get Prison Terms, Fines." September 15, 2007. Available: http://hrw.org/english/docs/2007/09/15/egypt16883_txt.htm

———. "As Fragile as a Crystal Glass: Press Freedom in Iran." HR Watch Report, 1999. Available: http://www.hrw.org/reports/1999/iran/

———. "The Press under President Khatami," 1999. Available: http://www.hrw.org/hrw/reports/1999/iran990-02.htm.

IFEX. "Bahrain," July 4, 2008. Available: http://www.ifex.org/en/content/view/full/95099

———. "Freedom of Expression in Tunisia Still Under Siege Over One Year After WSIS." January 22, 2007. Available: http://www.article19.org/pdfs/press/tunisia-joint-action.pdf

Inquirer Staff [U.K.]. "Bush Admin to Fund Al-Jazeera Rival," April 20, 2003.

International Press Institute (IPI). "Algeria: World Press Freedom Review," 2002. Available: http://www.freemedia/at/wpfr/Mena/algeria.htm

———. "Bahrain: 2006 World Press Freedom Review." Available: http://www.freemedia.at/cms/ ipi/freedom_detail.html?country=/KW0001/KW0004/KW0089/

———. "Israel: 1998 World Press Freedom Review." Available: http://www.freemedia.at/cms/ipi/freedom_detail.html?country=/KW0001/KW0004/KW0094/&year=1998

———. "Kuwait: 2006 World Press Freedom Review." Available: http://www.freemedia.at/cms/ipi/freedom_detail.html?country=/KW0001/KW0004/KW0096/

———. "Libya: 2001 World Press Freedom Review." Available: http://www.freemedia.at/cms/ipi/freedom_detail.html?country=/KW0001/KW0004/KW0098/&year=2001

———. "Libya: 2006 World Press Freedom Review." Available: http://www.freemedia.at/cms/ipi/freedom_detail.html?country=/KW0001/KW0004/KW0098/

———. "Morocco." World Press Freedom Review, 2006. Available: http://www.freemedia.at/cms/ipi/freedom_detail.html?country=/KW0001/KW0004/KW0099/&year=2006

———. "Saudi Arabia: 1999 World Press Freedom Report." Available: http://www.freemedia.at/cms/ipi/freedom_detail.html?country=/KW0001/KW0004/KW0103/&year=1999

———. "IPI Releases Updated Report on Press Freedom Violations in Israeli/Palestinian Conflict," April 24, 2002. Available: http://www.freemedia.at/cms/ipi/statements_detail.html?ctxid=CH0055&docid=CMS1146660973687&year=2002

Internet World Statsistics Usage for Africa, March 2007. Internet World Stats. Available: http://www.internetworldstats.com/stats1.htm

Internet World Statistics Usage for the Middle East. December 2007. Internet World Stats. Available: http://www.internetworldstats.com/stats1.htm

Iran Analytical Report. Al-Alam and Iran's Expanding Media Influence. April 17, 2007. Available: http://www.iranreport.org/Weeklies/04-17-2007.htm

"Iran Confiscated Satellite Dishes: Create Cultural Immunity." Tehran Times, November 3, 2001.

"Iran Intends to Put Two Small Telecom Satellites into Orbit Within Next Few Months." Reuters, June 5, 2000.

"Iraqi Journalists under Fire, 2008." Available: http://www.aswataliraq.info/look/english/article.tpl?IdLanguage=1&IdPublication=4&NrArticle=30022&NrIssue=2&NrSection=1

Ismael, J., and Ismael, T. "Globalization and the Arab World in Middle East Politics: Regional Dynamics in Historical Perspective." *Arab Studies Quarterly* 21, No. 3 (Summer 1999). Available: http://find-articles.com/p/articles/mi_m2501/is_3_21/ai_57476495/print

Jarrah, N. "The Rise and Decline of London as a Pan-Arab Media Hub." *Arab Media and Society,* January 2008. Available: http://www.arabmediasociety.com/topics/index.php?t_article=174

Kraidy, M. "State Control of Television News in 1990s Lebanon," *Journalism and Mass Communication Quarterly* , 76(3) (1999), 485–498.

Kurd Net. "Iraq's Kurdistan President to Ask Parliament to Reconsider Media Law." December 20, 2007, 2–7. Available: http://www.ekurd.net/mismas/articles/misc2007/12/independentstate1856.htm

"Kuwaiti Minister of Information Resigns." Al-Sharq, October 19, 2000, 1.

Lancaster, P. "Syria Looks Forward." *The Middle East,* July/August 2000, 5.

Larson, L. Arabic Newspapers Choose Televisual for Online Publishing. December 2000. Available: http://www.newsandtech.com/issues/2000/12-00/int/12-00_televisual.htm

Layalina Productions. "Europe increases Arabic Broadcasts." March 30-April 12, 2007. Available: http://www.layalina.tv/Press/PR_III.8.asp

"Lebanon to Slash Private Broadcasters." Reuters, February 7, 1996.

Lehman-Wilzig, S., and Schejter, A. "Israel." In Kamalipour, Y., and Mowlana, H. (eds.), *Mass Media in the Middle East: A Comprehensive Handbook,* 109–125. Westport, CT: Greenwood Press, 1994.

Limor, Y. "The Printed Media: Israel's Newspapers," 1999. Available: http://www.mfa.gov.il/MFA/Facts%20About%20Israel/Culture/The%20Printed%20Media-%20Israels%20Newspapers

Lynch, M. "Young Brothers in Cyberpace." *Middle East Report* 245 (Winter 2007), 26–33.

Ma'an. About Us (2008). Available: http://www.maannews.net/en/index.php?opr=Content&Do =Aboutus

Merrett, A. "First Saudi Blogger, Fuad al-Farhan, Arrested." Blog Herald. January 2, 2008. Available: http://www.blogherald.com/2008/01/02/first-saudi-blogger-fouad-al-farhan-arrested/

Middle East Review of International Affairs, "Iran's 2000 Elections," Vol. 4, No. 1, March, 2000. Available: http://meria.idc.ac.il/journal/2000/issue1/jv4n1a1.html

"Minister urges to hasten private radios licensing." Syria, Politics, August 20, 2004.

Mofidi, B. "The Perils of Journalism in Iran." Editorial published by Iranian newspaper E'temed Web site on October 28, 2007. BBC Monitoring http://www.arabmediasociety.com/arab_media_wire/?item=463

Moubayid, S. "Syria Takes Long Hard Look at 'Primitive' Advertising Market." *Daily Star,* 2 October, 2000, 7.

Muhsen, M. *The Information War: Examples of Resistance Media in Lebanon.* Beirut: Dar al Nada, 1998.

Najjar, O. "Media Law in Jordan and Egypt: An Overview of Continuities and Changes." In Kai Hafez (ed.), *The Arab Media: Power and Weakness.* New York: Continuum, 2008, 183–196.

————."Communication Media Law and Policy, Middle East." In Donsbach, W. (ed.), *International Encyclopedia of Communication.* Malden, MA: Blackwell, 2008a.

————. "New Palestinian Media and Democratization from Below." In Philip Seib (ed.), *New Media and the New Middle East.* Palgrave Macmillan Series in International Political Communication, 2007, 191–212

————. "The West Bank and Gaza, Status of the Media in." In Donald Johnston (ed.), *Encyclopedia of International Media and Communications.* San Diego, CA: Academic Press, 2003.

———— ."Freedom of the Press in Jordan 1927–1998." In Hafez, K. (ed.), *Mass Media and Society in the Middle East: Impact for Political and Social Development.* Cresskill, NJ: Hampton Press, 2001, 77–107.

————."The Ebb and Flow of Press Freedom in Jordan, 1985–1997," *Journalism and Mass Communication Quarterly* 75, No. 1 (1998), 127–142.

Newman, D. "Israel: The Myth of Left-Wing Media Control." *World Press Review,* August 2002. Available: http://www.worldpress.org/Mideast/634.cfm

Ogan, C. *Communication and Identity in the Diaspora: Turkish Migrants in Amsterdam and their Use of Media.* Lanham, MD: Lexington Books, 2001, 1–22.

OpenNet Initiative Blog. Archive for the "Surveillance" Category. (2007). http://opennet.net/blog/?cat=23

Oppel, R., Jr. "Iraqis Get the News but Often Don't Believe It." *New York Times,* August 5, 2003.

Osman, A. "Rude Awakening: Dream Drops Top Talkers." TBS 12, Spring/Summer 2004. Available: http://www.tbsjournal.com/Archives/Spring04/dream.htm

Parsons, C. "Turkey's EU reform laws passed by parliament. Turkish MPs Vote for Kurdish TV." Istanbul, August 3, 2002 (Reuters). Available: http://www.theturkishtimes.com/archive/02/08_01/f-eureform.html

Phillips, M. "How the Arab World Sees Bush Trip." CBS News. January 13, 2008. Available: http://www.cbsnews.com/stories/2008/01/13/sunday/main3705683.shtml?source=mostpop_story

"Police Will Not Enter Houses to Seize Satellite Dishes." *Payrant's Iran News,* November 15, 2001.

Press Release. "First Russian TV Channel in Arabic Launched." 5 September, 2007. Available: http://www.ameinfo.com/130979.html

Press Release: BBC appoints Arabic TV News Editor. 14 March 2006. Available: http://www.bbc.co.uk/pressoffice/pressreleases/stories/2006/03_march/14/arabic.shtml

Prusher, I. "In volatile Iraq, US Curbs Press." *The Christian Science Monitor,* June 19, 2003.

Quest, M. "The Lessons of the Bandung Conference: Reviewing Richard Wright's *The Color Curtain* 40 Years Later." Available: http://www.spunk.org/library/pubs/lr/sp001716/bandung.html

Quilty, J. "Arabic film, financed in the Emirates?" *The Daily Star.* December 31, 2007. Available: http://www.dailystar.com.lb/article.asp?edition_id=10&categ_id=4&article_id=87736

Reporters Without Borders. Bahrain–Annual Report, 2007. Available: http://www.rsf.org/article.php3?id_article=20752

———. Jordan—Annual Report 2007. Available: http://www.rsf.org/article.php3?id_article =20765

———. Libya—Annual Report 2007. Available: http://www.rsf.org/article.php3?id_article =20770

———. Morocco—Annual Report 2007: Available http://www.rsf.org/article.php3?id_article =20772

———. Palestinian Authority—Annual Report 2007. http://www.rsf.org/article.php3?id_article =20774

———. Syria—Annual Report 2007. Available: http://www.rsf.org/article.php3?id_article =20777

———. Tunisia—Annual Report 2007. Available: http://www.rsf.org/article.php3?id_article =20780

———. 2006. "Israel Again Strikes at Media Installations." August 11, 2006. Available: http://www.rsf.org/article.php3?id_article=18341

———. "Enemies of the Internet," 2000.

———. Saudi Arabia–Annual Report, 2007. Available: http://www.rsf.org/article.php3?id_article=20775

———. "Three Years of Slaughter in Iraq." December 27, 2007. Available: http://www.rsf.org/special_iraq_ en.php3 (RSF, Iraq Annual Report 2007).

———. Iraq–Annual Report 2007. Available: http://www.rsf.org/article.php3?id_article=20761

———. Iran–Annual Report, 2007. Available: http://www.rsf.org/article.php3?id_article=20758&Valider =OK

———. Egypt–Annual Reports, 2001, 2002. Available: http://www/rsf.org.

———, "Conservatives Renew Attacks With the Suspension of Two Reformist Papers," September 16, 2002.

———. "Cyber-dissident Arrested and His Online Newspaper Censored," June 5, 2002.

———. "The Only Satirical Paper Suspends Its Publication," January 22, 2002. Available: http://www.rsf.org/article.php3?id_article=202

———. Turkey–Annual Report, 2002. Available: http://www.rsf.org/article.php3?id_article=1789

———. "The Iraqi Media Three Months After the War: A New but Fragile Freedom," July 23, 2003.

Risen, J. "C.I.A. Tried, With Little Success, to Use U.S. Press in Coup" (online), April 16, 2000. Available: http://www.nytimes.com/library/world/mideast/041600iran-cia-media.html

Rugh, W. A. *The Arab Press,* 2nd ed. Syracuse, NY: Syracuse University Press, 1987.

Russell, R. "First Newspaper to Hit Baghdad's Streets Is Red." Reuters, April 21, 2003.

Sachs, S. "Arab Leaders' Choice: Unleashed Anger Can Bite Its Master." *New York Times,* October 22, 2000. http://query.nytimes.com/gst/fullpage.html?res=9403e2de1e3ef931a15753c1a9669c8b63

Sakr, N. *Satellite Realms.* London: I.B.S. Taurus and Co., 2002.

Salama, S. "Abu Dhabi: UAE Women Will Soon Be Able to Become Federal Court Judges." *Gulf News.* January 6, 2008. Available: http://www.zawya.com/Story.cfm/sidZAWYA20080106060613/SecIndustries/pag

"Satellite TV Reaches Iraq." Agence France-Press, October 11, 1999.

Schleifer, A. "The Dubai Digital Broadcasting Miracle." TBS, No. 5, Fall/Winter 2000. Available: http://www.tbsjournal.com/Archives/Fall00/Schleifer_Dubai.html

———. "Opening Speeches Call for Free Press at DMC." TBS, No. 6, Spring/Summer 2001. Available: http://www.tbsjournal.com/Archives/Spring01/dubai.html

———. "Business Unusual: CNBC Arabiya on a Roll." TBS, No. 12, 2004. Available: http://www.tbsjournal.com/cnbc.htm

Semati, M. (ed.). *Media, Culture and Society in Iran: Living with Globalization and the Islamic State.* London: Routledge, 2007.

Shahid, A. "Maverick Cleric Is a Hit on Arab TV." *Washington Post,* February 14, 2003, A01

Shahidi, H. "From Mission to Profession: Journalism in Iran, 1979–2004." *Iranian Studies.*

Silverman, J. "Is the U.K. Facing Up to Bahrain's Past?" BBC News, April 16, 2003. Available: http://news.bbc.co.uk/2/hi/uk_news/2842535.stm

"Syrian Comment," October 30, 2006. Available: http://joshualandis.com/blog/?p=70&print=true

The Arab Press Network, Young Jordan Daily Relies on Subscribers. March 28, 2006. Available: http://www.arabpressnetwork.org/rubriquesv2.php?id=72

The Brussels Tribunal. "Iraqi Media Killed in Iraq under US-Occupation" 2008. Available: http://www.brusselstribunal.org/Journalists.htm

Tryhorn, C. "We Have the Upper Hand in Iraq, Claims Al-Jazeera." *The Guardian,* March 27, 2003.

U.S. Department of State: Background Note, Algeria, October 2007. Available: http://www.state.gov/r/pa/ei/bgn/8005.htm

Usher, S. "The Lie of Media Freedom in Jordan: ATV as an example." August 24, 2007. Available: http://www.jordanwatch.net/archive/2007/8/301680.html

Wardam, B. "Drawing a New Map for Journalism in the Mideast." January 5, 2008. Available: http://www.nytimes.com/2008/01/05/world/middleeast/05rashed.html?

Wheeler, B. "Al-Jazeera's Cash Crises." C, April 7, 2003.

Whitaker, B. "Al-Jazeera Causes Outcry with Broadcast of Battle Casualties." *The Guardian,* March 24, 2003.

White, J., and Graham, B. "Military Says It Paid Iraq Papers for News." *Washington Post,* December 3, 2005, A01.

Worth, R. "Drawing a New Map for Journalism in the Mideast." January 5, 2008. Available: http://www.nytimes.com/2008/01/05/world/middleeast/05rashed.html?

Yaghi, Z. "'The Event' on Abu Dhabi Station: Another Example of the Development of the Gulf Stations." *As-Safir,* October 6, 2000, 15.

Yavuz, M. H. "Media Identities for Alevis and Kurds in Turkey." Eikelman, Dale and Anderson, J. (eds.) *New Media in a Muslim World.* Bloomington, Ind.; Indiana University Press, 1999, 180–199.

Zahlan, R. *The Making of the Modern Gulf States.* London: Ithaca Press, 1998.

Arabic Sources

Abdul Karim, A. *The Iranian Press.* Baghdad: Ministry of Information, 1972.

Abdul Rahman Awatef. *Studies in the Contemporary Egyptian and Arab Press: Current Issues.* Cairo: Dar al-Isha'a, 1989.

Abu Saud, I. "Egypt in the Age of the Internet." *Media Studies* 100 (July–September 2000), 116–125.

Abu Zaid, F. *The Immigrant Arab Press.* Cairo: Madbouli, 1985.

Al-Alawi, H. "The Theory of National Investment in the Press and Abdul Nasser's Theory in Defensive Communication." Al-Siyassa (Kuwait), March 3, 1981. Reprinted in Bashir Al-Awf (ed.), *The Press: Its History, Development, Art and Responsibility,* 169–174. Beirut: Islamic Office, 1987.

Al-Ghareeb, M. *The Press: History and Present.* Beirut, Lebanon: Al-Kifah, 1978.

Al-Shalabi, J. *Mohammad Hassanein Heikal: Continuity or Change?* Translated from the French by Hayah Attiyyah. Beirut: Arab Institute for Printing and Publishing, 1999.

Al-Shamikh, M. *The Press in Hijaz, 1908–1941*. Beirut: Dar al-Amanah, 1971.

Arab Human Rights Organization. "Freedom of Expression and the Condition of Human Rights in the Arab World, 1999." *Media Studies* 100 (July–September 2000), 12–54.

Diliou, F. "The Print Press in Algeria: Between Authenticity and Alienation." *Arab Future* 255 (May 2000), 47–61.

Ismail, I. "The Investigative Report and Freedom." *Media Studies* 100 (July-September 2000), 55–69.

Izzat, M. *News Agencies in the Arab World*. Jeddah: Knowledge Library/Dar al Shurouk, 1983.

Jarrus, S. "The Party Press in Syria." *Media Studies* 100 (July–September 2000), 173–175.

16

Sub-Saharan Africa

MINABERE IBELEMA
University of Alabama, USA

TANJA BOSCH
Cape Town, South Africa

As the euphoria of democratization in the 1990s waned, the African press settled into the challenges of democratic consolidation. The fortunes of the press in the different countries have mirrored the quality and vagaries of their democratization. On one end of the spectrum, there are countries such as Benin and Ghana that are decidedly marching away from their autocratic past, and their press reflects the corresponding political culture. Kenya was solidly in this group when violence erupted in 2008 in the wake of presidential elections. On the other end of the spectrum are countries such as Cameroon, Equatorial Guinea, Eritrea, and Zimbabwe, where there is merely the veneer of democracy and the press is intensely repressed. The renewed civil unrest and war in Chad, also early in 2008, again underscored how fragile Africa's political dispensation is.

In between are countries of varying political health, democratic status, and corresponding media plight. Among them are the Democratic Republic of Congo (or Congo Kinshasa), Côte d'Ivoire, and Ethiopia which are still experiencing lingering civil or interborder wars. Not only do their journalists face the dangers inherent in wars, they also have to cope with the hypersensitivity of governments that see national security dangers in every unfavorable news story or commentary. Even in countries such as Angola, Liberia, and Sierra Leone, which have settled their civil wars, there is the lingering effect of prolonged anarchy and the militarization of civic culture. In all contexts, however, the growing independent press is spearheading the cause of democratic consolidation and valiantly asserting the right of unfettered reporting and commentary (Ibelema, 2008).

In general, the growth of the independent press, both print and broadcast, remains the most remarkable feature of Africa's current media systems. The independence of the press is especially notable with regard to its increasingly effective (or at least meritorious) role in shepherding elections. However, elections have also proven to be hazardous times for the press in many countries—before, during, and after balloting. Election-related violence and repression have affected the press to various degrees in both Congos, Ethiopia, Nigeria, and Zimbabwe, among other countries. In Kenya there was a live news blackout after the 2008 presidential election, but citizens found ways around it via new media technologies, especially using SMS.

In South Africa, perhaps one of the most stable democratic countries in the region, there were renewed efforts to silence critical press voices in the aftermath of the election of Jacob Zuma as chairman of the ruling African National Congress, after the ousting of the country's president, Thabo Mbeki, as party chairman.

Even as the African press strives to play its role in the consolidation—or introduction—of democracy, it continues to cope with economic pressures inherent in sub-Saharan Africa's underdevelopment. Yet, an independent press can hardly thrive without a robust economy that is driven by private enterprise. To varying degrees, that is what the press in sub-Saharan African countries is striving to do. It is a daunting challenge. Yet, the African press milieu has never been more promising. As summarized in the review of history that follows, journalists in most African countries did not even have the opportunity of independent operation until quite recently.

Historical Overview

In the introductory paragraph of her still very valid history of the African press, Rosalynde Ainslie writes:

> Until Africa is in uncontested control of its own communications, the struggle for full independence will still not be won. For he who controls communications controls more than the means to transmit messages. He has in his hands a terrible power, the power to create for his audience an image of the world, and, more important still, an image of itself (Ainslie, 1966:7).

Writing in the early years of independence for most African countries, Ainslie was referring to the colonial control of the mass media. However, her thesis soon became even more relevant to the struggle of control between the state and individuals and private enterprise. Much of what follows in this chapter is a rendition of how the two areas of contestation have played out, with an emphasis, of course, on the domestic dimension (also see De Beer, 2009).

The Print Press

In much of sub-Saharan Africa, the press played an important role as an agitator for independence. However, this role was more pronounced in West Africa. "In English-speaking West Africa, the Press is over 160 years old—as old as the Press in South Africa, and a hundred years older than the Press in East Africa, or in the French-speaking territories" (Ainslie, 1966:21). An important factor in the difference was the repatriation of freed slaves to Liberia and Sierra Leone, among them well educated people who embarked on journalism both as a business and as a means of advocacy. They ultimately inspired nationalists in neighboring African countries, including Ghana's Kwame Nkrumah and Nigeria's Nnamdi Azikiwe. It was not an accident, therefore, that Ghana became the first sub-Saharan African country granted independence—in 1957—and was followed soon after by other English-speaking West African countries.

In a number of those countries, several nationalists began their careers as journalists and publishers. Among them were Ghana's first president, Kwame Nkrumah, Nigeria's first president, Nnamdi Azikiwe, and independence-era opposition leader, Obafemi Awolowo. Thus the early West African press was largely political and partisan. There were notable exceptions. In Nigeria, for instance, the *Daily Times* was established in 1926 by a consortium of British and Nigerian entrepreneurs. It was purchased in 1947 by the British Mirror group. Its commercial, rather than political, orientation enabled it to grow to become one of Africa's largest newspapers. It maintained that status until its precipitous decline began in the late 1970s, after the federal government acquired it. In Ghana, the Graphic newspapers were also owned by the Mirror group, until they were acquired in 1962 by the government of Kwame Nkrumah—by mutual agreement.

The dominant orientation and pattern of ownership was reversed in the other regions of sub-Saharan Africa. "Whereas in West Africa, newspapers developed as a voice to express the protests of the ruled, in East Africa they were from the beginning vehicles for the culture and concepts of the rulers, with the considerable resources of white capital at their command" (Ainslie, 1966:99).

In Kenya in Eastern Africa, as another sterling work on African media shows (Bourgault, 1995:164), Asian entrepreneurs working with the colonial government used their accumulated capital to establish newspapers that were essentially colonial in orientation. The *African Standard,* which as the *Standard* remains one of the two dominant publishing houses in Kenya, was the first newspaper. Established in 1902 in the port city of Mombassa, "the staff was almost all white until 1965" (Bourgault, 1995:164). Kenya's other dominant paper, the *Nation,* was established in 1960 as a commercial enterprise by Aga Khan of the Ismaili Islamic sect (Bourgault, 1995). Given this dominant colonial and commercial orientation of the East African press, nationalists had to rely on less widely circulated papers for their agitation. Among those publications were local language and regional newspapers.

The Southern African press has a long history. What is considered sub-Saharan Africa's first English-language newspaper, the *Cape Town Gazette and African Advertiser,* began publishing in 1800 (Martin, 1983). The most significant papers in South Africa's early press history, however, were the *Cape Argus* and the *Cape Times,* which were established in 1857 and 1876, respectively (Ainslie, 1966). A third paper of note, the *Rand Daily Mail* was established in 1902, and it became "the pioneer of modern popular journalism in South Africa" (Ainslie, 1966:45).

The *Argus* would subsequently establish sub-Saharan Africa's first newspaper chain. Part of its growth was its acquisition in 1889 of *The Star* newspaper in Johannesburg, which became "the newspaper with the highest circulation in South Africa, and indeed one of the highest in sub-Saharan Africa" (Martin, 1983:200). As the *Star's* primary competitor, the liberal *Rand Daily Mail* would also lead other newspapers to form the Associated Newspapers of South Africa to more effectively compete against the Argus group. The *Rand Daily Mail* folded in 1985 during the state of emergency under which the apartheid government embarked on severe press repression.

A significant factor in the development of the press in Southern Africa was the pattern of European settlement there and especially the resulting politics of racial separation and white-minority government. In South Africa, for instance, the major European settlers were Dutch and English. Therefore, newspapers there began publishing in English and Afrikaans, the language of the Dutch settlers (Martin, 1983). The Afrikaans papers were generally more supportive of the policies of the apartheid government and that gave them greater access to government news. Indeed, the government was known to assist in the establishment of English language newspapers to counter the relatively liberal editorial orientation of the others (Jackson, 1993).

Although the Afrikaners were the larger of the two major settler groups and were entrenched in power since 1948, the English papers were greater in number and circulation. Most of the country's ethnic groups, especially the black majority, had an aversion for the Afrikaans language because of its embodiment of the oppressive politics of the time. Therefore, they almost exclusively read the English-language papers, though many black ("coloured" in apartheid nomenclature) readers read the special or extra editions Afrikaans newspapers. In 1981, the Argus group established the *Sowetan* as a black-oriented newspaper. It was during the peak of the anti-apartheid struggle; however, the paper was required to stay clear of politics. It began to stray from that orientation as the end of apartheid seemed increasingly imminent. In the post-apartheid era, it has become one of the largest circulating dailies in South Africa, but since then it has been overtaken by the tabloids aimed at black readership, and published by both former Afrikaans and English publishing houses.

The South African media landscape changed dramatically after apartheid ended in 1994. In addition to lifting press laws that repressed opposition to apartheid, the new government also pursued the policy of empowerment for the black majority. The private sector pursued similar policies. One of the results was the acquisition of the *Sowetan* by black entrepreneurs from its then owner, Anglo American (for an overview of the South African press, see inter alia Hadland, 2005; Jackson, 1993. For the Cameroon, see Nyamnjoh, 2005; and Peterson, 2000, for Somalia, Sudan and Rwanda).

The Broadcast Press

Broadcasting in sub-Saharan Africa generally began in the early 1930s, often in the form of radio relay of Western stations such as the BBC and the Voice of America. For the most part, it was intended to advance colonial goals or government interests. In some cases, they served to counter the success of newspapers as the voice of the colonized. The first broadcast in Nigeria, for instance, was in 1932 and it was a re-diffusion service of the BBC. Even after the Nigerian Broadcasting Service was established in 1951, it primarily retransmitted BBC programs. In South Africa, radio broadcasting was introduced in 1936 when the South African Broadcasting Corporation was established by the Broadcasting Act. It remained a government enterprise until 2004, when it was converted into a limited liability enterprise by the Broadcasting Amendment Act of 2002. Before then, the South African broadcast landscape changed dramatically in 1994, with the end of apartheid. Under the black empowerment policy, the South African Broadcasting Corporation's stronghold on broadcasting was broken with new stations opened to black businesses, though by 2008

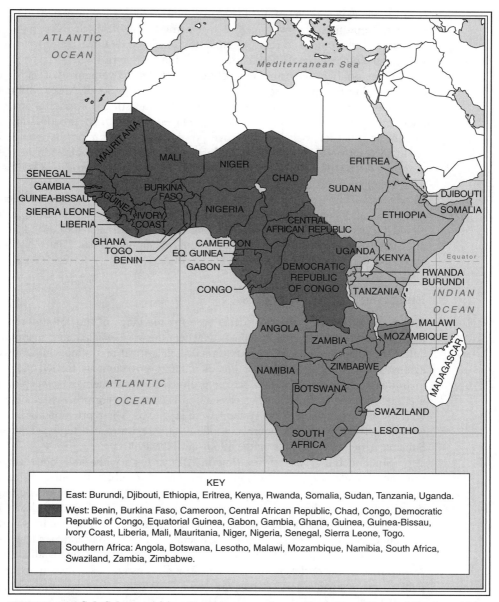

FIGURE 16.1 Sub-Saharan Africa. Countries grouped according to East, West, and Southern Africa.

there was much misgiving about the influence of the ANC government on broadcasting (see Tomaselli, 2002).

Television broadcasting reflected the same pattern of political realities in much of Africa, beginning mostly in the 1960s. The first television station established in sub-Saharan Africa, for instance, was by the Western Nigerian Broadcasting Service, in 1959.

It still reminds its viewers of this history with the slogan "First in Africa." That a regional, rather than the federal, government was the first to establish television in Nigeria was a reflection of the clout and relative autonomy of Nigeria's three regions at the time. The federal government established its own television service in 1962.

Other political and economic realities affected the development of television in other countries. Sub-Saharan Africa's most advanced country, South Africa, did not establish television until 1975, when the South African Broadcasting Corporation broadcast in the major cities; it went national in 1976. The delayed entry into TV broadcasting was related to concerns that its socially integrative power would undermine the apartheid order. It could be said that TV broadcasting in South Africa came to full circle in July 2007, when Soweto—the teeming black township that was the hub of anti-apartheid activism—got its own TV channel on the digital DStv subscription service. In Tanzania TV broadcasting came even much later than in South Africa. Tanzania's first president, the socialist Julius Nyerere, saw television as a luxury that the country could hardly afford, a luxury that would further privilege the rich. Therefore television was not introduced into Tanzania until the 1990s, and even then it was by the private enterprise. That made Tanzania an exception to the pattern of television history in Africa.

Emerging Independent Press

The postindependence press in Africa bore the markings of the colonial era of overt or indirect political orientation. In countries where the press was a major instrument of anti-colonial agitation, newspapers soon turned their critical and often vituperative attention against their political opponents. For their parts, governments treated the press not as instruments of democracy, but as weapons directed against them or as weapons they could use against their opponents. Thus censorship became the norm in African countries, and with few exceptions, the press systems were repressed. The repression became even more widespread following the emergence of military regimes in a high percentage of sub-Saharan African countries from the 1960s until the 1990s.

Since then and for the first time in African history, the independent press in both print and broadcasting has become a major factor of public discourse. With few exceptions, privately run newspapers now offer independent news coverage and opinions that are not directly or overtly the platform of governments or political parties. Governments also began to license private broadcasting. Today there are few African countries in which independent radio, if not television, does not operate. The growth of independent broadcasting has also forced state-run broadcasters to reconsider their propagandistic orientation. "Some state media outlets have . . . undertaken reforms aiming at their transformation into public service broadcasters" (Khan, 2007:vi). They were, of course, supposed to be public service broadcasters in the first place. However, they typically served as mouthpieces for the government and some continue to do so.

Government repression and media freedom is still a major concern for the African press. Colonial antipress libel and sedition laws are still entrenched in the penal codes of most countries, and governments use these laws to harass journalists (Mundua, 2007). Some governments are starting to enact new broadcast regulation laws. When all broadcasters were state-run, regulation was more or less as civil service protocol. The advent of private broadcasters has meant the establishment of broadcasting commissions that are ostensibly independent of the government. In some cases, private broadcasters are regulated by the Ministry of Information, bringing them under direct government oversight.

Press Freedom and Government/Media Relations—An Overview

The African press overall continues to enjoy the unprecedented levels of freedom that began in the 1990s. One dimension of the political liberalization in Africa is the strengthening of constitutional provisions for press freedom (Berger, 2007). In the past, there was no lack of such constitutional provisions, but they were usually nullified in the same documents by "clawback clauses" (Ogbondah, 2003:119). Though such clauses remain in the constitutions of a number of countries, they are usually not enforced in the countries with the freer press systems. However, there is continuing tension among press freedom, press responsibility, and government transparency. With a few exceptions, African governments continue to resist attempts to pass and implement laws on press access to information. Yet, "Freedom of information is a closely related right to freedom of expression, in the sense of being the other side of the same coin" (Berger, 2007:9). Often in disregard of the connection between access to information and accuracy in reporting, governments frequently berate and prosecute the press for inaccurate reporting.

What is notable, in any case, is that African governments are increasingly resorting to the judicial process for dealing with perceived press transgressions. That is a significant improvement over the years of widespread practice of long-term detentions of journalists without trial. With some exceptions, the increasing independence of the judiciary ensures some protection against repression. However, there is also the counterdevelopment of increasing threat from shadowy groups. Over the past several years of democratization, a number of African journalists in countries such as the Ivory Coast in the west, and war stricken countries of the northeast, such as Somalia, Sudan, and Rwanda, have been killed in circumstances that suggest vigilante action. And in a number of these cases, the murders were of journalists who reported or commented critically on their governments. The number of murders per se does not tell the full story. It is the environment of fear that is created that makes the greater difference.

The introduction and growth of non-state-run broadcasting has introduced a new dimension to government-press relations. State-run broadcast operations were the norm in African countries, and so were their fare of sanitized programming and the typically sycophantic news coverage. That has changed considerably, and many African governments are uneasy about the unprecedented scrutiny from the airwaves. News and views that are routinely published in newspapers and magazines draw the ire of government officials when broadcast. A plausible explanation is that African governments have become more accustomed to the independence of the print press. Nongovernment stations are relatively new. Given the propagandistic fare that dominated and continues to dominate on state-owned stations, government officials are yet to become used to critical reporting by the broadcast press. Therefore, even in countries such as Nigeria, with a history of freedom for the print press, independent broadcasters face greater scrutiny and sanctions.

Three Levels of Press Freedom—Country Classification

We have differentiated African countries in their scope of press freedom by grouping them as high, medium, and low (Table 16.1). This grouping relies considerably on the reports of various monitoring agencies, including Reporters Without Borders (RWB), the Committee to Protect Journalists (CPJ), and the International Press Institute (IPI). We have relied especially on RWB's annual ranking of countries by press freedom. However, our grouping does not necessarily correspond with RWB's rankings, which we believe is unduly skewed by particular incidents. As RWB notes about its method of ranking, "It is based solely on events between [the dates under consideration]. It does not look at human rights violations in general, just press freedom violations." In categorizing countries, we have considered the overall robustness of the press system, rather than particular actions against the press that do not substantively affect general press operations. As has been argued, emphasis on actions against the press fails to reflect the actual efficacy of the marketplace of ideas (Ibelema, Powell, and Self, 2000).

Of course, the categorization is not an exact science. Some countries such as Senegal and Tanzania that we have grouped among the most free could be moved to the medium category. And the case could be made for countries such as Liberia and Mozambique to be moved from medium to most free. The grouping is based on our best judgment, all things considered.

The countries we have categorized as high level in press freedom are those that manifest a robust media environment in which a diversity of opinions is allowed full expression in both the print and broadcast media. These countries are not without incidents of censorship, as will be discussed below. However, such acts are generally isolated, and their effects on the overall vibrancy of the press are minimal or fleeting.

Table 16.1   Selected African Countries Grouped by Level of Press Freedom

High Level	Medium Level	Low Level
Benin	Burkina Faso	Angola
Ghana	Congo (Brazzaville)	Burundi
Botswana	Congo (Kinshasa)	Cameroon
Kenya	Gabon	Côte d'Ivoire
Mali	Liberia	Djibouti
Namibia	Mozambique	Equatorial Guinea
Nigeria	Uganda	Eritrea
Senegal	Zambia	Ethiopia
South Africa		Gambia
Tanzania		Guinea
		Niger
		Rwanda
		Somalia
		Zimbabwe

The countries we have categorized as medium level in press freedom have some of the characteristics above; however, the scope of censorship is greater, as is the impact on the marketplace of ideas. In these countries, the government tends to play a significant or dominant role in press ownership, both print and broadcasting, but especially the latter. These countries tend to face pressures not only from government, but also from vigilante or militarized groups. In several instances, the overall insecurity gives rise to a high level of self-censorship.

Countries in the low-level category are those in which government control is at a high level and instances of press repression are pervasive and severe. In some instances, there may be few instances of press censorship during a given period of time, and therefore such countries may rank high in RWB's index of press freedom. Yet, the press system is considerably constricted because of an existing climate of fear and self-censorship. In comparison with the medium-level countries, government ownership of print and broadcast press tends to be even more dominant in the low-level countries.

High-Level Freedom of the Press

As noted above, the countries classified as having a high level of press freedom are not without incidents. In some cases, some of the incidents are very serious. Yet they maintain robust press systems.

Benin Perhaps nowhere else in sub-Saharan Africa has democratization had as profound an impact on the growth of the independent press as in Benin. Following a stretch of Marxist rule from 1974 to 1989, Benin embarked on a democratization process that culminated in a presidential election in 1991. President Ahmed Kerekou, who officially abandoned Marxism two years earlier, lost that election but won the subsequent one in 1996. Benin has been a model African democracy ever since. Kerekou was replaced by Thomas Boni Yayi, who won the presidential election run off in 2006.

When Reporters Without Borders first issued its ranking of press systems in 2002, Benin was ranked highest among all African countries. Overall, it was ranked no. 21 out of 139 countries in the world. That was a tie with Great Britain and several places ahead of the Western European democracies Austria, Spain, and Italy. By 2007, Benin had dropped to No. 8 among African countries and 53 overall. The drop resulted from a number of incidents in which journalists were arrested for articles that were deemed libelous or seditious. The arrests were based mostly on a law instituted in 1997 that made libel a criminal offense. For periods of time, the law was hardly enforced. However, since 2006 there has been a flurry of arrests, most of them connected with reportage on the transition in government.

Unlike what obtains in countries in the lower categories of press freedom, most of the government actions against the press in Benin were related to substantive concerns. As the International Press Institute notes in its assessment of Benin's press, "Poorly paid journalists and media in economic difficulty have led to a form of journalism often lacking accuracy and fairness; this is especially true of the more sensational tabloids" (International Press Institute-Benin, 2006).

Botswana   "Botswana, one of Africa's most stable countries, is the continent's longest continuous multiparty democracy. It is relatively free of corruption and has a good human rights record" (BBC Country Profile: Botswana, 2007). Indeed, Botswana has long been ranked among the world's freest press systems (see, for instance, Stevenson, 1995). Its enduring democratic ethos has been traced to its Kgotla traditional system of governance through an assembly of the people (Kerr, 2001). Even the government broadcasting system is mandated by law to practice independent journalism, and it does so to a considerable extent. However, opposition parties complain of not getting sufficient access (BBC Country Profile: Botswana, 2007).

Recent incidents suggest that the government is overly protective of its image. In 2005, for instance, it deported Kenneth Good, an Australian lecturer in political science at the University of Botswana, relying on an immigration law passed in 1986 when South African forces were launching raids against anti-apartheid guerrillas in Botswana. Good had written critically on human rights in Botswana. Journalists in Botswana working for government media have also been pressured to refrain from unfavorable coverage of government officials and national affairs and to avoid embarrassing questions to visiting dignitaries. In 2007, the government introduced a bill that is ostensibly intended to ensure fair press coverage, but would give considerable power to the Botswana Press Council. The press in Botswana and the Media Institute of Southern African have vigorously protested the pending bill.

Ghana   "The Ghanaian media is remarkably one of the most unfettered and freest on the continent of Africa" (Commonwealth Press Union, 2007). It has not always been that way. Press freedom in Ghana suffered considerably soon after independence, when the government of Kwame Nkrumah became despotic and hypersensitive. That right was further curtailed during a series of military governments, including the prolonged regime of Flt. Lt. Jerry Rawlings, who ultimately transformed himself into an elected president in 1992. As part of that transition, Ghana adopted one of Africa's more liberal constitutions with regard to the protection of press freedom.

As in other countries', the Ghanaian constitution includes a clause that could have been used to nullify the provisions of press freedom and other liberties. Article 162 (2) states that, "Subject to this Constitution and any other law not inconsistent with this Constitution, there shall be no censorship in Ghana" (Berger, 2007:38). To preempt the misinterpretation of these exceptions, the constitution also stipulates in Article 165 that, "For the avoidance of doubt, the provisions of this chapter shall not be taken to limit the enjoyment of any of the fundamental human rights and freedoms guaranteed under Chapter 5 of this Constitution."

President John Agyekum Kufuor, who succeeded Rawlings in 2000, has come to personify the spirit of the constitution. Kufuor owes his presidency in part to the independent press, much of which resented Rawlings because of his repressive actions against the press during his military government. Not surprisingly, Kufuor has courted the press rather than repress it. One of his first gestures was to have the legislature repeal the criminal libel laws that Rawlings used against the press. Kufuor also donated a building to the Ghana Journalists Association, "a move that not only demonstrates his extraordinary support of independent media in general but also perhaps his gratitude to the private press in particular" (Hasty, 2005:166).

However, the Ghanaian press is not without its problems. Though national authorities are more respectful of press freedom, journalists are more likely to be assaulted by local security officials, party operatives, and even thugs acting on behalf of drug dealers on trial (International Press Institute, 2006b).

Namibia   Reporters Without Borders ranks Namibia 2nd in Africa and 25th in the world in its 2007 index of press freedom. That is a monumental record for a country that up to 1990 was mired in a war of independence from South Africa, which defied the United Nations' demand that it give up a World War II mandate to govern the German colony. Namibia's liberal press environment evolved after its independence in 1990.

Namibia's free press system, however, is in the context of a virtual one-party state. The South West African Peoples Organization (SWAPO), which fought a guerrilla war of independence, transformed itself into Namibia's dominant party. It hardly has opposition in the parliament. However, it was not a matter of law; it was a choice of the people.

Nigeria   The Nigerian press continues to be one of the most robust in Africa. Yet, the press has borne some of the country's burden of political disorder, including electoral irregularities and violence. As with Benin, the Nigerian press system has received considerably reduced ranking in press freedom from Reporters Without Borders (RWB). Between 2002 and 2007, it fell from 7th among African countries to 34th, and from 49th in the world to 131st. The lower rankings reflect RWB's undue reliance on incidents rather than the actual robustness of the press system.

Between 2006 and early 2007, however, there were significant developments against the press. Among them were the harassment of DAAR Communications (the parent company of Africa Independent Television) and the apparent assassination of a columnist for the newspaper *This Day*. These developments took place in the context of an extremely strained relationship between the press and President Olusegun Obasanjo, who tried unsuccessfully to extend his constitutionally mandated term limit.

These serious incidents have not had noticeable effects on the resilient Nigerian press, however. The press has, after all, been through much worse days without succumbing to the pressures. In 1986, the editor of the weekly newsmagazine, *Newswatch,* was assassinated with a parcel bomb while the magazine was investigating corruption in the military government. Then from 1993 to 1998, the military government undertook an unprecedented campaign of repression of the press. Several journalists were arrested and jailed, some were executed for alleged complicity in an attempted coup, newspapers and magazines were shut down for up to 18 months, and copies were routinely confiscated. During that period, several journalists and publications went underground or on exile. Yet the press remained largely defiant (Ibelema, 2003).

Not surprisingly, the Nigerian press withstood the recent harassment without losing its robustness. Its uncompromisingly critical reporting on the elections of 2007 is testimony to its continued strength. The newly elected president, Umar Musa Yar'Adua, has more solid democratic credentials than Obasanjo, a former army general. He is unlikely to authorize or condone the kinds of punitive measures undertaken during the last years of the Obasanjo presidency.

South Africa   South Africa itself was only a quasi-democracy or oligarchy until 1994, when its whites-only apartheid government was replaced through open elections. In 1996, with Nelson Mandela as president, South Africa passed one of the most liberal constitutions in the world. Today the South African press is regularly ranked among the world's freest. Reporters Without Borders ranks South Africa 4th in Africa and 43rd in the world in its index of press freedom. However, there are many tell-tale signs that freedom of the press has not (yet) been won. Being the freest press in Africa does not safeguard the media from government actions, such as the proposed (1997) media tribunal and a growing list of official restrictive conduct against the media (Louw, 2008).

The South African Broadcasting Corporation (SABC) was one of the most independent state-run media in Africa. That independence was further enhanced in 2004 when SABC became a limited liability enterprise. However, since the new Board of Directors took over in 1993, there was a gradual move towards the ruling African National Congress. By 2008 the SABC has all but forsaken its role as a public broadcaster, and in following the 'typical African tradition' has all but become yet another state broadcaster. This situation was driven to almost a comedy of errors when the SABC CEO, Dali Mpofu, first suspended long-time Bulgarian-trained ANC political commissar Snuki Zikalala as head of news. Mpofu was then suspended by the Board, with the ANC let committee (who appointed the Board.) Underlying these tensions was the power struggle between SA President Thabo Mbeki and ANC President Jacob Zuma and factions within the SABC structures supporting one or the other, and trying to get a stranglehold on especially news programming. In between these political scuffles, there were numerous allegations of corruption (e.g. Haffajee, 2008).

South Africa has also become—due to unbridled crime—one of the most violent countries in the world, and the press and other people in the communication/creative professions are affected. In October 2007, for instance, Lucky Dube, the internationally renowned reggae star and social critic, was gunned down in Johannesburg during an apparent carjacking. Two of the pacifist singer's children were with him in the car. Although such random violence does not necessarily inhibit press freedom, it results in significant logistical cost (Ibelema, Powell, and Self, 2000).

At the same time, South Africa has by far the most sophisticated and technologically advanced media system in Africa. Its media holds high regard for the Constitutional Bill of Rights, including free speech and a free press, and has effective self-monitoring bodies, the SA Press Ombudsman and the SA Broadcast Complaints Commission (though the ANC government proposal in November 2007 to set up a statutory body to oversee the work of these organizations was met with vehement protest by the SA media).

Since the democratic elections of 1994 the country has seen:

■ The unbundling of formerly mainly white-owned media groups, black empowerment in the media, and the setting up of new solely black-owned media houses.

- The growth of community media and the implementation of the Media Diversity Development Agency to aid black entrepreneurs in print and broadcast media.
- An explosion in the tabloid market, with newspapers such as the *Sun* reaching sales of 400,000 and more per day and a daily readership of more than 1.5 million.
- The media market's continued segmentation according to language/ethnicity in broadcasting, but also in print with numerous niche magazines in English and Afrikaans, and to a lesser extent in certain African languages.
- The media's strengthening of its professional journalism fraternity, the South African National Editors' Forum, which deals with issues such as ethical codes and with media-government relations when tensions arise.

(See: www.sanef.org.za; journalism.co.za; and *Ecquid Novi: African Journalism Studies* at http://ajs.uwpress.org/)

Kenya   Even during the one-party regimes of Jomo Kenyatta and Daniel arap Moi, the Kenyan press managed to maintain a degree of vibrancy. The domination of the print press by two media houses of foreign origins had both positive and negative consequences. On the one hand, as commercial enterprises, both newspaper groups were more interested in profitability than in political advocacy. That facilitated their viability and their independence. On the other hand, their perception as foreign operations also made them vulnerable to government suspicion of lack of patriotism (Bourgault, 1995). The result was a degree of self-censorship. The liberalization of the polity in the 1990s, which made possible the first ever transfer of power from one party to another, has further opened up the press system.

Still, there have been recent incidents of press repression. In March 2006, the government of President Mwai Kibaki had security personnel raid the offices of the *Standard* newspaper. The unusual action "shocked many Kenyans and alarmed Western donors" (BBC, 2006). In August 2007, the parliament passed a bill that, among other things, would empower courts to force journalists to reveal their sources. Under pressure from journalists and civil society, who staged protests, President Kibaki declined to sign the bill as proposed. The government has, however, taken actions against unregistered newspapers. In the beginning of 2008, the country was in turmoil after the presidential elections.

At least one instance of attempted censorship turned into a farce. Late at night on May 2, 2005, First Lady Lucy Kibaki stormed the premises of the *Nation* newspapers with her security personnel. It was on the eve of the observation of press freedom day around the world. As the rival newspaper the *Standard* reported the affair on May 3, "She stayed in the newsroom for about five hours, during which she confiscated notebooks, mobile phones, tape recorders and cameras from reporters covering her protest." Mrs. Kibaki even slapped a cameraman for Kenya Television, who was recording the scene. Before leaving she delivered a long tirade to the newsroom about what she called lies in the press about herself and her husband. Mrs. Kibaki wanted the security personnel to arrest the journalists, but they balked. Rather than inhibit the press, the incident merely added to a list of incidents that established Mrs. Kibaki as Africa's foremost mercurial first lady.

Mali   Mali is one of Africa's poorest countries, and for much of its postindependence history it was under military dictatorship. Now, it is one of Africa's most democratic countries and has one of the most pluralistic media. The transition began in 1991 when General

Amadou Toumani Toure overthrew a violently repressive military government and handed over power to an elected government the following year. Appreciative of this singular action, Malians elected Toure president in 2002 and reelected him in 2007. Like Benin, Mali retains its criminal libel laws, but they are rarely enforced. However, there are occasional actions of repression. In August 2006, for instance, an opposition broadcast station, Radio Kayira, was shut down for operating without a license, and the staff members were sentenced to one month in prison and fined (International Press Institute, 2006c). The station operators had applied for a license in 2005 and were denied. Still, the most pressing challenge facing the press in Mali is the country's impoverishment.

Senegal   Senegal is another poor country that enjoys considerable press freedom. It was ranked No. 6 among African countries and 47th in the world in the index of press freedom issued by Reporters Without Borders in 2002. By 2007, however, it had fallen to 18th and 83rd, respectively. The fall resulted from a number of developments in the intervening years. In December 2005, the National Council for the Regulation of Broadcasting was established with broad powers to monitor the broadcast media and punish offenders. In addition, tension created by Islamist and separatist insurgency has created unusual government sensitivity. The government has taken punitive actions against the press when it deems its coverage of the insurgents too favorable. However, Senegal plans to decriminalize libel laws, though the plan is yet to be implemented. In general, the press system is quite free, and various opinions find expression.

Tanzania   If the legal basis for censorship were the basis for ranking a country's press system, Tanzania's would be one of the least free. However, though its newspaper and broadcast licensing statutes would seem repressive, their actual applications are sufficiently lax to place Tanzania's among Africa's freest press systems. In 2002, Reporters Without Borders ranked Tanzania 12th in press freedom among African countries and 62nd in the world. By 2007, it had moved up to 9th in Africa and 55th in the world, reflecting its continued liberalization. Tanzania is unusual in having a primarily private television broadcasting system.

Medium-Level Freedom of the Press

Any of the countries categorized as medium level in press freedom could readily move into the high-level category, except for structural or systemic factors. The following countries illustrate this point.

Burkina Faso   There is considerable press freedom in Burkina Faso. Reporters Without Borders ranks it No. 11 among African countries and 68th in the world in its 2007 index of press freedom. However, there are considerable systemic constraints, especially politically inspired violence. In April 2007, for instance, the host of an FM music program received a chilling e-mail with this warning (as translated from French, grammatical hitches and all): "Just inviting you to stop your nonsense at radio Ouaga FM. You must know that you will be gunned down very soon and nothing will happen. We have gunned down Norbert Zongo, nothing happened. You also your turn isn't very far" (Committee to Protect Journalists, Burkina Faso, 2007). The warning was issued to Karim Sama, who uses his reggae radio program as a forum for social and political criticism. Among other things, he often plays socially conscious reggae, makes comments on social injustice, and allows callers to do the same.

Democratic Republic of Congo The DRC or Congo-Kinshasa has one of the liveliest presses on the continent, though the press is still affected by the country's lingering civil war. A measure of order was established in 2003, when a settlement with the rebel groups culminated in elections in 2006. Still, armed rebellions still flare up. As recently as December 2007, the armed forces of Joseph Kabila's government were battling the soldiers of a dissident general, Laurent Nkunda, in eastern Congo. The violence and related insecurity have continued to compromise an otherwise robust press system. Journalists are routinely arrested by security personnel or assaulted by individuals and groups for political differences. In October 2007, the government shut down 38 radio stations, ostensibly for administrative infractions such as not paying license fees. Twenty-two of the stations were allowed to reopen in December 2007.

Not surprisingly, Reporters Without Borders ranks the DRC as one of the lowest countries (133rd in the world) in its index of press freedom. However, the DRC, like Nigeria, has structural and systemic buffers against repression. It is an ethnically and geographically diverse country with strong constituencies whose political interests cannot be repressed. Thus, even in the face of hostilities, the DRC's press remains one of the most robust in Africa.

Republic of Congo Reporters Without Borders ranks the Republic of Congo highly (17th in Africa and 80th in the world) in its index of press freedom in 2007. That is far ahead of its much bigger namesake to the east. Like the DRC, the Republic of Congo has undergone considerable political upheaval. Unlike the DRC, however, Congo has attained a greater degree of stability. The press correspondingly has a high level of freedom. The excision of criminal libel laws in 2001 was particularly significant. However, the Congo's recent history has also resulted in considerable self-censorship. The state-run radio and TV stations essentially broadcast to promote government policies. In any case, the state is the primary broadcaster of television; radio broadcasting is split between state and private ownership. Unlike many African countries, newspapers in Congo are all privately owned, though several have obvious political interests.

Mozambique Mozambique has substantially put its postindependence civil war and Marxist politics behind it. The independent press has a strong presence both in print and broadcast, though government radio broadcasting remains the one source of news that reaches most of the people. The press is quite free, ranked 14th among African countries and 73rd in the world in RWB's index of press freedom. However, as the BBC notes in its country profile, "criminal libel laws deter total freedom of expression." There is, of course, no such thing as total freedom of expression. However, the deterrent effect of criminal libel laws keeps Mozambique from the first tier of press freedom in Africa.

Uganda Uganda was a one-party state under President Yoweri Museveni from 1986 to 2005. The first multiparty elections in 25 years took place in 2006, after Museveni yielded to internal and external pressures to liberalize the polity. Like most of the region, Uganda's media were under state control until liberalization in the early 1990s. Live call-in radio programming is one the manifest elements of the liberalization. However, the government has taken actions to rein in the freewheeling broadcasts.

Zambia Zambia is another country that could be considered in the first tier of press freedom, if not for the continued domination of both the print and broadcast press by state-run operations as well as government intimidation and application of criminal libel laws. However, the independent press has continued to assert itself. When in 1991 the labor unionist Frederick Chiluba defeated Kenneth Kaunda, ending Kaunda's 37-year tenure as Zambia's president, the independent press took some credit. However, the same press ensured the failure of Chiluba's attempt to change the constitution to extend his tenure in 2001.

Low-Level Freedom of the Press

Angola Although Angola's constitution guarantees press freedom, the structural constrictions on the press, recent enforcement of libel laws, and other forms of harassment make Angola a relatively low-level country in press freedom. The dominance of the press by the formerly Marxist government is a major factor constricting the press. Private ownership of newspapers was not allowed until 1995. The liberalization was subsequently extended to radio and later still to television. In 2006 legislation opened up TV broadcasting to private enterprise, while making provisions for community radio and TV. But the monopoly on shortwave radio broadcasting by the national radio broadcaster has not been addressed (Pereira, 2007).

The only daily newspaper in the country, *Jornal de Angola,* is state-owned, as is all national broadcasting. That leaves little room for truly independent journalism. What there is of the independent press operates under a considerably intimidating environment in a country that only recently emerged from 27 years of civil war. "[A]fter decades of conflict, self-censorship is a rule of thumb, and true gauges of public sentiment are rare" (LaFraniere, 2007). Moreover, Angola's criminal libel laws are quite harsh. In October 2007, for instance, the director of the independent weekly *Semanário Angolense* was sentenced to eight months in prison and a fine the equivalent of $250,000 (Committee to Protect Journalists, 2007a). The fine alone would be debilitating for a media operation in any African country.

Still, the Angolan press is not at all passive. In 2003, for instance, the weekly newspaper *Angolese Samanario* put the spotlight on public corruption by publishing a list of Angola's wealthiest people. The list showed that 17 of the top 20 richest were current or former government officials. The revelation prompted the government to become more transparent by opening up financial records that were hitherto kept from press scrutiny (LaFraniere, 2007). As the vestiges of the civil war and Marxism further recede, the Angolan press system is likely to become one of Africa's most robust.

Burundi Burundi is emerging from a 12-year long ethnic-based civil war, after being plagued by tension between the dominant Tutsi minority and the Hutu majority. Out of 22 newspapers appearing regularly in Burundi at the end of 1994, 15 had been created after the October 1993 coup d'état and were committed to extremist solutions with an aggressive and defamatory approach, openly inciting to racial hatred and murder and playing heavily on ancestral fear (Philippart, 2000). As a result, resentment permeated print and broadcast media alike. Much of that has been toned down now. The media have been subject to self-censorship and occasional government censorship, but there is a strong, though sporadic, opposition press, and diverse political views are aired. Radio is the main source of information as newspaper readership is limited by low literacy levels. Reporters Without Borders ranks Burundi 127th out of the 159 countries in its 2007 index of press freedom.

Côte d'Ivoire Côte d'Ivoire has been immersed in civil war since 2002 and considerable unrest even before then. The press system has reflected the turbulence. In many areas of the country, journalists are more concerned about their safety than their press freedom. Several Ivorien journalists have been killed, among other reasons for allowing the wrong side to express their views. There is perhaps no better illustration of the state of the press than an incident in 2006. A member of parliament walked into the room where three journalists were being interrogated by the police and told them: "even if the police force lets you go, I will kill you" (International Federation of Journalists, 2007). The threat was issued to three top editors of the newspaper *Le Rebond* for articles it carried on wasteful government expenditures and the accumulation of wealth by several members of the ruling party, the Front Populaire Ivoirien.

Djibouti The constitution makes provision for media freedom, but government owns the main newspaper (*La Nation*) and also owns and operates television and radio stations, all of which are heavily progovernment. The Arabic-language newspaper *Al Qaran* is published by the ruling Popular Rally for Progress (RPP). The country's only Internet service providers are also controlled by government. There are no private broadcasters. A powerful medium wave/AM transmitter broadcasts U.S.-sponsored Arabic-language Radio Sawa programs to East Africa, while local FM stations carry the British Broadcasting Corporation and Voice of America (BBC Country Profile, 2007).

Eritrea Eritrea is the only African country with no privately owned news media and has been described as one of the world's leading jailers of journalists (BBC Country Profile, 2007). After the war of independence ended in 1993, Eritrea plunged into military conflict again, first with Yemen and then with Ethiopia. The private press was shut down by government in 2001, and 10 journalists were arrested for alleged national security violations. This was after the country's new private newspapers began publishing critiques of the president and the conflict with Ethiopia in 2000 and early 2001. A 1996 press law also banned foreign funding of indigenous press, the contravention of which was the government's unofficial rationale for the press closures.

Ethiopia Ethiopia has not known democracy until recently, and even now it is only marginally democratic. After the 2005 elections, government raided newsrooms, blocked newspapers from publishing, and expelled two foreign reporters. Ethiopia is currently the third-leading jailer of journalists in the world. Today, there are fewer than 10 private newspapers published in Addis Ababa, compared with more than 20 before the violence in November 2005 (Freedom House, 2007). The OpenNet Initiative, a group dedicated to open access to Web sites, states that the Ethiopian government has censored antigovernment Web sites and blogs, although the government denies the allegation (Freedom House, 2007).

Ethiopia typifies the formerly prevalent practice of having constitutional provisions for press freedom but then nullifying them in the same or other clauses. Ethiopia's constitution of 1994 includes lofty guarantees that people have the right to hold and express opinions, and that the press—even government-run press—should reflect a diversity of opinions. Article 29, Clause 4, states: "In the interest of free flow of information, ideas, and opinions which are essential to the functioning of a democratic order, the press shall, as an institution, enjoy legal protection to ensure its operation independence and its capacity to entertain diverse opinions" (Berger, 2007). However, Article 29, Clause 6, protects the "honour and reputation of individuals." It also prohibits "the public expression of opinion intended to injure human dignity." These clauses essentially wipe out the lofty provisions that precede them.

Contributing to the restrictive environment of the Ethiopian press system is the fact that the prime minister is almost directly responsible for broadcast regulation. In any case, though private broadcasting began in 2002, "the two supposedly private [radio] licenses were held by a company connected to the ruling party" (Berger, 2007:30).

Gambia   Like other countries in this category, Gambia criminalizes press infractions. In his first press conference after he was reelected in September 2006, President Yahya Jammeh announced that he would continue to prosecute and jail journalists for inaccurate reporting. He justified his stance by warning journalists: "['If you report that] Yahya is a thief,' you should be ready to prove it in a court of law. If that constitutes lack of press freedom, then I don't care" (International Press Institute, Gambia, 2006).

Niger   In some of the worst cases of lingering press repression, journalists continue to be prosecuted just for expressing critical opinions. On July 28, 2006, for instance, Niger's weekly newspaper *Le Républicain* carried an editorial criticizing the government for cultivating relations with Iran and Venezuela and risking a rupture in relations with the United States and Europe. One week later, two of the paper's staff members, including Editor-in-Chief Mamane Abou, were arrested and detained. They were charged with publishing false information and defaming the government (International Press Institute, Niger, 2007).

Rwanda   The Rwandan media is still grappling with the role that some media outlets played in the 1994 genocide. The repercussions of the involvement continue to shape attitudes toward media policy, most notably high government regulation. In general, there is considerable self-censorship by both government-run and privately owned radio stations. The licensing of the latter began in 2004 for the first time after the killings (BBC Country Profile: Rwanda, 2007). The current regime has used allegations of ethnic "divisionism" to silence critics, and such allegations have been used against the country's only independent newspaper *Umuseso* (The Dawn).

More recently, one of Rwanda's biggest independent media groups and the publisher of *Newsline, Umuseso,* and *Rwanda Championi* suspended all publishing for at least two weeks from October 23, 2007 (Bizcommunity, 2007). This came soon after the *Weekly*

Post was deregistered by the government in July for allegedly being funded by Rwanda's enemies. The media group is using the suspension as a means of protesting allegations by President Paul Kagame that they were funded and controlled by external negative forces. The president also authorized advertising in newspapers that cover government favorably. Rwanda is ranked 147th out of the 169 countries in Reporters Without Borders' index of press freedom for 2007.

Somalia Omar Faruk Osman, the secretary general of the National Union of Somali Journalists (NUSOJ), said in November 2007: "Somalia became the worst country for press freedom and security of journalists in Africa and the second most dangerous place for journalists in the world after Iraq, because political groups do not like the Somali media's role of disseminating useful, impartial and objective information to the public" (National Union of Somali Journalists, 2007). That is hardly surprising in a country that has been what political scientists call a failed state since the early 1990s. A political vacuum was created in January 1991 when President Siad Barre fled the country after a 21-year-long dictatorship. Somalia has been a country with no real government ever since, and the press has borne the brunt of the anarchy and violence.

After an Islamist group forced out the weak government in Mogadishu, Ethiopia sent in forces to oust them. Mogadishu has been wracked by violence ever since, as the new government's forces—backed by Ethiopian troops—battle Islamist insurgents (Duhul, 2007). Independent journalists are under attack by all sides. In November 2007 the Somali government shut down three independent radio stations: Radio Simba, Radio Banadir, and Shabelle Media Network.

Zimbabwe Zimbabwe is without question one of the most repressive press systems in Africa and in the world. The press is a victim of President Robert Mugabe's dogged resolve to remain in office despite the country's economic collapse because of his policies. The independent press has been under the onslaught of the Zimbabwe Intelligence Organization (CIO) and other security agencies. They have routinely shut down newspapers, imprisoned journalists, and forced others into exile. In some cases, editors are just kept from entering their newsrooms and told they have been fired. Publishers are forced to go along under the blackmail of being shut down.

The CIO even infiltrates newspapers to ruin them. In a press release in March 2007, Reporters Without Borders observed as follows: "Unable to live with a free press, casting suspicion on the publications they manipulate and paying little heed to the journalists they employ, the intelligence agencies have just helped to undermine the already moribund press even further." The government also uses its requirement of journalist accreditation via the Media Information Commission to punish journalists and editors.

Cultural Context and Issues

With Africa's democratization and enhanced freedom of the press, a number of social and cultural issues surrounding media operations are beginning to gain salience. Among them are the tug between press freedom and cultural proprieties and the pressures of global synchronization on national values. Related issues include the preservation of local languages and their use as the language of the media despite the economic imperatives that suggest an urban focus and the use of official languages. Problems facing indigenous-language media in Africa reflect problems facing the languages of the continent in general. Communication in local languages has been adversely affected by the use of colonial languages as the official languages (Salawu, 2006). The exception is in East Africa, where English often operates together with Kiswahili.

A related concern in much of Africa is the need to improve the culture of reading. Along with financial constraints, it is a major factor of newspaper and magazine readership. Low literacy rates remain a problem in some countries. But in a number of countries, the adult literacy rate is approaching or has exceeded 70 percent, and youth literacy rate is even higher. Yet readership remains depressed. To cultivate a culture of reading, there are suggestions that primary schools begin to integrate newspaper reading and discussion into their curricula (Babalola, 2002).

A particular concern in this regard is the rapid decline in the readership of local language newspapers. In his research on readership of Yoruba-language newspapers in Nigeria, for instance, Salawu (2004) finds that the young and the highly educated are less likely to read such publications. The findings are of significance not just for the press. They reinforce predictions that several African languages will become extinct by the end of the twenty-first century. Salawu points to studies that note also that African youth are increasingly unable to speak a native language.

All across Africa, the broadcast media are more effectively used to reach people in their native languages and to promote the languages and local culture. In East Africa, for example, TV has been used to promote local indigenous music, with youth also using this music to address social issues via the entertainment–education strategy. While public broadcasting has declined and become more commercial, East African Community (EAC) media are attempting to offer content that preserves the cultural and social interests of the member states. One example is the introduction of Kiswahili (the main language in Kenya and Tanzania) on Ugandan-based WBS TV, in an attempt to cater to more audiences in the region (Mundua, 2007).

The media's role in enhancing the status of women is another cultural issue. The press is generally critical of the harsher dimensions of women's conditions. When, for instance, a Nigerian woman was sentenced to death in 2001 for adultery under the sharia law of an Islamic state, the press roundly condemned it and galvanized opposition that ultimately saved the woman's life. However, lesser forms of disenfranchisement, such as traditional practices on property rights that privilege men, are much less vigorously challenged. That the press and the mass media industry as a whole remain dominated by men may be a factor. A study of bylines in the major Nigerian news magazines found, for instance, that 91 percent of the bylines in the sample were of men (Okunna, 2005).

The following discussion of culture-related matters in the African press is intended to highlight the manifestation of these issues in a variety of countries.

Burundi   The news media in Burundi use French, along with a number of native languages. The state-run daily *Le Renouveau du Burundi* and the weekly *Burundi Chrétien* are notable newspapers published in French. Several periodicals, including a weekly newspaper, *Ubumwe,* are published in Kirundi. The government-run Voice of the Revolution broadcasts in Kirundi, Swahili, French, and English.

Kenya   In Kenya the nationalist struggle was responsible for the development of the indigenous language press in the country, with the establishment of *Muigwithania* in 1928 (Salawu, 2006). Despite this rich history, today *Taifa Leo* is Kenya's only Swahili language daily, published by the Nation Media Group. The state-owned Kenya News Agency uses English, and the dominant major publishing houses, the *Nation* and *Standard,* both use English primarily. The Kenyan Broadcasting Corporation (KBC) offers services in English, Swahili, and 15 other indigenous languages. Coro FM, Inooro FM, and Kaneme FM are private Kikuyu-language stations. Radio Ramogi broadcasts in Luo, and Rehema Radio broadcasts programs in Kalenjin. The region is also served by Radio Mang'elete, a community radio station operated by the East African Community Media Project, a program of EcoNews Africa. Ethnic groups in Southeast Kenya speak Kikamba (not the more widely spoken national language of Kiswahili), and community radio is the only source of mass media information in the area (Yusuf, 2007).

Tanzania   Tanzania was one of the first African countries to use a local language (Kiswahili) as the language of parliament and as the primary language of national business, as part of Julius Nyerere's nation-building policies. However, with the rise of the information age and increasing access to the Internet, the limited number of Web sites in Kiswahili means that Tanzanians are surfing the Web using English, which is fast becoming the language of the Tanzanian elite (Mafu, 2004). A large number of Kiswahili titles are published in Tanzania, but ironically the newspaper *The Express* conducts interviews in Kiswahili and then translates them into English (World Association of Newspapers, 2003).

Several new FM stations broadcast and promote local music, mostly in Kiswahili. That is part of the reason radio listening is high, with 60 percent of households owning a radio set (Tanzania National Web site). However, much of the television content is imported, primarily from the South African Digital Satellite Television Network (DStv). That is because of the recency of TV broadcasting in Tanzania, as well as the expense of local production.

In terms of cultural issues surrounding the media, gender and HIV/AIDS feature strongly in Tanzania. The press has been criticized for its lack of a gender policy for recruitment and reporting, and its consequent inadequate coverage of women. A 2003 study showed that women featured mostly as sex workers and beauty contestants (Nkya, 2003). Still, radio has been widely used for promoting messages about HIV/AIDS via the entertainment–education strategy.

Uganda   In Uganda state radio is mandated to broadcast in as many indigenous languages as possible, and as a result one might hear up to 27 languages on Radio Uganda (now the Ugandan Broadcasting Corporation, UBC) (Salawu, 2006). Across the broadcast media, English is most used, followed by Luganda, with all other languages on Kampala-based stations appearing only as fillers during entertainment-based shows (Chibita, 2006).

The use of indigenous languages also reflects the realization that they have a role to play in HIV/AIDS prevention, as many people in the targeted groups do not understand English or Luganda (Gulere, 1998).

Economic Context of the Mass Media

An important factor in the condition of any media system is the economy. For the African media, it has been a hindrance. There are indications, however, that the African economy is poised for expansion. The African Development Bank and the Organization for Economic Cooperation and Development reported in May 2007 that "Africa has experienced its highest economic growth in the last two decades, with the GDP growth rate, which averaged about 5 percent annually in the past six years, rising to 5.5 percent in 2006, and is expected to reach 6 percent in 2007" (African Development Bank, 2007).

Similarly, in an editorial on November 2, 2007, the *New York Times* sums up sub-Saharan Africa's economic situation as follows: "Nobody can know for certain whether Africa south of the Sahara might be on the cusp of shaking its endemic destitution and starting up the ladder of development. But it has its best chance in decades." The paper credits "rising prices of raw materials" for "helping the region achieve its best economic performance since independence." The major beneficiaries of the prices are the oil exporting countries, including Nigeria, Angola, Cameroon, and Equatorial Guinea. Non-oil exporting countries have also benefited from improvements in other exports. Ghana's increased cocoa production and export, for instance, has been one of the factors in its remarkable economic recovery and growth.

Governments have privatized state-owned corporations, and opened up other areas of the economy that used to be state monopolies including broadcasting. The liberalization of African polities resulted in the emergence of commercial and community broadcasting projects challenging the prevalent monolithic broadcasting systems in most countries. Among other things, this development has enhanced the adoption of new technologies and the pursuit of technological convergence (Banda, 2006). Yet, the possibilities also pose several economic challenges related to tabloid explosion, audience fragmentation, the impact of pay-per-view services, and regional television, among others.

In East Africa, there are predictions that the media market will most likely be monopolized by a single conglomerate in the future, with the expansion of media giants such as the Kenya-based Nation Media Group—which owns several newspapers and radio and TV stations—into Uganda and Tanzania (Mundua, 2007). There is an emerging notion of an East African Community (EAC) media identity, which is promoting the region's sociopolitical, cultural, and economic way of life.

The situation and experience of the following selected countries illustrate the overall outlook and challenges.

Angola   The Angolan economy is expanding rapidly following the end of a protracted and bloody civil war. "The International Monetary Fund projects a 24 percent economic growth this year [2007]—one of the fastest rates in the world" (LaFraniere, 2007). Still, the press, like much of the populace, is under economic pressure. Paper and printing costs are high, pushed up by the lack of economies of scale; advertising revenue is thinly spread, and the only daily paper, the state-owned *Jornal de Angola,* is heavily subsidized (Pearce, 2007).

Angola especially illustrates the economic challenges of the growing private broadcasting. Private radio stations now broadcast in several cities, and they are competing with six independent newspapers in a limited market. A 2006 press law includes a provision to end the state monopoly over television broadcasting and news agencies and the establishment of community radio and television. Many Angolan journalists see the promised independent TV station as a lucrative opportunity for well-connected businesspeople. Because of the economic pressures, independent newspapers are expensive and depict community issues from a national angle. Magazines have been of poor quality due to lack of resources and skilled staff. Three community newspapers were formed in 2006, but community radio stations are on hold until the Regulation of the Press Law is tabled and approved.

Malawi In Malawi, the opposition-dominated parliament cut funding to public broadcasters, claiming that they were being used by government for propaganda. The Malawian Broadcasting Corporation (MBC) and Television Malawi (TVM) were each allocated US$0.01 out of a budget of US$670 million to satisfy a law that makes it illegal to provide no allocation at all, and the two stations will now have to compete with private broadcasters for advertising (MISA, 2007).

Mozambique Most print media in the country survive on income they generated, but they also face restrictions in terms of expanding their circulations outside of Maputo. Newspaper penetration in the interior is still quite limited (only 5 out of 1,000 people had access to a newspaper in 2000), and the average print run for the main daily paper, *Noticias,* was just 12,793 in 2003 (Limbobo, 2006). Between 1992 and 2002 there was a boom in the newspaper sector as a result of the new Press Law, with independent media and donor support to assist in the setup of new media houses. Alfredo (2006) highlights the main issues facing independent or private media in Mozambique as including high telecommunications costs and high taxation. Most printing presses use outdated printing equipment. Many new private radio stations were formed in 2003, and radio and TV stations are limited in terms of advertising, as this is still in the hands of the public service stations. Limited financial resources also affect access to technology. A study by Berger (2005) shows that access to the Internet in newsrooms is restricted, there is no digital photography, Web sites are few and unsophisticated, and hardware and software are often out of date, particularly at the public broadcaster.

South Africa In South Africa, the reform and restructuring of the broadcasting and telecommunications sector has been characterized by an increased role for private capital and the market. Barnett (1999) identifies the emerging policy question of how liberalization can be regulated and made consistent with the "promotion of nation-building, reconciliation, democratization and cultural diversity" (Barnett, 1999:650). However, the Independent Broadcasting Authority (IBA) (now Independent Communication Authority of South Africa, ICASA) acknowledged that market forces in the media sector could be a threat to diversity of ownership and opinion. It consequently promoted a framework that encouraged a plurality of independent broadcasters, "implying both the de-concentration of media industries and the separation of media from the state" (Thompson, 1995:240).

Key issues facing the South African economy, and consequently its media, are privatization, unbundling, and black economic empowerment. The selling off of the South African Broadcasting Corporation's (SABC) commercial radio stations obliged white-owned capital to forge partnerships with black empowerment groups (Barnett, 1999). Hailed as the "first privatization deal in South African history" (*Mail and Guardian,* September 20, 1996), it ended the SABC's monopoly of ownership, and though the SABC was repositioned as the national public broadcaster, it is dependent on commercial advertising for revenue.

In fact, both unbundling and privatization are most advanced in the media industry, with ownership of the South African press restructured after the introduction of international capital and domestic black empowerment groups. Some argue that the SABC has become too dependent on cheap American entertainment programs (Berger, 2001), while Banda (2006) argues that this commercial imperative could not be avoided in an environment where state resources were constrained as a result of competing demands. Before the end of apartheid, South Africa had been largely disconnected from the international capital markets. The dismantling of apartheid and the deregulation of the media landscape resulted in the inflow of foreign direct investment (Tomaselli, 2002).

With regard to the print media, the segmentation of South Africa's newspaper markets by class and language, means that "there are too many low circulation newspapers feeding off a relatively small advertising cake" (Sparks, 2003:92 in Collins, 2004). The consequent shortage of revenue means that newsrooms are understaffed. In fixed-line telecommunications, Telkom still enjoys a monopoly in the provision of services despite the suggestion of a second national operator.

Zambia   In Zambia, the issue of commercialism was more important than privatization, as the latter was avoided because it would involve loss of state control over the ZNBC. Some units of the state broadcaster were commercialized and a new commercial radio channel (Radio 4) was introduced (Banda, 2006). Deregulation resulted in licenses being given mostly to Christian applicants and international media business interests, primarily from South Africa. Multichoice Africa obtained a license to establish subscription Digital Satellite Television (DSTV), with 30 percent of the shares held by the state broadcaster (Banda, 2006). The ZNBC is also funded by advertising, sponsorships, and shares.

Mass Media Growth and Reach

The mass media have grown phenomenally in Africa in the past two decades, and much of that growth is attributable to the growth of the independent press and private broadcasters. Political liberalization opened up press systems to private enterprise with both commercial and political interests. Independent newspapers have sprouted in countries where any hardly existed before. So has private broadcasting. As noted earlier, the licensing of private broadcasting in African countries is generally a recent phenomenon. The expansion of broadcasting is particularly notable since the 1990s when governments began to relinquish monopolies. Countries such as Ghana and Nigeria began such licensing in the 1990s; others began even later, including Ethiopia in 2002 and Guinea in 2006. For Ethiopia, the enabling laws had been in place since the 1990s but were not effected.

FM radio has witnessed the fastest growth of all broadcast media. Until the 1980s, radio broadcasting in African countries was dominated by shortwave and AM radio. Much of the millennial expansion of broadcasting has been in FM radio. The growth has had both positive and negative ramifications. FM radio is of higher quality and, unlike AM and shortwave radio, is less subject to interference. On the other hand, FM radio has limited range for comparable transmission power. Therefore, their greatest impact has been in the urban centers. Remote villages in expansive countries such as Congo-Kinshasa do not benefit from the variety of options, when they receive any signals at all. Following is a digest of the scope of the mass media in selected countries.

Newspapers and Magazines

Despite unfavorable advertising environments in most sub-Saharan African countries, the number of newspapers and magazines in various African countries has grown. However, after the spurt at the onset of liberalization in the 1990s, there has been a decline in some countries, as a number of the small papers were just not viable. In general, there is considerable fluidity in the number of publications. Some newspapers are sponsored for the sole purpose of political advocacy, including the promotion of candidates for elections. Such papers often fold when their advocacy runs its course or when the financial burden on the sponsors becomes untenable.

In general, newspapers and magazines in Africa remain largely for the educated urban dwellers. There are a number of hindrances to wider circulation of newspapers. First, there is the logistical challenge of distributing papers in distant rural communities. Then there is the limitation of literacy. Although the adult literacy rate has risen considerably in the past two decades, as will be discussed below, illiteracy is still widespread, especially in the rural areas. Then there is the economic factor. The purchase price for African newspapers and magazines is very high. Faced with rising costs of newsprint and constricted advertising environments, African newspapers and magazines resort to price increases. That in turn reduces the number of likely purchasers. In Nigeria, for instance, the leading dailies cost N100, or about US$0.80. Few American dailies cost this much, and the gross national income per capita in the United States ($43,740) is about 78 times that of Nigeria ($560).

Literacy Rates

There has been a phenomenal rise in adult literacy rates (for people ages 15 and above) in many African countries (United Nations Development Programme, 2004). The youth literacy rates (for people 15–24 years old) are significantly higher. Countries with the highest adult and youth literacy rates by 2002 include Zimbabwe (90, 97.6), South Africa (86, 91.8), Kenya (84.3, 95.8), Democratic Republic of Congo (82.8, 97.8), Zambia (79.9, 89.2), Botswana (78.9, 89.1), Tanzania (77.1, 83.1), Ghana (73.8, 81.8), and Nigeria (66.8,

88.6). Countries in the low end include Niger (17.4, 24.5), Senegal (39.3, 52.9), and Benin (39.8, 55.5). Even for these countries, the figures still represent substantial growth within the past decade.

Daily Newspaper Circulation

Daily newspaper circulation rates in these countries (culled from the Lexis-Nexis Statistical Database) generally reflect the adult literacy rates. Among the countries with relatively high circulation rates per thousand population as of 2004 are South Africa (32), Botswana (27), Nigeria (24), Zambia (22), Zimbabwe (19), and Ghana (14). These figures are much lower than what obtains elsewhere in the world, but they stand out in comparison with the figures for low-circulation African countries such as Niger (< 0.1), Uganda (2), Senegal (5), and Benin (5.6 in 1998). Two countries, Kenya and Democratic Republic of Congo, are notable for much lower circulation figures than suggested by their high adult literacy rates. Congo's circulation rate per thousand in 1998 was 6.4 and Kenya's in 2004 was 9.

Despite the much greater reach of the broadcast media, especially radio, the print media remain very influential. Even with the growth in independent broadcasting, newspapers and magazines still set the agenda of political discourse for the most part (Kayanja, 2002, Hasty, 2005). They are not as encumbered as the broadcasters to pursue investigative stories and to publish exposés. Although the print and broadcast media operate in the same economic and political environments, the broadcast media are more vulnerable to both. They rely almost exclusively on advertising for revenue, and their licensing status makes them more subject to government leverage. The following cases illustrate the general pattern.

Print Press: East Africa

Ethiopia   Of the 125 newspapers in Ethiopia, 108 are in Amharic, two in Oromo, and one in Tigre. Ethiopia is one of three African countries (the others being Tanzania and Somalia) where a local language is used as a medium of instruction, as well as for official and administrative purposes. Most of the papers publish weekly and are small in size and circulation. The *Daily Monitor,* which was a thrice-weekly paper until September 2000, prides itself as Ethiopia's first private daily newspaper. It was established in 1993.

Kenya   The Kenyan print press is dominated by the Nation and Standard group of newspapers, with the Nation being the larger of the two. Its leading flagship newspaper, the *Nation,* is estimated to have a circulation of 200,000, and that is by far the largest in the country. Among papers in the Nation group are the *East African* and the Swahili-language paper, *Taifa Leo.* The formerly dominant party, the Kenya African National Union, owns the daily *Kenyan Times.*

Somalia   No newspapers are distributed nationally, and circulation figures for individual papers are estimated at only a few thousand (Somalia Media Guide, February 2007). However, several newspapers are produced in major cities, but the skills level is low (IREX, 2007). Several media outlets are unable to regularly pay salaries. Most newspapers serve political purposes (Media Sustainability Index).

Uganda For a long period of time, Uganda was one of the most media-poor African countries. Economic, geographic, and infrastructural factors all contributed to the stunted growth. "But perhaps most detrimental to independent media development is Uganda's authoritarian history" (Kayanja, 2002:155). In fact, until recently the Ugandan press was virtually an all-government affair. The state-owned *Uganda Times* was for long the dominant newspaper. Then the private press "was allowed to emerge in 1986" (Kayanja, 2002:162). There soon would be 30 newspapers in Uganda, both government and private. The increase in media outlets led to competition for audiences and a focus on profit, with several media companies listed on the stock exchange. By 1999, however, only two English-language dailies were publishing regularly: the state-owned *New Vision* and the independent *Monitor*. The *New Vision* replaced the Uganda *Times* after Yuweri Museveni came to power. The *Monitor* was established in 1992 by journalists who left the *New Vision* after falling out with the management. "[It] is now Uganda's only independent daily publication with an average daily circulation of 29,000" (Kayanja, 2002:63). The *New Vision* and its sister regional newspapers have a combined circulation of about 30,000.

Print Press: West Africa

Ghana The number of newspapers grew from the 1990s, after the end of military rule. About 20 independent newspapers were soon established, "most of them critical of the government" (Asante, 1996:111–112). "Though primitive in layout and journalistically poor, their arrival marked the end of over a decade of media silence" (Asante, 1996:112, quoting a Ghanaian journalist). "Currently, there are up to 50 newspapers, journals and periodicals which appear regularly on the newsstands" (Commonwealth Press Union, 2005).

State-owned newspapers remain a major part of the print press. Among the government-owned newspapers in Ghana are the *Daily Graphic* (circulation 100,000), *Ghanaian Times* (50,000), and its sister daily *The Evening News* (10,000). Though state-owned, the *Daily Graphic* and the *Ghanaian Times* do not receive subsidies or tax exemptions from government, and the government makes no deliberate attempt to supplement them through discriminatory advertising. With the exception of the *Daily Graphic* and some staff employed by private broadcast media, salaries and conditions of service for journalists are generally bad, which encourages corruption. The government-sponsored newspapers face competition from privately owned dailies such as *Accra Mail,* the thrice weekly *Ghanaian Chronicle,* and the weeklies *Public Agenda, Palavar,* and *The Independent.*

Liberia There is a widespread perception that the print media market in Liberia is saturated, but newspapers remain relatively weak with little impact on the economic, social, and political life of the country. Most newspapers reportedly sell less than 3,000 copies a day across the country (with a population of over 3 million people.) In addition, newspapers are poorly funded and undercapitalized. They often lack basic infrastructure and communication facilities, they have inadequate management capacities, and the staff have little formal professional training.

The existing monopoly on the printing press has resulted in indirect control over the editorial content of newspapers by a commercial printer. The limited capacity of the printing press has hindered the growth of the newspaper industry, not allowing newspapers that want to move from being bi-weeklies to dailies to do so, because it allegedly cannot handle the additional printing (UNESCO, 2004).

Nigeria   By African standards, Nigeria is a media-rich country. More than 100 newspapers and magazines are in circulation at any time, with the actual numbers varying in between elections and subject to the vagaries of the economy. At least 12 of these publications are nationally circulating dailies with typical per-issue page numbers ranging from 32 to 96. Circulation figures are not readily available, but on the upper levels are the dailies—the *Guardian,* the *Punch,* and the *Vanguard.*

The growth of the independent press in Nigeria began in the early 1980s, a few years after the federal government acquired a majority share of the *Daily Times* group, then Nigeria's most successful publishing house. The subsequent decline of the *Daily Times* group spurred the establishment of privately owned newspapers and magazines, among them the dailies the *Concord,* the *Guardian,* and the *Vanguard,* and the weekly news magazine *Newswatch.* The growth continued in the 1990s during a period of draconian-military rule, spurred in part by opposition to the dictatorship. Among the notable publications established during this period were the daily *This Day* and the news magazines *Tell, TheNews,* and *Tempo* (a sister magazine and sometime reincarnation of *TheNews*). These publications were among the most strident in resisting military rule and defying censorship between 1994 and 1998, Nigeria's most perilous years since the 1967–1970 civil war.

Print Press: Southern Africa

Botswana   For a country of about 1.7 million people, Botswana is media rich. It has at least two dailies and several weeklies. The *Daily News* is government owned, and the other daily, the *Mmegi* (or Reporter), is privately owned, along with the weeklies.

The other papers of note include the *Guardian, Gazette, Standard, Midweek Sun,* and *Voice.* However, Botswana is a sparsely populated country, and that makes media coverage difficult, especially for rural areas.

Democratic Republic of Congo (DRC)   DRC or Congo-Kinshasa is a media-rich country. The print press is predominantly privately owned. However, readership is surprisingly low for a country with a high literacy rate. The country's high poverty and unemployment mean that few people buy newspapers. Therefore, only about 3,000 copies of newspapers are printed daily. In addition, newspapers are often photocopied by individuals, who then sell the copies at reduced prices (Kabemba, 2005).

Most media owners are more interested in profit than in quality reporting. The media do not have the necessary infrastructure and resources for high-quality journalism. The country's socioeconomic difficulties are reflected in the media's poor infrastructure and equipment. Many newspapers still use printing equipment left behind by the Belgians, equipment that is not only outdated but is too old to be maintained. Many journalists do not have access to computers and telephones. Moreover, journalists receive low salaries, which are not paid regularly. And so they are susceptible to the culture of *"le Coupage,"* the practice of paying journalists in exchange for desired news stories.

Namibia   Namibia represents one of the extreme cases of urban media bias in Africa. That results from its geography. With a population of about 2 million people, it occupies an area of more than 328,000 square miles. That is about two-thirds the size of neighboring South Africa (population 46 million) and about 90 percent of the area of Nigeria (population 130 million). The resulting dispersion of the Namibian population poses a special challenge for the circulation of newspapers and magazines, which are almost all based in the capital city of Windhoek. There are four notable dailies, including the state-owned *New Era,* which was established in 1992 about two years after its independence from South Africa. The other papers are almost all privately owned. Notable among them are the *Namibia Economist, Die Republikein,* and *Allgemeine Zeitung.* There are several weeklies. Most papers are published in English, but *Die Republikein* and *Allgemeine Zeitung* are published in Afrikaans and German, respectively.

South Africa   The South African press is very diverse and the newspapers and magazines are virtually all private. "South Africa has 20 daily and 13 weekly newspapers, most in English. Some 14.5 million South Africans buy the urban dailies, while community newspapers have a circulation of 5.5 million" (International Marketing Council of South Africa, 2007). However, four media conglomerates dominate ownership of the newspapers: Naspers, Times Media Limited, Independent Newspapers (an Irish Chain), and New Africa Publications.

Naspers owns the *Daily Sun,* which has overtaken the *Sowetan* as South Africa's largest circulating daily, partly by attracting a sizable component of the Sowetan's black base. "[The] Daily Sun is the first South African tabloid aimed at the black working class. Initially met with disdain by the established press, its huge sales—and the fact that it has made new newspaper readers out of millions of South Africans—have earned it some respect" (International Marketing Council of South Africa, 2007). Established in 2002 by Media24—Naspers' newspaper/magazine publishing component—the *Sun* quickly grew in circulation through aggressive marketing and a tabloid fare that is heavy on scintillating news. The paper's "audited paid circulation. . . of over 500,000, [is] three times its nearest daily competitor" (*Wall Street Journal,* August 17, 2007). Among its marketing strategies is a per-copy sale price that is only half that of the competitors, a strategy that hearkens to that of the U.S. penny press of the 1830s. The *Sun* also attracts readers by paying writers whose letters to the editor are selected as the best on any given day, and readers who identify themselves in the *Sun's* photos.

The Independent group now owns some of South Africa's most historic newspapers, including the *Star, Cape Argus,* the *Daily News,* and *Cape Times.* Naspers owns the other major and historical newspapers, *Die Burger* and *Beeld,* both of which are published in Afrikaans.

Broadcasting: East Africa

Eritrea   EriTV began broadcasting in Asmara in 1993, and Dimtsi Hafash (Voice of the Masses radio) broadcasts in six languages. Some radio programs are run by party-controlled social organizations (women, workers, youth); and a party-controlled Web site, Shaebia.org. The Ministry of Information uses the media for propaganda and no opposing views are allowed to be published or broadcast (Freedom House, 2007).

Kenya   Kenyan broadcasting has expanded considerably during the period of liberalization. The major step in private broadcasting began when the then dominant political party, the Kenya African National Union, established a television network in collaboration with the British company Maxwell Communications. The Nation and Standard group of newspaper companies have since established private broadcasting. In its annual report of 2005/2006, the Communications Commission of Kenya (CCK) reported developing a plan that made possible "the introduction of an additional 23 FM frequencies" and the "assignment of 64 FM sound and 17 television frequencies during the year under review" (Communications Commission of Kenya, 2007:8).

Government is moving toward restricting cross-media ownership, though the two most popular TV channels in the country, Nation TV and KTN-TV, are owned by the Nation Media Group and Standard Group, both of which have holdings in other media sectors. There has been little growth in satellite subscriber numbers because the cost is still too prohibitive for most people. Another reason for the lack of regional or local TV services and the slow growth of the TV sector is the low level of TV ownership in the country.

Somalia   Privately owned media outlets were established in 1991 after 21 years of a state monopoly during Somalia's military regime. In early 2000 the number of privately owned radio stations increased rapidly and TV stations began broadcasting. There are seven TV operators in Somalia: three in Somaliland, two in Puntland, and two in Mogadishu (African Media Development Initiative Research Project 2006—www.bbcworldservicetrust.org/amdi). The two in Mogadishu are HornAfrik (a cable service) and Global, though services remain limited with restricted operating hours, low presentation standards, little locally made programming and much airtime filled with poorly made local advertisements and relays of foreign satellite services such as Al Jazeera. As a result, many Somalis use satellite dishes to watch foreign Arabic or English channels.

Tanzania   Tanzania is an exceptional country in Africa in having its broadcast press—including television—dominated by private operations. It was also one of the last African countries to establish television broadcasting. Its first president, the socialist Julius Nyerere, considered television "a luxury that would widen the gulf between the rich and the poor" (BBC, 2007). Its first television operation, Independent Television (ITV), was launched in 1994 by IPP Holdings. The state-run Televisheni ya Taifa (TVT) began broadcasting about seven years later in 2001. But it is generally dwarfed by ITV and three other private TV networks, along with similar radio operations.

Uganda   The state monopolized broadcasting in Uganda until 1993, when liberalization policies were introduced. The subsequent increase in privately owned FM stations gave Ugandans an opportunity to participate in and through radio (Chibita, 2006). The Ugandan Broadcasting Corporation (UBC) was formed in 2005 as the country's first public broadcaster, though according to Chibita (2006) it still falls short of the basic criteria outlined by the 2005 African Charter on Broadcasting for conversion of a state broadcaster to a public broadcaster. The UBC remains fully owned by government but has to compete for advertising with commercial media.

Broadcasting: West Africa

Ghana A large number of radio stations broadcast in Ghana, most of them privately owned. The state-owned Ghana Broadcasting Corporation (GBC) broadcasts on two radio stations. Though most stations are based in the three largest cities of Accra, Kumasi, and Takoradi, especially the capital city of Accra, they reach much of the country. A major challenge in this regard is that the country's largest cities are all coastal, while much of the country juts northward.

That geography has a greater impact on television reach. The GBC's Ghana TV is the only national television service. Metro TV, which was founded in 1999 as a joint venture of the government and private enterprise, is said to reach about 60 percent of Ghanaians (Kafewo, 2007). Two wholly private broadcast stations reach an even smaller percentage of Ghanaians. One, TV3, reaches people primarily in Kumasi and Takoradi. The other, Fontomfrom TV, broadcasts from Accra and reaches a radius of about 31 miles (AfricaFilmTV.com). A handful of cable and satellite services supplement the free-to-air services. A major dimension of the growth of Ghanaian television is the involvement of foreign entrepreneurs and businesses, including the Lebanese and Malaysians.

Liberia The press in Liberia was decimated by the long civil war and government repression. Several broadcast stations have since emerged, but they are struggling financially. Even the state-run Liberian Broadcasting System has not been able to restore national television broadcasting (BBC Country Profile: Liberia, 2007). Most broadcast stations are owned by private enterprise or religious and international service organizations. Frequency allocation procedures are still being worked out, and license fees are prohibitively high.

Nigeria Until the 1990s, broadcasting in Nigeria was a state monopoly. However, unlike most other African countries, state monopoly never meant homogeneity in Nigeria. Except during military regimes, the different regions and states have had their own political orientations, which may correspond with or differ from the federal government's. In fact, depending on the political parties in control, the regional or state-government-run stations sometimes engage in editorial feuds with the federal stations.

The Nigeria Television Authority (NTA) promotes itself as the largest television network in Africa. It has at least one TV station in all of Nigeria's 36 states and the federal capital, Abuja. Its radio counterpart, the Federal Radio Corporation of Nigeria (FRCN), operates from the federal capital and four zonal headquarters, with affiliated stations all over the 36 states. The federal TV and radio stations reach virtually every part of the country. Each state also has its own broadcast operations, though not all are yet to operate their own TV stations.

Independent radio and television became a significant component of Nigeria when DAAR Communications launched its operations in 1994, with RayPower FM Radio. About five years later, DAAR Communications launched Africa Independent Television (AIT) and RayPower 2 FM. Private radio has since proliferated. However, they operate under considerable financial pressure. Private TV stations, in particular, face high costs and limited revenues from advertising, particularly because legislation requires a 60 percent local content quota (BBC Country Profile: Nigeria, 2007).

A major source of funding for all TV stations is religious programming. In Southern Nigeria, which is predominantly Christian, evangelists and churches buy hours of airtime everyday to proselytize and recruit members. In Northern Nigeria, which is predominantly Muslim, Islamic clerics and mosques do the same. So regular are such paid programming that an uninformed visitor could readily conclude that Nigeria is a theocratic state.

Broadcasting: Southern Africa

Botswana   Botswana has had several radio stations over the years; however, internal TV broadcasting did not begin nationally until the government launched Botswana Television in 2000. Before then, the privately owned Gaborone Television broadcast for the capital city and its environs. Television broadcasts are also received from South Africa and satellite services.

Namibia   To overcome the urban bias in media reach and orientation, the Namibian Broadcasting Corporation (NBC) adopted the policy and slogan, "We must take radio to the people" (Mulongeni, 1998). That policy has resulted in the extension of radio service to much of Namibia. By 1998, radio was reaching 97 percent of the population (Mulongeni, 1998). Television broadcasting, however, is a different matter. The state-owned Namibian Broadcasting Corporation is the only national service that is striving to expand its reach. The privately owned Desert TV broadcasts in the capital city, Windhoek.

South Africa   Like the print press, the broadcast media are vast and diverse. "Listeners in Johannesburg alone can choose from among some 40 radio services, from the national broadcasts of the state-owned South African Broadcasting Corporation (SABC) to community stations targeting local neighborhoods or ethnic groups" (BBC Country Profile: South Africa, 2007). Rural areas are not left out either. South Africa is ahead of most other African countries in the development of community and rural radio. There are as many as 100 community radio stations in South Africa (International Marketing Council of South Africa, 2007). The growth reflects the policy of the regulatory and licensing agency, the Independent Communications Authority of South Africa, to ensure that all segments of the population has a radio voice.

Despite the relatively belated arrival of television in 1976, television services have expanded beyond that of most African countries. The South African Broadcasting Corporation (SABC) alone broadcast four national services, with variations in programming. A commercial network, e.tv, is the privately owned broadcast network. Satellite and cable television is provided by M-Net and DStv.

Zambia   The state-run Zambia National Broadcasting Corporation broadcasts the country's only television service as well as several radio stations. They are joined by several privately owned FM stations. Media groups in Zambia welcomed government's promise to review its 1996 media policy (Chikale, 2007). The 1996 media policy provided for the liberalization of broadcasting, but provisions such as the establishment of an independent broadcasting authority and revisions to the public broadcaster act still have to be implemented. Local journalists complain that the high tax on newsprint and broadcasting equipment is slowing down the growth of the information sector. The government has prioritized the roll-out of radio transmitters to improve reception via its Fifth National Development Plan (Chikale, 2007).

Internet and Related Communication Technologies

As of September 2007, Internet penetration in Africa was at 4.7 percent of the population, according to figures provided by the International Telecommunication Union (www.internetworldstats.com). That compares with 21.3 percent penetration for the rest of the world. However, the growth rate in Africa outpaces that of the rest of world. Between 2000 and 2007, Internet penetration grew at a rate of 874.6 percent. That compares with a growth rate of 236.8 percent for the rest of the world.

Within Africa, countries vary considerably in the extent of their integration into the cyber world. However, hardly any country is unconnected. The adoption of new communication technologies is, of course, a function of the overall economic and technological advancement. The islands of Seychelles (34.1%) and Mauritius (23.2%) have Internet penetration rates that exceed the global average. Within continental sub-Saharan Africa, countries in the high end of penetration include South Africa (10.3%), Zimbabwe (9.8%), Benin (9.1%), and Kenya (7.9%). In the middle range are Senegal (5.9%), Togo (5.8%), Gabon (5.5%), Nigeria (4.9%), and Zambia (4.4%). Countries with minimal penetration include Ethiopia (0.2%), Sierra Leone (0.2%), Democratic Republic of Congo (0.3%), Liberia (0.3%), Central African Republic (0.4%), Malawi (0.5%), Guinea (0.6%), Madagascar (0.6%), and Mali (0.6%).

Despite the relatively low Internet penetration in Africa, the technology is already having an impact on public discourse. There is perhaps no greater evidence of this than that repressive governments now target cybercafes as part of their campaign against the press. The Internet connections are especially important politically because they provide an effective linkage with citizens living abroad, as Langmia (2008) illustrates with regard to Cameroon.

In general, telephone and online penetration in Africa has grown dramatically and continues to improve. In Kenya, for instance, "mobile network connections grew by 81%" as subscriptions grew from 2.5 million to 4.6 million between the 2004/2005 and 2005/2006 annual review periods (Communications Commission of Kenya, 2007:8). "Overall teleaccessibility (mobile and fixed) improved from 8.8% to 14.7%" (Communications Commission of Kenyan, 2007:8). However, in a country of about 34.3 million people, that still leaves a lot of people without telephones.

General Policy Issues and Initiatives

In general, the technological issues in African countries include matters of convergence, fiber optics, Web 2.0 and social networking sites, digital migration, digital radio and TV frequencies, community television, and e-government. Convergence has emerged as one of the major issues facing Southern African broadcasters. It can be defined from a number of perspectives, but the most common understanding is usually of technological convergence, which refers to the trend for technologies to overlap, or the merging of delivery technologies (e.g., video on cell phones), while convergence in the media refers to the removal of entry barriers across the IT, telecoms, media, and consumer electronics industries. Southern African countries have recognized the strategic importance of responding to the challenge of convergence within the context of broad regulatory reform (Wild, 2006).

The main technological issue facing the Central and East African region is the Eastern Africa Submarine Cable System (EASSy), an initiative to connect the countries of East Africa to the rest of the world via a high bandwidth fiber-optic cable system. These countries will no longer depend on expensive satellite systems to carry voice and data services, and the project is due to be completed in 2008.

The newsrooms of Africa's elite newspapers and magazines from Johannesburg to Nairobi are well furnished with desktop computers and online access. However, that is not the case across the board, certainly not until recently (Agbese, 2006; Hasty, 2005). By the 1990s, most journalists in Africa had little familiarity with the use of computers or online technology. For newsrooms that had computers, they were operated by typists. Reporters merely submitted their handwritten stories. That is still the case for newsrooms that are shoestring operations. Were it not for cell phones, even telephones would remain in short supply at such operations. As Jennifer Hasty narrates from her experience as a participant-researcher in 1999 at a Ghanaian newspaper, "The only telephone at the *Independent,* located upstairs in the typists' office, is guarded by a secretary and requires a key" (Hasty, 2005:125).

Here then are summaries of situation and policy issues on Information and Communication Technology (ICT) and other new media technologies in selected countries.

East Africa

Kenya   Kenya has a draft ICT policy, which was drafted by government, without consultation with stakeholders. Kenya was one of the first countries in the world to roll out Digital Video Broadcast-Handheld (DVB-H) technology, which enables the broadcast of DStv channels to a special mobile phone. DVB-H allows the digital terrestrial broadcast of live television channels to cell phones, using scarce bandwidth more effectively than 3G technologies (Kimutai, 2007). More recently, the Africa Interactive Media Foundation has been involved in the training of mobile reporters, as part of its Voices of Africa Project. Each reporter is equipped with an advanced cell phone, keyboard, telephone credit, and a monthly stipend. The reporters produce articles, photographs and videos and upload the content using their phones (www.Africa-Interactive-Foundation.com).

Somalia   Internet penetration is still very low in Somalia, but cell phone service is well developed. A call from a Somali cell phone, for instance, is usually cheaper and clearer than a call from anywhere else in Africa. After the toppling of the Barre regime in 1991, a number of private telecommunications companies were set up. Today there are at least six privately owned telecommunications companies offering cheap calling rates and high-quality connections compared to most other African countries. With regard to the Internet, there are at least three ISPs, and Somali diaspora communities are avid consumers of Somalia media services online (BBC World Service Trust, 2006).

Tanzania Like Somalia, Internet penetration in Tanzania is below average in Africa; however, cell phone services are growing rapidly. The Tanzania Telecommunications Company Ltd. (TTCL) and Zanzibar Telecommunications Ltd. (Zantel) have introduced the Division Multiple Access (CDMA) system, which is more advanced than the global system for mobile communications (GSM). CDMA is widely used in the United States and Japan, and transmits simultaneous signals over a shared portion of the spectrum. It uses fewer cell sites than GSM, with a calling capacity of between three and five times more (www.digitalopportunity.org).

West Africa

Ghana By 2004, Ghana had registered 140 Internet service providers, 100 of which where registered just that year. Among the Internet service providers in Ghana are Broadband4U, Internet Ghana, and Network Computer Systems (NCS), and Ghana Online. Broadband4U is a service of Ghana Telecom, the formerly state-run corporation that was privatized in 1996. Online television and radio services have also taken off with the Internet Protocol Television (IPTV) and radio Web site, which offers on-demand viewing (Nyarko, 2007). Nearly one-third of Ghanaians have access to the Internet, and mobile telephones are becoming a significant source of news (BBC Country Profile: Ghana, 2007).

The government of President Kufour is among the more aggressive in Africa in pursuing policies to integrate Internet technology into primary education. In 2003, it established a program with Internet Ghana that provided free Internet services at selected secondary schools nationwide.

Nigeria Internet penetration in Nigeria is low relative to the more developed countries; however, it is above average in Africa. Most Nigerians who access the Web do so at cyber-cafes, which have sprouted around major cities and on university campuses. Initially expensive, the cost has fallen dramatically as competition increased and the economy of scale improved. Cybercafes charge as little as 40 cents for 30 minutes of use. Though that is still expensive relative to average income, Nigerian youth and professionals crowd the strategically located cybercafes, sometimes waiting for up to an hour for terminals to become available.

The rapid penetration of cell phones in Nigeria since 2001 illustrates the stifling effect of state monopoly on the adoption of new technologies. In 2001, about two years after the transition to democracy, the government licensed private operators to provide cell phones or GSM services. Overnight, telephone services in Nigeria leaped into the modern era. "The transformation of Nigeria's telecommunications landscape since the licensing of three GSM networks in 2001 and a fourth one in 2002 has been nothing short of astounding. The country continues to be one of the fastest growing markets in

Africa with triple-digit growth rates almost every single year since 2001" (Internet World Stats, 2007).

Democratic Republic of Congo ICTs have not been considered an important part of media reconstruction in DRC and have not been included in development schemes for the country. One of the main challenges is a lack of infrastructure, with a poor landline telephone network, no national fiber-optic backbone, and the absence of a broadband connection (Gjerstad, 2007). The Ministry of Post and Telecommunications and the Post and Telecommunications Regulatory Authority (ARPTC) signed the broadband protocol for the New Partnership for Africa's Development (NEPAD), including the DRC in the Eastern Africa Submarine Cable System (EASSy) project. But it is mobile phones that have experienced the highest growth, with over 70 percent of people owning at least one mobile phone in 2005 (Gjerstad, 2007).

Southern Africa

South Africa South Africa is one of Africa's most advanced countries in communication technologies. The Cape Town-based Naspers, for instance, provides Internet services not just in Africa, but in parts of Asia and Europe. "The media group has been investing in the Internet for 10 years and has previously been building up a presence across Africa, in China, and in Russia" (BBC Naspers, 2007). In order to expand to central and Eastern Europe, Naspers in November 2007 made a $1.9 billion bid to purchase Tradus, a UK-based company that specializes in Internet auctioning. "Tradus has sites in most central and eastern European nations, as well as Denmark, Norway and Switzerland and the UK" (BBC Naspers, 2007).

The rise of Web2.0 technologies and social networking sites such as Facebook.com has affected newsrooms. In South Africa the *Mail and Guardian* newspaper created an application to allow Facebook users to add headlines to their profile pages. Despite shallow Internet penetration, recent statistics show Facebook users in South Africa to be around 350,000, with recruiters such as the Metropolitan Health Group calling for prospective graduates to sign up for their development programming on the Web site (Pather, 2007).

With regard to fiber optics, the Eastern Africa Submarine Cable System, a 9,900-km long undersea fiber-optic cable, was scheduled to be finished in 2008 and will considerably enhance capacity for telecommunications by lowering the cost of connectivity and improving access to high-speed bandwidth (SouthAfrica.info).

The roll-out of digital migration in South Africa is managed by a body called the Digital Dzonga (meaning South), and the switch is scheduled for November 1, 2008. The analog signal is to be switched off on the same date in 2011. The Broadcasting Digital Migration Policy was gazetted in June 2007, and the National Electronic Media Institute of South Africa (NEMISA) plans to establish a digital content hub to produce animated and e-learning products and services (Warby, 2007). The switch from analog to digital transmissions will mean better-quality images and sound, and also result in more frequencies for new broadcast and data services.

Zambia Zambia is about average in Internet penetration in Africa, about 4.4 percent by September 2007. The development of policy to regulate the sector of new communications technologies has been slow. The final draft of the Zambian Information and Communication Technology (ICT) policy was signed off in 2005 (Zambia, 2005), and the development of the broadcasting and telecommunications regulatory bodies was still "un-converged" (Banda, 2006).

Zimbabwe In Zimbabwe, a $100 million project to construct an inner-city fiber-optic network was launched in 2003 by Zimbabwe Express Services to link the country's main cities (World IT Report. 2003).

Journalism Education

Journalism education has advanced considerably in Africa. In several countries, there are universities that offer degrees in journalism or mass communication. In these and other countries, diplomas or associate degrees are also awarded by polytechnics and two-year colleges. The scope of journalism education in Africa is suggested by the fact that in their study of the topic, for instance, Berger and Matras (2007) examined about 100 programs, of which they identified 12 as potential centers of excellence. Berger and Matras conclude that "Africa does not need new or more journalism schools. Instead, the continent needs a core of excellent facilities that make a real impact." (For a recent overview of journalism education in Africa, see De Beer, 2007).

Nigeria and South Africa have several universities and other postsecondary institutions that offer at least the bachelor's degree in journalism or mass communication. Among the notable universities in Nigeria are the University of Lagos, the University of Nigeria, Nsukka, and Bayero University. Among the notable institutions in South Africa that offer degrees in journalism are Rhodes University, Stellenbosch University, and the Tshwane University of Technology. The journalism school at Rhodes University, with its state-of-the-art IT facilities and extended teaching and research programs housed in a modern media building, is arguably the top journalism school in Africa and would compare well with some of the best schools elsewhere (Botha and De Beer, 2007).

Other notable institutions of journalism education in Africa include Makerere University (Uganda), Mozambican School of Journalism, and Centre d'études de sciences et techniques de Information (Senegal).

Although Berger and Matras identify most of these programs as potential centers of excellence, they note that a common deficiency is in modern amenities. "Many African journalism schools are forced to operate in the pre-Internet age" (Berger and Matras, 2007: 41). Others are unable to optimize their potential because of financial constraints. For instance, although Nigeria's premier mass communication department, at the University of Lagos, owns a printing press, it is not operational because of broken parts that have not been replaced.

Still, more than ever before, African journalists are receiving professional education before going into the profession. Others acquire formal education in journalism through seminars and short-course programs while they are already on the job. Some African governments take particular interest in journalism education with the expectation that it would result in more responsible journalism.

Challenges and the Future

As sub-Saharan African countries consolidate their democracy, a number of issues remain with regard to the role and performance of the press. Among them are the continued criminalization of journalistic infractions, the need for information access laws, and the corollary need to improve journalism professionalism.

Decriminalizing Press Infractions

The continued criminalization of journalistic infractions in many countries is readily the most pressing problem facing the press in many African countries. The laws provide the legal basis for arresting, detaining, and imprisoning journalists for everything from irreverent comments to erroneous claims. Governments see such laws as a necessary check on journalistic irresponsibility. However, the application of such laws more often reflects the hypersensitivity and insecurity of the government than the gravity of the press's infractions. Civil proceedings provide more than adequate restraint on the press. In fact, excessive fines in civil cases can have an even more chilling impact on the press. At least they do not constitute as much of an assault on human dignity and freedom as do jails and prisons. Still, governments that recognize the value of press freedom put in place judicial mechanisms that ensure that even civil awards against the press are reasonable.

Facilitating Access to Information

Access to information is a major issue in most African press systems. Left to themselves, governments everywhere would keep their processes secret, revealing only those things that earn them praise or project their authority. Yet, it is the role of the press to ensure that governments are as transparent and accountable to the people as is possible. Attempts to pass laws that guarantee such rights have been resisted by governments in most African countries, including some of the more democratic. In Nigeria, for instance, a freedom of information bill was ultimately passed in 2006 after years of deliberation and negotiation in the National Assembly. However, after stalling for months, President Obasanjo formally announced—at the end of his tenure in 2007—that he would not sign the bill into law. Among his reasons was that the name "Freedom of Information Bill" was inappropriate.

It is not unusual, of course, for presidents to fret about the consequences of laws that grant access to government records. In the United States, President Lyndon Johnson was anything but eager to sign the Freedom of Information Act. He expressed strong reservations to his aides about the consequences of allowing journalists so much access to government information. Ultimately, he was persuaded of the necessity and, perhaps, inevitability. The press in a vast majority of African countries still has to persist to get such rights.

Press Professionalism and Responsibility

Although the tenets of libertarianism place few constraints on the press, in practice an irresponsible press invites the abridgement of its freedom. Though much of the continued censorship in African countries results from government hypersensitivity, political instability, and general disorder, one cannot discount the aspect of journalistic irresponsibility or excesses.

One reason for the excesses is the steam effect—the natural outburst that results when a long repressed press system is opened up (Ibelema, 1994). An article for allafrica.com in November 2007 illustrates the double-edged sword of this outburst in the context of Liberia. Drawing from experience monitoring the Liberian press and hosting a youth-oriented program on a United Nations radio, Boakai M. Fofana cites instances of serious but unsubstantiated claims and irreverent language. Fofana surmised, therefore, that "Although this new openness is welcome, it is alien to some Liberians, who sometimes abuse their rights in the name of free speech" (Fofana, 2007). Liberia is not alone in this regard.

Sometimes political partisanship and ethnic bating drive coverage. During his presidency in the 1990s, for instance, Jerry Rawlings was referred to as a half-caste and mulatto, terms that suggested that he was not fully Ghanaian (Hasty, 2005). Sometimes, there is disregard for cultural sensibility. In its issue of November 3, 1996, for instance, the Ghanaian opposition newspaper the *Statesman* carried the front-page tabloid headline: "NANA KONADU'S SECRET SEXUAL PROBLEMS OUT." It was a reference to President Rawlings's wife, published by a major newspaper while Rawlings was running for reelection (Hasty, 2005:149). Such Fleet Street-type of exposés on personal matters is familiar to readers of London's tabloids. In Africa, they are still shocking, even if they are of scintillating appeal to some readers. They certainly engender little goodwill toward the press from the discerning public and the judiciary.

Even more problematic in the African context is the press's role in inciting ethnic passions. In countries that are experiencing conflict, the press would ideally serve as an arbiter, or at least the vehicle of informed public opinion. It is often not the case, as illustrated by the experience of Rwanda and Côte d'Ivoire, among others. Also, the press generally has professional and technical limitations in its coverage of conflicts. The professional standards and economic and technical capabilities of the press in countries in conflict were usually low even before the conflicts. The conflicts merely exacerbate the deficiencies and further comprise judicious coverage (UNESCO, 2004).

As to professionalism, that is growing. Studies indicate a strong commitment to professional standards and social responsibility among African journalists. A survey of Tanzanian journalists, for instance, shows that they rate journalistic functions such as accuracy, analysis, and investigation highly (Ramaprasad, 2001). Yet, they perceive the role of the press from the perspective of civic or community journalism, thinking of news as a social good for national development. An earlier study of Nigerian journalists reports similar findings (Pratt and McLaughlin, 1990).

Conclusion

The prospects of the African press and Africa's democratization are intertwined. A vibrant press is necessary to consolidate democracy in Africa, regardless of the press's short-comings. Governments that are displeased with the performance of their countries' press—and that is typical everywhere—will be better served to pursue policies that strengthen the press. Among such policies is the improvement of journalism education, as recommended by Berger and Matras (2007), the facilitation of journalism professionalization through self-regulation, and improvements in working conditions for journalists. Repressive policies ultimately backfire, as Rawlings found out in Ghana. They only retard the professional maturity of the press and the consolidation of democracy.

BIBLIOGRAPHY

AfricaFilmTV.com: Ghana. www.africafilmtv.com/pages/profiles/Ghana.htmGhana. Accessed December 24, 2007.

African Development Bank. "Continent Records Highest Growth in Two Decades." Press Release, May 16, 2007. allafrica.com/stories/200705160823.html. Accessed May 24, 2007.

Agbese, A. *The Role of the Press and Communication Technology in Democratization: The Nigerian Story*. New York: Routledge, 2006.

Ainslie, R. *The Press in Africa: Communications Past and Present*. New York: Walker and Company, 1966.

Asante, C. E. *The Press in Ghana: Problems and Prospects*. Lanham, MD: University Press of America, 1996.

Babalola, E. T. "Newspapers as Instruments for Building Literate Communities: the Nigerian Experience." *Nordic Journal of African Studies* 11, No. 3 (2002), 403–410.

Banda, F. "Negotiating Distant Influences: Globalization and Broadcasting Policy Reforms in Zambia and South Africa." *Canadian Journal of Communication,* 31, No. 2 (2006), 459-467.

Barnett, C. "The Limits of Media Democratization in South Africa: Politics, Privatization and Regulation." *Media, Culture and Society* 21, No. 5 (1999), 649–671.

BBC   Country Profile: Botswana. Available: news.bbc.co.uk/2/hi/africa/country_profiles/1068674.stm. Accessed December 22, 2007

———. Djibouti. Available: http://news.bbc.co.uk/2/hi/africa/country_profiles/1070579.stm. Accessed November 16, 2007.

———. Eritrea. Available: http://news.bbc.co.uk/2/hi/africa/country_profiles/1070813.stm#media. Accessed November 16, 2007.

———. Ghana. Available: http://news.bbc.co.uk/1/hi/world/africa/country_profiles/1023355.stm#media. Retrieved November 27, 2007.

———. Liberia. Available: http://news.bbc.co.uk/2/hi/africa/country_profiles/1043500.stm. Accessed December 26, 2007.

———. Nigeria. Available: http://news.bbc.co.uk/1/hi/world/africa/country_profiles/1064557.stm. Retrieved November 26, 2007.

———. South Africa. Available: http://news.bbc.co.uk/2/hi/africa/country_profiles/1071886.stm. Retrieved December 21, 2007

———. Tanzania. Available: http://news.bbc.co.uk/1/hi/world/africa/country_profiles/1072330.stm. Retrieved November 22, 2007.

BBC Naspers. "African Media Group Buys Tradus," December 18, 2007. Available: http://news.bbc.co.uk/2/hi/business/7149434.stm. Accessed December 22, 2007.

BBC World Service Trust. "African Media Development Initiative: Somalia Context." Available: http://downloads.bbc.co.uk/worldservice/trust/pdf/AMDI/somalia/amdi_somalia8_support.pdf (2006). Retrieved November 22, 2007.

Berger, G. (ed.). "Absent Voices, Missed Opportunity: The Media's Silence on ICT Policy Issues in Six African Countries." Highway Africa. Rhodes University, Grahamstown, 2005.

———. (ed.). *Doing Digital Journalism: How Southern African Newsgatherers Are Using ICT.* Cape Town: Mega Digital, 2005.

———. "De-Racialization, Democracy and Development: Transformation of the South African Media 1994–2000." In Tomaselli, K., and Dunn, H., (eds.), *Media, Democracy and Renewal in Southern Africa,* 151–180. Colorado Springs, CO: International Academic Publishers, 2001.

Berger, G., and Matras, C. *Criteria and Indicators for Quality Journalism Training Institutions and Identifying Potential Centres of Excellence in Journalism Training in Africa.* Paris: UNESCO, 2007. Available: http://unesdoc.unesco.org/images/0015/001514/151496E.pdf.

Berger, G. *Media Legislation in Africa: A Comparative Legal Survey.* Grahamstown, South Africa: School of Journalism and Media Studies, Rhodes University (published for UNESCO), 2007.

Bizcommunity. "Rwandan Media Group Halts Own Publications." October 29, 2007. Available: http://www.bizcommunity.com/Article/414/15/19259.html. Retrieved November 7, 2007.

Botha, N., and De Beer, A. S. "South African Journalism Education: Working towards the Future by Looking Back." *Ecquid Novi: African Journalism Studies,* 28, nos. 1&2, 2007, 198–206.

Chibita, M. "Indigenous Language Programming and Citizen Participation in Ugandan Broadcasting: An Exploratory Study." Unpublished doctoral dissertation, University of South Africa, June 2006.

Chikale, E. "Zambia Plans Review of Media Policy." Available: http://www.journalism.co.za. Accessed November 17, 2007.

Collins, R. "From Monopolies, Virtual Monopolies and Oligopolies . . . to What? Media Policy and Convergence in South Africa and the UK." LINK Centre. Wits University Graduate School of Public and Development Management, 2004. Available: http://link.wits.ac.za/papers/rc040421.pdf. Article retrieved October 16, 2007.

Committee to Protect Journalists. "Angola: Prominent Journalist Sent to Jail in Libel Case." Available: www.cpj.org/news/2007/africa/angola05oct07na.html, 2007a. Accessed November 25, 2007.

———. "Benin: CPJ Condemns Jailing of Two Journalists for Criminal Libel." Available: http://www.cpj.org/news/2006/africa/benin04dec06na.html. Accessed November 11, 2007.

———. "In Nigerian Capital, Government Demolishes Broadcaster's Offices." Available: http://www.cpj.org/news/2007/africa/nigeria22jun07na.html, (2007b). Accessed November 11, 2007.

———. "Nigerian Publisher Charged with Sedition over Story Critical of Governor." Available: http://www.cpj.org/news/2007/africa/nigeria17oct07na.html (2007c). Accessed November 11, 2007.

Commonwealth Press Union. "Ghana." Available: www.cpu.org.uk/focus_africa.html. Accessed November 14, 2007.

Communications Commission of Kenya. "CCK Annual Report 2004/2005." Available: www.cck.go.ke/statistics_annual_reports, 2006. Article retrieved November 5, 2007.

De Beer, A. S. (ed.). Project Leader and Editor: Research Report—"Journalism Education in Africa," prepared for the First World Journalism Education Conference (Singapore) and published in *Ecquid Novi* 28, Nos. 1–2 (2007), 156–197 as: Fackson Banda, Catherine M. Beukes-Amiss, Tanja Bosch, Winston Mano, Polly McLean, and Lynette Steenveld, "Contextualising Journalism Education and Training in Southern Africa," *Ecquid Novi: AJS* 28, Nos. 1–2 (2007), 156–175; Terje S. Skjerdal and Charles Muiru Ngugi, "Institutional and Governmental Challenges for Journalism Education in East Africa," *Ecquid Novi: AJS* 28, Nos. 1–2 (2007), 176–190; Folu F. Ogundimu, Olusola Yinka Oyewo, and Lawrence Adegoke, "West African Journalism Education and the Quest for Professional Standards," *Ecquid Novi: AJS* 28, Nos. 1–2 (2007), 191–197.

De Beer, A. S. 2009. "Communication in Africa." In W. Donsbach (ed.-in-chief), *The International Encyclopaedia of Communication.* Oxford: Blackwell. Editorial phase.

Duhul, S. "Somali Government Cracking Down on Media." November 13, 2007. The State.com. Available: http://www.thestate.com/372/story/228312.html

Encyclopedia of the Nations. Available online at www.nationsencyclopedia.com/Africa/Uganda-MEDIA.html. Retrieved November 22, 2007.

Fofana, B. M. "Free Speech Emerges under New Rule," allAfrica.com, November 30, 2007. Accessed November 30, 2007.

Freedom House. *Countries at the Crossroads 2007—Eritrea,* September 25, 2007. UNHCR Refworld. Available: http://www.unhcr.org/cgi-bin/texis/vtx/refworld/rwmain?docid=47386924c. Accessed November 16, 2007.

Freedom House. *Countries at the Crossroads 2007— Ethiopia,* September 25, 2007. Online. UNHCR Refworld. Available: http://www.unhcr.org/cgi-bin/texis/vtx/refworld/rwmain?docid=4738692464. Accessed November 16, 2007.

Gjerstad, L. Democratic Republic of Congo. Global Information Society Watch, 2007. Available: http://www.globaliswatch.org/files/pdf/GISW_DRC.pdf. Retrieved November 21, 2007.

Gulere, C. "The Role of the Indigenous Languages in HIV/AIDS Prevention." *International Conf AIDS* 12 (1998), 689.

Haffajee, F. "The SABC go-around." *Mail&Guardian,* June 6–12., 2008, 4.

Hasty, J. *The Press and Political Culture in Ghana.* Bloomington: Indiana University Press, 2005.

Ibelema, M. "Professionalism as Risk Management: A Typology of Journalists in Developing Countries." *Journal of Development Communication* 5, No. 1 (1994), 22–32.

———. "The Nigerian Press and June 12: Pressure and Performance During a Political Crisis." *Journalism and Communication Monographs* 4, No. 4 (2003), 161–209.

———. *The African Press, Civic Cynicism, and Democracy.* New York: Palgrave Macmillan, 2008.

Ibelema, M., Powell, L., and Self, W. "Press Freedom as a Logistical Notion." *Free Press Yearbook* 38 (2000), 98–115.

Independent Communications Authority of South Africa (ICASA). "Inquiry into Regional Television." Discussion paper. August 22, 2003.

Independent Online. "Eritrea Accuses Ethiopia of Jamming Media." October 9, 2007. Available: http://www.iol.co.za. Retrieved November 15, 2007.

International Marketing Council of South Africa. "The Press in South Africa." Available: www.southafrica. info/ess_info/sa_glance/constitution/news.htm. Accessed December 22, 2007.

International Press Institute "World Press Freedom Review 2006—Benin." Available: http://www.freemedia.at/ cms/ipi/freedom_detail.html?country=/KW0001/KW0006/KW0141/. Accessed September 14, 2007.

———. "World Press Freedom Review 2006—Gambia." Available: http://www.freemedia.at/cms/ipi/ freedom_ detail.html?country=/KW0001/KW0006/KW0156/&year=2006

———. "World Press Freedom Review 2006b—Ghana." Available: http://www.freemedia.at/cms/ipi/ freedom_detail.html? country=/KW0001/KW0006/KW0157/. Accessed September 14, 2007.

———. "World Press Freedom Review 2006c—Mali." Available: http://www.freemedia.at/cms/ipi/ freedom_detail.html? country=/KW0001/KW0006/KW0165/. Accessed September 22, 2007.

———. "World Press Freedom Review 2006—Niger." Available: http://www.freemedia.at/cms/ipi/freedom_ detail.html?country=/KW0001/KW0006/KW0170/&year=2006

Internet World Stats. "Nigeria: Internet Usage and Marketing Report." Available: http://www.internet-worldstats.com/af/ng.htm. Accessed on December 9, 2007.

IREX. International Research and Exchanges Board. Media Sustainability Index Africa. Available: http://www.irex.org/programs/MSI_Africa/Somalia.asp. Accessed on November 16, 2007.

Kabemba, C. The State of the Media in the Democratic Republic of Congo. Electoral Institute of Southern Africa (EISA) Occasional Paper no. 30, March 2005. Available: http://www.eisa.org.za/PDF/OP30. pdf. Retrieved November 21, 2007.

Kayanja, R. D. "The Current State of Media Reform in Uganda." In Price, M. E., Rozumilowicz, B., and Verhulst, S. G. (eds.), *Media Reform: Democratizing the Media, Democratizing the State,* 155–179. New York: Routledge, 2002.

Kafewo, S. "Ghana AMDI Research Report," December 21, 2006. Available: http://www.bbc.co.uk/world-service/trust/reserchlearning/story/2006/12/061206_amdi_ghana.shtml. Retrieved July 17, 2008.

Kenya Country Report. Available: http://downloads.bbc.co.uk/worldservice/trust/pdf/AMDI/kenya/ amdi_kenya6_television.pdf

Khan, A. W. "Foreword to *Media Legislation in Africa: A Comparative Legal Survey,*" by Guy Berger. Grahamstown, South Africa: School of Journalism and Media Studies, Rhodes University (published for UNESCO), 2007.

Kimutai, C. "Kenya Gets Mobile TV." Available: www.bizcommnity.com/Article/111/66/19189.html. Retrieved November 22, 2007.

LaFraniere, S. "As Angola Rebuilds, Most Find Their Poverty Persists." *New York Times,* October 14, 2007.

Langmia, K. *The Internet and the Construction of the Immigrant Public Sphere: The Case of the Cameroonian Diaspora.* Lanham, MD: University Press of America, 2008.

Limbobo, A. *The Media Landscape in Mozambique. A Country Audit Commissioned by AMARC.* MISA, Mozambique, 2006.

Mafu, S. "From the Oral Tradition to the Information Era: The Case of Tanzania." *International Journal on Multicultural Societies* 6, No. 1 (2004), 53–78.

Martin, L. J. "Africa." In Merrill, J. C. (ed.), *Global Journalism: A Survey of the World's Mass Media,* 190–248. New York: Longman, 1983.

Media Watch. Media Council of Tanzania. Available: www.mct.or.tz/full.asp?id=164. Retrieved November 22, 2007.

MISA. "Malawi Slashes Funding for Broadcasters." September 13, 2007. Available: http://www.bizcommunity.com/Article/410/59/18025.html

Mulongeni, B. "Media and Broadcasting in Namibia." Workshop on National Information and Communication Infrastructure (NICI) for Namibia, May 11–13, 1998. Available: www.uneca.org/aisi/nici/country_profiles/namibia/nampap4.htm. Accessed December 24, 2007

Mundua, S. "The East African Community. Global Journalist: The Online Magazine for the International News Business." Available: http://web.missouri-edu/~umcjourglobjourwww/web-content/stories/2007_07/02EAC/page1.html

National Union of Somali Journalists. "Popular Radio Station Silenced, NUSOJ Strongly Protests." Press Release, November 12, 2007. Available: www.nusoj.org/. Accessed November 12, 2007.

Nkya, A. "Media Still Treats Women as Sex Workers, Mothers, Wives." September 3, 2003. Available: http://www.warmafrica.com.

Nyarko, E. "Online Television and Radio Service Begins Operating in Ghana." Available: http://www.bizcommunity.com/Article/83/23/15578.html. Article retrieved on November 27, 2007.

Ogbondah, C. W. *State-Press Relations in Nigeria (1993–1998): Human Rights and Democratic Development.* Ibadan: Spectrum Books, 2003.

Okunna, C. S. "Gender and Communication in Nigeria: Is This the Twenty-first Century?" *International Journal of Media and Cultural Politics* 1, No. 1 (2005), 127–130.

Pather, S. "Recruiters Employ Facebook." *The Times,* September 21, 2007, 18.

Pearce, J. "Angola in 2007." *Rhodes Journalism Review,* September 27, 2007, 44.

Pereira, A. "A Brief Look at the New Press Law." *Rhodes Journalism Review,* September 27, 2007, 45.

Philippart, M. Media Status Report: Burundi, 2000. Available: http://www.gret.org/parma/uk2/ressource/edm/pdf/burundi.pdf

Pratt, C. B., and McLaughlin, G. W. "Ethical Dimensions of Nigerian Journalists and Their Newspapers." *Journal of Mass Media Ethics* 5, No. 1 (1990), 30–34.

Ramaprasad, J. A. "Profile of Journalists in Post-independence Tanzania." *International Communication Gazette* 63, No. 6 (2001), 539–555.

Salawu, A. "Rich History, Uncertain Future." *Rhodes Journalism Review* 26 (September 2006).

———. "Social Status as a Factor for the Readership of Yoruba Newspapers in Nigeria." *Nordic Journal of African Studies* 13, No. 2 (2004), 200–215.

Somalia Media Guide. Available: http://www.redorbit.com/news/technology/834036/somalia_media_guide_february_2007/index.html?source=r_technology.

SouthAfrica.info reporter. African fiber-optic cable on track. January 24, 2006. Available: http://www.southafrica.info/doing_business/economy/infrastructure/ecfibreoptic.htm.

Stevenson, R. L. "Freedom of the Press around the World." In Merrill, J. C. (ed.), *Global Journalism: Survey of International Communication,* 3rd ed., 63–76. White Plains, NY: Longman, 1995.

"Tanzanian Phone Firms Adopt New CDMA Technology." Available: http://www.digitalopportunity.org/article/view/125150/1/. Retrieved November 21, 2007.

Tomaselli, K. "Media Ownership and Democratization." In Hyden, G., Leslie, M., and Ogundimu, F. (eds.), *Media and Democracy in Africa,* pp. 129–155. New Brunswick, NJ: Transaction Publishers, 2002.

UNESCO. "The Partnership for Media and Conflict Prevention in West Africa. Supporting the Media in Liberia: A Review of the Media Landscape for the Post-Conflict Transition Period, 2004." Available: http://portal.unesco.org/ci/en/files/18570/11128868501supporting_media_liberia.pdf/ supporting_media_liberia.pdf. Retrieved November 27, 2007.

United Nations Development Programme. *Human Development Index 2004.* New York: United Nations Development Programme, 2004.

Warby, V. "High-def TV satellite for 2010." 2007. Available: http://www.news24.com

Wild, K. "The Importance of Convergence in the ICT Policy Environment." Association for Progressive Communications Issue Papers Series.

World Association of Newspapers. "The Challenge of Local Languages" [2003]. Available: http://www. rap21.org/article1664.html. Retrieved on November 15, 2007.

World IT Report. "Optic Fiber Project Launched in Zimbabwe." April 9, 2003. Available: http://findarticles.com

Yusuf, H. "Using Tech to Talk Back." MIT Center for Future Civic Media, October 29, 2007. Available: http://civic.mit.edu/?m=20071031

Zambia. Ministry of Transport and Communications. *National Information and Communications Policy.* Lusaka, Zambia: Ministry of Transport and Communications, 2005.

CHAPTER

17 Asia and the Pacific

JIAFEI YIN

Central Michigan University, USA

A Continent in the Eye of the World

Perhaps more than any other continent, Asia, and especially China, is catching the attention of the world in the first decade of the twenty-first century. In the 1990s, a ten-videocassette series of educational video was produced by the Annenberg/CPB Project entitled, "The Pacific Century." The cover story of *Newsweek*'s May 9, 2005 edition carried the title, "China's Century," while *Time* magazine's January 22, 2007 edition's cover was titled, "China: Dawn of a New Dynasty." The rise of Asian economies led by China and India on the heels of economic miracles of Japan, and the "four little dragons"—Singapore, South Korea, Hong Kong and Taiwan—has awakened the rest of the world to the impact of such breathtaking growth on global trade, the global labor market and global environment.

Just by its sheer size, Asia is an impressive continent. It is perhaps best known for the size of its population. It occupies 29.5 percent of the world's land area but supports 60 percent of its population. Of the ten most populous countries in the world, six are in Asia, and seven metropolises in Asia make it to the top 10 list of the world's most populous cities. Together, China and India account for more than one-third of the world's population, while Indonesia is the largest Muslim country in the world. A large population provides a mass market for the media but puts enormous stress on the environment. Three Asian countries ranked the second, third, and fourth of the world's largest economies in 2007, measured in GDP's purchasing power parity—China with a GDP of $10 trillion, Japan $4.2 trillion, and India $4.1 trillion. The United States was number one with GDP of $13 trillion. Measured by GDP per capita, Japan, Singapore, Hong Kong, Macao, and South Korea were also among the top 36 countries and regions.

However, diversity defines Asia and the Pacific region and its mass media, and contrasts among Asian countries sometimes can be disturbing. In the South Pacific, many island nations have small populations. While some countries in Asia are at the top of the GDP ranking list, other less developed and often smaller nations such as Afghanistan, Nepal, Bhutan, East Timor, Laos, Cambodia, and Bangladesh are located toward the bottom of the list and often overshadowed by their neighbors with faster economic growth.

Such extreme contrasts in wealth come from the much-diversified economic systems practiced in Asia, including *laissez-faire* capitalism, state-guided capitalism, rigid communism, and communist systems undergoing major reforms, such as in China and Vietnam. Different levels of economic development help explain the varied pace of media development on the continent.

Asia's political systems are as varied as its economic ones. They range from constitutional monarchy in Japan and Thailand to parliamentary democracies, quasi-democracies, communism, authoritarian governments, and governments with civilian and military leaders taking turns, as in Pakistan. However, the general trend on the continent is toward liberalization, with new democracies appearing, such as in Indonesia, the Philippines, South Korea, and Taiwan, and more countries opening up, such as China, India, Vietnam, and Laos even though there are still setbacks occasionally, such as the military coup in Thailand in 2006. The political system in any given Asian country determines the level of government control of the media, but culture also plays a big role in the control of news.

Asia has a rich and diverse cultural heritage. Two of the world's four ancient civilizations are in Asia—Chinese and Indian. The Chinese language is the only ancient language still used in the world today, and the ancient Chinese philosopher-educator Confucius still has a strong and widespread influence on politics, business, and culture in East Asia and parts of Southeast Asia. India is the birthplace of Buddhism, which is popular throughout Asia and has been spread to other continents as well. All the major religions in the world today originated in Asia and the Middle East. As a result, different religions coexist on the continent. The ethnic and religious mix adds to the strength and vitality of Asia, but it also poses challenges to stability in the region and to the Asian value of harmony. In some countries, such as Malaysia and Singapore, it is a tough issue for the news media. The countries of Asia and the Pacific are shown in Figure 17.1.

Media Overview

One major characteristic of the Asian media is its uneven development across the continent. With the support of commercial advertising and the high literacy rate in more developed societies such as Japan, South Korea, and Singapore, the news media have become highly profitable businesses, and several major media corporations dominate the industry in the respective countries. In China and India, the news media have taken off, benefiting from the expanding economies. But in economies that are still struggling to provide a basic living standard for its people, the news media lack the resources and audience base to develop; in many cases, they have become easy targets of government control as some of them have to depend on the government for subsidies, government advertising, or newsprint (e.g. see McNicol, 2005).

In contrast, economic reforms and open policies in China and Vietnam have led to a more relaxed political environment for the news media. In East and Southeast Asia, the wind of freedom has swept through the Philippines, Indonesia, South Korea, and Taiwan as dictators or military governments have been overthrown and martial law has been ended. Taking advantage of the new opportunities, the news media in these countries experienced phenomenal growth, as if releasing pent-up energy. The number of newspapers and maga-

FIGURE 17.1 Asia, Australasia and the Pacific

zines doubled or even trebled, and reporters are allowed to explore new territories that used to be taboo.

But the progress of press freedom on the continent is mixed, and democracy is still fragile where it was newly restored. In Hong Kong, the press remained free, dynamic and diverse 10 years after its return to the Chinese mainland, despite criticism of central government pressure. In China, the government was hypersensitive to political coverage in the days leading up to the Seventeenth Party Congress in 2007. In Indonesia and the Philippines, governments restored some control of the media, while in Nepal, Sri Lanka,

Thailand, and Pakistan, freedom was in retreat due to tightened government control as a result of resumed civil war, military coup, or deteriorating security in these countries.

Self-censorship remains a major concern in Asian journalism. The self-interest of the media and concern for national development and image often lead the news media to practice self-censorship. After all, development journalism originated in Asia, more specifically India and the Philippines, and it still represents the mainstream journalism in Asia today, even though it is practiced in different ways and in different environments. Sadly, however, much of the mainstream media in Asia caters to the elite while ignoring the needs of the poor in their societies.

News media in Pacific island countries are still developing and, to a great extent, depend on foreign aid and expertise for the operation of some of the media and for the training of the staff. Most of the countries in the Pacific have a democratic political system. However, governments in the region occasionally take actions to silence the media when news coverage of government corruption becomes too critical.

Historical Highlights of the Asian Press

Sizable, diverse, and with a long history, the Asian press has traveled an amazingly similar path in various countries across the continent—indigenous press started early, introduced to modern newspapers by Western Christian missionaries, and vernacular papers springing up to lead revolutionary struggles for national independence. Notable exceptions were Japan, which invaded and occupied many of the Asian nations before and during World War II, and Thailand, which is the only Asian nation that has never been invaded or occupied by a foreign power.

The Ancient Asian Press

Asia hosts two of the four ancient civilizations—India and China. Paper was invented by Ts'ai Lun in China in A.D. 105, and in 610 the technology was introduced to Japan. By 800 it reached Egypt and from there it spread to Morocco. It was the Moors who brought paper to Europe (Brackenburg, 2005). But despite the fact that both the paper and the printing press were invented in China, indigenous, official, but primitive papers, called *Dibao,* had dominated the Chinese press scene for about a thousand years until foreign missionaries established modern newspapers in China in the early nineteenth century. They were the earliest newspapers in China and among the earliest newspapers in the world. There are disagreements among scholars as to when exactly they first appeared as only two copies of them printed in the Tang Dynasty (A.D. 618–907) still exist today; one is housed in the British Library in London and the other in the National Library of France in Paris. Those two copies are the earliest primitive newspapers left in the world today. They carried mostly information concerning government affairs (Fang, 1996). During the Song Dynasty (960–1279) *Dibao* was also called *Chaobao.* For the next three dynasties (1279–1911)—Yuan, Ming, and Qing—*Dibao* and *Chaobao* continued without major changes.

Nonofficial underground papers, called *Xiaobao* (little paper), also existed in China. By the late Ming Dynasty, the government allowed nonofficial papers to be printed, hence the birth of the earliest legal nonofficial papers, *Jingbao* (capital paper), which carried not only official information, but also stories by their own reporters. By the Qing Dynasty, most of these *Jingbao* were dailies and had their own names. *Jingbao* was the most developed of the indigenous papers in China.

The history of the Japanese press, though shorter, resembled that of China—a tradition of indigenous publications followed by modern newspapers introduced from the West in the nineteenth century. Research on early newspapers in Japan mostly started with *kawara-ban* broadsheets, which, according to *Encyclopedia Britannica-Macropaedia,* appeared continuously throughout the Tokugawa period (1603–1867), reporting popular festivals, personal scandals, natural disasters, and important events.

Both Japan and Korea were heavily influenced by the ancient Chinese culture and the early beneficiaries of Chinese inventions such as paper and movable type printing. Today's Japanese language still contains Chinese characters in their earlier forms. In Korea the first script materials (through A.D. 313) used in reading and writing were Chinese texts and characters, and surviving printed works in Chinese script date back to the Koryo Dynasty (935–1392) (Gilmore-Lehne, 2007). Korea also has a long history of newspaper publishing. The first known paper was published in A.D. 692.

Missionary and Colonial Press in Asia in the Nineteenth Century

Modern newspapers were first introduced to China by foreign missionaries during the early nineteenth century when European colonialists led by Great Britain were trying to force open the door of China. As the number of foreign merchants, missionaries, and officials in China increased, foreign newspapers were published with the purpose of "protecting the public interest of the foreign community" (Fang, 1996:23.) At the time there were more foreign-language newspapers in China than newspapers in Chinese. Other than newspapers published by missionaries, there were also mercantile papers published by foreigners. From 1815 to the late nineteenth century, foreigners published more than 200 newspapers in China, accounting for more than 80 percent of the total.

Missionary papers promoted Christianity and the superiority of Western civilization. The first such publication in Chinese, *Chashisu Meiyue Tongjizhuan* (the *China Monthly Magazine*), was published in 1815 in Malacca outside China because the government banned missionaries at the time. The magazine tried hard to appeal to Chinese readers by citing Confucian teachings and Chinese classics in explaining Christian values. The first modern publication in Chinese published inside China, *Dongxiyangkao Meiyue Tongjizhuan* (the *East West Monthly Magazine*), appeared in Canton in 1833. *Wanguo Gongbao,* a weekly, founded in 1868 in Shanghai, was the most influential, the longest lasting (about 40 years), and the most widely circulated (peaking at 54,000 copies) among religious publications after the Opium War.

After the Opium War, China's doors were forced open, and trade followed. The mercantile press replaced missionary papers as the dominant press run by the colonialists. The foreign-language press flourished in Hong Kong, and in Shanghai the *North China Daily News* (formerly *North China Herald*) was the most influential. Among Chinese-language mercantile papers in Shanghai, *Shenbao,* started in 1872, had the longest history and the most influence. *Zhaowen Xinbao,* launched in 1873, was the first newspaper published by the Chinese even though it lasted only several months. The most influential Chinese-run paper was *Xunhuan Daily,* founded by Wang Tao, who was known for his political commentary promoting reforms in China.

The nineteenth century also witnessed the development of modern newspapers in Japan. As in China, English-language newspapers predated modern vernacular papers in the country. The first English-language newspaper, *The Nagasaki Shipping List and Advertiser,* was launched in 1861. Six years later in 1867, the first modern Japanese paper, *Koko Shimbun,* appeared. The decade also saw the birth of several other giants of contemporary Japanese newspapers. The first daily newspaper, the *Yokohoma Mainichi,* was started in 1870. Four years later the leading national daily in modern Japan, *Yomiuri Shimbun,* was born. Also, the *Osaka Nippo* (1876) and the *Ssaka Asahi* (1879) were to become, respectively, the *Osaka Mainichi* and the *Asahi Shimbun* (Encyclopaedia Britannica).

Two financial resources supported the development of modern Japanese newspapers—advertising and political patronage. The rise in the literacy rate and the growth of the advertising industry spurred development of the press industry. Between the 1870s and 1900s, newspaper circulation jumped from several thousand to more than a million (Moeran, undated).

Newspapers appeared a little later in Korea in 1883 when the first Korean newspaper was launched, but it lasted only three years (Lankov, 2007). In 1896 Korea's first privately-published modern newspaper, *The Independent* (*The Tongnip Shinmun*), was born, and it closed three years later after a series of run-ins with the royal court. In 1898 Korea saw its first daily newspaper, the *Maeil Shinmun.* Before *The Independent,* most of the papers in Korea were published in Chinese, which had long been the language of the educated and privileged minority.

In India, researchers credited the *Bengal Gazette* or *Calcutta General Advertiser* published in 1780 as the first modern newspaper in the country, which was earlier than its counterpart in East Asia because of the presence of the East India Company (Natarajan, 1962.) Most of the early publications were short lived and small in circulation. Four weeklies and one monthly existed around 1786, but only the *India Gazette* survived in 1799.

The nineteenth century saw the birth of many of India's great English-language newspapers, including the *Times of India,* the *Bombay Statesman,* the *Indian Economist,* the *Statesman,* the *Englishman,* the *Bombay Times,* the *Bombay Gazette,* and the *Native Herald.* But the Indian press developed slowly. In 1871 there was only one Indian daily newspaper in the English language, the *Indian Mirror.* In 1878 the *Hindu* was launched as a weekly, which was soon recognized as a leading voice of the Indian opinion. Given the sensitive political situation in the colony, newspapers assumed different political positions. In Calcutta, the *Statesman* espoused Indian causes; the *Englishman* opposed them; and the *Indian Daily News* pursued a middle policy.

In Sri Lanka, the *Government Gazette* marked the beginning of the press in the country in 1802 (Desai, 2002). The first paper that actually carried news was *Colombo Journal,* published in 1832. Two other newspapers followed, the *Observer and Commercial Advertiser* and the *Ceylon Times,* which later became the famous *Times of Ceylon.* The vernacular press began in 1860 with the publication of *Lankaloka* in Galle, and the first Sinhala weekly newspaper, *Lakminapahana,* appeared in 1862.

In Indonesia the Dutch published the first newspapers also in the nineteenth century. Most publications printed news from Europe instead of local events. The first local general interest paper, the *Bataviasche Courant,* was founded in 1816, and the name was later changed to the *Javasche Courant,* which continued publication until the Japanese occupation in 1942 (Yoder, 2002). By the middle of the century, there were about 30 Dutch newspapers published in Indonesian islands. The first Indonesian periodicals, which started to appear in the mid-1800s, were also financed by the Dutch. Real Indonesian newspapers did not appear until the early twentieth century when the nationalist movement was about to start.

The Asian Press in the Struggle for National Independence

Around the turn of the century much of the Asian press was leading the fight for national independence. In China reformist papers mushroomed in Beijing, Shanghai, Tianjin, and other major cities in China, which was reduced to a semifeudal and semicolonial state with major Western powers carving out concessions in the major cities of China. A total of around 120 Chinese publications were in circulation in 1895–1898. Kang Youwei and Liang Qichao were among the pioneers of the reformist movement, and both published papers of their own. Kang published *Zhongwai Jiwen* in Beijing and *Qiangxuebao* in Shanghai. Because of their political commentary, both papers were banned. A more radical press was the Chinese revolutionary press led by Dr. Sun Yat-sen, who advocated the overthrow of the imperial government and the establishment of a republic. One such paper, *Subao,* was also shut down, and five of the main contributors were arrested. There were other patriotic but nonrevolutionary papers, such as the *Dagongbao* in Tianjin and the *Shibao* in Shanghai.

During the early days of the republic, the press experienced unprecedented freedom. The number of newspapers increased sharply, totaling more than 500. But the brief restoration soon ended the free press. One of the most well-known journalists during this period was Shao Piaoping, who devoted his whole life to journalism and was executed for his antirestoration views in his paper. But more radical papers, such as *Xinqingnian* (the New Youth), spearheaded the New Culture Movement in China under the banners of "Mr. Democracy" and "Mr. Science," and later started to introduce the Bolshevik revolution and Marxism. Nonpartisan commercial papers, such as *Shenbao, Xinwenbao,* and *Dagongbao,* continued their success stories of expansion.

In 1931 the Japanese invasion and occupation of northeastern China shocked the whole country. One patriotic journalist, Zou Taofen, distinguished himself in rallying the people against the Japanese invasion and criticizing the Nationalist government for busily fighting the Communists instead of the Japanese invaders. Another journalist, Fan Changjiang, made a name for himself by reporting exclusively for *Dagongbao,* rated the best international newspaper in 1941 at The School of Journalism, University of Missouri-Columbia, on the Long March of the Communists. *Shenbao* also called for fighting the Japanese invaders and opposed the civil war. As a result, its publisher, Shi Liangcai, was assassinated (Fang, 1996). In 1937, the Japanese expanded the war inside China and occupied Beijing, Tianjin, and Shanghai. The anti-Japanese press in the Nationalist-controlled part of the country was heavily censored (Fang, 1996; MacKinnon, 1997), while in

Communist-controlled areas, Communist media continued to expand, including the establishment of the Xinhua news agency. The Communist media played a big role in the victory of the Communists in China in 1949.

In Korea there was a newspaper boom in the late 1890s and early 1900s. In 1898 four new papers were launched (Lankov, 2007). In 1905, Korea became a Japanese dependency. During the two world wars, the Japanese occupiers closed down nearly all Korean-language periodicals and encouraged the spread of Japanese-language newspapers. In 1910–1919, most Korean newspapers were published outside Korea in Russia and China (Lankov, 2007). In 1919 the funeral of the last independent king, King Kojong, sparked an outbreak of mass anticolonial demonstrations, which effectively ended the harsh colonial rule in the country. The press became the first beneficiary of the relaxed political rule and was well on its way to develop and play a significant role in the fight for national independence.

In India conditions in the colony were getting grimmer in the mid-1890s, and the Indian press protested discriminatory laws despite sedition laws (Natarajan, 1962). Outside India, there were the *Free Hindustan* in America and the *Indian Sociologist* in London and Paris. The widening gap between the British administration and the Indian people led to a national awakening to colonial rule in 1910s. The Anglo-Indian papers hardened into the defender of the government. Indian newspapers, however, reflected Indian public opinion. The movement for national independence was in full swing, and the press played a key role in the struggle. Among the papers at the time, the *Pioneer* served as the voice of the British official. The *Times of India* half-heartedly supported the moderate leaders of the Indian National Congress, and the *Statesman* shifted from vigorous support of Indian opinion to its advocacy of British commercial interests.

In 1919 the Sedition Committee Report sparked a nationwide fire. Gandhi led a campaign to protest against the laws. The Jallianwala Bagh massacre and martial law in Punjab followed in quick succession. Indian newspapers condemned the crackdown. The *Independent* launched by Motilal Nehru in 1919 was considered an organ of extreme Indian opinion. With the expansion of the movement for national independence, the Anglo-Indian press began to lose ground except in Bombay and Calcutta. The *Mail* of Madras lost to the *Hindu;* the *Pioneer* to the *Leader;* the *Daily Gazette* of Karachi to the *Sind Observer;* and the *Civil and Military Gazette* to the *Tribune.*

From 1923 to 1930, encouraged by the relaxed political climate, S. Sadanand built his media empire with the establishment of the Free Press of India News Agency, and more than a half dozen newspapers in the major cities. The history of Sadanand ventures is the history of the Indian press (Natarajan, 1962). In contrast to the proliferation of the Indian press, the British press in India was in retreat. The *Pioneer* was passed into Indian hands in 1933; the *Englishman* merged into the *Statesman.* Party presses started to appear. In Bombay there was a Congress newspaper, the *Bombay Chronicle.* The start of World War II was the last straw for British rule in India. The *National Herald* launched an all-out campaign against the colonial Indian government. With the help of the Indian press, which gained strength during the war, the "Quit India" movement prevailed.

Pakistan as an independent country had a much shorter history. When the country became independent in 1947 from British India, only four major Muslim-owned newspapers existed in the area. They were the *Pakistan Times,* the *Zamindar,* the *Nawa-I-Waqt,* and the *Military Gazette,* all located in Lahore. As the partition of India was caused by religious conflicts, a number of Muslim papers moved to Pakistan, including *Dawn,* the *Morning News,* and the Urdu-language dailies *Anjam* and *Jang.*

The Indonesian press traveled a similar route. The first Indonesian-language and Indonesian-sponsored newspaper, the *Medan Prijaji,* began publication in 1907, and soon more Indonesian publications followed. With little advertising, these early vernacular papers became instruments of communication for the early nationalist movement and rallied people to the Budi Utomo (High Endeavor) movement founded in 1908 (Yoder, 2002). When the Japanese invaded the islands in 1942, all Dutch and most Indonesian newspapers were banned. The independence fight for the Indonesians was a long one, first against the Dutch, then the Japanese. In both, the press played an indispensable role in helping set the country free.

In contrast to declining newspaper circulations in the West, Asia hosts a large number of mass-circulating daily newspapers, and most of them concentrated in East Asia. Of the top 10 circulating newspapers in the world today, nine are from East Asia, seven of which are published in Japan and two in China. *Yomiuri Shimbun* of Japan tops the list with a combined circulation of morning and evening editions of 14 million, according to a 2005 report by the World Association of Newspapers. It was listed in the *Guinness Book of Records* as the largest daily newspaper in the world. *Asahi Shimbun* also of Japan follows closely with a circulation of 12 million. Of the next ten largest newspapers in the world, six are printed in Asia—three in South Korea, two in Japan and one in India.

The wonder of the press industry in Asia does not stop at the mass-circulation numbers. The readership in Asia is much larger than the circulation numbers, which are only the tip of the iceberg. For example, *Thai Rath* of Thailand has a circulation of 1.2 million, but its readership is six times higher (Ekachai, 2000:440). The same is true of *Kompas* of Indonesia, which has a circulation of around 525,000 but a readership of 2.04 million (Gunaratne and Wattegama, 2000:291). One reason can be the high population density in these countries. Another reason may be social. In China, institutions subscribe to newspapers for their employees. Pass-along readership is typically high across the region.

Asians are avid newspaper readers because the Asian culture values reading and education, and also because of its large population. The potential for the growth of newspaper circulation is still huge if literacy rates continue to improve: India is currently at 61 percent and Pakistan at 43 percent. Strong and rising economies in Asia also support the expansion of the press industry in the region.

Many of the leading dailies in Asian countries are conservative, elitist, and powerful. Because of the Asian cultural tradition and their self-interest, they often do not challenge the government as vigorously as their Western counterparts do. But despite their phenomenal success, Asian newspapers face tough competition from their domestic rivals, international publishers, and the new media.

East Asia

Today any foreign visitor to China expecting to be exposed to monolithic and tightly controlled Communist media would have a big surprise in store for them. The media in China today are increasingly driven by market pressure since the country has started the economic reforms. With the national economy substantially decentralized and increasingly market-oriented, the Chinese media today are quite diversified and commercialized. With access to the Internet widely available with a monthly fee, complete control of information is no longer technically feasible.

The print media in China has experienced an explosive growth as people have realized that newspapers and magazines can be moneymakers. One journalism scholar, Fang Hanqi, said the industry had become "a pillar of the national economy" (International, News Media Seminar, 2000), while it used to be regarded mostly as a political tool. In 2006 there were 2,200 newspapers and 9,500 magazines published in China. Newspapers using the languages of ethnic minorities total 84. To prepare for the competition with foreign media as China is now a member of the World Trade Organization, 16 newspaper groups have been formed. The first and the largest by advertising revenue, the Guangzhou Daily newspaper media group, owns seven subsidiaries and 14 publications in addition to the namesake flagship. Established in 1996, the group has print centers across China. Other groups include the China Daily News Group, the Guangming Daily Group, the Economic Daily Group, and the Wenhui-Xinmin Group.

Besides the *Reference News* (circulation at 2.6 million) and the *People's Daily* (circulation at 2.5 million), top-circulating papers include many of the metropolis evening papers, such as the *Yangtse Evening Post* in Nanjing (circulation at 1.7 million), the *Yangcheng Evening News* in Guangzhou (1.3 million), the *Xinmin Evening News* in Shanghai (1 million), and the *Beijing Evening News* (950,000). Major metropolis dailies also have large circulations, such as the *Guangzhou Daily* (1.6 million), the *Southern Metropolis News* (1.4 million), and the *Chutian Metro Daily* in Wuhan (1 million). TV guides in major cities, like evening papers, are also popular as they are less political and more entertainment-oriented. Newspapers in China today have to stay competitive and profitable by appealing to their readers. They need to make themselves viable economic entities now that the government has ended subsidies for most of them.

To be competitive as a result of market pressure, some newspapers and magazines are pioneering investigative journalism in China despite fierce resistance from local governments. Corruption is rampant in China, and it causes public discontent. It is so bad that the head of the State Administration for Production Safety, Zhang Baoming, encouraged the media to investigate major industrial accidents, almost every one of which, he said, was connected with corruption (Giving the Media a Greater Voice, 2002). One financial magazine, *Caijing,* made a name for itself for muckraking the financial service sector. Other papers resort to sensationalism to sell papers, which has severely damaged the credibility of news reporting. Tabloids are no longer rarities in China.

Reference News published by the official Xinhua news agency is the largest newspaper in China. It is a Chinese translation of news stories published in the foreign media. The leading position of the paper is likely to hold when the percentage of the population who can read a foreign language expands. *People's Daily* remains the voice of the Communist Party. *China Daily* is a product of China's economic reforms. Started in 1981, it is the only national English-language daily newspaper in China. Its Web site ranks among the top 10 most visited sites hosted in China. Many of the major Chinese newspapers can be accessed on the Internet today, including the *People's Daily,* which also has an English online version.

The magazine market in China has witnessed even bigger changes and expansion. Before the reforms, the "consumer magazine" was a novel concept, and the magazine titles were limited. Today an amazing number of consumer magazines are found in bookstores and libraries and are sold at the newsstands on the curbside, at subway stations, and in the post offices. There is a title for almost every demographic group, interest, or hobby, with more titles on sports, as well as Chinese versions of fashion, and women magazines, such as *Elle* and *Vogue*. News magazines are on the rise as well.

In Hong Kong, the tenth anniversary of the transfer of sovereignty to China was marked by a still diverse and flourishing media ("Hong Kong Marks," 2007), although a survey of Hong Kong journalists showed increased self-censorship (Cheung, 2007). Hong Kong is a media-saturated society, which was known in the 1970s as "a city of a hundred newspapers" (*China Journalism Yearbook,* 1998:717). Hong Kong's print media is fiercely competitive with nearly 50 daily newspapers ("HK Press Freedom," 2007) and around 700 magazines and journals. About 30 of the newspapers are in Chinese, 10 in English, and the rest are in other languages or bilingual. Around 20 papers cover mostly local and world news; three focus on financial news, and the rest comprise the popular press or tabloids, which lead circulation in Hong Kong and thrive on sensationalism, gossip, crime, and pornography (e.g. see Kubiske, 2000 on press freedom in Hong Kong).

The elite press in Hong Kong today, including the *South China Morning Post, Ming Pao Daily News,* the *Hong Kong Economic Journal,* and the *Hong Kong Economic Times,* is depoliticizing its news coverage (So et al., 2000:533) because of the economic pressure brought on by *Apple Daily*'s sensationalism and self-censorship after 1997. *Ming Pao Daily News* and the *Hong Kong Economic Journal* are the most read newspapers among intellectuals and the best quality Chinese newspapers in the territory. The conservative, influential, and very profitable *South China Morning Post* and *Ming Pao Daily News,* both opinion leaders despite small circulations compared with the popular press, caught media attention when both were bought by Chinese-Malaysian tycoons who have heavy investment in China (So et al. 2000:535).

Leading the press market in circulation are the *Oriental Daily* with a reported circulation of 400,000 and the *Apple Daily* with a reported circulation of 340,000. It is hard to verify circulation numbers in Hong Kong as they are seldom audited. In 1997–1998 the two tabloids commanded 75 percent of the newspaper market. The duo was locked in price wars in 1995 and 1997 that drove several smaller papers out of the market and made serious papers less serious.

In Taiwan, the media were not free until 1987 when martial law was ended and the freeze on newspaper license applications was lifted in 1988. The press industry took off to enjoy the newfound freedom. The number of newspapers jumped from 31 to 360 in 1998 including nondailies (Wang and Lo, 2000) and remained at that level in 2007 after fluctuations over the years. Magazines in Taiwan, numbering around 6,640, never experienced a freeze on license during the martial law years and became the favorite medium for political dissidents. After the martial law was lifted, dissident magazines recorded major growth.

A slowing economy in the new millennium negatively impacted the press industry in Taiwan. The expansion of cable television, declining readership, and competition for advertising, which accounts for about 70 percent of newspaper revenues, contributed to the industry's woes ("Slumping Economy," 2001). The saturation of media was one more negative factor. With a population of 23 million, the market perhaps was too small for 21 national newspapers.

In 2003 the entry of the *Apple Daily* has shaken up the newspaper industry in Taiwan by focusing on "tabloid journalism, entertainment and nihilism" ("Tabloid Journalism," 2005) and appealing to the younger generation. In two years it reached the leading position among Taiwan newspapers. In a 2005 A.C. Nielsen survey, *Apple Daily* led Taiwan in readership at 28 percent, beating the former leader, the *Liberty Times*. The two traditional large newspapers—the *United Daily News* and the *China Times*—were reduced to third and fourth positions as their primary news coverage was still politics.

North of Taiwan, Japan is a newspaper giant, sweeping the top five of the ten largest newspapers in the world. There are five national daily newspapers, all of which are based in Tokyo—*Yomiuri Shimbun* (14 million), *Asahi Shimbun* (12 million), *Mainichi Shimbun* (5.6 million), *Nihon Keizai Shimbun* (4.6 million), and *Sankei Shimbun* (2.7 million). The five national dailies, together with an additional 117 daily newspapers, give Japan a combined daily newspaper circulation of over 72 million, which also tops world statistics. Major newspapers in Japan publish both morning and evening editions, and 90 percent of the newspapers printed are delivered to homes.

There are many explanations for the large circulation of newspapers in Japan, including the country's 99 percent literacy rate, population density, homogeneous population, sizable middle class, coast-to-coast home delivery system, and long commuting hours. After a tour of Japan, Al Neuharth, founder of *USA Today,* concluded that Japan's dailies do better because they provide more news, and they are more reader-friendly, fair, and more polite in their editorial comments or criticisms (Neuharth, 2004).

The *Yomiuri* is a general interest, conservative and pro-establishment national daily newspaper. More than 60 percent of its readers live in the Tokyo metropolitan area. When a scandal involving Hidenao Nakagawa, a top official of the ruling Liberal Democratic Party (LPD), broke out in 2000, the paper was slow in reporting it. And when it did, it sounded like the spokesman of the party (Nomura, 2002). The mainstream press in Japan maintains a cozy relationship with the government and is rewarded with privileged access to government information through an exclusive press club system.

The *Asahi* is a more liberal paper. The *Nihon Keizai* is the largest financial daily in the world. With 1,300 reporters and editors, it is almost twice as large as *The Wall Street Journal.* Some Japanese readers resented Nikkei's close ties with big business and called *Nihon Keizai* the "Japan Company Daily." The other two mass-circulating national dailies are the *Mainichi Shimbun* and the *Sankei Shimbun.*

Besides the five national dailies, there are also a large number of sports newspapers or tabloids. There is also an English daily, the *Japan Times,* serving the international community in Japan.

Newspapers in Japan are highly profitable with retail prices for newspapers guaranteed by the law but profits limited by government regulations. Japanese newspapers are conglomerates owning publications, national TV networks, sports teams, amusement parks, and travel agencies. They also sponsor sports events. The five national commercial networks are owned by each of the five national dailies. The newspapers have become major cultural, social, economic, and political institutions in the Japanese society.

The cross-ownership of national newspapers and national TV networks creates powerful media synergy in political coverage. For the 2001 prime minister race, all the newspapers focused on LDP candidates, while ignoring opposition parties. The spotlight on LDP candidates was in sharp contrast to public opinion poll results showing that only 25 percent of the voters supported the LDP (Nomura, 2002). As a result, the party's PR chief, Eita Yashiro, actually expressed his gratitude on national television for the media coverage of the race.

The press in South Korea shares many of the characteristics of the Japanese press—large circulation numbers, elitist, conservative, pro-establishment, and practices of self-censorship. Similar to Taiwan, after decades of rule under military governments, South Koreans finally ushered in a new era of freedom in 1987. Once freed from government control, the press industry witnessed a phenomenal growth, and new newspapers and magazines mushroomed. Even Japanese magazines are allowed to be circulated in the country today.

Twenty years later, the South Koreans have choices among 116 daily newspapers and 6,500 periodicals, 2,000 of which are weeklies, 3,300 monthlies, and 1,200 quarterlies, each targeting its own niche market (Lee, 2002). All the major publications are based in Seoul. There are 10 national general-interest dailies, and they set the news agenda in the country. Three of the 10 national dailies—the *Chosun Ilbo,* the *Joongang Ilbo,* and the *Dong-A Ilbo*—have a circulation of more than 2 million each, accounting for 74 percent of Korea's total daily newspaper circulation of around 9.4 million. They are also among the top 20 largest newspapers in the world. But South Korea only has a little more than one-third of the Japanese population and less than one-sixth of the U.S. population. The explanations for the large circulations are the affluent Korean economy and the homogeneous society.

The *Chosun Ilbo,* is the largest and most influential and conservative newspaper in South Korea. Its political coverage is a must read for anyone interested in Korean politics. It's a huge media complex, publishing not only the paper, but also all kinds of general interest or specialized papers and magazines. The company also owns an art gallery and a tourist hotel. Like other leading dailies in the country, the *Chosun* is a family-owned media group. The *Joong-ang Ilbo,* which is the second largest daily in the country, is also conservative in its editorial content but progressive and innovative in its management and editorial design. The paper distinguishes itself for its business and financial news coverage and appeals to career-minded professionals.

The *Dong-a Ilbo* is a leading liberal paper, which still tries to act as a watchdog of the government. It used to be the major critic of Korea's military and dictatorial regimes, and today it still engages in diligent investigative reporting. The *Hankook Ilbo* used to enjoy similar status with the other three. But it started to decline in the 1990s after the death of its founder-publisher Chang Key-young. The paper is strong on soft news and foreign news. It has a huge following among the younger generation. It also publishes the *Korean Times,* one of the two English dailies in the country. The other one is the *Korean Herald*, subsidized by the government.

In addition to the general-interest national dailies, there are other specialized papers such as five business-financial dailies, children's dailies, and sports dailies. There are also 39 local dailies mostly based in provincial capital cities and other urban areas. Developed as they are, the Korean newspapers face tough competition from rival papers, free morning papers, and the new media.

Compared with the overwhelming changes taking place in China and Vietnam, the Communist press in North Korea has remained mostly the same over the decades—rigid party control of the press. Of the daily newspapers in the country, the *Rodong* (or *Nodong*) *Shinmun* (Labor News) published by the party and the government's *Minju Choson* (Democratic Korea) have the largest circulations. North Korea also has newspapers and periodicals for specific occupational and demographic groups, such as the workers, the military, the farmers, women, and the youth. The monthly, *Kulloja* (Workers), is one of the most influential periodicals.

News coverage in North Korea is much focused and predominantly positive. Three topics dominate the news agenda in the country—the personality cult of Kim Jong Il, praise of the army, and criticism of the country's foes, especially South Korea, the United States, and Japan. In the *Rodong Shinmun,* commentaries carry greater weight than news (Kim, 2002). All the publications in North Korea are strictly censored. The press in North Korea does not print any advertisements except government notices (Gunaratne and Kim, 2000).

South Asia

India presents a unique spectacle in the landscape of Asian press as the country is the largest democracy in the world and has one of the freest presses in Asia. The growth of the Indian press in recent years has been breathtaking. The sharp increase in the number of newspapers and in circulation numbers presents a contrast to the steady decline of newspaper circulation in the West. According to India's Registrar of Newspapers, the country has the largest number of daily newspapers in the world, and the total number of registered newspapers reached 62,483 in 2006. Newspaper circulation in India rose 33 percent from 2001 to 2005. Advertising was also expected to grow by 15 percent in 2007 (Dolnick, 2007). Roughly 11 million English newspapers were sold every day in 2007, while three times as many Hindi papers, nearly 34 million, were sold, ending the long-time dominance of English-language papers. According to the Registrar, total circulation of newspapers in the country reached 180 million in 2006, in a nation of 1.1 billion people.

In India it is common for people to read up to four or five newspapers a day because of the low prices of the papers and a slower-paced lifestyle. According to the World Association of Newspapers, the press currently reaches about 35 percent of the country's adults, which means that there is still tremendous potential to grow, especially in the rural areas. As a result, newspaper companies continue to launch new papers and new editions. HT Media, one of the major media companies in India, reported a revenue increase of 28 percent in 2007. In New Delhi, newspapers are published in 15 different languages. One popular New Delhi newspaper store can offer up to 117 dailies (Dolnick, 2007).

Of the impressive growth in the newspaper industry, regional language newspapers registered the fastest growth. Advertisers used to flock only to the English-language papers. That has changed as local language papers blossomed, and their reach and quality improved. National advertisers began to realize the value of regional markets (Jeffrey, 2000), as most of the vernacular newspapers in the country are regional papers while most of the English-language papers are national newspapers. Desktop publishing also gave the development of local language papers a boost as printing in the Indian languages had never been easy. Computer technology finally enabled local language papers to reach beyond state capitals. Content in local language papers was also localized, and its impact was dramatic and sometimes unexpected. Locals used to be terrified of the presence of a single police officer in their village. Now six policemen may enter a village, and the people are not afraid as they now know that the police are not supposed to beat them (Jeffrey, 2000). "I'll go to the newspapers" has become an effective deterrent.

The expansion of the Indian press industry is propelled by the liberalization and the development of the Indian economy, the growth of the middle class in India, and its culture of reading, as two-thirds of households with TV sets still buy newspapers. And ironically, it can also be attributed to the slow and uneven development of the Internet and cable TV. Only 8.5 million of Indians use the Internet, according to government statistics (Dolnick, 2007). While cable TV is expanding its reach in the country, it is still very expensive for most Indian families, especially when compared with newspapers, which cost less than a cup of tea. Private radio stations are not allowed by law to broadcast news, giving newspapers one more advantage in covering news.

According to the 2006 statistics released by India's Registrar of Newspapers, the largest-circulated multiedition daily newspaper was *The Times of India,* which publishes six editions and had a circulation of 2.5 million. The second largest multiedition daily was *Dainik Jagran* in Hindi, which publishes 15 editions and had circulation of 2.1 million. The largest single-edition daily newspapers included *Ananda Bazar Patrida* in Bengali, and *The Hindu* and *Hindustan Times* in English. The largest periodical, *The Hindu* weekly, had a circulation of 1.1 million. Other top mass-circulating newspapers are mostly in regional languages. India's growing affluence also led to the growth of the business media. In 2007 at least five national daily business papers competed to satisfy a growing demand for financial news.

While advertising ensured the independence of the Indian press and provided financial resources for its dazzling growth, it also drove it to sensationalism. An article in the *Hindustan Times* criticized the press's excessive coverage of lavish weddings while ignoring stories of rape ("Not Fine Print," 2007). The paper warned that another one of those weddings could be the funeral of the press. Another article in the paper (May 30, 2007) warned against the race of commercialism.

The press in Pakistan today, however, faces tough challenges of a weak economy, an increasing threat of terrorism, low circulation rates, and a low literacy rate at only 43 percent. There are around 1,330 newspapers in Pakistan, even though only 1 percent of the population buys a newspaper (Isa, 2001:137). A slightly larger number buys a magazine, which totals 1,623.

The print media in Pakistan are independent of the government and influential as newspapers help mold public opinion on important issues despite their low circulation. Given the long absence of democracy and government's control on TV and radio, newspapers in Pakistan have become important instruments for social change. However, covering politics is a complex and sometimes dangerous job in the country, considering the competitive political parties and issues of religion and terrorism. Islamic beliefs are widely reflected in the news media. The press is forbidden to criticize Islam, although leaders of religious parties and movements are not off limits to public scrutiny and criticism (Pstein,

2002). As Pakistan is on the front line in the War on Terror, the government has instructed newspapers to stop publishing photos and sermons of al-Qaeda chief Osama bin Laden and elusive Taliban chief Mulla Omar (Sehar, 2004).

Pakistan is a multilingual society, and its press reflects this language diversity. Newspapers that publish in Urdu have a broader reach than the English-language press (Pstein, 2002). Leading newspapers in the country include *Jang, Nawa-e-Waqt, Dawn, The Nation, The News International,* and *Business Recorder.* English dailies are more conservative than the vernacular press, which is more vocal in public debates and more popular among average readers.

Three main media groups dominate the Pakistan press industry—the Jang Group, the Herald Group, and the Newa-e-Waqt Group. Jang Publications is the largest media group in the country and holds a virtual monopoly of Urdu readership. According to its Web site, the group controls almost 65 percent of the total urban newspaper readership in Pakistan. Its flagship *Jang* is the country's largest national daily with a circulation of 800,000 and claims a readership of more than 7 million. The group also publishes Pakistan's largest English-language newspaper, *The News,* which has a circulation of 140,000, as well as morning and evening papers and weekly magazines.

The Herald Publications Ltd. publishes the well-established *Dawn,* which has a moderate editorial policy. However, in 2004, the paper offended the government by covering political crises, which led to suspension of government advertising. The group also publishes other English papers and magazines, targeting the elite of the Pakistani society. The Nawa-e-Waqt Group publishes *Nawa-e-Waqt, The Nation,* an English daily, and the *Family,* an Urdu weekly. Other publication groups, independent publications, and a couple of major newspapers published by political parties in the country contribute to the diversity of the press in the country.

The young nation of Bangladesh traveled a tough road. Decades of political instability and frequent natural disasters resulted in a poor economy and many repressive laws controlling the press. Its low literacy rate of 43 percent limits readership in the country. Religion also has a major impact on the press, which is not allowed to criticize Islam as in many other Islamic countries. The country is also homogeneous; thus, most of the publications are also in Bengali. There are 201 dailies (188 Bengali and 13 English) and 415 weeklies in the country. The English press, mostly newspapers and weeklies, accounts for around only 10 percent of the total press circulation (Desai, 2001), but it has a powerful influence because its readers are the elites in the Bangladeshi society.

Dailies both in Bengali and English are published in Dhaka, Chittagong, and other major cities and towns. *Prothom Alo* is the country's largest Bengali-language daily (Karlekar, 2005), which is still brave enough to publish a series of investigative reports on militant Islamist activities. Main English newspapers are the *Bangladesh Observer, the Daily Star, the Financial Express, the Daily Independent, New Age,* and *the Holiday* (weekly). There are two major privately owned and well-financed publication groups in the country—the Ittefaq Group and the Inquilab Group (Desai, 2001).

In contrast to its neighbors, Sri Lanka has a high literacy rate of 90 percent (Desai, 2002). Press freedom suffered in recent years as the civil war resumed between government troops and the separatist Tamil Tigers. In addition to English publications, Sinhala and Tamil newspapers comprise the bulk of the publications in the island nation, reflecting the two sides of the conflict.

Three media groups dominate the press industry—the Associated Newspapers of Ceylon Ltd. (ANCL), the Upali Newspapers Limited (UNL), and Wijeya Newspapers Limited (WNL). ANCL is the only government-owned newspaper-publishing group, whose *Ceylon Daily News* is the country's leading national daily newspaper. It is also the only publishing group that publishes newspapers in all of the three languages—in Sinhala, it publishes the *Dinamana* and *Sunday Silumina;* in English, *The Daily News,* the evening *Observer,* and the *Sunday Observer;* and in Tamil, the *Thinakaran.*

UNL claims to be independent of political groups in the country and often adopts a critical attitude in its coverage of them (Desai, 2002). UNL publishes the daily *Divayina* and the *Sunday Divayina* in Sinhala, and the *Island* and *Sunday Island* in English.

The third major media group, WNL, publishes the Sunday *Lankadipa* and the daily *Lankadipa* in Sinhala, and the *Sunday Times,* the *Midweek Mirror,* and the *Daily Mirror* in English. Other notable newspapers outside of the three groups include the *Sunday Leader,* the *Weekend Express,* and *Veerakesari* in Tamil. In Sri Lanka, circulation numbers are not made public by newspaper groups because of the intense competition for advertising.

Lagging far behind Sri Lanka, Nepal is another underdeveloped country in South Asia with a little more than half of Sri Lanka's literacy rate, at 48.6 percent. There are approximately 60 daily newspapers published in the country, and about 80 percent of Nepalese newspapers are weeklies (Schafer, 2001). Newspapers and journals have low circulation rates. Most of the people in Nepal, about 85 percent, live in rural areas, but the mainstream press mostly ignores issues specific to them.

The *Gorkhapatra* in Nepalese, owned by the government's Gorkhapatra Corporation, is the largest newspaper in the country with a circulation estimated at 75,000 (Schafer, 2001). The corporation also publishes *Rising Nepal,* an English daily. The Nepalese media frequently feature the royal family. Nongovernment leading newspapers published in Kathmandu include the *Annapurna Post,* the *Kantipur, Nepal Samacharpatra,* and the *Rajdhani.* Nongovernment English newspapers printed in the country include *The Himalayan Times,* the leading English daily in the country, *The Independent, The Kathmandu Post,* the *Nepali Times,* and *The Telegraph.*

Bhutan is a small traditional country, which is slowly modernizing but makes a conscious effort to resist Western influence. The literacy rate of the country stands at 42.2 percent, and 90 percent of the people in the country live in rural areas. As the media are only a fledgling industry in the country, Bhutan had only one TV station, one radio station, two Internet providers, and one weekly newspaper, the *Kuensel,* until 2006 when two more publications appeared—the *Bhutan Times* and the *Bhutan Observer,* both privately owned. *Kuensel* is published by the government in three languages—Dzongkha, the national language, English, and Nepalese. It has a circulation of about 10,000 (Sharma, 2002).

In Afghanistan, years of fighting have reduced the media infrastructure to practically nothing. Even before the Taliban came to power, fighting in the early 1990s damaged buildings and equipment. American bombing in late 2001 destroyed more communication facilities. Journalism also suffered greatly as many skilled journalists left the country. The press industry under the Taliban was underdeveloped and subject to heavy censorship by religious fundamentalists (Warren, 2002). Press circulation and readership were low because of the low literacy rate of 31.5 percent, among the lowest in Asia.

After the U.S.-led war in Afghanistan drove out the Taliban, the new government of Hamid Karzai eased restrictions on the news media. The new 2004 constitution provides for freedom of the press and of expression, and the new government granted approximately 300 licenses to independent publications (Freedom House report, 2007). However, national and local governments continue to own or control several dozen newspapers, and some warlords or political factions do not allow independent media in the areas under their control. The poor economic environment of the country still leaves most media outlets dependent on the financial support from the state, political parties, or international donors.

Southeast Asia

The press industry in Thailand is fairly developed. The leading national Thai-language dailies are the *Thai Rath,* the largest in the country with a circulation of 1.2 million; the *Daily News,* the second largest in the country with a circulation of 900,000; the *Kom Chad Luek,* the third largest with a circulation of 850,000; and the *Matichon* and the *Khao Sod,* each with a circulation of 600,000, according to statistics compiled by the World Association of Newspapers in 2005. Other national Thai-language dailies include the *Siam Rath,* the *Naew Na,* and the *Thai Post.* Thailand also has some well-established leading English-language dailies, such as the *Bangkok Post,* the *Nation,* and a specialized business daily, the *Business Day.* Six Chinese-language dailies and three Japanese weekly newspapers add to the choice of newspapers in the country.

The press in Thailand covers a wide range of topics and issues in the country and provides different perspectives on news topics as the media in the country generally enjoy a considerable degree of freedom. But they are forbidden from publishing negative stories about the royal family or the country's international image (Paquette, 2002). The government is also sensitive to reporting on government affairs and internal security matters. Coverage of politics is often less than neutral or balanced as the media in the country often have ties with families of government officials. In Thailand the press market is very competitive, and as a result the press often resorts to sensationalism to sell papers.

In Indonesia, after the dictatorial Suharto regime ended in 1998, the press is becoming more diverse, dynamic, and rapidly urbanizing due to the interplay of the press and political institutions, and the changing economy (see Eng, 1998). During the early days of freedom, press outlets proliferated, with high expectations for the role of the press. Approximately 1,000 newspapers had registered and begun publishing, although some of them had to shut down within several months as the market could not support all the newcomers. Tabloids also began to appear and constituted about one-quarter of the number of the newspapers published in 2002.

On top of the rapid growth of the press industry, leading newspapers in Indonesia can further expand their circulation as none of the major newspapers in Indonesia ranks among the 100 largest newspapers in the world, considering the fact that Indonesia is the fourth most populous country in the world and the world's largest Muslim country. The diversity of the Indonesian press and of its people, and the fact that it is an oral culture, may provide part of the explanation. Also, the cost of buying a newspaper or newspaper subscription can still be a barrier. When times are difficult, the number of newspapers sold declines. A single newspaper issue bought from a newsstand can cost as much as a simple meal

(Yoder, 2002), and an annual subscription to a major newspaper costs more than a modest TV set. Further development of the newspaper industry in Indonesia depends on the more rapid growth of its economy.

There are three types of newspapers in Indonesia (Yoder, 2002)—the "establishment" press, such as the *Kompas* with a circulation of 750,000 in 2006 and the *Republika;* the more "aggressive" press, such as the *Rakyat Merdeka* and the *Jawa Pos,* and the "extreme" Islamic press, such as the *Sabili.* Compared with the more conservative newspapers of the past, the aggressive press may seem insensitive and crude, but more papers seem to be going in this direction. Other major newspapers in the country include the *Pos Kota,* a low-priced Jakarta newspaper popular among blue-collar workers, and the *Suara Pembaruan,* which is considered a serious newspaper.

Of the three English-language newspapers published in Jakarta, the *Jakarta Post* has the largest circulation. The paper's Web site claims that the paper carries independent views and bold coverage of various national and international events. The other two are the *Indonesia Times* and the *Indonesian Observer,* the oldest of the three.

As suggested earlier, the press in Indonesia is very diverse because of the diversity of its people and culture. Predominantly Muslim, the country has also been influenced by Indian, Arabic, Malay, Chinese, Melanesian, and European cultures. Indonesia is made up of a wide geographical area of islands, most of which have their own culture and language, totaling 583 in the spoken form (Yoder, 2002). Diversity in the press provides Indonesian readers with an array of viewpoints. Even within the Islamic press, readers can tell clear differences between the *Media Dakwah,* which promotes an Islamic state and Middle Eastern political ideals, and the *Republika,* which is more cosmopolitan. Diverse perspectives in the news sometimes end in physical attacks on the reporters. Journalists in Indonesia are under constant threat from mobs, the police and security forces, Islamic extremist groups, rebels, and political activists.

The Philippine press is reputed to be one of the freest in the developing world and does not require licensing of either newspapers or journalists. The press is mostly privately owned and has been vibrant and outspoken since the ouster of the Marcos regime in 1986. The Philippine press is also known for being rowdy because of its sometimes less than accurate reporting and "tendency toward innuendo and sensationalism" (Freedom House report, 2005.) The press is also powerful. Its exposés of corruption and crime have prompted many government investigations and ended numerous political careers.

Like the Indonesian press, newspapers in the Philippines are quite diverse. The top English papers include the *Manila Bulletin,* one of the largest newspapers in the country and a quality daily that has earned wide respect, the *Philippine Star,* a major national daily, and the *Philippine Daily Inquirer,* also a leading newspaper. Major Filipino papers are the *People's Tonight,* the *Pilipino Ngayaon,* and the *Taliba.* Indonesia also has Taglish- and Chinese-language publications in the country. The largest Taglish papers include the *People's Journal,* the *Headline Manila,* and the *News Today,* and top Chinese papers are the *World News,* the *United Daily News,* and the *China Times.* Other well-established newspapers in the country include the *Manila Times* and the *Daily Tribune.* Major business newspapers are the *Business World,* a Manila business daily, and the *Chinese Commercial News of Manila.* There are also some weeklies published in the country.

Because of the free press environment, investigative reporting supported by its center of investigative journalism is effective and powerful, and is unmatched in Asia other than in Taiwan and Hong Kong. Its stories uncovering political corruption and wrongdoing, such as money laundering involving politicians, and crimes including drug trafficking and illegal logging led to resignations of powerful officials and a Supreme Court justice and to government investigations of crimes. But such relentless crusades also resulted in reprisals against the news media and journalists. In 2004 alone, 13 journalists were killed, one of the deadliest years on record for newsmen (Freedom House report, 2005). Outside influences and pressure—such as politicians and businessmen who bribe journalists—sometimes work to deter investigative reporting.

In contrast to the Philippine press, the press in Singapore is controlled and mostly follows government guidelines. The "soft authoritarianism" (Unnithan, 2001) practiced by the Singaporean government tames the press through the promotion of Asian values, clever management control mechanisms, and court cases against the press. In India and Pakistan, the government often loses court battles against the press; in contrast, in Singapore the court often vindicates the government. Asian values often result in a notable absence of coverage of political controversy in the country, and in self-censorship.

The press industry in Singapore is a virtual monopoly by the Singapore Press Holdings (SPH), which is publicly traded, so it is not government owned, even though it is government controlled. It publishes 14 newspapers and 25 magazines according to its Web site. The English flagship daily of the company, the famed *The Straits Times,* has a circulation of 385,690 and is the largest daily newspaper of the country. The paper has 16 bureaus in major cities around the world. The largest Sunday newspaper is *The Sunday Times,* the Sunday edition of *The Straits Times,* with a circulation of 400,865. *The Business Times* is the only financial daily in the country with a circulation of 29,461. The paper claims to be a key source of business intelligence for investors, managers, and businessmen in Singapore and the Asian region.

The New Paper, Singapore's only afternoon tabloid, is Singapore's *"USA Today,"* and it has a circulation of 114,034. Established in 1988, it tries to "present complex issues in an easy-to-read, pop style for young and busy readers." "It catches readers' attention with bold and colorful designs, exciting layouts and punchy headlines," according to SPH's Web site. The paper has developed a huge following for its sports and entertainment sections. It entered *The Guinness Book of Records* in 2000 for organizing the largest walk in the world, its annual mass-fitness walk. The Sunday edition of the paper has a circulation of 145,365.

The *Lianhe Zaobao,* the only Chinese morning daily in Singapore, has the largest circulation among Chinese papers in the country—around 184,476 copies on weekdays and 187,678 on Sundays. It is regarded as an important source of political and economic news on East Asia, especially China, according to the paper's Web site. The paper has an extensive correspondent network in Beijing, Chongqing, Shanghai, Guangzhou, Hong Kong, Taipei, Seoul, and Tokyo, and stringers in the Philippines, Japan, Europe, and America. Besides Singapore, the paper is also circulated in Indonesia, Brunei, Hong Kong, Vietnam, and major cities in China such as Beijing and Shanghai. The *Lianhe Wanbao* is the evening edition of the Zaobao and one of two evening Chinese papers in the country. It sells 126,172 copies on weekdays and 125,958 copies on weekends. It distinguishes itself by using the simpler form of Chinese characters adopted on the Chinese mainland.

Other papers published by the group include *My Paper,* the *Shin Min Daily News,* the *Friday Weekly,* the *Thumbs Up,* the *Berita Harian,* the *Berita Minggu,* and the *Tamil Murasu.* SPH also publishes about 25 magazines, most of which target women and young people on topics ranging from health and parenting to fashion.

For a short period of time, SPH's monopoly was broken when the government allowed the monopoly broadcaster, Media Corporation of Singapore, to publish newspapers. At the same time, SPH was also permitted to own some TV and radio stations. But a megamerger was agreed upon in 2004 to end four years of cutthroat competition, restoring the Singapore media to the days of monopolies. Newspapers in Singapore are well financed, and the bulk of press earnings come from advertising. Unlike the situation in most developed economies, newspapers in the country continue to dominate in terms of advertising revenue. *The Straits Times* is so popular that it has found itself turning away advertisers.

Surveys in the country have repeatedly shown that most Singaporeans are happy with press coverage of their country and do not necessarily want aggressive, combative, or crusading journalism (Unnithan, 2001). But there are signs that the younger generation growing up in an affluent society wants more rights and freedom.

The Malaysian press bears much resemblance to the press in Singapore, emphasizing national unity and development and practicing editorial self-censorship. Like its neighbors in the Southeast Asian region, Malaysia is a diverse country. But ethnic diversity and economic disparity are sensitive issues in the country. To preserve order and stability and to prevent violence against any ethnic group or religion, the government has defined the role of the press as promoting nationalism and development.

Most of the country's major newspapers are in four languages—Malayan, Chinese, Tamil, and English. *The New Straits Times,* a well-established progovernment paper, derived from *The Straits Times.* It claims to be the "newspaper of the nation," focusing on political and financial news reporting. The newspaper group publishes five publications and has bureaus all over the country. The *Utusan Malaysia* is a top news provider in the country in both English and Bahasa Melayu. *The Malay Mail,* which earned its reputation as "a paper for the small man," highlights human interest stories, campaigns for the aggrieved, and serves as a voice for the man-in-the-street, according to the paper's Web site. *The Daily Express* claims to be the independent national newspaper of East Malaysia. It is published in three languages—English, Bahasa Malaysia, and Kadazan—and it is by far the largest circulating daily newspaper in Sabah. *The Star* and *The Sunday Star* are two of the largest newspapers in Malaysia, outselling *The New Straits Times. The Star* was the first tabloid newspaper published in Malaysia and the first English paper to launch its Web edition. Major newspapers in the country are owned by political parties and their investment companies, some of which are connected with the ruling parties in the coalition government.

Distribution of national publications is slowed down by the sea separating the two parts of Malaysia. Press circulation in Malaysia also reflects ethnic and geographic divisions: English papers are popular in metropolitan areas, while the rural population is mostly conservative and prefers reading Malay newspapers that cater to Muslims (Johnson, 2002). Malaysia with a Chinese minority does not allow the circulation of Singaporean papers in the country, nor does Singapore with a predominantly Chinese population allow the circulation of Malaysian papers in Singapore.

The press in Vietnam in many ways resembles the changing Chinese press. Since Vietnam started its economic reforms and began reintegrating itself into the world market in 1986, more and more people in Vietnam came to the realization that in today's business world, information is crucial to any enterprise. As a result, the country's information industry experienced a boom in the 1990s. At that time, almost every province, ministry, and industry had its own newspapers and magazines, which led Vietnamese lawmakers to complain about a "publication glut" ("Publication Glut," 1999). Most of the news media outlets in Vietnam today are still owned by the state, even though they are commercial in nature as the government abolished subsidies for the press. To survive on the market, the press rediscovered sensationalism as a marketing tool.

Major newspapers in Vietnam include the *Nhan Dan,* which is the "central organ of the Communist Party of Vietnam" and serves as "the voice of the party, the state and the people of Vietnam," according to the paper's Web site. It is a comprehensive newspaper with news, life, business, travel, culture and sports sections, and it is published in both English and the local Vietnamese language. The *Quan Doi Nhan Dan* is the "organ of the central military commission and the Vietnamese Ministry of National Defense" and serves as "the voice of the armed forces and the people. It has three main sections—Vietnam, the world, and the army. In the Vietnam section, readers can find stories concerning Vietnamese politics and society, the economy, culture and sports, the overseas Vietnamese community, and travel. The army section is split into two subcategories—internal affairs and external affairs. Both of these papers are published in Hanoi. Other publications also published in the city include the *Ha Noi Moi,* the *Le Courier du Vietnam,* and the *Vietnam News.* Publications printed in Ho Chi Minh City (formerly Saigon) include the *Ho Chi Minh Globe,* the *Lao Dong,* and the *Saigon Times Weekly.*

Laos is the least-known Communist country in Asia bordering Vietnam. It has a rudimentary economy dominated by fishing, forestry, and agriculture. Despite a remarkable annual GDP growth rate of 6 percent in the past 20 years, today's Laos still has only a primitive road system and limited telecommunications facilities. The level of economic development in the country has severely limited the development of its news media, while government control of the media further restricts the growth of the press industry. The government owns all domestic newspapers, which tend to reflect official views in their news reporting. One sensitive news topic that is avoided in the press is the issue of the rebelling Hmong communities in the hills of northern Laos.

Laos has three major daily newspapers, two in the local language of Lao and one in English. The *Pasason* is the national newspaper, while the *Vientiane Mai* serves the capital, Vientiane. The *Vientiane Times,* the first English newspaper in Laos, was officially launched as a weekly tabloid in 1994. By 2007 the paper had become a daily, publishing Monday to Saturday. The newspaper covers a wide range of news stories and provides information reflecting on government policies and socioeconomic development in the country. The *Vientiane Times* is part of the Lao Press in Foreign Languages, which is a specialized agency of the Ministry of Information and Culture. The press agency has 60 staff members. All three dailies have small circulations. One French-language weekly—*Le Renovateur*—is also published in the country.

The Cambodian press operates in a similar environment—lack of financial resources and government control. But the major difference between Cambodia and Laos is the political system. Today's Cambodia is a multiparty democracy under a constitutional monarchy. However, that democracy is in name only, as the nature of the government is still authoritarian. Suspension of newspapers and harassment of journalists, including beatings, detentions, and forced confessions, still occur in the country. Many of the print media outlets in the country are either aligned with or subsidized by the three main political factions. They do offer diverse views and provide some criticism of government policies and senior officials.

The *Rasmei Kampuchea* is the largest daily newspaper in Khmer in the country. With help from the United Nations, a group of English newspapers and publications also appeared, including the *Phnom Penh Post,* the *Phnom Penh Daily,* the *Cambodia Daily,* and the *Cambodia Times.* The *Cambodia Daily* is the main English-language newspaper in the country. The paper dared to challenge the authorities and engage in independent and investigative reporting by covering the refuge-seeking Vietnamese minority group in Cambodia, the Montagnards. The consequences of such reporting included the arrest and detention of, and forced confession to human trafficking, by its editor Kevin Doyle. Other papers include the *Koh Santepheap* and the *Commercial News.*

Like Laos, the country's economy is not strong enough to provide sufficient advertising funding to support the press industry, much less the truly neutral or independent media. Newspaper circulation in Cambodia is also small.

The Myanmar (Burma) media are among the most tightly controlled in the world, according to the Freedom House 2005 report. The government is led by a military junta and tolerates no opposition or different views in the media. It owns all daily newspapers in the country, while there are other privately owned publications, which have to apply for annual licenses and accept prepublication censorship by the government. The stagnant economy, which has resulted from the lack of foreign investment and from policy failures, also hampers the development of the press industry, which lacks an adequate supply of newsprint and advertising financing.

The *Myanmar Times* is the best-known English-language publication in the country and also the country's first international weekly. Started in 2000, it is like no other newspaper in Myanmar in that it is not forced to comply with junta press regulations (Schafer, 2001) inasmuch as it is published by an Australian journalist, Ross Dunkley. The paper was permitted to carry exclusive articles about talks between the junta government and Nobel Peace Prize winner and opposition leader Aung San Suu Kyi, who was jailed and then put under house arrest after winning a landslide victory in the 1990 national election. It was speculated that the junta allowed the paper more freedom in order to gain international acceptance and attract foreign investment to help alleviate the country's dim economic prospects.

Other papers in the country include the *New Light of Myanmar* in English, the *Myanmar Alin,* and the *Kyehmon.*

The Pacific

Most newspapers in the Pacific region have small circulations. But since the late 1990s, thanks to desktop publishing, increased literacy, citizen interest in voting rights, and better coverage, circulations of newspapers have registered rapid growth in the Solomon Islands,

New Guinea, Vanuatu, Fiji, and the Samoas (Lael, 1997). In Pacific countries, government media are giving way to private enterprise, and the viability of private media has been made possible through desktop publishing. A case in point is the *Solomon Star,* which has grown in circulation from 1,000 to 6,000 in its decade of independence with the help of the new technology (Lael, 1997).

Papua New Guinea, located north of Australia in the Pacific, has the most developed press industry among Pacific countries. Its press is free and dominated by foreign companies. The impact of the press on the country's politics is, however, rather limited because access to the press is limited to mostly urban areas, while 85 percent of the population lives in remote villages with little contact with the modern world. The ancient cultures and languages of its isolated people also slow down the spread of newspapers. Political advertising and election coverage are absent from the press, and no candidate accepts a newspaper's offer of free publicity (Tindall, 2002).

The country hosts the largest-circulation daily in the South Pacific, the *Papua New Guinea Post-Courier,* whose majority shareholder is Rupert Murdoch's News Corporation, while private local investors own about one-third of the stocks. One of the nation's two daily newspapers, the *Post-Courier* had a circulation of 26,262 in 2006 and is the most influential paper in the country. It targets both native and expatriate communities. It features short articles, large sensational headlines, and plenty of photos and graphics to compensate for the high illiteracy rate and lack of a common language in the region (Tindall, 2002). It is a comprehensive newspaper published Monday through Friday, covering international news, business, and sports. Since 1988, the *Post-Courier* has also published two magazines targeting the high-income groups—the weekly general-interest *Papua New Guinea (PNG) Magazine* and the *Newagewoman,* a monthly woman's magazine. The group also publishes the first Braille newspaper in the region, *The South Pacific Braille News.*

A competing daily, *The National,* started by a Malaysian logging interest in 1994, had a circulation of about 23,500 in 2002 and, like the *Post-Courier,* was also in English. The paper was often criticized for lack of independence and for avoiding controversial topics concerning the country's foreign-dominated logging and forestry industry. But on other topics, the paper's coverage was mostly unbiased. Other publications in the country include the weekly *Wantok Niuspepa,* the English-language biweekly *Eastern Star,* and the monthly *Niri Nius,* which prints government news in all three languages.

In Fiji, military or civilian-led coups, the last of which took place in 2006, cast a long shadow over the country's political stability, economy, and development of its press. Successive governments tried but failed to control the press because of strong resistance from an organized Fiji media community. But despite such uncertainties about the country's future, the press in Fiji remained largely free and robust. The media have vigorously reported many treason and mutiny trials associated with the attempted coup in 2000 and its aftermath.

The country has three daily newspapers, all published in English—the *Fiji Times,* the *Daily Post,* and the *Fiji Sun.* Both the *Times* and the *Sun* are privately owned and represent the oldest and the newest in the press industry. The *Times* is the largest of the three. The *Daily Post* used to be partially owned by the government. Some weekly publications include the *Nai Lalakai* and the *Shati Dut,* both published by the Fiji Times Group. The weekly *Fiji Republic Gazette* focuses on local business issues.

Tonga has two weeklies, the independent *Times of Tonga* and the government-owned *Tonga Chronicle,* with circulation of around 8,000 and 5,000, respectively. Other newspapers in the region include *Pacific Daily News* of Guam, *Cook Island News* and *Samoa News* of American Samoa, *The Island Tribune* of Micronesia, *Samoa Observer* of Samoa, and *Saipan Tribune* of the Northern Mariana Islands.

Electronic Media

Radio broadcasting started to appear in Asia before World War II, while television was introduced to the continent after most of the former colonies of Western powers in Southeast Asia became independent nations following the end of the Japanese occupation. In the Philippines, Thailand, South Korea, and Japan, countries that were most closely associated with the American economic and anti-Communist policies, television was established in the early 1950s and reflected the commercial character of America's decentralized system (Kitley, 2003). In Hong Kong, market forces drove the growth of the industry.

But elsewhere television was seen as essential to the economic development and therefore, a protected national resource (Thomas, 2006). In Malaysia, Singapore, Indonesia, India, and China, television was developed as an important tool in the political and cultural processes of nation-building, which was the main motivation for establishing state-owned, public television services. To support their nationalistic agendas, Indonesia, China, and India launched their own communication satellites to reach far-flung corners of their states with public television broadcasts. Only in the 1990s did governments in Asia face the intrusion into their media space of transnational broadcasts via both satellite and cable (Thomas, 2006). That explains why in many Asian countries such as India, Pakistan, Bangladesh, Malaysia, Indonesia, and Taiwan, radio and television networks are publicly owned, whereas the press is privately owned. Japan has one of the biggest public broadcasting services in the world, and in Hong Kong radio broadcast is also a public service.

Today electronic media in most parts of Asia are highly developed; only some isolated Pacific islands lack TV service. In some areas of electronic media, Asia is the leader. In Singapore, the whole country is wired for cable and Internet access. In fact, Singapore was the first country in the world to set up a national Internet Web site, Singapore InfoMap (Kuo and Ang, 2000:414). Malaysia is a strong contender with Singapore to be the center of communications in the region.

Asia has the highest television penetration worldwide: 500 million television households at the start of the twenty-first century, which is expected to reach 700 million within a decade (Thomas, 2005). But the development of electronic media in Asia is rather uneven, with East Asia far ahead of South Asia in general. Within Southeast Asia, development is also unbalanced: there are huge differences between Singapore and Cambodia, for example. The differences in electronic media penetration are surprising, with South Korea's radio and TV receiver penetration rates at 103.9 and 34.8 per 100 people, respectively, in contrast to the radio and TV receiver penetration rates for Myanmar of, respectively, 9.6 and 0.59 per 100 people.

For the electronic media industry, Asia is an ideal regional market, because Asians, especially Chinese, Indians, and Filipinos, have the tradition of immigrating to neighboring countries. And some cultural influences reach beyond borders, such as Confucianism, Buddhism, and Islam. Diversity and common influence make Asia receptive to regional or transnational media, whose explosive growth in the 1990s, achieved by utilizing commercial satellites, took Asia by surprise. The 1991 Gulf War opened the eyes of the Asian audience to live news broadcast by CNN through satellite transmissions. Other global television broadcasters followed suit, such as BBC World, Discovery, National Geographic, MTV, ESPN, TNT, HBO, MGM, Disney, and specialized business services such as CNBC Asia-Pacific and Bloomberg. Regional commercial broadcasters include ABN, CTN, Channel News Asia, ZeeTV, and Asian Business News. Public broadcasters such as China's CCTV and India's Doordarshan also decided to go regional or even global (Thomas, 2005).

But the real pioneer broadcaster to target Asia and the star player in catching the Asian audience is the Hong Kong-based StarTV, started by Hong Kong billionaire Li Ka-Shing and later purchased by Rupert Murdoch's News Corp. StarTV broadcasts programs in many different languages to not only different parts of Asia but also Europe and North America. In 1992–2001, the number of its entertainment channels increased from two to 11, news and sports channels from two to 14, music and movie channels from five to 38. Being one of the most prominent regional satellite and cable television operations in the world, StarTV takes programming from a number of sources, mainly the United States, Hong Kong, China, Taiwan, India, and Japan (e.g. see Cooper-Chen, 1994).

East Asia

China has more than 10,000 radio stations, covering 90 percent of the population, and more than 3,000 television stations, covering about 88 percent of the population. By June 2007, the number of Internet users in China had reached 162 million, soon to overtake the Unites States (with 165 million net users) as the largest Internet user in the world. The growth rate of Internet users in China in 2006 was 23 percent. TV has become the richest and the most popular medium in China because of its impact and power and its entertainment programming. A survey by A.C. Nielsen Media International showed that in 2001, China's television stations reaped $8.1 billion in total advertising revenue, $5.2 billion more than newspapers and $7.9 billion more than magazines.

Television stations in China, like radio stations, are set up along administrative lines: national, provincial, municipal, and county. They provide news throughout the day and entertainment programs, the most popular of which are TV show series, a genre similar to soap opera but with a faster pace, and imported TV programs. Some interactive quiz shows have also become popular. News programs invariably start with official meetings. But other news shows can be uncomfortable for some government officials, such as Jiaodian Fangtan on CCTV, which is a kind of talk show that focuses on hot issues, mainly dealing with problems people face in their daily lives, such as official corruption, shoddy products, etc. The show has developed a large following and has attracted the attention of government officials.

CCTV is the most powerful and influential television station in China. It can make or break an enterprise. Many enterprises and local governments are ready to pay television stations to do a favorable story about them. Paid news is a serious problem in the industry.

There are rules and regulations banning such payment, but often the financial temptation proves too strong to resist. Regulated access to foreign media is a welcome change for the Chinese audience, which today can watch programs ranging from ESPN to movies on HBO, but only five-star hotels and newsrooms such as the one at *China Daily* have access to CNN. Government regulations ban satellite dish receivers from rooftops or balconies, but many people still install them. China is a large country, and it is difficult to implement the law to the letter.

Radio is still a popular source of news for people in both urban and rural areas because of its convenience. Morning radio news is the most popular. Only in some remote mountainous areas do rural residents still depend solely on radio for news and entertainment. The development of electronic media in China has been rather uneven, with coastal areas far ahead of the inland regions. Overseas, China Radio International, formerly known as Radio Beijing, represents the voice of the Chinese government. The radio station broadcasts news in 43 languages to the whole world. It has a wide following as well. In 1997, when the station sponsored a knowledge contest on tourism and investment in Sha'anxi, about 260,000 listeners from 155 countries sent in their answers.

The next big challenge for China's TV and radio industry involves the country's commitment to the World Trade Organization to open up markets. To prepare for competition with foreign media, a state radio, film, and television conglomerate was established in 2001 that includes all the major players in the industries.

Internet use is expanding rapidly in China as the number of net surfers and domain names keeps rising. Foreign capital is trying to get into the fast-developing sector as well. Online recruitment took off in 2001 as college graduates found it a convenient means to hunt for jobs. The net has also been used for sex education because the topic is an embarrassing one for Chinese parents and children, even at schools. There are many regulations regarding the use and operation of the Internet, especially concerning news, politically sensitive material, and violence and sexual content. Details of regulations are discussed in the government–media relations section.

The electronic media in Hong Kong are very well developed, and Hong Kong's TV entertainment programs are popular not only in Asia but in Chinese communities across the world. Every household in Hong Kong has access to television, totaling about 2 million. Hong Kong has more than 55 television stations and several influential regional TV broadcasters as well, such as StarTV, Chinese Television Network, which was founded in 1994 and was the first fully digitalized television station in Asia, and China Entertainment Television, a Chinese-language satellite television channel in the Greater China region. The "Phoenix" channel run by StarTV was the first to broadcast in Mandarin in 1996. Hong Kong has two commercial radio broadcasters, and each has three channels. Compared with TV popularity in Hong Kong, less than half of the people in Hong Kong listen to radio every day. The Internet is easily accessible in Hong Kong with the island's advanced telecommunications technology.

In Taiwan, for a long time the government, the army, and the KMT (the Nationalist Party) each owned a television station. In 1993 the government lifted the ban on new TV stations and approved additional radio frequencies for applicants. Since then there has been substantial growth in the number of television and radio stations. Today there are 169 radio stations, and cable and satellite television is widely available in Taiwan, numbering about 100 channels. Media expansion has improved diversity but has cut the profit margin. Broadcasting is even more saturated than the print media in Taiwan ("Slumping Economy," 2001). With the politically independent National Communications Commission replacing the Government Information Office in 2006, the government's influence in the sector was reduced to the minimum

In Japan, the electronic media operate under a dual broadcasting system: the public broadcaster (NHK) and commercial broadcasters (Saito, 2000). NHK is Japan's sole public broadcaster. It is independent of both government and corporate sponsorship and relies almost entirely on household reception fees. Therefore, it carries no commercial advertisements. Commercial broadcasters are affiliates of national networks, which are owned by the major national newspapers in the country. NHK has more advanced broadcasting technologies and more staff compared with commercial networks. Its terrestrial services offer two channels—a general service and an educational channel (Hirano, 2003). The general service channel presents news, documentaries, sports, drama, operas and concerts. The educational channel delivers programs to both children and adults. The network also operates two satellite channels, one for general news and information and the other for entertainment and culture.

Nippon Television (NTV), started in 1953, was the first commercial broadcaster in Japan. One unique characteristic of the Japanese media is the alliance between commercial television networks and national newspaper companies, which own the five commercial television networks in the country. NTV is owned by the *Yomiuri Shimbun,* TV Asahi by the *Asahi Shimbun,* TBS by the *Mainichi Shimbun,* Fuji TV by the *Sandei Shimbun,* and TV Tokyo by the *Nihon Keisai Shimbun* (Hirano, 2003). All of these national papers have circulations in the millions and, thus, can provide capital, personnel, and advertising contacts for the networks, which return the favor by generating high profits on the investment. There are more than 100 commercial television broadcasters in Japan, each of which belonged to one of the major networks based in Tokyo and owned by big newspaper companies.

The programming of commercial networks is very similar, parallel to the uniformity of content in the country's press; thus competition for ratings is fierce. TV Asahi pioneered a news program called "News Station," which became very popular and prompted other networks to copy the program format, leading to a fundamental shift in programming focus from entertainment to news. In entertainment TV shows, particularly animated cartoon shows for children, Japan is a world leader. Japanese television is different from television fare elsewhere in the world, where shows are dominated by Hollywood productions. Perhaps mindful of protecting its culture, Japan has mostly stopped importing television series. Instead, its networks rely on their own programming, which is in sharp contrast to the programming strategy of the Hong Kong-based StarTV.

Japan's broadcast law reflects both political needs and cultural values. It stipulates that domestic broadcast programs should not disturb public security, good morals, or manners; should be politically impartial; should broadcast news without distorting facts; and should clarify points of views on controversial issues from different perspectives.

South Korea has two public broadcasting networks, KBS and MBC, and one commercial network, SBS. Nationwide, there are also nine regional private television broadcasters providing services in the nine largest cities in the country. South Korea also has one government-owned educational broadcasting network, EBS, and cable television companies, which started in 1995 with 29 channels (Kwak, 2003). Satellite broadcasting in the country was delayed owing to the absence of a legal structure to protect the interests of operators and regulate activities. The 2000 Broadcast Law allowed the operation of satellite television starting in 2001 (Kwak, 2003). Foreign ownership and investment in the Korean media were prohibited until 1995, when the government partially lifted the ban on foreign ownership of cable television because of financial difficulties.

South Korean broadcast programming focused on national and political interests until the 1980s, when programs became more commercial (Heo, Uhm, and Chang, 2000). In 2001, the credibility of public broadcasting was cast into doubt when it supported the government's "newspaper directives," which initiated outside regulation of newspaper sales and advertising (Jin, 2001; Kim, 2001). In the broadcast sector, the Korea Broadcasting Advertising Corporation, a government agency that sets the advertising rates, has maintained a monopoly over the entire broadcast advertising industry in South Korea since its establishment in 1981 (Heo, Uhm, and Chang, 2000), which means all South Korean and foreign advertisers have to deal with the government agency if they want to buy airtime.

Like all Communist and developing countries, the government of North Korea has long recognized the importance of the mass media, particularly radio and television. The broadcast media in the country have played a major role in ideological indoctrination. Radio broadcasts reach every corner of the country as almost all North Korean households have loudspeakers connected to village receivers as a result of a government project, very similar to the program in rural China in the 1970s. Television broadcasting in North Korea is also available all across the country, and the number of television sets in the country has also increased despite economic difficulties in recent years.

Radio and television programming in the country has to be approved by the Radio and Television Broadcasting Committee. The Korean Central Television Station in Pyongyang, the AM stations—Radio Pyongyang and the Korean Central Broadcasting Station—and Pyongyang FM Pangsong are the major domestic broadcasters (Schemer, 2002). Smaller stations air local programming to individual communities. Some large stations issue international broadcasts.

Inside North Korea, little outside broadcast programming is available as all the radio sets manufactured in the country have fixed dials to receive only domestic programs. Radio sets that were purchased outside the country have to be fixed to function the same way. Despite the fact that relations between the North and the South have relaxed in recent years, there is still little television fare from the South on the screens of the North.

South Asia

Radio plays a uniquely important role in South Asian countries as the region represents the lesser-developed part of Asia. Radio is popular in this part of the world, particularly its rural areas, because its technology is relatively simple and inexpensive and because the audience does not have to be literate to understand the message. As development journalism plays a positive role in South Asian societies, community radio is also very popular. It broadcasts programs relevant to the needs of its audience, very different from the mainstream elite and commercial media in urban centers. Community radio in the region obtains support from local universities and UNESCO. The 1990s witnessed a revolution in the broadcast industry in South Asia. Over the decade, the television sector was transformed from single-dominant public broadcasters having virtual monopolies of each country to a system whereby there are over 100 transnational and regional channels available across borders (Thomas, 2005).

India has experienced a rapid proliferation of television broadcasters, most of them private, since 1986 when the country hosted the Asian Games. Satellite television has also established its presence and power over the Indian market. Out of 70 million TV households of the country in the early 2000s, about 37 million receive satellite channels (Joshi, 2000). Although multiple players are an indication of democracy and plurality, the vast majority of the Indian population and their interests are underrepresented in the mainstream media. It is not surprising that programming is targeted at a small segment of the urban middle class, which wields significant buying power.

Milestones in the development of the Indian broadcast industry include the first satellite broadcasting, in 1975, which helped take television signals to remote areas of the country. The Gulf War of 1991 provided another opportunity for the television industry when CNN was the first to beam transnational signals on the war. These CNN transmissions inspired young entrepreneurs in the country, who initiated the present mode of distributing satellite signals through a cable network to individual households. Then Rupert Murdoch's StarTV network followed CNN into the market in India in 1992, offering more choices in entertainment programs.

Doordarshan now faces real competition. Gone are the days of monopoly, as this national television authority of the government has to reorient itself to compete with its rivals. In the 1980s it adopted color transmission and shifted its programming focus from social-educational to commercial and entertainment programs (Thomas, 2005). To compete with transnational broadcasters, Doordarshan launched five new satellite channels in 1993 and started 10 ethnic language channels in addition to three national channels. At the start of the 2000s, Doordarshan had 47 program production centers, 19 satellite transponders, 1,056 terrestrial transmitters, and 19 channels. It was watched by about 450 million people in the country (Thomas, 2005). After more than 30 years in operation, Doordarshan has grown into a giant network. All India Radio remains a dominant radio broadcaster in the country, continuing its longtime tradition of development and community journalism and programming.

In Pakistan, the government decided to free the electronic media from government monopoly in 2000 when a framework was being developed to allow Pakistan Television (PTV) and Radio Pakistan to compete with private channels ("Government to Free," 2000). But PTV and the Pakistan Broadcasting Corporation will continue functioning in the public sector. The government has no plans to privatize radio and television in Pakistan, but private individuals will be able to set up their own TV and radio stations ("Private Radio," 2000).

In late 2000, PTV lost its 36-year monopoly on television news when the government of Musharraf launched Pakistan News Network (PNN) (Thomas, 2005). Broadcasting in Hindi, Bengali, and Chinese, PNN was started with the intention of ending the regional dominance of Indian news channels. It was believed that viewership of ZeeTV and other Indian channels was very high as Urdu is similar to Hindi except in the written script.

Trying to limit the influence of Indian broadcast media and expand its own regional influence seem to be the top priorities in the development strategy of Pakistan's broadcast industry. In 1992 PTV launched a transnational service to compete with the Pakistani private channel, Shalimar, and Indian public television (Thomas, 2005). In 1998 another satellite channel called PTV World was started, targeting Pakistanis elsewhere in Asia, and Prime TV was established to transmit PTV programs to Pakistani seasonal workers in Europe. A year later, the PTV Mid-East channel was launched to provide home television fare to expatriate Pakistanis in the Persian Gulf region.

In addition to opening up the broadcast media, the Pakistani government also reduced Internet connection charges for Internet service providers by more than 50 percent in an attempt to boost use of the Internet and the information technology industry.

Radio broadcasters in Pakistan continue to play a community radio role by providing information relevant to community and economic development. Pakistani radio also offers regular news and entertainment programs. Given the relatively low literacy rate of the country, radio remains an important source of information, especially in the rural areas.

The same is true in Bangladesh, where the government-owned Radio Bangladesh, with its eight regional stations, covers 95 percent of the country's land and people (Bhuiyan and Gunaratne, 2000). Radio Bangladesh functioned as an independent government department until 1984 when it was merged with Bangladesh Television. Its programming consists of 65 percent entertainment, 9 percent cultural and religious programs, 5 percent educational programs, 3 percent news, and a variety of other programs. Its shortwave service broadcasts in more than six languages to South Asia, the Middle East, and Europe. In 1975 the country opened its first satellite radio station with financial assistance from the Canadian International Development Agency.

Television in Bangladesh began in 1964 when Bangladesh Television (BTV) was established with the help of the NEC of Japan (Bhuiyan and Gunaratne, 2000). Even after nationalization in 1971, when Bangladesh became independent, NEC has remained a major stockholder. More than 50 percent of the programming on BTV was entertainment, most of which was locally produced, while only about 21 percent was imported.

Both radio and television in Bangladesh remained under government monopoly until 1999, when the government allowed the establishment of the country's first private television station, Ekushey TV, granting it a 15-year license (Thomas, 2006). In the 1990s, cable TV also entered the country and has become a popular medium for entertainment as it provides dozens of channels from India and regionally. The country has more than one million cable and satellite homes with about 2,000 cable operators providing services. All cable operators need a license from the BTV (Desai, 2002). In Bangladesh, television still remains a privilege for the elite—there were only 1.5 million licensed sets in the country in the late 1990s (Bhuiyan and Gunaratne, 2000), which compares to the country's population of 150 million in 2007. Most of the television sets in the country were imported and beyond the means of a majority of the people.

Public radio and television in Bangladesh are financed through license fees, advertising, and government funding. The country also has eight Internet service providers, and quite a few Bangladeshi publications can be accessed on the Web.

Community radio is a major characteristic of Sri Lankan radio broadcasting, which began as a government monopoly in 1925 and remained so until the 1984. Private radio broadcasters emerged after the government relaxed the monopoly of the Sri Lanka Broad-casting Corporation (SLBC) (Gunaratne and Wattegama, 2000). There were 11 private radio broadcasters in the country in the early 2000s.

In contrast, television was started as a private enterprise with the establishment of the Independent Television Network in 1979. But in less than two months, the government took over the network. The government-run Sri Lanka Rupavahini Corporation (SLRC) and ITN dominated the television industry in the country. Government monopoly of the sector was relaxed in 1992 when four private companies introduced six television chan-nels. In 1999, the government's Telecommunications Authority allowed two more private television broadcasters. Both SLBC and SLRC are public corporations whose funding comes from license fees and advertising.

Nepal's broadcast environment has changed radically since the country's transition to multiparty democracy in 1990. New broadcast policies, legislation, and regulations allowed for public interest, community, and commercial FM stations, as well as satellite TV distribution via cable and some limited local TV broadcasting. The first private radio station was on the air in 1991 funded by UNESCO as a model for community radio, while the first private endeavor in television came in 1994 when satellite television entered Nepal in 1994 (Rao and Koirala, 2000).

The government owns the influential Radio Nepal and one of several television stations. Political coverage on Radio Nepal is progovernment, and private radio stations are required to broadcast Radio Nepal news at least once daily in addition to their own news programming. Unlike many other countries in the region, policies regarding access to outside broadcast programming are very liberal, as Nepalese have unrestricted access to cable and satellite television, foreign broadcasts, and the Internet. But private Internet service providers have blocked access to the Maoists' Web site since 2004 (Freedom House report, 2005).

In Bhutan, both radio and television stations are run by the government's Bhutan Broadcasting Service, and they do not carry antigovernment programs or statements. Bhutan had no domestic television service until 1999 (Conlon, 2000), when the government believed that the country was ready to produce its own programs. Concern exists that the popularity of foreign films may undermine traditional Bhutanese values and culture. In the absence of television, urban Bhutanese watched rented foreign movies.

Cable television services in the country are privately run and provide uncensored foreign programming today. Cable TV is very popular in the cities, but its growth has been slowed by a high sales tax and the lack of a broadcasting law. Internet access is expanding and unrestricted. In 2004 a second Internet service provider started operation.

In Afghanistan, years of fighting and repression have destroyed the infrastructure of the broadcast industry. American bombing in November 2001 destroyed radio and televi-sion transmitters. As a result, the broadcast industry in Afghanistan had to start from scratch. The need for public service broadcasting in Afghanistan has never been greater, as it should be concerned about even the nonconsuming classes. It needs to determine and meet the needs of the illiterate, poverty-stricken villager watching TV or listening to radio on a community set in some far-away corner of the country. It also needs to provide serv-ice for minorities—ethnic, religious, linguistic, class, or caste.

Afghanistan's new 2004 constitution provides for freedom of the press and of expression. It allows Afghan citizens, political parties, organizations, and the government of Afghanistan to set up audiovisual establishments, bringing an end to government monopoly in the sector.

Southeast Asia

The government of Thailand has a unique way of managing the broadcast media in the country—government and army ownership of radio and television stations that are leased long term to private business groups for daily operations. Radio was introduced to Thailand as early as 1907, and there are more than 500 radio stations in the country today. The Broadcasting Directing Board determines all aspects of radio broadcasting, such as hours of operation, content, advertising, and technical requirements (Ekachai, 2000).

In 1955, Thailand was the first country in continental Asia to start regular television broadcasting, which remained a state monopoly until 1996 when the first nongovernment television station, Independent Television, was started with promises of in-depth and aggressive news coverage. ITV quickly established a reputation for critical journalism, but financial woes following the Asian financial crisis forced it to sell 40 percent of its shares in 2000 (Lewis, 2003). The financial difficulties also dashed the hopes for broadcasting reform prompted by the new liberal constitution of 1997. Despite the setback, the Thai television industry continues to diversify, totaling 111 television stations in the country today.

Throughout Asia, radio is a very important, popular, and effective mass medium for national unity and development. It is even more so in the case of Indonesia as the country is still developing and its landmass and people are widely scattered. Broadcast media in the country underwent major transformations after dictator Suharto was overthrown in 1998. The number of broadcast media outlets jumped, totaling more than 50 RRI broadcasting stations, 780 commercial stations, and 133 local government stations among others (Idris and Gunaratne, 2000).

The Asian Games held in Indonesia in 1962 boosted the development of television broadcasting in the country, as it did for other Asian countries, and marked the debut of its new Televisi Republik Indonesia (TVRI). Television in Indonesia experienced three growth spurts: the exponential growth in television households after the launch of its satellite in 1976, the rise of commercial television in the early 1990s, and the expansion of the sector as a result of *reformasi* following Suharto's forced resignation (Kitley, 2004).

After Suharto, there was a sharp increase in the number of broadcasters and in the diversity of content. In 2002 the percentage of local programming increased due to audience preference despite the popularity of licensed program formats, such as quiz shows (Kitley, 2004). The localized version of *Who Wants to Be a Millionaire?* glued over a third of Indonesian television households to their screens at 7 on Saturday nights. The program was just one of a number of quiz and game show formats screened across all channels in the country.

Unlike most other countries on the continent, broadcast media in the Philippines are mostly privately owned and free from government controls. The National Telecommunication Commission (NTC) indirectly controls the quality of performance and standards of radio and television stations.

Radio was introduced to the Philippines in 1922, only two years after the establishment of the first American radio station in Pittsburgh. After World War II, radio broadcasting expanded rapidly. By 1972, when Marcos declared martial law, there were about 350 radio stations in the country (Maslog, 2000). Commercial television broadcasting started in 1953. During the 1960s and 1970s the growth of television caused overcrowding. The rule by martial law from 1972–1986 put an end to a free media that was sharply critical of government corruption and human rights abuses. After Marcos, free and private media returned and thrived. In the Philippines, radio set ownership was relatively high at 88 percent of the households in Metro Manila, and 81 percent elsewhere in the country (Maslog, 2000). Television set ownership was a little lower at 87 percent.

ABS-CBN is a leading television broadcaster in the country, with its Channel 2 commanding one of the highest ratings. Its locally produced fare dominated weekday programming—about 77.5 percent of a 20-hour airing day (Santos, 2004). Its programs, representative of other higher-rating channels, ranged from news and public affairs, game and variety shows, to talk shows, movies, sitcoms and soaps, and midnight Christian-evangelist programs. Latin American telenovelas and foreign children's shows in the morning and afternoon accounted for 22.5 percent of the daily airtime. The emphasis on locally produced programs was due to earlier criticism of the "colonial mentality" and Americanized culture as a result of foreign programming. Channel 7 of GMA Network, a fast-rising broadcaster, also had a wide variety of locally produced programs with a slightly higher foreign content. Channel 4, a government-owned channel, broadcast two hours of Fox News five days a week.

In Singapore, the government was directly involved with the start of radio and television services in the country. The Ministry of Communications and the Singapore Broadcasting Authority (SBA) control much of what occurs in television and radio in the country. The SBA's purpose is supposed to regulate and promote the broadcasting industry in Singapore. The SBA stipulated that no person could hold more than 3 percent of shares in a broadcasting company, that the CEO and at least half of the board of directors must be Singapore citizens, and that foreign funding was not allowed to exceed 49 percent of a company's capital (Kuo and Ang, 2000). The Singaporean government has always been wary of foreign influence on its media.

Singapore had 18 radio channels in the early 2000s. Radio Corporation Singapore (RCS) operated major radio stations to serve both local and international audiences and owned and managed 10 local and three international channels.

In 1980 a statutory organization, the Singapore Broadcasting Corporation (SBC), was formed with the charge of improving the quality of radio and television programming. In 1999 it was renamed the Media Corporation of Singapore (MCS). There were nine terrestrial television stations controlled by just two large local media networks—MCS and SPH MediaWorks, a subsidiary of Singapore Press Holdings (Lim, 2004). MCS had two television networks under it—MediaCorp TV Singapore and MediaCorp STV12—which were in direct competition with channels owned by SPH. The main contenders for serious industry competition were the four entertainment channels. As a result of the competition, the overall television audience reach expanded from 77.3 percent in 2001 to 90 percent a year later. But in 2004 a megamerger between SPH and MediaCorp TV ended four years of cutthroat competition and diversity in the Singapore media.

Singapore is also home to most of the key international satellite broadcasters and many production companies such as HBO Asia, ESPN Star Sports, Discovery Asia, MTV Southeast Asia, and BBC Worldwide, solidifying its position as a hub of communication in the region.

Like Singapore, the broadcast media in Malaysia are characterized by the advanced level of communication technologies and the direct involvement of the government, which tends to rely on the mainstream media as a tool for national integration and economic development. The state-owned Radio Television Malaysia (RTM) has a virtual radio monopoly ("Malaysia," 2007). Four government radio networks broadcast in the various languages—Bahasa Melayu, Chinese, English, and Tamil. In 2007, the Malaysian National News Agency, Bernama, began the dry run of the country's first 24-hour news radio, Radio24. The test run was the prelude to the official launch of the latest radio station by the information ministry. Radio24 would air "info-capsules" and community service messages interspersed with patriotic songs, according to Minister Zainuddin Maidin. It would also broadcast hourly news bulletins and cover national and international news with support from Bernama bureaus. In Malaysia, not only state media but private media including radio and television were asked to assist the government in its nation-building efforts, including the promotion of independence, which has its own theme and official song for each campaign. The songs were aired on all RTM stations ("Private Media," 2007).

There are four nationwide television channels in the country—two RTM channels (TV1 and TV2) and two privately run channels (TV3 and NTV7). There is also an additional private television station, MetroVision, which only operates in the Klang Valley. A cable network, MegaTV, is also available in the country. As in many developing countries, RTM is funded by receiver license fees and government subsidies, as well as advertising revenues (Thomas, 2006). In order to compete for advertising, in the 1980s RTM began to import more recent, higher quality foreign programming, catering to ethnic minorities, particularly the Chinese, who had greater purchasing power. Such imports lowered the standards of television programming on sex and violence.

Satellite dishes used to be illegal in the country. But in 1996 the Broadcasting Act was amended to license its use to receive the domestic pay-TV services MegaTV and Astro, which carried transnational and domestic channels. However, all foreign programming was censored before rebroadcast locally (Thomas, 2006).

Vietnamese radio and television are still government monopolies, owned, operated, and mostly financed by the state. The Voice of Vietnam is the major official radio station in the country, serving both a domestic and an international audience. Its national service is carried by three networks—one on news, current affairs, and music; another on the economy, culture, and education; and the third serving the minority population in the country (Panol and Do, 2000). Its international service is quite ambitious, targeting the whole world. As elsewhere in Asia, the Voice of Vietnam remains a tool for national development and education. In 2007, it embarked on a three-year project, making use of a serialized radio drama of 104 episodes to improve the awareness and change behavior regarding HIV/AIDS prevention.

The television market in Vietnam is expanding rapidly with 90 percent of Vietnamese households owning television sets (Lee, 2006) and attracting the attention of international broadcasters such as the Disney channel, whose 24-hour kid-driven, family-inclusive channel was expanding its reach in the country and was available in 75 percent of all the pay-TV households in 2007 (Tatoy, 2007). Even though television in Vietnam is still state-run, there are increasing opportunities for private companies to participate in program production. For example, Fremantle Media and Endemol not only license program formats but also offer program production assistance.

Until 2006, television game shows had been very popular with eight major television stations in the country airing more than 50 of them, many in prime time (Lee, 2006). Among the most popular were Vietnamese versions of American shows such as *The Price Is Right* and *Wheel of Fortune,* which captured 35 to 40 percent of the viewers in Hanoi. Unlike in the United States where game shows tend to draw an older audience, in Vietnam the biggest fans were the young people. By 2007 talk shows and reality programs replaced game shows as major ratings boosters.

Limited by its level of economic development and state control of the media, the broadcast media in Laos are far from being developed. The main radio station in the country is Radio Vientiane, and the major television service provider is Lao National Television, which began in 1983. The major task of the broadcast media in the country is to disseminate party policies to its people. Countries including Vietnam, Australia, and Japan, and organizations such as UNESCO provided assistance in improving the infrastructure of the Lao broadcast media.

In Cambodia the broadcast media remain controlled by the state, and programming reflects government views. More Cambodians acquire information from radio than from any other media (Schafer, 2001). There were 19 radio stations and an estimated one million radios in the early 2000s in the country, where broadcasts are accessible in all provinces. As in Laos, people who do not own radios can hear broadcasts on loudspeakers. The Voice of Cambodia is a major radio station in the country. There are also nine television stations today in the country, where the number of television sets is also limited. More urban dwellers than rural ones have access to television broadcast.

Myanmar (Burma), known for its opposition leader and Nobel Peace Prize laureate Aung San Suu Kyi, remains an impoverished and isolated country. Electrical services are available in about only 10 percent of the country's territory, thus the use of radio and television is rather limited (Schafer, 2001). By 2004, there were only two television stations, one AM radio station, and one FM radio station, in the country. Government radio broadcasting, Burma Broadcasting Service, reaches urban populations only. Radio stations play only approved programs, which exclude Western songs. Shortwave radio broadcasts including the Voice of America and the BBC are, however, available. The government-owned television station broadcasts only a few shows on evenings and weekends. Internet access in Myanmar is rare. However, Internet journalism is developing a substantial presence in the region, including Singapore, Malaysia, Thailand, the Philippines, and Indonesia.

The Pacific

Many Pacific radio stations are still under the control of the governments, either directly or indirectly, and are heavily influenced by their colonial history—the influence from Europe, Australia, and New Zealand (Craddock, 2000). But despite the many obstacles in the development of the electronic media in the Pacific region, radio remains the only timely link between the islands in the region and the rest of the world.

The Cook Islands Broadcasting Corporation incorporates public broadcasting goals into its radio objectives. In the Marshall Islands, the radio system is a mixture of public service radio, commercial broadcasting, and automated satellite radio feeds for United States military personnel and families. A number of radio and television stations in the South Pacific broadcast "stale news," because "to try and be the first with the news is more the exception than the rule" (Craddock, 2000). To beef up news coverage, Radio New Zealand International and Radio Australia supply much of the up-to-date news on Pacific events. The Australian station has several reporters around the Pacific; the New Zealand station relies on a few freelancers and telephone interviews.

As a commercial venture, radio is unlikely to be sustained by market forces in the small Pacific countries. Radio Tonga and the Solomon Islands Broadcasting Corporation run side businesses to bring in money for their station funds, such as selling electric appliances and servicing other electronic equipment (Seward, 1999). Other stations supplement their operation funds with payments for broadcasting birthday calls, pending events, and death notices, adding a unique flavor to Pacific radio through the broadcasting of personal family histories.

In Papua New Guinea, there are eight AM radio stations, 19 FM stations, 28 short-wave radio stations, and three television stations. Fiji is quite a contender, hosting 13 AM and 40 FM radio stations. In Samoa, five radio stations and two television stations serve a population of 214,265, while in Tonga a population of 116,921 is served by six radio stations and three television stations.

News Services

Given the uneven development of the news media in Asia, ownership forms and the role of news agencies vary widely in the region. Most Asian nations have national government news agencies, while many also have private news agencies. In democratic and media-rich societies, private news agencies compete with each other and with government news agencies, while in government-controlled or poor-media societies, government agencies play a dominant role in disseminating news and in setting the tone of news coverage.

There are two regional news services in Asia. The Asia News Network is a network of national daily newspapers, while Depthnews, a development news service established in 1969, caters to clients throughout the Asian region and serves as a voice for Asian development journalism. Depthnews stands for development, economics, and population themes.

East Asia

China has two news agencies: the well-known Xinhua and the lesser-known China News Service, targeting the overseas Chinese population. Both are owned by the government. For domestic news, Xinhua has more than 30 bureaus across the country, employing nearly 3,000 people. Overseas, Xinhua has 101 bureaus in 92 countries, employing more than 500 people. In 35 other countries, Xinhua hires locals as its editorial staff. Outside the country, Xinhua correspondents and editors are classified as diplomats and enjoy diplomatic immunity. News from Western news agencies usually goes through Xinhua before it reaches local papers. To be competitive economically, Xinhua has added several publications of its own: the *Xinhua Daily Telegraph, Economic Reference News, Outlook,* and *Semimonthly Talk.*

China News Service also has bureaus inside and outside China, employing about 500 people. The agency claims to be the first in Asia to put a Chinese-language media outlet on the Internet.

The only news agency in Hong Kong is the Hong Kong China News Agency, established in 1956. Its target audiences are overseas Chinese media and people in Hong Kong, Macao, and Taiwan.

Kyodo News Service and Jiji Press are Japan's largest news services. Kyodo is a nonprofit cooperative organization run on an annual budget, which is primarily made up of membership dues and revenues from nonmember subscribers, according to the Web site of Kyodo. Kyodo's Japanese-language news service is distributed to almost all newspapers and radio-TV networks in Japan. The combined circulation of newspaper subscribers is about 50 million. Kyodo's English-language news service reaches news media outlets around the world. Kyodo News has a U.S. subsidiary, Kyodo News International, Inc. (KNI), based in New York. It also has an affiliate, K.K. Kyodo News, which serves as its business arm. Kyodo has some 1,000 journalists and photographers. More than half of them are posted at the Tokyo head office. For international newsgathering, some 70 full-time correspondents and 40 stringers are posted outside Japan. News coverage focuses on the Asia-Pacific region and North America, followed by Europe, the Middle East, Latin America, and Africa.

Jiji Press specializes in business news. It also publishes Jiji Press News on the Web, which is an Internet-based English news service, providing news about important policy decisions in Japan and up-to-the-minute information on Japan's economic and corporate activities. Major economic statistics are also available, along with financial market information and charts. The site claims to have more than 100 news items on a daily basis.

South Korea, North Korea, and Mongolia all have government news agencies. The Korean Central News Agency of North Korea acts as the spokesman of the government and the gatekeeper of the country's news media.

South Asia

The privately owned Press Trust of India (PTI), a nonprofit-sharing cooperative owned by the country's newspapers, is one of Asia's best-known news agencies. PTI subscribers include 450 Indian newspapers and scores of foreign newspapers. All major television and radio channels in India and some international broadcasters, including the BBC, receive the PTI Service. With a staff of over 1,300 including 400 journalists, PTI has over 80 bureaus across the country and foreign correspondents in major capitals of the world. It also has about 475 stringers contributing to its news pool.

As is conventional with major international news agencies, PTI has exchange relations with the Associated Press (AP), Agence France-Presse (AFP), and Bloomberg for distribution of their news in India, as well as with the Associated Press for its Photo Service and International Commercial Information. PTI exchanges news with nearly 100 news agencies of the world as part of bilateral and multilateral arrangements, such as the Non-Aligned News Agencies Pool and the Organization of Asia-Pacific News Agencies. PTI also provides specialized services in photo and financial information and contributes to Asia Pulse, which provides a package of four weekly features on topical national, international, and general events.

Another strong contender is the United News of India (UNI), which serves more than 1,000 subscribers in more than 100 locations in India and abroad, according to its Web site. UNI has bureaus in all the major cities of the country and correspondents in major cities of the world. It also has more than 325 staff journalists and more than 250 stringers. It claims to be the first Indian news agency to serve subscribers abroad in 1981 and the first news agency in the country to launch a financial service, a stock exchange service, and a national photo service.

There are three major news agencies in Pakistan. News Network International (NNI), established in 1992, is the largest independent international news agency in the country. Besides providing services to more than 100 national and regional newspapers in English, Urdu, and Sindhi languages, NNI has subscribers in America, Europe, the Far East, South Asia, Central Asia, the Gulf States, and the Middle East. NNI has a network of 700 correspondents, reporters, and stringers throughout Pakistan. The other two news agencies are Pakistan Press International (PPI) and the Associated Press of Pakistan (APP).

Sri Lanka has two news agencies, Lankapuvath (National News Agency of Sri Lanka) and Sandesa News Agency. Nepal's news agency, the Rashtriya Samachar Samiti, is owned by the government, and its chairman is appointed by the government.

Southeast Asia

Most of the countries in the region have a national news agency, providing news feed and sometimes guidelines for news reporting within their national boundaries.

One of the largest national news agencies in the region is the Malaysian National News Agency or Bernama, a statutory body set up by an Act of Parliament in 1967. The agency has its offices throughout Malaysia and correspondents in Singapore and Jakarta and stringers or retainers in Washington, London, Manila, New Delhi, Dhaka, Melbourne, and Vancouver. It provides general and economic news services and screen-based real-time financial information services to subscribers in Malaysia and Singapore. With the launching of its audiovisual unit known as BernamaTV in 1998, news is now available in the form of visuals as well. Its Web site provides easy access to news and visuals.

Indonesia's major national news service is Antara, founded in 1937 to serve the struggle for national independence from the Dutch colonizers and Japanese occupation. Antara has bureaus in all provinces, manned by nearly 200 correspondents who cover news from provincial capitals down to the villages. The agency also has bureaus in New York, Canberra, Kuala Lumpur, Cairo, and Sana'a. It has also teamed with news agencies in the world, such as Bernama, AAP (Australia), Reuters, AFP (France), DPA (Germany), Xinhua, and Kyodo. It is a member of the ASEAN News Exchange, Organization of Asia-Pacific News Agencies, and Non-Aligned News Agencies Pool. It distributes more than 250 stories covered by its own reporters and 3,000 stories received from its foreign partners to its clients on a daily basis. Aside from providing news and photos, Antara also offers real-time data from stock and money markets and press release distribution. Antara is also a partner in running Asia Pulse and Asia Net.

The Philippines News Agency (PNA) is a division of the News and Information Bureau of the Philippines government. It is the primary news source on the Philippines for the domestic and international media, as well as all levels of the government.

The Thai News Agency (TNA) is operated by the Mass Communication Organization of Thailand (MCOT), which is a Thai media conglomerate and which was partially privatized in an initial public offering in 2004, with the Thai Ministry of Finance retaining a 77 percent stake. TNA news stories are distributed via MCOT television and radio networks and the Internet.

The Vietnam News Agency is the official national news service of Vietnam. As in China, it is directly attached to the government, serves as the voice of the government, and is authorized to report on national and international events, setting boundaries of news reporting for news media outlets in the country.

The Pacific

PACNEWS, the Pacific News Agency Service, is perhaps the only news agency in the region. Its members include almost all the Pacific island countries. The news agency provides comprehensive coverage of regional events and issues for members and commercial clients. News is gathered from both broadcasting and stringers, and is then provided every weekday through facsimile or by e-mail. Its standard service features three separate Pacnews bulletins every weekday. Each bulletin contains between 6 and 10 stories concerning the Pacific Islands region.

Media Freedom and Government–Media Relations

Asia is a very diverse continent in terms of political system. Government–media relations vary from country to country. Of the major theories of the press regarding global press systems, namely, authoritarian, libertarian, Communist, social responsibility, development, and democratic-participant (Downing, 2002:22), examples of each can be found in Asia.

If there is one commonality regarding the media in Asia, it is their role in nation-building. Many of the Asian countries were colonies of Western powers before World War II. They became independent only after the war, which devasted many of these countries. High on the agenda of national governments across Asia was economic development, which is a long-term goal, given the low starting point and large populations. It is no coincidence that development journalism originated in the Philippines and India.

East Asia

In China, the news media are owned by the state. The media are expected to follow Communist Party and government policies. News media are regarded as a tool for national development, education, information, and entertainment. Media are supposed to be a bridge between the party and the people. The government keeps the media in line mainly through regulations and through the appointment or removal of editors.

Ding Guangen, former head of the Publicity Department of the Central Committee of the Chinese Communist Party, emphasized in one speech that under no circumstances can the news media alter its role as the voice of the party and the people ("Party Publicity Chief," 2001). He said that the news media should help promote reform, safeguard social stability, and create a sound environment for the socialist cause with Chinese characteristics. Interestingly, he also stated that journalists should listen to public opinion in order to tell the truth and write news stories that can stand the test of time.

In China there is still no press law, even though it was proposed at the National People's Congress in 2000. The need for the law arose when some government officials refused interviews by the media. In other cases, journalists' video cameras were broken, and some reporters were even manhandled by local governments. Anhui Province took the lead in issuing a regulation in 2000 banning its government from refusing interviews with the press ("Press Law," 2000). Other provinces and cities followed suit as the government now needs the media to fight corruption. In Shanghai, a reporter, based on a city ordinance mandating the disclosure of public information, sued the municipal planning department for repeatedly declining interviews (Zhou, 2006).

To regulate news on the Internet, the Netnews Bureau of the China Internet Information Center declared in 2000 that commercial Web sites without traditional news background could not engage in news coverage. The government often blocks some Western news sites for politically sensitive material and other sites for content deemed objectionable, such as sex and violence. But on a regular day, Fox News, MSNBC, the *New York Times, Washington Post, Christian Science Monitor, USA Today,* and ABC can be accessed inside China. There does not seem to be consistent guidelines on what sites to block. In September 2002, the search engine Google was briefly blocked, resulting in a worldwide uproar over control of the Internet in China. The block was believed to be prompted by the unflattering information retrieved about former President Jiang Zemin.

Relations between the government and media in Hong Kong have been in the spotlight of the world media since 1997. In the 10 years after the turnover, China has kept its promise of "one country, two systems" regarding Hong Kong affairs. Today Hong Kong remains a free society, and its media are still diverse and dynamic despite concerns of increased self-censorship.

Ironically, freedom of the press and freedom of expression were clearly enshrined and entrenched in Hong Kong's written constitution for the first time after 1997 (Cheung, 2002:191). The colonial government in Hong Kong had "notoriously illiberal ordinances" to control the press, even though it seldom used them (So, Chan, and Lee, 2000:542). Many of these laws were repealed after 1985 when Britain and China signed the treaty to return Hong Kong to China.

Hong Kong law professor Anne S. Y. Cheung called for attention to the threat to press freedom from the judiciary branch (Cheung, 2002). She said, "The problem is that most of the Hong Kong SAR judges are trapped in the pre-constitution mindset" (2002:215). Professor Cheung stated that the judges value deference to authority more than the respect of civil liberties, and she concluded that unless there is an awakening in the judicial attitude, the struggle to protect press freedom in Hong Kong will be a constant uphill battle (2002:193).

In Taiwan, successive governments have embarked on a road of liberalization since 1987, lifting martial law, repealing the ban on new licenses for newspapers, television, and radio stations, and relaxing policies of control over the media in general. Discussions of Taiwan's independence used to be off limits in the press. Now encouraged by a government promoting independence, papers are openly advocating it. To further reduce government influence on the media, the politically independent National Communications Commission replaced the government regulatory body, the Government Information Office, in 2006. A new law approved in 2003 barred the government and political party officials from holding positions in broadcast media companies. Government agencies and political parties were also required to pull their investments out of all broadcast companies by December 2005. In 2006, the government donated its majority share in China Television System to the Public Television Service, according to the 2007 Freedom House report.

Japan and South Korea are both democracies, and their media legally are free from government intervention or influence. But the media in both countries are described as a "lapdog" rather than a watchdog (Freeman, 2000). Confucian thought is a dominant influence in Japan and South Korea, even though the Chinese philosopher-educator lived more than 2,000 years ago. Confucius believed that a strong state is the ultimate goal and that all individual interest should give way to national interest. He hoped that the government would be strong and kind and would take care of its people. Confucian philosophy clearly prescribed a patriarchal role for the government. Japan and South Korea prospered under state-guided capitalism. For purposes of the "national interest," media in Japan and South Korea exercise heavy self-censorship.

In Japan, controversial media bills—laws to protect personal data and human rights—are being introduced. Ignoring protests from newspapers and broadcasters, Prime Minister Junichiro Koizumi's cabinet approved a bill aimed at outlawing "excessive reporting activities" and "violations of privacy" by reporters (Whymant, 2002). Japanese legislators and critics pointed out that the bills would put unreasonable restraints on the media ("Media Bills Require Changes," 2002).

Since South Korea returned to civilian government in the late 1980s, the media in South Korea have finally been free. However, mainstream media in South Korea have always been progovernment except for the flare-up between the government and the media in 2001 over alleged tax evasion by major newspapers. The Chosun Ilbo (Nam, 2001) contended that the government crackdown occurred because of the paper's criticism of government policy toward North Korea. The South Korean government also controls the media through advertising. In recent years there have been signs that the news media are moving away from a collusive to a more adversarial press (Gunn, 2007).

South Asia

Most of the governments in South Asia are democratically elected and thereby claim to uphold their constitutions guaranteeing freedom of speech and of the press. But given the harsh economic realities of the region, most governments try to influence news coverage along the line of nation-building. Another area of grave concern to governments in the region is national security, some involving internal conflicts and others relating to external relations and the issue of terrorism. When security issues or social order are involved, some governments in the region, such as Sri Lanka, Bangladesh and Nepal, often exercise direct censorship while others often resort to the court system. Other means of control include allocating newsprint and advertising quotas, stipulating registration rules, and directly operating the broadcast media.

In Sri Lanka, the government approved the reintroduction of state-controlled regulation of the media after a more hard-line government led by President Rajapakse was elected into office in 2005. Later in the year emergency regulations were established giving government wide powers of prior restraint against the media. The Tamil media in the country operate under very difficult conditions. Tamil correspondents face challenges such as refusal of the police and the military to confirm information, interference in the editorial policies, late night police and military visits to the newsroom, violent threats on the phone, physical assaults and murder, and the denial of distribution of the print media ("Struggle for Survival," 2007). But in areas controlled by the Tamil Tigers, press freedom was also described as severely restricted.

Press freedom in Sri Lanka is often upheld by an independent judiciary system, and political writings, even if they are critical of government policies, receive far more tolerance than those affecting religion or family values (Desai, 2002). Other than censorship and control of access to information, another major threat to press freedom in the country comes from assaults on journalists. In some cases, army officers and the police were involved.

The War on Terror has put the media in Pakistan in a spotlight. The absence of a specific freedom of information law leaves press freedom at the mercy of the government. For example, the election of more liberal state leaders such as Prime Minister Mohammad Khan Junejo and the first woman Muslim Prime Minister Benazir Bhutto in the 1980s and 1990s allowed the media more freedom to grow. But the election of former Pakistani prime minister Nawaz Sharif turned back the clock as he used heavy-handed methods in dealing with journalists critical of his government and put tremendous pressure on independent journalists (Pstein, 2002).

In the early days of his administration, President Musharraf enjoyed a cooperative relationship with the media as his government followed a more liberal policy toward the press. But by 2007 the press was locked in a looming battle against the increasingly frustrated government under Musharraf as the War on Terror and the hunt for bin Laden intensified. Aside from security concerns, Pakistan is a relatively open society where independent courts often strike down government attempts to restrain the media.

The government in Nepal controls the independent media by restricting access to information and firing reporters who write stories contrary to government media dictates (Schafer, 2001). A partisan press dominates the media scene in Nepal, where 90 percent of Nepalese newspapers do not sell advertisements and instead, rely on sponsors, usually politically related. Journalists often are active members of political parties, and editors and publishers gain their positions through political appointments.

The press suffered a major setback in 2005 when King Gyanendra declared a nationwide state of emergency and dissolved the parliament. Within one year, there were 400 cases of arrests and attacks on the media ("WAN Joins," 2006). Repression of the media and crackdowns on freedom of expression were common and increasing. The government introduced a series of new laws dramatically restricting freedom of expression and changing the regulatory environment for the print, broadcast, and online media. It also substantially increased the license fees for radio stations, especially independent and community radio stations. As a result of these measures, newspaper circulations declined and media organizations had to lay off hundreds of journalists ("Founding Father," 2005). The emergency rule produced a backlash and ended three months later.

In Afghanistan, effective government and the rule of law are still an issue. The new 2004 constitution and a press law revised in 2005 guarantee the right to freedom of expression and prohibit censorship, but do retain certain restrictions such as registration requirements and overly broad guidelines on content, according to the 2007 Freedom House report. It also established five commissions to regulate media agencies and investigate complaints of misconduct. In 2006, intelligence officials issued instructions to restrict media coverage of security issues, terrorist incidents, and the conduct of foreign troops. Media diversity and freedom are markedly higher in Kabul, and some warlords display limited tolerance for independent media in the areas under their control. Some journalists were threatened or harassed by government officials, the police, and security services as a result of their reporting. Many practice self-censorship on topics relating to Islam, national unity, or crimes committed by specific warlords.

In Bangladesh there is no direct government restriction on press ownership or content, but the government influences the press through economic means such as the allocation of government advertising and newsprint. Government advertising is the largest source of revenue for the press, taking about 50 percent of the press space (Desai, 2001). To avoid economic penalties, many newspapers apply self-censorship. Some newspapers are highly partisan in their political coverage, while a growing number of newspaper owners are either members of, or are affiliated with, parties in the government (Freedom House, 2005). But there are still independent newspapers that present a variety of views and actively engage in investigative reporting of government corruption. A 2005 corruption database report by the Transparency International Bangladesh studied the reporting of 26 newspapers, 19 of which were national dailies and 7 of which were regional dailies, and found a total of 2,128 incidents of corruption in the press coverage.

India has prided itself on its democracy and its tradition of a free press. The only exception was the Emergency Rule under Indira Gandhi. The press in India plays a significant watchdog role. Newspapers and news magazines are constantly engaged in aggressive reporting exposing corruption. Almost all leading papers have been critical of the government in power. Like many other Asian nations, the Indian government is still trying to control access to information by introducing a new Freedom of Information Bill in early 2001. Cusbrow R. Irani (2001) criticized the bill by charging that the bill was drawn up by bureaucrats for the benefit and protection of bureaucrats.

Southeast Asia

Southeast Asia is the most diverse part of Asia with regard to government-media relations. The region has Communist governments, authoritarian governments, and democratic governments. However, democracy in Southeast Asia is still young and fragile and in a state of flux. Because of the coup in Thailand, the attempted coup in the Philippines, and attempts at Islamization in Malaysia and Indonesia, the extent of press freedom allowed by the governments in these countries varies widely from year to year. Ironically, authoritarian and Communist governments are the more stable ones, where control of the media is constant.

The transition in national leadership in Singapore and Malaysia after decades of strongman rule did not bring about reforms toward more liberal governments. In Singapore, Lee Hsien Loong, the son of former Prime Minister Lee Kuan Yew, became prime minister in 2004. Singapore, where a majority of the country's citizens are Chinese, is one of the countries in Asia that is most heavily influenced by Confucius's teachings, even more so than China (Yin, 2003). Confucius believed in a strong and just government, and the Singaporean government practices meritocracy and is known for its transparency and relative lack of corruption. Confucius also believed in a patriarchal government, and the Singaporean government makes sure that the people receive only the right kind of information. Journalists in the country face pressure from the government not to oppose the government's nation-building goals and to avoid reporting on sensitive topics, such as race and religion, for the sake of social order and stability, leading them to practice self-censorship.

The Singaporean government controls the news media mainly through legislation and the court system. Singapore's constitution limits the right to freedom of speech and expression to citizens in Singapore, thus banning foreign media from covering Singapore's politics. The Newspapers and Printing Presses Act of 1974 requires annual licensing of daily newspapers. A 1986 amendment to the act gives the government the power to restrict the circulation of foreign publications that discuss domestic politics. In 2006 the *Far Eastern Economic Review* was banned following an interview with Singapore Democratic Party (SDP) leader Chee Soon Juan. In Singapore, the government won most of its libel cases against the media, which sometimes calls the independence of the judiciary system into question. The Singapore government fiercely guards not only its political system, but also its culture (Kuo and Ang, 2000). Soft porn and alternative lifestyle publications are prohibited under the Undesirable Publications Act.

Broadcasting is licensed as well, including the Internet, despite the fact that all domestic television channels and radio stations are operated by government-linked companies. The government monitors and sometimes censors the media for sex, violence, and drug references, and all political films are banned unless they are sponsored by the government. In Singapore satellite dishes are banned except for the international and financial communities.

The Malaysian government controls the press directly through several restrictive laws and punitive measures, including closing down newspapers, revoking licenses, denying the renewal of permits, arrests, jail time, and fines. The stepping-down of Mahathir in 2003 as prime minister of the country after 22 years of rule has not brought about much change. The Islamization of Malaysia and the Malay supremacy promoted by some cabinet ministers has crystallized a racial divide, and political corruption remains a serious issue, according to the 2007 Freedom House report.

Facing these potentially explosive social issues, the Malaysian government tightened control over the news media, banning coverage of racial and religious issues. In 2006 two publications were suspended for reprinting infamous Danish cartoons of the prophet Muhammad. Internet editions of newspapers are not currently required to obtain permits, but some government ministers call for extending the licensing requirement to cover online media in 2006. Privately owned television stations have close ties to the ruling party, and they censor programming according to government guidelines (e.g. see Saski, 2000).

The news media in Indonesia were set completely free after the dictatorial Suharto regime was overthrown in 1998. All the control mechanisms of the government or regulations were dismantled, and the number of media outlets rose sharply. However, cases of press freedom abuse prompted calls for some of the government controls to be reinstalled (Yin, 2003). Alerted by the push for a greater Islamization of Indonesia, exposés of government corruption, coverage of the 2004 tsunami, and continued cases of press freedom abuses, the government restored some of the control mechanisms of the past.

In 2006 the government promulgated a new set of broadcasting regulations restricting access to information, which reminded Indonesians of the censorship under Suharto. Libel laws and political pressure restrict the areas journalists can report on, according to the Freedom House. In the aftermath of the 2004 tsunami, Aceh was closed to the foreign media. In 2006, online editor Teguh Santosa was detained for republishing one of 12 controversial Danish cartoons of the prophet Muhammad. But the Internet remains a free medium in the country. There are more than 62,000 Internet hosts in Indonesia, an estimated 10 million users, and no reported government restrictions on access.

In the Philippines, after Marcos was forced to leave the country in 1986, the news media were freed from restrictive laws and regulations. But a lack of government regulation does not necessarily equal a free press (Kadrich, 2002), as newspapers are primarily driven by commercial and political interests, which often are tied to the government. However, such commercial ties do not deter the government from interfering in media operations. In 2001, President Arroyo tied the media's hands by ordering a blackout on coverage of the conflict between the army and Abu Sayyaf rebels in the southwestern part of the country. And in 2006 an alleged coup attempt prompted President Gloria Macapagal-Arroyo to declare a week-long state of emergency, during which some newspaper offices were raided, other newspapers placed under surveillance, some journalists charged with incitement to rebellion, and others arrested, according to the Freedom House. After emergency rule ended, the Supreme Court ruled that the administration's clampdown on the press was unjustified.

But on the whole, the news media in the Philippines are free to express a wide range of opinions, but journalists can pay a high price for their work, sometimes that price being their life. The Internet is widely available and uncensored in the country, which is home to more than 110,000 Internet hosts.

In Thailand the new military government applied tighter restrictions on media freedom in 2006 following a successful coup, which ousted Prime Minister Thaksin Shinawatra, dissolved parliament and the Constitutional Court, abrogated the constitution, and banned political gatherings. The new military government banned public discussion of the coup on government-run broadcast stations in order to silence opposition. Broadcast outlets in Thaksin strongholds were also targeted, and more than 300 radio stations in three provinces were closed down in just a few days, according to the Freedom House. Prior to the coup, Thaksin was also cracking down on the media by continuing in 2006 to launch criminal and civil defamation suits against harsh media critics.

Under civilian rule, Thai governments influence the media mainly through media ownership ties and economic means, such as channeling government advertising to pro-government press outlets. As a result, the media practice self-censorship and avoid political controversies and investigative reporting, even though corruption in the government and the military is widespread. The Thai government generally censors the Internet mainly to prevent circulation of pornography or illegal products and continues to block sites considered a threat to national security. Following the coup, the focus of Internet censorship shifted to potentially disruptive political messages.

Since the economic reforms in the mid-1980s, Vietnamese journalists have sought and achieved more freedom of expression (Schafer, 2002). The media have become livelier and more diverse in content. Investigative reporting of government corruption appeared and was even encouraged by the government as the problem became more serious. In 2006 as part of the anticorruption campaign, the government allowed the media greater freedom to report on graft and corruption following major bribery and corruption scandals involving officials in the Ministry of Transportation and the national soccer team.

However, the media are still mostly owned and controlled by the government, who often order the detention of reporters who disobey state rules and print anti-Communist materials (Schafer, 2002). The most unique piece of Vietnamese legislation is a 1999 law that requires journalists to pay damages to groups or individuals found to be harmed by press articles, even if the reports are accurate. Under a 2006 decree, journalists face large fines for transgressions of censorship laws. Satellite television is officially restricted to senior officials, international hotels, and foreign businesses, but many Vietnamese homes and businesses install satellite dishes anyway. More than two million Vietnamese have access to the Internet, which the government tightly controls.

Laos is the only other Communist country in Southeast Asia. Corruption and abuses by government officials are widespread. New laws aimed at curbing corruption are ineffective. Freedom of the press in the country is severely restricted. Any criticism of the government or discussions on controversial political topics will result in punishment. The state owns all the media, both print and broadcast. Some residents can access foreign broadcasts from Thailand. Internet access is heavily restricted and content is censored.

In Cambodia the end of Khmer Rouge rule did not usher in an era of freedom and democracy. Today's Cambodia is a constitutional monarchy with Prime Minister Hun Sen and his party dominating national and local politics and controlling the security forces, officials at all levels of government, and the state-owned media, according to the Freedom House. However, there are media owned by opposition parties, and there are no restrictions on privately owned satellite dishes.

The government exercises tight control of local broadcast media, which serve as the primary source of information for most Cambodians. Newspapers reach only about 10 percent of the population, according to the Freedom House. While print journalists are freer to criticize governmental policies and senior officials, their impact is limited. Since 2005 the government has used defamation suits to harass journalists and indefinitely detain and imprison them. The Internet is free of government control, but high cost and lack of connectivity outside the capital and a few major cities limit access.

In Myanmar, the harsh rule by a military junta sparked mass prodemocracy demonstrations by monks in 2007, which led to a bloody crackdown. The regime rules by decree, and controls all executive, legislative, and judicial powers as efforts at drafting a new constitution are stalled. In a system that lacks both transparency and accountability, official corruption is rampant at both national and local levels, according to the Freedom House.

To control its image, the junta restricts press freedom and either owns or tightly controls all daily newspapers and broadcast media. It subjects private periodicals to prepublication censorship and restricts the import of foreign news periodicals, according to the Freedom House. Under the new censorship rules of 2005, media are allowed to criticize government projects as long as the criticism is considered "constructive." While some people have access to international shortwave radio or satellite television, those caught can face jail time. The Internet, which operates in a limited fashion in the cities, is tightly regulated and censored.

In the aftermath of the cyclone that killed tens of thousands of people in 2008, Myanmar's military government tried to keep out international aid workers in an attempt to hide the reality of the country from the international community.

The Pacific

Often accused of adding fuel to the fire in its coverage of crises, the media in Pacific nations face constant government pressure. In Fiji, Papua New Guinea, and Tonga, the constitutional freedom of expression guarantees are under assault as the role of the media in promoting good governance has been an emerging theme (Singh et al., 2004). In Fiji, Tonga, and the Solomon Islands, the media play a key role in promoting multiracial, multiparty, and fairer political systems by covering popular discontent and mass demonstrations against the ruling elite (Singh and Prakash, 2006).

The governments of Pacific nations rely mostly on traditional powers in dealing with the media and sometimes allow critical coverage of the government. But still Pacific news media remain a vital barometer of the region's well-being, as chiefs and politicians in the Pacific use influence drawn from tradition, custom, and honor of authority as a shield for immunity from criticism and unlawful actions (Seward, 1999).

The new Port Vila-based regional newspaper said: "In the Pacific, there is a general acceptance of the need for a free press, which can help in nation-building and in creating open and accountable governments." But incidents threatening press freedom often occur. The paper called on governments not to use the War on Terror as an excuse to crack down on freedom of expression.

The threat to press freedom in the region is vigorously alive (Seward, 1999). The Tongan Crown Prince once said that there is no need for democracy to flourish. Many of the government officials in Pacific island countries regard democracy and freedom as Western concepts that do not suit their society. Even though globalization and world culture do have an impact on media in the region, when an event is covered by the media, it is most likely explored by a journalist outside the region. The most typical news from Pacific commentators is silence (Seward, 1999).

Concepts of Media Freedom

Media freedom is available to more people in Asia today than 20 years ago, and media responsibility and ethics have become a big concern in new democracies. The credibility of the media is in serious crisis because of sensationalism, the self-interest of the press owners, self-censorship, a partisan press, and government pressure (e.g. see Chuensuksawadi, 2001; Kubiske, 2000; Singh, 2002; Sussman and Karlekar, 2005; Yu, 2002).

On the topic of press freedom in Asia, *Four Theories of the Press* (Siebert, Peterson, and Schramm, 1956, 1963), which have now been expanded into five or six theories (Hachten, 1987, 1992; Downing, 2002), can serve as a helpful starting point. But media researchers have to remind themselves that they are borrowing a yardstick developed in the West to measure media systems in the East, and they may run the risk of pigeonholing media systems in theory concepts that do not fit. The same caution should be exercised when Freedom House's rankings of press freedom around the world were consulted. How accurately do those indexes reflect the reality of press freedom in those countries?

For example, Freedom House's 2006 report rated Japan as having the freest press in Asia. But with the increasing outcry against the restrictive "press club" system from the nonmainstream media in Japan and from foreign correspondents in the country, with criticism of uniformity in content in the media, and with a conspicuous lack of rigorous investigative reporting in the mainstream media, questions should be asked: does Japan have the freest press in Asia? What standards and methodology does the Freedom House use in measuring press freedom?

Self-Censoring Libertarianism

To a certain extent, all journalists, including Western journalists, censor themselves. But self-censorship in Asia has reached a scale of its own, particularly the institutionalized self-censorship in Japan and the widespread and increasing self-censorship practices in Hong Kong, Thailand, and South Korea.

Both Japan and South Korea are now democratic societies, but their culture is clearly Asian and deeply rooted in Confucianism. Media would censor themselves to be pro-government and/or at the same time be in favor of big business, rather than muckrake both due to cultural traditions and economic considerations. The press clubs, which have just been phased out in South Korea but which are still solidly planted in the Japanese press system, play a unique policing role.

The Japanese press club system provides exclusive access to government information to the mainstream media and discourages independent and investigative reporting in order to keep that privilege. It also discourages competition or scoops among media organizations so that every media company can be profitable. As a result of the press club system, the mainstream media rarely expose scandals in the government. Instead, such scandals are often uncovered by nonmainstream media and independent journalists, who together with foreign correspondents are barred from the press clubs. When the Asian financial crash occurred in 1997, the media in Japan were criticized for ignoring coverage of irregularities in the financial sector. As most mainstream media outlets tend to be conservative, progovernment, and probusiness, there is a "uniformity of content" (Saito, 2000). Freedom House rated Japan as having the freest media in Asia perhaps because there is little government intervention in media operations. But the institutionalized self-censorship or professional control by the press clubs serves the same purpose of taming the media and leads to the same result as a marketplace of fewer ideas. Control by the press clubs also saves the government the trouble of disciplining the media.

Laurie Anne Freeman (2000) has reported that the media cartels in Japan are composed of the unholy trinity of press clubs, industry associations, and media conglomerates, which make it possible to muzzle the press, restrain competition within the media, and abuse the public trust. The media in Japan want to keep the status quo because the industry is doing very well financially.

The media in South Korea is in a very similar situation as in Japan, even though the press club system has been phased out in recent years. The mainstream media tend to keep cozy relationships with the government and big businesses. Much of what is going on inside the government and big corporations does not appear in the media. The South Korean government banned publication of the size of foreign reserves and foreign debt, considering such information as national security concerns. The media do not challenge such claims and instead accept such assertions (Neumann, 1998). It has become a tradition for the South Korean media not to report critical and important information. But there are signs that the South Korean media are becoming more aggressive in covering the government as competition with other media companies is heating up.

In Hong Kong and Thailand, journalists censor themselves when it comes to politically sensitive stories, but they resort to sensationalism when they are covering non-political stories.

Ten years after Hong Kong was returned to China, former British Prime Minister Margaret Thatcher told BBC that worries about Hong Kong's future "have largely proved groundless." (Foreman, 2007). *The South China Morning Post* declared that "one country, two systems" has been a success and that Hong Kong's core values have remained intact (Ruwitch, 2007). For the most part, the media in Hong Kong have remained free, diverse, and dynamic. They are free to cover any topic or story, and the media reflect the diverse opinions of the territory.

At the same time, a survey conducted in 2007 by the Hong Kong Journalists' Association showed that 58 percent of the journalists believed press freedom in Hong Kong had worsened since 1997 due to increased self-censorship and tighter government control (Cheung, 2007). About 30 percent of the journalists said they had censored their reports, while 40 percent said their colleagues had censored themselves.

Jimmy Lai, owner of the *Apple Daily,* a best-selling newspaper with a strong prodemocracy line, said, "In the last 10 years, I do think Hong Kong media still has its freedom of speech. At least no one has been arrested. We have never been threatened by anyone." But he said his paper's views have cost it advertising, and that media bosses concerned for their investment in China make their publications censor themselves (Foreman, 2007:35).

In Thailand, the royal family is off limits to the media. And much of government corruption is kept out of the press. Like Japan and South Korea, Thailand has a culture of secrecy. Thai journalists are not vigorously using the freedom they have. Roderick Macdonell, director of the World Bank's investigative journalism program, called on the media in Thailand to step up investigative journalism to help curb corruption and keep the public better informed (Changyawa, 2001). However, journalists sometimes abuse that freedom in competition for market share and in inserting bias in covering local controversies ("News That," 2001).

Anarchist Libertarianism

In Indonesia, Taiwan, and the Philippines, the news media are enjoying unprecedented freedom after decades of government repression as strongmen were replaced by democratically elected but weak governments, which have yet to establish trust and credibility among their people. With the absence of regulations and management mechanisms, the media operate in a regulatory void, free to chase profits and free to launch political attacks. The sharp increase in media outlets resulting from lifting the licensing requirement added to the chaos. Battles among the partisan press and commercial press often result in a sacrifice of accuracy and balance in the news.

In Indonesia, now that the media enjoy so much freedom, the main problem is a lack of ethics among journalists. More and more journalists are violating the most sacred principle of the profession: tell the truth ("Press Credentials," 2000). Journalists in Indonesia today are accountable to no one but themselves and their proprietors. The Ministry of Information was abolished, and gone also is the licensing mechanism. In 1999, a new press law was put in place to guarantee freedom and promise punishment for those who obstruct the profession.

Free as they are, Indonesian journalists still face violence and intimidation in their profession. The government also is still trying to intervene in the business as well. It reversed almost four years of relaxing media restrictions by banning one of the highest-profile foreign correspondents working in the country (Aglionby, 2002). Freedom is still vulnerable and fragile in Indonesia.

In Taiwan, the partisan press is being replaced by tabloid journalism with the entry of the *Apple Daily* to Taiwan, which has been catapulted to the leading position among all Taiwan newspapers with colorful photos and front-page headlines such as "Father Tortures 10-Year-Old Daughter; Taken around with a Dog Leash." The paper practices a tabloid journalism that highlights scandals and celebrities ("Tabloid Journalism," 2005). Profitability is the ultimate goal of the paper. It drives the paper to its leading position, and it also seems to drive the Taiwan press to the ground. Intense competition in a crowded market led the media to spend a lot more energy on crime stories or the private lives of public figures than investigating the government.

A magazine, the *Scoop Weekly,* included a VCD of an alleged sexual encounter of a female legislative candidate. The magazine argued that the VCDs were given to the readers as "evidence" supporting the veracity of its investigative reporting ("Freedom," 2001). Reporters in a rush to be the first to get the story out sacrifice accuracy in their reporting, rather than finding credible sources to check out the facts. Sometimes newsgathering gets in the way of solving kidnapping cases. "The freedoms that were so hard to obtain, ironically, now threaten some parts of a society that considers the press the enemy because of its influence and power" (Luwarso, 2002.) "Freedom of the press" has been condemned as the "freakdom of the press."

The Philippine press claims to be one of the freest in Asia, even though broadcasting is still subject to more regulation. Sheila S. Coronel (2000) described the Philippine press as "rowdy," "vibrant," "pluralistic," and "anarchistic." She describes Filipino journalists as noisy and powerful. Media exposés have ended political careers and raised public awareness about important issues. Because of their recent past, Filipino journalists guard their freedom fiercely and believe strongly in the adversarial role of the press as the watchdog of the government.

Yet, press freedom in the Philippines has been pushed to the extreme and is often abused. Media are being criticized for irresponsible and sloppy reporting, for "checkbook journalism," and for using their freedom to commercially exploit the public's taste for the sensational (Coronel, 2000). The news media have also used their freedom to outdo rivals in the race to peddle newspapers and television programs. Media owners sometimes use their newspapers to defend and advance their business and political interests.

Confucian Authoritarianism

Authoritarianism has a long history as a political system and a press system. Thus, it is no coincidence that authoritarianism meshes well with Confucius's teachings, which have influenced parts of Asia for more than 2,000 years. Singapore and Malaysia may be the loudest voices among Asian nations in promoting "Asian values," which emphasize putting the interest of the country, the family, or the group above the interest of the individual, in contrast to Western values of individual rights and freedom. Luwarso (2000) said that Malaysia, Singapore, and Brunei frequently resort to "Asian values," where government controls press freedom and political activity in order to guarantee economic growth. He calls Asian values a thinly veiled pretext for authoritarianism and states that Southeast Asia sees its press as a government tool, a "free and responsible" press.

However, these governments emphasize responsibility more than freedom. The press is constantly asked to account for itself. Heads of government keep a close eye on the press because they believe that press freedom will lead to anarchy, conflict, and instability. Threats to press freedom come mostly in the form of licensing, lawsuits, and intimidation directed at journalists.

In Singapore, all forms of imported material must first pass the censors of the Films and Publications Department. All compact disks and electronic mail are also censored. Singapore's Internet service providers and one cable television operation all have links to the government. The People's Action Party, Singapore's ruling party, dominates ownership of the mass media through the state enterprise, Singapore Press Holdings (Luwarso, 2000).

The mainstream media in Malaysia are mostly tame and compliant, and thus lack credibility among the public. The government makes sure that the media pursue the goal of a strong nation rather than the bottom line or press freedom. Access to information in both Malaysia and Singapore is limited by many existing laws, including colonial-era laws, the Official Secrets Acts, Internal Security Acts, and Printing Presses and Publications Acts ("Regional Overview," 2002).

Not all authoritarian media in Asia have Confucian roots. Pakistan is a relatively open society (Isa, 2001:146). The press enjoys a lot more freedom than the electronic media. The constitution in Pakistan prohibits the ridicule of Islam, the armed forces, or the judiciary. The country has a strong and an independent court system, which often becomes the guardian of press freedom and the integrity of public discourse. In one such case Pakistan's Supreme Court struck down an order by the central government prohibiting the publication of a periodical, *The Mirror* (Isa, 2001:142). But the government still has strong influence over the media by providing guidelines.

The press in most Pacific island countries belongs more to the authoritarian press model than to the libertarian model, even though it generally enjoys more freedom than many of the papers on the Asian continent. Despite the existence of a critical press and sometimes even radio, governments often take actions against the media, such as the expulsion from Fiji of two German PACNEWS personnel, the relocation of this news service to New Zealand to circumvent editorial control by the Fiji government, and the banning of the Samoa opposition leader from the government-owned Apia radio station 2AP (Seward, 1999). There is no live news from this radio station. After the news is written, it is cleared by the prime minister's office.

Reforming Communism

Of the five remaining Communist countries in the world, four except Cuba are located in Asia: China, Vietnam, North Korea, and Laos. Although North Korea has changed little despite the transition of power from the father to the son, communism in China, Vietnam, and, to a lesser extent, Laos, has taken a new direction as Vietnam and Laos are following China's example in implementing economic reforms.

The changes in the Chinese and Vietnamese media are overwhelming, even though some descriptions of the Communist media still apply. News media in both China and Vietnam are still mostly state owned, while state ownership in other industries is on a sharp decline, accounting for less than 50 percent of the national economy in China. The government still emphasizes the nation-building and educational role of the media and promotes positive stories while trying to black out or downplay some negative stories, such as labor unrest, major cases of police brutality, or corruption by top government officials. Sensitive topics such as the 1989 student movement and the passing of former Party General Secretary Zhao Ziyang have only one version of the story, the official Xinhua version.

The media in China today, however, particularly local media, are much more aggressive in news reporting than the media in the past, given their financial independence and the competitive media environment. In the Chinese media today, there is no lack of negative stories, such as exposés of official corruption, crime, industrial accidents, or natural disasters. Official corruption has become so widespread that government actually encourages the media to help expose and reduce it. Some publications known nationally for their aggressive reporting and bold political commentary, such as *the China Youth Daily,* the *Southern Metropolis Daily,* and the financial magazine, *Caijin,* seem to have earned special rights in news reporting. As they are well known in the country, any action taken by the government against them becomes a high-profile case, which can serve as a deterrent to harsh punishment by the government. With the rising economic clout and political influence of China in world affairs, government officials are more sensitive to China's international image, which helps the cause of pushing for greater press freedom in the country. Some journalists in China claim that there is plenty of press freedom in China today, especially for local papers, as long as the press does not print anything against the party or the political system.

The Internet in China provides a freedom forum for the Chinese. The Chinese Web sites Sina.com, Sohu.com, and China.com all offer free and spirited discussions on hot issues in China. Stories that are turned down by the traditional media often surface on the Internet. In some cases the traditional media had to publish a story they had turned down earlier because the story turned up on the Internet and caught national attention. Discussions on some Chinese Web sites can also be sharp and bold, which the editorial and opinion pages of the traditional media would not publish. The new media in China is spearheading the push for more freedom in the country despite government efforts at taming it.

News media in Vietnam are also changing, even though they remain an arm of the government and extol the virtues of the party. But media in Vietnam are also opening up, and the press is freer than it was a decade ago (Lamb, 2002). In terms of freedom, the press has been getting better and more aggressive. Hong Phuong, a local journalist, said: "We are now having debates more on 'responsibilities and morals of journalists' than on free press." ("News Often Wounds," 2001).

In the Vietnamese press today, readers can find stories on official corruption, slumping exports, the sluggish pace of economic reforms, or the widespread use of drugs. The country's 7,000 journalists routinely report on issues ranging from smuggling to prostitution.

Development Media

In India, government officials lauded the role of the press in exposing scams and corruption, strengthening democracy, and guiding society ("Stress on Free," 2007). That is a reminder of development journalism, for which the Indian press is known. Most South Asian governments provide guidance for their news media and use the media as tools for national development. Perhaps development media are popular in South Asia because the economies in the region are still developing.

Communication in India means not only the transfer of information, but also the participation in the society and the community (Namra, 2004). The Indian brand of development journalism aspires to focus on the needs of the poor and their effective participation in development planning. Some journalists in the country believe that the media should not only publish stories about the prevention of AIDS, but also discuss issues that are important for a civil society, such as democracy, social and economic justice, national integration, and economic progress. People in India expect the newspapers to "don a steering mantle when the need may arise," according to Vivek Goenka, chairman and managing editor of *The Indian Express*. Goenka (1996) maintains that Indian newspapers cannot be passive disseminators of news. They have to reflect plurality of opinion and encourage debate, with an objective to serve society and uplift falling societal values.

The Indian Express covers socially relevant issues, such as the environment, health, and the development of women and children, and has organized cancer detection camps and races against pollution. The paper also created campaigns against dowry and female feticide, and covered these campaigns in its group publications. The paper also had its readers constitute special action groups under the banner "Express Citizens Forum," which directly took up civic and other issues of their city. In this way the paper turned its readers into active information users and agents of change within their communities.

In Sri Lanka, the mass media play a role as a channel and means for environmental education. A recent environment awareness study showed that most people in both urban and rural areas cited different organs of the media as their primary source of environmental education, especially the print media. Television was the next major source of information for the urban population, while radio was for the rural population.

Media Economics and Special Problems

As Asia is host to some of the richest and some of the poorest countries in the world, the economic realities the media in various Asian countries have to face are very different. In successful and thriving media markets such as Japan, South Korea, India, and China, large circulations of leading papers produce an income that can only be envied by their Western counterparts. And the mass media are generating huge profits when an increasing amount of advertising revenue flows to the media as a result of the rapid economic growth in some of these countries.

But even the hugely profitable top-circulating Japanese and South Korean press have problems. The new media have posed strong challenges by luring away the younger generation. For the first time in a long time, the Japanese press has felt the uncertainty of its future (Shiraishi, 2003). Tough competition has forced newspaper publishers to expand their news distribution services to digital media such as the Internet, cell phones, and satellite data broadcasting. Stakes are high with such new digital services because of their lower profitability. A major concern for newspapers is how to recover the cost incurred in setting up Internet businesses.

In 2000, the Internet services of the *Yomiuri Shimbun* were still in the red as the advertising market failed to grow as anticipated. Among national dailies, the *Nihon Keisai,* the national financial newspaper, was the only newspaper that made a profit from its online business. The Japanese media are hoping that their news distribution services on cell phones will make up for their losses on the Web, as the *Yomiuri* reaped profits from the second-hand use of news stories originally edited for its own Web site.

In South Korea, there has been an explosion of competition since the early 1990s, including challenges from the new media. Nine of the biggest newspapers experienced a 4.4 percent drop in earnings in 2004, a 17 percent decline since 2002 ("Korea: Circulation," 2005). Only four stayed in the black. And Korea's three main sports dailies incurred losses totaling 45.2 million won (about 49,093 U.S. dollars). Bottom lines have taken a significant hit from the sudden increase of free morning newspapers. In 2004 four of the free dailies—*AM7, Good Morning Seoul, Metro,* and *Focus*—issued a total of 1.75 million copies in Seoul and Kyonggi Province, eating into the advertising market.

To stop the trend, the importance of new media is emphasized in South Korea, as it is in Japan, too. Some have suggested that the mobile media will accelerate the renaissance of newspapers, using strategies such as sending out text message announcements of breaking news, inviting participation in opinion polls, and adding still photography and video feed to supplement written content. Others have stressed the importance of building readership among young people by learning the market ("Korea: Circulation," 2005). During the 2004 tsunami crisis, text-messaging services beat both online and wire services in getting the news to readers.

In Cambodia, Laos, Nepal, Myanmar, and Bangladesh, the news media lack basic resources for development, such as advertising funding, adequate technology and equipment, trained journalists, and even an adequate rate of literacy. Newspaper circulation in these countries is low. In Nepal, there was only one television station by 2001 (Schafer, 2001). There was one television set for every 200 people, and 2.8 people out of every 1,000 had a computer. The quality of journalism staffs was not high as they needed better training. The lack of advertising revenue left plenty of room for the government to influence media operations by providing government subsidies for the media. Independent journalism is out of the question. Elsewhere, in India, Thailand, Pakistan, and Bangladesh, governments still indirectly influence news coverage through the allocation of newsprint, which is imported in many of these countries (see Downie, 2000).

Intense competition often drives the quality of media products down instead of up. One problem for the Hong Kong press is that competition for circulation sometimes results in price wars, lower editorial standards, and the rise of sensationalism. In Hong Kong, tabloids represent the mainstream press. The same problem plagues Indonesia, Thailand, the Philippines, Taiwan, and even China and Vietnam. Journalism ethics is, to a great extent, compromised in the pursuit of market share.

The Chinese media learned fast how to compete once government subsidies ended. The official and commercial media in China are reaping big profits. But they face challenges unique to media in Communist countries—they have to be commercially successful and politically correct at the same time. To attract larger audiences, investigative reporting has appeared in both China and Vietnam. But how far the media can go is the real test.

The Chinese media are also bracing for competition from foreign media now that China has joined the WTO. On the newsstand in China today, popular foreign consumer magazines are displayed prominently on the sidewalks. Foreign capital has entered the Internet sector in China. To get ready for the challenge, Chinese media are speeding up the establishment of mega-media groups to pool media resources against competition. To China, WTO is not only an economic issue. Already media in the country are talking about the possible "corrosive role" of transnational media on local culture.

Similar to the West, a concentration of ownership in the form of media conglomerates, monopoly, or oligopoly characterizes much of the Asian press. The Singapore Press Holdings is a major publishing group in Southeast Asia and a press monopoly in Singapore. In Hong Kong, Sing Tao Holdings gets the word out and in more than one language. In Japan, media conglomerates form an oligopoly that controls news flow and discourages diversity in content. The cross ownership of major newspapers and television networks in the country further reduces the independence of the media. In South Korea, the trend toward monopoly ownership of the media is speeding up. In India, a few major national newspaper chains dominate the system.

Across Asia, and especially in new democracies such as Indonesia, the Philippines, Taiwan, and South Korea, a historical shift in control of the media from the government to powerful media owners is occurring. The media owners mostly look out for their own economic interests and bow to government pressure to protect those interests. Typical examples also include Singapore and Malaysia.

The self-interest of media owners is not the only factor compromising the integrity of the journalism profession. Corruption of journalists is widespread in Asia because the salaries of reporters in the region are mostly low, as in China, Indonesia, Thailand, the Philippines, Vietnam, and Cambodia. Envelopes stuffed with cash are handed out at press conferences. Even in higher-income societies such as South Korea, corruption among journalists is not rare. Gifts in the form of stocks, free trips, and free meals are also available in some of these countries. In Vietnam, one serious case shocked the public when it was revealed that one journalist received a bribe of up to $200,000 ("News Often Wounds," 2001).

For the Pacific island nations, funding has always been tight for media operations and training. In 1996, the Pacific Islands News Association was declared financially insolvent and was revitalized in 1997 (Lael, 1997). Financial independence is a hard-to-reach goal for most of the media in the region, which depend heavily on foreign aid.

Journalism Education and Training

The quality and availability of journalism education in Asia depend to a large extent on development of the media in a country and on the resources available. In some parts of Asia, universities offer prestigious programs and degrees in journalism, while in others very little formal education in journalism is available. Some have to depend on international or foreign assistance, such as short-term journalism workshops run by the UNESCO.

East Asia

There is a boom in journalism education in China as the government supervision of the press loosens, and journalism in China is getting more competitive and professional. The fact that both Beijing University and Tsinghua University, two of the most prestigious universities in China, set up their own journalism schools in 2001 and 2002, respectively, testifies to the popularity of the programs and the need for trained journalists. Some of the more prominent master's programs in journalism are offered by the Graduate School of the Chinese Academy of Social Sciences, People's University, Beijing Broadcast College, School of Journalism of China (run by the Xinhua news agency), Fudan University, Nanjing University, Jinan University, and Wuhan University.

South Asia

Of all the countries in South Asia, India has the largest number of universities and colleges, more than 50 in total, that offer journalism and mass communication programs, and many of the programs are quite comprehensive. Some of these academic programs offer doctoral degrees in communication. India also has quite a few education and research centers in journalism and communication, which are the best equipped in the region, including the Indian Institute of Journalism and New Media (IIJNM), the Sri Sri Center for Media Studies, and the Indian Institute of Mass Communication in New Delhi. With India's resources in journalism education, it provides training not only for journalists in the country, but also for journalists in neighboring countries.

Southeast Asia

The need for trained journalists in the region is acute. In 2000 Medialink, a global corporate media communications services company, organized a workshop in Bangkok for journalism teachers from Cambodia, India, Indonesia, Laos, Malaysia, Philippines, Thailand, and Vietnam. Journalism education in Southeast Asia can be as emerging as short-term courses or workshops in Cambodia and Laos or as comprehensive and advanced as Singapore's Asian Media Information and Communication Center (AMIC), which is a premier communication center for information, research, education, and promotion of mass communication in the Asia-Pacific region. The center has a close working relationship with the School of Communication and Information at Nanyang Technological University (NTU) of Singapore.

The Pacific

The two more important journalism programs among the Pacific island countries are offered by the University of Papua New Guinea and the University of the South Pacific based in Suva, capital of Fiji. Australia and New Zealand both assist with the training of journalists in the region.

Prospects for the Future

News media in Asia face tremendous challenges and opportunities. They have the potential to rise above yellow journalism and self-interest, shake off the shackles of self-censorship, and wean themselves from corruption to reach real greatness, and perhaps they can help redress the unbalanced flow of information between the North and South with their technological capabilities and their position as a world leader in newspaper circulation.

Or the media in Asia can pass up this historic opportunity by continuing the downward spiral of sensationalism and self-censorship to remain a lapdog. Freedom of the press is fragile in Asia. If it continues to be abused rather than guarded, it can easily be lost.

The media in Asia have never had a better opportunity to fully develop, given the sweeping liberalization trend across the continent, the increasing economic strength, and the vast readership base. The key to the success of Asian media lies in the maturing of the media in exercising press freedom and in pushing for the frontier of press freedom. In the case of China, the hope lies in the younger generation of Chinese leaders and the enactment of a press law that protests the right to newsgathering and reporting.

Globalization of the media is no longer a vision; it is a reality, even for a country like China. There are already strong and successful regional media in Asia, such as STAR TV, and some leading newspapers and magazines, which have a regional circulation. The next step is going global. Asian media are fully equipped, both in their hardware and software, to take the next step. The question is whether the editors and journalists in the region have the vision and the will to take that step.

In Pakistan, journalists are calling for and being trained in "peace journalism" in regard to the coverage of conflicts in Kashmir ("Realistic," 2000). In today's world, peace journalism is more urgently needed than at any other time in human history, and it points to the future role of the ubiquitous global news media.

BIBLIOGRAPHY

Aglionby, J. "Indonesia Bans Foreign Journalist." *The Guardian,* March 18, 2002.
Bangladesh Basic Information and Media Guide. Bangladesh: Ministry of Information, 1993.
Bhuiyan, S. I., and Gunaratne, S. A. (2000). "Bangladesh." In Gunaratne, S. A. (ed.), *Handbook of the Media in Asia.* New Delhi: Sage Publications.

Brackenburg, A. "The Historical Paper Trail." *Geographical* 77, No 8 (August 2005), 32–33.

Changyawa, P. "Journalists Reminded of Role to Help Curb Corruption." *Bangkok Post,* December 13, 2001. Retrieved from the LexisNexis database.

Cheung, A. S. Y. "One Step Forward, Two Steps Back: A Study of Press Law in Post-Colonial Hong Kong." *Journalism Communication Monographs* 3, No. 4 (Winter 2002), 189–226.

Cheung, J. "Press Freedom Declining". *South China Morning Post.* July 9, 2007, 3.

China Journalism Yearbook. Beijing: China Journalism Yearbook Press, 1998, 2001.

Chuensuksawadi, P. "Freedom of Information in Thailand: Tentative Beginnings." In Iyer, V. (ed.), *Freedom of Information: An Asian Survey.* AMIC, 2001.

Clark, J. "Training Journalists in an Emerging Democracy: The Case of Cambodia." *Asia/Pacific Media Educator* 8 (January–June 2000), 82–98.

Conlon, C. J. "Bhutan." In Gunaratne, S. A. (ed.), *Handbook of the Media in Asia,* 67–83. New Delhi: Sage, 2000.

Cooper-Chen, A. *Games in the Global Village: A 50-Nation Study of Entertainment Television.* Bowling Green, Ohio: Popular Press, 1994.

Coronel, S. The Philippines: After the Euphoria, the Problems of a Free Press. Paper presented at a conference, *Transparency, Asian Economic Crisis and the Prospects of Media Liberalization.* University of Sydney, Australia: Research Institute for Asia and the Pacific, 2000.

Craddock, P. "Review: Unique Flavor of Pacific Public Radio." *Pacific Journalism Review* 6, No. 1, January 2000, 121–132.

Desai, D. S. "Bangladesh Press, Media, TV, Radio, Newspapers." 2001. Retrieved July 26, 2007 from http://www.pressreference.com/A-Be/Bangladesh.html

————. "Sri Lanka Press, Media, TV, Radio, Newspapers." 2002. Retrieved July 16, 2007 from http://www.pressreference.com/Sa-Sw/Sri-Lanka.html

Dolnick, S. "Newspaper Business Thriving in India." *The Associated Press.* Section: Business News, May 28, 2007.

Downie, S. "Journalism Training in Laos, Cambodia and Vietnam." *Asia/Pacific Media Educator* 8 (January–June 2000). Available: http://www.uow.edu.au/crearts/journalism/APME/contents8/Downie.html

Downing, J. D. H. "Drawing a Bead on Global Communication Theories." In Kamalipour, Y. R. (ed.), *Global Communication,* 21–39. Belmont, CA: Wadsworth/Thompson Learning, 2002.

Ekachai, D. "Thailand." In Gunaratne, S. A. (ed.), *Handbook of the Media in Asia,* 429–461. New Delhi: Sage, 2000.

Eng, P. "Economic Woes Pummel Thai, Indonesia Media." *Columbia Journalism Review* 37, No. 2, July/August 1998, 58–59.

Fang, X. *Zhongguo Xinwen Jianshi.* (A Brief History of Chinese Journalism). Nanjing, China: Nanjing Normal University Press, 1996.

Foreman, W. "Hong Kong Marks Decade of Chinese Rule". June 23, 2007. *The Associated Press Online.* Retrieved July 9, 2007 from the LexisNexis database.

"Founding Father of Independent Media in Nepal Remains Hopeful, Despite Continued Restrictions." June 2005. World Association of Newspapers. Retrieved July 16, 2007 from http://www.wan-press.org/print.php3?id_article=7574

"Freedom Comes with Responsibilities" (editorial). *Taipei Times,* December 19, 2001. Retrieved from the LexisNexis database.

Freedom House report 2007: Press Freedom. Retrieved July 1, 2007 from http://www.freedomhouse.org/template.cfm?page=251&year=2007

Freeman, L. A. *Closing the Shop: Information Cartels and Japan's Mass Media.* Princeton, NJ: Princeton University Press, 2000.

"Gandhi to Gandhi: Views on Press." *India Abroad,* August 25, 1989, 13.

Gilmore-Lehne, W. J. "Communication Systems in Korea: Writing, Printing, Movies & Broadcasting (Radio and Television). 2007. Retrieved July 9, 2007 from http://www.stockton.edu/~gilmorew/consorti/teasia.htm

"Giving the Media a Greater Voice." *People's Daily,* March 31, 2002. Available: http://english.peopledaily.com.cn/200203/31/eng20020331_93207.shtml

Goenka, V. "Journalism in India: A Changing Perspective." *Editor & Publisher* 129, June 22, 1996, 68.

"Government to Free Electronic Media" *Dawn*, April 4, 2000. Retrieved from the LexisNexis database.

Gunaratne, S. A., and Kim, S. D. "North Korea." In Gunaratne, S. A. (ed.), *Handbook of the Media in Asia.* New Delhi: Sage, 2000.

Gunaratne, S. A., and Wattegama, C. L. "Sri Lanka." In Gunaratne, S. A. (ed.), *Handbook of the Media in Asia.* New Delhi: Sage Publications.

Gunn, G. C. "Journalism and Democracy in Asia" (Book review). May 1, 2007. *Journal of Contemporary Asia.* Retrieved September 28, 2007 from http://goliath.ecnext.com/coms2/summary_0199-6563124_ITM

Hachten, W. *The World News Prism,* 2nd ed. Ames: Iowa State University Press, 1987.

————. *The World News Prism,* 3rd ed. Ames: Iowa State University Press, 1992.

Heo, C., Uhm, K.-Y., and Chang, J.-H. "South Korea." In Gunaratne, S. A. (ed.), *Handbook of the Media in Asia,* 611–637. New Delhi: Sage, 2000.

Hirano, C. "Profiles: National Television Systems in Asia and Australia—Japan." In Kitley, P. (ed.), *Television, Regulation and Civil Society in Asia.* London: RoutledgeCurzon, Taylor & Francis Group, 2003.

"HK Press Freedom Weaker Since Handover: Report." July 8, 2007. *Reuters.* Retrieved July 9, 2007 from http://www.reuters.com/articlePrint?articleId=USSP19628320070708

"Hong Kong Marks Anniversary Amid Fears for Press Freedom." June 30, 2007. *Radio Free Asia.* Retrieved July 9, 2007 from http://www.rfa.org/english/china/2007/06/30/china_hongkong/

"Hu Calls for Study of Theories." *Ximhua* News Agency, September 3, 2002. Available: http://www.16congress.org/cn/english/features/41290.htm

Idris, N., and Gunaratne, S. A. "Indonesia." In Gunaratne, S. A. (ed.), *Handbook of the Media in Asia,* 263–295. New Delhi: Sage, 2000.

International News Media Seminar Starts. *People's Daily,* October 21, 2000. Avalable: http://fpeng.peopledaily.com.cn/200010/21/eng20001021_53221.html

"International Media Seminar in Afghanistan." BBC World Service, September 24, 2002.

Irani, C. R. "Freedom of Information in India: Some Reflections." In Iger, V. (ed.), *Freedom of Information: An Asian Survey,* 125–134. Singapore: Asian Media Information and Communication Center, 2001.

Isa, Q. F. "Freedom of Information in Pakistan: Pressing Need for Action." In Iger, V. (ed.), *Freedom of Information: An Asian Survey,* 135–148. Singapore: Asian Media Information and Communication Center, 2001.

Jeffrey, R. *India's Newspaper Revolution: Capitalism, Politics and the Indian-Language Press, 1977–99.* New York: St. Martin's Press, 2000.

Jin, S. "Newspaper Self-Regulatory Committee Resigns en Masse." *Chosum Ilbo,* April 24, 2001. Available: http://srch.chosun.com/cig-bin/english/search?did=35960&OP=;5&word=NEWSPAPER%20

Johnson, L. "Malaysia Press, Media, TV, Radio, Newspapers." 2002. Retrieved July 16, 2007 from http://www.pressreference.com/Ky-Ma/Malaysia.html

Joshi, S. "25 Years of Satellite Broadcasting in India" (columns in English), October 2000. Available: Orbicom.uqam.ca

"Journalists Face Violence, Intimidation." *Jakarta Post,* May 3, 2001, 2.

Juan, C. S. Media in Singapore. Presented at a conference: Transparency, Asian Economic Crisis and the Prospects of Media Liberalization. University of Sydney, Australia: Research Institute for Asia and the Pacific, 2000.

Kadrich, B. "Philippines Press, Media, TV, Radio, Newspapers". 2002. Retrieved July 16, 2007 from http://www.pressreference.com/No-Sa/Philippines.html

Karlekar, K. D, ed. Freedom House. *Freedom of the Press 2005: A Global Survey of Media Independence.* New York: Rowman & Littlefield Publishers, 2005.

Kim, J. "Strayed Broadcasting." *Chosum Ilbo,* April 26, 2001. Available: http://srch.chosun.com/cgibin/english/search?CD=333554431&SH=1&FD=1&OP=3&q=strayed+broadcasting

Kim, M. "The Workings of a Party Mouthpiece: The Rodong Shinmun." *The Chosun Ilbo.* February 27, 2002. Retrieved September 1, 2002 from http://srch.chosun.com

Kitley, P. "Closing the Creative Gap—Renting Intellectual Capital in the Name of Local Content: Indonesia in the Global Format Business." In Moran, A. and Keane, M. (eds.), *Television across Asia: Television Industries, Programme Formats and Globalization.* London: RoutledgeCurzon, Taylor & Francis Group, 2004.

Kitley, P. "Introduction: First Principles—Television, Regulation and Transversal Civil Society in Asia." In Kitley, P. (ed.), *Television, Regulation and Civil Society in Asia.* London: RoutledgeCurzon, Taylor & Francis Group, 2003.

"Korea: Circulation Up but Papers Still Hurting." May 30, 2005. *The Korean Times.* Retrieved July 9, 2007 from http://www.asiamedia.ucla.edu/article.asp?parentid=24959

Kubiske, D. "Press Freedom in Hong Kong: No Easy Answers." *Quill* 88, No. 3 (April 2000), 38–40.

Kuo, E., and Ang, P. H. "Singapore." In Gunaratne, S. A. (ed.), *Handbook of the Media in Asia,* 402–428. New Delhi: Sage, 2000.

Kwak, K.-S. "Profiles: National Television Systems in Asia and Australia—Korea." In Kitley, P. (ed.), *Television, Regulation and Civil Society in Asia.* London: RoutledgeCurzon, Taylor & Francis Group, 2003.

Lael, M. "South Pacific Circulation Grows." *Quill* 85, October 1997, 7.

Lamb, D. "Free Enterprise But Not Freedom of the Press." *Nieman Reports* 56, No. 2, Summer 2002, 69–71.

Lankov, A. "The Dawn of Modern Korea: Hold the Presses!" *Korea Times,* February 15, 2007. Retrieved July 9, 2007 from http://www.asiamedia.ucla.edu/article.asp?parentid=63781

Lee, D. "Final Answer: Vietnam." *Los Angeles Times,* October 17, 2006. The World section, col. 1.

Lee, J. "South Korea Press, Media, TV, Radio, Newspapers." 2002. Retrieved July 16, 2007 from http://www.pressreference.com/Sa-Sw/South-Korea.html

Lewis, G. "Thailand." In Philip Kitley (ed.), *Television, Regulation and Civil Society in Asia.* London: RoutledgeCurzon, Taylor & Francis Group,2003.

Lim, T. "Let the Contests Begin! 'Singapore Slings' into Action." In Moran, A. and Keane, M. (eds.), *Television Across Asia: Television Industries, Programme Formats and Globalization.* London: RoutledgeCurzon, Taylor & Francis Group, 2004.

Luwarso, L. "'Freakdom' of the Press: Keeping Indonesia Free for All." *Taipei Times,* April 5, 2002, 13.

———. "The Paradox of Freedom in Southeast Asia." *Jakarta Post,* May 3, 2000, Retrieved from the LexisNexis database

MacKinnon, S. R. "Toward a History of the Chinese Press in the Republican Period." *Modern China* 23, No.1 (January 1997), 3–32.

Malaysia. "Quest Economics Database: World of Information Asia & Pacific Review World of Information." July 30, 2007. Retrieved August 23, 2007 from the LexisNexis database.

Maslog, C. "Philippines." In Gunaratne, S. A. (ed), *Handbook of the Media in Asia,* 372–401. New Delhi: Sage, 2000.

McNicol, T. "Drawing on Politics." *Japan Media Review,* July 14, 2005. Retrieved July16, 2007 from http://www.japanmediareview.com/japan/stories/050715mcnicol/print.htm

"Media Bills' Require Changes." *Japan Time*s, May 25, 2002. Available: http://www.japan-times.co.jp/cgi-bin/getarticle.pl5?ed20020525al.htm

"Media Freedom Day 2002 Focuses on Corruption." *Post-Courier,* May 2, 2002, Local Section 5.

"Media in Constant Battle over Press Freedom." *Pacific Weekly Review,* 3 September 30, 2002–October 6, 2002.

Moeran, B. (undated). "Newspapers, Advertising and the Japanese Economy: Early Developments." Retrieved July 9, 2007 from http://ep.lib.cbs.dk/download/ISBN/x656124309.pdf

Namra, A. "Development Journalism vs. "Envelopment" Journalism". 2004. *Countercurrents.org,* April 19, 2004. Retrieved July 25, 2006 from http://www.countercurrents.org/hr-namra190404.htm

Natarajan, S. *A History of the Press in India.* Bombay, India: Asia Publishing House, 1962.

Neuharth, Al. "Why Are Newspapers So Popular in Japan?" November 25, 2004. *USAToday.com* Retreived July 16, 2007 from http://www.usatoday.com/news/opinion/columnist/neuharth/2004-11-25-neuharth_x.htm

Neumann, A. L. "High Price of Secrecy." *Columbia Journalism Review* 36 (1998), 50–51.

"News Often Wounds, But More Often It Heals." *Saigon Times*, October 5, 2001. Retrieved from the LexisNexis database.

"News That Didn't Make News." *Bangkok Post,* August 30, 2001. Retrieved from the LexisNexis database.

"Newsman Urged to Follow Code of Ethics." *Dawn,* July 8, 2002. Retrieved from the LexisNexis database.

"Newspaper Circulation Set for Asian Rise." *Irish Examiner,* July 31, 2002. Retrieved from the LexisNexis database.

Nomura, T. "The Press in Japan: Job Security versus Journalistic Mission." In Atkins, J. B. (ed.), *The Mission: Journalism, Ethics, and the World.* Ames: Iowa State University Press, 2002.

"Not Fine Print." *The Hindustan Times.* March 12, 2007. Retrieved from the LexisNexis database.

Panol, Z. S., and Do, Y. "Vietnam." In Gunaratne, S. A. (ed.), *Handbook of the Media in Asia,* 462–486. New Delhi: Sage, 2000.

Paquette, W. A. "Thailand Press, Media, TV, Radio, Newspapers." 2002. Retrieved July 16 from http://www.pressreference.com/Sw-Ur/Thailand.html

"Party Publicity Chief on China's Media Work." *People's Daily,* October 29, 2001.

"Press Credentials." *Jakarta Post,* July 14, 2000.

"Press Law Needed to Protect Reporters." *China Daily,* December 25, 2000.

"Private Media Asked to Help Promote Independence." *Bernama,* The Malaysian National News Agency. August 8, 2007. Retrieved August 23, 2007 from the LexisNexis database.

"Private Radio, TV Stations to Go on Air Next Year." *The News,* April 26, 2000.

Pstein, B. W. "Pakistan Press, Media, TV, Radio, Newspapers." 2002. Retrieved July 12, 2007 from http://www.pressreference.com/No-Sa/Pakistan.html

"Publication Glut a Waste of Vietnam's Press, Say Deputies." *Saigon Times,* May 10, 1999.

Rao, S., and Koirala, B. "Nepal." In Gunaratne, S. A. (ed.), *Handbook of the Media in Asia,* 132–154. New Delhi: Sage, 2000.

"Realistic Approach on Kashmir Stressed." *Dawn,* April 10, 2000.

"Regional Overview." *Bangkok Post,* April 1, 2002.

Republic of China Publication Yearbook. Taipei: Government Information Office, 1999.

Ruwitch, J. "Hu, Protests Mark HK's First Decade under Chinese Rule." July 1, 2007. Reuters.

Saito, S. "Japan." In Gunaratne, S. A. (ed.), *Handbook of the Media in Asia.* New Delhi: Sage, 2000.

Saksi, a Web site of independent journalism in Malaysia, no. 8, June 2000.

Santos, J. M. C. "Reforming the Format: Philippines in the Global Television Format Business." In Moran, A and Keane, M. (eds.), *Television across Asia: Television Industries, Programme Formats and Globalization.* London: RoutledgeCurzon, Taylor & Francis Group, 2004.

Schafer, E. D. "Cambodia Press, Media, TV, Radio, Newspapers." 2001. Retrieved July 16, 2007 from http://www.pressreference.com/Be-Co/Cambodia.html

———. "Myanmar Press, Media, TV, Radio, Newspapers." 2001. Retrieved July 16, 2007 from http://www.pressreference.com/Ma-No/Myanmar.html

———. "Nepal Press, Media, TV, Radio, Newspapers." 2001. Retrieved July 16, 2007 from http://www.pressreference.com/Ma-No/Nepal.html

———. "Vietnam Press, Media, TV, Radio, Newspapers." 2002. Retrieved July 16, 2007 from http://www.pressreference.com/Uz-Z/Vietnam.html

Schemer, E. D. "North Korea Press, Media, TV, Radio, Newspapers" 2002. Retrieved July 16, 2007 from http://www.pressreference.com/Sa-Sw/North-Korea.html

Sehar, E. "Pakistan: Newspaper Barred from Printing Bin Laden Sermon." World Editors Forum. 2004. Retrieved July 12, 2007 from http://www.editorsweblog.org/print_newspapers/2004/12/pakistan_newspaper_barred_from_printing.php

Seward, R. *Radio Happy Isles: Media and Politics at Play in the Pacific.* Honolulu: University of Hawaii Press, 1999.

Sharma, M. "Bhutan Press, Media, TV, Radio, Newspapers." 2002. Retrieved July 26, 2007 from http://www.pressreference.com

Shiraishi, K. "Is the Japanese Press a Dinosaur in the 21st Century?" *Japan Media Review,* March 19, 2003. Retrieved July 16, 2007 from http://www.ojr.org/japan/research/1048098923.php

Siebert, F., Peterson, T., and Schramm, W. *Four Theories of the Press.* Urbana: University of Illinois Press, 1956.

———. *Four Theories of the Press,* 2nd ed. Urbana: University of Illinois Press, 1963.

Singh, S., and Prakash, S. "Politics, Democracy and the Media: Case Studies in Fiji, Tonga and the Solomon Islands." In David Robie (ed.), *The Pacific Journalism Review* 12, No. 2, September 2006, 67–85.

Singh, S., Pamba, K., and Moala, K. "Media Ownership in Oceania: Three Case Studies in Fiji, Papua New Guinea and Tonga." *The Pacific Journalism Review* 10, No. 2, September 2004, 47–68.

Singh, S. "Bad Governance 'Root Cause' of Pacific Woes, Says Chandra." Wansolwara Online, June 12, 2002. Retrieved from http://www.usp.ac.fj/journ/docs/news/wansolnews/2002/2002june/wansol1206021.html

"Slumping Economy Hits Taiwan's Crowded Media Market." *People's Daily,* June 5, 2001.

So, C., Chan, J. M., and Lee, C.-C. "Hong Long SAR (China)." In Gunaratne, S. A. (ed.), *Handbook of the Media in Asia,* 527–551. New Delhi: Sage, 2000.

Statistical Yearbook 2001. Geneva: UNESCO, 2002.

Struggle for Survival. "International Press Freedom and Freedom of Expression Mission to Sri Lanka." January 2007. Retrieved July 16, 2007 from http://www.wan-press.org/IMG/pdf/1148_SriLanka.vers4.pdf

Sussman, L., and Karlekar, K. *The Annual Survey of Press Freedom.* New York: Freedom House, 2002.

"Tabloid Journalism Trumps Politics in Taiwan." August 16, 2005. Retrieved September 27, 2007 from http://zonaeuropa.com/20050816_1.htm

Tatoy, M. "Disney Channel Expands Its Audience Reach in Vietnam." *Asia Pulse,* June 27, 2007. Retrieved September 6, 2007 from LexisNexis database.

Tindall, B. "Papua New Guinea Press, Media, TV, Radio, Newspapers." 2002. Retrieved July 16, 2007 from http://www.pressreference.com/No-Sa/Papua-New-Guinea.html

Thomas, A. O. *Transnational Media and Contoured Markets.* New Delhi: Sage Publications, 2006.

———. *Imaginations and Borderless Television: Media, Culture and Politics across Asia.* New Delhi: Sage Publications, 2005.

"Two Pacific Winners of New PIMA/AUT Scholarships." *Pacific Media Watch,* October 5, 2002. Retrieved from http://www.asiapac.org.fj/cafepacific/resources/aspac/reg3782.html

Unnithan, N. P. "Singapore Press, Media, TV, Radio and Newspapers." 2001. Retrieved July 16, 2007 from http://www.pressreference.com/Sa-Sw/Singapore.html

"USP Academic Tells of Crisis of Conscience." *Pacific Journalism Online,* January 23, 2001, 3162. Retrieved from http://www.usp.ac.fj/journ/docs/news/usp32crisis.html

"Vice-Premier Calls for Wider Radio, TV Coverage in Inland Regions." *People's Daily,* January 9, 2002.

"WAN Joins International Organizations in Condemning a Year of Media Repression in Nepal." February 2006. World Association of Newspapers. Retrieved July 16, 2007 from http://www.wan-press.org/print.php3?id_article=9075

Wang, G., and Lo, W.-H. "Taiwan." In Gunaratne, S. A. (ed.), *Handbook of the Media in Asia,* 660–681. New Delhi: Sage, 2000.

Warren, C. "Afghanistan Press, Media, TV, Radio, Newspapers." 2002. Retrieved July 26, 2007 from http://www.pressreference.com/A-Be/Afghanistan.html

Whymant, R. "Japan Bill to Curb Press." *The Statesman,* March 9, 2002. Available: http://www.thestatesman.net/page.arcview.php?clid=8&id=31896&usrsess=1

Yin, J. "Press Freedom in Asia: New Paradigm Needed in Building Theories." Paper presented at the 2003 Annual Convention of the Association for Education in Journalism and Mass Communication, Kansas City, Missouri, July 30–August 2, 2003.

Yoder, L. "Indonesia Press, Media, TV, Radio, Newspapers." 2002. Retrieved July 26, 2007 from http://www.pressreference.com/Gu-Ku/Indonesia.html

"Your Nambawan Newspaper Wins International Award." *PNG Post-Courier,* August 16, 2002.

Yu, R. "Hong Kong Media Reported More Freedom of Speech after Turnover" (translated from Chinese). Chinanews.com.cn, July 4, 2002.

Zhou, K. "Shanghai Reporter Sues Municipal Planning Bureau for Withholding Information." *China Youth Daily.* June 1, 2006. Retrieved July 29, 2006 from http://zqb.cyol.com/content/2006-06/02/content_1404266.htm

18 Australasia[*]

STEPHEN QUINN
Deakin University, Australia

JOHN TIDEY
Australia

Australia and New Zealand are home to some of the hungriest media consumers in the world. On a per capita basis newspaper and magazine readership in Australia is one of the highest in the world. Australian homes have an average of two television sets and five radios. Internet penetration is high, with almost universal adoption in offices and almost 11 million people using the Internet from home, as of June 2007, in a population of 21 million. The Australian information and communications technology market was worth about US$38 billion in 2007, the third largest in the Asia Pacific region after Japan and China. New Zealand's information technology (IT) goods and services sector was estimated at almost US$9 billion. New Zealanders are also major media consumers. This chapter looks first at Australian media and journalism, and then New Zealand before looking briefly at the Pacific.

Australia

Australia inherited the traditional English view that freedom of speech is best protected by common law. Australia's press has traditionally been regarded as free. But no provision in either the federal constitution or any of the state constitutions explicitly guarantees freedom of speech. Some unsuccessful attempts have been made to incorporate a guarantee of free speech into the Australian constitution, either alone or with other human rights. But the constitution is difficult to amend because change requires a national referendum with a two-thirds majority.

Media Regulation

The Australian Journalists' Association and the country's major publishers established the Australian Press Council in 1976. Its main aims are to help preserve the traditional freedom of the press within Australia, and to ensure that the free press acts responsibly and

---

[*] For a map of Australasia, see Figure 17.1 on p. 339.

ethically. The council investigates and deals with complaints about press conduct. Funding comes from its members. The council provides an independent and free service. Members are not obliged to publish the council's findings.

Major changes to media ownership laws occurred in Australia in May 2007. Companies are able to own two of the three media platforms—commercial radio or TV or newspapers. In the past, a newspaper could not own a television or radio outlet in the same city. The changes in the law produced one of the most frenzied buying and selling periods in Australia's media history. Media analyst Alan Kohler wrote that the government's notion that the new ownership laws would promote greater media diversity and not lead to a wave of consolidation, was looking "as threadbare as that other idea that the Iraq war is going well and is not leading to more terrorism." Communications Minister Senator Helen Coonan said that media mergers would only be allowed if metropolitan markets had five independent media voices, with four in regional markets. This "diversity rule" would prevent acquisitions, Senator Coonan insisted.

Changes to Australia's media ownership laws last occurred two decades earlier. At the time the country had 19 metropolitan daily newspapers and 13 Sunday papers. Within five years of the change, the number of metropolitan dailies had fallen to 12, and the country had three fewer Sunday papers. It will be interesting to see if the 2007 laws produce a further decline in the number of Australian newspapers.

Print Media Ownership

By world standards, Australia has a high concentration of ownership. News Ltd., a subsidiary of Rupert Murdoch's News Corporation, controls almost 70 percent of the capital-city and national newspaper market by circulation, three quarters of the Sunday newspaper market, almost half of the suburban newspaper market, and 23 percent of the regional newspaper market.

John Fairfax Publishing merged with Rural Press in May 2007 to become Fairfax Media. After further acquisitions of radio and television channels, Fairfax Media has emerged as the biggest media company in Australia and New Zealand. Fairfax bought Southern Cross Television, which gave the publisher one metropolitan and four regional television licenses with a potential audience of 21.5 percent of Australia's population. Fairfax Media publishes four metropolitan dailies, four regional and country newspapers, and controls about half the suburban newspaper circulation in Sydney and Melbourne. Its New Zealand holdings are described later in the chapter.

Australian Provincial Newspapers publishes 14 regional daily newspapers in Queensland and northern New South Wales, plus a host of weekly country newspapers and suburban newspapers in Melbourne. West Australian Newspapers publishes the Perth daily, *The West Australian,* a regional daily, and a number of country newspapers, and has a large interest in most of the Perth suburban newspapers.

Print Media

Australia has 49 daily newspapers for a total population of 21 million. Analysts distinguish between capital-city (or metropolitan) dailies, and dailies in smaller population centers (usually referred to as regional newspapers). Ten metropolitan and two national dailies are published in the capital cities of the five states and two territories. Half of that dozen are published in the two largest population centers, Sydney (4.3 million) and Melbourne (3.7 million). All other capitals have one daily paper.

Another 37 dailies publish in the regional centers. Their circulation tends to be much lower than the metropolitan dailies. Each weekday 2.2 million people read the two national and 10 metropolitan dailies, compared with 0.6 million who read the 37 regional dailies. Circulation is generally higher on weekends. About 100 weekly or twice-weekly newspapers, mostly free, circulate in city suburbs. Another 250 country newspapers publish one to three times a week.

Magazines

Australians consume magazines at a prodigious rate relative to other English-speaking nations: Every person aged 14 or older buys an average of 13.6 magazines a year. About 4,500 magazine titles are available in Australia, and those publications sell more than 300 million copies a year. In 2006, magazine advertising was worth US$1.05 billion a year. Nine in 10 magazines are purchased at retail outlets such as newsagents and supermarkets rather than through subscription. This love affair with magazines is driven by the wide choice of titles that cater to almost every interest, hobby, and activity.

News Agencies

In terms of content for Australia's media, the main news agency is Australian Associated Press (AAP), headquartered in Sydney. All of the major international agencies—Associated Press, Reuters, and Agence France-Presse—cover the country and region from offices in Sydney and other state capitals. AAP bases reporters in all capital cities and London.

Broadcast Media

Commercial radio started in Australia in 1923 in Sydney, spreading to other cities the next year. In 1932, then Prime Minister Joseph Lyons inaugurated the Australian Broadcasting Company, modeled on the BBC. News was first broadcast on the ABC in 1947. It became the Australian Broadcasting Corporation (ABC) in 1980. Over time the ABC has grown to become the country's largest broadcaster. The ABC employs about 1,000 domestic journalists, plus correspondents in 14 foreign bureaus. The ABC's editorial and programming independence is guaranteed by legislation.

The Australian Communications and Media Authority (ACMA) was established on July 1, 2005 through the merger of the Australian Broadcasting Authority and the Australian Communications Authority. ACMA has effectively become the main media regulator in Australia, looking after broadcasting, the Internet, and telecommunications. It works closely with relevant industries to achieve "active self-regulation" while ensuring industry compliance with license conditions, codes, and standards. A total of 261 commercial radio stations were on air in 2007, and 257 were members of Commercial Radio Australia Ltd. (CRA). CRA said commercial radio accounted for 70 percent of listening in Australia.

The Special Broadcasting Service (SBS) began in 1975 with radio stations in Sydney and Melbourne, broadcasting four hours a day in eight languages. SBS was established to define and foster Australia's cultural diversity in accordance with its charter obligation to provide multilingual and multicultural radio and television services that inform, educate, and entertain all Australians and reflect Australia's "multicultural society." As of late 2007 it was broadcasting in more than 60 languages other than English, more than any other network in the world. SBS Radio produces news bulletins in 36 languages every day. SBS Online provides text, video services, and audio-on-demand in 68 languages, making it the most linguistically diverse Web site in the world.

Television

Commercial television started in Australia in 1956, though it took about a decade before TV reached all areas of the nation. By the early 1990s, most people had access to five free-to-air channels: the national broadcaster, the ABC; a network that reflects Australia's multicultural background, SBS Television; and three national commercial networks: Seven, Nine, and Ten. The Australian Broadcasting Corporation (ABC) was discussed earlier. SBS Television draws its mostly international programs from more than 400 national and international sources. The three national commercial networks are described below, along with the major regional broadcasters. Like much of Australia's media, the commercial TV channels are tending to converge their assets.

Seven Network Seven is Australia's largest commercial television network. It also runs one of Australia's two largest magazine publishers—Pacific Magazines, which publishes more than one in five magazines sold in Australia. The Seven Network controls five metropolitan and one regional television license, with a potential audience reach of 98 percent of the population. Seven joined forces with Yahoo! in the United States in January 2006. The aim was to combine the strengths of Yahoo!'s search and communications capabilities and its global Internet network with Seven's media and entertainment content and marketing capabilities. The joint venture is driving the online, mobile, and IPTV businesses of both companies in Australia.

Nine Network Until the media laws changed in 2007, Australia's richest man, James Packer, ran a family-owned empire called Publishing & Broadcasting Ltd. (PBL). Packer sold three-quarters of PBL to CVC Asia Pacific, a private equity company, and pocketed about US$ 4.5 billion in cash, which he used to buy casinos in places like Macau and Las Vegas. PBL owns the Nine Network and a major magazine publisher, Australian Consolidated Press (ACP). PBL controls three metropolitan and one regional television license, giving it a reach of 51.5 percent of the potential audience. ACP publishes 60 magazines, which sell about 109 million copies a year, about a third of total sales. It has a joint online venture (ninemsn) with the Microsoft Corporation.

Network Ten Network Ten consists of commercial television stations in Brisbane, Sydney, Melbourne, Adelaide, and Perth, with a potential audience reach of 64.9 percent of the population. The largest shareholder is Canada's CanWest group of companies with a holding of about 56 percent. Network Ten pioneered e-trading in Australia, making it the first commercial television network to allow clients to book advertising campaigns online.

WIN Corporation Pty Ltd WIN is the largest regional television broadcaster in Australia and the fourth largest in Australia behind Nine, Seven, and Ten. It controls one metropolitan and nine regional television licenses, with a potential audience of 26 percent of the population. WIN also has a radio station. The major shareholder is chairman Bruce Gordon.

Prime Television Ltd Prime broadcasts in Australia and New Zealand. It has eight regional television licenses in Australia, with a potential audience of a quarter of the population. In New Zealand Prime covers the entire country with a free-to-air signal, which can also be received by Sky viewers via satellite.

New Zealand

Freedom of expression has statutory endorsement in New Zealand and is one of the 29 provisions of the country's Bill of Rights Act of 1990. Section 14 declares: "Everyone has the right to freedom of expression, including the freedom to seek, receive and impart information and opinions of any kind in any form." Sir John Jeffries, former chairman of the New Zealand Press Council, has noted that independent international studies on freedom of expression usually rate the country in the top bracket.

Regulation

The New Zealand Press Council has operated since 1972 as a voluntary dispute-resolution body with the function of maintaining the professional standards of the NZ press. The first independent review of its activities and objectives, performance, resources, and governance was conducted early in 2007 and was expected to report later that year.

A Broadcasting Standards Authority was established in 1989 to encourage broadcasters to develop and maintain program standards "that respect human dignity and reflect current social values." The authority has drawn up four codes: Free-to-Air Television, Pay Television, Radio, and Election programs. Each code has a series of standards or principles that are supported by guidelines.

Print Media Ownership

New Zealand's two biggest media groups are Australian companies—Fairfax Media and APN News & Media. Fairfax Media purchased the publishing assets of Independent Newspapers Ltd. (INL) in 2003. Through a series of acquisitions INL (founded in 1906) became New Zealand's largest media company.

NZ assets of Fairfax Media include the capital city daily *The Dominion Post,* the major South Island daily, *The Press,* seven regional dailies, two national Sunday newspapers, magazines, community newspapers, the major online news site http://www.stuff.co.nz, and Trade Me, an auction and classified advertising site. After its merger in 2007 with Rural Press Limited (RPL), Fairfax Media is now the largest integrated metropolitan, rural, and regional print and online digital media company in Australasia.

APN News & Media publishes the country's biggest daily newspaper, *The New Zealand Herald,* as well as eight regional dailies, community newspapers, and magazines. Through its Australian Radio Network (a joint venture with Clear Channel Communications of the United States), it also operates 120 radio stations in New Zealand as The Radio Network (TRN). APN News & Media is an Australian company whose major shareholder is Independent News & Media PLC, a Dublin-based company with media interests in many countries including Ireland, the UK, India, and South-Africa.

Print Media

The print media environment in New Zealand has two unique features. One is the foreign ownership by two companies of 78 percent of the country's daily newspapers (18 out of 23); the other is the large number of provincial evening dailies that survive despite the world trend to morning publication. Neighboring Australia, for example, has no paid evening daily newspapers.

New Zealand's four metropolitan dailies—in Auckland, Wellington, Christchurch, and Dunedin—are all morning newspapers. The country's last traditional metropolitan evening paper, *The Evening Post* in Wellington, closed in 2002. But of the 19 dailies published in regional centers no fewer than 14 appear in the afternoon. It should be noted that some are very small. On the west coast of New Zealand's South Island, for example, *The News* in Westport has a paid circulation of 2,200. The paper was established in 1871.

Several factors go some way to explaining this afternoon newspaper phenomenon in New Zealand. The national news agency, the New Zealand Press Association, provides a great deal of content aimed at an afternoon paper schedule. "Its enormous domestic and international output is both affordable and critical for the survival and relevance of evening newspapers" (Tidey, 2002:144). Another factor is the intense parochial focus of local communities along with the fact that nowhere in the country are daily newspapers in serious head-to-head contest.

Only one major NZ daily, the *Otago Daily Times* in Dunedin, remains independent of the two big groups, along with a handful of local dailies. The country's major business weekly *National Business Review* is also independently owned.

Magazines

Magazines are extremely popular in New Zealand, where they enjoy one of the highest readership figures in the world according to one estimate cited by Rosenberg (2007:9). The Magazine Publishers Association (MPA) of New Zealand estimates that the country has more than 5,000 titles; of these about 1,000 are actually published in NZ. There are four principal magazine publishers, and the MPA lists more than 60 member organizations and companies. Two of the big four magazine publishers are owned by the dominant newspaper groups Fairfax Media and APN News & Media. The largest magazine publisher is ACP Media, a subsidiary of ACP Magazines Limited in Australia. ACP Media publishes some of New Zealand's most popular magazines, including *Woman's Day* and *The Australian Women's Weekly,* as well as iconic monthly titles such as *Metro* and *North & South.*

Business-to-business magazine publishers cover a wide range of industries from marketing, medical, and local government to rural, hospitality, travel, and computing. The

New Zealand Audit Bureau of Circulation (ABC) covers more than 300 publications including all paid daily and weekly newspapers, virtually all community newspapers, and more than 160 magazines.

News Agency

The New Zealand Press Association (NZPA) was founded in 1879, and until 2005 much of the copy distributed around its national network was supplied by member newspapers on a cooperative basis. Since that time, it has operated on a more commercial basis. NZPA is owned by the two main newspaper companies and a number of smaller ones. It employs more than 40 journalists in its Wellington headquarters as well as in Auckland and Sydney, Australia.

In addition to reporting and distributing domestic news, the agency also edits foreign news agency copy for distribution to its member newspapers, as well as handling up to the minute pictures and graphics of news, sport, and entertainment events in NZ. The news agency also provides material to government, corporate, and other nonmedia customers and operates a media release distribution service.

Broadcast Media

Historically, government provided most broadcasting services in New Zealand. Radio broadcasting began in 1925. For a long time public broadcasting was seen as a social service designed to reflect and develop the country's identity and culture. New Zealand was a relative latecomer to the television age with the first official transmission, in Auckland, in June 1960.

Sweeping changes from the late 1980s resulted in an "open entry" policy in which economic restrictions were relaxed to provide for new television and radio services. Restrictions on overseas ownership of broadcasters were also removed. There are no longer restrictions on which technologies may be used to broadcast services.

Television New Zealand (TVNZ), a government-owned television broadcasting corporation, is today the country's biggest free-to-air broadcaster. It operates two channels, TV One and TV2, and about 90 percent of its revenue is from commercial activity such as advertising and merchandising.

Major commercial TV operators in New Zealand are TV3 and C4 (a youth music format channel) owned by Media Works NZ and controlled by the Australasian private equity company Ironbridge Capital; and Prime Television, a national free-to-air network purchased in 2006 by Sky Television. The latter is part of Rupert Murdoch's News Corporation. Pay TV in the form of Sky Television entered the NZ market late relative to international trends, in 1990.

New Zealand has a number of small regional TV stations, a Maori Television Service and a racing network. In 2006 the New Zealand government announced the introduction of two new noncommercial digital television services, to be operated by TVNZ and offering drama, arts, documentary, and children's programs.

Radio New Zealand, the country's public service broadcaster, has two main national networks—Radio New Zealand National (news, current affairs and arts) and Radio New Zealand Concert (classical music and jazz). A third network broadcasts parliamentary debates, and there is an international service aimed particularly at neighboring countries in the Pacific.

New Zealand has a very large commercial radio sector dominated by two groups: TRN (The Radio Network) operates about 120 stations and is jointly owned by U.S. and Australian interests. The other is Radio Works (part of Media Works NZ), which by 2007 had grown to a network of more than 180 frequencies throughout the country, including six network brands.

Journalism Education

Oddly enough, despite the similarities between the Australian and New Zealand media industries (and the ownership of much of the latter by Australian companies), their approaches to journalism education are quite different. In Australia most "new" reporters start work after graduating from one of the country's 37 universities. Many have a degree in journalism or communication: According to the Australian Press Council's *State of the News Print Media in Australia,* journalism is taught at the undergraduate level at 26 Australian universities. "What is not in dispute," it adds, "is that universities are graduating many more potential journalists than there are jobs available in the mainstream media" (2006:57). Many of the larger organizations prefer to hire graduates in areas such as law, science, and business and to conduct in-house training programs for them in, for example, reporting, media law, and media ethical issues.

Journalism as an occupation has long been regarded by many journalists as *sui generis,* and no particular qualifications are demanded before a person can describe himself or herself as a journalist. A journalist is simply someone who is employed as such.

In New Zealand journalism education has traditionally been more practical and more structured. All major media employers belong to the NZ Journalists Training Organisation (JTO), a voluntary organization funded by newspaper, magazine, radio, and television companies. The JTO's brief is to "guide and foster" training. It helps accredit training schools, writes training standards, runs short courses, and publishes materials. The news media industry recognizes 10 tertiary level schools in New Zealand, and these conduct programs for qualifications in print (newspapers and magazines), radio, television, and new media. Industry input and views are strong and influence educators' teaching methods. These arrangements result in about 80 percent of journalism graduates finding news media work.

Ownership

Concentration of ownership is a serious issue in both countries, as is the very high level of foreign ownership in New Zealand. Academic Bill Rosenberg in his paper *News Media Ownership in New Zealand* points out that "four companies, all overseas owned, dominate the New Zealand news media" (2007:1). The growth of Internet-related competition is another major issue for all media, especially newspapers.

The outsourcing of editing and page design is a major issue in New Zealand. Most of the *New Zealand Herald*'s editing and page makeup was being outsourced by September 2007 after the changes were announced at the start of the year. It was run by a subsidiary of the Australian Associated Press, Pagemasters, in the largest city, Auckland. In-house editing at the paper was mostly restricted to front-of-sections. Most of APN's New Zealand regional dailies were expected to follow suit by the end of 2007.

Toward the Future

The future outlook for Australia and New Zealand is rather unclear because of the myriad factors at play. What can safely be said is that further expansion of digital media is highly likely. Many newspaper and broadcast companies are consolidating their print and free-to-air activities, and expanding into the digital realm. The percentage of advertising done online in Australia rose from 2.1 percent in 2002 to 10.4 percent in 2007. Granted, the total spent was much bigger because of a booming economy. Total advertising was worth A$7.8 billion in 2002, but had grown to A$11.1 billion only half a decade later. What will happen if the economy goes into recession is not known, but it obviously would have an impact on the media's potential growth and would force media managers to allocate resources more carefully.

BIBLIOGRAPHY

Australian Press Council. *State of the News Print Media in Australia*. Sydney. October 2006, Chapter 8.
Rosenberg, B. *News Media Ownership in New Zealand,* 66. July 15, 2007. Available: http://www.indymedia.org.nz. Accessed September 15, 2007
Tidey, J. "Death in the Afternoon." *Australian Journalism Review* 24, No.1 (July 2002), 141–145.

RELATED WEB SITES

APN News & Media: http://www.apn.co.nz
Audit Bureau of Circulation (NZ): http://www.abc.org.nz
Australian Associated Press: http://aap.com.au
Australian Broadcasting Corporation: http://www.abc.net.au
Australian Communications and Media Authority http://www.acma.gov.au
Australian Consolidated Press http://www.acp.com.au
Australian Press Council: http://www.presscouncil.org.au
Commercial Radio Australia http://www.commercialradio.com.au
Fairfax Media NZ: http://www.fairfaxnz.co.nz
Journalism Training Organisation (NZ): http://www.journalismtraining.co.nz
Magazine Publishers Association (NZ): http://www.mpa.org.nz
Magazine Publishers of Australia: http://www.magazines.org.au/
Media Works: http://www.mediaworks.co.nz
New Zealand Press Association (NZPA): http://www.nzpa.co.nz
New Zealand Press Council: http://www.presscouncil.org.nz
Newspaper Publishers Association of NZ: http://www.npa.co.nz
NZ Broadcasting Standards Authority: http://www.bsa.govt.nz
Otago Daily Times: http://www.odt.co.nz
Prime Television: http://www.primetv.co.nz
Radio New Zealand: http://www.radionz.co.nz
Radio New Zealand: http://www.rnz.co.nz
Special Broadcasting Service http://www.sbs.com.au
Television New Zealand (TVNZ): http://www.tvnz.co.nz
Ten Network http://ten.com.au
WIN Corporation: http://www.wintv.com.au/wincorp/

19 Latin America

RICK ROCKWELL
American University, USA

Despite facing a variety of institutional and political challenges, as Latin American media moved into the twenty-first century, they seemed poised to make considerable contributions to the wave of democratization breaking across the hemisphere (Tilson and Rockwell, 2004). However, what analysts did not anticipate was a backlash against both the media and democratic reforms that would have increased free expression in the region in the first part of this century. Dubbed by some as a "pink tide," the election of left-leaning leaders in some parts of the region (BBC, 2005) opened the door to a reemergence of centralized Latin American states seemingly bent on controlling communication and diminishing the role of alternative media voices (Lauría, 2006).

Before moving into this era of the so-called pink tide, journalists such as Peru's Gustavo Gorriti explained the role the media played in the region:

> In most of Latin America there is a true yearning for transparency, a true yearning for freedom also, and for true accountability. So in this . . . sometimes purely cosmetic democracies . . . the judiciary or the legislators do not fulfill their roles. It has been the press, the independent press, that has taken those larger roles, and taken of course the costs that that implies. (Smith, 1998)

As Gorriti notes, this positioned journalists as the tip of the spear in the battle for democratization. With globalized news influencing the region, and as journalists began making inroads toward more free expression, these trends undercut the traditional role of the state in Latin America as the central font of information (Waisbord and Morris, 2001). The result has been a backlash against independent media often led by leftist leaders in the region.

On the other side of the spectrum, in countries where conservative leaders have tended to look the other way as powerful media conglomerates in the region have further consolidated their power (such as Mexico), the fight between the state and supranational criminal organizations (drug cartels or criminal gangs) for order has often left the media as vulnerable and lucrative targets for attacks. In Colombia, Mexico, and elsewhere, countries have had to deploy elements of their armed forces to guard investigative journalists or to keep news organizations operating without facing violent attacks.

The relationship between communication systems and the state remains paramount in Latin America, partially because of how these systems were influenced by the shared experience of colonialism and European views of the media from the time of the conquests of the region through much of the nineteenth century. Although Latin America—stretching from the Caribbean and Mexico southward through Central America, and through South America to the tip of Tierra del Fuego—shares the experience of Spanish and Portuguese culture, the nations of the region are quite diverse in their outlooks toward the media, governance, and culture. That diversity can be seen when we compare countries such as Costa Rica—the nation with the oldest democracy in the region dating from the nineteenth century—to authoritarian Cuba, even with changes becoming possible in February 2008 with president Fidel Castro stepping aside for his brother Raul to take over.

The Historical Context

Communication in what became Latin America did not begin with colonization and European philosophies, however. The Mayans, Aztecs, Olmecs, and Incas all carried on sophisticated communication and recorded the histories of their dynamic cultures before the conquests (Ferreira, 2006). Indeed, millions of descendants of the Mayans, Aztecs, and Incas display the cultural remnants of those earlier times today in countries such as Guatemala, Mexico, Bolivia, and Peru. To understand Latin American media, communications, and culture is to know that the foundation of the region begins with these indigenous cultures. These various indigenous cultures were mixed with European influences just as the population became mainly *mestizo,* although important minorities of indigenous groups and elite European *criollos* remain to this day.

Although Latin America imported its first printing press about a century before a press would start working at Harvard College in New England (Ferreira, 2006), the history of censorship from the Spanish crown to its colonies and the Catholic Church's concerns about publications, influenced by the Inquisition, slowed the advance and culture of free expression in the region. The first printing presses came to the region in the 1530s to Mexico City, the governmental hub of New Spain. The first news item published in the region was likely from the printer Juan Pablos, whose description of an earthquake in Guatemala was carried to Europe in 1541 (Soruco and Ferreira, 1995).

The first regular newspaper published in Latin America was the *Gaceta de México,* which was published by the Catholic Church, beginning in 1722 (Ferreira, 2006). Other researchers note that single-edition trials of the *Gaceta de México* were published as early as 1666 (Fromson, 1996), but unlike the editions from 1722, these were occasional, not regular weekly publications. Although Latin American publishing began in Mexico, Peru had its own printing press by 1580. Slowly, the Church, in concert with Spanish governors, would bring independent printing to other areas of the region: Guatemala in 1660; Argentina in 1700; Paraguay in 1705; Cuba in 1707; Colombia in 1737; Ecuador in 1750; and Venezuela in 1808 (Ferreira, 2006). Within three years of the Venezuelan press's founding and the regular printing of the *Gaceta de Caracas,* the newspaper became a vehicle for those seeking independence from Spanish rule. In Brazil, an independent printing operation had been established in 1747, but it was soon closed after the Catholic Church asked

FIGURE 19.1 Latin America and the Caribbean

the Portuguese crown to order the press shuttered. Another printing operation would not open in Brazil until 1808, when the Portuguese royal court in exile asked to open a printing operation so that it could issue decrees criticizing Napoleon's occupation of Portugal.

   After most of Latin America became independent of colonial rule in the wake of the Napoleonic Wars in Europe, much of the nineteenth century was marked by violent struggles between conservative and liberal forces. Liberals favored international trade and secularization, while conservatives clung to the ideas of the Church as a dominant force in both family and political life, and protectionism. For more than 150 years after independence, much of the region often turned to *caudillos,* military strongmen or authoritarian rulers, as a way to guarantee security. These *caudillos* often carried on the tradition of media censorship and repression that had begun under colonial rulers (Van den Heuvel and Dennis, 1995).

The Media Landscape

Today, television and radio have developed as the dominant forms of media in Latin America. Although television is ascendant, in some countries, such as Honduras and Guatemala, radio remains the most important medium with nearly universal market penetration compared to television, which has an influence that is sometimes limited to urban centers in these developing nations (Rockwell and Janus, 2003).

Because of problems in developing media infrastructure in rural areas, and because of its cheap cost to consumers, radio remains the dominant medium in much of the region, with penetration rates surpassing television in most countries. Before television had *telenovelas,* radio developed a unique form of Latin American serial drama called *radionovelas* (or merely *novelas*) in the 1940s. As with *telenovelas,* the creative centers for these dramas were in Mexico and Cuba (Hayes, 2000), but Argentina also provided a number of influential dramas during the era when radio gained its dominance throughout the hemisphere. In the twenty-first century, AM radio remains an important mechanism for communication throughout the region, and although FM radio is fully developed, it remains more of a dominant force in Latin America's urban centers.

Latin America is home to some of the largest television syndication firms in the world: Televisa of Mexico; Venevision of Venezuela; and Globo of Brazil (Sinclair, 1999). Until 2006, Televisa and Venevision were minority stakeholders in the largest Spanish-language television network in the United States, Univision.

Often these television giants are vertically and horizontally integrated concerns. For instance, Globo (Organizaçoes Globo), besides its Brazilian television network operations (likely the world's fourth or fifth largest television operation) and global syndication, also owns one of Brazil's leading newspapers *O Globo,* and Globo Cabo, the country's top cable firm (Tilson and Rockwell, 2004). Globo recorded a $1.97 billion profit in 2005 (InvestNews, 2006).

Grupo Cisneros, the conglomerate that owns Venevision, has 37,000 employees, investments and syndication concerns in at least 40 countries, and revenues of $3.7 billion (Mayorbe, 2002). At one time, Grupo Cisneros also had significant holdings in mining, supermarkets, sporting goods, and the conglomerate-owned Coca-Cola distributorships in Venezuela, Puerto Rico, and other locations in Latin America. As of 2007, Grupo Cisneros owns music production companies, cosmetic firms, breweries, and sports teams in Venezuela, along with telecommunications firms, including cell-phone companies distributing phones and providing service in the United States (Grupo Cisneros, 2007). Besides its flagship network in Venezuela, Grupo Cisneros also has television holdings in Chile (Sinclair, 2004) and was lobbying to expand into Colombia.

Along with Globo and Venevision, Televisa of Mexico continues its dominance as one of the most important television networks and syndicators in the world. Although Grupo Cisneros and Globo compete strongly with this Mexican media conglomerate, Televisa is considered the broadcaster that reaches the largest number of people in Latin America, producing more than 44,000 hours of programming annually and syndicating about 61,000 hours in 2001 (Hillman, 2003). Televisa's production of *telenovelas* (the unique Latin American version of the soap opera created in the 1950s in Mexico, Cuba, and

Brazil) for export worldwide, along with its news and other syndication services, makes it a force in the dynamic world of global television. The company listed a profit of $750 million in 2007 on sales of $3.9 billion (Bernstein-Wax, 2008). Televisa has about 13,000 employees in its various divisions including its four network channels in Mexico (Malkin, 2004).

During the 1990s, Televisa expanded into direct and partial ownership of various networks outside of Mexico, including partnerships in Peru, Chile, and Guatemala (Tilson and Rockwell, 2004). Although the Mexican government encouraged the formation of a new challenger to Televisa in the 1990s in the form of TV Azteca, the older network found a way to revamp its programming to win the ratings challenge, often making it the choice of 70 percent of Mexican viewers (Malkin, 2006). In Mexico, Televisa controls four national broadcast networks (the 70 percent of Mexican viewers is measured across all four of these network channels), the top cable TV distribution firm in the country, the only satellite TV company, one of the leading radio chains, the leading magazine distributor, soccer teams, sports venues, and production studios for radio, television, and film.

Significantly, backed by its owners NBC in the United States and General Electric, in 2007, Telemundo claimed to have advanced to the position of the second-largest syndicator of Spanish-language programming in the world, surpassing even Venevision (Waldman, 2007). This shows the continued strength of U.S. exports in the region, although U.S. broadcasters have adapted now to not only reselling dubbed English-language programming, but also providing original Spanish-language programming to the region. Telemundo has production facilities to produce this programming not only in Los Angeles and Miami in the U.S., but also in Mexico and Colombia.

Although not on the same level of influence as the big three Latin American conglomerates or U.S. concerns in the region, Mexico's secondary commercial broadcaster TV Azteca has also made inroads in the region through both syndication and television ownership. TV Azteca established Azteca America to syndicate its programming to Latino audiences in the United States, and the firm has established key partnerships as minority network owners in Guatemala and direct network ownership in El Salvador. Until it spun out Azteca America, TV Azteca also had a strategic partnership with Telemundo.

Another Mexican influence on the region is businessman Angel Gonzalez, who operates a small empire of television networks and production facilities throughout the region from his headquarters in Miami (Rockwell and Janus, 2003). Besides six local television affiliates in Mexico (for Televisa), as of 2006, Gonzalez owned at least 20 television affiliates and networks in at least eight countries in the region, including a new strategic partnership to enter into a joint venture ownership deal in Argentina (*El Cronista,* 2006). Gonzalez is also involved in syndicating television programming, films, and other television fare and he has also invested in various radio chains, including ownership of a significant portion of Guatemala's radio stations. Gonzalez also owns a four-network television monopoly in Guatemala.

These various conglomerates and television holdings serve 95 million television households in the region, out of a population estimated at 420 million people (Sinclair, 2004). Over-the-air or terrestrial broadcasting remains dominant as most people, outside of the elite class, cannot afford cable television. Cable only has a penetration rate of 13 percent in the region.

Various conglomerates, including Grupo Cisneros, Televisa, and the telecommunications holdings of Carlos Slim (who made his billions after securing the Mexican telephone concession Telmex), have begun competing strongly to provide Internet services to the region, both through Web sites and Internet connectivity. However, the leaders in the region for providing Internet communication are generally from the Southern Cone.

Argentina embraced the Internet as an early adapting nation and has generally led the region in connectivity and high-quality Web information. Governments in both Chile and Argentina intervened aggressively to spur Internet connectivity growth in the 1990s by mandating reduced costs for calls connecting to the Internet (Ryan, 1999). Grupo Clarin of Argentina has often been regarded as a pioneer of the Internet in Latin America. The media company also publishes what it says is the newspaper with the highest circulation in Latin America, Argentina's *El Clarin,* which distributes 550,000 copies daily (Paxman, 1999). Grupo Clarin also owns the top cable television firm in Argentina. Besides providing various Web portals, Grupo Clarin owns the region's third largest Internet service provider (ISP). Spain's Telefonica and Argentina's Arnet Telecom are the top ISPs in Latin America. With its leadership in Internet communications, and its holdings in print and electronic media (the company also has various radio holdings and a stake in film production beyond its television investments), Grupo Clarin challenges both Televisa and Globo as a regional information leader.

Brazil has also been one of the leaders in the region for Internet use, spurred on by the competition between Globo, which also provides one of the top Internet portals besides its dominance in television, and Grupo Folha, the top Internet firm in the country. Grupo Folha also publishes Brazil's second largest newspaper, *Folha de São Paulo* (Straubhaar, 2003). In a joint venture, Grupo Folha and Editora Abril, the publisher of Brazil's most popular magazine, provide the country's most popular ISP.

Miniwatts Marketing of Colombia, which tracks marketing trends and Internet usage throughout Latin America, lists Chile as the country with the highest Internet penetration rate at 42.8 percent in 2006 (Rockwell, 2007). In Chile, *El Mercurio,* the leading conservative daily, runs the country's most popular Internet portal. Following Chile are Argentina at 39.7 percent and Costa Rica at 29.4 percent. The difficulty with providing a higher connectivity rate to the Internet is that in many countries landline phones are still considered a luxury. Some countries, such as Brazil, El Salvador, Peru, and Chile, have turned to public kiosks or other communal systems to provide Internet service, especially to rural areas. With the lowered cost of cell phones in the region, Internet service provided via cell phone or other wireless connectivity holds great potential for the future, but as of yet, the region lags behind the United States and Europe in Internet connectivity rates and service. In many parts of the region, less than 10 percent of the populace are connected to the Internet, reflecting how elites are able to access this media platform and that a digital divide exists in Latin America that is reflective of the region's problems with poverty and class divisions.

Some also see newspapers as an elite medium in the region, often limited in their reach due to geography, transportation, and other infrastructure problems, poor literacy rates, and cost. However, newspapers remain very influential in the region, as they connect elites. Often other media depend on newspapers, especially radio and television, which may be cheaper and easier for consumers to use, but often don't have the staffs to provide rich content. As in other parts of the world, often the popular Internet portals of the region borrow liberally from the content of the region's newspapers and news services. Although *El Clarin* is regarded as the most circulated newspaper in the region, Argentina also boasts other newspapers respected for their content, including *Pagina/12,* which was influential in uncovering scandals during the presidency of Carlos Menem.

Although hailing from smaller countries, Costa Rica's *La Nación,* and Nicaragua's *La Prensa* are often noted in the region as quality newspapers (Rockwell and Janus, 2003). In Venezuela, *El Universal* has often led the media battles against President Hugo Chávez's administration and his antimedia policies. In Mexico, a group of conservative dailies, including *El Norte* of Monterrey, *Reforma* of Mexico City, *Mural* of Guadalajara, and *Palabra* of Saltillo, led the way toward political reform that ushered in Mexico's democratic movement and President Vicente Fox in 2000 (Rockwell, 2003). In Brazil, besides *Folha de São Paulo,* various newspapers, including *Jornal do Brazil* and *O Estado de São Paulo,* are admired by journalists for providing quality journalism (Calmon Alves, 2003). In Colombia, *El Espectador* became a legendary newspaper for its reporting on the country's drug cartels: the paper survived a bombing by those cartels in 1989. Although its reporters have been killed, attacked, and harassed, the paper continues investigating the drug gangs and critiquing the country's president.

Media and the State

Traditionally, much of the media of Latin America have supported elite or oligarchic structures and strong centralized states. In return, many media outlets have depended on the state for their existence. For example, in some poorer countries in the region without well-developed economies, government subsidies, both official and unofficial, may spell the difference between profitability and bankruptcy. For example, in Nicaragua, many media outlets depended on state subsidies. Official handouts from the state and state advertising represented 70 percent of the media revenue stream (Jones, 2001), and this remains so. In some countries, such as Mexico, this legacy of media dependency is still present despite attempts at modernization both by the state and the media. During the elections in Argentina in 2007, the level of state advertising became a major issue as some accused President Nestor Kirchner of using official advertising and state subsidies as a fulcrum to leverage the media in favor of his wife Cristina Fernandez's presidential campaign (Lauría, 2007).

In some countries, this media dependency has changed in an era of globalization and state moves toward privatization and less use of subsidies. In some parts of the region in the 1990s, these changes yielded an era of consolidation. The results in Mexico, Venezuela, Brazil, Guatemala, Argentina, and Brazil have produced Televisa, Grupo Cisneros, Globo, Grupo Clarin, and the media holdings of Angel Gonzalez. Importantly, the state in these various countries reacted differently to this media evolution based on both the historic political evolution of each nation and the political economy present in each. The approaches of conservatives and left-leaning leaders to this evolution have proved to be starkly different. Indeed, dynastic media conglomerates, often built upon multigenerational family commitments to the enterprise often outlived the regimes that promoted these media as a way to catalyze the message of the state. The continued dominance of Televisa in Mexico, despite the end of the rule of the Institutional Revolutionary Party (PRI, by its

Spanish acronym) and the continued ratings triumphs of Globo (although the Brazilian military's rule is a memory of a different generation) are but two examples. The rise of the media conglomerate or media enterprise that can challenge the state's power is also often due to the ties these conglomerates have to powerful elite forces. Beyond Televisa and Globo, Venevision (Grupo Cisneros) is certainly another example of that relationship between the media and the powerful.

The wave of leftist reformers who have won electoral victories in the new century, the so-called pink tide, campaigned vigorously against powerful oligarchies or conservative elites to gain office. This naturally pitted populist reformers against those who once controlled the state. And although these often conservative elites had lost the reins of state power, their alliances with the media gave them tools to oppose reform. What this has meant however, is that populist leftists have often resorted to the traditional methods of the state to make the media come to heel.

These methods have varied. In Argentina and Nicaragua, leftist presidents have attempted to bar reporters who did not pass an ideological litmus test from attending government events and government news conferences, along with axing them from the list of those to receive media credentials or even press releases from the government (Rockwell, 2007). In Venezuela, President Chávez has frequently called the critical media enemies of the state and obstacles to progressive change (Lauría, 2006); he moved against one of the more powerful television networks, taking their broadcast frequency and forcing their migration to cable television and, ultimately, a considerably reduced audience.

In Bolivia, Ecuador, and Uruguay, the relationship between the media and leftist reformers has been contentious and sometimes openly hostile.

Even in Brazil, although President Luiz Inácio Lula da Silva (commonly called merely "Lula") has been less aggressive in striking out against the media than others, he too has shut out media access to the government or his election campaign (Lauría, 2006). After Lula's election victory in 2006, many of his supporters carried signs saying his party had defeated not the opposition parties but the media. Lula's relationship with Globo and various newspapers, including the international media (the *New York Times* famously labeled Lula as "a drunk"), has been rocky (Kingstone, 2004).

To blunt the informational force of private media, the state will turn not only to subsidies and advertisements to buy influence but also to its own media. In Argentina, Bolivia, and Venezuela, often the state has adopted an aggressive media policy to employ state television as a counterbalance to private media (Lauría, 2006).

As history shows, these are not new battles. The leftist populists of the new century are leaning on a history of media repression that stretches back to colonial times. This is a repressive culture not just stitched into the fabric of the region by the state, but also by a conservative Church, and carried forth into the nineteenth and twentieth centuries by abusive authoritarian dictators.

Chávez and Venezuela

Few Latin American politicians have made as great an impact on the global news scene since the beginning of the 2000s as President Hugo Chávez. He has been at odds with the media almost since his election in 1998, arguing that "he has been the victim of unfair coverage by the opposition-aligned news media" (*The Miami Herald,* 2002). Chávez has framed himself as a populist reformer against large conglomerates in league with oligarchic forces which have ruled Venezuela, even under the guise of democratic forms, for the past half-century. As Chávez faced off against large conglomerates such as Grupo Cisneros—in the form of Venevision—and the powerful Phelps family with the oldest network in the country, RCTV (Radio Caracas Television), many Venezuelans believed their president was indeed in a fight with powerful entrenched interests of the elite.

Even before the watershed events of a brief coup in 2002, world press freedom groups and other supranational forces had expressed concern about free expression in Venezuela (González Rodríguez, 2002). Overall, during the Chávez era these problems have unfolded for the media: (a) At least four journalists have been assassinated, although many of those cases may relate to reporting on drugs or local corruption; (b) at least 38 journalists have been attacked in a variety of incidents by Chavistas, the military, and antigovernment protestors; (c) the state has filed at least a dozen high-level criminal defamation cases against journalists; (d) several journalists went into exile rather than face legal proceedings aimed at muzzling them; (e) at the president's urging, the National Assembly expanded the scope and penalties attached to so-called disrespect laws (*desacato*), which are a cause of self-censorship; and (f) the Chávez government has admitted to spying on journalists and tapping phone conversations. After producing critical reports, some journalists have reported members of the military made intimidating visits to their newsrooms (Rockwell, 2007).

Supporters of Chávez have defended this record saying it is an improvement on the relationship between the media and the Venezuelan state of the past (Lauría and González Rodríguez, 2007). For example, in 1992, after Chávez failed to gain power in an unsuccessful coup, President Carlos Andrés Pérez cracked down on the media using censors installed in newsrooms after government raids. He also ordered newspapers that had escaped the censors' hands confiscated. However, this was part of a state tradition of censorship stretching back through Venezuela's history to colonial times. In the twentieth century, if presidents weren't using censors directly, they were threatening the media by withholding subsidies or state advertising or by denying requests for the importation of newsprint for newspapers. During the February 1992 coup, President Andrés Pérez had actually outsmarted Chávez and his co-plotters by escaping their attempts to capture him and holding up in the studios of Venevision. From Venevision, Venezuela's top network, Andrés Pérez was able to broadcast a message to the nation, saying that although a coup attempt was underway, he was still in charge and the coup leaders would be defeated. In a battle for the Venezuelan airwaves that would be echoed in later coups, Chávez's allies were unable to broadcast their own message using captured state television VTV (Sanchez, 2007). Although he had seized the presidential palace, Chávez agreed to surrender after losing this media war, and he did so on live television.

The tables would be reversed on Chávez in 2002. After serving prison time, winning a pardon, and then an election, Chávez faced a growing opposition movement as he moved to consolidate his executive power against the entrenched interests of the oligarchy who still controlled the state oil concern PDVSA. Working with renegade elements of the military, the opposition colluded against Chávez, and leading members of the media became involved in a plot to overthrow the president (Dinges, 2005). When protestors were killed by snipers during competing marches by Chavistas and the opposition, the leading

Venezuelan networks manipulated the news and the video of the incident to make it seem as if Chávez's followers and the military were behind the shooting. Led by Venevision and RCTV, the Venezuelan media began calling for Chávez to resign over the shooting incident. Then rogue elements of the military moved against Chávez and set up business leader Pedro Carmona as the president. Chavistas took to the streets in protest. During these protests, the leaders of Venevision and RCTV gave orders that they should not be covered: Venezuela's networks were showing cartoons and films (including *Pretty Woman*) as elements of the military still loyal to Chávez and his supporters regained control (Klein, 2003). Many analysts labeled the unsuccessful overthrow of Chávez "a media coup," partially because some of the planning for the plot had occurred at the Venevision studios or the home of Diego Cisneros. However, no media owners were ever formally charged, and Venezuela's Supreme Court actually ruled that the incident was not a coup (Lauría and González Rodríguez, 2007).

After his brief removal from office in 2002, Chávez would sharpen his policies against the media. Beginning in 2000, he had begun the radio program *Aló Presidente* (Smeets, 2001), which eventually also became a television program. He had also used *cadenas,* legal orders for Venezuela's networks to turn over time to him for speeches, to establish a strong presence on the country's airwaves. But those were countermeasures of the state to balance against the anti-Chávez messages of the Venezuelan networks, which Chávez often characterized as "the four horsemen of the Apocalypse" (Lauría and González Rodríguez, 2007). In 2004, Chávez proposed the Law of Social Responsibility, which aimed directly at the powerful television networks and which applied directly to all electronic media. Dominated by Chávez's supporters, the National Assembly passed the law. Human rights and press freedom groups have criticized the law as vague. The law directly restricts content but leaves open to government interpretation what is meant by content that is "disrespectful" or that incites war or that "disrupts the public order" (Karlekar, 2005c:218). In 2005, again aided by the National Assembly, Chávez pushed through changes in the country's *desacato* laws, which increase criminal penalties for defamation and which widen the definition of speech that may be covered by these so-called respect laws (Lauría and González Rodríguez, 2007:13). These restrictive media laws were passed after Chávez triumphed over the Venezuelan opposition, which tried unsuccessfully twice to recall him with petition campaigns and a plebiscite.

Besides creating a legal framework to better control the media, Chávez also created institutions to better transmit the government's message. This began with the formal creation of an Information Ministry in 2002 to better monitor the media but also to manage the government's growing sophistication in the use of state radio and television (Tilson and Rockwell, 2004). In 2005, Chávez and Venezuela were the driving force behind establishing TeleSUR, a 24-hour satellite network supported by a consortium of Latin American governments. Andres Izarra heads the network (Bruce, 2005). Izarra is a Venezuelan journalist who had exposed the complicity of the Venezuelan commercial broadcasters in the 2002 coup. Before taking over TeleSUR, Izarra had also served as Venezuela's minister of information. Venezuela, Cuba, Argentina, Uruguay, Bolivia, Ecuador, and Nicaragua all contribute to the consortium that operates the network (Associated Press, 2007). Venezuela provides the lion's share of operating capital for the network, and the network's headquarters is in Caracas. The aim of the network is not only to provide a voice for some of these left-leaning governments, but also a counterhegemonic information frame to counterbalance the influence of U.S. cable and satellite information—available throughout the region (via NBC and CNN in Spanish)—and the largely conservative broadcasting conglomerates of the region.

The Chávez government also greatly expanded licenses and the broadcast spectrum for small community broadcasters in Venezuela, as another competitor against the large established commercial broadcast concerns. Beginning in 2002, the Venezuelan government granted licenses to 193 low-power radio and television stations licensed to communities and nonprofit groups. In 2007, Venezuela budgeted an additional $1 million to further develop community radio and television (Lauría and González Rodríguez, 2007). Although these programs did provide a wealth of opportunities for many new voices to gain access to the Venezuelan airwaves, some of these new stations proved to be dependent on the state for continued financing and for programming.

Although far from over, the contentious relationship between Chávez and the media reached near-crisis status again in 2007 in a dispute over RCTV's license. RCTV is owned by Empresas 1 BC, which is controlled by the Phelps-Granier family. Although not on the same level as Grupo Cisneros on the international broadcasting scene, Empresas 1 BC also owns the Miami-based Coral Pictures, which distributes programming in 42 countries. RCTV and its other broadcasting concerns are significant enough that, despite the existence of other broadcast networks, many experts referred to Venezuela's broadcasting scene as a duopoly, putting RCTV on a par with Venevision (Fox, 1997). The Phelps family emigrated from the United States to Venezuela and was involved in retail sales and manufacturing before branching into broadcasting in the twentieth century (Sinclair, 1999). When RCTV's broadcast license was up for renewal in 2007, the Chávez government decided to take and use the broadcast frequency for a new state television operation TVes.

The government cited RCTV's role in the 2002 coup, along with a variety of violations of the Law of Social Responsibility, as reasons for declining the license renewal. In addition, the government seized RCTV's transmitters so that it could guarantee a smooth transition to its broadcast of TVes. Various press freedom groups and human rights organizations, along with the Inter-American Commission on Human Rights, protested this broadcast change, noting RCTV was not given due process or the right to appeal the government's decision (Lauría and González Rodríguez, 2007). The closure sparked violent street demonstrations and awakened a nascent student protest movement in the country. While it was knocked off of Venezuela's airwaves, RCTV took its programming to the Internet: the network produced more than 500 videos for YouTube, and the most popular attracted more than 113,000 views. However, this was far from the millions of viewers the network had commanded as Venezuela's second most popular network. Eventually, after two months off the air, RCTV returned to Venezuelan (and Caribbean) viewers as a cable and satellite station. This move still left the network's audience at less than 30 percent of what it had been when the government seized its transmitters.

The Chávez government reacted against RCTV a second time when the network refused to air the president's *cadena* messages on cable and satellite. The Information Ministry moved to close RCTV again. However, RCTV appealed to Venezuela's Supreme Court, arguing that because RCTV was now an international broadcaster on cable and satellite beyond Venezuela, the law giving the president the power to commandeer networks no longer applied. The court agreed with this argument. Although Chávez and the Venezuelan state had succeeded in diminishing the power of one of the country's media conglomerates, some of this struggle may have backfired. At the end of 2007, Chávez called for a plebiscite on constitutional reforms, which would have allowed him to rule indefinitely. The student movement that was formed to defend the rights of RCTV organized opposition to Chávez, and ultimately to defend the constitutional reforms, lost at the polls. This was the first defeat of Chávez at the polls in a decade.

The Venezuelan Template

For those on the left, the battles between Chávez and the media provided a lesson for how to advance a populist cause. Although some might see this as new, international media organizations criticized these actions as just a modern example of a *caudillo* suppressing media critics (Lauría, 2006). Indeed, many of the current methods of media coercion in Latin American, both subtle and direct, can be traced to the mid-twentieth century in Argentina, Brazil, and Mexico (Rockwell and Janus, 2002). Some media researchers have noted that strongman Juan Perón seemed to perfect this style of confrontational populism.

Following the Venezuelan example, in Nicaragua, President Daniel Ortega has declined to give interviews to media outlets not directly aligned with his political party, the FSLN (Sandinista National Liberation Front, by its Spanish acronym). In addition, Ortega has cut subsidies for media outlets not connected with his party, and independent media are often left off the credentials list for state news conferences or official events. Nicaraguan journalists complain that they are being harassed and that Ortega uses radio and television channels allied with the Sandinistas almost exclusively. In 2007, Ortega sacked Nicaragua's ambassador to France for giving an exclusive interview to *La Prensa,* the longtime conservative opposition paper. Ambassador Oscar Rene Vargas wasn't just fired for breaking the FSLN ban on interviews to independent media, but because he told the paper these days it was "dangerous to think" if you were a high-level Sandinista (Rockwell, 2007).

In Bolivia, President Evo Morales has clashed with the powerful television network Unitel (Lauría, 2006). Unitel newscasts often referenced Morales's indigenous background with unflattering and racist terms. The media are "discriminating against the indigenous people," Morales told a delegation from the Committee to Protect Journalists (CPJ) in 2007. "Journalists sympathize with me, but the media owners are aligned in a campaign against my government," he added (Lauría, 2007). The Bolivian government has issued a list of journalists it believes are enemies of the state, and Morales has threatened to nationalize hostile media outlets. Bolivian journalists complain they have become targets for violence, and violence against journalists has increased during the Morales administration. Morales is supporting constitutional reforms that would increase the breadth of defamation laws and limit the holdings of media owners. As in Venezuela, Morales is reviewing broadcast licenses, and he has poured state funds into improving state media outlets, along with funding 24 new community radio stations, which are now linked by a new state network, Radios de los Pueblos Originarios de Bolivia (Radios of the Native People of Bolivia). Some of the funding for these new initiatives in Bolivia has come from Venezuela.

In Argentina and Uruguay, leftist governments have been less confrontational, but still manipulative when it comes to media policies. Opponents of the Kirchner government in Argentina accused the president of using the state's media funds to sway an election, in effect allowing Kirchner to appoint his wife as a successor (Lauría, 2007). In Uruguay, the media also accuse the government of treating them like the political opposition, rather than the Fourth Estate, by using state subsidies as a tool to reward friendly media outlets and as a weapon against critics.

The Conservative Democracies

But not all states in Latin America were following the Venezuelan path in the relationship between government and the media at the beginning of the twenty-first century. Two of the hemisphere's cornerstone states, Colombia and Mexico, confronted the issue of media violence, but with different tacks. Both ruled by conservative governments, Colombia and Mexico often approached the media and media conglomerates with a *laissez-faire* economic attitude. Both states were often confronted with larger questions threatening these governments: the rise of powerful drug groups, which often rivaled the state for power in some areas, and the continued tug of guerrilla groups to splinter the power of the state.

In Mexico, the authority of the state was undercut by a controversial election in 2006, which was ultimately decided by Mexico's Supreme Court. Although Felipe Calderon of the conservative PAN (National Action Party, by its Spanish acronym) was installed as president, the controversy over the election sparked a left-wing movement that challenged his presidency at almost every turn. Mexico's virtual television duopoly of Televisa and TV Azteca, nominally aligned with the PRI (Institutional Revolutionary Party, by its Spanish acronym) focused on President Calderon's difficulties almost as if this was a new amusing telenovela. Although not as openly contentious with this coverage as his predecessor Vicente Fox, Calderon was forced to defend the media in strong ways against violent forces. Calderon often ordered Mexican army troops to guard reporters or newspapers due to threats: a policy, which followed on the work of Fox, to protect journalists in the face of repression by drug cartels (González Rodríguez and Lauría, 2006). Although Fox had ordered the protection of journalists almost from the beginning of his term in 2001, the highest profile case came in 2006 when drug cartels attacked *El Mañana,* a newspaper in the border city of Nuevo Laredo.

Gunmen working for one of Mexico's four drug cartels used grenades and assault rifles to attack the newspaper offices, severely injuring one reporter. This was the start of attacks not just on individual reporters but on entire news organizations. In 2007, the entire newsroom of the regional paper *El Imparcial del Istmo* in Oaxaca resigned after three of the newspapers' delivery workers were targeted and executed by drug gangs. Journalists were not the only targets. Singers of the popular *narcocorridos* (ballads glorifying or condemning drug dealers) became particular targets of the drug gangs too, with a string of killings of musicians beginning in 2006 (Tobar, 2006). President Calderon responded by sending thousands of troops to the border regions where the cartels are especially strong, to the state of Michoacan, and other regions.

As Mexico entered one of its most violent and unstable periods since the Mexican Revolution, the media were also undergoing radical changes. Fox's victory in 2000 meant the end of decades of official state subsidies for most of the country's media outlets, a system that kept most media outlets tethered to a particular information line approved by the Mexican government and the PRI (Rockwell, 2003). One of the legacies of the Fox government was a new open records law passed in 2003, which some analysts called the most progressive in Latin America (Karlekar, 2005b). Although Mexico's media under the Calderon government were freer and served as a greater balance to the state in the country's young democracy than perhaps any time in the country's history, the media were also more restrained by violence, self-censorship, and their vulnerabilities if they chose to report on the growing power of the cartels.

In Colombia, the years 2007 and 2008 saw perhaps the country's biggest offensive against leftist guerrillas at any time in the country's civil war, which has stretched over 44 years (Forero, 2008). Along with Mexico, Colombia remained one of the most dangerous countries in the hemisphere for reporters, with at least 30 reporters killed, most by drug gangs, in the decade between 1995 and 2005 (Mitchell, 2005). Under the government of President Alvaro Uribe, Colombia's Interior Ministry had often granted funds to critical journalists to hire bodyguards, or the ministry dispatched police or troops to guard investigative journalists. However, Uribe's views toward journalists have evolved as more critical reports about him and his government have appeared in his second term in office. Beginning in 2002, some of the most powerful media owners began spiking reports critical of Uribe, his government, or Uribe's handling of the civil war.

The nation's two leading radio and television networks, RCN and Caracol, deleted a variety of reports saying they would not be helpful in the government's ongoing struggle against terrorism. However, some critical journalists did manage to publish or broadcast reports linking the president to the Medellín cartel and to uncover links between Colombia's Congress, its military establishment, and the country's right-wing paramilitary organizations, which often operate outside the law. For the past five years, Uribe has fought accusations that he had ties to deceased cartel leader Pablo Escobar. In 2007, the president launched a media offensive and openly issued declarations against various reporters. Some of those reporters went into self-imposed exile after death threats followed the president's protestations. International media and human rights groups denounced Uribe's actions. Despite this recent record, Uribe selected Francisco Santos, a former journalist, as his vice president. The former editor of *El Tiempo,* Colombia's most influential daily, Santos had been a kidnap victim of Escobar in 1990. Some Colombian journalists have noted that with Santos as vice president, Uribe's ties to the country's conservative establishment and right-wing media owners are quite obvious. And Santos is also not above criticizing the media despite his past vocation. In 2005, Santos said that media outlets criticizing how the government was carrying out its plan against a guerrilla bombing campaign had become "a sounding board for terrorist actions that, without a doubt, was more effective than the use itself of the explosives" (Mitchell, 2005).

Cuba: Authoritarian Control

Although some of the leftist governments of the hemisphere are portrayed as authoritarian, Cuba remains the only truly authoritarian government in Latin America, and its media system is the least free of any in the region. Notably, Cuba has the second largest number of journalists imprisoned for political reasons in the world, behind China. Freedom House, a U.S.-based prodemocracy organization, ranked Cuba as having the second worst system for media freedom in the world behind North Korea (Karlekar, 2005a). Cuba had 24 journalists imprisoned as of 2007. The Cuban government also employs arbitrary arrest for short periods to intimidate and coerce would-be dissidents and to maintain an atmosphere of self-censorship and fear (Boadle, 2008).

Almost all media on the island are directly controlled by the state. The government publishes three national newspapers (*Granma, Trabajadores,* and *Juventud Rebelde*) and a number of regional newspapers. The Cuban government also runs two news agencies (which have Web sites along with the country's newspapers), two national television networks, and a number of radio networks. However, dissident journalists operate on the island by phoning reports to Radio Marti, the U.S. propaganda apparatus in Florida. Radio Marti beams such stories back into Cuba when its signal can get around the Cuban government's jamming. Dissident journalists also send telephone, e-mail, and written reports to Latin American and European media outlets with varied rates of success. One of the most successful efforts to publicize different viewpoints came from the Catholic Church's *samizdat* publication *Vitral*. However, the Church changed the direction of *Vitral* in 2007, focusing it more on religious discussions rather than politics. For a time, Omar Rodriguez Saludes was part of a group that ran the *samizdat* publication *De Cuba,* however, Cuban authorities shut the publication down in 2003 and jailed Rodriguez Saludes (Marrero, 2008). Rodriguez Saludes is currently serving a 27-year sentence for violating Cuban laws restricting independent journalists. The Cuban government also limits access to the Internet and attempts to block many Web sites, as numerous Web sites critical of the government are operated in the United States, Spain, and locations throughout Latin America. Dissident journalists on the island are sometimes successful at publishing their reports on such Web sites.

In February 2008, Fidel Castro officially transferred power to his brother Raul as the head of the Cuban state. Although many noted this would make little difference in the Cuban government's attempts at maintaining control of the media, some international media groups and human rights organizations were hopeful that a change in power would eventually mean liberalization of communication policy. The Cuban government signaled this potential change with discussions about the release of some of the imprisoned dissident journalists (CPJ, 2008).

The Cuban government also expelled journalists from the BBC, the *Chicago Tribune,* and Mexico's *El Universal* in 2007 for reports the government deemed to be too negative.

Institutionalized Censorship and Violence

As delineated here in the discussions of Cuba, Colombia, Mexico, Nicaragua, Bolivia, and Venezuela, the culture of media oppression—directly, through state means, or indirectly through violence—is ever present in Latin America. The state's interventions, and repression by the Church in colonial times, laid the cultural and political groundwork for such problems (Ferreira, 2006). During the region's swing toward democracy in the past 20 years, however, various media outlets have led the way in attempting to shatter this culture of oppression.

One of the first newspapers to lead this wave of opposing authority was Venezuela's *El Nacional.* This newspaper faced the wrath of Venezuela's President Andrés Pérez in the early 1990s; he closed the paper on numerous occasions due to its critical reporting (Van den Heuvel and Dennis, 1995). However, *El Nacional* was crucial in exposing the corruption scandal that eventually unseated Andrés Pérez. Although *El Nacional,* known since its founding in 1943 as a left-wing paper, supported President Chávez initially, it began to shift its political stance in 2002, and now it is one of the leading critics of Chávez, taking a more moderate line.

Also during the 1990s, in Brazil, a number of newspapers worked to expose corruption and with it also brought down a president who had been supported by another powerful media entity, Globo. Publications such as *Veja, Jornal do Brasil,* and *Folha de São Paulo* used their pages to begin the debate about entrenched political corruption that led to the end of the presidency of Fernando Collor de Mello (Lins da Silva, 2000).

Other countries throughout the region also provided examples of courageous journalism that fed a growing movement for free expression. In Argentina, the corruption investigations started by *Pagina 12* took a decade to gain momentum and eventually snuffed out the political career of former President Menem (Waisbord, 2000). In Guatemala, beginning in the mid-1990s, various publications also took on the corruption of presidents (Rockwell and Janus, 2003). The investigative reporting by reporters at *Prensa Libre* and *elPeriodico* revealed the corruption scandals of the administration of Alvaro Arzú: these revelations did not hound Arzú from office, but were instrumental in the dismantling of his political party after he left power. Intrepid editor Jose Ruben Zamora of *elPeriodico* also focused his newspaper's reporting on the corruption in the next administration of President Alfonso Portillo. Armed members of an elite Guatemalan intelligence unit terrorized Zamora and his family at gunpoint, attempting to silence him (Rockwell, 2003). Instead, the incident focused more attention on Portillo. One member of the intelligence unit was eventually found guilty of attacking Zamora (although 10 others would face no penalty), and former President Portillo eventually fled to Mexico to avoid prosecution for the corruption Zamora and other journalists had exposed during his administration.

Although direct censorship, the blunt instrument of the state, is mostly gone from the hemisphere, as noted earlier, more discreet forms of coercion continue to plague the media: manipulation of state subsidies, threats of state takeovers, and competition from state media all influence the culture of self-censorship in the region. Violence remains a potent weapon against free expression. Although mostly not wielded by agents of the state, with notable exceptions, drug cartels, guerrillas, paramilitaries, and other criminal elements seek to silence or limit investigative reporting by using violence. Although violence against journalists in Colombia was receding, it was still one of the most dangerous countries in the region to work as a journalist, perhaps only temporarily eclipsed by Mexico, which has had more incidents of murder and kidnapping in the past several years (Campbell, 2007). Governments throughout Latin America also continued to use a variety of legal mechanisms to hem in the media. Beyond reviewing broadcast licenses, governments have used controversial *colegio* laws, requiring practicing journalists to be certified by the state by matriculating through an approved institution of higher learning and belonging to an approved organization of journalists. Various gag laws and *desacato* laws remain on the books in Panama, Chile, and Venezuela, among other countries in the region, and have been used to punish or silence critical reporters (Tilson and Rockwell, 2004).

Media Corruption and Collusion

Although many in the media have looked to various publications and media outlets in Latin America as operations to emulate, the media in the region have often been spawned from corrupt beginnings. For example, Mexico's current media duopoly evolved over decades. However, until the 1990s, Mexico was considered a monopolistic system with Televisa dominating and the only television competition coming from a weak public television system. The founder of the Televisa empire, Emilio Azcarraga Vidaurreta, began an alliance with Mexico's powerful PRI near the beginning of that party's grip on power of more than 70 years (Sinclair, 1999). Azcarraga began the Televisa empire with radio stations and music recording studios, a cultural reach the PRI needed for its modern message. By the television age, his son Emilio ("El Tigre") Azcarraga Milmo was declaring, "I am a soldier of the PRI" (Vanden Heuvel and Dennis, 1995:22). Consequently, Televisa was censoring the news in favor of the ruling party and slanting its programming to further guarantee the PRI's hold on all levels of power. Even during a privatization phase in the 1990s, when President Carlos Salinas de Gotari sold off one of the state's underperforming networks to investor Ricardo Salinas Pliego (no relation to the president), the corruption and collusion of the Mexican broadcast system was revealed. After Salinas Pliego started the TV Azteca network, investigative reports surfaced that showed Salinas Pliego had paid a kickback to the president's brother in order to get the television concession (Rockwell, 2003). The Fox era ended the PRI's reign and this collusion with the media. Although these media firms have since evolved, this history illustrates the corrupt methods often employed by the media working in league with the state, rather than representing independent interests and the advancement of democratic concerns.

In Peru, the end of the corrupt rule of Alberto Fujimori in 2000 arrived as a television special report. Canal N, a cable firm, which had made a mark with its investigations of judicial impropriety, obtained hidden camera footage of presidential advisor Vladimir Montesinos bribing a member of the opposition's congressional delegation (Peirano, 2002). The footage also showed the vice president of what was Peru's largest television network taking part in the bribery scheme, and Montesinos advised the television executive on the tape on how to slant the news in the government's favor. A series of videos played by Canal N would reveal that Fujimori had bribed many owners of Peru's leading networks, often paying in the hundreds of thousands of dollars for their complicity. Journalist Luis Iberico obtained the key tape of Montesinos. Iberico said one of Montesinos's disgruntled aides had leaked the video (Fuguet, 2001). After the Fujimori regime collapsed, investigators uncovered thousands of Montesinos's videos, revealing the extent of the government and media's corruption.

The culture of media corruption, though retreating in some parts of the region, including Mexico, is so well developed that often the slang for journalistic bribery varies depending on the type of bribe. In Central America, the slang for journalist bribes varies from country to country (Rockwell and Janus, 2003). In some countries, such as El Salvador and Mexico, unlabeled advertisements masquerade as front-page stories in newspapers or as prominent radio reports.

Poverty and Economic Oligarchies

In many countries of the region, media conglomerates are not just vertically integrated enterprises but family businesses. Televisa, Globo, and Venevision are just the three largest examples of that longtime trend. In Mexico, less than 40 families own most of the media in the country (Vanden Heuvel and Dennis, 1995). In Central America, this concentration of media ownership can be even smaller: in Nicaragua and El Salvador, four families account for the ownership of most of the leading newspapers and television outlets (Rockwell and Janus, 2003). These family ownership structures often retain control of the media over various generations despite existing in dynamic media environments, and often these media families also represent the views of conservative economic oligarchies. The history of the region also shows that both the economic oligarchies of the region and the conservative media oligarchies have frequently allied with dictators or military regimes (Rockwell, 2007). The Chamorro family of Nicaragua, owners of *La Prensa,* among various other media outlets, is a notable exception to this trend.

Throughout Latin America, weak democratic institutions that should be shoring up accountability, representation, and the rule of law have instead left strong executive power in place, with few exceptions. As noted, some media have stooped to corrupt practices. Many media outlets, though, are guilty of negligence in a democratic system: they have shirked any sense of a public service mission in favor of the pursuit of profits. Consequently, they aim very little reporting of consequence at the immense poverty of the region (Tilson and Rockwell, 2004). The stark contrast between the super-rich billionaires (Mexico's telecom entrepreneur Carlos Slim is the world's third richest man) and the dirt-poor peasants of the region are evident. In most countries of the region, the average person lives on less than $2 per day.

Taken at face value, relatively free media systems may appear to be cornerstones of democracy and important institutions for building democratic systems. However, the history and cultural development of the region has revealed that the media are often part of the economic oligarchies of the region, and are less effective at bolstering democracy than some may theorize. Media systems, which have adopted the predominant tabloidism of the United States and other northern nations—a problem that is apparent in the sensational news products that are available throughout the region—often are not interested in the public service needs of a populace transitioning to democracy. These relatively free media systems provide yet another façade that hides the lack of democratic advancement, in the same way that multiparty systems and elections sometimes mask the true power structures that underpin systems that are really polyarchies, although they are labeled emerging democracies.

Some analysts have noted that liberal economic theory, especially when applied to Latin America, promised that free and open markets alone would transform the region into a vibrant hotbed of democracy (Hallin, 2000). Although that may have been the analysis in the post-Cold War years of the 1990s following waves of privatization, it did not account for the inevitable backlash when democratic systems could not produce reforms quickly. The populists of the left in the region have seized upon that disaffection with democracy. Will they change these polyarchies masquerading as young democracies, or will they just become a new generation of *caudillos*? Their interactions with the media are clues to what is to come.

One of the institutional ingredients for a democratic system that both the media and governments of the region have neglected is stronger support for a civil society movement (Tilson and Rockwell, 2004). Truly, more nongovernmental and nonprofit institutions have sprung up in the region than ever before, many to aid in a transition from more authoritarian forms of government employed in the region in the past. However, the caution is that these new institutions be indigenous to the region and not carry the cultural imprint of the United States or other nations. Likewise, the ethical practices and journalistic norms of the region need to be shaped by those from the region rather than transplanted. In this way, the media can begin to bring about democratic change by creating public space for the necessary discussions of institution-building, and to free the region of media manipulation from all sectors (public and private). By creating such public space for discussions, the media may begin to bridge the gap between the oligarchies of conservatism and the populist leaders of the left. If not, the region may be doomed to another cycle of destructive and violent turbulence, as opposing ideological forces battle for control rather than finding a compromise that may be best for the various societies of the region.

Journalism Education[1]

In an extensive overview, Ferreira, Tilson, and Salwen (1999) argue that "[s]ince its origins in the 1930s, journalism and mass communication education in Latin America and the Caribbean has been the topic of heated regional and even international debates. Discussions have concerned matters such as secular or religious values in education, domestic or transnational journalistic values, humanistic or behavioral science training and freedom of the press." Ferreira, Tilson, and Salwen (1999) argue that the critical approaches of the Latin American journalism schools moved away from a neo-Marxist base, even before the the end of the Cold War.

"Journalism education in the region traces its roots to Argentina, Brazil and Mexico. These nations had the most developed universities and the most advanced media systems. Aside from Brazil, Argentina and Mexico, no other Latin American country had a journalism program before World War II."

Unlike countries in the North (e.g., in the UK), media organizations and governments in the region required journalists to have a journalism degree and were eventually "accredited," or more precisely, "licensed" to practice as journalists (e.g., in Brazil). This process formed part of different systems of censorship in the region (Knudson, 1987).

As Ferreira, Tilson, and Salwen (1999) show,"[f]or years, especially after the Cold War, media organizations and professionals have been critical of the region's communication

---

[1] Section on 'Journalism Education' added by the Editor.

education programs. Many of these criticisms mirror those of professional communicators in the U.S. and Europe who prefer jobs skills to theory. In Latin America, professionals often view the critical theory-social communication orientation (taught in journalism schools) as a remnant of the region's Marxist past."

According to *Journalism Educator* (41:4), there were about 275 journalism schools in the early 1990s in the region, namely, in Argentina (18); Bolivia (7); Brazil (64, with some indications that there are presently more than 200); Chile (27); Colombia (12); Costa Rica (2); Cuba (2); Dominican Republic (5); Ecuador (9); El Salvador (2); Guatemala (2); Haiti (1); Honduras (2); Jamaica (1); Mexico (89); Nicaragua (1); Panama (2); Paraguay (2); Peru (12); Puerto Rico (6); Trinidad & Tobago (1); Uruguay (2); and Venezuela (5). (see Ferreira, Tilson, and Salwen, 1999). According to a more recent list presented to the World Journalism Education Conference in 2007 in Singapore, there are now about 320 recognized university journalism degree programs in the region.

Prospects for the Future

Given the corruption and oligarchic media power evident in many countries, some analysts have questioned the nature of democracy in the region (Robinson, 2000). Do the new governments of Latin America reveal themselves as true democracies, or are these fledgling democracies or protodemocracies really something like Robert Dahl's polyarchy, where the poor and large swaths of the population have no real hope of leveraging power through democratic institutions? This may explain the rise of the leftist and populist movements throughout the region, and why these populist governments are naturally aligned against entrenched media interests that often represent older conservative oligarchies.

Taken at face value, relatively free media systems may appear to be cornerstones of democracy and important institutions for building democratic systems. Also, media systems, which have adopted the predominant tabloidism and sensationalism of the media in the United States and other northern nations—a problem that is apparent in the sensational news products that are available throughout the region—often are uninterested in the public service needs of a populace transitioning to democracy. These relatively free media systems provide yet another façade that hides the lack of democratic advancement, in the same way that multiparty systems and elections sometimes mask the true power structures that underpin systems that are really polyarchies, although they are labeled as emerging democracies.

BIBLIOGRAPHY

Associated Press. "Ecuador Inks Deal to Acquire Five Percent of Venezuela's Telesur Network." August 31, 2007.
BBC News. "South America's Leftward Sweep." BBC News Online. Available: http://news.bbc.co.uk/1/hi/world/americas/4311957.stm, March 2, 2005.
Bernstein-Wax, J. "Mexican Media Giant Televisa Reports 17 Percent Increase in Fourth Quarter Net Profits." Associated Press, February 22, 2008.

Boadle, A. "Cuba Rights Abuses Continue but Fewer Prisoners." Reuters, January 16, 2008.

Bruce, I. "Venezuela Sets Up CNN Rival." BBC News Online. Available: http://news.bbc.co.uk/1/hi/world/americas/4620411.stm, June 28, 2005.

Calmon Alves, R. "Status of the Media in Brazil." In Johnston, D. (ed.), *Encyclopedia of International Media and Communications,* Vol. 1, 129–138. Amsterdam, Netherlands: Elsevier Science, 2003.

Campbell, M. "A New Front in Mexico." Committee to Protect Journalists [online database]. Available: http://www.cpj.org/mexiconewfront/index.html, November 7, 2007.

Committee to Protect Journalists (CPJ). "CPJ Welcomes the Impending Release of Two Cuban Journalists." [online database]. Available: http://www.cpj.org/news/2008/americas/cuba15feb08na.html, February 15, 2008.

El Cronista (Argentina). "Argentina: Mexican Money to Come in Handy at Channel Nine." December 18, 2006.

Dinges, J. "Soul Search." *Columbia Journalism Review* [online edition]. Available: http://cjrarchives.org/issues/2005/4/dinges.asp, July/August 2005.

Ferreira, L. *Centuries of Silence: The Story of Latin American Journalism.* Westport, CT: Praeger, 2006.

Ferreira, L., Tilson, D. J., and Salwen, M. B. "Sixty-Five Years of Journalism Education in Latin America." Paper read at the Association of Journalism and Mass communication Education Convention, 1999, New Orleans, USA. Available: http://66.102.9.104/search?q=cache:Mc75zzApz_4J:list.msu.edu/cgi-bin/wa%3FA2%3Dind9909a%26L%3Daejmc%26P%3D202+%22latin+america%22+journalism%2Beducation&hl=en&ct=clnk&cd=3

Forero, J. "Latin American Crisis Resolved." *The Washington Post,* March 8, 2008, A9.

Fox, E. *Latin American Broadcasting: From Tango to Telenovela.* Luton, UK: University of Luton Press, 1997.

Fromson, M. "Mexico's Struggle for a Free Press." In Cole, R. R. (ed.), *Communication in Latin America: Journalism, Mass Media, and Society,* 115–138. Wilmington, DE: S. R. Books, 1996.

Fuguet, A. "This Revolution Is Being Televised." *New York Times Magazine,* February 24, 2001.

González Rodríguez, S. "Cannon Fodder." The Committee to Protect Journalists [online database]. Available: http://www.cpj.org/Briefings/2002/ven_aug02/ven_aug02.html, August 2002.

González Rodríguez, S., and Lauría, C. "Dread on the Border." Committee to Protect Journalists [online database]. Available: http://www.cpj.org/Briefings/2006/nuevo_laredo/nuevo_laredo.html, February 24, 2006.

Grupo Cisneros. "About the Group." [official corporate web database] Available: http://www.cisneros.com/(en)AboutUs.aspx, 2007.

Hallin, D. C. "Media, Political Power and Democratization in Mexico" In Curran, J. and Park, M. (eds.), *De Westernizing Media Studies*, 97–110. London: Routledge, 2000.

Hayes, J. E. *Radio Nation: Communication, Popular Culture, and Nationalism in Mexico, 1920–1950.* Tucson: University of Arizona Press, 2000.

Hillman, L. "Televisa Still Scanning Markets for Acquisitions." *Broadcasting & Cable TV International* 11, No. 6 (March 14, 2003), 10, 14.

InvestNews (Brazil). "Media: Globo Posts $1.9 Billion in 2005." March 27, 2006.

Jones, A. "The Death of *Barricada*: Politics and Professionalism in the Post-Sandinista Press." *Journalism Studies* 2, No. 2 (2001), 243–261.

Journalists [online database]. Available: http://cpj.org/attacks06/americas06/americas_analysis_06.html, 2006.

Karlekar, K. D. (ed.). "Cuba." *Freedom of the Press 2005,* 67–68. New York: Freedom House and Rowman & Littlefield, 2005a.

———. "Mexico." *Freedom of the Press 2005,* 139–140. New York: Freedom House and Rowman & Littlefield, 2005b.

———. "Venezuela." *Freedom of the Press 2005,* 217–219. New York: Freedom House and Rowman & Littlefield, 2005c.

Kingstone, S. "Lula may Sue over Boozing Claims." BBC News Online. Available: http://news.bbc.co.uk/1/hi/world/americas/3702953.stm, May 11, 2004.

Klein, N. "Venezuela's Media Coup." *The Nation* [online edition]. Available: http://www.thenation.com/doc/20030303/klein, February 13, 2003.

Knudson, J. W. "Journalism Education's Roots in Latin America Are Traced." *Journalism Educator* 41, No. 4, 1987, 22–24, 33.

Lauría, C. "Bolivia's Historic Moment." Committee to Protect Journalists [online database]. Available: http://cpj.org/boliviahistoric/index.html, September 25, 2007.

_____. "Leftists Lean on the Latin American Media." Committee to Protect Journalists [online database]. Available: http://cpj.org/attacks06/americas06/americas_analysis_06.html, 2006.

_____. "News for Sale." Committee to Protect Journalists [online database]. Available: http://www.cpj.org/Briefings/2007/argentina_07/index.html, October 23, 2007.

Lauría, C., and González Rodríguez, S. "Static in Venezuela." *Dangerous Assignments* [the quarterly of the Committee to Protect Journalists] (Spring/Summer 2007), 2007, 10–17.

Lins da Silva, C. E. "Journalism and Corruption in Brazil." In Tulchin, J. S. and Espach, R. H. (eds.), *Combating Corruption in Latin America,* 173–192. Washington, DC: Woodrow Wilson Center Press, 2000.

Malkin, E. "Mexican Media Mogul Follows the Money." *New York Times,* February 27, 2004, W1.

_____. "Mexico's Televisa Likely to Add to Its Dominance." *The International Herald Tribune,* March 31 2006, 16.

"Marchers Hail Chávez, Who Faces Recession, Revived Foes." *The Miami Herald,* August 25, 2002, 15A.

Marrero, I. "A Future beyond Fidel?" washingtonpost.com [online news]. Available: http://www.washingtonpost.com/wp-dyn/content/article/2008/02/22/AR2008022202203.html, February 23, 2008.

Mayorbe, J. A. "Venezuela and the Media: The New Paradigm." In Fox, E. and Waisbord, S. (eds.), *Latin Politics, Global Media,* 176–186. Austin: University of Texas Press, 2002.

Mitchell, C. "Untold Stories." Committee to Protect Journalists [online database]. Available: http://www.cpj.org/Briefings/2005/DA_fall05/colombia/colombia_DA_fall_05.html, October 29, 2005.

Paxman, A. "Grupo Clarin." *Variety,* August 23, 1999, A60.

Peirano, L. "Peruvian Media in the 1990s: From Deregulation to Reorganization." In Fox, E. and Waisbord, S. (eds.), *Latin Politics, Global Media,* 153–163. Austin: University of Texas Press, 2002.

Robinson, W. I. "Polyarchy: Coercion's New Face in Latin America." *NACLA Report on the Americas* 34, No. 3, November–December 2000, 42–48.

Rockwell, R. "Guatemala: Stop Attacks on Journalists." *The Miami Herald,* October 27, 2003.

_____. "Privilege, Conservatives & the Internet." *iVoryTowerz* [internet media blog]. Available: http://ivorytowerz.blogspot.com/2007/03/privilege-conservatives-internet.html, March 20, 2007.

_____. "Status of the Media in Mexico." In Johnston, D. (ed.), *Encyclopedia of International Media and Communications,* Vol. 3, 143–148. Amsterdam, Netherlands: Elsevier Science, 2003.

_____. "The Chill Wind from Managua." *iVoryTowerz* [internet media blog]. Available: http://ivorytowerz.blogspot.com/2007/08/chill-wind-from-managua.html, August 13, 2007.

_____. "Venezuela: Why Political Activists Don't Get Freedom of Expression." *iVoryTowerz* [internet media blog]. Available: http://ivorytowerz.blogspot.com/2007/05/venezuela-why-political-activists-dont.html, May 9, 2007.

_____. "Vestiges of Authoritarianism: Monopoly Broadcasting in Central America." In Blankson, I. A. and Murphy, P. D. (eds.), *Negotiating Democracy: Media Transformations in Emerging Democracies,* 35–50. Albany, NY: SUNY Press, 2007.

Rockwell, R., and Janus, N. *Media Power in Central America.* Champaign, IL: University of Illinois Press, 2003.

_____. "The Politics of Coercion: Advertising, Media, and State Power in Central America." *Journalism* 3, No. 3 (December 2002), 331–353.

Ryan, J. "In Spanish and Portuguese, Web Growth Spurt." *New York Times,* June 1999, G1. 3.

Sanchez, M. "The Truth behind Chávez' Media Obsession." washingtonpost.com [online news]. Available: http://www.washingtonpost.com/wp-dyn/content/article/2007/06/08/AR2007060801228.html, June 8, 2007.

Sinclair, J. "Latin American and Spanish Television." In Sinclair, J., and Turner, G. (eds.), *Contemporary World Television,* 87–90. London: British Film Institute Publishing, 2004.

_____. *Latin American Broadcasting: A Global View.* Oxford: Oxford University Press, 1999.

Smeets, M. "Venezuela: Radio Chávez." Committee to Protect Journalists [online database]. Available: http://www.cpj.org/Briefings/2001/Ven_feb01/Ven_feb01.html, February 2001.

Smith, T. "Rewarding Courage." Online NewsHour [online transcript database]. PBS. Available: http://www.pbs.org/newshour/bb/media/july-dec98/gorriti_11-25.html, November 25, 1998.

Soruco, G., and Ferreira, L. "Latin America and the Caribbean." In Merrill, J. C. (ed.), *Global Journalism: Survey of International Communication,* 329–354. White Plains, NY: Longman, 1995.

Straubhaar, J. "Status of the Media in South America." In Johnston, D. (ed.), *Encyclopedia of International Media and Communications,* Vol. 4, 217–226. Amsterdam, Netherlands: Elsevier Science, 2003.

Tobar, H. "Mexican Singer Dead, Ambushed after Concert." *The San Francisco Chronicle* [newspaper online database *SFGate*]. Available: http://www.sfgate.com/cgi-bin/article.cgi?f=/c/a/2006/11/26/MNGEBMK1U81.DTL, November 26, 2006.

Tilson, D., and Rockwell, R. "Latin America." In de Beer, A. S., and Merrill, J. C. (eds.), *Global Journalism: Topical Issues and Media Systems,* 409–429. 4th ed. Boston: Pearson Education, 2004.

Vanden Heuvel, J., and Dennis, E. *Changing Patterns: Latin America's Vital Media.* New York: Freedom Forum Media Studies Center at Columbia University, 1995.

Waisbord, S. *Watchdog Journalism in South America: News, Accountability, and Democracy.* New York: Columbia University Press, 2000.

Waisbord, S., and Morris, N. "Rethinking Media Globalization and State Power." In Morris, N., and Waisbord, S. (ed.), *Media and Globalization: Why the State Matters,* vii–xvi. Lanham, MD: Rowman & Littlefield, 2001.

Waldman, A. J. "Business Built on Original Content." *Television Week,* November 26, 2007, 16.

North America[*]

WILLIAM BRIGGS

San José State University, USA

Introduction: Two Neighbors Moving beyond 9/11

Canada and the United States share the world's longest borders, more than 5,000 miles, largely unguarded (Figure 20.1). They are also each other's leading trading partner. In 2005 Canada–U.S. merchandise trade totaled $461 billion. Canada–U.S. trade supports 7.1 million U.S. jobs. Every day 260,000 businesspeople, tourists, and commuters travel between Canada and the United States. More than $1.5 billion crosses this border daily (Retrieved from, http://www.Connect2Canada.com, 2007). However, since the terrorist attacks of September 11, 2001, the United States has treated security as paramount in its relations with its neighbors, steadily increasing checks at the borders. The recent rise in protectionist and anti-immigrant sentiment in the United States has stalled efforts to deepen the North American Free Trade Agreement (NAFTA), linking Canada, Mexico, and the United States. With almost a million tourists annually traveling to and from Alaska via Canadian ports, the new U.S. passport requirement completely logjammed the U.S. Passport Office and adversely affected hundreds of thousands of vacations and business trips. But that's just one way in which the terrorist attacks on the United States on September 11, 2001, changed the relationship between these two North American democracies overnight, and changed everything else as well, including the media ("Diverted by Jelly Beans...," *The Economist*, 2007)

    According to Orville Schell, former dean of the Graduate School of Journalism at the University of California at Berkeley, the terrorist attacks and the ensuing War on Terror have been a wake-up call for how negligent the West has been covering the news of the rest of the world. "The great paradox is that the word globalization is on everyone's lips while the American media, at least, has been in great default mode in terms of covering it. I think September 11 was a shocking reminder that we literally did not know what was going on between Tel Aviv and Hong Kong. There's very little by way of permanent [media] presence out there" ("Q&A" *Newsweek*).

---

[*] The author wishes to thank former student and San José State alumna Catherine Frazier (2000, B.A. Public Relations) for research and editing assistance.

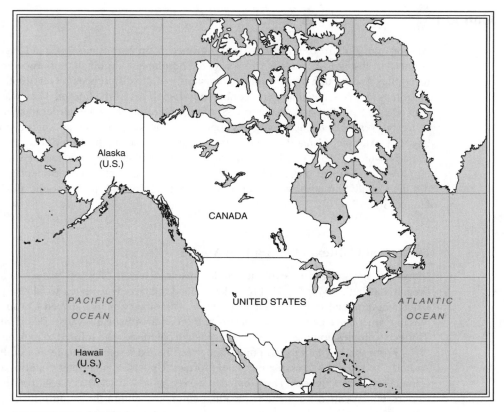

FIGURE 20.1 North America

In the ensuing interval, the United States and Canada have grown closer than ever, participating in military and intelligence activities and with greater economic integration and with increased calls for a customs union or an open border for workers and visitors. The media in both countries recognize the anniversary of the terrorist attacks with days of high-quality news coverage focusing on how the societies had changed, each from its own national perspective.

At the end of the day, however, Canada has withstood the economic, security, and media onslaught from its neighbor and has focused on core Canadian values like civil liberties and multiculturalism. Meanwhile, the United States continues to debate in the press the trade-off between personal liberty and collective security as it fights off the psychological effects of the attacks and the effects of a protracted war in Iraq. More similar than different, the two North American media systems nevertheless are the products of different philosophies and historical backgrounds. This chapter explores the evolution and character of those parallel systems that so greatly influence the media of the entire world.

Canada

Author and global observer Pico Iyer summed it up by saying, "[Canada is] the only country in the world that sits right next to the planet's dominant superpower, which it resembles just enough to be reminded constantly of the differences" (Iyer, 2000:158). The great majority of Canadians live within a hundred miles of the border. They watch American (i.e., U.S.) television, listen to U.S. radio, and often cross the border to shop or attend sporting events. But much energy is spent trying to keep that same American culture at bay. For example, Canadian content laws require broadcasting to air at least 30 percent Canadian-made programming, and U.S. filmmakers making movies in Canada must employ a percentage of Canadians to be eligible for attractive government grants. How did the Canadian media evolve out of a colonial empire and the economic shadow of the United States?

Historical Context of Canadian Media

Modern Canada began its evolution as the result of a pair of wars. British victory in the French and Indian War (1754–1763) determined that North America would be part of the British Empire and largely English speaking. The other war that shaped Canada's destiny was the American Revolution, when tens of thousands of British loyalists fled north from the Thirteen Colonies, joining the indigenous French colonists, who refused to join the rebellion.

From the beginning, the population was divided along language and cultural lines. As early as 1791, the British government formed Upper Canada (later Ontario) and Lower Canada (modern Quebec). The provinces were reunited in 1840 as a result of the Durham Report, which called for greater Canadian autonomy within the empire. Dominion status followed in 1867, with new provinces added as the country expanded westward across North America. Canada's vast size, distinct population groups, and proximity to the United States have often made it a challenge to create a unified Canadian identity. Centuries of attempts at integrating the cultures of the two founding groups, English and French (or perhaps of assimilating the French into the English), have proved unsuccessful. Regionalism, influences from Britain and France, and the need to fend off an expansionist United States have all influenced the character of Canadian media.

It is impossible to dismiss the role of geography in Canada's development. All major geographic features—mountain ranges, rivers, plains, prairies, and coastlines—run north to south and are shared with the United States. Thus, many Canadians identify more strongly with their regional counterparts in the lower 48 states or Alaska than with their fellow citizens across the country. Canada is also thinly populated, and three-quarters of the population lives within a few hundred miles of the U.S. border, mostly along the corridor from Windsor and Toronto to Montreal and Quebec City. Creating a national identity across this vast continent required superhuman feats of engineering, transportation, and communication. Even today, communication holds the far corners together, overcoming geographic barriers, distance, and weather.

As with the population, the early media were transplanted from the American colonies when Boston editor John Bushnell established the *Halifax Gazette* in 1752. The first paper in Quebec, the bilingual *Quebec Gazette* (1764), survives today as part of the *Quebec Chronicle-Telegraph,* arguably North America's oldest surviving newspaper. The short-lived *Nova Scotia Magazine and Comprehensive Review of Literature, Politics and News* was the first British North American periodical.

Newspaper development in the eastern provinces was temporarily interrupted by war with the United States in 1813. An enlarging business community requiring advertising outlets made the press more self-sufficient and less dependent on the government for subsidies. It also made the press more critical of government.

This tension marked the period between the Constitutional Act of 1791 and the Rebellions Losses Act of 1849. Libertarian press principles were asserted when Joseph Howe was found guilty of seditious libel but was nevertheless acquitted. With the arrival of the first iron printing press in 1839, the layout of newspapers changed and became more inviting.

The dominion expanded from the original four provinces of New Brunswick, Nova Scotia, and Upper and Lower Canada with the addition of Manitoba (1870), British Columbia (1871), and Alberta and Saskatchewan (1905). The Yukon Territory was established in 1898 to help administer the gold fields of the Klondike Gold Rush. These decades saw considerable emigration into the western provinces, much of it from the United States. But the press came from eastern Canada. The *Victoria Gazette* and the French-language *Le Couriler de la Nouvelle Caledonie* were both established in British Columbia in 1858. The *Edmonton Bulletin* began in Alberta in 1880. By 1900, 1,266 newspapers served Canada, accompanying settlers and gold seekers into the west. The telegraph facilitated east-west news flow, and coverage was further improved with the founding of the Canadian Press Association in 1859.

Technological innovations, such as the rotary press, helped attract mass audiences. Advertising revenues climbed. Daily publications increased from 23 in 1864 to 121 in 1900. In the twentieth century, population growth, urbanization, immigration, the Great Depression, and technological change all contributed to the growth of newspapers, particularly in the western provinces and Canadian north. The trend toward media consolidation and single-newspaper cities began, so that by the 1960s, seven publishing interests controlled half of the 110 daily papers. The three major groups were Free Press Publications, Southam Company, and Thompson Company. Papers began looking better, but their content was duller, less localized, less personalized.

Canadian broadcasting arrived with the granting of the first license for sound broadcasting to the Marconi Wireless Telegraph Company. Canadian Reginald Fessenden had been the first person to transmit voice and music over the air, on Christmas Eve 1906. Three federal broadcasting acts (1932, 1936, and 1958) created the Board of Broadcast Governors, the broadcast regulatory agency, and the Canadian Broadcasting Corporation (CBC). Private television stations formed their own network in 1961, linking stations in 80 cities. The Broadcasting Act of 1968 replaced the Board of Broadcast Governors with the Canadian Radio-Television and Telecommunications Commission (CRTC) and established a mixed system of public and private broadcasting with a single regulatory agency. Canadian broadcasting enjoys ownership protection with the requirement that 80 percent of voting shares be held by Canadians and that directors and chairpersons be Canadian. The CRTC also established minimum requirements for radio, ensuring a level of Canadian broadcast programming and stimulating the industry. While broadcasting ascended, Canadian magazines, never flourishing, continued to struggle against U.S. competition. When the O'Leary Commission (Royal Commission on Publications) was established in 1960, Canadians read U.S. magazines three-to-one over domestic publications, and two U.S. publishing companies, Time Inc. and Reader's Digest, controlled 40 percent of Canadian newsstand sales.

Legal Environment of Canadian Media

Canada is a fully independent nation but remains the subject of the British monarch. A governor general is appointed by the queen and acts in her stead as head of state, but not of government. Canada remains a member of the British Commonwealth. If the United States is built upon the fundamental principles of life, liberty, and the pursuit of happiness, then Canada is founded upon the principles of peace, order, and good government. Canada embodies elements of both the British and American governmental systems. Cabinet ministers, responsible to a parliament, serve at both national and provincial levels. Federalism holds the provinces together and assures each a degree of local independence.

Until passage of the Canada Act in 1982, whereby the British Parliament granted Canada control of its own constitution, Canadian press freedom was not part of its constitution and could be applied only to federal laws. The courts generally asserted press freedom but based their decisions on technicalities. With the Canada Act came a Charter of Rights and Freedoms that includes "freedom of thought, belief, opinion and expression, including freedom of the press and other media of communication." However, this freedom is not absolute. Such freedoms are "subject only to reasonable limits prescribed by law as can be demonstrably justified in a free and democratic society."

Canada has long been skeptical of American-style populism and has long viewed government as benign. As Canada became more Americanized, it adopted more notions of press freedom, but it has never abandoned the legitimate rights of government to prevent the press from going too far. The Canada Act leaves it to the courts to decide the extent to which limits on fundamental freedoms can be justified. A pair of laws enacted in 1983 delineates press behavior. The Privacy Act protects citizens from invasion of privacy. The Access to Information Act provides access to governmental records, with five mandatory and 12 discretionary exemptions. The act is limited to citizens and declared permanent residents of Canada. The various provinces have passed similar statutes.

Part of Canada's inheritance from Britain is a long tradition of secrecy. Receipt and divulgence of classified information is actionable in court, although high-profile cases in 1978 and 1989 were unsuccessful. The Emergencies Act allows government to suspend civil liberties during times of emergency, such as the separatist civil unrest in Quebec in 1970. The Canadian press is also more restricted in it coverage of crime and criminal trials. The media are proscribed from releasing information about a defendant's prior criminal record, or other information that might interfere with his or her right to a fair trial. But Canada's long-standing practice of protecting certain parties in court cases is coming under increasing criticism from the media and may be rendered obsolete by technology. For example, the 1996 Manitoba murder case of George Mentuck, who was accused of the second-degree murder of Amanda Cook, underwent much scrutiny in the Canadian

Supreme Court, with the Court seeking to protect the identity of police investigators whose abilities to work in covert operations would have been jeopardized (Canadian Newspaper Association, 2001). If the court sides with the media, it will alter the balance between police protecting their secrets and the public's right to know. The Internet and satellite TV make it increasingly difficult to use publication bans to protect police techniques. The identity of juveniles in trials is protected. The British Columbian Supreme Court allows journalists to record the proceedings for accuracy, but not for broadcast. Libel and defamation cases are usually tried in civil court. As in the United States, truth, fair comment, and privilege are allowed as media defenses. However, Canada has no statute regarding reporting on public officials. In the area of obscenity law, the Canadian Supreme Court ruled in 1982 that obscenity provisions in the criminal code do not violate the guarantee of freedom of expression in the Charter of Rights and Freedoms. Voluntary press councils exist at provincial or regional level but have no legal authority. The Canadian Broadcast Standards Council oversees broadcasting, maintaining a strong relationship with the CRTC.

Canada faces many of the same difficult and complicated issues related to the rapidly changing media and communications industries as the United States does. But prior to the Canada Act of 1982, the operating constitution was similar in principle to that of the United Kingdom, and courts were primarily concerned with jurisdictional decisions between the provinces and the federal government. In the last two decades, the Canadian Supreme Court has had to tackle myriad issues defining the relationship between government, the media, and society, issues the United States has had two centuries to wrestle with. Much of the Canadian media policy over the past century has been the formulation of laws to protect and develop Canadian media and cultural industries and to foster national unity and cultural identity. Now, Canada must also face new technologies, such as the Internet and satellite delivery systems, that increasingly make national borders—and national media policy—irrelevant.

Print Media in Canada

Canada is a nation of concentrated media ownership. Today, fewer than 100 dailies circulate just under 5 million copies, down from a peak of 105 dailies and 5.18 million circulation in 1999. Circulation has slowly declined over the past decade. The major cities of Canada all support more than one daily newspaper. Edmonton, Calgary, and Vancouver have two papers, while Montreal and Ottawa claim three. Toronto, Canada's largest city, has five daily papers: the *Toronto Star* (2006 weekly circulation 3.25 million), *The Globe and Mail* (2 million), *The National Post* (2.05 million), the *Toronto Sun* (1.35 million), and *Metro Today,* a free commuter paper that circulates 200,000. Together these papers reach 75 percent of Toronto's households. *The Globe and Mail* is considered Canada's national newspaper and maintains a number of foreign correspondents as well. It compares with the *New York Times* as a paper of record and is aimed at educated, affluent readers, particularly the business class. *The Star* is considered the more liberal paper, *The Post,* the more conservative.

If Canadians read newspapers for their distinctive political stance, they also bemoan a certain sameness in their papers. CanWest Global, for example, owns a third of the English-language market. Bell Globe Media, the telephone concern, now owns Thompson

Corporation of Toronto, once Canada's largest communications company, and is now publisher of *The Globe and Mail*. Bell Globe Media also owns CTV, the largest private TV network. The chains tend to homogenize the news for wide distribution, creating a certain dullness in the press.

The Canadian Press Wire Service, a cooperative, contributes to the sameness of Canadian publications, since the same papers contribute and publish the wire service copy. The CPWS does not maintain a large foreign correspondents network and is dependent on Associated Press (AP), Reuters, and Agence France-Presse (AFP) for international news, adding to the notion that Canada sees the world through U.S. reporting.

In 1997, Conrad Black, former chief executive officer of Hollinger International Inc., purchased the 14-newspaper Southam chain and launched the *National Post* to compete with *The Globe and Mail*. The National Post was never financially successful, and in 2000 Black divested all of his communication holdings to CanWest Global Communications, creating an unprecedented media conglomeration. The CanWest empire includes media in Australia, Northern Ireland, and New Zealand, as well as 14 English-language metropolitan dailies, television stations, a news portal, and scores of community newspapers in Canada. In 2001, CanWest instituted a policy of corporately written national editorials for all its dailies. Letters to the editor and columns contrary to the corporate viewpoint were discouraged, producing a single (conservative) viewpoint across the nation. Prominent journalists were let go or resigned. Media observers questioned the heavy-handed tactics, censorship, and aggressiveness of the owners so soon after being awarded cross-media ownership. A national debate has ensued over concentration of ownership and the role of political objectivity. In 2007, CanWest Global and the American financial firm Goldman Sachs Capital announced purchase of Alliance Atlantis Communications' 13 specialty TV stations, expanding the media empire and further concentrating Canadian media. Clearly, CanWest sees itself as a global player and envisions expanding its playing field to the United States and the rest of the world (Canadian Media Guild, 2007).

In 2007, Conrad Black was convicted in a U.S. court of defrauding Hollinger International of $60 million. At its peak, Hollinger, now called Sun-Times Media group Inc., trailed only News Corp. and Gannett Co. in publishing English-language newspapers, including the *Chicago Sun-Times,* the UK's *Daily Telegraph,* Canada's *National Post,* the *Jerusalem Post,* and hundreds of community newspapers. Black had renounced his Canadian citizenship to enter the British House of Lords (Retrieved from, http://www.Bloomberg.com, 2007).

The number of Canadian community newspapers continued to grow during the 1990s but plateaued as advertising revenues dried up during the recessionary first years of the 2000s. Nevertheless, more than five million Canadians receive a community newspaper. In addition, Canada has a wide variety of ethnic newspapers, specialized newspapers, supplements, and shoppers.

In general, the Canadian magazine industry lacks the critical population mass to support a vibrant magazine industry editorially or with advertising. The Canadian magazine industry has been continually affected by direct U.S. competition, and substantial federal intervention has kept it afloat.

Most of the 1,500-plus Canadian magazines are consumer publications, with the balance divided between business and specialty publications. Canada's largest circulating English-language magazine is the general interest *Maclean's,* with a circulation of 512,000.

When the Royal Commission on Publications (O'Leary Commission) determined in 1960 that three-quarters of magazines read in Canada were American, and that *Time* and *Reader's Digest,* in Canadian editions, controlled 40 percent of newsstand sales, legislation followed disallowing income tax deductions for advertising aimed at the Canadian market but placed in non-Canadian publications. However, this 1966 law exempted *Time* and *Reader's Digest* until it was amended in 1975. At that point, *Time* abandoned its Canadian edition, and *Reader's Digest* spun off a Canadian affiliate company. Canadian advertising revenues increased by more than a third.

By the end of the 1990s, however, Canadian magazines were still looking to the government for help, and the government was still responding with cultural initiatives. Rather than close its borders to American magazines, which still represent about 80 percent of newsstand sales, Canada has sought to penalize magazines that publish split runs (parallel editions of the same publication with minor editorial differences and different advertising content) and the Canadian companies advertising in them. In 1997, the World Trade Organization ruled that Canada remove an earlier, similar law. The law seems particularly aimed at *Time Canada,* the split run with the largest circulation (320,000). For multinational advertisers, it is even simpler to reach the Canadian market (for free) by simply advertising in border-crossing U.S. magazines. These magazine wars represent a skirmish in the larger globalization wars of free trade versus protectionism.

Canadian book publishers are more keenly aware of their need to serve a Canadian market than U.S. publishers. And while healthy, Canadian publishing is nevertheless dominated by the United States. Two-thirds of titles in Canadian bookstores are published in the United States. Thus, some publishers are more determined to seek out Canadian authors and themes.

Electronic Media

Writing in *The Cultural Industries in Canada,* Michel Filion concludes:

> In Canadian radio's first phase, American airwave imperialism posed a serious threat to the Canadian radio industry. Since direct state involvement began in 1932, American influence has become subtler. . . . [The] last phase of evolution has seen the competition from private stations become official, while regulatory mechanisms are put in place to contain American influence and promote a Canadian cultural identity. This remains the ultimate objective of state intervention in broadcasting. (Dorland, 1996:138)

Canadian radio is ubiquitous. From the birth of the technology, the airwaves have been considered public property, and the state has held regulatory authority over them. The Broadcasting Act of 1932 created the Canadian Radio Broadcasting Commission (CRBC), ushering in the golden age of public radio in Canada. In reality, Canadian broadcasting has always been a compromise between nationalism and commercial interests. By 1958, the private sector was allowed to create its own networks in parallel with public radio. Adapting to the arrival of television, radio moved into automobiles and became transistorized. The evolution of FM radio coincided with radio's transition to a largely music format medium.

Today, Canadian commercial radio provides music, news-talk, and sports programming. Public CBC radio offers a noncommercial music and alternative programming option, called Radio 1, and a higher culture (classical music, opera) station, Radio 2. Public radio is in reality state radio and is not dependent on the larger mass markets of its commercial cousins. Commercial stations tend to serve local markets. Licensing regulations require that music programming contain a percentage of Canadian products, although the amount varies, depending on the musical genre. Rock music stations must play the most Canadian music, 30 percent, under a formula called the MAPL (Music, Artist, Producer, Lyrics) System. Music meeting two of those four criteria, such as a Canadian singer and songwriter, is considered Canadian. In reality, the appeal of American popular culture and the relative paucity of Canadian product undermine attempts at managing cultural programming.

Canadian broadcasting has developed as a hybrid, shifting toward privatization but with a private sector increasingly reliant on public subsidies and government regulation. The Canadian Broadcasting Corporation remains the centerpiece of Canadian broadcasting. The CBC produces radio and television programming in both English and French, and produces the internationally distributed 24-hour Newsworld. Both noncommercial radio and commercial TV strive to be distinctive rather than competitive. The distinction between CBC and independent broadcasting is, however, increasingly blurred.

A small market, dual-language requirements, and easy cross-border reception of U.S. programming have always made it more economic for Canadian broadcasters to import U.S. programs and sell them to Canadian audiences rather than to produce comparable programming at home.

In its 2007 report, the Canadian Radio-Television and Telecommunications Commission (CRTC) concluded that Canadian broadcasting is continuing to expand and that new media are becoming increasingly important. Among its findings are the following:

- In 2006, Canadians enjoyed 1,252 different radio services, including 929 English-language service and 286 French-language services. Of the 662 television services, 445 are English language, 104 French language, and 113 third language TV services.
- Canadians listened to 18.6 hours of radio weekly in 2006, a slight decline from the previous year. Eighty percent of the radio listenership was to commercial stations; the CBC 11.6 percent; satellite radio 1 percent and a fraction of a percent over the Internet. Television viewership in 2006 averaged 27.6 hours—about a half-hour decline from 2005.
- Commercial radio revenues increased nearly 6 percent to $1.4 billion in 2006.
- Canadian radio stations paid $24 million for development of Canadian content; conventional television broadcasters paid $624 million on Canadian content, while specialty broadcasters spent $890 million.
  - Canadian television services captured 79 percent of total viewership in 2006. TV revenues reached $2.6 billion for traditional service and another $2.5 billion for on-demand services, both an increase. Digital services represented only 5 percent of television revenues.
  - Despite the increased spending on Canadian programming by the country's largest private broadcasters, CTV and Global, viewership of those shows is in decline. Both TV networks had made large commitments to spending on Canadian production as conditions of recent acquisitions (Retrieved from, http://www.crtc.gc.ca/eng/newsreleases/2007/r070731.htm, 2007).

There are more than 1,800 cable systems operating in Canada, offering customers dozens of channels. In 2006, 7.4 million Canadians subscribed to cable services. Cable operators and broadcasters alike have engaged in a decade-long period of consolidation and expansion through takeovers, new channels, and new technologies. While Canadians are intrigued with the new digital channel offerings coming online, only about a tenth of them are willing to pay for the new bundled programming. Currently, about 2.6 million Canadians subscribe to direct-to-home (DTH) satellite distribution. Subscriptions to digital systems rose by 10 percent from 2005 to 2006, to 5.8 million subscribers. The uncertain future direction of the CBC keeps everyone else perpetually jockeying for position in a changing broadcast environment. One of the players looking to expand globally is the previously mentioned CanWest Global Communications Corp. Another global television network combining commercial and public approaches is WETV, a publicly funded attempt to counterbalance the developed world's stranglehold on television by providing production and distribution for underrepresented countries and indigenous cultures worldwide. Canadian, foreign, and United Nations development funds financed its 1996 start-up. Small audiences in partnership countries view WETV worldwide.

Minority broadcasting is a significant issue in a country where multiculturalism is official policy. The Aboriginal People's Television network (APTN) began in 1999 to better serve Inuit and various other aboriginal peoples. Not only does it broadcast specialized programming, but native peoples largely staff it, and much of the programming is in native languages.

Clearly, the overriding cross-cultural challenge for Canadian media is its dual-language responsibility. Quebec declined to sign Canada's new constitution in 1982 for lack of special consideration for Quebec's linguistic and cultural differences, and two other provinces declined to ratify a subsequent agreement giving Quebec unique status. Quebec nearly approved a referendum to secede. Thus, Canada walks the tightrope of national disintegration. The existence of the North American Free Trade Agreement (NAFTA) makes Quebec separation even more possible, if not probable. French-language broadcasting has reinforced the Francophone identity, in addition to providing programming and commercial messages.

Ironically, the CBC produces more English-language programming than any of the U.S. networks and more French programming than the national system of France. Francophone programming is available in all metropolitan areas, although its reach is not as strong as in English. All Anglophone Canadian schoolchildren study French in school, but the crossover market is not large. Research shows a slightly different CBC news agenda for French and English audiences. Francophone audiences tend to be more parochial, more provincial, and more interested in other Francophone countries. Three French networks serve the Francophone audience: Société Radio-Canada, TVA, and Television Quatre Saisons. While much of Quebec can easily access U.S. media, especially in Montreal, the preference is to import French, rather than U.S., programming.

Convergence and New Media

Canada is recognized as a world leader in Internet penetration, with 70 percent of all Canadians having Internet access in 2006. High-speed connections have penetrated to the 60 percent level. This contrasts with almost universal television penetration and cable or satellite subscription rates above 80 percent. So, while not an immediate threat to traditional media, the Internet is nevertheless siphoning off some of the viewership. Half of Canadians surveyed say they are spending less time watching television, listening to radio, or reading newspapers, books, and magazines. Young Canadians spend 2.5 hours more per week online than their U.S. counterparts and are 95 percent more likely to use a high-speed Internet service. The most popular use of the Internet by Canadians is for electronic mail. But the desire for news and other information is also strong. A quarter of Canadians listen to the radio over the Internet, while 6 percent watch TV that way. Internet access by cell phone, Web cam, PDA, Blackberry, or iPod are all increasing. And at this point, traditional and new media can converge (Retrieved from, http://www.crtc.gc.ca/eng/newsreleases/2007/r070731.htm, 2007).

Internet use by French-speaking Canadians, however, is substantially less, 44 percent compared to 58 percent of Anglophone Canadians, suggesting that the digital divide between the nation's two language groups is likely to widen.

The idea of convergence underlies many of the decisions being made by Canadian corporations and regulatory agencies, as Canada moves into the fast lane on the information superhighway. Convergence in its technical, functional, and corporate manifestations is the most important policy issue Canadian communication faces. "This is because convergence relates closely to such basic geopolitical trends and issues as the erosion of national sovereignty and the concomitant growth in transnational corporate power; the controversy over whether government should be a major policy planner as opposed to merely a market facilitator; the debate over whether information/communication are to be treated as instruments of social/political/cultural policy, or merely as commodities; questions of continued universal access to telecommunications and information in the context of widening gaps between the information rich and the information poor" (Babe, cited in Dorland, 1996:284–285).

Historically, information has been afforded public good status, but this is in opposition to the deregulated, market-driven forces of globalization. Canada has always treated its media as a public resource, not as a commodity (in contrast to the U.S. decision to withdraw from UNESCO over the commodity issue.) Squaring convergence with traditional Canadian values will be a delicate maneuver.

Movies and Film

From the early days of motion pictures, Canada has spun in the orbit of Hollywood. From Canadian stars such as Mary Pickford to Hollywood-made movies about survival in the Yukon, Canada has seen itself in the movies through the filter of California sunglasses. In 1939, the federal government established the National Film Board of Canada to produce and distribute Canadian films that would positively interpret Canada to the world. Telefilm Canada was established in the 1960s to support the television and feature film industry. The majority of these government-subsidized projects are made for television, many of them documentaries or otherwise of significant social content. The rise of private-sector companies, most small but several eventually offering public-sector shares, signals a shift in the Canadian film industry. These companies, such as Cineplex, Alliance, and Alias, have benefited from a government-stimulated environment and Hollywood's (as well as other nations') desire for cost-effective partnerships. The formerly weak Canadian dollar, good locations, lots of "American" actors and extras, and an insatiable hunger for product sent U.S. production companies into Canada in droves. Today, more than nine out of ten movies in Canadian theaters are foreign. As with much of its media, Canadian film has witnessed the collision of an industry in the marketplace with Canadian cultural public policy initiatives.

Currently, the competition for foreign film production in Canada has sparked a "tax-credit war" between provinces, with Quebec boosting its labor tax credit to 18 percent. British Columbia, for example, with a viable motion picture industry of its own, is feeling the competition (Retrieved from, http://www.taxpayer.com/main/news.php?new_id=1889, 2007).

Media Education

Journalism and mass communication education in Canada has developed in its own special way. While early models included Columbia University and other U.S. institutions, today media students receive specialized journalism training at a dozen major institutions across English and French Canada. Leading institutions include Carleton University, Ottawa, and Ryerson University, Toronto, which offer baccalaureate programs; the University of Western Ontario, London, and the University of British Columbia, Vancouver, which offer graduate-level programs; and the Université du Quebec, in Montreal, and the Université Laval, Quebec City, which offer French-language programs.

Canadian education tends not to stream its communication programs. The market is too small, and students tend to be more broadly trained across different media platforms. Public relations and advertising are frequently taught at the community college level, which is considered a terminal qualification. In a tightening, competitive marketplace, many baccalaureate degree holders are returning to the community colleges for hands-on training. Many of the degree-granting institutions also provide continuing education and professional development seminars and courses.

"Journalism education in Canada is at a crossroads," says Stephen J.A. Ward, director and professor of journalism ethics at the School of Journalism at the University of British Columbia. "Major schools are enriching their programs with additional courses, new graduate programs and online journalism instruction. But the tendency is to add elements to a traditional and outdated vocational model of journalism education. What is needed are not more courses and workshops, but an entirely new approach to how journalism programs are conceived and structured. The vocational paradigm, like journalism itself, is under siege. The challenge is to fundamentally restructure them." (Ward, 2007)

Toward the Future

A core democracy with a sophisticated media system, Canada enters the twenty-first century full of hope and promise, but with British and French baggage and one eye on the United States. Driven by the psychological need for a unique national identity and culture, and tempered by the need to pay for it in a globalizing world, Canada juggles the public and the private to maintain a media culture all its own.

The United States

When, centuries from now, archaeologists (or interplanetary visitors) examine the remains of the U.S. civilization, it well may be that they declare the American media empire to be the dominant feature of our times. Media from the United States offer the most far-reaching news and entertainment options available in the world. U.S. media are particularly global, as domestic programming and copy are exported to, viewed or read, imitated, and smuggled into every corner of the globe. Domestic U.S. stories often dominate international headlines. American popular culture is admired or despised worldwide. Proponents of globalization point to American media as messengers of liberal democracy. Opponents assail the surge of cultural imperialism. Characteristically, American media is big. More than half of the largest global media conglomerates are American owned. Those archaeologists may be right.

At home, Americans are truly a mediated society: they spend an average of nine hours daily with media, watching one of their multiple television sets or listening to their car radio while negotiating clogged highways, or increasingly interacting with their computers by playing games, downloading music, exchanging e-mail messages, or surfing the World Wide Web. Fueling all this media activity is an enormous advertising industry representing hundreds of billions of dollars as it relentlessly dominates a consumer society.

It is also a free society—arguably the freest in the world. This is in large measure due to the watchdog function of the American press, warily guarding the democracy against abuse and corruption in government, business, and society, and protected by the guarantees of the First Amendment of the Constitution, ensuring freedom of speech and of the press. Balancing the needs for corporate profits with fairness, accuracy, and responsibility in an atmosphere of permissive commercialism is the challenge for U.S. media in the twenty-first century.

In many ways the press of the United States mirrors the republic it serves. From its colonial beginnings it has been assertive, rebellious, and independent-minded. No less an observer of American society than Alexis de Tocqueville marveled at the widespread nature of the frontier press and saw it as the cement between an exuberant population and their youthful democracy. The trend toward global media hegemony today is in many ways a natural continuance of the themes of manifest destiny that tamed a continent and became an industrial and commercial force long before world wars pulled the United States into global involvement. Press systems reflect the societies that house them. A look at the historical context of the American press helps explain its current state.

Historical Context of the U.S. Media

The press in America developed right along with the country. From colonial beginnings, through revolution, westward expansion, civil war, industrialization, world wars, cold war, and superpower status, the press has reflected, critiqued, and cheered on the United States.

Like its British antecedents, the press in colonial America was licensed by the government and subject to prior restraint and penalties for printing seditious libel. Evolving from pamphlets and handbills, the first newspaper was Benjamin Harris's *Publick Occurrences Both Foreign and Domestick,* in 1690. It lasted but a single issue. The first continuously published newspaper was John Campbell's *Boston Newsletter,* begun in 1704. A competitor, *The Boston Gazette,* began in 1719, and in turn, its printer, James Franklin, launched his own paper, *The New England Courant.* While Franklin was in jail for seditious libel, his younger brother, Benjamin, ran the paper, beginning his own illustrious career as a journalist and publisher. The 1735 acquittal of publisher John Peter Zenger in a seditious libel case did not establish legal precedent, but it did allow truth as a defense and became a symbolic victory for emerging press freedom.

Increasingly emboldened, the press became highly partisan as the rift with England widened. Tory (pro-British) publishers were often persecuted. Colonial revolutionaries such as Thomas Paine and Samuel Adams used the press to mold public opinion toward independence, often using woodcut illustrations by Paul Revere and other artisans. The Stamp Act (1765), a tax on legal documents and newspapers, infuriated editors. The press was in large measure responsible for forging an "American identity" among colonists. During the Revolutionary War, the colonial press traded news throughout the colonies and helped hold the colonies together.

Following independence, the new nation operated under the Articles of Confederation. A constitution was developed in 1787, and its supporters, called Federalists and led by Alexander Hamilton and James Madison, wrote and published an extensive series of essays, known as the Federalist Papers, explaining the new Constitution and urging ratification. Anti-Federalists, championed by Thomas Jefferson, also published highly partisan essays and political attacks. With the inclusion of a Bill of Rights, whose First Amendment guarantees freedom of speech and press, the Constitution was ratified by the states. A highly partisan political press marked the early years of the new nation.

Though closely aligned with political patronage through the early decades of the nineteenth century, the press gradually became a more commercial enterprise, relying on advertising and subscriptions instead of political parties. The arrival of the "penny press" with Benjamin Day's *New York Sun* (1833) shifted the audience to the emerging middle class and immigrants in large cities. James Gordon Bennett's *New York Herald* (1835) signaled the arrival of reporter-generated stories and news beats, such as police news. Emphasis was placed on human interest and local stories. Along the frontier, small papers borrowed stories freely from one another for a news-hungry population. By 1844, the development of the telegraph separated communication from its dependence on transportation. Reporters covering the Mexican War (1846–1848) made use of the new telegraph. By 1861, the telegraph linked the Atlantic and Pacific coasts.

With the election of Abraham Lincoln as president in 1860, Southern states sensed a shift in political power to the North and a threat to their slavery-based economy, and began to secede from the union. Civil War followed. Abolitionists had long used the press for antislavery essays. William Lloyd Garrison's *Liberator* was absolute in its demand for the end of slavery. Elijah Lovejoy, a white editor murdered by a proslavery mob, became a martyr. Harriet Beecher Stowe's *Uncle Tom's Cabin* became the most widely read book in the world after the Bible and brought the issue of slavery to the forefront of national debate.

The ensuing war (1861–1865) saw brigades of correspondents compete to cover the battles and profile the generals, with varying degrees of accuracy and objectivity. Military censorship was rampant. The new technology of photography allowed artists to make woodcuts for publication from photographs, and the public flocked to see the actual photographs of battlefield carnage taken by Mathew Brady and other photographers, bringing the horror of war home to thousands.

Post-Civil War industrialization brought with it advances in printing production and expansion of newspapers, magazines, books, and other printed material. The press reflected the growing urbanization of the country, and crusading—if sensationalist—publishers such as Joseph Pulitzer and cartoonist Thomas Nast targeted big city corruption. Pulitzer's excesses peaked during a circulation war with William Randolph Hearst and their coverage of the Spanish American War (1898). A cartoon character of the day gave rise to the expression "yellow journalism." The century ended with a wave of reform journalism, including "muckraking" that attacked social ills and influenced government legislation.

Government persuasion techniques during World War I were transferred to the private sector as a way to burnish the image of big business. Ivy Lee and Edward Bernays helped pioneer a new media industry of public relations. Meanwhile, Lee De Forest and his audio tube had advanced the early efforts of Marconi in radiotelephony. The war stimulated research, and civilian applications became possible with the cooperation of government and industry in creating the Radio Corporation of America in 1919, headed by David Sarnoff. Radio networks soon followed as advertisers discovered a way to reach mass audiences relatively cheaply.

Radio and moving pictures became the entertainment mainstay during the 1920s and 1930s, when government also used its tremendous reach to soften the effects of the Depression and prepare the nation for eventual entry into World War II. The Federal Communications Commission was established in 1934 to help ensure that broadcasting operated in the public interest. Photojournalism came of age with the advent of large-format, glossy magazines such as *Life* in 1936.

Allied victory in World War II ushered in a period of prosperity, and the acquisition of choice was a television set. Television technology had been adapted to military use during the war, but its civilian popularity was unprecedented. Veteran war correspondents, led by Edward R. Murrow, set a high standard for television news, and many of America's favorite entertainers made the transition to television. Radio, the movies, and print publications all had to adjust to the arrival of television, as TV would later have to adjust to the arrival of cable and the Internet. Some of the more recent developments are detailed in the sections that follow.

Government–Press Relations and the Law

The United States is a nation of laws, and all law is tested against the Constitution, which reigns supreme. When the original states ratified the Constitution, there was much debate and concern about specific protection against government infringement on individual liberties. The first ten amendments, known as the Bill of Rights, placed restrictions on the power of the federal government and remanded much authority back to individual states.

The First Amendment to the Constitution is the bulwark of press freedom. It states:

Congress shall make no law respecting an establishment of religion, or prohibiting the free exercise thereof, or abridging the freedom of speech, or of the press, or the right of the people peaceably to assemble, and to petition the government for a redress of grievances.

For over 200 years, journalists have thrived under the protection of the First Amendment and rallied to its defense at every challenge. Nevertheless, there has endured a tension between the government and its unofficial "fourth estate," the press. Prior restraint was precluded by the First Amendment, and after a brief reintroduction of laws against seditious libel, primarily in the form of the Alien and Sedition Act (1798–1801), the federal government yielded to scrutiny by an aggressive press playing its role in the democracy by informing the people about the workings of their government.

In recent years, landmark court decisions have reinforced the notions of press freedom in the United States, notably in *New York Times v. Sullivan* (1964) and *New York Times v. U.S.* (1971), commonly known as the Pentagon Papers case (Emmert, 2002).

In *Times v. Sullivan,* the U.S. Supreme Court turned back efforts by a state government official to bring a civil libel suit against the press. The decision has made it difficult for civil officials to bring defamation lawsuits against their critics as a means of silencing them. Writing in the Sullivan decision, Justice William Brennan wrote, "[There should be] a profound national commitment to the principles that debate on public issues should be uninhibited, robust and wide open." And, the court argued, citizens not only have the right but also the duty to criticize government. However, a steady stream of libel cases over the years demonstrates that many courts are sensitive to the special First Amendment issues involved in the constantly evolving area of libel law.

In 1971, the *New York Times* published stories based on leaked classified material about U.S. involvement in Vietnam. The U.S. attorney general brought an injunction against the *Times* on the grounds of national security. It was a case of prior restraint that went quickly to the Supreme Court. The Court ruled that "Any system of prior restraints of expression comes to this Court bearing a heavy presumption against its constitutional validity."

In 1972, another collision occurred between the press and the administration of President Richard Nixon. Burglars had been caught breaking into the Democratic Party headquarters at the Watergate apartment complex in Washington, D.C. Reporters for the *Washington Post* connected them to the Republican Party's presidential reelection committee. Over the ensuing months, a trail of lies and cover-ups was disclosed that eventually ended its way back to the office of the President himself.

When altered tapes of Nixon's conversations in the White House were disclosed during Senate hearings before a national television audience, the Nixon presidency unraveled and ultimately, in 1974, he resigned. It was a high-water mark for the press, although its role in bringing down a sitting president has been exaggerated. A generation of young journalists modeled themselves after investigative *Post* reporters Carl Bernstein and Bob Woodward. The reputation of the government, however, was at low ebb. The cynicism of the American public, already heightened by the Vietnam War, became complete. Public mistrust and antipathy toward government—and by some toward the press—endures to the present.

More recently, the Supreme Court has generally been reluctant to hear major press freedom cases. U.S. libel laws remain more protective of the press than anywhere in the world, although those protections are not likely to be expanded greatly in the near future. There is an area, however, that bears watching as the press and government continue to almost literally cross swords—war coverage.

Wars make big stories. Audiences are captivated and crave information, especially when U.S. service personnel are involved. The Vietnam War was fully covered by its own battalions of journalists, who ignored the military press handouts and covered the war at will. Vietnam was the first television war, and the sight of body bags and other carnage did not sit well with the American public. When respected television newsman Walter Cronkite expressed misgivings about U.S. involvement in Vietnam during a newscast, there was a perceptible shift in American public opinion, and President Lyndon Johnson is said to have remarked that was when he lost the backing of the American people.

Some military and government officials believe the press "lost Vietnam." In subsequent American military operations, such as Grenada (1983), Panama (1989), and the Persian Gulf War (1990–1991), the government has increasingly made it difficult for the press to have access to the war zones and otherwise has placed obstacles in reporters' way. In the current Bush administration, Vice President Dick Cheney and former Secretary of State Colin Powell had been part of the command structure during the Gulf War. They seem even more inclined to keep the press under control now during this new era of war against terrorism. Following the Gulf War, the American press subjected itself to close scrutiny and found itself lacking. Since then, the press has called for greater access during times of hostilities, pointing out that in only a very few instances has the press acted irresponsibly with sensitive stories.

Michael Getler, ombudsman for the *Washington Post,* said:

> The press will always find ways to cover the story. If the military seriously restricts coverage, reporters will find other sources and other ways to cover the war, as they should. The public's best interests are served by an enlightened relationship between the military and the media, when both sides make an honest stab at solving some of the problems that naturally arise in a way that does not interfere with military operations and security, but allows an independent account of America at war to be recorded. (Getler, 2001:26).

During the Iraq War, in a dramatic change of policy, the Pentagon authorized U.S. and foreign journalists to be "embedded" with military units throughout the theater of war. Viewers and readers got first-hand battlefield accounts, often in real time, unparalleled in the history of reporting. However, critics pointed out that such coverage was often disjointed and lacked context and worried that the journalists traded objectivity for such unprecedented access. Had the military cleverly co-opted the press to its advantage, or had the public been better served than ever? In addition, more than a thousand journalists covered the Iraq conflict in the more traditional "independent" mode. As the Iraq War continues, becoming one of the nation's longest military engagements, it has dwarfed all other topics in the U.S. news media by a factor of three. However, less than a third of the coverage has been about Iraq itself or the plight of Iraqis. More than half of the coverage has been about the political debate in Washington or has focused on Americans in Iraq.

Although the print media in America operates free from government regulation, the same cannot be said for broadcasting. Broadcasting operates in the public interest, under licensure from the Federal Communication Commission. The FCC, established in 1934, regulates ownership and allocates frequencies to broadcast operations, since the broadcast spectrum is a finite resource. An FCC license for a radio or television station is a lucrative property. Challenges to ownership, from underrepresented community groups, for example, have been largely unsuccessful. FCC forays into influencing programming have been met with resistance. Broadcasting enjoys the same First Amendment protection as its print relatives.

In the 1980s, a wave of deregulatory thinking accompanied the arrival of the Ronald Reagan Administration in the United States (and the Thatcher government in the United Kingdom.) Broadcasting was among the industries opened up to market forces (although broadcasting had always been a commercial venture in the United States.) Deregulation brought about a reduction in record keeping, streamlined license renewal, and increased the number of media holdings an individual could own. These free-market policies have continued into the present, generating a rash of media mergers and consolidation, as well as the Telecommunications Act of 1996. One victim of deregulation was the Fairness Doctrine.

Debate over the Fairness Doctrine illustrates a sea change in media thinking. For almost 40 years, the Fairness Doctrine had mandated that broadcasting air opposing sides of controversial issues. In the spirit of government deregulation, and mindful of developing new technologies such as cable, the FCC moved to rescind the Fairness Doctrine. By the turn of the century, the Fairness Doctrine had withered away, including the equal-time provision for political candidates. Stations are now free to present controversial issues unilaterally, and the government is further removed from programming decisions.

The Telecommunications Act of 1996 replaced an older court order that had broken up the telephone monopoly, AT&T. It forced local telephone companies to open their networks to competition, while letting them compete in the long-distance market and compete in areas they were formerly denied by law or regulation. Thus broadcasting, cable, and telephone companies began jockeying for position in an ever-changing marketplace and a yet-to-be-determined technological environment. Ownership opportunities were further expanded. A V-chip to block objectionable programming was mandated, and provisions against pornography and other indecent material on the Internet were instituted. A portion of the broadcast spectrum was reserved for digital television services. In signing the legislation, President Bill Clinton said:

> For the past three years, my administration has promoted the enactment of a telecommunications reform bill to stimulate investment, promote competition, provide open access for all citizens to the Information Superhighway, strengthen and improve universal service and provide families with technologies to help them control what kinds of programs come into their homes over television. As a result of this "act", consumers will receive the benefits of lower prices, better quality and greater choice in the television and cable services, and they will continue to benefit from a diversity of voices and viewpoints in radio, television and the print media. (Scherr, 1996:2)

Currently, federal regulators are considering loosening rules limiting ownership of radio and television stations and newspapers even further in a natural extension of deregulation. Expected revisions would make cross-ownership of media in a given market much easier and would facilitate mergers of large media firms. Critics charge that this will limit diversity of media ownership and opinion even more.

Among other issues likely to receive Supreme Court attention is the loosening of advertising restrictions under political campaign finance reform legislation. As Chief Justice John Roberts said, "Where the First Amendment is implicated; the tie goes to the speaker and not the censor" (Greenhouse, 2007).

Big media will continue to press for support of the Copyright Term Extension Act of 1998 and to withhold creative products, such as music or Disney's Mickey Mouse, from passing into the public domain (Cohen, 2007).

Contemporary Media Industries

Print Media—Newspapers   The newspaper industry in the United States stands at a crossroads as it tries to balance shrinking circulation and advertising defection to the Internet with increasing production costs and rising shareholder expectations. This problem was illustrated in 2006 by the forced sale of Knight-Ridder, then the country's second largest newspaper chain, to McClatchy for $4.5 billion, and the subsequent spin-off of several of the former K-R assets to Media News. Though profitable, and though it had arguably done as much as any chain to adapt to the new technologies, Knight-Ridder was taken down by shareholders demanding more profitability than the newspaper environment could produce. While its sign still dominates the corporate headquarters building in the San José, California skyline, the company no longer exists. Its former papers have seen massive layoffs and budget cuttings. As the papers shrink, the subscribers and advertisers continue to flee. And the downward spiral continues. Other newspaper companies face the same pressures.

A different scenario played itself out in 2007 as News Corp. media lord Rupert Murdoch made a successful $5 billion bid for Dow Jones Corp. and its crown jewel, the *Wall Street Journal*. By offering an overvalued purchase price (a 67 percent stock premium) and promising a hands-off editorial stance, Murdoch was able to convince the family-controlled Dow Jones to sell, further enhancing the Murdoch empire and legend (Ellison and Karnitschnig, 2007).

According to *The State of the News Media 2007,* published by the Project for Excellence in Journalism, newspaper circulation fell sharply in 2006 for the third year in a row. The likely explanation: competition from free dailies, online news consumption, and decline in seven-day-a-week subscribers. "Not only is circulation threatened by online products, so is advertising. Competition from online advertising companies like Google, Yahoo!, Monster and Craigslist continue to detract from newspapers' classified advertising. Though newspaper revenue growth online helps, the rate of growth is slowing, and newspapers have yet to figure out how to tap into the potential there. In response, Wall

Street now appears to value newspapers less than many private investors do, which could lead to a change in the ownership model of America's largest newsrooms" (Project for Excellence in Journalism, 2007).

In 2006, newspaper circulation in the United States was down 2.8 percent daily and 3.4 percent on Sunday over the previous year. The largest circulation papers suffered the greatest decline. Readership has declined over 5 percent since 2000. Share prices of publicly traded newspapers have declined nearly 35 percent since 2005. Many newspapers have reduced the format of the paper to save money. Newspapers have lost approximately 3,000 full-time news staff jobs since 2000. Metropolitan dailies are taking a more local orientation. Newspapers are more targeted to older, more educated readers. Alternative weekly newspapers seem to have peaked. But loyal readers still depend on newspapers for their political news, and most say they think newspapers have improved.

The trends seem to break down squarely along generational lines. For readers over age 50, newspapers are the most read medium. Newspaper readers seem to be more interested in national and international news than young people, who read other things. The challenge for newspapers is to find other subjects that attract young readers. But young readers are not news averse. On the contrary, they express interest in religion, entertainment, business, sports, and health news and follow the news in other media. The future viability of newspapers depends to no small extent on attracting these younger readers. While circulation may remain stable for the short term, due to legions of loyal baby boomers, the aging population of readers will eventually have to be replaced.

During the period of deregulation, many media companies merged and went public. Corporate earnings began to vie with the public interest as the rationale for media efforts. With companies publicly traded on the stock exchanges, editors were faced with stockholder ownership as demanding as any nineteenth-century publisher. And as news became more of a corporate enterprise, the nature of the product changed in an ongoing effort to attract readers. Newspapers created more special-interest sections; news became "softer," with more emphasis on lifestyle issues, celebrities, and features. Today, three out of four American newspapers are chain-owned. Few American cities are served by more than a single daily newspaper, usually a morning paper. Many chains have diversified into other communication activities such as magazines, broadcasting, or cable. In a triumph of market research, the Gannett Company launched *USA Today* as a national newspaper in 1982. Although criticized for lack of serious content, *USA Today*'s use of graphics, positive stories, and a carefully formulated editorial mix has defied the critics and attracted a wide readership over the past two decades.

Newspapers are increasingly relying on new technologies. New offset printing techniques have led to greater use of color. Many newspapers distribute their product online to customers, and offer computerized retrieval capability. *USA Today,* the *Wall Street Journal,* the *New York Times,* and the *Washington Post,* among others, transmit daily or weekly editions via satellite for global distribution. The *International Herald Tribune,* a joint venture between the *New York Times* and the *Washington Post,* is printed via satellite in 11 cities around the world and distributed in most of the world's countries.

The leading daily circulation newspapers in terms of circulation are shown in Table 20.1.

Magazines   Magazines have been a companion print medium to newspapers since before the American Revolution. They have provided space for many of the greatest writers and thinkers of their time and the most pressing issues of their day. Far from dying out, the magazine medium has proved extremely adaptable to economic trends and societal shifts, as well as to changes in media technology. From the political tracts of the eighteenth century through the literary journals, abolitionist essays, women's publications, and muck-rakers' exposés, magazines endured. With photography, magazines like *Life* brought pictures into the home long before television. After television, magazines evolved from general interest to special interest to niche. Many advances in graphic design and printing take form in magazines. Today, there are more than 12,000 consumer magazines and even more trade, technical, and professional journals. Of the hundreds of magazines launched annually, almost all fail within a couple of years for lack of capitalization or lack of audience appeal. Although many magazines struggle to survive, the ones successful at capturing advertising dollars prosper, such as the 600-page *Vogue*.

The news magazines are experiencing change. *Time* announced a new publication schedule, a new way of measuring audience, and a shift to a heavier reliance on the Web. *Time, Newsweek,* and *U.S. News & World Report* all experienced flat advertising revenues and made staff cuts. Smaller rivals such as the *Economist* and *The Week* grew their print circulations. *The New Yorker* was especially hard hit in 2006, with a 13 percent decline in ad pages. New magazines trail broadcasting when measured for believability but fare better than other print media. Spending on the Web has increased to a third of news magazine budgets.

Areas of current interest among consumer magazines include health and fitness, gardening, family leisure, computing, travel, fashion, and cooking. *Modern Maturity,* aimed at an aging, growing demographic, circulates well over 20 million. Pocket-sized publications such as *Readers' Digest* and Rupert Murdoch's *TV Guide* circulate upward of 15 million.

Table 20.1   Highest Newspaper Circulations

1. *USA Today*	(Gannett)	2.525 million
2. *Wall Street Journal*	(News Corp)	2.068 million
3. *New York Times*	(New York Times Co.)	1.627 million
4. *Los Angeles Times*	(Tribune Company)	1.173 million
5. *Chicago Tribune*	(Tribune Company)	941,000
6. *Washington Post*	(Washington Post Company)	930,000
7. *New York Daily News*	(Zuckerman)	776,000
8. *New York Post*	(News Corp)	741,000
9. *Denver Post/Rocky Mountain News*	(Media News Group, Inc.)	704,000
10. *Philadelphia Inquirer*	(Philadelphia Media Holdings, LLC)	689,000

Source: Statistics from Audit Bureau of Circulations for 2007.

Half of the top 10 magazines are women's publications such as *Better Homes and Gardens* and *Family Circle*. Many magazines make use of technology to publish international editions in several languages. Trade, technical, and professional journals offer industry-specific news and features of use to occupational markets. Many are widely circulated, though little known outside their specific industry.

Magazines enjoy anywhere between $10 and $15 billion in advertising revenues, depending on the overall economy. In the most recent recession, many magazines, particularly those targeting high technology, succumbed because of lack of advertising. In recent years, many magazines have added Web pages to their offerings, and a number of high-visibility Webzines have been published exclusively on the Internet. Despite the advantage of being online, Webzines are still in their infancy, searching out an audience and advertiser base. Countless thousands of "zines," small-scale, often home-produced hybrids between newsletters and magazines, are published for very specific, targeted markets.

Electronic Media

Broadcast media dominate American life. Radio, the senior medium, reaches 80 percent of the population daily, either at home, over one of an average of five receivers, increasingly in the car, or at some other venue. Radio revenues exceed $10 billion from the roughly 5,000 commercial AM stations, the nearly 5,000 commercial FM stations, and the approximately 1,600 public or noncommercial stations.

By 1920, what had been a hobbyist's experiment with radio technology had been transformed into an entertainment medium eagerly seized upon by a mass market. Differing opinions and criteria place the first radio station in San José, California, or Pittsburgh, Pennsylvania. But commercial broadcasters immediately took control, and the medium has been commercially driven almost since its inception. Within a decade almost half the households in America owned radio sets, over which they listened to popular entertainment and the calming messages of President Franklin D. Roosevelt during the Great Depression and the dark days of World War II. In postwar years, the new medium of television lured away both radio's audience and many of its biggest stars and most popular programs. Radio, in turn, adapted by seeking narrower audiences for music or news programming. The expansion of FM radio with its superior sound quality captured most of the music audience by the 1970s and 1980s, while AM radio increasingly relied on news and listener call-in talk formats. Despite television's popularity, radio remains the most versatile, portable medium, particularly in times of emergency (Emmert, 2002).

According to the Project for Excellence in Journalism, radio is being transformed into the broader concept of audio. "The use of iPods, portable podcasting, satellite signals, HD radio, internet streaming, and even phones as information devices all grew [in 2006]. But the traditional AM/FM dial still captures a large audience—93.7 per cent of Americans over 12 years old—who, on average, listen almost 20 hours [a] week, though this number is ebbing" (Project for Excellence in Journalism, 2007).

Television, the most popular medium in the country, has penetrated virtually every home in America. Consider these facts:

- Each week the average child spends 20 times more minutes watching television than talking with his or her parents.
- Teenagers spend 900 hours in school each year, but 1,500 hours watching television.
- The average American watches an equivalent of 52 days of TV per year.
- By age 65, the average American adult will have spent nine years of his or her life in front of the TV.
- Two-thirds of Americans watch TV while eating dinner.

Television technology, delayed during World War II, changed the lifestyles of millions of Americans, who clustered around small black-and-white screens to watch their favorite programs. Until the 1980s television was dominated by three major networks: ABC, CBS, and NBC which was headed by radio and television pioneer David Sarnoff. However, the advent of Community Access Television (CATV), now popularly called cable television, broke the networks' dominance. By the 1990s two-thirds of American homes were wired for cable television and a third of TV programming was nonnetwork (Emmert, 2002).

Other challenges came from new networks, including Rupert Murdoch's Fox Broadcasting Company; the WB Television Network, owned by Warner Bros.; and UPN, owned by Viacom. Though still attracting large audiences, the original three networks realized enough slippage that by the end of the 1990s, all three had been acquired by new owners: NBC by General Electric, CBS by Viacom, and ABC by Capital Cities (Disney). In addition, the Corporation for Public Broadcasting, created by Congress in 1967, provides about 20 percent of the budgets for more than 600 public, noncommercial radio and television stations. The balance of their funding comes from foundations, corporate underwriting, and viewer pledges. Much of public television's daytime programming, such as Sesame Street, is aimed at children.

Viewership of network news programming dropped more than 3 percent during 2006 for both morning and evening shows. After two decades, NBC relinquished its ratings leadership and suffered steep budget cuts. Viacom spun off CBS into a separate company in 2005 and saw its stock value rise. Disney enjoyed a very profitable 2006, offsetting poor performance in its motion picture division. Despite its believability by the viewing public, network news is shrinking as it struggles to make the best use of digital content and multimedia platforms (Project for Excellence in Journalism, 2007).

Meanwhile, local television viewing remains healthy in a business sense, with increased profits and advertising revenues in 2006, along with the majority of local stations changing ownership during the year. However, viewership is eroding and viewers are going elsewhere for their news.

Cable television has expanded from providing reception in mountainous or remote locations to providing a hundred or more channels over coaxial or fiber-optic cables. Once considered merely a common-carrier public utility, cable now represents many of the innovations in broadcasting, such as Home Box Office (HBO) and Ted Turner's Superstation, which distribute their programming via satellite. Turner also founded the Cable News Network (CNN), the first 24-hour, all-news station, which came into its own with nonstop live coverage of the events of the Gulf War in 1991. Today, many people unable to access cable television or who want even more programming choices can install their own satellite receiving dish from companies, such as DirecTV, using direct broadcast satellites (DBS).

The notion of broadcasting has been recast as narrow casting, where smaller, special-interest audiences can have their own channels, while allowing the cable operators and content providers to still make a profit through advertising and subscriptions. Concern over rising monthly cable rates in a deregulated marketplace caused Congress to partially deregulate the cable industry, again treating it as a public utility. With substantial penetration into American households, cable TV manages to make healthy profits, but by 2006 evidence started to suggest that cable TV news was losing its stronghold in news on demand. To compensate, cable increasingly depends on personality and opinion programming. One significant development is Fox News pulling even or ahead of CNN in profits for the first time.

In terms of news programming, networks and local stations differ significantly. According to the Project for Excellence in Journalism, network news is more abstract, with defense, foreign affairs, and the economy accounting for a large portion of the newscast. A lone anchorperson fields reports from a cadre of correspondents. Local news is presided over by a family-like grouping of male and female anchors, a weatherman, and a sports anchor, who engage in small talk and present short news stories. The study suggests more community coverage, more enterprise reporting, better sourcing of stories, longer stories, and more reporters with longer lead times as a way of regaining viewers siphoned off by the Internet and other activities. The terrorist attacks of September 11, 2001, temporarily brought viewers back to their local stations. But will they stay?

Existing technologies are converging and new technologies are emerging, but America remains a television culture. It is the primary source of news for most Americans, a habit, an escape, perhaps even a necessity. It has been critiqued and criticized unlike any other industry. Its effect on children has been hotly debated. It has been called too violent, too bland, too lowbrow, and too much of everything else. A former chairman of the FCC called it "a vast wasteland." But amid the clutter of advertising, the reruns, the banality, and the boosterism, there are nuggets of entertaining, enlightening, and uplifting programming that make TV the most popular medium in history.

News Services

The Associated Press (AP) is the dominant news service in the United States. Founded in 1848 as a way to share the cost of international reporting, AP is uniquely owned as a not-for-profit member cooperative. Today, AP's World Services provides news and features in six languages to some 8,500 international print, photography, and broadcasting customers in more than 110 countries. This membership cooperative is a counterpoint in a highly competitive industry. Members pay for the content they receive and, in turn, agree to share the news with other members. This concept hastened the development of objective reporting.

A second news service, United Press International (UPI), has experienced a long downward spiral in its business fortunes in recent years. Once an aggressive competitor with AP, today UPI has sold off its broadcasting arm (to AP), has been acquired by the Unification Church, and is struggling to find an Internet presence.

Several U.S. newspapers or newspaper chains and broadcast companies maintain a somewhat lesser degree of intermedia cooperation and often syndicate their own product to subscribers. Notable is the availability of the various CNN broadcast services on a 24-hour basis. The federal government is also a major player in the distribution of news and information. In 1998, the United States Information Agency was restructured, and the newly created International Broadcasting Bureau (IBB) is responsible for disseminating news and public affairs programming through the Voice of America, WORLDNET Television and Film Service, and Radio and TV Marti, aimed at Cuba. The Cold War rhetoric of these propaganda arms has been tempered by an increased emphasis on trade and commerce issues. However, public diplomacy efforts in both print and broadcast media aimed primarily at the Middle East were enhanced by the U.S. Department of State in response to the terrorist attacks of 2001 (Kamalipour, 2002).

Internet and Interactive New Technologies

Each successive technological innovation has expanded the reach of the media while forcing existing media to adapt and perhaps change. The telegraph, radio, movies, television, cable, satellite, and now digital communication have all shaped the direction of mass communication. Today, well over half of U.S. homes have computers, and most enjoy access to the Internet. Many others use computers on the job. However, research suggests that unlike the democratizing effect of radio or television, the wired revolution remains largely the tool of the more educated and more affluent. President Bill Clinton called it the "digital divide." Taking the society as a whole, the heavily computerized United States (along with other industrialized nations) represents the "haves" in a world increasingly characterized by the disparity between the haves and the have-nots.

The Internet, relying on widely separated but interconnected computer systems, was originally designed as a military solution to the threat of communication disruption due to nuclear attack. By the end of the twentieth century, the Internet was being used for everything from news to shopping, entertainment, and distance learning. The Internet was siphoning customers from traditional media. At the same time, traditional media were embracing Internet technology to complement their original print or broadcast product.

While some people were bypassing traditional media reporting by using the World Wide Web, other consumers were simply using the Web to access traditional media services in a new technological format. Major media companies, such as AOL Time-Warner, competed with technology giants, such as Microsoft, to maximize audience share and retain competitive advantage in a constantly changing technological marketplace, as well as occasionally in the courts. Competition looms fierce between computer, coaxial cable, and fiber-optic service providers for access to the consumer's household hookup and subscription revenues. Today nearly 20 percent of online adults watch or download Internet video on a typical day, according to a Pew Internet & American Life Project study.

"While news websites are improving, and some are gaining in popularity, the best evidence suggests that online mews consumption overall leveled off in 2006 . . . it is clearer now that the growth in advertising revenue online is beginning to slow down—earlier than many people expected" (Project for Excellence in Journalism, 2007). However, the media seem to have embraced digital journalism. News outlets are devoting more time, staff, and resources to their digital efforts.

Global Mass Culture and Media Imperialism

American media is big business and getting bigger. Propelled by deregulation at home and the worldwide trend of merger-mania, U.S. media firms have engorged themselves on smaller competitors and now dominate the globe. The largest media conglomerates, along with nationality, and their most recent available revenues (in billions) are shown in Table 20.2.

Most top-grossing conglomerates have diversified into other ventures beside media. TimeWarner is the largest media corporation, owning America Online, Netscape, Time-Warner publications, CNN, HBO, Turner Entertainment, cable, film, music, and TV production, as well as major league sports franchises. By any measure, the United States dominates the news and entertainment production and flow for the world.

Domestically, mainstream media reflect the interests and mores of the large majority of citizens, and this is the group advertisers most desire to reach. Go, too, globally, Western media, led by the United States, reflect the capitalistic, democratic values of the more developed nations of the Northern Hemisphere. The effect of this media dominance is as complex as the debates over globalization. Do U.S. values subvert and swamp the cultural traditions of less developed nations that are unable to compete against media empires? Or do exported U.S. media offer a lifestyle of consumer choice and political freedom that will advance the lives of millions? Why does Western news largely ignore the developing world, except in times of crisis? From marketing to programming to satellite technology, the rest of the world has little choice but to avail itself of U.S. media. When cries of media imperialism reached a crescendo in the 1980s, the United States withdrew from UNESCO, and only recently has it announced plans to rejoin that world body. But the debate continues in a new century of change.

Advertising and Public Relations

The decade of the 1990s represented a period of considerable growth and profitability for the advertising industry and its quieter but equally effective partner in persuasion, public relations. Riding the crest of the runaway bull market economic expansion, advertising and pub-

Table 20.2 Media Conglomerates

General Electric	United States	$163.391 (2006)
News Corp.	Australia	$71.43 (2007)
Sony	Japan	$70.303 (2007)
AT&T	United States	$63.055 (2007)
TimeWarner	United States	$44.70 (2006)
The Walt Disney Company	United States	$35.3 (2006)
Vivendi Universal	France	$28.6 (2006)
Bertelsmann	Germany	$27.5 (2006)
Comcast	United States	$24.966 (2006)
National Amusements (includes Viacom and CBS)	United States	$24.15 (2005)

Source: Individual Web sites for each media conglomerate

lic relations helped drive share prices to dizzying heights, launching entrepreneurial start-up companies and then taking them public. It was a period that saw revenues rise and ad rates climb to more than $1 million for a 30-second television commercial during the National Football League Super Bowl. Agencies grew, merged, and provided plenty of employment.

But as all good things seem to end, the Internet company bubble burst by the year 2000. Share prices tumbled. Companies folded. And with the steep decline in advertising revenue, media constricted. Small publications went out of business. Layoffs beset advertising and public relations agencies and media firms alike. Many blamed advertising and public relations for artificially hyping the value of start-up companies that still lacked any products to take to market. Even large global communication conglomerates felt the impact. Cash rich, many had acquired big public relations agencies as a way to offer broader services to their clients and as a hedge against an advertising downturn. Some had proved profitable investments. Other public relations agencies, however, had been overvalued, and the parent companies found themselves servicing high levels of acquisition debt in a soft business climate. Currently, three-quarters of the top grossing public relations agencies, including such U.S. firms as Weber Shandwick, Fleishman-Hillard, Hill & Knowlton, and Burson Marstellar, are owned by global diversified holding companies, such as Omnicom, Interpublic Group (IPG), or WPP, which also own such major advertising agencies as BBDO Worldwide, DDB Worldwide, FCB Worldwide, McCann-Erickson, J. Walter Thomson, Ogilvy& Mather, and Y&R Advertising (see below). Independent firms with major U.S. operations include Edelman (2006 fee income of $324.5 million), Ruder Finn Group, Waggener Edstrom, APCO Worldwide, and Text 100 Int'l (Retrieved from, http://www.odwyerpr.com, 2007).

A significant trend in recent years has been the consolidation of advertising and public relations functions under the umbrella term of integrated marketing communication (IMC). In IMC, all activities designed to move goods and services in the marketplace, such as advertising, publicity, sales promotion, direct mail, trade shows, and special events, are coordinated under a single management function. This trend has been implemented in corporations and agencies alike.

Advertising is no longer just about media placement of advertising messages aimed at a mass audience. Today's advertising practitioner must know niche marketing, interactive media, relationship marketing, and brand development. Advertising is a worldwide business, but the United States is the largest advertising market and New York is the capital. Domestic advertising expenditures for all media are in the neighborhood of a quarter of a trillion dollars per year, with daily newspapers, broadcast television, and direct mail responsible for nearly two-thirds of that total. In recent years, however, cable television and newer technologies such as the Internet have been claiming larger shares of the media pie. This new technological revolution has changed advertising significantly, moving it away from reliance on mass media toward more specialized media aimed at smaller audiences with select interests. Of course, technology has also provided the tools for the audience to skip over the commercials altogether. However a 2007 study by the Nielsen Company found that people who own a digital video recorder, or DVR, still watch, on average, two-thirds of the ads. And Arbitron, another audience measurement company, found that two-thirds of movie theater viewers don't mind onscreen commercials.

Half of all U.S. advertising billings are generated by the largest 500 agencies. Many of these in turn are owned by giant global holding companies. The top 10 advertising agencies (and parent companies) by 2006 revenues (in millions) are shown in Table 20.3.

Worldwide estimates for advertising spending in 2007 total $630 billion; U.S. expenditures represent almost half of that total, or about $300 billion (Elliott, 2007).

By providing full client services with global reach, these giant agencies obtain an economy of scale and greater efficiency. However, critics argue that they restrict competition and monopolize the media, while overwhelming nascent advertising industries in developing markets.

Advertising adds desirability to the products it promotes. It adds value to brands, stimulates competition, and gives the consumer higher quality and more choice. But advertising also continues to face social criticism for campaigns aimed at children; advertising in schools, such as the Channel One project; and for health-related issues such as tobacco and alcohol advertising. By the end of the 1990s, settlements in a series of lawsuits against the tobacco industry resulted in severely curtailing tobacco advertising efforts. When Seagram, the Canadian liquor conglomerate, defied a 60-year-old voluntary ban by reintroducing liquor advertising into American broadcasting, state and federal governments as well as consumer groups moved to restrict alcohol advertising. However, the Federal Trade Commission, the government's watchdog on advertising, was substantially downsized during the Reagan administration's era of deregulation, making advertising monitoring more problematic. Generally, the First Amendment of the U.S. Constitution protects commercial speech. A case involving Nike Corporation currently before the U.S. Supreme Court may possibly further define the limits of commercial speech protection and affect the practices of advertising and public relations communicators in the future.

Public relations in its many forms and functions is an estimated $10 billion per year industry in the United States and enjoys a growth rate roughly equal to the country's gross domestic product (GDP). As many as a quarter of a million people work in public relations in the United States. Public relations practitioners handle media research and media relations, counseling, public affairs, fundraising, publications, and creating positive relationships with a variety of publics, such as the government, the community, employees, or shareholders. Practitioners work for corporations, public-sector organizations, and not-for-profit firms. The federal government is the single largest employer of public relations personnel.

Table 20.3   Top 10 Advertising Agencies by Revenue

JWT	WPP	$445.4
BBDO Worldwide	Omnicom	$444.2
McCann Erikson Worldwide	Interpublic	$443.4
Leo Burnett Worldwide	Publicis	$312
Ogilvy & Mather Worldwide	WPP	$290
DDB Worldwide Communications Group	Omnicom	$277.9
Y & R	WPP	$250
Grey Worldwide	WPP	$235.7
Saatchi & Saatchi	Publicis	$212.6
DraftFCB	Interpublic	$210

Source: Adage.com

Media Diversity in a Changing Environment

Demographically, California signals the future of America. The majority in the state is now Spanish speaking. The most common surnames are Rodríguez and Gonzáles. In San Jose, the 10th largest city in the United States, the most common surname is Vietnamese: Nguyen. Nationally, companies are retooling their branding, marketing, and advertising campaigns to tap the estimated $1.3 trillion—20 percent of the national total in minority spending power. Mainstream media is diversifying into these markets with bi- or trilingual pages, supplements, and separate publications. Local broadcasting is also targeting the ethnic communities, though not as quickly as cable, where entire channels are devoted to ethnic news and entertainment programming. Non-English Internet content is growing.

At the same time, a small, tenacious group of ethnic publishers and broadcast owners struggle to meet the diverse needs of their communities and compete for advertising revenue. Media directories list ethnic publications of various groups in the hundreds. Broadcast outlets are far fewer. The black press, for example, has functioned since the end of the Civil War. The ethnic press has accompanied each successive wave of immigration into the United States. The audience for the ethnic press is still growing as the minority population increases. But the growth is not even. Most Latinos in the United States are now second or third generation and slightly less likely to rely on foreign-language media. Asian media habits incorporate English-language outlets sooner, while the black press is generally flat or in decline, and embracing new media more slowly.

Media employment for minority journalists, broadcasters, and other communicators is a priority in industries anxious to effectively serve and sell to the growing minority communities. Qualified applicants are highly sought after and recruited. But the applicant pool is small. Women fare better than ethnic minorities in finding media jobs, filling one-third to two-thirds of positions, depending on media segment. Women still encounter the so-called glass ceiling in their attempts to infiltrate upper management. Launching their own publication or agency is a common tactic to advance careers. Ethnic practitioners make up about 20 percent of the workforce, but very few are represented in the executive suite (Project for Excellence in Journalism, 2007).

Preparing Tomorrow's Journalists and Communicators

Communication education in the United States remains healthy, despite a recessionary economy and chronically low starting salaries in the industry. More than 400 colleges and universities offer degrees in mass communications. There has even been a slight upturn in journalism enrollment since the terrorist attacks of September 11, 2001. Communication students are roughly equally distributed between print and broadcast journalism, public relations, and advertising. More than 10 percent of communication students are pursuing advanced degrees. Virtually all communication industries require a college degree for entry-level positions. About a quarter of college and journalism programs are accredited by the Association for Education in Journalism and Mass Communication (AEJMC), meeting standards in curriculum, faculty scholarship, diversity, budget, facilities, and public service.

Communications graduates find jobs in advertising and public relations, broadcasting, and print. About a quarter of graduates continue their education or work outside of communications. As in the industries they are preparing students for, the primary issue of the twenty-first century for U.S. schools of mass communication is convergence. Nationwide, journalism schools are increasingly teaching students how to present news in more than one medium, repurposing print journalism for the Internet and beyond. Thus students are being prepared for multimedia careers. Since the audience already seeks out news in a multiplatform environment, schools are adapting to the new reality.

While some media and some educational programs simply transfer their print content to the Web, others have embraced convergence seriously, using and teaching streaming video, Web production, and cross-platform publishing, after teaching research, writing, and critical thinking. Similarly, public relations and advertising programs are cross-training their students to meet the needs of contemporary agencies and integrated communications departments. Not only does convergence challenge the students to learn multiple platforms, it also challenges the curriculum to make hard choices of what to teach and what to expect students to learn elsewhere. Faculty members are also challenged to upgrade their own skills, and increasingly skills courses are being taught by working professionals. Curricular change is evolutionary. A new dean at the Medill School of Journalism at Northwestern University was given carte blance to impose a new curriculum; most universities espouse shared governance and change slowly over time.

Reporting back from a Poynter Institute seminar, Larry Pryor wrote in the *Online Journalism Review*:

> [Educators] said their deans, provosts and college presidents were now pushing them to teach new media topics, were offering to build facilities and were willing to consider interdisciplinary approaches. . . .The choices in this seminar were more about "what," "how," and "how soon," rather than "whether" or "why." And most of the good ideas this year came from educators. Clearly a lot had been learned. If this seminar is representative, we in academia are much further down the road toward solutions for out-of-date instruction. (Pryor, 2007)

Toward the Future

A core democracy with a sophisticated media system, Canada enters the twenty-first century full of hope and promise, but with British and French baggage and one eye on the United States. Driven by the psychological need for a unique national identity and culture, and tempered by the need to pay for it in a globalizing world, Canada juggles the public and the private to maintain a media culture all its own.

Unfettered by regulation and fueled by huge quantities of advertising revenues, U.S. media act out the global role one would expect of a superpower. Often the media play a lead in formulating the public agenda and participating in public diplomacy. Media are the major form of "white propaganda" on behalf of liberal capitalist democracies in a world characterized by globalization. Driven by technological innovation, U.S. media constantly merge and evolve into new organizations, seeking media convergence and market dominance. While its critics are many, both foreign and domestic, U.S. media will continue to exert an enormous influence over the entire world for a long time to come.

BIBLIOGRAPHY

"A Chronicle of Freedom of Expression in Canada (Part 1, 1914–1994)." Available: http://www.hackcanada.com/canadian/freedom/freedomchron/chronicle.htm. Accessed August 24, 2002.

"A Chronicle of Freedom of Expression in Canada (Part 2, 1995–present)." Available: http://www.hackcanada.com/canadian/freedom/freedomchron/recent.html. Accessed August 24, 2002.

Akin, D. "Canadian Youth Online More Than Americans: Survey by Forrester." *Financial Post,* January 31, 2001.

"Alliance Atlantis sale: bigger is better for whom?" Canadian Media Guild, January 11, 2007.

Annenberg Public Policy Center. "Media Usage by Families and Children for 2000." June 26, 2000. Available: http://www.media-awareness.ca/eng/issues/stats/usetv.htm#meduse. Accessed August 24, 2002.

Bass, W. "Silence of the Press: Canada's Horrific Unreported Trial." *Columbia Journalism Review* (September/October 1993). Available: http://www.cjr.org/year/93/5/canada.asp. Accessed August 16, 2002.

Barnouw, E. *A History of Broadcasting in the United States. Vol. 1, A Tower of Babel (to 1933).* New York: Oxford University Press, 1966.

———. *A History of Broadcasting in the United States. Vol. 2, The Golden Web (1933–53).* New York: Oxford University Press, 1968.

——— . *A History of Broadcasting in the United States. Vol. 3, The Image Empire (From 1953).* New York: Oxford University Press, 1970.

Beattie, E. "In Canada's Centennial Year, U.S. Mass Media Influence Probed." *Journalism Quarterly* 44, No. 4 (Winter 1967), 667–672.

Beauchesne, E. "Internet Clicking with Youth: Nine of 10 Teenagers Have Been Online, Overall Use Soars: Survey." *The Standard.* March 27, 2001.

Blanshay, M. "Canadian TV Sucks: Six-Year-Old Repeats of Drivel, Lumberjack Contests—No Wonder So Many People Want U.S. Satellite TV, Which Is Now Illegal Here." *Montreal Gazette,* May 27, 2002.

"Broadcasting Policy Monitoring Report, 2007." Canadian Radio-television and Telecommunications Commission. July 2007. Available http://www.crtc.gc.ca/eng/publications/reports/PolicyMonitoring/2007/bpmr2007.htm. Accessed September 29, 2007.

Brown, B. "Canada, Land of Newspaper Barons." *Media Life.* August 16, 2002. Available: http://www.medialifemagazine.com/news2002/aug02/aug12/5_fri/news5friday.html. Accessed August 16, 2002.

"Cable TV Subscribers Dip While DHT Demand Rises." *The Vancouver Province.* June 21, 2001, A32.

Campbell, R. *Media and Culture,* 2nd ed. Boston: Bedford/St. Martin's, 2000.

Canada: A Portrait. Ottawa, Ontario: Minister of Supply and Services, 1992.

Canada, Communications Division. *Canada Year Book 1994.* Ottawa, Ontario: Statistics Canada, 1993.

Canadian Association of Internet Providers. "Copyright & Other Policy Issues." Available: http://www.caip.ca/issues/copyright/aug1501-2.htm. Accessed August 21, 2002.

Canadian Newspaper Association. "Supreme Court agrees with CNA on publication ban." Available: http://www.cna-acj.ca/client/cna/cna.nsf/newsengMB/ABF8AEAB13FC8EB285256C3200646747?OpenDocument. Accessed June 5, 2008.

Canadian Radio-Television and Telecommunications Commission. Retrieved August 5, 2007. Available: http://www.crtc.gc.ca/end/newsreleases/2007/r070731.htm.

"Canada Will Put Different Spin on 9/11." *The Kitchener-Waterloo Record.* August 20, 2002, B5.

Canam—Supreme Court of B.C. October 12, 1999. Available: http://www.scacanada.com/bcsupreme-court.html. Accessed August 23, 2002.

Christians, C. G., Ferré, J. P., and Fackler, P. M. *Good News, Social Ethics and the Press.* New York: Oxford University Press, 1993.

Cobb, C. "Divas Lead Cultural Export Surge: Pop Superstars Help Put Canada's Balance of Cultural Trade in the Black." *The Ottawa Citizen.* June 21, 2001, A1.

Cohen, N. "Taking the Copyright Fight into a New Arena." *New York Times.* July 2, 2007.

Commission on Freedom of the Press. *A Free and Responsible Press.* Chicago: University of Chicago Press, 1947.

"Conrad Black, Three Codefendents Convicted of Fraud". Retrieved July13, 2007. Available: http://www.Bloomberg.com.

Cornacchia, C. "Gimme Shelter: Publications Devoted to Home Comforts—the Shelter Magazines Are Doing Surprisingly Well in a Troubled Economy." *The Vancouver Sun.* February 1, 2002, E6.

"Coverage a Balancing Act for Media." *The Regina Leader-Post.* November 2, 2001, A3.

"The CRTC Releases Its Annual Report on Canadian Broadcasting." Canadian Radio-television and Telecommunications Commission. July 31, 2007. Available http://www.crtc.gc.ca/eng/NEWS/RELEASES/2007/r070731.htm. Accessed September 29, 2007.

Desbarats, P. *Guide to Canadian News Media.* Toronto: Harcourt Brace Jovanovich, Canada, 1990.

Diekmeyer, P. "Little Long-term Effect on Ad Sales: But Terrorist Attacks Have Distracted Public, Making It Hard for Advertisers to Make Impact." *Montreal Gazette.* October 9, 2002, C2.

"Diverted by Jelly-Beans: No Sight Yet of a North American Union." *The Economist.* August 25, 2007.

Dordick, H. S., and Wang, G. *The Information Society: A Retrospective View.* Newbury Park, CA: Sage, 1993.

Dorland, M. *The Cultural Industries in Canada.* Toronto: James Lorimer, 1996.

Downey, K. "Movie Theater Spots Earn a Thumbs Up. Arbitron Study Finds Most Patrons Don't Mind Ads." *MediaLife.* March 13, 2007. Available: http://www.medialifemagazine.com/artman/publish/article_10744.asp. Accessed September 29, 2007.

Elliott, S. "Another Turn in Spending for '07." New York Times, June 27, 2007.

Ellis, D. *Split Screen.* Toronto: Friends of Canadian Broadcasting, 1993.

Ellison, S., and M. Karnitschnig. "Murdoch Wins His Bid for Dow Jones." *Wall Street Journal.* August 1, 2007. Available: http://online.wsj.com/public/article_print/SB118589043953483378.html.

Emery, M., E. Emery, and N. L. Roberts. *The Press and America: An Interpretive History of the Mass Media,* 9th ed.. Boston: Allyn and Bacon, 2000.

Emmert, F. A. "U.S. Media in the 1990s: Part I. Overview and the Print Media." Available: http://usinfo.state.gov/usa/infousa/media/media1cd.htm. Accessed August 23, 2002.

———. "U.S. Media in the 1990s: Part II. The Broadcast Media." Available: http://usinfo.state.gov/usa/infousa/media/media2cd.htm. Accessed August 23, 2002.

———. "U.S. Media in the 1990s: Part III. The Media and Society." Available: http://usinfo.state.gov/usa/infousa/media/media3cd.htm. Accessed August 23, 2002.

Eng, D. "Targeting New Markets." *Presstime.* June 2002.

"Federal Government Reminded That Advertisers Are the Engine Driving Canadian Broadcasting System; Advertising Associations Present Case to Standing Committee on Canadian Heritage." *Canada NewsWire.* April 18, 2002.

Ferguson, M. "Invisible Divides: Communication and Identity in Canada and the U.S." *Journal of Communication* 43, No. 2 (1993), 42–57.

"Film Credit Follies." Canadian Taxpayers Federation. January 18, 2005. Available: http://www.taxpayer.com/main/news.php?news_id=1889. Accessed September 29, 2007.

Folkerts, J., and Teeter, D. L., Jr. *Voices of a Nation: A History of Mass Media in the United States,* 4th ed. Boston: Allyn and Bacon, 2002.

Getler, M. "Challenges: The Press and the Pentagon." *Columbia Journalism Review* 40, No. 4 (November/December, 2001), 26.

"Global National Wins Awards for Sept. 11 Coverage." *Calgary Herald.* May 28, 200, B11.

Greenaway, N. "52% of Us Saying No to the Net." *Montreal Gazette.* June 12, 2002, A1.

Greenhouse, L., and Kirkpatrick, D. D. "Justices Loosen Ad Restrictions in Campaign Finance Law." *New York Times.* June 26, 2007. Available: http://www.nytimes.com/2007/06/26/washington/26scotus.html?_r=2&hp=&adxnnl=1&oref=slogin&pagewanted=print&adxnnlx=1191096037-LqYEFWSB17IQQjZkQKPqQQ. Accessed September 29. 2007.

Gwyn, R. "No Need to Fear Closer Ties to the U.S." *Toronto Star.* June 23,2002. Available: http:// friendscb.ca/articles/torontoStar/torontostar020623-2.htm. Accessed August 19, 2002.

Hackett, R. "Covering Up the War on Terrorism: The Master Frame and the Media Chill (Top Ten Questions Undercovered by the Dominant U.S. Media)." *Canadian Business and Current Affairs* 8, No. 3 (Fall 2001), 8–11.

Halberstam, D. *The Powers That Be.* New York: Knopf, 1979.

Haggett, S. "Newspapers Turn the Page after Slump." *Calgary Herald,* April 24, 2002, C1.

Harris, A., and Schneider, J. "Conrad Black, Three Codefendants Convicted of Fraud." *Bloomberg.com.* Available: http://www.bloomberg.com/apps/news?pid=20670001&refer=home&sid=alPnXOCSW9SU. Accessed September 29, 2007.

Head, S. W., and Sterling, C. *Broadcasting in America,* 5th ed. Boston: Houghton Mifflin, 1987.

Holmes, H., and Taras, D. *Seeing Ourselves: Media Power and Policy in Canada.* Toronto: Harcourt Brace Jovanovich, Canada, 1992.

Innis, H. A. *The Bias of Communication.* Toronto: University of Toronto Press, 1951.

Iyer, P. *The Global Soul.* New York: Vintage Departures, 2000.

Jobb, D. "Fighting Publication Bans." *Canadian Business and Current Affairs* 8, No. 4 (Winter 2002), 12–14.

Johansen, P. Personal interview by William Briggs. September 25, 2002.

Joyce, G. "B.C. Supreme Court Allows Recorders Inside Courtroom, But Not for Broadcast." Yahoo! Headlines. June 5, 2002. Available: http://ca.news.yahoo.com/020605/6/mv7v.html. Accessed August 24, 2002.

Kamalipour, Y. R. *Global Communication.* Belmont, CA.: Wadsworth, 2002.

Kesterton, W. H. *A History of Journalism in Canada.* Toronto: McClelland and Stewart, 1967.

Kohut, A. "Young People Are Reading, Everything But Newspapers." *Columbia Journalism Review.* (July/August 2002).

Leonard, T. C. *The Power of the Press: The Birth of American Political Reporting.* New York: Oxford University Press, 1986.

Levy, L. W. *Emergence of a Free Press.* New York: Oxford University Press, 1985.

MacAffee, M. "Six Out of 10 Canadians Say Culture Is Threatened by Americans: Poll." *Canadian Business and Current Affairs.* June 30, 2002.

McMurray, S. "Less TV Is Net Gain." Available: http://www.pollara.ca/new/LIBRARY/surveys/net_gain.htm. Accessed August 19, 2002.

McPhail, T. L. *Global Communication: Theories, Stakeholders, and Trends.* Boston: Allyn and Bacon, 2002.

Martin, R., and Adam, G. S. *A Sourcebook of Canadian Media Law.* Revised ed. Ottawa, Ontario: Carleton University Press, 1991.

Marzolf, M. *Up from the Footnote: A History of Women Journalists.* New York: Hastings House, 1977.

Merrill, J. C. *The Dialectic in Journalism: Toward a Responsible Use of Press Freedom.* Baton Rouge: Louisiana State University Press, 1989.

Miller, S. M. (ed.). *The Ethnic Press in the United States: A Historical Analysis and Handbook.* Westport, CT: Greenwood Press, 1987.

Moore, A. J. "A Chill in Canada." *Columbia Journalism Review* (July/August 2002). Available: http://www.cjr.org/year/02/2/moore.asp. Accessed August 16, 2002.

Mott, F. L. *American Journalism: A History, 1690–1960.* New York: Macmillan, 1962.

Newspaper Association of America. "Canadian Daily Newspapers." Available: http://www.naa.org/info/facts00/28.html. Accessed August 3, 2002.

———. "Employment of Women and Minorities." Available: http://www.naa.org/info/facts00/32.html. Accessed August 25, 2002.

———. "Journalism Graduates." Available: http://www.naa.org/info/facts00/25.htm. Accessed August 25, 2002.

———. "Highlights: The Year in Review." 2000. Available: http://www.naa.org/info/facts00/33.html. Accessed August 25, 2002.

———. "Newspaper, Voice and Online Services." Available: http://www.naa.org/info/facts00/ 18.html. Accessed August 25,2002.

"Newspaper Industry Rebounding, Says CAN." *Windsor Star,* April 24, 2002, A15. LexisNexis. Accessed September 24, 2002.

New York Times Co. v. Sullivan, 376 U.S. 254 (1964).

New York Times Co. v. United States, 713 U.S. 403 (1971).

O'Neill, J. "Net Users No Recluses, Study Finds." *Montreal Gazette,* December 12, 2001, A1.

Peterson, T. *Magazines in the Twentieth Century.* Urbana: University of Illinois Press, 1964.

Pollard, J. E. *The Presidents and the Press.* New York: Macmillan, 1947.

Project for Excellence in Journalism. "Gambling with the Future." *Columbia Journalism Review* 40, No. 4 (November/December 2001, supplement).

Project for Excellence in Journalism. "The State of the News Media 2007." An Annual Report on American Journalism. Available: http://www.stateofthenewsmedia.org/2007/. Accessed September 29, 2007.

Pryor, L. "Teaching the Future of Journalism. Educators Turn a Critical Eye to the Curricula of Convergence: a Report Back from a Poynter Institute Seminar." *Online Journalism Review*. February 12, 2006. Available http://www.ojr.org/ojr/stories/060212pryor. Accessed September 29, 2007.

"Q & A: How 9/11 Changed Media Coverage." *Newsweek* Web Exclusive. May 12, 2002. Available: http://www.msnbc.com/news/695680. Accessed May 12, 2002.

Raboy, M. *Les Média Québécois: Presse, Radio, Télévision*. Gaëtan Morin (ed.). Boucherville, Québec: Câblodistribution, 1992.

Regan, T. "Courtroom Secrecy Is under Fire in Canada." *The Christian Science Monitor,* July 3, 2001. Available: http://www.csmonitot.com/durable/2001/07/03/p7s1.htm. Accessed August 24, 2002.

Roberts, J. L. "A Tale of Two Dynasties: The Bancrofts Are the Most Important Family You've Never Heard of. With the Murdochs in the Hunt for Dow Jones, a Media Saga Takes a New Turn." *Newsweek*. June 11, 2007. Available: http://www.msnbc.msn.com/id/19002792/site/newsweek/. Accesed September 29, 2007.

Romanow, W. I., and W. C. Soderlund. *Media Canada*. Mississauga, Ontario: Copp Clark Pitman, 1992.

Scanlon, J. "Putting Terrorism and Its Aftermath into Context: The Quality of News Reports after the September 11 Attacks." *Canadian Business and Current Affairs* 8, No. 3 (Fall 2001), 16–17.

Schecter, B. "Homegrown Viewing Falls, CRTC Data Show: CTV, Global Spend More." *National Post,* February 22, 2002, C4.

———. "You Expect Us to Pay More for That: TV Viewers Aren't Clamouring for More." *National Post,* June 21, 2001, C1.

Scherr, E. F. "Fact Sheet: Telecommunications Act of 1996." Available: http://usinfo.state.gov/usa/infousa/media/telecomc.htm. Accessed August 23, 2002.

Schudson, M. *Advertising: The Uneasy Persuasion*. New York: Basic Books, 1984.

Scotton, G. "Media Integration a Work in Progress: Publishers Agree Convergence Way of Future." *Calgary Herald,* April 25, 2002.

Shaw, D. "Foreign News Shrinks in Era of Globalization." *Los Angeles Times,* September 27, 2001. Available: http://www.commondreams.org/headlines01/0927-03.htm. Accessed April 19, 2002.

Shaw, M.-L. "Holding the Line: Two Neighboring Nations Try to Raise Their Defenses While Staying Friends." *Milwaukee Journal Sentinel,* March 10, 2002, 1A.

Singer, B. D. *Communications in Canadian Society*. Scarborough, Ontario: Nelson Canada, 1991.

Smith, A. *Goodbye Gutenberg: The Newspaper Revolution of the 1980s*. New York: Oxford University Press, 1980.

Smith, J. A. *Printers and Press Freedom: The Ideology of Early American Journalism*. New York: Oxford University Press, 1988.

Soderlund, W. C., Gedelovsky, P., and Lee, M. F. "Trends in Canadian Newspaper Coverage of International News, 1988–2000: Editors' Assessments." *Canadian Journal of Communication* 27 (January 2002), 73–87.

Steffens, L. *The Autobiography of Lincoln Steffens*. New York: Harcourt Brace Jovanovich, 1931.

Stein, N. "Magazine Trade Wars." *Columbia Journalism Review* (January/February 1999). Available: http://www.cjr.org/year/99/1/canada.asp. Accessed August 16, 2002.

Steinhart, D. "Canadians Top Net Bankers, U.S. Leads Shopping Stakes: Ipsos-Reid Poll." *National Post,* August 22, 2002, C7.

Stephens, M. *History of News from the Drum to the Satellite*. New York: Viking, 1988.

Stevenson, R. L. *Global Communication in the Twenty-First Century*. New York: Longman, 1994.

Steward, G. "Is There Any Room for Stories Unrelated to the September 11 Attacks? Convergence Has Made That Difficult to Answer." *Canadian Business and Current Affairs* 8, No. 3 (Fall 2002), 20–21.

Stothart, P. "A Culture Strong and Free: The Doomsayers Predicted That a Trade Deal with the U.S. Would Spell the End of the Cultural Sovereignty. They Were Wrong." *The Ottawa Citizen,* A13.

Taras, D. *The Newsmakers: The Media's Influence on Canadian Politics.* Scarborough, Ontario: Nelson Canada, 1990.

Tibbetts, J. "French Isolated in 'Digital Divide,' Report Finds." *National Post,* March 26, 2002, A9.

Tolusso, S. "Broadcast Policy Report: Good News for Producers." *Playback,* November 27, 2002.

"Top 200 Newspapers by Largest Reported Circulation." Audit Bureau of Circulations. Available: http://www.accessabc.com/products/top200.htm. Accessed September 29, 2007.

Trade and Security Partnership Map. Retrieved February 2007. Available: http://www.Connect2Canada.com.

"TV Facts." Available: http://www.girltech.com/Sports/SP_hfacts.html. Accessed August 23, 2002.

Vanderburg, G. "Couch-Potato Time Falling—Maybe: Albertans Watch Television the Least, StatsCan Study Says." *Edmonton Journal.* January 26, 2001, A3.

Von Jenna, Y. "Navigating Turbulent Waters." Interactive Multimedia Arts and Technologies Association. Available: http://www.imat.ca. Accessed August 23, 2002.

Wall, B. "Review of Key Legal Decision in 2000." December 15, 2000. Available: http://www.gannett.com/go/newswatch/2000/december/nm1215-5.htm. Accessed August 24, 2002.

Walsh, S., and Fogg, P. "Editing the Mission." *Chronicle of Higher Education* 48, No. 40 (August 9, 2002).

Ward, S.J.A. Interview by William Briggs. August 9, 2007.

Weaver, D. A., and Wilhoit, G. C. *The American Journalist: A Portrait of U.S. News People and Their Work.* Bloomington: Indiana University Press, 1986.

Wilcox, D. L., Cameron, G. T., Ault, P. H., and Agee, W. K. *Public Relations: Strategies and Tactics.* Boston: Allyn and Bacon, 2003.

Wolseley, R. E. *The Black Press, U.S.A.* Ames: Iowa State University Press, 1990.

"Worldwide fees of Independent Firms with Major U.S. Operations." (2007) Available: http://www.odwyerpr.com.

Contributors

Oliver Boyd-Barrett (*Chapter 3, Global and National News Agencies*) is director of the School of Communication Studies at Bowling Green State University in Ohio and holds a joint professorship in the Department of Journalism and in the Department of Telecommunications. He is author of *The International News Agencies* (1980), joint author (with Michael Palmer) of *Le Trafic Des Nouvelles* (1981), joint author (with Daya Thussu) of *Contra Flow in Global News,* joint editor (with Terhi Rantanen) and contributor to *The Globalization of News* (1998), and contributing editor of *Communications Media, Globalization and Empire* (2006). [oboydb@bgsu.edu]

Lee B. Becker (*Chapter 5, Freedom of the Press Around the World*) is director of the James M. Cox Jr. Center for International Mass Communication Training and Research in the Grady College of Journalism and Mass Communication at the University of Georgia. He earned his doctorate from the University of Wisconsin-Madison and has written extensively on the journalism and mass communication labor market, journalism education, evaluation of postemployment training, and media development. [lbbecker@uga.edu]

Tanja Bosch (*Chapter 16, Sub-Saharan Africa*), is a lecturer at the Centre for Film and Media Studies at the University of Cape Town, South Africa. She teaches radio journalism, health communication and media theory and research methodology. She has worked with community radio stations in South Africa and the Caribbean, and completed her Ph.D. as a Fulbright scholar at Ohio University. She publishes and conducts research on talk radio, community radio, youth culture and new media. [tanja.bosch@uct.ac.za]

William Briggs (*Chapter 20, North America*) is director of the School of Journalism and Mass Communications at San Jose State University, San Jose, California, where he was the founding director of both the Pacific Rim Institute and Global Studies Institute. He has lectured *inter alia* in Taiwan, Hong Kong, China, Singapore, the Philippines, Thailand, Vietnam, Australia, New Zealand, South Africa, Belgium, the United Kingdom, Canada, and Mexico. He is a Fellow of the Salzburg Global Seminar, teaches graduate seminars in international communication, and has published on globalization issues and organizational communication in times of crisis. Briggs has been an active communication consultant, broadcast and print journalist. [bbriggs@casa.sjsu.edu]

Arnold S. de Beer (*Chapter 12, Global News*) is professor extraordinary in the Department of Journalism, Stellenbosch University, South Africa, as well as in the Media and Law Research

Initiative (Malri), Faculty of Law, University of the Western Cape, South Africa. He is the founding editor, and now managing editor, of *Ecquid Novi: African Journalism Studies*. He has published and co-published on media and democracy; media ethics and journalism education in Africa. [asdebeer@imasa.org] [www.imasa.org]

Mark Deuze (*Chapter 9, Global Journalism Education*) holds a joint appointment at Indiana University's Department of Telecommunications in Bloomington, United States, and as professor of journalism and new media at Leiden University, The Netherlands. Publications of his work include five books—including *Media Work* (Polity Press, 2007), and articles in journals such as the *International Journal of Cultural Studies, New Media & Society, Journalism Educator, Asia Pacific Media Educato,r* and *Journalism Studies*. [http://deuze.blogspot.com] [mdeuze@indiana.edu]

Paul Grosswiler (*Chapter 8, Continuing Media Controversies*), is an associate professor of journalism, University of Maine, and teaches on international mass communication, history of mass communication, media ethics. and media ecology. His Ph.D. in journalism is from the University of Missouri, and he was a senior Fulbright scholar in China. He has published *inter alia* on journalism in China and Tanzania; the press and foreign policy, cultural studies and postmodernism, media ecology, critical media theory, and political communication and new technology; recently in *Journal of Human Subjectivity, Explorations in Media Ecology,* and *Canadian Journal of Communication*. He authored a book on the media and social theories of Marshall McLuhan (1998). [paul_grosswiler@umit.maine.edu]

Minabere Ibelema (*Chapter 16, Sub-Saharan Africa*) holds a Ph.D. from Ohio State University and is an associate professor of communication studies at the University of Alabama at Birmingham (USA). He is the author of *The African Press, Civic Cynicism, and Democracy* (2008) and co-

author of *Afro-Optimism: Perspectives on Africa's Advances* (2003). His articles have appeared in *Journalism & Communication Monographs, Free Speech Yearbook, Newspaper Research Journal,* the *Journal of Development Communication,* as well as in several books. [mibelema@uab.edu]

Beate Josephi (*Chapter 10, Journalists, International Profiles*) is in charge of the coursework Masters program in the School of Communications and Arts at Edith Cowan University in Perth, Western Australia. She is the former head of the Professional Education Section (now the Journalism Research and Education Section) of the IAMCR (International Association of Media and Communication Research). Her research publications are on journalism, journalism education, young journalists' socialization processes, and the journalistic professional model. She is the editor of the forthcoming book on *Journalism Education in Challenging Environments,* which deals with journalism education in countries such as China, Cambodia, Tanzania, Palestine, Oman and Russia. [b.josephi@ecu.edu.au]

Richard Landesberg (*Chapter 4, Barriers to Media Development*) is an assistant professor in the School of Communications at Elon University in North Carolina. Landesberg was a visiting professor at Southeast University in Nanjing, China in the summer of 2007. His Ph.D. is from the University of North Carolina at Chapel Hill. Landesberg spent more than 20 years as a broadcast journalist working for Mutual/NBC Radio and CNN Television. He was European Bureau Chief for Mutual/NBC Radio, stationed in London. Landesberg is on the editorial board of *Electronic News* and is on the executive board of the Radio Television News Directors Association of the Carolinas. [rlandesberg@elon.edu]

Eric Louw (*Chapter 11, Reporting Foreign Places*) has a Ph.D. from the University of Natal, South Africa, and is director of communication programs, School of Journalism and

Communication, University of Queensland, Australia. He previously taught at a number of South African universities and worked as a journalist on the *Pretoria News*. During the 1980s, Louw was the chair of a nongovernment organization engaged in development communication work in South Africa. He has published widely in the areas of political communication and the South African media. His books include *The Media and Political Process*; *The Media and Cultural Production*; *New Voices over the Air*; *The Rise, Fall and Consequences of Apartheid*; *South African Media Policy* and *The Alternative Press in South Africa*. [e.louw@uq.edu.au]

John C. Merrill (*Preface and Chapter 1, Introduction to Global Western Journalism Theory*) is professor emeritus at the School of Journalism, University of Missouri. He has taught at some half dozen universities for 60 years, has edited and written about 30 books, and has lectured in at least 50 countries. His newest book (forthcoming) is *Call to Order: Plato's Legacy of Social Control*. [merillj@missouri.edu]

Orayb Aref Najjar (*Chapter 15, the Middle East and North Africa*) is associate professor at the Department of Communication, Northern Illinois University, DeKalb, Illinois. Her publications center on media law in the Middle East and North Africa, as well as new technology, and include book chapters such as, "Media Policy and Law in Egypt and Jordan: Continuities and Changes." In Kai Hafez (Ed.). *Arab Media: Power and Weakness*. New York: Continuum, 2008, and, "New Palestinian Media and Democratization from Below," in *New Media and the New Middle East,* edited by Philip Seib, New York: Palgrave Macmillan 2007, as well as articles in journals such as *Rethinking Marxism* (2007), and *Journal of Communication Inquiry* (2007). [onajjar@niu.edu]

Doug Newsom (*Chapter 7, Global Advertising and Public Relations*) holds a Ph.D., is an APR, and a Fellow of the PRSA. She is the author of

Bridging Gaps in Global Communication and co-author of four textbooks: *Media Writing* (with the late James Wollert); *This Is PR* (with Judy VanSlyke Turk and Dean Kruckeberg), and *Public Relations Writing* (with the late Bob Carrell, and now with Jim Haynes.) She is co-editor of a book of women's colloquium papers, *Silent Voices* (also with Bob Carrell). She is a professor at Texas Christian University in Fort Worth and a public relations practitioner. [d.newsom@tcu.edu]

Allen Palmer (*Chapter 14, Eastern Europe, Eurasia, and Russia*) is a professor of media studies and a journalist. He holds a doctorate in communication theory and research from the University of Utah. He is director of International Media Studies at Brigham Young University in Provo, Utah. He has also taught as a visiting professor in Mauritius, Namibia, Kosovo, and the Philippines. His research has been published inter alia in *Media and Society, Science Communication, Communication Law & Policy, Gazette,* as well as numerous chapters in books and anthologies. [allen_palmer@byu.edu]

Paul Parsons (*Chapter 4, Barriers to Media Development*) is a professor and dean of the School of Communications at Elon University in North Carolina. He was a Fulbright professor at the China School of Journalism, Beijing (1992–1993) and a visiting professor at Nanyang Technological University, Singapore (1999–2000). He holds a Ph.D. from the University of Tennessee. He spent 10 years as a reporter and editor with the *Arkansas Democrat,* United Press International, and the Associated Press. He has authored two university press books, numerous book chapters and articles on international news framing, comparative studies, and other global perspectives. [pparsons@elon.edu]

Stephen Quinn, Ph.D. (*Chapter 18, Australasia*), an associate professor at Deakin University in Australia, has taught journalism in Australia, New Zealand, the UK, the United Arab Emirates, and the United States. He has worked for regional newspapers in Australia; the *Bangkok Post*; the Press Association, BBC-TV, Independent Television News, and *The Guardian* in London; the Australian Broadcasting Corporation in Sydney; Television New Zealand; and the Middle East Broadcasting Centre in Dubai. Since becoming a university academic in 2006, he has written 11 books on links between journalism and technology. Another four books are due for publication in 2008 and 2009. [stephenq@deakin.edu.au] [http://www.deakin.edu.au/~stephenq]

Terhi Rantanen (*Chapter 3, Global and National News Agencies*) is professor and director of the MSc Program in Global Media and Communications at the London School of Economics and Political Science. It is a pioneer joint program between three universities: LSE, University of Southern California in Los Angeles, and Fudan University in Shanghai. Her publications include *The Globalization of News* (with O. Boyd-Barrett, 1998), *The Global and the National Media and Communications in Post-Communist Russia* (2002), *The Media and Globalization* (2005), and *When News Was New* (2008). She is a founding editor of Sage's *Global Media and Communications* (2005–). [t.rantanen@lse.ac.uk]

Rick Rockwell (*Chapter 19, Latin America*), associate professor of broadcast journalism at American University, is the co-author of the book *Media Power in Central America*, which won an American Library Association *Choice* magazine award in 2004. Rockwell began working extensively as a journalist in Central America and Mexico in the 1980s. In addition to his book, he has authored or co-authored 18 book chapters, government reports and peer-reviewed journal articles on Latin America, including a chapter in the recently released book *Negotiating Democracy: Media Transformations in Emerging Democracies*. [rockwell@american.edu]

Byron T. Scott (*Chapter 13, Western Europe*) is professor emeritus of journalism and director of the European Union Center at the University of Missouri-Columbia. In the past two decades he has lectured at universities and taught professional workshops in 47 nations. In 1986 he came from the Scripps School of Journalism at Ohio University to take the first endowed chair at Missouri, the world's oldest journalism school. He was the school's first international programs director. Prior to teaching, Scott was a newspaper and magazine journalist in five major U.S. cities. [scottbt@missouri.edu]

Glenn W. Scott (*Chapter 4, Barriers to Media Development*) is an assistant professor in the School of Communications at Elon University. He specialized in international mass communication while earning his Ph.D. at the School of Journalism and Mass Communication at the University of North Carolina at Chapel Hill. He also studied for one year as a fellow in the Asian Studies Program for Journalists at the University of Hawaii at Manoa. Scott worked for 20 years as a journalist for newspapers in California, Hawaii, and Japan. Among his research interests is the study of media practices in the Asia-Pacific region. [gscott3@elon.edu]

John Tidey (*Chapter 18, Australasia*) is an Australian journalist who has also worked in East Africa, China, and the United Kingdom. He holds a master's degree from Monash University; is a former president of the Pacific Area Newspaper Publishers Association, and was for five years an adjunct professor at Deakin University in Australia. Tidey is co-author of a book on newspaper management and has contributed articles on newspaper issues in New Zealand and Australia to books and academic journals. [tidey@brd.com.au]

Tudor Vlad (*Chapter 5, Freedom of the Press around the World*) is associate director of the James M. Cox Jr. Center for International Mass Communication Training and Research, Grady College of Journalism and Mass Communication,

University of Georgia. His doctorate is from Babes-Bolyai University, Cluj-Napoca, Romania, where he was chair of the Department of Journalism. He has authored two books, *The Interview: From Plato to Playboy* and *The Romanian Writers' Fascination with Film,* numerous studies, scholarly materials and articles published in the United States and Europe, and four novels. Vlad is co-editor of *Copyright and Consequences.* [tvlad@uga.edu]

Herman Wasserman *(Chapter 2, Critical and non-Western Press Philosophies; Chapter 6, Global Journalism Ethics)* is a senior lecturer in journalism studies at the University of Sheffield, UK, as well as an associate professor extraordinary of journalism, Stellenbosch University, South Africa and a former Fulbright scholar at the School of Journalism, Indiana University, USA. He has previously worked as a newspaper journalist. He is editor of *Ecquid Novi: African Journalism Studies,* associate editor of the *Journal of Global Mass Communication,* and editorial board member of the *Journal of African Media Studies,* and *Journal of Mass Media Ethics.* His publication and research interests include media and journalism in Africa, media ethics and postcolonial theory. [hwasserman@imasa.org]

Jiafei Yin *(Chapter 17, Asia and the Pacific)* is professor of journalism at the Central Michigan University, teaching and doing research in the areas of international and cross cultural communication—more specifically, topics concerning theories of world press systems, press freedom in Asia, the changing media in China, and the coverage of international news. She was a 2003 fellow at the Institute for Journalism Excellence sponsored by the American Society of Newspaper Editors. She conducted seminars in Hong Kong and Beijing for the staff of the *China Daily,* China's only national English-language daily newspaper, where she had worked as a chief copyeditor. She has started an exchange program between her department and the *China Daily.* [jiafei.yin@cmich.edu]

Index